THE THEATER OF OPERATIONS

THE THEATER

OF OPERATIONS

NATIONAL SECURITY AFFECT FROM THE COLD WAR TO THE WAR ON TERROR

JOSEPH MASCO

DUKE UNIVERSITY PRESS

DURHAM AND LONDON 2014

Library of Congress Cataloging-in-Publication Data
Masco, Joseph
The theater of operations : national security affect from the Cold War
to the War on Terror / Joseph Masco.
pages cm
Includes bibliographical references and index.
ISBN 978-0-8223-5793-3 (cloth : alk. paper)
ISBN 978-0-8223-5806-0 (pbk : alk. paper)
1. Terrorism—United States—Prevention—History—20th century.
2. Terrorism—United States—Prevention—History—21st century.
3. National security—United States—History—20th century.
4. National security—United States—History—21st century. I. Title.
HV6432.M3795 2014
363.325'60973—dc23   2014007343

Cover: Trevor Paglen, STSS-1 and Two Unidentified Spacecraft over
Carson City (Space Tracking and Surveillance System; USA 205) (detail),
2010. C-print, 50 × 50 in. (127 × 127 cm). Courtesy of Metro Pictures,
New York; Altman Siegel, San Francisco; Galerie Thomas Zander,
Cologne.

CONTENTS

THE "NEW" NORMAL

In the fall of 2001, the United States inaugurated a new project to secure the American future, and did so in the name, and language, of counterterror. The very real terrorist violence of September 2001 was quickly harnessed by U.S. officials to a conceptual project that mobilizes affects (fear, terror, anger) via imaginary processes (worry, precarity, threat) to constitute an unlimited space and time horizon for military state action. By amplifying official terror and public anxiety, the U.S. security apparatus powerfully remade itself in the early twenty-first century, proliferating experts, technological infrastructures, and global capacities in the name of existential defense. Counterterror constitutes itself today as endless, boundless, and defensive—a necessary means of protecting American interests in a world of emergent and violent dangers. The resulting security state apparatus no longer recognizes national boundaries or citizenship as the defining coordinates of its governance; rather, it constitutes a dangerous future as its object of concern. The motivating force behind this radical renewal and expansion of the national security state in the twenty-first century is a vision of a world without borders, generating threats without limit. The goal of the counterterror state is to produce and administer a U.S.-centric world, one in which American interests can never be surprised by external events, let alone shocked by them (see U.S. White House 2002a). Always already in crisis and failing, this aspirational image of American power has nonetheless been hugely productive in its first decade, generating new expert worlds devoted to counterterror as a planetary project while rewriting the domestic social contract in fundamental ways.

The relationship between affect, technological capacity, and political agency in U.S. national security culture is the central concern of this book, which investigates the conditions of possibility for the most powerful military state in human history to declare war on an emotion. In particular, it traces how the affective politics of the Cold War nuclear state both enabled, and—after 2001—were transformed into those of the counterterror state. *Terror*, as we shall see, has a specific genealogy in the United States after 1945, one that is deeply structured by the revolutionary effects of military technoscience on American society and governance. But existential terror (after 1945, of the atomic bomb; after 2001, of the WMD) not only empowers the most radical actions of the security state; it also creates ideological barriers to dealing with a vast set of everyday forms of suffering and vulnerability that Americans experience, now rejected in favor of warding off imagined catastrophes. The escalating violence of neoliberal economics in the twenty-first century (poverty, bankrupt municipal governments, spectacular white-collar crime, energy scarcity) and of an increasingly destabilized biosphere (affecting health, agriculture, city infrastructures) generate an intensifying experience of precarity in the United States but rarely rise to the level of a formal national security concern. Although cities lost to storm surges and bankruptcies create terrors of the most visceral and immediate kind for citizens, such events do not activate the attention of the counterterror state.[1] The state security apparatus today sets aside these everyday insecurities endured by citizens to pursue a specific, if expansive, universe of terroristic potentials. American insecurity may derive from many sources, but it can be affectively channeled to enable a state project with specific logics and coordinates. Put differently, the United States is a global hyperpower that increasingly produces the conditions for its own instability (politically, economically, environmentally) and then mobilizes the resulting vulnerability of its citizens and systems to demand an even greater investment in security infrastructures. Counterterror has thus become recursive and self-colonizing, replacing the social commitment to building a prosperous collective future and a stable international order with the project of warding off a field of imagined and emergent dangers.

Given the wide-ranging global violence (involving wars, covert operations, and drone strikes) as well as the extraordinary costs of counterterror, its incompatibility with democratic governance, and its overwhelmingly

2

negative vision of citizens, international relations, and the future, it is important to consider how and why counterterror has become so American. What a national community fears and how it responds to those fears are cultural forms as well as technologically mediated processes, the basis for a domestic politics as well as a geopolitics. The affects and infrastructures of the contemporary security state, as we shall see, have both a history and an emerging logic and purpose. This book explores why American society, at the very height of its global military, economic, and cultural power, has been so receptive to a state program that offers little in the way of material everyday security in exchange for increasing public docility, private excitability, and the promise of unending war. *The Theater of Operations* is ultimately an examination of American self-fashioning through technoscience and threat projection, of how fear and terror have been domesticated as a primary national resource and projected out globally as a twenty-first-century American project.

Threatening Histories

One of the very first formal acts of the War on Terror was a purge of the U.S. national archives. After the suicide-hijacker attacks on New York and Washington in 2001, researchers at the U.S. National Archives and Records Administration, myself included, began to notice the disappearance of long-available files or the absence of documents within them, sometimes marked with a withdrawal notice stating that "this item was removed because access to it is restricted" (figure I.1; see Aid 2006; U.S. Information Security Oversight Office 2006). Specific historical materials related to national intelligence estimates, emergency response planning, nuclear policy, and covert actions dating back to World War I were pulled from public access and reclassified. Documents that had been in the public domain for years and, in some cases, already published in official government histories were nonetheless inexplicably recategorized as official secrets. Codified in secret legal agreements with U.S. intelligence and defense agencies, this reclassification program extended from the National Archives to the presidential library system, involving records from the State Department, National Security Council, Central Intelligence Agency (CIA), and Department of Defense (DOD), as well as from agencies that no longer officially exist—such as the Atomic Energy Commission, Defense Nuclear Agency, and Chemical Warfare Service. Thus, before the United States invaded Afghanistan on October 7, 2001 (which inaugurated the George W. Bush administration's global War on Terror), or adopted the U.S.A. Patriot Act

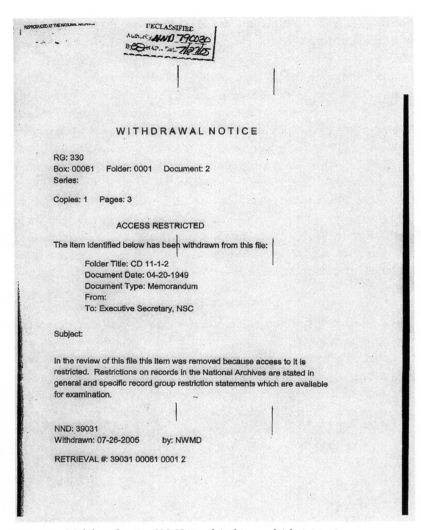

DECLASSIFIED
Authority *NND 790030*
By *CH* NAP.. Date *7/2/05*

WITHDRAWAL NOTICE

RG: 330
Box: 00061   Folder: 0001   Document: 2
Series:

Copies: 1   Pages: 3

ACCESS RESTRICTED

The item identified below has been withdrawn from this file:

    Folder Title: CD 11-1-2
    Document Date: 04-20-1949
    Document Type: Memorandum
    From:
    To: Executive Secretary, NSC

Subject:

In the review of this file this item was removed because access to it is restricted. Restrictions on records in the National Archives are stated in general and specific record group restriction statements which are available for examination.

NND: 39031
Withdrawn: 07-26-2005   by: NWMD

RETRIEVAL #: 39031 00061 0001 2

FIGURE I.1. Withdrawal notice, U.S. National Archives and Administration.

on October 26 (which profoundly redefined the concept of U.S. citizenship through search, seizure, surveillance, and detention policies), a war on public memory was already well under way.

We might well ask: Why would national security policy documents, particularly those of the long-dead Cold War, be of such immediate concern to U.S. officials, appearing to undermine the War on Terror at its very founding? And if American history began anew with the violence of September

2001, as White House officials reiterated over and over again in their public statements, declaring the end of Cold War security logics of deterrence and a "new normal" of preemptive counterterrorism, then why was it so important to control the deep history of the national security state?

We should begin by recognizing that the official declaration of a "new" counterterror state in 2001 was actually a repetition, modeled in language and tone on the launch of the national security state in 1947. Both projects involved the designation of new insecurities, new institutions to fight them, a public mobilization campaign grounded in fear, and above all, official claims that a new kind of war (a cold war or a war on terror) was a multigenerational commitment, constituting a new mode of everyday life rather than a brief intensity of conflict. The former cold warriors in the George W. Bush administration intended the War on Terror to be as powerful as the Cold War in realigning citizen-state relations and defining American geopolitical objectives, constituting a renewed commitment to state and nation building through confronting an existential danger. Nonetheless, official desires for a newly militarized consensus, and a reliance on a prior model of state and nation building, still do not explain the immediate anxiety about the public history of the national security state in the fall of 2001.

Consider the following two instances of War on Terror reclassification of Cold War materials.[2] A "top secret" memo from April 27, 1951 (originally declassified in 1996), on the subject of "Chinese Communist Intentions to Intervene in Korea" seems to have been reclassified because it documents a failure to predict the future. The CIA intelligence estimate states that the Chinese would not invade Korea in 1950, as they in fact did in November of that year (U.S. Central Intelligence Agency 1951). It was pulled for reclassification on October 16, 2001. A CIA report to the National Security Council from April 1949 (originally declassified in 1996 and reclassified in 2005) on the subject of the "Atomic Energy Program of the USSR" also attempts to engage the future, stating that "in order to estimate the capability of the USSR to wage atomic warfare, it is necessary to know, not only the events that preceded the date when the first bomb is detonated, but also the capability for bomb production thereafter" (U.S. Central Intelligence Agency 1949, 1). It calls for a comprehensive effort to study Soviet capabilities in nuclear weapons science, including "special intelligence," "interrogations," "covert operations," attention to "Soviet technical literatures," as well as the production of a "detection system" to discover when a nuclear explosion has occurred (ibid.). The document suggests that in spring 1949 the CIA was unaware that the Soviets would test their first atomic bomb on August 29 of that year. Today,

5

these documents show how the newly formed U.S. intelligence agencies of the mid-twentieth century calculated Communist activities and nuclear threat at the very start of the Cold War. However, the documents also reveal something else that is deeply important to national security professionals to this day: the value—and the shame—of strategic surprise.

In their historical moments, the shock of the first Soviet nuclear test and of the Communist revolution in China and later actions in Korea were driving forces for a massive expansion of the national security state in the 1950s, a radical investment in militarism not to be repeated until the first decade of the twenty-first century, when the nuclear security state, shocked by suicide-hijacker attacks on two American cities, remade itself under the logics of counterterror. The politics of shock are central to the conceptualization of the national security state as a distinctly American form of power. We might think of the reclassification project as not only a sign of the deep commitment of the counterterror state to official secrecy and covert action in all its forms, but also as an effort to purge evidence of the inability of the national security apparatus to perfectly predict the future—to anticipate and mediate crisis and thereby produce a normalized everyday, unbroken by trauma. It is as if the failure to prevent the suicide hijackers in 2001 created a reverberating anxiety not only about the attacks but also about the concept of national security itself, connecting seemingly disparate and historically distinct expert judgments within an alternative understanding of American power, an infrastructure of failure rather than success. The failure to predict global events, let alone protect U.S. citizens and cities from violence, haunts U.S. security culture today, creating the constant drive for new technical capacities and the increasing militarization of American life. It also generates professional desires for revenge against those who have revealed the institutional weakness of the global hyperpower. These administrative commitments fuse the problem of futures, infrastructures, expertise, and international competition with affect in a new way, one that creates the expectation of a total anticipatory control of the future even as that possibility breaks down from one second to the next, producing the grounds for serial shocks (and thus, perpetual trauma).

During the Cold War constituting, mobilizing, and exploiting existential danger was a central domain of national politics, with each federal election in part based on how prospective leaders would handle the production of nuclear technologies as well as manage the minute-to-minute threat of nuclear attack. Evoking existential threat became the core vehicle for building a military-industrial state, pursuing rivalries between political parties, and mobilizing ideological campaigns on both the Right and the Left. Nuclear fear was thus a total social formation in the second half of the twentieth century, mobilizing all aspects of American society through specific images of the end of the nation-state. This negative view of the future was balanced by investments in a welfare-state apparatus devoted to improving the conditions of everyday life for citizens in terms of health, education, and the environment (Light 2003). Thus, the catastrophic as well as the utopian potentials of the nuclear state were explicit terms of public discourse, making both panic and promise the basis for the domestic political sphere. Americans now live in a postwelfare state society, which is no longer so formally invested in improving the qualities of collective life through social programming; thus, terror has increasingly become the primary domain of everyday politics in the early twenty-first century. The lack of a positive vision of the collective future is pronounced in the United States today, and it is amplified by the increasingly blurred public memory of the historical evolution of the security state itself. Indeed, the proliferation of Cold War nuclear panics is rarely discussed as a model for contemporary counterterror politics, leaving largely unexamined the truth or falsity of official claims of Soviet nuclear advantage: the 1950s bomber gap, the 1960s missile gap, the 1970s window of vulnerability, and the 1980s Soviet first-strike capability. But it is important to recognize that these domestic productions, as iconic moments in American politics, were emotional recruitments before they were technological or military claims of fact. These episodes were domestic political campaigns of threat proliferation before, and sometimes even after, the technological and scientific reality of Soviet military capabilities had been determined. From this perspective, terror has a specific American logic and domestic history, one that since 1945 has drawn on the destructive capacities of nuclear weapons to focus social energies, unlock resources, and build things. In the twentieth century, the United States remade itself through the atomic bomb, using nuclear fear as a coordinating principle for U.S. institutions, citizen-state relations, and geopolitics alike (Masco 2006).

The counterterror state, like the countercommunist state before it, attempts to install through domestic affective recruitments a new perception of everyday life that is unassailable. The campaign to normalize threat is the flip side of identifying and articulating new kinds of danger, allowing new forms of governance to be pursued as a necessary counterformation.

Consider, for example, the following official statements about insecurity in the United States framed in the future conditional:

> This situation will continue as far ahead as anyone can foresee. We cannot return to "normalcy." This is the "new normalcy." Only by winning what at best will be a long war of endurance can we hope to avoid . . . the very possible destruction of civilization itself. (quoted in Chernus 2002, 44)

> Homeland security is not a temporary measure just to meet one crisis. Many of the steps we have now been forced to take will become permanent in American life. They represent an understanding of the world as it is, and dangers we must guard against perhaps for decades to come. I think of it as the new normalcy. (Cheney 2001)

As far as anyone can foresee. The first statement—from July 1953—is by Eisenhower administration official James Lambie, who was charged with developing a national communications strategy to mobilize citizens in the thermonuclear age. In response, he helped craft one of the largest public education campaigns in U.S. history (a program that we remember today as civil defense), devoted to teaching citizens to fear the bomb in a specific way so as to prepare them for a potentially short nuclear or long cold war. The second evocation of a "new normal"—from an October 2001 speech to the Republican Governors Association—is by Vice President Dick Cheney, who also attempts to standardize danger and to create a new psychic infrastructure capable of accommodating a permanent, imminent danger. In both cases, existential threat is presented as both novel and emergent and is then positioned as the baseline reality for a new kind of everyday American life. Future crisis is projected—as concept—to be the basis for life at institutional, technological, and affective levels, reordering domestic politics and geopolitics in a startlingly economical gesture.

Declaring a "new" normal is thus anything but new as a state security practice in the United States. However, the objects, logics, and consequences of defense have significantly changed with the shift from the twentieth century's nuclear "balance of terror" to the twenty-first century's "War on Terror."[3] Interrogating the links between the first decade of the Cold War and the first decade of the War on Terror is a central project of this book, which pays specific attention to how technological revolution, surprise, normality, and terror have been used to orchestrate a new kind of security culture. I pursue these comparisons not because they are absolutely symmetrical or simply code shifts from nuclear fear to terrorism, but because each iteration of the national security state announces itself through acts of normalization and naturalization (see Der Derian 2002). It is increasingly important to understand how historically crafted images and logics of imminent danger allow feelings to be nationalized and directed to produce antidemocratic actions and policy. These affective logics constitute a specific zone of interaction between citizens and the state, one that is the very basis for the social contract (which Hobbes once defined as the exchange of public obedience for collective security). As we shall see, national security affect is a special kind of collective experience, one that is central to enabling the technological and administrative capacities of the security state. Infrastructures—affective, imaginative, and material—are linked in the production of American power today, creating an unprecedented global projection of American fears and desires in the name of existential defense.

The Threat Matrix

Since the atomic bombings of Hiroshima and Nagasaki, surprise and its opposite, anticipation, have been foundational concerns of the U.S. national security state. A formal rationale for the 1947 National Security Act (which created the Department of Defense, the National Security Council, and the CIA) was to prevent a nuclear Pearl Harbor—to prevent strategic surprise in the nuclear age.[4] U.S. policy makers immediately understood the power of the atomic bomb to be revolutionary, enabling U.S. leaders to threaten rival nations with "prompt and utter destruction," as President Harry Truman did in July 1945, or with "shock and awe," in the language of Secretary of Defense Donald Rumsfeld on the eve of the U.S. invasion of Iraq in 2003.[5] The ability to shock (at both psychic and material levels) and not experience shock, in other words, became a primary goal of the American security state after 1945. The national security state also sought right from the beginning to politically exploit the psychological effects of nuclear fear as much as the destructive physical capacities of nuclear weapons. This formulation of security makes the near future as well as the human nervous system specific objects of state scrutiny, with perceptions and temporalities of danger the guiding administrative logics of the security state.

At the start of the Cold War, the United States transformed an anticipated Soviet nuclear capability into the rationale for building a global technological system, which became the always-on-alert infrastructure of mutual assured destruction. The nuclear strategist Albert Wohlstetter (1958) famously called this the "delicate balance of terror," a phrase that underscores the Cold War's affective logics but not always its material reality. Indeed, the era of most acute nuclear paranoia in the United States was a largely self-generated effort to mobilize and coordinate citizens, officials, military personnel, and major social institutions through a new concept of nuclear terror. In the first decade of the War on Terror, the United States also committed to building an ever-expanding, always-on-alert global security apparatus, but one that had an astonishing new range of interests (weapons, people, data, microbes). This is a broad-based effort to create a kind of American power that can administer the global future, prevent rivals from amassing threatening power, and is never deterred or shocked. Counterterror is a project subject to constant failure, and precisely because it fails constantly, it energizes a hyperactive, and increasingly planetary, U.S. security apparatus, one that is forever striving to realize its imaginary potential.

For defense experts, the challenge of the September 2001 attack was not only its spectacular violence but also the shocking display of American vulnerability (see RETORT 2005). The fact that the global nuclear hyperpower could still suffer strategic surprise—and by suicide hijackers armed not with atomic bombs and state-of-the-art bombers, but with simple box cutters and commercial airplanes—challenged the existing rationale for the massive multigenerational investment in defense. The U.S. nuclear complex alone has cost over $6 trillion since 1943, a federal expenditure exceeded only by those for the nonnuclear military and social security (S. Schwartz 1998). Rather than enjoying the end of history with the demise of the Soviet Union and the start of a new, unipolar American century, U.S. security experts were shocked and shamed by the ease with which the attacks were carried out. Indeed, the attacks transformed the most powerful security apparatus in the world into a nervous system in a state of global panic (Taussig 1992). Immediately after the attacks, President Bush ordered that all potential threats made to U.S. interests around the world be routed directly to the White House. This unfiltered "threat matrix" became a daily exercise in expanding the field of imminent danger for decision makers, as unvetted threats piled on top of one another to create a world of seemingly endless and varied forms of danger, with verifiable information mixed in with rumor, error, and hearsay (Mayer 2008, 5).

By embracing an amplifying economy of fear, policy makers became the most terrified of American subjects. When a second wave of attacks hit on September 18, 2001, in the form of anthrax-filled letters aimed at top elected officials and figures in the news media, the result was a spectacularly consequential dislocation: the U.S. Congress moved into improvised facilities while its members deliberated some of the most important security legislation in U.S. history; at the same time, prominent media figures who might otherwise have been reporting on those deliberations instead focused on securing their work spaces from biological agents, while generating a proliferating and hysterical media narrative of imminent attack. In this context, key White House officials came to believe they had been victims of a chemical warfare attack when a "sensitive, specialized sensor, designed to alert anyone in the vicinity that the air they were breathing had been contaminated by potentially lethal radioactive, chemical, or biological agents" sounded (Mayer 2008, 3). This alarm led Vice President Cheney, Secretary of State Colin Powell, and others to believe that they might have been lethally infected by nerve gas. A faulty White House bioweapons sensor played a significant role in the evolution of the War on Terror, creating an affective atmosphere of immediate danger to officials huddled in their most secure facilities. At this moment of vulnerable uncertainty, every worst-case scenario might have been playing out in real time—a cascading set of imagined horrors and potentials. The ever-expanding threat matrix created both escalating responsibilities and new institutional opportunities to pursue specific visions of American power, which in turn allowed a vast range of interests to quickly agree on "terror" as the operative principle for a renewal and expansion of American power in the twenty-first century.

The inability to perfectly predict and preempt low-tech terroristic violence in 2001 enabled a new vision of the future to emerge among security experts, one in which nearly every aspect of American life was potentially at risk from unknown forces, requiring not only a conceptual remaking of the concept of "security" but also a new global apparatus to achieve it. Identifying threat, in all its myriad forms and temporalities, transformed the state security project from a focus on capabilities—that is, an expert effort to identify existing technological capacities of known enemies—to a world of *what ifs*. A key innovation of the counterterrorist state is this commitment to using the imaginary to locate danger. Since 2001 scenarios, speculations, and hypotheticals have been endowed with the power to drive American policy across the spectrum of government agencies, which are now charged not only with administering a day-to-day lived reality but also with responding to threatening probabilities, potentials, and possibilities *before* they become fact.

Consider, for example, how one branch of the Department of Defense (DOD) currently defines both its mission and U.S. national security:

> The Defense Advanced Research Project Agency (DARPA) was established in 1958 to prevent strategic surprise from negatively impacting U.S. national security and create strategic surprise for U.S. adversaries by maintaining the technological superiority of the U.S. military. To fulfill its mission, the Agency relies on diverse performers to apply multi-disciplinary approaches to both advance knowledge through basic research and create innovative technologies that address current practical problems through applied research. DARPA's scientific investigations span the gamut from laboratory efforts to the creation of full-scale technology demonstrations in the fields of biology, medicine, computer science, chemistry, physics, engineering, mathematics, materials sciences, social sciences, neurosciences and more. As the DOD's primary innovation engine, DARPA undertakes projects that are finite in duration but that create lasting revolutionary change. (Defense Advanced Research Project Agency n.d.)

To prevent strategic surprise at home while creating it for others through revolutionary technological change. DARPA announces itself programmatically here as an unending series of Manhattan Projects, using the full spectrum of scientific inquiry for U.S. national advantage. The success or failure of U.S. national security is thus determined by the register of surprise—a highly slippery term whose negation requires a specific ability to read the future, as well as the capacity to anticipate intentions, accidents, and opportunities on a global scale. DARPA's mission statement also assumes nothing less than a permanent war posture and a planetary field of action.

When amplified across the global U.S. national security apparatus, the logics of threat designation and preemption transform counterterrorism into a project of constant affective recruitment and capacity generation. The Congressional Research Service estimates the formal costs of the first decade of the War on Terror at $1.4 trillion (Belasco 2011)—a vast U.S. expenditure that is in addition to the costs of maintaining the largest formal military budget in the world, which has almost doubled since 2001 (Stockholm International Peace Research Institute 2011). The Watson Institute at Brown University estimates that total costs of the first decade of counterterror come closer to $4 trillion (Costsofwar.org 2013). The first decade of the War on Terror has produced multiple fronts: many Manhattan Project–like research programs located across the military sciences (from drones to cyberwar to biosecurity); the creation of a second defense department in the Department of Homeland Security; and a vast new commitment to intelligence gathering, data mining, global digital communications systems, and, above all, new forms of expert threat perception. Dana Priest and William Arkin have shown that since 2001 a new intelligence apparatus has been built that is too big for any single person to understand its reach, level of redundancy, or output. The authors found that over 850,000 people now have security clearances in counterterrorism alone, and generate some 50,000 reports a year. Priest and Arkin were able to identify "1,271 government organizations and 1,931 private companies" working on "programs related to counter-terrorism, homeland security, and intelligence at over 10,000 locations across the United States" (Priest and Arkin 2010, 1; see also 2011). Committed to recognizing vulnerabilities in the global web of U.S. interests and imagining proliferating vectors of foreign and domestic threat, the catastrophic terrorist future is now a competitive domain for security experts at multiple agencies and companies—making disaster calculation the major growth industry of the new century. The worst-case terrorist scenario is produced across this spectrum of expert activity, dictating the terms of the counterterror formation, and maintaining a charged hold on the concept of security as well as the future. The paradox is that despite this commitment to preemption and the fact that the United States outspends almost all other countries combined on its security, Americans in the twenty-first century are caught in multiple forms of crisis (economic, environmental, and political).

Counterterror is a mode of global engagement that attempts to extend U.S. military dominance but one that paradoxically generates new forms of insecurity: by installing technological and bureaucratic capabilities to preempt imagined threats, counterterror simultaneously creates new forms of uncertainty, ripple effects from expert practices that create their own realities and retaliations and threats. Every system has built into its infrastructure a future crisis: the counterterror state is loading new capacities into the future as well as the conditions of possibility for new nightmares not yet realized (Cazdyn 2007; see also Berlant 2007). This is not quite the epistemic murk that Michael Taussig (1987) encounters in the mutual terror of colonial-native encounters in rubber-boom Colombia, as its domain is the future instead of the present. But by allocating conceptual, material, and affective resources to ward off imagined but potentially catastrophic terroristic futures, the counterterror state also creates the conditions for those catastrophic futures to emerge. It does so by generating new arms races; increasing international blowback from war, covert actions, and drone strikes; and by not responding to existing suffering at home and abroad with the same urgency as it addresses real and imagined terrorist acts. A perverse effect of the counterterror system is that failure and disaster, like surprise and shock, can be absorbed as part of its internal circuit, authorizing an expansion of the number of objects to be surveilled and secured, empowering expert speculation about the various forms of danger that might emerge from an ever-shifting landscape of information and potential threat. Thus, for defense experts most of all, an affective recruitment to constant crisis is one of the chief effects of the counterterror formation—which is self-colonizing, opening a potentially endless conceptual space of worry and projected dangers.

Counterterror thus approaches the American future as both already ruined—a boundless source of violence—and as perfectible—a conceptual universe requiring radical social and technological engineering and intervention. One powerful effect of these administrative logics is that demilitarizing becomes increasingly impossible to imagine, as potential dangers pile up for experts, while citizens *feel* increasingly insecure with the diversion of funds and psychic energies from everyday welfare to anticipatory defense (see Gusterson and Besteman 2009). Counterterror, then, constitutes itself as an endless horizon, providing a self-justifying rationale for radical expenditures and action—offering a potentially eternal project for the security state. For when can the future ever be perfectly secured? When can terror ever be eradicated from both thought and action? Threat, as an imaginary engagement with the future, is limitless, offering an ever-expanding field of potentials, possibilities, and fears for counterterror governance.

Gaming Death

Perceptions of the future are affectively laden, as well as tied to expert judgment and information; they are based on feelings and intensities that can be nonrational but that link people together through threat-based projection. Put differently, one can be afraid only of that which one knows to fear. Fear requires a kind of familiarity with danger that the future does not allow us full access to. In the realm of esoteric military technologies—weapons of mass destruction, for example—the general public has no expert knowledge to draw on and must instead be educated to think and *feel* a particular way about technological capacities and worst-case outcomes. Rehearsing the end of the nation-state at the level of imagination has consequently been a core American project since the U.S. atomic bombings of Hiroshima and Nagasaki, with each generation embracing its own concept of nation-ending apocalyptic danger, consolidated most powerfully in the image of the mushroom cloud.

The innovation of the War on Terror is that it formally rejects *deterrence*, with its focus on global stability, as an objective in favor of *preemption*—an unending manipulation of the future for national advantage. The counter-terror state is devoted to locating and/or conjuring up images of dangers from an unrealized future and then combating each of those alternate fu-tures *as if* they were material and imminent threats. In this way, imagined futures and the affects they produce have become institutionalized as na-tional security policy, creating a form of expert judgment that is at war with its own apocalyptic imaginary before it meets the real world, creating a massively productive form of militarization that is easily delinked from evidence, facts, or the observable in the name of confronting and eliminat-ing potentially cataclysmic future danger. How did this kind of governance come to be?

The origins of the preemptive, counterterror state reside in the logics and lessons of the Cold War. The nuclear arms race, with its minute-to-minute calculation of threat and advantage and the always ready-to-launch nuclear war machine, was an effort to stabilize the present by loading nuclear de-struction into the everyday and continually displacing it by a few minutes into the future. Mutual assured destruction promised that any state that started a nuclear war would only minutes later be destroyed by it, an unpre-cedented compression of time, space, and destructive capability in the name of global defense. To make this system work, U.S. defense experts not only built nuclear weapons and delivery systems that could function in any en-vironment, launch within minutes, and operate on a planetary scale, but they also gamed, modeled, and fantasized future war scenarios incessantly (see Ghamari-Tabrizi 2005). Locating security in intercontinental missile systems that were never fully tested and trusting a vast web of machines, institutions, and people to respond perfectly in the first moments of global crisis, the nuclear war machine was designed first and foremost to produce fear of the near future in adversaries and to harness that fear to produce a stable bipolar world. The Cold War system was therefore saturated with affective and imaginary recruitments as well as anticipatory logics. Deter-rence, however, restrained both sides of the conflict, putting a break on both U.S. and Soviet desires and aggressions. The Cold War focus on nu-clear weapons and delivery systems also set material parameters for the speculative expert imaginary; it focused experts' attention on the numbers and types of Soviet weapons, their deployments and machinic capabilities (speed and force), as well as on the psychologies of nuclear command and control. These technoscientific forms were never free of political calculation but had a material basis: Donald MacKenzie (1990) has shown how the accuracy of intercontinental missiles was determined in the United States not by exacting experimental proof but rather by a political consensus among all the interested scientific, military, and industrial parties (adding an unacknowledged uncertainty to nuclear targeting going forward). Similarly, Lynn Eden (2004) has shown how the urban consequences of fire from nuclear explosions fell out of formal nuclear war planning in the 1960s, enabling the development of nuclear war and civil defense concepts that vastly underestimated the material effects of each detonation and allowed far greater numbers of U.S. weapons to be deployed globally (see also Gusterson 2008).

In other words, although nuclear war remained at the conceptual stage after the bombings of Hiroshima and Nagasaki in 1945, it was fought incessantly at the level of the imagination, with an unending state-based commitment to trying to model, game, intuit, and assess the likely actions of all parties in a nuclear conflict. By contrast the future imagined by counterterror officials today is an endless spectrum of threat, with a proliferating set of objects, vectors, scales, and possibilities—a spectrum that is literally not bounded by time, space, technology, or the rules of evidence. By defining terror as constantly emergent, the counterterror state also assumes an open-ended futurity that cannot be deterred by external forces. As Secretary of Defense Rumsfeld (2002) famously put it in a press conference about the (ultimately fictional) threat of Iraqi weapons of mass destruction before the U.S. invasion, the counterterror state needs to make not-yet-visible dangers its central concern because:

Reports that say that something hasn't happened are always interesting to me, because as we know, there are known knowns; there are things we know we know. We also know there are known unknowns; that is to say we know there are some things we do not know. But there are also unknown unknowns—the ones we don't know we don't know. And if one looks throughout the history of our country and other free countries, it is the latter category that tend to be the difficult ones. And so people who have the omniscience that they can say with high certainty that something has not happened or is not being tried, have capabilities . . . they can do things I can't do.

"Unknown unknowns" can now be the basis for war. Here, Rumsfeld transforms a catastrophic future at the level of the speculative imaginary into an urgent problem of counterterror. Security is thus constituted as both a necessity (to defend against catastrophic shock) and as an unachievable goal (as the future is an inexhaustible source of threat), a perverse logic that the counterterror state uses to drive increasing calls for resources, technical capacities, and agency. In the first decade of counterterror, a strategic mobilization by security officials of the unknown, not yet emergent, or invisible danger has powerfully overturned long-standing American democratic values about the rule of law, the treatment of captives, the surveillance of citizens, and the necessity of covert actions. It has transformed intuitions and desires into policy, invalidated long-standing forms of expert judgment that worked to constrain official fears by attending to material reality, and—as a result—has enabled deadly actions in the absence of facts. Rumsfeld's vision—precisely because it transforms the unknown into a space of terror requiring immediate action—simultaneously validates and eliminates the possibility of factual evidence, creating both a rationale for unrestrained American power and a security apparatus of constantly expanding capacities and infrastructures. This logic renders security itself obsolete, replacing it with a constant conceptual agitation and physical mobilization. Threat (as pure potential) is used to enable a radically active and ever emerging counterterror state, allowing action to be favored over restraint, possibilities over capabilities, hypotheticals over knowledge.

Excitable Subjects

The uniquely destructive capabilities of nuclear weapons and the speed of their potential delivery constituted a new kind of technologically mediated existential threat after 1945, one that made feelings (fear, terror, shock, aggression, futility, revenge) a new national project. I argue in this book that the first and most powerful effect of the nuclear revolution in the United States was the constitution of a new affective politics, one that informs the evolution of the national security state to this day and that is key to the formation of the counterterror state. Put differently, in the age of thermonuclear war, the security state became a committed affect theorist, investing substantial multidisciplinary resources in efforts to understand public morale, contagious affects (panic, fear, terror), resilience, resolve, and the long-term effects of stress. The nuclear balance of terror was always an all-encompassing formation, creating a new executive (a president preauthorized to start a nuclear war any second of the day) and a new citizen-subject (recruited to reorganize everyday life around the minute-to-minute reality of nuclear danger). Military science funded extensive research on affects, feelings, and emotions with the goal of both psychologically strengthening and militarizing American society, using nuclear fear to calibrate officials and citizens alike through a new image of collective death.

National security affect has thus become a new kind of infrastructure—a "structure of feeling," to use Raymond Williams's felicitous phrase (1978, 132)—that is historically produced, shared, and officially constituted as a necessary background condition of everyday life (see Stoler 2009). It is based on fears that are officially sanctioned and promoted as a means of coordinating citizens as members of a national security state. It can be a specific and negative form of what Kathleen Stewart calls "ordinary affects" (2007), in the sense that certain kinds of fear are now coded into social life as potentials that can be triggered by small events—fear of the unattended suitcase in the airport, for example—or directly recruited by official statements, such as terrorist alert warnings. National security affect also relies on a specific political aesthetic, one that rehearses certain forms and images to produce what Jacques Rancière calls a "sensuous shock" that limits thought as much as expands it (2009, 6; see also M. Hansen 2004). The goal of a national security system is to produce a citizen-subject who responds to officially designated signs of danger automatically, instinctively activating logics and actions learned over time through drills and media indoctrination. An individual's response to this kind of emotional call (in either the affirmative or negative) reveals his or her membership in a national community. Indeed, the production of a fearful and docile public in the nuclear age has been historically matched by the rise of vibrant activist movements (across the antinuclear, peace, justice, and environmental spectrum), counterpublics that mirror the intensities of officially sanctioned nuclear terror in pursuit of different collective futures.[6]

An affective atmosphere of everyday anxiety (Anderson 2009), grounded in an understanding that accidents, disasters, and attacks can happen at any moment of the day, is transformed into individualized emotion by specific events, becoming a personalized and deeply felt experience. As Stewart puts it, "what affects us—the sentience of a situation—is also a dwelling, a worlding born from an atmospheric attunement" (2011, 449). I argue in this book that national security affect has a specific form in the United States, one that is tied to a deep structural investment in the atomic bomb and that has been recalibrated and expanded since 2001 to address a new concept of terror (consolidated in the logic of the WMD). American citizens have been taught through official and mass-media campaigns to attune themselves to the possibility of terroristic violence as an unlimited daily potential. This new concept of terror maintains the minute-to-minute threat made familiar by decades of Cold War nuclear culture, but it is different in that it is an open-ended concept, one that links hugely diverse kinds of threats (nuclear, chemical, and biological weapons to be sure, but also attacks on the public image of the United States, computer hacking, infectious disease, and disruptions to daily life, to name but a few) and treats them all as equally imminent, equally catastrophic.

Counterterror today requires a continual expansion of the security state, reaching a limit only when its key objects attain planetary scale (exhausting space) or when federal monies run out (exhausting resources). That is, counterterror sets no conceptual or territorial limit to defense, scaling its problems up to the ultimate spatial unit—the earth—while offering an unlimited call for resources to secure life from the species to the population to the individual to the microbe. In this manner, counterterror produces a highly mobile sovereignty, one that uses the potential of catastrophic future events as a means of overcoming legal, ethical, and political barriers in the here and now and that is endlessly searching for new objects of concern. However, this commitment to total security—and the constant failure to achieve it—creates an unending bureaucratic circuit where shock requires ever more militarization and normalization in the name of warding off future shock.

A war on shock, like a war on terror, locates national security within the human nervous system itself, constituting a peculiarly embodied psychopolitics (Orr 2006) that fuses an energetic apocalyptic imagination with both an immediate and deep future. Conceptually, a national security project of this kind would seem to offer only two means of achieving stability: first, by changing the nature of the individual at the level of emotions, senses, and psychology so that he or she experiences threat in a different manner—a project of normalization through militarization; and second, by changing the global environment in the hope of eliminating the possibility of danger. The Cold War state and the counterterror state in specific formulations have attempted to do both: endeavoring to produce a new citizen who is tuned to the specific threats of the age and psychologically capable of supporting permanent war, while simultaneously mobilizing U.S. economic and military power to change the international system, in the hope of eradicating threat on a planetary basis. However, the impossibility of this dual effort to produce a completely compliant citizen incapable of resisting the national security state or to eliminate danger on a planetary scale creates an endless feedback loop of shock, normalization, and militarization. We could say that this recursive system is what constitutes the United States as a global hyperpower, but an increasingly fragile one—as experts see danger coming in all physical dimensions (land, sea, air, space, and cyberspace) as well as in all temporal conditions (past, present, and future). This requires a new kind of expert psychopolitics that is not grounded in the effort to establish facts but rather is committed to generating speculative futures (imagined dangers of cataclysmic scale) that it will then need to counter. Security thus becomes a highly conceptual enterprise, one that moves past statistical, fact-based, or capability-based assessments of risk (see Collier 2008; De Goede 2008). Threat assessment—with all its imaginative, affective recruitments—becomes the chief domain of counterterror.

The inability to perfectly predict and counter threat creates in the American security system the opportunity to constitute nearly every domain and object of everyday life as a potential vector of attack, creating a national security project that performs as a nearly perfect paranoid system, but one with planetary reach. Peter Sloterdijk has noted that a nervous condition is an attribute of globalization, which he sees as:

> the establishment of the system of synchronous stress on a global scale. This has progressed to such an extent that those who do not make themselves continuously available for synchronous stress seem asocial. Excitability is now the foremost duty of all citizens. This is why we no longer need military service. What is required is the general theme of duty, that is to say, a readiness to play your role as a conductor of excitation for collective, opportunist psychoses. (Sloterdijk and Henrichs 2001, 82)

Excitability is now the foremost duty of all citizens. The circulation of affect, the ability to be coordinated as subjects through felt intensities rather than reason at a mass level, is a core aspect of modern life (see Mazzarella 2010; Clough 2007, 19; Orr 2006). The atomic bomb is one key origin of this kind of governance (see Lutz 1997, 247), a WMD that greatly expanded American power but that also created a world of constant existential danger, one that was quite formally managed for generations by suturing collective life to an imminent destruction located in each minute of the day. A security culture of existential threat was embedded quite thoroughly in American society and U.S. security institutions by decades of Cold War, allowing national politics of every kind (domestic, international, activist) to be positioned as a matter of collective life or collective death. From this perspective, *terror* is a familiar mode of governance in the United States, one that was merely reconstituted in 2001 with a new set of objects, ambitions, and concerns.

Living Code Orange

National security affect is productive whether it is reinforced by material or verifiable dangers or simply exists as a background register in everyday life. It is an atmosphere (Stewart 2011; Anderson 2009) that can become a deeply felt emotional structure when directed by mass media or official declarations into a collective event. It can start from the top down, creating lines of intensity between the national leadership and the citizenry, or short circuits in the democratic process by raising the stakes of critiquing official action. Citizens can also opt out of the national security public sphere all together by nonattention or generate specific counterpublics to it. Official White House statements, however, draw on a classified universe of information that citizens know exists but cannot interrogate, making counterterror often a one-way communication. After the 2001 attacks, the classified threat matrix and the mass media combined to generate a national nervous system, one that promoted a growing sense of vulnerability in the United States and transformed the basic structures of everyday life into vectors of possible terrorist attack. Mass transit systems, nuclear power plants, electrical grids, the banking system, food, air, and water all became objects of mounting hysteria as possible targets of the next strike. White House officials incited this affective environment as part of a larger political strategy that would culminate in the invasion of Iraq in 2003 to rid that country of fictitious weapons of mass destruction. Nonetheless, it is important to recognize that when the national security leadership appears scared and tells citizens to be scared, there are few options open to the public.

The ability to shape public fears—to give image and form to threat—is one of the key powers of the counterterror state today, and one of its primary domains of sovereignty. When security state officials announce an imminent, existential threat based on classified material who, or what, can push back on that statement in real time? In such moments, citizens are left with only two options: acquiescence or denial. This on-off structure of engagement inevitably works to enable security state actions, as it functions to disable political resistance and countermobilizations (easily dismissed by officials as uninformed about the true nature of risk in the world and working on vastly slower time scales). National security affect, however, also requires cultural work to maintain; its intensities decay over time, and the rehearsal of specific forms of threat can become normalized, a background condition of everyday life. Counterterror attempts to turn feelings—the ability to be called to an image of danger and be excited by it—into a national infrastructure, a set of ideas, images, and affective intensities that can be instrumentalized.

From this perspective, the Homeland Security Advisory System announced by presidential directive on March 11, 2002, was a remarkably straightforward effort to calibrate public fear at the national level—a technology designed to synchronize citizens via terror (see figure 1.2). The color-coded system attempts to fine-tune institutions, officials, and citizens through an escalating scale of terroristic danger, moving from green (low), to blue (guarded), to yellow (elevated), to orange (high), and finally to red (severe). Backed by official promises that the warning level would be elevated only in response to specific credible information (always classified), the system nonetheless raises immediate questions: Why five levels? And how is a "guarded" threat to be technically distinguished from an "elevated" one? The goal of this system is explicitly to provide a matrix or grammar for threatening potentials, installing terror as a permanent condition of American life. Enabling affective escalation is its chief project. Code Green, the first threat level, for example, marks a "low risk of terrorist attacks," not the absence of terror, and from 2002 to 2011, the national threat level was never less than Code Yellow (elevated). Although the threat level had immediate implications for transportation security, police, and first responders, announcements of shifts in the system were rarely accompanied by discussions of actual sources of information, as officials sought to protect their sources and methods of intelligence during wartime.

On December 22, 2003, for example, the new Homeland Security Secretary Tom Ridge raised the national alert level to orange. In his announcement of the change, he stated that "information indicates that extremists abroad are anticipating near-term attacks that they believe will rival, or exceed, the attacks in New York and at the Pentagon," but he then noted that U.S. officials had no specific information on where or when an attack might be planned and advised citizens to simply "continue with your holiday plans" (quoted in Mintz 2003). Thus, a near-term catastrophe is officially announced, one that could come from anywhere on the planet, take any form, and involve any region of the United States or its vast range of global interests. This is an official appeal to participate in being generally terrorized, followed by an appeal not to alter one's life in any significant manner. It is an invitation to pure excitement. Ridge activates here a terror-

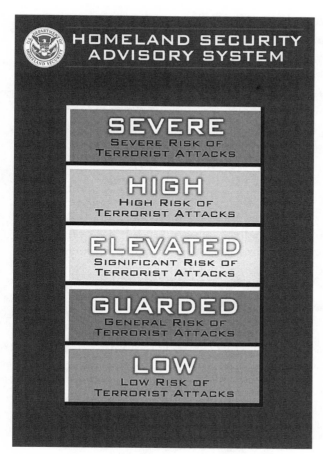

FIGURE I.2. Homeland Security Advisory System chart, U.S. Department of Homeland Security.

normalization circuit that the security state has relied on since the invention of the atomic bomb to mobilize citizens by evoking an inchoate existential danger as normative everyday reality. A pure technology of fear generation, the alert attempted to distill, purify, and amplify menace through all instruments of state power. The color-coded warning system was a central tool in building the national state of anxiety leading up to the U.S. invasion of Iraq on March 17, 2003, when the threat level repeatedly jumped back and forth between Yellow and Orange in anticipation of the U.S. attack. An affective atmosphere was cultivated via alerts and mass-media speculations in which any kind or scale of violence was deemed possible, allowing rumor and fantasy to amplify pressure on the public to support, or at least not resist, counterterror activities. The alert system addressed citizens not as thinking subjects capable of evaluating information but as raw nerve endings, part of a national nervous system that could be excited to enable a U.S. invasion of Iraq (see Prados 2004). The threat advisory system became a central part of a highly sophisticated mass-media campaign by White House and Pentagon officials to implicitly link the 2001 attacks to Saddam Hussein and thus justify the U.S. invasion as a legitimate form of defense and national revenge. The failures to find weapons of mass destruction in Iraq or a link between Saddam Hussein's government and Al Qaeda are irrelevant to the affective politics promoted here, because counterterror can use feelings alone as a justification for radical action.[7]

The logics of preemption rely on affect to suture a potential future to a current reality at the level of feeling. Commenting on President Bush's postwar argument that invading Iraq was the only course of action, despite the ultimate failure of each of the rationales used to justify the invasion, Brian Massumi suggests that the anticipatory logics of preemption are locked in a perfect affective and temporal spiral:

> The invasion was right because *in the past there was a future threat.* You cannot erase a "fact" like that. Just because the menace potential never became a clear and present danger doesn't mean that it wasn't there, all the more real for being nonexistent. The superlative futurity of unactualized threat feeds forward from the past, in a chicken run to the future past every intervening present. The threat *will have* been real for all eternity. It will have been real because it was *felt* to be real. Whether the danger was existent or not, the menace was felt in the form of fear. What is not actually real can be felt into being. Threat does have an actual mode of existence: fear, as foreshadowing. Threat has an impending reality in the present. This actual reality is affect. Fear is the anticipatory reality in the present of a threatening future. It is the felt reality of the nonexistent, loomingly present as the *affective fact of the matter.* (2010, 53–54)

What is not actually real can be felt into being. In other words, the feeling of existential threat is enough to justify any response to it. As the human organism is designed for self-preservation in the face of danger, one cannot but respond to an overpowering threat (even an imaginary one). By locating the rationale for radical action not in material facts but in feelings, this type of thinking installs a permanent alibi for official actions that are otherwise unjustifiable.[8] It also constitutes the fullest form of a war on, and through, emotion, since anticipatory defense constitutes the potential of feeling terror as the enabling reality, rather than expert judgments of technologically verifiable, material dangers.

For it to be possible to declare war on terror, terror must be made manifest as a structure one can feel with some regularity; for an emotion to be an enemy, it must be made ever present. For the first decade of the War on Terror, Americans lived mostly at Code Orange—the level denoting a *high risk* of terrorist attacks.[9] This elevated call to a militarized alertness eventually became normalized for many citizens, appearing primarily in the endlessly repeated security announcements of terroristic danger in U.S. airports, a form of background noise that nonetheless amplified the policing powers of a wide range of security personnel including the Transportation Security Administration (founded in 2001), the Department of Homeland Security (founded in 2002), the FBI, and local police. But normalizing specific kinds of potentials to enable counterformations has always been a primary goal of the national security state. The federal government first considered a color-coded warning system at the start of the Cold War. It was initially proposed in *Report of the Project East River* (Associated Universities 1952), a monumental study of how to redesign American domestic life (cities, suburbs, industries, emotions) in light of the nuclear revolution (see Galison 2001; Oakes 1994). Intended to alert Americans to potential Soviet nuclear attack, the proposed warning system was a specific early effort to devise a means of calibrating and mobilizing citizens through nuclear fear. A decade before the Soviet Union actually had a nuclear arsenal capable of producing an existential threat to the United States, U.S. policy makers launched a civil defense campaign with three goals: teaching citizens to fear the bomb as an imminent danger, giving them enough information about nuclear war and emergency measures to enable them to act at a time of crisis, and teaching them emotional self-discipline in the attempt to modulate the difference between fear (constituted as a productive state) and terror (imagined as an unsustainable, paralyzing condition).[10] The rehearsal of national destruction through a national media culture was crucial in cultivating the affective atmosphere of nuclear crisis a decade before the technological infrastructure to fight a global nuclear war actually existed (see Fenrich 1997; Oakes 1994). Nuclear fear has been a highly effective organizing principle of American life for generations. It has produced not only a deeply militarized society but also many forms of resistance among citizens, who have felt not only fear and terror but also anger and the need for collective mobilization on a wide range

25

of issues involving war, civil rights, and the environment. Indeed, locating oneself along the spectrum of fear to terror has been the basis for an emerging social contract in the nuclear age—one that today seeks less to mobilize citizens through calibrated fear than to immobilize them by confronting them with multiplying terrors.

By the 1960s, the technological infrastructure of the Cold War constituted a very real existential threat to humanity, one that could easily have rendered much of the planet lifeless in only a few hours of nuclear warfare. Stateless terrorist groups today can cause much damage, mayhem, and death, but they are not an existential threat in the same way that thousands of always-on-alert nuclear weapons loaded into intercontinental missiles, bombers, and submarines are, and of course were, during the height of the Cold War. Thus, although American understandings of existential threat are informed by decades of Cold War, providing a set of images and logics well honed by decades of nuclear politics, there is a significant difference in the kinds of danger informing counterterror today. The War on Terror—precisely because the threats are potentially hyperviolent but not existential—mobilizes many of the techniques of emotional management used in the Cold War system but redirects them to new ends. Specifically, the counterterror state proliferates danger rather than regulating it, rehearsing vulnerability in public to amplify threat rather than establishing a psychosocial space of sustainability located somewhere between fear and terror—as the Cold War system attempted to do. The War on Terror is ultimately an inflationary regime, one that attempts to exhaust the field of danger by recruiting new objects and possibilities and that engages the category of threat as existential as a matter of principle. Counterterror transforms governance from the improving of populations into the administration of negative potentials. Thus, the counterterror state grounds many of its core programs, desires, and concepts in Cold War notions of nuclear threat and emotional management—and specifically attempts to merge the existential threat of the atomic bomb with many new objects in the ever expanding category of the WMD—but it is also a new state formation, one that is producing a distinct national security culture in the twenty-first century.

Infrastructures, Critical and Otherwise

The Theater of Operations is an examination of the affective and imaginative logics of the national security state. It focuses particularly on how the institutions (cultural, material, and expert) supporting the Cold War balance of terror were transformed after 2001 into a global War on Terror, a seemingly nonsensical attempt to eliminate a primal emotional state. In this regard, there is a paradox at the center of U.S. national security: despite the vast commitment to security and proliferating objects of official concern, the counterterror state does not recognize the terrorizing effects of collapsing national infrastructure (roads, highways, levies, and dams), the devastating effects of unregulated capitalism (on jobs, housing, and pensions), or the destabilizing effects of toxic industrial substances on the environment (from polluted air and water to climate change). Thus, a foundational logic of the security state is that it recognizes those threats that allow it to produce a militarized counterformation and ignores everyday forms of violence that require other, nonmilitarized forms of governance. The security apparatus, in other words, determines what constitutes *terror* to enable its own field of action. The increasing vulnerability of citizens to environmental disasters, health crises, and economic volatility does not engage the counterterror apparatus, although these crises can feed its affective conditions of possibility.[11] Indeed, national security culture tries to affectively redirect the fears and injuries produced by collapsing infrastructure, unregulated finance, and toxic environments by giving the ultimate danger a name. In the twenty-first century, the "terrorist with a WMD," to use President Bush's favorite formulation, is the perfect image of an unlocatable menace with apocalyptic potential, one that requires an unrestrained national security state to combat it in perpetuity. The slow violence of capitalism, industrial toxicity, or aging infrastructure is no match for this image of threat, which is at once everywhere and nowhere, invisible until it is suddenly catastrophic. As we will see, the *terrorist* as well as the WMD are highly elastic categories, subject to constant modification. Together, they offer perhaps the purest form of threat projection imaginable, one devoid of specific content (and thus able to be filled with nearly anything) but nonetheless capable of being felt as existentially consequential. Counterterror offers an almost pure emotional appeal, one that seeks to engage a larger affective culture produced by generations of nuclear crises but that does so by amplifying it from a specific formulation, a concern with the atomic bomb, to one that views technology itself as a source of fear (including weapons, planes, computers, viruses, and box cutters). This formulation creates a terroristic menace of nearly infinite scope and capabilities, enabling a counterformation that seeks to be equally total, one that obviates borders and assumes a planetary field of action in the name of defense (see Siegel 1998).

This book unpacks the evolution of counterterror in American security culture but also underscores how the constitution of a pure threat (the "terrorist with a WMD") works to leave unaddressed the increasing vulnerability and insecurity of everyday American life at the level of health, welfare, economy, and environment. The War on Terror is both a massive drain on the U.S. economy and a huge distortion in American politics. For example, in addition to the $4 trillion already spent on the War on Terror, the United States operates as many as a thousand U.S. military bases around the world—a material footprint requiring constant maintenance, protection, and support.[12] Concurrently, the nonmilitary infrastructure of the United States—its roads, bridges, levies, dams, schools, airports, sewers, and water systems—achieve mostly D grades from the American Society of Civil Engineers (2012) in its annual report card on structural integrity and public safety. Thus, when the latest homeland security campaign quite rightly asks citizens "If You See Something, Say Something" (see figure 1.3) as a form of collective security, it also limits the things citizens can report, rejecting a wide variety of objects that are also quite capable of producing fear and terror: homelessness and poverty, decaying infrastructure and toxic environments, and extreme weather, to name but a few. Social structures of abandonment (Povinelli 2011), including the physical wearing out of a population (Berlant 2007) or rendering a class of citizens expendable via slow violence (Nixon 2011), also reveal a submerged "state of emergency" that the security state's concept of sovereignty does not address (see also Weston 2012; Gusterson and Besteman 2009). How the national security state acknowledges, calculates, engages—and/or ignores—danger is, then, a complicated matter, one that each chapter of this book attempts to address from a specific vantage point.

Infrastructure is a key concept in this book, referring here not only to the material structures that support social life in complex urban societies but also to the imaginative and affective contexts that enable fear to be nationalized on specific terms. Infrastructures (material, imaginative, and affective) reveal the priorities of a given historical moment. The Cold War state built not only atomic bombs but also a national highway system, not only a military-industrial complex but also a welfare state. The War on Terror has been enormously productive in the sense of building a new global war machine, a second defense department (the Department of Homeland Security), new biosecurity and cybersecurity programs, and so on, but it has not considered crises in the domains of health, finance, and the environment to be a security matter. Nonetheless, infrastructure is a

NTAS: National Terrorism Advisory System
www.DHS.gov/alerts

Report suspicious activity
to local law enforcement
or call 9-1-1 in case
of emergency.

if you
SEE
something
SAY
something™

If You See Something Say Something™ used with permission of the NY Metropolitan Transportation Authority.

NTAS
National Terrorism Advisory System
www.DHS.gov/alerts

FIGURE I.3. National Terrorism Advisory System poster, U.S. Department of Homeland Security.

central concern of the counterterror state. In its 2003 *National Strategy for the Physical Protection of Critical Infrastructures and Key Assets*, the Bush administration committed itself to preventing terrorist actions that would:

1) Impair the federal government's ability to perform essential national and homeland security missions and ensure the general public's health and safety;
2) Undermine state and local government capacities to maintain order and to deliver minimum essential public services;
3) Damage the private sector's capability to ensure the orderly functioning of the economy and the delivery of essential services; and

4) Undermine the public morale and confidence in our national economy and political institutions. (U.S. Department of Homeland Security 2003, 11)

This list defines a break in the seamless quality of everyday life, across services and perceptions, as the domain of terror. It also implicitly promises to deliver a world without such events, projecting a vision of an everyday life unbroken by surprise, let alone trauma.

Counterterror constitutes a significant shift from the kind of state security that Michel Foucault (2003) theorized as the basis for the modern era. The new focus on creating a resilient critical infrastructure immune to disruption circumvents an older form of the security state that was devoted to statistical reasoning, population governance, and that sought to define and improve the citizenry across a wide spectrum of interests (health, wealth, life span, education, and so on) while protecting the territorial borders of the state from external danger.

Under the current logics of counterterror, it is now a national infrastructure (made up of experts, technologies, capabilities) that is essential to the security state, not its citizenry. But because acts of terrorism are so rare in the United States, not even registering statistically in relation to other forms of death and injury, they must be conjured to be countered. Simulated disaster (hypotheticals, war games, scenarios) becomes a ritual performance that both makes counterterror governance visible and establishes its technical limits (see Adey and Anderson 2012; Beck 2007, 11; Schoch-Spana 2004). Andrew Lakoff has productively named this "vital system security" (2008a, 37), a new modality of governance that focuses on the continuity of systems over populations. The goal of vital systems security is a resilient society that can preempt or absorb any kind of trauma and maintain its basic functions. Vital systems security promises to secure the infrastructure of society by attending to everyday forms of vulnerability, but its primary effect is to manage both experts and the national community at the level of affect and emotion. As Ulrich Beck notes, "nobody can appeal solely to an external reality in dealing with risks," for "the risks which we believe we recognize and which fill us with fear are mirror images of our selves, of our cultural perceptions" (2007, 13; see also Furedi 2006).

Critical infrastructures and the related commitment to *disaster preparedness*, however, are ever emerging projects evoking no consensus definitions (see Falkenrath 2001). The security of the citizen is replaced here by a focus on the survival and operability of the institutions that make up society, which immediately raises the issue of how to coordinate the vast range of public, private, and military structures, networks, and institutions that exist in twenty-first-century America. Consider, for example, the outline of critical infrastructures recognized by the 2003 *National Strategy* (see figure 1.4). This list is a recipe not for security but for a full-spectrum paranoia, since nearly 2 million farms, 137 million postal delivery sites, 590,000 highway bridges, 2 billion miles of cable, as well as 5,000 airports, 5,800 hospitals, 80,000 dams, 104 nuclear power plants, 460 skyscrapers, and 5,800 historic landmarks all need to be protected every second of every day from every imaginable vector of attack. What is striking about this list is its diversity and range: critical infrastructure involves the railroads as well as the tracks they run on, not simply nuclear power plants but the electrical grid itself, not only emergency services but the "250,000 firms in 215 distinct industries" that make up the "Defense Industrial Base." A vast spectrum of risk here becomes a singular form, since terrorism directed against any object in society is constituted as equally meaningful, equally terroristic, equally catastrophic. This is nothing less than a domestic version of the global threat matrix—a field of proliferating potentials, each of which requires programmatic scrutiny by the counterterror state, creating in practice an endless opportunity for threat selection, amplification, and exploitation.

This concept of critical infrastructure flattens risk across radically different objects and domains from emergency rooms and sewage treatment facilities to objects of national pride (like parks and urban monuments) and symbols of American power (such as the World Trade Center and the Pentagon). Not many of these items constitute the ground for an existential risk, yet the critical infrastructure concept as a counterterrorism provision positions them *as such*, which allows for radical new forms of policing at home and new militarism abroad. For example, the electrical grid is increasingly positioned not as a public utility but as a critical infrastructure to be protected by official secrecy (National Research Council 2012), and simply taking tourist photographs of historical landmarks—such as the Hoover Dam, the Statue of Liberty, or the Pentagon—can now be interpreted as a form of potential terror requiring preemptory police action (Simon 2012). Thus a new kind of security state is emerging in the twenty-first century, one that treats all endangered objects equally at the level of expert analysis and that considers a potential disruption of the system (at the level of institutions, thoughts, or emotions) as equivalent to its destruction.

The opposite of danger in this concept of security would be nothing less than a *world without events*—an elimination of accidents, malfunctions,

THE PROTECTION CHALLENGE

Agriculture and Food	1,912,000 farms; 87,000 food-processing plants
Water	1,800 federal reservoirs; 1,600 municipal waste water facilities
Public Health	5,800 registered hospitals
Emergency Services	87,000 U.S. localities
Defense Industrial Base	250,000 firms in 215 distinct industries
Telecommunications	2 billion miles of cable
Energy	
Electricity	2,800 power plants
Oil and Natural Gas	300,000 producing sites
Transportation	
Aviation	5,000 public airports
Passenger Rail and Railroads	120,000 miles of major railroads
Highways, Trucking, and Busing	590,000 highway bridges
Pipelines	2 million miles of pipelines
Maritime	300 inland/costal ports
Mass Transit	500 major urban public transit operators
Banking and Finance	26,600 FDIC insured institutions
Chemical Industry and Hazardous Materials	66,000 chemical plants
Postal and Shipping	137 million delivery sites
Key Assets	
National Monuments and Icons	5,800 historic buildings
Nuclear Power Plants	104 commercial nuclear power plants
Dams	80,000 dams
Government Facilities	3,000 government owned/operated facilities
Commercial Assets	460 skyscrapers

*These are approximate figures.

FIGURE I.4. U.S. critical infrastructure "Protection Challenge" list, U.S. Department of Homeland Security.

acts of terror, or surprise. Rather than balancing a national security apparatus with a welfare state, as in the Cold War model of state and nation building (matching images of nuclear destruction with the promise of a constantly improving society), the counterterror state folds governance into the rubric of existential risk and asks experts and citizens alike to remain perpetually agitated and tuned toward an announced spectrum of potential violence. It performs *care* by proliferating discourses about vulnerability rather than building better infrastructure, which in many domains is today much more likely to collapse from aging and structural fatigue than from a terrorist attack. In this way, the critical infrastructure concept creates a mode of governance that works primarily at the affective level to create a universe of endangered objects and institutions, and to focus administrators on the problem of managing the complexity and vulnerability of those institutions during a terrorist attack, instead of simply rebuilding and securing aging American infrastructures.

Infrastructure is the enabling architecture of a system (Larkin 2013; Star 1999). As such, it is also a lived structure, offering the naturalized conditions of possibility for everyday life. Historically, however, the United States builds, rebuilds, and extends its security apparatus during times of national panic—mobilizing a perceived crisis to install new technological capacities and expand administrative commitments. One key innovation of the War on Terror has been to transform U.S. domestic defense into a planetary project, with agencies from the FBI and the Drug Enforcement Agency to the Centers for Disease Control and Prevention reconstituted as counterterrorism agencies with a global mandate. Consider, for example, the FBI's internal assessment of its changing mission in the first decade of counterterror (Federal Bureau of Investigation 2011), revealing a new "global footprint" consisting of 56 field offices, 381 resident agencies in the United States, and 76 international offices (see figure 1.5). Note how the strategic vision of the FBI as a counterterror agency has become *threat driven* and not crime driven, *global* instead of domestic, *networked* rather than insular, and now focused primarily on *national security* and only secondarily on law enforcement. Four days after the 2001 suicide-hijacker attacks, the director of the CIA, George Tenet, presented to President Bush a "Worldwide Attack Matrix" that described "covert operations in 80 countries either underway or that he was now recommending" consisting of everything from "routine propaganda to lethal covert action in preparation for military attack" (Woodward 2003, 68). This worldwide attack matrix may have been the first act of the U.S. war on Al Qaeda, but it was merely the start of a

FBI Strategic Shifts

We have defined our strategic vision through the Strategy Management System. Our vision takes shape in the FBI's Strategic Shifts, which describe how the FBI will transform to meet the challenges of the 21st century.

Law Enforcement	Roles	National Security and Law Enforcement
Case-Driven	Focus	Threat-Driven
Quantitative Evaluation (Case-Based)	Measurement of Success	Qualitative Evaluation (Threat-Based)
"Restrict; and Share What You Must"	Information Sharing	"Share; and Restrict What You Must"
Contributor	Intelligence Community	Full Partner
Domestic	Scope	Global
Tactical	Senior Management	Strategic
Ineffective Communications	Internal Communications	Effective, Relevant, and Timely Communications
Operational Silos	Organization	Integrated Team Approach
Inefficient and Ineffective HR Processes	Human Capital	Highly Efficient and Effective HR Processes
Agent/Support	Culture	Team of Professionals
Antiquated and Disparate IT Systems	Information Technology	Mission-Enhancing Integrated IT Systems; Productivity Tools
Applying Developed S&T	Science & Technology	Developing and Applying Optimal S&T
Budget Drives Strategy	Resource Management	Strategy Drives Budget

FIGURE I.5. "FBI Strategic Shifts, 2001–11," Federal Bureau of Investigation.

more systematic global response, one that would soon proliferate objects of concern—moving from specific governments to military technologies, to transportation networks, to communication systems, to named terrorists, and eventually to microbes.

Thus, one structural effect of anticipatory defense is an ever-expanding universe of objects to secure, scaling the problem of security up increasingly from the territorial boundaries of the state to the planetary level. This advances the Cold War security state's concern with military logistics and the establishment of global knowledge systems (see Farish 2010; Edwards 2010) by seeking the capacity to intervene anywhere on the planet a threat might arise, before it materializes. It also militarizes infrastructure itself: if you use the Internet, go to the hospital, fly on a plane, send a letter, or use a cell phone, you become part of a counterterror system that is interested in comprehensively archiving telecommunications, identifying travelers, monitoring infectious diseases, scanning letters, and accruing detailed knowledge about over 800,000 people on an ever-growing global watch list (see Dilanian 2013). It is impossible today to use modern infrastructure—including anything related to communication, transportation, public health, or finance—in the United States and not become the object of state surveillance and data archiving, which is one of the most profound achievements of the War on Terror. A fundamental change in the nature of individual privacy has been but one foundational effect of counter-terror, which attempts to "connect the dots" of potential threats by capturing and mining digital information for anticipatory signs.

One of the perplexing questions about a war on terror, therefore, is how to define its boundaries, battlefields, and home fronts. All wars have theaters of engagement that define battle spaces, and the boundary between the foreign and the domestic has historically been a central way of establishing law and setting limits to the scale of officially sanctioned violence. For Samuel Weber, "theatricality is defined as a problematic process of placing, framing, situating," or as an "imposition of borders" in a disputed space (2004, 315). One important aspect of counterterror is that its theater of operations has been construed from the beginning as planetary, meaning that there is no space, object, or person that cannot be construed in some fashion as on the front line of this new kind of conflict, and thus of potential concern to the U.S. security apparatus. The complexity of this world-without-borders approach to counterterror ensures immediate and constant slippage between the desire for a planetary theater of operations and the very real limitations on American power. As Carlo Galli has argued, the War on Terror is the end of a Schmittian politics in which friend-enemy distinctions supported the territorial security of a state (see also Dillon 2007); it is instead a war fused with the logics of globalization in such a way that the demarcation between foreign and domestic is no longer the crucial definition of security:

> Politics, in the global age, is the coincidence of real insecurity and illusory security; it is the concurrence of real conflict and the specter of peace. In general, the State-operated distinction between secure internal space and dangerous external space has vanished, leaving us with our current "risk society." Globalization is the epoch in which the State no longer protects its citizens from external turbulence. The principle of *protego ergo obligo* ("protection, therefore obedience") was the load-bearing column of modern politics, but in the global

age, anything can happen anywhere, at any moment, precisely because the State no longer filters disorder from the external environment (terrorist acts, migratory flows, the movement of capital) and is no longer capable of transforming it into internal peace. In this context, the "public" no longer assumes the traditional institutionalized form of politics, the State; it is now the event that, for better or for worse, immediately touches the lives of many "private" individuals with particular importance and intensity. (Galli 2010, 158)

It is now the intensity of the event that matters. The "intensity" of the event is the language of affective politics, one in which the visual event—the televised image of the World Trade Center in flames, the "shock and awe" bombing of Iraq, or the abandoned citizens of New Orleans awaiting rescue after Hurricane Katrina—can be a global structure, gathering different individuals, cultures, and motives around the psychosocial force of highly mediated, but brutally real, violence (Massumi 2011; see also RETORT 2005; S. Ahmed 2004).

The collapsing of time and space, together with the anticipatory preemption of catastrophic futures, remakes the question of security into a postnational formation, even as the counterterror state (across the administrations of both George W. Bush and Barack Obama) has sought to extend and secure American power through it. There is a profound disconnect between threat as a global condition necessitating a state security apparatus and the counterterror state's commitment to extending U.S. hegemony through an ever-evolving state of emergency. The formal merging of offense and defense animates the most destructive aspects of American power and underscores why counterterror as a global project is perpetually undermined by a continual slippage between threat perceptions and material conditions. As Anne McClintock (2009) has pointed out, the U.S. counterterror state was established through a simultaneous commitment to attaining absolute military power and recognizing totalizing threat, a foundational contradiction that makes the War on Terror both violent on a new scale (as danger is perceived to be everywhere) and a paranoid system ultimately at war with itself. This is because anticipatory preemption begins with imaginative projection and cannot be exhausted through taking action in the world or by factual accumulation: there is always another level to the imaginary, more potential dangers to preempt, other nightmares to locate and eliminate.[13]

WMDs, or "The Nature of the World We Live In"

The "terrorist with a WMD" formulation is at the center of the new counterterror state, a crucial reworking of long-standing American nuclear fears
and security logics that both establishes an imminent, if inchoate, threat
and makes that threat a future-oriented, conceptual infrastructure whose
scope is ever expanding. The atomic bomb became the organizing fetish
of the security state after 1945, linking technoscientific, military, political,
and psychosocial projects under the image of the mushroom cloud.[14] The
nuclear revolution not only "drastically altered statecraft" and the very
concept of war, as Robert Jervis (1989, 2) has shown, but American society largely built itself through the bomb, remaking its geopolitics, cities,
environment, and institutions via nuclear fear (Masco 2006). Garry Wills
argues that the bomb altered American life "to its deepest constitutional
roots" (2010, 1), creating a new concept of unchecked authority in the form
of a president with command and control of a global nuclear arsenal and
distorting other American institutions—including the courts, Congress,
and the military—in favor of a nuclear-powered commander in chief. Wills
argues that the United States has been in a state of perpetual emergency
since the start of World War II and has built a national security apparatus
for the nuclear age that exists largely outside of constitutional law (237).
The logics of nuclear terror are thus deeply embedded in American society,
providing institutional, ideological, and cultural resources to the War on
Terror (see Gusterson 2004 and 1998; see also Oakes 1994). But although
the twentieth-century nuclear security state was focused on the specific technologies (bombs, warheads, missiles, planes, submarines, and so on) enabling global nuclear war, the twenty-first-century counterterror state is
devoted to preempting a new kind of ultimate danger—the "terrorist with
a WMD"—a figuration that converts specific and long-standing American
nuclear fears into an emerging danger of potentially infinite form and du-
ration.[15] In crucial ways, the War on Terror is thus the ideological fulfill-
ment of the Cold War state project, creating an institutional commitment
to permanent militarization through an ever-expanding universe of threat
identification and response.

The "terrorist with a WMD" combines two poorly defined concepts
into an image of total danger, one that cannot be deterred but only preempted through anticipatory action. Without linkage to the WMD category the terrorist of the early twenty-first century could not rise to the

level of an existential danger that requires a total state mobilization or a global American security apparatus. But, like terrorism itself, the WMD is an emerging concept, one that in a single decade has undergone a radical redefinition and expansion.[16] The term *weapon of mass destruction* was coined by Cosmo Gordon Lang, the archbishop of Canterbury, who first used it to comment on the German aerial bombing of civilians at Guernica, Spain, in 1937, but it took on lasting nuclear connotations with the U.S. use of the atomic bomb at Hiroshima and Nagasaki in 1945. It was codified by the United Nations as a nuclear referent in 1948, when weapons of *mass* destruction were identified as those weapons (radiological, biological, or chemical) that have "characteristics comparable in destructive effect to those of the atomic bomb" (UN Commission for Conventional Armaments 1948). Although the term *WMD* occasionally appeared in arms control negotiations through the second half of the twentieth century, it was rarely used by U.S. security experts, who preferred to designate specific technologies, and with them specific degrees of threat and ideal countermeasures (see Perkovich 2004; Vogel 2007). The Cold War security state apparatus, in other words, relied on a kind of precision in calculating threats that the concept of WMD does not allow.

When the Bush administration switched, in the late fall of 2001, from a discussion of the actual attacks—that is, suicide-hijackers and anthrax letters—to the general category of the WMD in its public discourse, it was a strategic decision to expand the potential field of danger and endow a wide range of objects with the existential threat culturally identified with the atomic bomb (see Mayer 2008). In its *National Strategy to Combat Weapons of Mass Destruction*, the Bush administration declared:

> Weapons of mass destruction (WMD)—nuclear, biological, and chemical—in the possession of hostile states and terrorists represent one of the greatest security challenges facing the United States. We must pursue a comprehensive strategy to counter this threat in all of its dimensions. . . . We will not permit the world's most dangerous regimes and terrorists to threaten us with the world's most destructive weapons. We must accord the highest priority to the protection of the United States, our forces, and our friends and allies from the existing and growing WMD threat. (U.S. White House 2002b, 1)

A comprehensive strategy to counter threats in all dimensions. Although this document seems to articulate a familiar kind of existential threat to the nation (one evoking the multigenerational Cold War nuclear arms race), the category of the WMD articulated here provides an expansive new frame for danger itself. Only two years later, for example, the new Department of Homeland Security offered the following definition in its first *National Response Plan*:

> Weapon of Mass Destruction (WMD). As defined in title 18, U.S.C. 2332a: (1) any explosive, incendiary, or poison gas, bomb, grenade, or rocket having a propellant charge of more than 4 ounces, or missile having an explosive or incendiary charge of more than one-quarter ounce, or mine or similar device; (2) any weapon that is designed or intended to cause death or serious bodily injury through the release, dissemination, or impact of toxic or poisonous chemical or their precursors; (3) any weapon involving a disease organism; or (4) any weapon that is designed to release radiation or radioactivity at a level dangerous to human life. (U.S. Department of Homeland Security 2004, 74)

Explosives, toxins, diseases, radiation—any . . . similar to . . . more than four ounces. The WMD category, despite its seeming precision (measured down to the ounce), scales endlessly here and becomes an open-ended concept capable of grabbing future technologies via the "any weapon" language. It includes any intentional chemical or biological attack (raising immediate questions about insecticides as well as sexually transmitted diseases as potential WMDs), but it also scales explosive dangers in a surreal manner. Under this definition, a partial stick of dynamite (containing a few ounces of explosive power) is in the same category as the atomic bomb that destroyed Hiroshima (equivalent to 13,000 tons of TNT) or a hydrogen bomb (holding a force measured in the millions of tons of TNT) whose total destructive effects could involve hundreds of square miles (see Eden 2004). This is not a definition that makes sense from a technical or military point of view, but it is a key affective political tool of the War on Terror. Like the figuration of the *terrorist*, the WMD acronym activates more than simply a technical or administrative description of fact; it is now a phantasmatic force in American society, gaining meanings and intensities over time, operating primarily on psychosocial and political levels.

After a decade of counterterror, it is now impossible to know what the term WMD refers to in everyday official usage, except that the threat might be lethal—potentially massively so.[17] A terrorist alert concerning a WMD remains a deployment of the signifier of ultimate crisis (drawing on the nation-ending potential of the atomic bomb) but it may well reference a kind of danger that not long ago would have been considered a routine police matter, not a subject for collective national emergency. Evoking the WMD is, therefore, both an emerging logic and a calculated means of enabling maximal state agency without actually designating the degree or kind of threat. This is a profound shift in U.S. security logics, one that has important legal, institutional, and military consequences. It is also iconic of the counterterror state form, which seeks to maximize executive power under emergency conditions as a basic principle. When questioned about the limits of executive power in conducting the War on Terror by Fox News in 2008, Dick Cheney—former vice president and the chief architect of the counterterror state—replied:

> The President of the United States now for fifty years is followed at all times, 24 hours a day, by a military aid carrying a "football" that contains the nuclear codes that he would use and be authorized to use in the event of a nuclear attack on the United States. He could launch a kind of devastating attack the world's never seen. He doesn't have to check with anybody. He doesn't have to call the Congress. He doesn't have to check with the courts. He has that authority because of the nature of the world we live in. (Cheney 2008)

Because of the nature of the world we live in. Here, Cheney uses nuclear threat as a means of rationalizing all lesser forms of executive action in the world, constituting an all-powerful commander in chief beholden to no one in the domain of national security because he or she has been preauthorized to launch a nuclear war. This notion of power draws, as Wills (2010, 3) has described at length, on the conceptual power of the bomb in American society (see also Masco 2006; Hecht 2012). The subsuming of nuclear danger into the even broader category of a WMD threat has significant consequences not only for the War on Terror as a global military campaign but also for American society writ large. It has enabled radical actions in the name of defense, while also masking a startling fact about the War on Terror and WMDs.

The 2001 attacks on the United States—and the expansive U.S. operations in Afghanistan, Iraq, Pakistan, Yemen, and Somalia in response to them—are profound acts of violence. However, it is important to recognize a disturbing reality, one that is visible only by looking back across the first ten years of the War on Terror: the WMDs responsible for escalating the 2001 terrorist attacks from terrible mass violence to something that could be constituted as an existential threat to the nation-state were all made—

either literally or imaginatively—within the U.S. national security complex itself. From the anthrax letters, now attributed by the FBI to a U.S. biological warfare expert, to the fictitious WMDs from Saddam Hussein's Iraq produced rhetorically inside the Pentagon—these twenty-first-century dangers have been homemade, using material and imaginary resources produced by the U.S. security apparatus itself. To be direct: in the first decade of counterterror, the "terrorist with a WMD" has been a "made in the U.S.A." production at affective, imaginative, and material levels. This fact reveals the extraordinary power of deeply structured nuclear fear a half century after Hiroshima and Nagasaki, and of military-industrial capacities to mobilize the U.S. public as well as the war machine. As such, this book assesses not only the new material (scientific, political, military) capacities supporting the counterterror state but also the affective and imaginative infrastructures that are required to build a permanently militarized society.

Overview of the Book

The Theater of Operations investigates the cultural logics, technological fears, and political ambitions that had to be in place for a (literally nonsensical) War on Terror to be thinkable. It traces how the Cold War balance of terror was remade into the War on Terror as a means of extending American hegemony into the twenty-first century. The book traces the remaking of the nuclear security state as a counterterror state and assesses the resulting shifts in a variety of domains of American national security culture enabled by the politics of shock. It theorizes a new modality of citizen-state relations mediated by a shock-terror-normality circuit that produces two things: the promise of a world without events—that is, a perfectly secure every day unbroken by surprise, and, with the inevitable failure of that project, the continual drive to expand the security project in the name of producing a world without shock. This circuit is a key feature not only in defining a national security state after World War II; it also helps explain why non-militarizable threats—relating to climate, finance, domestic infrastructure, and health—fail to rise to the level of a national security problem despite the widespread destruction and terrors that they produce. To this end, *The Theater of Operations* addresses the following questions: How does a nuclear hyperpower—perhaps the most secure and powerful state in human history—come to embrace vulnerability and fear as the basis for its political order? How does a country commit to a permanent war posture grounded in covert actions, existential threat, and preemption while maintaining an ideology of openness, law, and democracy? And finally, how does a society define and limit its security project when the future is anticipated to be filled with emerging terrors, presenting a proliferating field of objects and spaces to be militarized in the endless pursuit of defense?

The chapters that follow mobilize methodological techniques drawn from science studies, ethnography, historical anthropology, media studies, and critical theory. Informed by two decades of ethnographic work in the national security sciences, each chapter offers a genealogical assessment of a set of practices (technological, imaginary, affective) that I think of now as infrastructural to U.S. national security as a distinctly American formation. I emphasize throughout the political and cultural force of threat identification in American society, and I focus on the ways in which specific logics and practices of insecurity are transformed into collective events in the domestic sphere. My project is ultimately a consideration of American self-fashioning through terror, interrogating the specific forms of fear that have enabled a new kind of state security apparatus to emerge, one that all too readily rejects democratic commitments in favor of perpetual trauma and militarism.

Chapter 1, " 'Survival Is Your Business,' " is an examination of the emotional management projects of the early Cold War—and specifically, the legacy of civil defense drills and visual image campaigns that installed a distinct concept of existential danger in American culture. I suggest that the multigenerational project of instilling fear of the atomic bomb created the terms for the affective politics of disaster that follow, and I interrogate the repetition of certain images of atomic destruction that now circulate in American culture as unrecognized citations of nuclear propaganda. I argue that one of the central achievements of civil defense in the early Cold War was to nationalize images of the end of the United States and to transform them into a strange new form of nation building, thereby investing nuclear ruins with a counterintuitive national affect.

In chapter 2, "Bad Weather," I ask how, and when, does it become possible to conceptualize a truly planetary crisis? The Cold War nuclear arms race installed one powerful concept of planetary crisis in American culture, in the form of global nuclear war. But the science enabling the U.S. nuclear arsenal also produced unintended by-products: notably, a radical new investment in the earth sciences. Cold War nuclear science ultimately produced not only bombs but also a new understanding of the earth as an integrated biosphere. Thus, the image of planetary crisis in the United States was increasingly doubled during the Cold War—the immediacy of nuclear threat matched by concerns about rapid environmental change and the cumulative effects of industrial civilization on a fragile biosphere. This chapter examines the evolution of (and competition between) two ideas of planetary crisis since 1945: nuclear war and climate change. In doing so, it offers an alternative history of the nuclear age and considers the U.S. national security implications of a shift in the definition of planetary crisis from warring states to a changing climate in the twenty-first century.

Chapter 3, "Sensitive but Unclassified," tracks the conversion of the United States from a countercommunist to a counterterrorist state formation via an examination of the expanding logics of state secrecy. Starting with an analysis of a new category of state information known as "sensitive but unclassified," the chapter theorizes a secrecy/threat matrix as a core project of the national security state. In doing so, the chapter assesses the ideological linkages between the WMD and the secret from the Cold War through the War on Terror. This chapter argues that the long-term effect of compartmentalized state secrecy is to fundamentally devalue knowledge and expertise, and it assesses the impact of such devaluation on the democratic state form. The result of the secrecy/threat matrix is a world where affect and desire, regardless of verifiable facts, become the rationale for military action.

In chapter 4, "Biosecurity Noir," I examine the emerging logics of biosecurity as an emblematic project of the counterterror state. Here I explore the strange fact that in response to anthrax attacks by a U.S. bioweapons expert in September 2001, the United States built a new biosecurity infrastructure, one that proliferates exponentially the numbers of experts and types of research on dangerous biological agents. I argue that biosecurity installs capacities in the future that are unknown, setting the stage not only for the potential preemption of a deadly virus but also for creating new kinds of danger. Thus, the chapter considers how the expert recognition of danger in a world without borders and the desire for a world without events frames the evolution of a major new security infrastructure. It also explores the expansion of the WMD concept to include biological threats that are naturally occurring, allowing an emerging biosecurity apparatus to see potential terror in every biological organism on the planet. This chapter documents the full conversion of the Cold War system—the management of emotions, enemy formations, planetary threats, and state secrecy—into a counterterrorist state formation—installing new expert capacities as well as new structures of emergency into a deep future.

I conclude with "Living Counterterror," an evaluation of the first decade of the War on Terror, which focuses on the new material, imaginary, and affective infrastructures informing U.S. national security. Engaging a group of national security professionals in Nevada, who were once known as nuclear weapons specialists but were remade after 2001 as homeland security, counterterrorism, and wMD experts, I explore the ongoing trauma of the 2001 suicide-hijacker attacks for members of the security state. I show how the 2001 terrorist acts have been constituted as a permanent injury within the defense world, a kind of loss that can never be overcome despite a hyperactive planetary theater of counterterror operations. I consider how expert national security affect informs the production of an ever-emerging security apparatus, demonstrating how terror, in all its proliferating forms, continues to dominate American visions of the twenty-first century.

ONE

"SURVIVAL IS YOUR BUSINESS"
Engineering Ruins and Affect in Nuclear America

Has any nation-state invested as profoundly in ruins as Cold War America? Although many societies have experienced moments of self-doubt about the future, perhaps even contemplating the ruins that might be left behind as testament to their existence, it took American ingenuity to transform ruination into a form of nation building. In this regard, the invention of the atomic bomb proved to be utterly transformative for American society: it not only provided the inspiration for a new U.S. geopolitical strategy—one that ultimately enveloped the earth in advanced military technology and colonized everyday life with the minute-to-minute possibility of nuclear war—but it also provided officials with a new means of engaging and disciplining citizens in everyday life. For U.S. policy makers, the Cold War arms race transformed the apocalypse not only into a technoscientific project and a geopolitical paradigm, but also a powerful new domestic political resource.

Put differently, a new kind of social contract was formed in the first decade of the nuclear age in the United States, one based not on the protection and improvement of everyday life but rather on the national contemplation of ruins. Known initially as *civil defense*, the project of building the bomb and communicating its power to the world turned engineering ruins into a form of international theater. Nuclear explosions, matched with large-scale emergency response exercises, became a means of developing the bomb as well as of imagining nuclear warfare (see, for example, Vanderbilt 2002; Glasstone and Dolan 1977; Kahn 1960). This test program would ultimately transform the United States into the most nuclear-bombed country on earth, distributing its environmental, economic, and health effects to each and every U.S. citizen.[1] By the mid-1950s it was no longer a perverse exercise to imagine one's home and city devastated, on fire and in ruins; it had become a formidable public ritual—a core act of governance, technoscientific practice, and democratic participation. Indeed, in early Cold War America it became a civic obligation to collectively imagine, and at times theatrically enact, the physical destruction of the nation-state.[2]

It is this specific nationalization of death that I wish to explore in this chapter, assessing not only the first collective formulations of nuclear fear in the United States but also the residues and legacies of that project for contemporary American society. Today we live in a world populated with newly charred landscapes and a production of ruins that speaks directly to this foundational moment in American national culture (see Stoler with Bond 2006). The notions of danger, preemption, and emergency response that inform the U.S. War on Terror derive meaning from the promises and institutions made by the Cold War security state. Indeed, the logics of nuclear fear informing that multigenerational state- and nation-building enterprise exist now as a largely inchoate, but deeply embedded, set of assumptions about power and threat. How Americans have come to understand mass death at home and abroad has much to do with the legacies of the Cold War nuclear project, and the peculiar psychosocial consequences of attempting to build the nation through the contemplation of nuclear ruins.

What follows is largely a study of visual culture, and specifically the domestic deployment of images of a ruined United States for ideological effect. I argue that key aspects of U.S. security culture have been formed in relation to images of nuclear devastation: the constitution of the modern security state in the aftermath of World War II mobilized the atomic bomb as the basis for American geopolitical power, but it also created a new citizen-state relationship mediated by nuclear fear. This chapter considers the lasting effects of nation building through nuclear fear by tracking the production and ongoing circulation of nuclear ruins from the Cold War's balance of terror through the current War on Terror. It is not an exercise in viewer response but rather charts the development and circulation of a specific set of ideas and images about ultimate danger. I begin with a discussion of the early Cold War project known as civil defense and track how the specific images created for domestic consumption as part of that campaign continued to circulate as afterimages in the popular films of the 1980s and 1990s.[3] I show that the early Cold War state sought explicitly to militarize U.S. citizens through contemplating the end of the nation-state, creating in the process a specific set of ideas and images of collective danger that continues to inform American society in powerful and increasingly complex ways. In the aftermath of the terrorist attacks on New York and Washington in 2001, the affective coordinates of the Cold War arms race provided specific ideological resources to the state, which once again mobilized the image of a United States in nuclear ruins to enable war. Ultimately, this chapter follows Walter Benjamin's call to interrogate the aestheticized politics that enable increasing militarization and that allow citizens to experience their own destruction as an "aesthetic pleasure of the first order" (1969, 242).[4]

Be Afraid but Don't Panic!

The disaster ruins everything, all the while leaving everything intact. . . . To think the disaster (if this is possible, and it is not possible inasmuch as we suspect that the disaster is thought) is to have no longer any future in which to think it.

—**Maurice Blanchot**, *The Writing of the Disaster*

Nuclear ruins are never the end of the story in the United States—they always offer a new beginning. In the early Cold War period, ruins become the markers of a new kind of social intimacy grounded in highly detailed renderings of theatrically rehearsed mass violence. The intent of these public spectacles—nuclear detonations, city evacuations, duck-and-cover drills—was not defense in the classic sense of avoiding violence or destruction but rather a psychological reprogramming of the American public for life in a nuclear age. The central project of the early nuclear state was to link U.S. institutions—military, industrial, legislative, academic—for the production of the bomb, while calibrating public perceptions of the nuclear danger to enable that project.[5] As Blanchot suggests, this effort to think through the ultimate crisis colonized everyday life as well as the future, while fundamentally missing the actual disaster. The scripting of disaster in the imagination has profound social effects: it defines the conditions of insecurity, renders other threats invisible, and articulates the terms of both value and loss. In the United States, civil defense was always a willful act of fabulation, an official fantasy designed to promote an image of nuclear war that would be above all other things politically useful. It also installed an idea of an American community under total, immediate, and unending threat, creating the terms for a new kind of nation building that demanded an unprecedented level of militarism in everyday life as the minimum basis for collective security.

After the Soviet Union's first nuclear detonation in 1949, U.S. policy makers committed themselves to a new geopolitical strategy that would ultimately dominate American foreign policy for the remainder of the twentieth century. The policy of containment, as formalized in a report to the president by the National Security Council, known as NSC 68, proposed as a response to the Soviet bomb a total mobilization of American society based on the experience of World War II.[6] NSC 68 articulates the terms of a permanent wartime posture funded by an ever-expanding domestic economy, transforming consumerism into the engine of a new kind of militarized geopolitics. The report identifies internal dissent as perhaps the greatest threat to the project of the Cold War and calls for a new campaign to discipline citizens in preparation for life under the constant shadow of nuclear war. Thus, in the White House, nuclear fear was immediately understood to be not only the basis of American military power, but also a means of installing a new normative reality in the United States, one that could consolidate political power at the federal level by reaching into the internal lives of citizens. Nuclear danger became a complex new political ideology, both mobilizing the global project of the Cold War (fought increasingly on covert terms internationally) and installing a powerful means of controlling domestic political debates about the terms of security. By focusing Americans on an imminent end of the nation-state, federal authorities mobilized the bomb to create the Cold War consensus of anticommunism, capitalism, and military expansion.

Defense intellectuals in the administrations of presidents Harry Truman and Dwight Eisenhower, however, worried that nuclear terror could become so profound under the terms of an escalating nuclear arms race that the American public would be unwilling to support the military and geopolitical agenda of the Cold War.[7] The immediate challenge, as U.S. nuclear strategists saw it, was to avoid both an apathetic public (which might just give up when faced with the emerging destructive power of the Soviet nuclear arsenal) and a terrorized public (which would be unable to function cognitively) (Oakes 1994, 34; see also George 2003). For example, a highly influential civil defense study from 1952, *Report of the Project East River*, argued that civilian response to a nuclear attack would be all-out panic and mob behavior: American society, the report concluded, would not only be at war with the Soviets but also at war with itself as society violently broke down along race and class lines (Associated Universities 1952). A long Cold War consequently required not only a new geopolitics powered by nuclear weapons, but also new forms of psychological discipline at home. One of the earliest and most profound projects of the Cold War state was thus to deploy the bomb as a mechanism for accessing and controlling the emotions of citizens.

As Guy Oakes has documented, the civil defense programs of the early Cold War were designed to "emotionally manage" U.S. citizens through nuclear fear (1994, 47). The formal goal of this state program was to transform "nuclear terror," which was interpreted by U.S. officials as a paralyzing emotion, into "nuclear fear," an affective state that would allow citizens to function in a time of crisis (Oakes 1994, 62–63; see also Associated Universities 1952). By militarizing everyday life through nuclear fear, the Cold War state sought to both normalize catastrophic danger and politically deploy an image of it. Rather than offering citizens an image of safety or of a war that could end in victory, the early Cold War state sought instead to calibrate everyday American life to the minute-to-minute possibility of nuclear warfare. In addition to turning the domestic space of the home into the front line of the Cold War (see McEnaney 2000; Elaine May 1990), civil defense officials argued that citizens should be prepared every second of the day to deal with a potential nuclear attack. The civil defense program thus shifted responsibility for nuclear war from the state to its citizens by making the enemy public panic, not nuclear war itself. It was, in other words, up to citizens to take responsibility for their own survival in the nuclear age.

Val Peterson, as director of the new Federal Civil Defense Administration (FCDA), argued:

> Ninety percent of all emergency measures after an atomic blast will depend on the prevention of panic among the survivors in the first 90 seconds. Like the A-bomb, panic is fissionable. It can produce a chain reaction more deeply destructive than any explosive known. If there is an ultimate weapon, it may well be mass panic—not the A-bomb. . . . War is no longer confined to the battlefield. Every city is a potential battleground, every citizen a target. There are no safe rear areas. Panic on Main Street can be as decisive as panic in the front lines. (1953, 1–2)

Panic is fissionable. Indeed, Peterson argued that Americans were particularly "susceptible to panic" and offered a checklist on how citizens could become "panic stoppers" by training themselves for nuclear attack and becoming like "soldiers" at home (V. Peterson 1953, 17; see figure 1.1). Thus, the official message from the early Cold War state was that extreme self-control was the best way for citizens to fight a nuclear war, revealing a national project to both colonize and normalize everyday life with nuclear fear. By declaring a war on panic, as Jackie Orr (2006, 14) has so powerfully shown, the national security state remade the individual as a permanently militarized, if insecure, node in the larger Cold War system. Civil defense planners sought ultimately to saturate the public space with a specific idea about nuclear war, one that would nationalize mass death and transform postnuclear ruins into a new American frontier, simply another arena for citizens to assert their civic spirit, fortitude, and ingenuity. At the heart of the project was an effort to install psychological defenses against the exploding bomb, as well as a belief in the possibility of national unity in a postnuclear environment—all via the contemplation of nuclear ruins.

Indeed, as the Eisenhower administration promoted an Atoms for Peace program around the world to emphasize the benefits of nuclear energy and provide a positive vision of atomic science, it pursued the opposite emotional management strategy within the United States (Osgood 2006; Craig 1998; Hewlett and Holl 1989). The domestic response to the growing Soviet nuclear arsenal was a new kind of social engineering project, pursued with the help of social scientists and the advertising industry, to teach citizens a specific kind of nuclear fear while normalizing the nuclear crisis. The goal, as one top-secret study put it in 1956, was an "emotional adaptation" of the citizenry to nuclear danger, a program of "psychological defense" aimed at "feelings" that would unify the nation in the face of apocalyptic everyday threat (Panel on the Human Effects of Nuclear Weapons Development 1956, 10–11).[8] This took the form of the largest domestic propaganda campaign to date in American history.[9] Designed to mobilize all Americans for a long Cold War, the civil defense effort involved town meetings and education programs in every public school; it also sought to take full advantage of mass media—television, radio, and particularly film. By the mid-1950s, the FCDA saturated newspapers and magazines with nuclear war advertisements and could claim that its radio broadcasts reached an estimated audience of 175 million Americans each year.[10]

As the campaign evolved, the FCDA turned increasingly to film, creating a library of short subjects on nuclear destruction and civil defense that were shown across the country in schools, churches, community halls, and movie theaters. The FCDA concluded: "Each picture will be seen by

PANIC STOPPERS

How to keep from being a victim of panic

Face the Facts — The more you learn, the safer you are. Insulate yourself against panic by finding out all you can about the enemy's weapons — A-bombs, germ and gas warfare, sabotage and rumor war. Misinformation and lack of information breed panic.

Get Ready at Home — Preparedness is good preventive medicine against panic. Prepare and train your family so that the members can perform their duties like trained soldiers under fire. Here's how:

1. Talk to your family about the dangers you face. Work out practice drills so you all know what to do—at home, at work or at school.

2. Get a civil defense emergency first-aid kit together and learn how to use it.

3. Put away a three-day emergency supply of food and water—enough to take care of the whole family and its special needs.

4. Build a home shelter if you live near a target area. If you can't build one, pick out the safest shelter area in your home. Personal shelter can help save your life.

5. Be sure you have a workable AM Radio, preferably battery-operated, in your shelter area. Remember the Conelrad frequencies—640 and 1240—where in an emergency you can get official news and civil defense instructions.

6. Take a Red Cross first-aid course as soon as possible. In the meantime, study the civil defense booklet, Emergency Action to Save Lives. You can get it at your local defense office or at the Government Printing Office, Washington 25, D.C. It costs five cents.

7. Practice fireproof housekeeping; learn how to fight small fires in your home before they can become big ones. There's a nickel government manual for that, too: Fire-Fighting for Householders.

8. Learn the simple steps your family should take to protect themselves against germ warfare. That calls for one more government pamphlet: What You Should Know about Biological Warfare. Cost: 10 cents.

Get Leadership Training — Invest a few hours a week in basic training for one of the organized civil defense services so that you will be ready for group action in any emergency.

Make Fear Work For You — Don't be ashamed of being scared. If an attack comes, you will be scared and so will everyone else. It is *what you do* when you are afraid that counts. Fear can be healthy if you know how to use it; it can make you more alert and stronger at a time when you and your neighbors must act to protect yourselves.

Spike That Rumor — Don't swallow everything you hear. Recognize wartime rumor and gossip for what they are—enemy weapons of the most dangerous kind. Don't let the enemy play you for a sucker — don't pass on rumors. Check any story you hear. Make sure that the facts are from official sources before you repeat them.

FIGURE 1.1. How to become a "Panic Stopper" in the Nuclear Age, Val Peterson (1953).

a minimum of 20,000,000 persons, giving an anticipated aggregate audience of more than half a billion for the civil defense film program of 1955" (Federal Civil Defense Administration 1956, 78). Thus, a key to winning the Cold War was to produce the bomb not only for military use but also in cinematic form for the American public. It is important to recognize that the circulation of these images relied on a simultaneous censorship of images from the atomic bombings of Hiroshima and Nagasaki in 1945. U.S. authorities made available images of destroyed buildings from Japan but withheld the detailed effects of the atomic bomb on the human body, as well as some firsthand accounts of the aftermath of the bombings.[11] Thus, an immediate project of the nuclear state was to calibrate the image of atomic warfare for the American public through the mass circulation of certain images of the bomb and the censorship of all others. In this way, officials sought to mobilize the power of mass media to transform nuclear attack from an unthinkable apocalypse into an opportunity for psychological self-management, civic responsibility, and, ultimately, governance. Civil defense officials sought to produce an "atomic-bomb–proof society" in which nuclear conflict was normalized alongside all other threats, making public support for the Cold War sustainable.

Civil defense theorists argued that citizens could achieve this contradictory state of productive fear (simultaneously mobilized and normalized) only by gaining intimacy with nuclear warfare itself, by becoming familiar with the language of nuclear effects from blast, heat, and fire to radioactive fallout. Irving Janis, a RAND analyst, concluded that the goal of civil defense was ultimately an "emotional inoculation" of the American public (1951, 220). This inoculation, he cautioned, needed to be finely calibrated: the simulated nuclear destruction in civil defense exercises, as well as the film footage of atomic tests released to the public, had to be formidable enough to affectively mobilize citizens but not so terrifying as to invalidate the concept of defense altogether (a distinct challenge in an age of increasingly powerful thermonuclear weapons, which offered no hope of survival to most urban residents). A central project of civil defense was thus to produce fear but not terror, anxiety but not panic, and to inform the public about nuclear science but not fully educate it about nuclear war. The goal was a micro regulation of a national community at the emotional level. In other words, alongside the invention of a new security state grounded in nuclear weapons was a new public culture of insecurity in the United States: figuring the United States as a global nuclear superpower was coterminous with a domestic campaign to reveal the country as completely vulnerable, creating a citizen-state relationship increasingly mediated by forms of inchoate but ever-present nuclear fear.

Indeed, one of the first U.S. civil defense projects of the Cold War was to make every U.S. city a target, and every U.S. citizen a potential victim, of nuclear attack. Through the 1950s the FCDA circulated increasingly de-

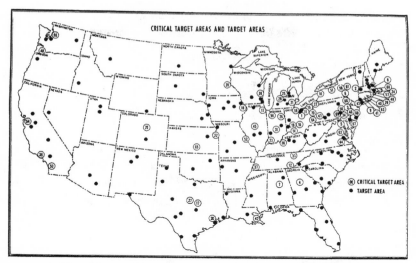

FIGURE 1.2. Map of Imagined Soviet Nuclear Targets in the United States, Federal Civil Defense Administration, 1955.

tailed maps of the likely targets of a Soviet nuclear attack, listing U.S. cities in order of population and ranking them as potential targets. In one 1955 FCDA map (see figure 1.2), the top seventy Soviet targets include major population centers as well as military bases in the United States—revealing not only the vulnerability of large cities to the bomb, but also the increasingly wide distribution of military-industrial sites across the continental United States. As the size of the U.S. and Soviet bombs grew and the means of their delivery improved (from bombers to intercontinental missiles), so did the highly publicized target lists. Thomas Martin and Donald Latham's 1963 civil defense textbook, *Strategy for Survival*, for example, presented a case for 303 ground zeros within the United States in case of nuclear war:

> No one can predict that any one or combination of these cities would be attacked in any future war. Thus, it might appear that we are trying to know the unknowable, to predict the unpredictable, to impose a logical rationale upon war which is, itself, illogical and irrational. But such an inference is incorrect. It was shown in Chapter 5 that there are good reasons to believe that a large fraction of these cities would be attacked in a future war—but what specific cities would be included in this fraction? Because there is no precise answer to this question, civil defense planning must assume that all could be potential targets.

"SURVIVAL IS YOUR BUSINESS"

Any other approach is thermonuclear Russian Roulette played with 100 million American lives. (Martin and Latham 1963, 182)

Thermonuclear Russian roulette. Marking every population center with over 50,000 residents a likely target of nuclear attack, Martin and Latham saw no safe area in the United States. From New York to Topeka, from Los Angeles to Waco, from Albuquerque to Anchorage—each community could increasingly argue that it was a *first-strike* target of Soviet attack. Given the expanding distribution of the nuclear weapons infrastructure (nuclear material production sites, scientific laboratories, command and control centers, and military bases) in U.S. territories, Americans not only increasingly lived beside nuclear facilities but also worked inside them. Indeed, citizens were informed from multiple media sources that their community was the literal front line of the Cold War, with Soviet thermonuclear warheads poised to attack.[12]

From 1953 to 1961, the yearly centerpiece of the civil defense program was a simulated nuclear attack on the United States directed by federal authorities (see T. Davis 2002; McEnaney 2000; Oakes 1994). Cities were designated as victims of nuclear warfare, allowing civic leaders and politicians to lead theatrical evacuations of the city for television cameras, followed by media discussions of blast damage versus fire damage versus fallout, and the expected casualty rates if the attack had been *real*. In 1955, for example, the scenario called Operation Alert involved sixty cities hit by a variety of atomic and hydrogen bombs, producing over eight million instant deaths and another eight million radiation victims over the coming weeks (figure 1.3). The scenario imagined twenty-five million Americans left homeless and fallout covering some 63,000 square miles of the United States (Federal Civil Defense Administration 1956; see also Krugler 2006, 126). In the first decade of the Cold War, Americans acted out their own incineration in this manner annually, with public officials cheerfully evacuating cities and evaluating emergency planning, while nuclear detonations in Nevada and the South Pacific provided new images of fireballs and mushroom clouds to reinforce the concept of imminent nuclear threat. The early Cold War state sought to install a specific idea of the bomb in the American imagination through these public spectacles, creating a new psychosocial space between the utopian promise of American technoscience and the minute-to-minute threat of thermonuclear incineration. It sought to make contemplating mass death an intimate psychological experience, while simultaneously claiming that nuclear war could be planned for alongside tornados, floods, and

FIGURE 1.3. Simulated Nuclear Attack, Operation Alert Exercise 1955," Federal Civil Defense Administration, 1955.

traffic accidents. Civil defense officials ultimately sought to make nuclear war a space for nation building and thereby bring this new form of death under the control of the state.

Here is how one of the most widely circulated U.S. civil defense films of the 1950s, *Let's Face It*, described the problem posed by nuclear warfare:

> The tremendous effects of heat and blast on modern structures raise important questions concerning their durability and safety. Likewise, the amount of damage done to our industrial potential will have a serious effect upon our ability to recover from an atomic attack. Transportation facilities are vital to a modern city. The nation's lifeblood could be cut if its traffic arteries were severed. These questions are of great interest not only to citizens in metropolitan centers but also to those in rural areas who may be in a danger zone because of radioactive fallout from today's larger weapons. We could get many of the answers to these questions by constructing a complete city at our Nevada Proving Ground and then exploding a nuclear bomb over it. We could study the effects of damage over a wide area, under all conditions, and plan civil defense measures accordingly. But such a gigantic undertaking is not feasible.

We could build a city to bomb it. The problem voiced here is ultimately one of scientific detail: how can the security state prepare to survive a nuclear attack if it does not know in detail how every aspect of American life would respond to the unprecedented effects of the exploding bomb and the resulting social confusion? But after denying the possibility of building an entire city in Nevada simply to destroy it, the narrator of *Let's Face It* reveals that the nuclear state has, in fact, done just that:

> Instead we build representative units of a test city. With steel and stone and brick and mortar, with precision and skill—as though it were to last a thousand years. But it is a weird, fantastic city. A creation right out of science fiction. A city like no other on the face of the earth. Homes, neat and clean and completely furnished, that will never be occupied. Bridges, massive girders of steel spanning the empty desert. Railway tracks that lead to nowhere, for this is the end of the line. But every element of these tests is carefully planned as to its design and location in the area. A variety of materials and building techniques are often represented in a single structure. Every brick, beam, and board will have its story to tell. When pieced together these will give some of the answers, and some of the information we need to survive in the nuclear age.

A weird fantastic city. The test city was also an idealized model of the contemporary American suburb, and by publicizing its atomic destruction the state was involved in an explicit act of psychological manipulation. As we shall see, the Nevada Test Site was the location of nuclear war "simulations" that involved real nuclear explosions and model American cities destroyed in real time for a national audience. Each ruin in these national melodramas—each element of bombed U.S. material culture–was presented as a key to solving the "problem" of nuclear warfare, a means of cracking the code for survival in nuclear conflict. But in this effort to control a specific idea of death, the civil defense strategy also forced citizens to confront the logics of the nuclear state, allowing many to reclaim and reinvest these same ruins with a counternarrative and critique.[13] Thus, real and imagined nuclear ruins became the foundation for competing ideas of national community, producing both resistance to and the normalization of a militarized society. But even if the early Cold War effort to produce an "atomic bomb–proof" society failed, we shall see that the psychosocial legacies of this moment continue to haunt and inform U.S. national culture.[14] In the remainder of this chapter, I offer a visual history of nuclear ruins in the United States as a means both of recovering the affective and imaginative coordinates of the nuclear security state and of exploring the lasting impacts of the Cold War strategy of emotional management on American society in the age of counterterror.

"Cue for Survival"

On May 5, 1955, a hundred million Americans watched a typical suburban community being blown to bits by an atomic bomb on live television (Federal Civil Defense Administration 1955a, 1956). Many watched from homes and apartments that were the explicit models for the test city, and saw mannequin families posed in casual everyday moments (at the kitchen table, on the couch, in bed—or watching TV) experience the atomic blast. Operation Cue was the largest of the civil defense spectacles staged at the Nevada Test Site: it promised not only to demonstrate the power of an exploding bomb but also to show citizens exactly what a postnuclear American city would look like (Federal Civil Defense Administration 1955b). In addition to the live television coverage, film footage was widely distributed in the years after the test, with versions shown in movie theaters and replayed on television. Some of the most powerful and enduring U.S. images of atomic destruction were crafted during Operation Cue and remain in circulation to this day. Thus, in important ways, the broken buildings, charred rubble, and scorched mannequins produced in Operation Cue continue to structure contemporary American perceptions of postnuclear ruins, constituting a kind of ur-text for the nuclear age.

As an experiment, Operation Cue was designed to test the effects of an atomic blast on residences, utilities, mobile housing, vehicles, warning systems, as well as a variety of domestic items and bomb shelter designs. Linked to each of these objects was a specific test program and research team drawn from the Los Alamos Scientific Laboratory, Atomic Energy Commission, and FCDA. A variety of civil defense exercises were conducted in the aftermath of the explosion, including rescue operations, fire control, emergency evacuations by airplane, communication and sanitation efforts, and mass feeding experiments. The test city was designed to resemble a "representative" American community: it was made up of an assortment of current building styles (ramblers and two-story brick houses, as well as trailers and mobile homes), a full range of public utility systems (from electronic towers to propane gas tanks), and numerous types of bomb shelters. There were experiments designed to protect paper records, including a variety of office safes located across the test city. Over 150 industrial associations participated in the test, ensuring that the very latest consumer items—cars, furniture, clothing, dishes, televisions, and radios—were installed in the

L. A. Darling Co., civil defense mannequin family.

FIGURE 1.4. "Civil Defense Mannequin Family," Operation Cue, Federal Civil Defense Administration, 1955.

model homes and streets. Hundreds of civilian participants were invited to inhabit not the pristine pretest city but the posttest atomic ruins: civilians were simultaneously witnesses and test subjects, serving as representative "Americans" to be tested by viewing the blast and participating in mass feeding and other emergency operations afterward. The formal inhabitants of Operation Cue were the mannequin families, dressed and theatrically posed to suggest everyday activities, communicating through their posture and dress that the bombing was an unexpected intrusion into an intimate, everyday home space (figure 1.4).

Operation Cue was designed to appeal to a domestic audience, and particularly to women.[15] Unlike previous civil defense films, *Operation Cue* (1955) has a female narrator—Joan Collins—who promises to see the test "through my own eyes and the eye of the average citizen." In its effort to produce a bomb-proof society, the FCDA was concerned with documenting the effects of the bomb on every aspect of white, middle-class, suburban life (a de facto recognition that urban centers could not be protected in a nuclear war; see Galison 2001). The media strategy involved recalibrating domestic life by turning the nuclear family into a nuclearized family, preprogrammed for life before, during, and after a nuclear war. Gender roles were reinforced by dividing responsibility for food and security in a time of nuclear crisis between women and men. Similarly, the civil defense campaigns in public schools were designed to deploy children to educate their parents about civil defense. Normative gender roles were used to reinforce the idea that nuclear crisis was not an exceptional condition, but one that could be incorporated into everyday life with minor changes in household technique and a "can do" American spirit.

Of particular concern in Operation Cue, for example, were food tests and mass feeding programs. In each of the model homes, the pantries and refrigerators were stocked with food. In her voice-over, Collins underscores Operation Cue's focus on women, announcing: "As a mother and housewife, I was particularly interested in the food test program, a test that included canned and packaged food." Additionally, food in various types of packaging was buried along the desert test site to expose it to radiation, and some of the mannequin families were posed as if they were involved in food preparation at the time of the detonation. Conceptually, the argument was that at any moment of the day—while enjoying one's breakfast, for example—the bomb could drop. Laura McEnaney argues that the FCDA sought to create a "paramilitary housewife" (2000, 109), emotionally and materially in control of her home and thinking about postnuclear social life. Formally, the FCDA was interested in whether or not food would be too contaminated to eat in the immediate aftermath of a blast, and how to feed large groups of homeless, injured, and traumatized people. Within this scheme for crisis management, food was positioned as a primary means of calming individuals' anxieties and establishing social authority (111). Informally, the goal was to saturate the domestic space of the home with nuclear logics and civic obligations and to militarize men, women, and children to withstand either a very long nuclear confrontation or a very short nuclear war.

Food for the test was flown in from Las Vegas, Chicago, and San Francisco to document the government's ability to move large quantities of food around the country in a time of emergency. The FCDA report, *Effects of Nuclear Explosions on Frozen Food,* concludes that "under emergency conditions similar to this exposure, frozen foods may be used for both military and civilian feeding" (Schmitt 1956, 3), but this conclusion only hints at the scale of this experiment. Frozen chicken potpies were a privileged test item and were distributed through the test homes as well as buried in large freezers. The pies were then exposed to nuclear blast and tested for radiation, as well as nutritional value, color, and taste. Thus, while building increasingly powerful atomic and thermonuclear weapons, the security state set about demonstrating to Americans that even if the nation-state disappeared under nuclear fire, its newly developed prepared foods would still be edible (making the chicken potpie a curious emblem of modernity in the process). Like these bomb-proof pies, all commodified aspects of American life were to be tested against nuclear blast, as the state sought to demonstrate not only that there could be a postnuclear moment, but that life in it could be imagined on largely familiar terms.

Indeed, documenting evidence of material survival after an atomic blast was ultimately the point of Operation Cue. The mass feeding project, for example, pulled equipment from the wreckage after the test, as well as the food from refrigerators and buried canned goods, and served them to assembled participants: this emergency meal consisted of roast beef, tomato juice, baked beans, and coffee (Federal Civil Defense Administration 1955b, 67). The destruction of a model American community thus became the occasion for a giant picnic, with each item of food marked as having survived the atomic bomb and each witness positioned as a postnuclear survivor. Additionally, the emergency rescue group pulled damaged mannequins out of the rubble and practiced medical and evacuation techniques on them, eventually flying several charred and broken dummies to off-site hospitals by charter plane. The formal message of Operation Cue was that the postnuclear environment would be only as chaotic as citizens allowed, that resources (food, shelter, medical) would still be present, and that society—if not the nation-state—would continue. Nuclear war was ultimately presented as a state of mind that could be incorporated into one's normative reality: it was simply a matter of emotional preparation and mental discipline.

The mannequin families that were intact after the explosion were soon on a national tour, complete with tattered and scorched clothing. J.C. Penney, which had provided the garments, displayed these postnuclear families in its stores around the country. Presenting a detailed before-and-after photographic record of damage to each figure, the exhibit stated: "These mannikins could have been live people, in fact, they could have been you."[16] Inverting the appeal of a standard advertising campaign, the exhibit did not make the blue suit or polka-dot dress the focal point for viewers. Rather, it was the mannequin as survivor, whose very existence seemed to show that you could indeed "beat the A-bomb," as one civil defense film of the era promised. Invited to contemplate life in a postnuclear ruin as the docile mannequins of civil defense, the national audience for Operation Cue was caught in a sea of mixed messages about the power of the state to control the bomb. This kind of ritual enactment did not resolve the problem of the bomb; instead, it used nuclear fear to focus citizens on emotional self-discipline. It asked them to live on the knife's edge of a psychotic contradiction—an everyday life founded simultaneously on total threat and absolute normality—with the stakes being nothing less than survival itself.

Indeed, although *Operation Cue* was billed as a test of "the things we use in everyday life," the full intent of the overall project was to nationalize nuclear fear and install a new civic understanding via the contemplation of mass destruction and collective death. Consider the narrative of Arthur F. Landstreet (the general manager of the Hotel King Cotton in Memphis, Tennessee), who volunteered to crouch down in a trench at the Nevada Test Site, about 10,000 feet from ground zero, and experience the nuclear detonation in Operation Cue. After the explosion he explained why it was important for ordinary citizens to be tested on the front line of a nuclear detonation:

> Apparently the reason for stationing civilians at Position Baker was to find out what the actual reaction from citizens who were not schooled in the atomic field would be, and to get some idea of what the ordinary citizen might be able to endure under similar conditions. This idea was part of the total pattern to condition civilians for what they might be expected to experience in case of atomic attack. . . . Every step of the bomb burst was explained over and over from the moment of the first flash of light until the devastating blast. We were asked to make time tests from the trench to our jeeps. We did this time after time, endeavoring to create more speed and less loss of motion. We were told that this was necessary because, if the bomb exploded directly over us with practically no wind, the fallout would drop immediately downward, and we would be alerted to get out of the territory. We would have about 5 minutes to get at least 2.5 to 3 miles distant, so it was necessary that we learn every move perfectly. (Federal Civil Defense Administration 1955b, 73)

The total pattern to condition civilians. Physical reactions to the nuclear explosion are privileged in Landstreet's account, but a corollary project is also revealed: that of training the participants not to think in a case of emergency, but simply to act. If the first project was an emotional management effort to familiarize citizens with the exploding bomb—to psychologically inoculate them against their own apocalyptic imaginations—the latter project sought simply to control those same bodies, to train and time their response to official commands.[17] The atomic bomb extended the docility of the citizen-subject to new levels, as civil defense sought to absorb the everyday within a new normative reality imbued with the potential for an imminent and total destruction.

This short-circuiting of the mind and willingness to take orders under the sign of nuclear emergency reveal the broader scope of the civil defense project: anesthetizing as well as protecting, producing docility as well as

"SURVIVAL IS YOUR BUSINESS"

agency. This effort to document the potentialities of life in a postnuclear environment met with almost immediate resistance. In addition to the mounting scientific challenges to the claims of civil defense, a "mothers against the bomb" movement started in 1959 when two young parents in New York refused to participate in Operation Alert by simply taking their children to Central Park rather than to a fallout shelter (Garrison 2006, 93–95). The widely publicized effects of radioactive fallout in the 1950s, as well as the move from atomic to thermonuclear weapons, provided ample evidence that Operation Cue was not, in the end, a "realistic" portrait of nuclear warfare.[18] Indeed, when *Operation Cue* was re-released in 1964, the following text was added to the introduction, minimizing the claims of the film:

> The nuclear device used was comparatively small. It had an explosive force of 30 kilotons, equivalent to 30,000 tons of TNT. Whereas some modern thermonuclear weapons are in the 20-megaton range—twenty million tons—more than 600 times as powerful as the bomb shown here, and with a much wider radius of destruction. In this test, many of the structures damaged by the 30-kiloton bomb were approximately one mile from "ground zero." With a 20-megaton blast, they probably would be obliterated, and comparable damage would occur out to a distance of at least 8.5 or 9 miles.

They probably would be obliterated. Thus, as a scientific test of everyday objects, Operation Cue had less value over time, as the effects of blast, fire, and radiation in increasingly powerful weapons rendered civil defense almost immediately obsolete as a security concept. In Cold War ideology, however, the promise of nuclear ruins was deployed by the state to secure the possibility of a postnuclear remainder, and with it the inevitable reconstitution of social order. The discourse of "obliteration" here, however, reveals the technoscientific limitations of that ideological project, as the destructive reality of thermonuclear warfare radically limits the possibility of a postnuclear United States.

After the 1963 Limited Test Ban Treaty, U.S nuclear testing went underground and the effects of the exploding bomb were no longer visible. The elimination of aboveground tests had two immediate effects: it changed the terms of the public discourse about the bomb, as the state no longer had to rationalize the constant production of mushroom clouds and the related health concerns about the effects of radioactive fallout on American society; and it locked in place the visual record of the bomb. Thus, the visual record of the 1945–62 aboveground test program, with its deep investment in manipulating public opinions and emotions, remains the visual record of the bomb to this day. As science, Operation Cue was always questionable, but as national theater it remains a much more productive enterprise: it created an idealized consumer dream space and infused it with the bomb, creating the vocabulary for thinking about the nuclear emergency that continues to inform American politics (see figures 1.5 and 1.6). Thus, the motto of Operation Cue—"survival is your business"—is not an ironic moment of atomic kitsch but rather reveals the formal project of the nuclear state, underscoring the links among the production of threat, its militarized response, and the Cold War economic program. As an emotional management campaign, civil defense proved extraordinarily influential, installing in American national culture a set of ideas, images, and assumptions about nuclear weapons that continued to inform Cold War politics and remain powerful to this day. I turn now to two afterimages of the 1950s civil defense program, each set roughly a generation apart, to consider the lasting consequences of this era's emotional management strategy, and to explore the psychosocial effects of deploying highly detailed depictions of the end of the nation-state as a means of establishing national community.

Afterimage 1: *The Day After*

The anticipation of nuclear war (dreaded as the fantasy, or phantasm, of a remainderless destruction) installs humanity—and through all sorts of relays even defines the essence of modern humanity—in its rhetorical condition.

—Jacques Derrida, "No Apocalypse, Not Now"

On Sunday, November 20, 1983, a hundred million Americans turned on their televisions to watch the United States destroyed by Soviet intercontinental ballistic missiles (ICBMs), and a few survivors in Lawrence, Kansas, negotiate everyday life in a postnuclear environment (see figure 1.7). Watched by half of the adult population in the United States, *The Day After* was a major cultural event, one that refocused public attention on the effects of radiation, mass casualties, and postnuclear life without a functioning state. Presented as a "realistic" portrayal, the blast and radiation effects depicted in the film were supported by statements from health experts and transformed into a moment of national dialog about the physical and biological effects of nuclear war (Rubin and Cummings 1989). Immediately following the film's broadcast on ABC, the network presented a roundtable discussion of the film and the current state of nuclear emergency. Public school teachers across

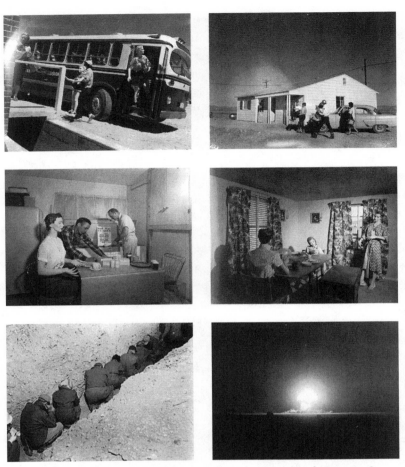

FIGURES 1.5 AND 1.6 (above and opposite). Photographic sequence of Operation Cue, U.S. National Archives and Records Administration.

the country advised students to watch *The Day After* in order to discuss its implications in class, thereby nationalizing the discussion. Even President Ronald Reagan, whose arms buildup and provocative nuclear rhetoric helped instigate the film, watched along with his fellow Americans, announcing after the program that he too had been terrified by its depiction of nuclear war. In synchronizing a hundred million viewing subjects, *The Day After* created a national community brought together by images of its own destruction. In doing so, the film also replayed the official program of Operation Cue with uncanny precision and demonstrated the enduring national and cultural legacy of the 1950s emotional management project.

The Day After follows several idealized Midwestern families, document-ing their lives before nuclear war breaks out and then attempting to survive in a postnuclear world. The first hour of the film is devoted to everyday life in Lawrence (against the backdrop of increasing international tensions); the second hour is devoted to the brief nuclear strike and then life in a postnuclear environment. The film rehearses the lessons of Operation Cue with an eerie fidelity: after nuclear attack, the state is absent, and it is up to citizens to step in to provide order, food, and medical care to survivors. The key difference between *The Day After* and Operation Cue has to do with the nature of survival: although Operation Cue argued that life was

FIGURE 1.7. Soviet nuclear attack in *The Day After* (1983).

possible after nuclear attack and promoted the idea that nuclear war was simply another form of everyday risk (alongside weather, fire, and traffic accidents), *The Day After* questioned whether life after nuclear war was worth living.[19] The central protagonist of the story, a doctor played by Jason Robards, is shown in the final scene dying of radiation sickness, collapsed in what might be the ruins of his former home, his wife and children long dead from the attack. No triumphal narrative of survival and reinvention here. Instead, the final moment of the film issues yet another warning:

> The catastrophic events you have witnessed are, in all likelihood, less severe than the destruction that would actually occur in the event of a full nuclear strike against the United States. It is hoped that the images of this film will inspire the nations of this earth, their peoples and leaders, to find the means to avert the fateful day.

Less severe than a full nuclear strike. Thus, the "realism" of *The Day After* is revealed in the end to be a deception—just as was the case with the *Operation Cue* film a generation earlier—as the filmmakers are forced to admit that the horror of nuclear war is ultimately beyond the power of cinematic representation.

The simulated realism of the film perfectly illustrates Derrida's claim that nuclear war is "fabulously textual" because until it happens it can only be imagined, and once it happens it marks the end of the human archive (1984, 23). As the only "remainderless event," nuclear war is thus in the realm of the sublime, ungraspable and subject only to displacements, compensations, and misrecognitions (28). Thus, by rehearsing nuclear war in the imagination or via civil defense exercises, one does not master either the event or its aftermath. Rather, one domesticates an image of a postnuclear world that stands in for the failure of the imagination to be able to conceive of the end. This postnuclear imagination is necessarily an arena of cultural work, as early Cold War officials immediately recognized—one that promotes an idea of order out of the sublime and often becomes a space of pure ideology. To this end, the consistency of the nuclear tropes presented in *The Day After* and the nationalization of the televised event document the multigenerational power of nuclear ruins in the American imaginary. A full generation after Operation Cue, filmmakers could rehearse with startling specificity the entire 1950s program of civil defense and provoke a national conversation about life after nuclear war. The state was no longer needed to enact this national melodrama of destruction because its terms were already deeply installed in American culture and subject to simple citation and repositioning. The entertainment industry could now provide the firestorm and fallout as "special effects," rehearsing the lessons of nuclear crisis that a live television audience first experienced in 1955 via a real nuclear detonation in Nevada. This time, however, the ruins were engineered not to "emotionally inoculate" Americans against nuclear war, but rather to shock them into action during the nuclear emergency of the early 1980s.

Put differently, the Reagan administration's escalating arms race and talk of "winnable" nuclear wars (Sheer 1982) produced a cultural return to the images and logics of Operation Cue, mobilized this time as a call to political action rather than normalization. Thus, the form and content of cinematic nuclear destruction remained largely unchanged from 1955 to 1983, but its emotional project was inverted from promoting the docility of the citizen-subject to mobilizing a national community before the bombs fall. *The Day After* reenacted the national melodrama articulated in Operation Cue twenty-eight years earlier with remarkable precision, but it did so not to produce a bomb-proof society but rather as a de facto form of nuclear critique. Similarly, activist groups (including Physicians for Social Responsibility and the Nuclear Freeze Campaign) used depictions of nuclear warfare—including targeting and blast damage maps of U.S. cities and medical analyses of radiation injuries—to counter the escalating military budgets and nuclear tensions of the late Cold War.[20] In other words, the calibration of the emotional management project was no longer controlled solely by the government, allowing counterformulations using the same texts and images that originally structured the Cold War cultural project. Nuclear ruins are revealed here to be the grammar of nuclear discourse in the United States—enabling both pronuclear and antinuclear projects— inevitably deployed to articulate the affective terms of national belonging. For despite its implicit nuclear critique and antiwar message, *The Day After* continues to mobilize a nuclear-bombed America as a call to community rather than as a marker of the end of sociability itself.

Afterimage 2: *Armageddon* and *Deep Impact*

There was a tacit agreement, equally binding on everyone, that the true state of material and moral ruin in which the country found itself was not to be described. The darkest aspects of the final act of destruction, as experienced by the great majority of the German population, remained under a kind of taboo like a shameful family secret, a secret that could not even be privately acknowledged.

—W. G. Sebald, *On the Natural History of Destruction*

Questioning the near total silence in German literature about everyday life in the bombed-out ruins of World War II, Sebald finds an "extraordinary faculty for self-anesthesia shown by a community that seemed to have emerged from a war of annihilation without any signs of psychological impairment" (2004, 11). He attributes this absence of commentary (about life in the ruins of Dresden and other German cities that were firebombed by the United States) to a collective understanding that it was Germany that had pioneered mass bombing years earlier, in Guernica, Warsaw, and Belgrade (104). Thus, the national repression he interrogates is double—that of life in the postwar ruins and that of a prior position as mass bomber— linking trauma and destruction as part of the same psychosocial legacy. I suggest that the United States—a country that did not experience mass bombings in World War II but that did conduct them, using both conventional and nuclear weapons—took an opposite national and cultural route in the Cold War. For while nuclear war did not occur after the destruction of Hiroshima and Nagasaki, rather than repress the bomb, American culture proliferated its meaning and influence. The bomb became an intimate part of American popular and political culture, incorporated into a set of ideas, images, and institutions that were installed in the 1950s and soon functioned outside the direct control of the national security state (see, for example, Brians 2006; Evans 1998; Sontag 1966). In other words, we live today in the world made by the Cold War, a global project that engineered everyday life—indeed, life itself—around the technological means of apocalyptic destruction (see Masco 2006).

What are we to make, for example, of the Hollywood films of the 1990s—the first period in the nuclear age in which U.S. national security was not structured in relationship to a nuclear-armed external enemy—that nonetheless repetitively enact the destruction of the nation on film? Although we no longer detonate atomic bombs on fabricated cities populated with mannequins, we do have yearly spectacles in which America's cities are reduced to smoldering ruins all in the name of fun. The Hollywood blockbuster—with its fearsome life-ending asteroids, alien invasions, earthquakes, floods, and wars—allows Americans to rehearse the destruction of their nation-state much as their parents and grandparents did in the 1950s and 1980s. These yearly technoaesthetic displays of finely rendered destruction are a unique form of American expressive culture. Only U.S. cinema deploys the cutting-edge technological achievements of computer-generated imagery to visualize the destruction of its cities in this way and does so with such fetishistic glee.[21]

Consider 1998, a year when the United States was twice attacked cinematically by asteroids—in *Armageddon* (directed by Michael Bay) and *Deep Impact* (directed by Mimi Leder)—the second and eighth most successful films of the year at the box office. In both cases, life on earth is threatened from outer space and saved only at the last minute by the heroics of Americans armed with nuclear weapons (see figures 1.8 and 1.9). While *Armageddon* uses the threat to the planet as a vehicle for promoting working-class males as protectors of the nation/planet (as oil riggers are sent via the space shuttle to destroy the asteroid with atomic bombs), *Deep Impact* is a study of civil defense and individual sacrifice right out of Operation Cue. In both cases, what is most striking is that the destruction of the United States is presented as a form of entertainment and redemptive play for American audiences. Part of a new genre of summer films in the 1990s that rehearse the destruction of the United States and demonstrate the necessity of U.S. nuclear weapons, I think we have to read this moment of popular entertainment as a space of psychosocial release from the Cold War arms race (cf. Mellor 2007; D. Davis 2001; Rogin 1998). In the 1990s, Hollywood could work out the details of nuclear war (and various allegorized

"SURVIVAL IS YOUR BUSINESS"

FIGURE 1.8. New York City under attack in *Armageddon* (1998).

FIGURE 1.9. New York City under attack in *Deep Impact* (1998).

nuclear threats) with new computer-generated precision—precisely because nuclear terror no longer had the meaning it had had for a previous
generation. In the immediate post–Cold War moment, in other words, life
did not hang so oppressively in the nuclear balance, and thus the cinematic
imagination was freed to explore the end of the United States in a new
way. Cold War nuclear cinema always had a moral point to make about the
nuclear state of emergency: nuclear war was not only always marked as an
object of distinct seriousness, but the detonation of the bomb was marked
as a political/ethical/technological failure of the Cold War system. In striking contrast, post–Cold War films have no purpose other than patriotism
and pleasure; they seek to reinstall American identity through aestheticized
mass violence, suggesting that only threat and reactions to threat can create
national community.[22]

Regardless of the form of existential danger (asteroids, tsunamis, alien
invaders), these apocalyptic spectacles function as nuclear texts because
they use mass destruction as a means of mobilizing the United States as a

global superpower. As allegories of nuclear war, they both reproduce the emotional language of nuclear danger (mass death as a vehicle for establishing national community) and allow a productive misrecognition of its political content. This filmic genre also inevitably reinforces through aestheticized politics the ever-present need for war, and the ubiquity of external enemies armed with apocalyptic power. And in doing so, these texts relegitimize the need for nuclear weapons in the United States, while offering an image of the United States as a reluctant superpower forced into global military action for the greater good. As a maelstrom of meteorites devastates New York in *Armageddon*, for example, a taxi driver yells to no one in particular: "We at war! Saddam Hussein is bombing us!" This fictional scene from 1998 prefigures the Bush administration's claim—widely believed but fabricated—that there was a link between the terrorist attacks on New York and Washington in 2001 and the Iraqi government of Saddam Hussein. Naming the enemy in this way (as science fiction or state propaganda) underscores the ideological alignment between the Hollywood blockbuster and the U.S. military, both of which rely on rehearsing threat as a means of stabilizing their industries.[23] Cinematic viewers, as Benjamin saw so early (1969), experience such ideological projects in a state of distraction, allowing both the covert habituation of ideas and a broader aestheticizing of politics in support of increasing militarization and war (see also Sontag 1966).

One afterimage of the Cold War campaign of emotional management is found in the continued commitment to, and pleasure in, making nuclear ruins and then searching the wreckage for signs of the collective future. The nuclear logics of the Cold War continue to haunt American society, informing how individuals experience acts of mass violence and how the security state then engages the world. Nuclear cinema in the 1990s transforms anonymous mass death into a vehicle for individuals to demonstrate their moral character and for the nation to be regenerated through apocalyptic violence. Indeed, the pleasure of post–Cold War nuclear cinema lies precisely in witnessing the destruction of the United States and then walking out of the theater into the unbroken world. Unlike viewers of *Operation Cue* in 1955 and *The Day After* in 1983, the viewers of *Armageddon* and *Deep Impact* were not addressed as citizens who needed to demonstrate their civic virtue by performing nuclear fear. Rather, the emotional management strategy was transformed into a form of post-traumatic play, with the destruction of the nation now presented as a diversion rather than a serious threat or opportunity for political mobilization. Nonetheless, it is important to recognize the remarkable coherence of the nuclear images from 1955 through 1998 to see the long-term effects of the Cold War strategy of emotional management. It is also important to interrogate the long-term effects on American national culture of rehearsing mass violence in this manner, of repetitively producing images of destroyed U.S. cities to constitute both pleasure and community.

Epilogue

Facing clear evidence of peril, we cannot wait for the final proof, the smoking gun that could come in the form of a mushroom cloud.
—**President George W. Bush, "President Bush Outlines Iraqi Threat," October 7, 2002**

In what has to be the most undiplomatic statement ever made, the Assistant Secretary of State . . . said we had to decide whether we were with America or with the terrorists, but that if we chose the terrorists, then we should be prepared to be bombed back to the Stone Age.
—**President Pervez Musharraf, *In the Line of Fire: A Memoir***

Reclaiming the emotional history of the atomic bomb is crucial today, as nuclear terror has been amplified to enable a variety of political projects at precisely the moment when American memory of the bomb has become impossibly blurred. In the United States, nuclear fear has recently been used to justify preemptive war and unlimited domestic surveillance, a worldwide system of secret prisons; and the practices of rendition, torture, and assassination. But what do Americans today actually know or remember of the bomb? We live not in the ruins produced by Soviet ICBMs, but rather in the emotional ruins of the Cold War as an intellectual, imaginative, and social project. The half-century-long project to install and articulate the nation through contemplating its violent end has colonized the present. The suicide-hijacker attacks on New York City and Washington in 2001 may have produced an immediate political consensus that the Cold War "was over" and a formal declaration of a counterterror project.[24] But American reactions to those attacks were structured by a multigenerational state project to harness the fear of mass death to divergent political and military industrial agendas. By evoking the image of the mushroom cloud to enable the invasion of Iraq, President Bush appealed directly to citizens' nuclear fear, a cultural product of the very Cold War nuclear standoff he formally disavowed in inaugurating the new counterterror state. The mushroom cloud imagery, as well as the totalizing immediacy of the threat in his presentation, worked to redeploy a cultural memory of apocalyptic nuclear threat (established during the four decades of the Soviet-American nuclear arms race) as part of the new War on Terror. The new color-coded terrorist warning system (based on a similar system proposed in Project East River [Associated Universities 1952] to deal with nuclear-armed Soviet bombers), as well as the more recent transformation of shampoo bottles on planes into an imminent threat by the Department of Homeland Security, are official efforts to install and regulate fear in everyday life through a public theater of insecurity.[25] In this regard, the War on Terror has been conducted largely as a campaign of emotional management within the United States, using the tropes and logics developed during the early Cold War to enable a new kind of American geopolitical project. The war redirects but also reiterates the American assumptions about mass violence, technology, and democracy I have explored in this chapter.

If the September 2001 attacks on New York and Washington felt strangely familiar to many U.S. citizens, it was because American society has been imaginatively rehearsing the destruction of these cities for more than three generations: in the civil defense campaigns of the early and late Cold War, as well as in the Hollywood blockbusters of the 1990s, which destroyed these cities each summer with increasing nuance and detail. The genealogy of this form of entertainment is traumatic, dating back to the specific way in which the United States entered the nuclear age as the perpetrator of the atomic bombings of Hiroshima and Nagasaki and to the specific propaganda campaigns informing nuclear threat throughout the four decades of Cold War. Indeed, the ease with which the suicide-hijacker attacks were nationalized as part of a nuclear discourse by the new counterterror state has much to do with this legacy (see Dower 2010; Kaplan 2003). Not coincidentally, the two graphic measures of nuclear blast damage most frequently used during the Cold War involved the Pentagon and the New York City skyline (see Eden 2004; Galison 2001). Figures 1.10 and 1.11, for example, are taken from the U.S. Atomic Energy Commission's campaign to document the size of the first U.S. hydrogen bomb test in 1952. Fourteen true-to-scale versions of the Pentagon (identified by the AEC as the largest building in the world) were placed inside the blast crater (the former Elugelab Island) to document its size, while the New York skyline is used to demonstrate the vast horizontal and vertical scope of the detonation. The attacks of September 2001 were easily nationalized and transformed into a nuclear discourse precisely because the U.S. security culture has imagined and rehearsed attacks on Washington and New York for generations, and because the specific symbols in the attacks (the Pentagon and the tallest building in the New York skyline) were also used by the nuclear state

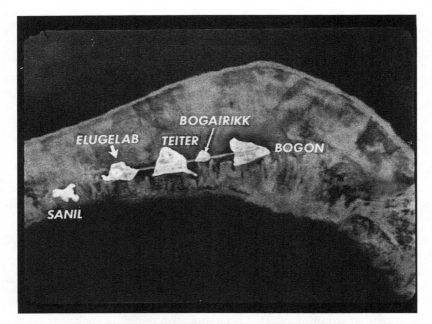

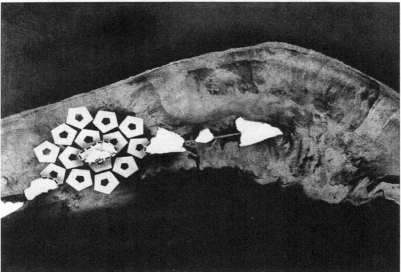

FIGURE 1.10. Before and after images of the first U.S. hydrogen bomb explosion, with true-to-scale replicas of the Pentagon in the blast crater, U.S. National Archives and Record Administration.

FIGURE 1.11. Blast radius of the first U.S. hydrogen bomb explosion set against the New York skyline, U.S. National Archives and Records Administration.

for three generations as part of its strategy of emotional management. In other words, the Bush administration mobilized a well-established logic of nuclear attack to pursue its policy objectives in Iraq, translating discrete, nonnuclear threats into the emotional equivalent of a global nuclear crisis.

Since the United States constructs itself via discourses of ruination, it should not be a surprise to see a corollary U.S. exportation of ruins on a global scale. As Pakistani President Pervez Musharraf clearly understood, the "with us or against us" stance of the Bush administration in 2001 left no ambiguity about the cost to Pakistan if it did not align itself with the sole remaining global superpower at the start of its War on Terror (2006, 201). The threat to reduce Pakistan to a "Stone Age" ruin is an alternative, international deployment of nuclear fear, constituting a U.S. promise to reduce that country to a prenational, pretechnological state. This threat of annihilation has its roots in the atomic bombings of Hiroshima and Nagasaki and is a recurring Cold War form, also expressed by U.S. officials in the mass bombing campaigns in Korea, Vietnam, and Cambodia. Thus, the United States enters the twenty-first century as a nation both fascinated by and traumatized by nuclear ruins. It transforms real and imagined mass death into a nationalized space and supports a political culture that believes bombing campaigns

"SURVIVAL IS YOUR BUSINESS"

can produce democracy. It simultaneously is terrorized by nuclear weapons and threatens to use them. The U.S. military both wages preemptive war over nascent WMD programs and is committed to maintaining state-of-the-art nuclear weapons for all future contingencies.[26] American society is today neither "atomic bomb–proof" nor capable of engaging nuclear technologies as a global problem of governance. Instead, U.S. citizens live today in the emotional residues of the Cold War nuclear arms race, which can address those citizens only as fearful and docile bodies. Thus, even in the twenty-first century, Americans remain caught between terror and fear, trapped in the psychosocial space defined by the once and future promise of nuclear ruins.

TWO

BAD WEATHER
On Planetary Crisis

Within the visual culture of the nuclear age, a very few sequences of film now constitute the core American cultural memory of the atomic bomb. This sequence of a forest experiencing a nuclear blast, for example, has attained a kind of iconic status, reproduced repetitively in documentary and fiction films for the past half-century to demonstrate the power of the exploding bomb (see figure 2.1). In presenting a forest bent to the breaking point, the intellectual value of these three seconds of film is to introduce viewers to an experience of the nuclear sublime.[1] The power of the blast, when mapped against one's own locality, also provides a rare point of physical reference in U.S. nuclear footage, offering a recognizable human scale that has informed official statements, antinuclear activism, and Hollywood productions alike. In the slow-motion footage of a dense forest blown back like a meadow of grass, viewers are confronted with a moment of pure ecological devastation, a kind of fury that is unprecedented and uncontrollable, and yet also oddly familiar. It is this notion of ecological risk mediated by national security concerns that I investigate in this chapter. For the iconic status of these bent and broken trees addresses multiple registers of American insecurity. Uncannily mirrored in the video footage of recent natural catastrophes—from the tsunami that hit Indian Ocean states in 2004 to the hurricane that submerged New Orleans in 2005 to the tsunami (and resulting nuclear crisis) in Fukushima in 2011, to the massive storm surge that submerged New York in 2013—

FIGURE 2.1. The trees of Operation Upshot-Knothole (stills from *Operation Upshot-Knothole*, U.S. Department of Defense).

this traumatized forest also allows us to interrogate the relationship of national security as a state project to the biosphere as the ultimate domain of human security. This sequence is undoubtedly a depiction of a crisis, but of what kind? It is a military experiment involving a weapon of mass destruction (WMD), but it is also a military test of a specific ecosystem—it appears as both a tool of war and as a war on nature—and thus a crisis of the future and of the now.

We live in an age of crisis—multiple overlapping crises, in fact, involving war, capital, ecology, governance—and in recent years have witnessed an extraordinary normalization of violence in everyday life via the War on

Terror. This cinematic depiction of ecological fury contains within in it a basic question about how to identify crisis, while expressing the conceptual power of war to override all other concerns. Revisiting these trees from a perspective of environmental risk reveals, I think, not only the technoscientific contribution of the Cold War arms race to our understanding of the biosphere as a fragile ecosystem but also the power of the bomb to block collective thought and action. For when, and under what conditions, does it become possible for citizens to imagine a truly planetary crisis? I argue here that the Cold War nuclear project enabled a new vision of the planet as an integrated biosphere, but that it is precisely the security state's reliance on nuclear weapons to constitute the United States' superpower status that blocks action on nonmilitarized planetary threats, and specifically on climate change. How the security state acknowledges terror—selecting specific fears and crises out of the multitude that exist and can be imagined, while ignoring other forms of existing violence—is a central concern of this chapter.

As we shall see, the Cold War nuclear arms race produced an unprecedented commitment to research in the earth sciences, enabling a new vision of the globe as an integrated political, technological, and environmental space. The U.S. nuclear project was linked very early on to concerns about weather, leading to new public fears and visions of planetary danger. But by elevating nuclear fear to the core instrument of state power, the Cold War arms race established a nationalized vision of planetary danger on very specific terms. In the early twenty-first century, the security state's effort to monopolize threat under a discourse of nuclear terror came into direct confrontation with the scientific evidence of rapid ecological change. For the counterterror state, the "terrorist armed with a WMD" trumps global warming as a planetary threat, underscoring the extraordinary politics involved in defining both *terror* and the *state of emergency*. The burned and breaking limbs of the postnuclear forest, however, not only offer an alternative genealogy of the nuclear age but also allow an assessment of the distorting effects of the bomb on contemporary American ideas of imminent danger.

In this chapter, I examine three moments (1953, 1983, and 2003) in which nuclear crisis and ecological crisis became linked objects of concern, and I assess the acts of political translation that allowed diverse forms of threat to be configured as a singular national security problem, one supporting the geopolitics of the U.S. security state. I am interested in the development of new infrastructures—technological, conceptual, and affective—and the unintended connections between the constant drive for new state capacities and future crises. I begin with the formal linkage between the atomic bomb and weather in the early Cold War earth sciences. I then explore how climate change was used to affect nuclear policy in the 1980s. Finally, I discuss how nuclear discourse has been mobilized in the 2000s to influence perceptions of climate change during the U.S. War on Terror. Attending to the ecological coordinates of the nuclear revolution in this way fundamentally challenges contemporary American ideas about planetary danger. It also reveals the conceptual and practical limits of a strictly "national" form of security.

Militarizing Nature, 1953

While seeming to portray an alpine forest, the film was actually shot in the desert landscape of the Nevada Test Site (see figure 2.2). Part of a nuclear test series in 1953 known as Operation Upshot-Knothole, the forest was constructed out of Ponderosa pines that were cut and transported from California to Nevada. Each of the 145 trees was sunk into concrete at the desert test site, creating a perfectly symmetrical, grid formation, forest. This synthetic forest was loaded with sensors and photographed from a variety of angles during the atomic blast. The goal, according to the once top-secret project report, was "to determine effects of blast wave and association winds on trees—in terms of tree breakage, branch breakage and defoliation—located in a forest area of such stand density that the shock front and its accompanying winds are influenced by the presence of the stand" (U.S. Department of Defense 1953, 36). As part of a larger techno-scientific effort to develop a comprehensive predictive capability for nuclear warfare and its material effects, this synthetic forest was constructed by the Department of Agriculture to be destroyed. Here is how the Department of Defense originally presented the experiment to nuclear war planners and other government officials in a formerly classified documentary film, *Operation Upshot-Knothole* (1953):

> A study of tactical importance: one hundred and forty-five Ponderosa pines set in concrete, approximately 6,400 feet from shot nine's zero. Instrumentation was thorough. A few major types being: pressure gauges at three heights, time-recording anemometers, phenotype dynamic pressure detectors, and snubber-wire arrangements to measure deflections. Pendulums were substituted for the lollipops of former operations, to provide mechanical simulation of tree response.

FIGURE 2.2. Building the test forest at the Nevada Test Site, U.S. National Archives and Records Administration.

As on many of these projects, camera stations were set up to provide high-speed motion picture coverage of blast effects. Thermal input: 18 calories per square centimeter—resulting in only mild charring on tree trunks since the normal ground litter that will ignite at around three calories was lacking. Static pressures around four psi. Post-blast surveys indicated that approximately twenty percent of the trees were broken and the missile hazard from falling trunks and limbs would be substantial.

A study of tactical importance. As a military science experiment, this event was part of a larger U.S. project to test the bomb against machinery, a variety of animal and human populations, as well as elements of the land, ocean, and atmosphere (see Masco 2006, 289). Part war fighting, part civil defense, part weapons science, the aboveground experiments conducted between 1945 and 1962 not only engineered the U.S. nuclear arsenal, they also produced and fixed American visual understandings of the technology on film. The technoaesthetics of the bomb were established for the American public in this period, as the U.S. nuclear test regime went underground in 1963, eliminating most visual evidence of the blasts (43). The visual record of the aboveground test period is thus more than simply an illustration of the logics of the security state—and the technoscience of producing atomic and thermonuclear explosions—it remains a primary conceptual means of understanding the destructive power of the bomb.

Aboveground nuclear experiments were labeled "tests", but the destruction was real, making each detonation an event with large-scale environmental consequences. The blast wave that bent this synthetic forest, for example, was only the most immediate of its environmental effects, as fallout from the explosion traversed the continental United States. Indeed, the eleven atomic detonations of Operation Upshot-Knothole produced substantial radioactive fallout in the United States, making it one of the most harmful Nevada test series in terms of public health (R. Miller 1986).[2] Today the remnants of this synthetic forest exist as a series of symmetrically aligned stumps in the Nevada desert, a cryptic marker of a moment when the Department of Agriculture was also a nuclear war–fighting agency (Johnson, Holz, and Jones 2000, 102). At its most basic, the lesson of "Project 3.19: Effects of Atomic Explosion on Trees in Forest Stands" was that a nuclear blast could profoundly damage a forest and ignite fires (see figure 2.3; U.S. Department of Defense 1953). The study did not investigate other kinds of nuclear effects on the trees, from radiation levels to potential mutation rates over time, as this forest was dead at the moment of its fabrication. Lost in the history of the Cold War—and in the technoscience of megatons and missiles that informed the nuclear "balance of terror"—is, however, this extraordinary new state commitment to atmospheric and earth sciences. In test ranges across the forty-eight contiguous states and in Alaska and the Marshall Islands, the development of the bomb not only produced unprecedented environmental damage, it also inaugurated a newly comprehensive scientific effort to understand the global biosphere as a postnuclear environment (Doel 2003). This synthetic forest remains important today because it reveals the official nuclear imagination in 1953, and registers an

FIGURE 2.3. The trees of Operation Upshot-Knothole after the atomic test, U.S. National Archive and Records Administration.

early effort to study ecological effects. The film footage of the trees under maximum stress has also become an iconic image of atomic devastation.

Indeed, the first decades of the Cold War turned the entire world into an experimental nuclear theater. The 215 aboveground and underwater nuclear detonations that the U.S. conducted between 1945 and 1962 produced a vast range of environmental effects that transformed both the globe and the earth sciences.[3] In the South Pacific, for example, two of the largest thermonuclear explosions—"Mike" in November 1952 (a 10.4-megaton blast) and "Bravo" in March 1954 (a 15-megaton explosion that was the single largest U.S. nuclear detonation of the Cold War, with more than a thousand times the explosive power of the bomb dropped on Hiroshima)—delivered vast radioactive material into the upper stratosphere (see figure 2.4). Noting that "for centuries meteorologists have thought of exploring large-scale atmospheric circulations by means of tracers," the meteorologists Machta, List, and Hubert mobilized the fallout to study global wind patterns in their 1956 *Science* article, "World-Wide Travel of Atomic Debris." Using data from the Mike and Bravo detonations, the researchers demonstrated that fallout entered the upper stratosphere and circled the earth, distributing fallout across the northern hemisphere. In the process of studying these nuclear effects, they also mapped stratospheric wind patterns (see figure 2.5).

FIGURE 2.4. The thermonuclear detonations "Mike" (November 1, 1952, Enewetak Atoll), top, and "Bravo" (March 1, 1954, Bikini Atoll), bottom, U.S. Department of Energy.

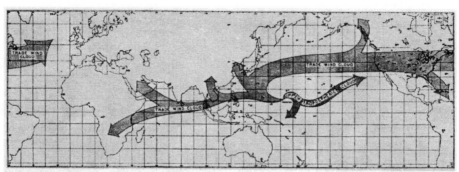

Fig. 2. Early history of the Mike cloud. The figures indicate the number of days between detonation and the first ground observation of fission products.

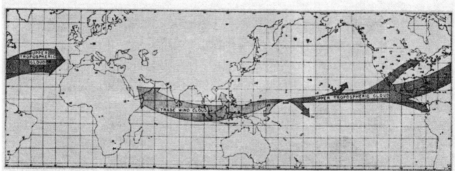

Fig. 3. Early history of the Bravo cloud. The figures indicate the number of days between detonation and the first ground observation of fission products.

FIGURE 2.5. Illustrations of atmospheric transport of radioactive materials from "Mike" and "Bravo" from Machta, List, and Hubert (1956).

Their work was part of a wide range of new research that used the effects of atmospheric nuclear testing to study ecological transport and circulation (see also Kroening 1965; Hare 1962; Odum and Odum 1955). For example, Comar, Russell, and Wasserman (1957) tracked the global distribution of strontium-90 from nuclear tests through the food chain, demonstrating that fallout deposited in the soil could be traced through plant and animal vectors into human beings.

By tracking the distribution of radioactive elements produced by atomic testing through the atmosphere and across plant, animal, and human populations, Cold War scientists were able to document the integration of the global biosphere. Mapping biology against geography and global wind patterns, for example, the RAND Corporation (1953) tracked the planetary distribution of strontium-90 from thermonuclear atmospheric weapons tests explicitly to determine its biological effects on people. Named "Project Sunshine" to dispel its gruesome implications, the RAND study found that fallout from the Marshall Island's nuclear tests were recorded at "44 stations in the United States" and "49 stations worldwide"; it also noted that there were "still large areas in the polar regions and the south of the equator, and of course, behind the Iron Curtain, that were not sampled" (1953, 30–33). Not only was the nuclear complex now a global enterprise, with U.S. laboratories stretching from the continental United States to the South Pacific, but the effects of nuclear explosions were increasingly recognized as planetary in scope, creating unprecedented health risks as well as new multidisciplinary cartographic opportunities. In an early moment in what was to become human genome science, RAND initiated a global project to collect human bones (with a focus on children) to study the absorption rates of strontium and possible genetic damage.[4] RAND also advocated the creation of a global project to monitor soils (as a central vector in spreading strontium-90 into the food chain) and speculated about the effects of nuclear testing on global weather patterns. Early Cold War scientists mapped the effects of radioactive fallout on human cells, plants, animals, landmasses, water systems, jet-stream patterns, and the atmosphere with increasing precision, using the bomb as health threat, economic resource, and experimental lens. In other words, the military commitment to understanding the full range of nuclear effects generated unprecedented levels of funding for the full spectrum of earth and atmospheric sciences.

Throughout the period of aboveground tests, Americans voiced increasing concern about the health effects of radioactive fallout, generating antinuclear and nascent environmental movements (see Rojecki 1999; Katz

1986; see also Wittner 1993, 1997, and 2003). Reading across the scientific literatures on fallout from this period, one discovers a constant concern about atomic tests changing the weather and destabilizing the seasons.[5] Indeed, the American public responded to the widely publicized U.S. nuclear testing and civil defense programs (which, as we have seen, were an explicit effort to psychologically and emotionally mobilize citizens as cold warriors) by attributing all manner of unusual natural phenomena—earthquakes, drought, floods, changes in agricultural cycles, hurricanes, insect plagues, changes in animal migration patterns, and strange weather patterns—to the bomb. The Atomic Energy Commission formed a special committee on Meteorological Aspects of the Effects of Atomic Radiation in 1956 to address these public concerns. In the journal *Science*, it offered the following conclusions:

> No statistically significant changes in the weather during the first 10 years of the atomic age have been found, yet careful physical analysis of the effects of nuclear explosions on the atmosphere must be made if we are to obtain a definite evaluation of this problem. Although it is not possible to prove that nuclear explosions have or have not influenced the weather, it is believed that such an effect is unlikely. (Committee on Meteorological Aspects of the Effects of Atomic Radiation 1956, 112)

In the first ten years of the atomic age. Despite the committee's declaration, the mounting evidence from biological, earth, and atmospheric sciences was that nuclear testing had a vast range of effects. Radioactive fallout not only traversed state territories (implicating nonnuclear states in the U.S. nuclear program) but also damaged ecosystems around the globe.

While previous generations of scientists imagined the experimental laboratory as a model of the world, in the early Cold War period the world itself became the laboratory. Experiments across a wide range of disciplines demonstrated that each biological being on the planet was increasingly marked by the trace elements of the U.S. nuclear testing program, as the earth, sea, and sky were transformed into experimental zones for nuclear science. Consider for a moment Shot Teak of the Hardtack test series conducted at Johnston Atoll on July 31, 1958. To study how the bomb would affect the upper atmosphere, scientists at the Los Alamos Scientific Laboratory detonated a 2.4-megaton warhead at 250,000 feet at 11:30 PM. The resulting nuclear flash was capable of temporarily blinding people in an area of 435 square miles; it also disrupted the Van Allen Belt, producing an aurora borealis that could be seen throughout the Pacific rim. This test knocked out electrical power stations from Hawaii to Australia, demonstrating both a new weapon—the electromagnetic pulse—and inaugurating a new generation of U.S. weapons research devoted to "hardening" military equipment against electrical disruption in nuclear warfare (see Hoerlin 1976). The first years of the Cold War, in short, were a period in which the global biosphere was quite literally militarized by the U.S. nuclear state, but as a result it was also positioned as a comprehensive object of research in the earth, ocean, atmospheric, and biological sciences (cf. Oreskes 2003). Ecological threat was publicly recognized by these projects, even if the arms race with the Soviet Union was prioritized at each step in U.S. Cold War policy. A nascent understanding of the impacts of technology on the biosphere was nonetheless established, generating the research questions that would ultimately inform understandings of climate change.

Producing experimental evidence of climate change, however, requires more than the accumulation of data sets in specific scientific disciplines; it requires a systematic means of measuring environmental conditions over time and of integrating diverse and huge data sets into a collective portrait of the biosphere. Many of the key scientific institutions that would ultimately provide the global infrastructure for climate change research were established in the early Cold War period.[6] The World Meteorological Association was formed in 1951 to standardize the collection of weather data across nation-states (Edwards 2006; C. Miller 2001). The World-Wide Network of Standard Seismographic Stations was established to detect nuclear explosions and enforce international treaties; it revolutionized seismology by creating the first real-time system for measuring movement in the earth, which enabled new understandings of continental drift, plate tectonics, and the constitution of the sea floor (see Barth 1998 and 2003; Oliver and Murphy 1971). The first ice core samples were taken from the poles by the U.S. military in the early Cold War period, as bombers and intercontinental missiles transformed the arctic zones into highly militarized spaces (see Doel 2003; Roucek 1983). Similarly, official concerns about biological and chemical warfare generated funds for new research in oceanography, meteorology, and space sciences as well as increasing long-standing military investments in predicting weather patterns during combat and in weather modification as a potential weapon.[7] (The Department of Defense, as recently as the 1990s, described weather as a "force multiplier" and considered the military value of weather modification as not unlike "the splitting of the atom"; it hopes to one day "own the weather" via the development of a "global, precise, real-time, robust, systematic weather modification capability" [House et al. 1996]; see also Fleming 2010.)

A central contribution of the Cold War state to a future understanding of climate change was its focus on cartography—on measuring and mapping all aspects of planet earth, from the oceans to the landmasses and from the ice caps to the airflows (Hamblin 2005; Cloud 2002; Hall 2002). After 1960, the Corona satellite system provided a top-secret new level of resolution to mapping operations, replacing the highly dangerous covert flights of U-2 spy planes over the Soviet Union (Ziegler and Jacobson 1995). Satellite surveillance systems increased exponentially in resolution and data collecting power during the Cold War, ultimately measuring weather, temperature, and ozone levels as well as identifying nuclear silos, military bases, and troop movements (see, for example, Mason, Massey, and Bedford 1968). Finally, the integration of these data sets into a comprehensive portrait of global climate was enabled by the long-term military investment in supercomputing (Edwards 1996 and 2000). The history of supercomputing in the United States is deeply intertwined with the history of U.S. nuclear weapons programs. Indeed, the complexity of modeling nuclear weapons explosions may only be exceeded by the complexity of modeling global environmental change. In sum, weather prediction, the study of ice caps, atmospheric and space sciences, satellite cartography, and supercomputing all derive their initial funding and substantial support through the twentieth century from the security logics of the nuclear state and its commitment to building the bomb—thereby establishing the early data sets and infrastructures for climate science.[8]

Nonetheless, throughout the first decade of the Cold War a structural confusion was installed in American culture about how to define *national security* in relation to *planetary threat*. The atomic bomb was the core technology involved in two rival notions of security—one in the form of a nuclear arsenal supported by deterrence theory; the other in the form of Cold War earth sciences which was producing increasing evidence of radiological damage from the nuclear test program itself. Key scientists who called for an end to nuclear detonations as a matter of public health were, at this moment, positioned as enemies of the state and subject to intimidation (Wang 1999; Hamblin 2007). In other words, those who offered an alternative definition of security based on a recognition of the accumulating industrial effects of the global nuclear complex were engaged as national security threats. Simultaneously enabled by Cold War funding and rejected by national security ideology, Cold War biological and earth scientists were both a resource and a threat to the evolving logics of the nuclear arms race. As a consequence, the regulation of military and nonmilitary planetary science was increasingly determined less by funding than by where scientists published—in the open or classified literatures. Ronald Doel insightfully argues:

> By the 1960s, two distinct "environmental sciences" had emerged: one biology-centered, focused on the problems in ecology and population studies, and funded in part by agencies and managers concerned about human threats to the environment; the other geophysics-centered, focused on the physical environment, and responsive to the operational needs of the military services that support it. Studies by biological environmental scientists often appeared in the open literature, while significant results from the physical environmental sciences were often "born classified." (2003, 653)

I would suggest that within these two sciences were two different concepts of planetary danger, one focused increasingly on issues related to the global environment and the cumulative effects of industrialized civilization, the other focused on how nature could be militarized for the benefit of the U.S. national security state.

Thus, although the emerging concept of the biosphere was shaped by the technoscience of the early Cold War state, the nuclear arsenal also severely distorted and limited the biopolitical lessons of Upshot-Knothole, Project Sunshine, or the Shot Teak. The nuclear state continued to privilege the military threat of state actors over that posed by a fragile biosphere. Nuclear policy makers did so by assuming a "worst-case scenario" form of military planning. Narratives of a surprise nuclear attack by the Soviet Union were affectively charged by fantasies of bomber gaps, missile gaps, and other forms of U.S. technological weakness. Predictions of large-scale genetic defects from radioactive fallout, contaminated food chains, and environmental damage on an unprecedented scale from the combined effects of nuclear industry and atomic tests were not constructed as "national security" problems, except as they threatened nuclear production. Both discovered as an object of state interest and repressed as a political project, the damaged biosphere was ultimately contained by early Cold War geopolitics. The worst-case scenario mode of official thinking was limited, in other words, to the realm of state actors (and thus located in international relations) and not radical environmental change (the biosphere), even as

Cold War technoscience was developing a portrait of the planet as a fragile and integrated system.

Perhaps the purest illustration of this structural linkage between the bomb and the biosphere in American political culture is revealed by the fact that the first nuclear arms control treaty is also the first international environmental protection treaty. The 1963 Limited Test Ban Treaty eliminated nuclear detonations in the oceans, on land, in the air, and in outer space. Sold in the aftermath of the Cuban Missile Crisis as a means of reducing international nuclear tension, the treaty was also a means of quieting public concerns about the effects of atmospheric fallout while continuing nuclear weapons production. The treaty is now remembered at Los Alamos predominantly as a public health initiative, one that took nuclear testing underground and stabilized its experimental regime from 1963 to 1992 (Masco 2006, 68). The containment of atmospheric fallout reduced the environmental urgency informing antinuclear movements, while also securing both an experimental test regime for weapons science and the power of the bomb within U.S. national security culture for the remainder of the twentieth century. The Limited Test Ban Treaty marks an important achievement for the environmental sciences as well: it demonstrated that industrial processes could damage the global biosphere, that negative environmental effects could be both cumulative and transnational, and that international agreements could be forged to limit future damage. Thus, although the treaty ensured thirty more years of the arms race, it also implicitly recognized a postnational form of security, one that was planetary in scope.

The early Cold War nuclear program thus enabled a changing understanding of the planet. Radioactive fallout and intercontinental ballistic missiles transformed specific kinds of threat into a global phenomenon, even as Cold War earth scientists were documenting the fragility of ecosystems within an integrated biosphere. This notion of a planet under ecological endangerment achieved a new kind of visual coherence with the first Apollo mission's photograph of earth rising above the moon in 1968 (see figure 2.6) and gained new detail with the first color portrait of the global biosphere in 1980 from a National Aeronautics and Space Administration (NASA) satellite (see figure 2.7), which showed plant life (on land and in the oceans) as a planetary phenomenon.[9] Within U.S. security culture, however, a basic conflict remained between nuclear threats and climate threats, between the bomb as a state technology and the cumulative effects of industrialized civilization on the global environment. As we shall see, an

FIGURE 2.6. "Earthrise" photograph by William Anders on Apollo 8 (1968), National Aeronautics and Space Administration.

evolving notion of planetary threat would eventually pit the national security logics of the state against a new, postnational view of security focused on a fragile biosphere.

A Nuclear Winter, 1983

Unlike most earlier studies, we find that a global nuclear war could have a major impact on climate—manifested by significant surface darkening over many weeks, subfreezing land temperatures persisting for up to several months, large perturbation in global circulation patterns, and dramatic changes in local weather and precipitation rates—a harsh "nuclear winter" in any season.

—Turco, Toon, Ackerman, Pollack, and Sagan, "Nuclear Winter" (1983)

After nearly four decades of life in the nuclear age—during which the United States rebuilt its economy, geopolitical strategy, military, and citizen-state relationship around the bomb, weaving potential annihilation

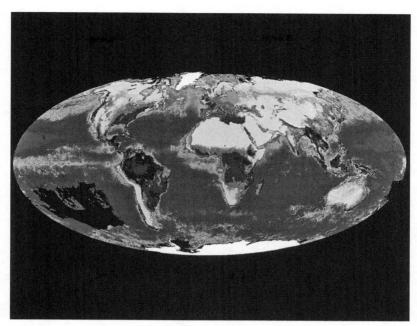

FIGURE 2.7. First satellite image of the global biosphere, 1980. National Aeronautics and Space Administration.

into the routine of everyday life—Americans discovered in the 1980s that they did not yet understand the full planetary costs of nuclear war. A research team headed by Luis Alvarez, a former Manhattan Project physicist and Nobel Prize winner, theorized in 1980 that the mass extinctions during the Cretaceous period had been caused by an asteroid hitting the earth, a collision so violent that it flooded the atmosphere with debris, blocking sunlight and radically cooling the global environment (Alvarez et al. 1980; see also D. Davis 2001; Mellor 2007). The theory, which seemed to explain the sudden extinction of the dinosaurs sixty-five million years ago, became a subject of enormous debate both inside and outside the academy. Paul Crutzen and John Birks (1982) soon pointed out that the massive fires ignited during a nuclear war might produce enough smoke to similarly affect the global atmosphere. The multidisciplinary team of Turco, Toon, Ackerman, Pollack, and Sagan (known as TTAPS) followed in 1983 with both an elaborated theory and an international research program, devoted to what they called "nuclear winter." Published in *Science*, the first article produced by the program presented a theory of radical climate change brought on by the combined planetary load of burning cities in a nuclear war (Turco et al. 1983), while the second article was devoted to the "long-term biological consequences of nuclear war" (Ehrlich et al. 1983). A scientific response to the Reagan administration's nuclear policy—which included a massive nuclear arms buildup, renewed confrontation with the Soviet Union, and official talk of winnable nuclear wars—the scientists offered the nuclear winter concept as a fundamental challenge to the nuclear security logics of the Cold War state (Badash 2001 and 2009). If the closed world sciences of the early Cold War state attempted to militarize the weather (Edwards 1996 and 2010), the scientific debate over nuclear winter in the 1980s explicitly mobilized a radically changing climate to promote nuclear disarmament.

Consider how Ehrlich et al. describe the biological effects of nuclear war in their second *Science* article on nuclear winter:

> Recent studies of large-scale nuclear war (5,000- to 10,000-MT yields) have estimated that there would be 750 million immediate deaths from blast alone; a total of about 1.1 billion deaths from the combined effects of blast, fire, and radiation; and approximately an additional 1.1 billion injuries requiring medical attention. Thus, 30 to 50 percent of the total human population could be immediate casualties of nuclear war. The vast majority of the casualties would be in the Northern Hemisphere, especially in the United States, the U.S.S.R., Europe and Japan. These enormous numbers have typically been taken to define the full potential catastrophe of such a war. New evidence presented here, however, suggests that the longer term biological effects resulting from climatic changes may be at least as serious as the immediate one. (Ehrlich et al. 1983, 1293)

Climactic effects at least as serious as war. This portrait of mass death relies on an understanding of nuclear war built up during nearly four decades of U.S. military planning and civil defense, a security discourse that frequently identified nuclear war itself as "unthinkable." Two decades after RAND nuclear war analyst Herman Kahn first asked "if the survivors would envy the dead" (1960, 40), the nuclear winter studies offered a portrait of a postwar environment almost as traumatic as the initial nuclear firestorm. Paul Erhlich and his coauthors summarized their report this way:

> Subfreezing temperature, low light levels, and high doses of ionizing and ultraviolet radiation extending for many months after a large-scale nuclear war could destroy the biological support systems of civilization, at least in the Northern Hemisphere. Productivity in

natural and agricultural ecosystems could be severely restricted for a year or more. Postwar survivors would face starvation as well as freezing conditions in the dark and be exposed to near-lethal doses of radiation. If, as now seems possible, the Southern Hemisphere were affected also, global disruption of the biosphere could ensue. In any event, there would be severe consequences, even in the areas not affected directly, because of the interdependence of the world economy. In either case the extinction of a large fraction of the Earth's animals, plants, and microorganisms seems possible. The population size of *Homo sapiens* conceivably could be reduced to prehistoric levels or below, and extinction of the human species itself cannot be excluded. (1983, 1293)

Nuclear war could destroy the biological support systems of civilization. Placing humanity firmly on the course of the dinosaurs moving towards extinction, the authors present the exploding bomb not simply as a military tool but as a transformational environmental event for the planet. There is a direct line of research connecting the early radioactive tracer studies of strontium-90 from aboveground nuclear detonations to this depiction of nuclear winter.[10] However, the political coordinates of the research have been inverted: although the fallout studies of 1950s were directly harnessed to the military expansion of the nuclear state, the nuclear winter concept was mobilized to reduce nuclear arsenals and diminish the geopolitical reliance on the bomb for the sake of environmental security.

Basing their models on the current U.S. and Soviet arsenals (59,959 total nuclear weapons in 1983), as well as likely nuclear war-fighting scenarios, TTAPS produced a series of computer simulations of the climatic effects of variously scaled nuclear wars.[11] They modeled the effect of nuclear wars with total loads of 100 to 25,000 megatons (the combined conventional explosive force used in World War II is commonly estimated to be 3–4 megatons, consolidated by 1954 into a single thermonuclear weapon). TTAPS concluded that a few hundred nuclear detonations, 100 megatons in all, could change the global climate, and they offered a detailed description of what a 5,000-megaton nuclear exchange would likely do to the biosphere. Cities would be transformed into soot and injected into the stratosphere, blocking the sun's light for months. Temperatures would drop dramatically and low light levels would affect photosynthesis, leading to widespread crop failures. Violent storms, unpredictable weather, and radioactive fallout would challenge life in all parts of the globe. A key finding of the study was that these effects would not be limited to the northern hemisphere—thus primarily affecting the nuclear-powered states in North America and Europe—but would have worldwide consequences. Calling for nuclear powers to recognize their shared dependence on a biosphere that is capable of being both damaged and radically destabilized, TTAPS sought to render nuclear national security an obsolete (and dangerously misguided) concept, rightfully superseded by concerns about transnational ecological and planetary sustainability.

With Carl Sagan as the chief spokesman, TTAPS not only addressed the scientific community and policy makers but also communicated the science of nuclear winter directly to the American public.[12] Sagan published an article in *Parade* (a Sunday supplement to most U.S. newspapers) on October 20, 1983, communicating in layman's terms the argument about nuclear warfare and climate change. His mass media strategy continued with the published proceedings of a 1983 conference, *The Cold and the Dark: The World after Nuclear War* (Ehrlich et al. 1984), which presented readers with a new graphic image of atomic conflict. Subverting the aesthetic perspective offered by the Apollo mission's photographs of the earth, the cover of *The Cold and the Dark* depicts a soot-blackened planet in which only the southern tip of South America remains exposed to sunlight (figure 2.8). Sagan and Turco extended this visual strategy in *A Path Where No Man Thought: Nuclear Winter and the End of the Arms Race* (1990), where they included a four-panel illustration of nuclear war and winter painted by Jon Lomberg (figures 2.9 and 2.10). Emphasizing the planetary scope of nuclear war, this pictorial sequence takes an extraterrestrial point of view, looking down first at the North Pole and then at the equator. What is immediately striking about the sequence is its temporal focus: nuclear war is presented in one frame, representing perhaps two hours of actual nuclear conflict, given the state of U.S. and Soviet weapons systems at the time (the left panel in figure 2.9), while nuclear winter continues on for weeks (the right panel in figure 2.9 and both panels in figure 2.10), only gaining in intensity. In their captions, Sagan and Turco underscore that from a polar perspective it is impossible to conclude who started the conflict. Indeed, they base their assessment of the environmental effects of nuclear war on the biosphere rather than the nation-state politics of the Cold War. The last three images show the atmospheric effects of thousands of nuclear explosions after seven days (figure 2.9, right), ten days (figure 2.10, left), and some months (figure 2.10, right). Ten days after the war, the soot has covered the northern hemisphere, and in the final image all but the south-

FIGURE 2.8. A soot-covered world, *The Cold and the Dark* (Ehrlich et al. 1984) depicts the earth after nuclear war.

ernmost continental spaces are covered in black smoke—blocking out sunlight.

By deploying an extraterrestrial perspective on the globe, instead of a portrait of nation-states, as the visual icon of nuclear winter, Sagan and Turco sought to change the terms of Cold War security debates. Relying on their computer simulations, they argued that the nuclear powers should reduce the number of nuclear weapons in their arsenals to beneath the threshold for a nuclear winter effect:

> If we define a city as having more than 100,000 people, then there are some 2,300 cities on the planet. This means that after START II

FIGURE 2.9. Temporal sequence of a nuclear winter, polar viewpoint at the start of a nuclear war (left) and one week later (right), paintings by Jon Lomberg. From *The Cold and the Dark* (Ehrlich et al. 1984).

is fully implemented, the USA or Russia could destroy every city on the planet and have 2,300 weapons left over. . . . If we wish to arrange a world in which no miscalculation, no technological error, no misunderstood orders, no fit of ethnic or religious passion, and not even a conspiracy of madmen could bring about a global environmental catastrophe, then we must arrange a world with fewer than several hundred nuclear weapons. (1993, 371)

No conspiracy of madmen could bring about a global environmental catastrophe. Here, we have a new definition of climate crisis mobilized to enable nuclear disarmament. The nuclear winter research undercut national security in favor of a new kind of planetary security, producing vigorous scientific and political debate.[13] The Scientific Committee on Problems of the Environment of the International Council of Scientific Unions (SCOPE), a group of two hundred scientists from thirty nations, participated in a nuclear winter study that reaffirmed the global threat of smoke-induced climate change as a result of nuclear warfare.[14] The SCOPE study also became a prototype of the multidisciplinary, multinational scientific collaborations that have informed recent science on carbon emissions and global warming, such as the Intergovernmental Panel on Climate Change. What the original nuclear winter theorists ultimately sought was a demilitarization of

FIGURE 2.10. Temporal sequence of the effects of nuclear winter, equatorial viewpoint, ten days after nuclear war (left) and some months later (right), paintings by Jon Lomberg. From *The Cold and the Dark* (Ehrlich et al. 1984).

the biosphere, avoiding international nuclear confrontation by focusing on a planetary notion of security—in effect, using one kind of catastrophe to critique another. Revising the dream of many Manhattan Project scientists that atomic weapons would make war obsolete, these researchers sought to use the science of climate change, as well as images of a damaged and destabilized biosphere, to promote global nuclear disarmament and an end to the Cold War arms race.

Global Warming as Nuclear War, 2003

Using the full commercial power of the Hollywood blockbuster formula, director Roland Emmerich gave audiences in 2004 an illustration of a biosphere radically out of balance. Intended to both entertain and raise people's consciousness, *The Day after Tomorrow* revisits the now long-standing link between nuclear war and ecological crisis, but it does so to highlight the threat of climate change. In the film, global warming produces sudden and severe ecological effects, which are presented with the latest computer-generated imaging technology and Hollywood panache: Los Angeles is destroyed by multiple tornados (see figure 2.11), while New York is both flooded by rising sea levels and then frozen solid (see figure 2.12), as the upper third of the United States enters a new ice age and surviving U.S.

FIGURE 2.11. Los Angeles destroyed by tornados, in *The Day after Tomorrow* (2004).

FIGURE 2.12. New York frozen, in *The Day after Tomorrow* (2004).

citizens are forced to flee across the Rio Grande into Mexico. A Hollywood response to early Bush administration claims that the contribution of industry to global warming was only a theory, the film drew openly on the tropes and history of Cold War atomic cinema to make a different kind of planetary security argument.

In atomic cinema, the apocalypse is harnessed directly to the power of the nation-state, promoting a perverse kind of nation building through images of collective sacrifice and death. For sixty years Hollywood has produced big-budget, special effects–driven stories about nuclear warfare (often allegorized), playing off of the civil defense promises and nuclear fears of the Cold War state (see Evans 1998; Edwards 1996; Derrida 1984; Sontag 1966). The cinematic destruction of New York—often codified in a ruined Statue of Liberty—has become an almost annual project in Hollywood and provides a precise genealogy of U.S. nuclear fears from *When Worlds Collide* (1951) to *The Planet of the Apes* (1968) (see figure 2.13) to *The Day after Tomorrow* (2004). The producers of *The Day after Tomorrow* are

FIGURE 2.13. Postnuclear New York, in *The Planet of the Apes* (1968).

particularly attuned to this filmic register, having established their careers by revisiting Cold War atomic cinema (in *Independence Day* [1996] and *Godzilla* [1998]). *The Day after Tomorrow* (a play on the title of the 1983 television event *The Day After*) is also a loose remake of the 1961 feature film *The Day the Earth Caught Fire*. In this British production, an aggressive series of thermonuclear tests by the United States and the Soviet Union knock the earth off its axis, causing the planet to spin closer to the sun and producing a nearly apocalyptic planetary heat wave. *The Day after Tomorrow* ultimately uses the devices of atomic cinema—a focus on the destruction of cities, collective sacrifice, and militarized response—to address a form of catastrophe larger than the national politics of the security state: radical climate change. Earning over $500 million in the global box office, *The Day after Tomorrow* was the seventh most successful movie of 2004 and was widely credited with increasing public recognition of climate change as a social issue (Leiserowitz 2004).

The Pentagon, perhaps not surprisingly, was thinking along very similar lines to Emmerich about the military implications of climate change in the early twenty-first century, despite its focus on the War on Terror. The Department of Defense hired the futurologists Peter Schwartz and Doug Randall to write a report on the national security implications of abrupt climate change. Positioning their report as an effort to "imagine the unthinkable" (2003, 1), Schwartz and Randall not only project an extreme vision of abrupt climate change into the next decade, but they also deploy almost all of the tropes of Cold War postnuclear planning to do so. The "unthinkable" as a national security discourse originates in the Cold War nuclear standoff, exemplified by Herman Kahn, who encouraged Americans to "think about the unthinkable" and plan for life in a postnuclear environment (1962 and 1960). In their scenario, Schwartz and Randall imagine a destabilized world reorganizing itself around radical scarcities of food and water. Arguing that "human civilization began with the stabilization and warming of the Earth's climate," they offer a sobering portrait of the "national security" threat posed by global warming:

> Violence and disruption stemming from the stresses created by abrupt change in the climate pose a different type of threat to national security than we are accustomed to today. Military confrontation may be triggered by a desperate need for natural resources such as energy, food, and water rather than by conflicts over ideology, religion, or national honor. The shifting motivation for confrontation would alter which countries are most vulnerable and the existing warning signs for security threats. (2003, 14)

Shifting vulnerabilities, changing threats. Climate change will thus redraw the geopolitical map on new terms, as states compete not just for prestige and power but also for food and energy. This new world of unpredictable weather will present both opportunities and challenges to the United States, calling for a new focus on national defense. In this future, the ecological crisis will lead some nations to build "virtual fortresses around their countries" in an effort to protect resources, while other nations fight one another for the remaining global stocks of food, water, and energy (2003, 18). Thus, the futurologists present nothing less than an internationalized version of the early Cold War fallout shelter debate: shelter owners were taught that their first act in a postnuclear world would likely be that of defending their property from their less prepared and highly traumatized neighbors (Grossman 2001). Preparation for disaster, rather than prevention, is the assumed role of government in this scenario, mimicking domestic nuclear emergency planning (Schwartz and Randall 2003, 7; see also Oakes 1994).

Indeed, although Schwartz and Randall's *Abrupt Climate Change Scenario* describes a radically destabilized biosphere, the primary problem the report addresses is how to manage people and resources, not how to deal with the causes of global warming. As in the civil defense programs of the 1950s, the central problem is presented as public panic—not nuclear warfare or the industrial origins of climate change. U.S. national security, in other words, does not include preventing climate change in this vision, only responding to it on terms that most benefit the counterterror state. Schwartz and Randall envision a radically changed, increasingly insecure world by 2020:

> As famine, disease, and weather-related disasters strike due to the abrupt climate change, many countries' needs will exceed their carry-

ing capacity. This will create a sense of desperation, which is likely to lead to offensive aggression in order to reclaim balance. Imagine eastern European countries, struggling to feed their populations with a falling supply of food, water, and energy, eyeing Russia, whose population is already in decline, for access to its grain, minerals, and energy supply. Or, picture Japan, suffering from flooding along its coastal cities and contamination of its fresh water supply, eyeing Russia's Sakhalin Island oil and gas reserves as an energy source to power desalination plants and energy-intensive agricultural processes. Envision Pakistan, India, and China—all armed with nuclear weapons—skirmishing at the borders over refugees, access to shared rivers, and arable land. Spanish and Portuguese fishermen might fight over fishing rights—leading to conflicts at sea. And, countries including the United States would be likely to better secure their borders. With over 200 river basins touching multiple nations, we can expect conflict over access to water for drinking, irrigation, and transportation. The Danube touches twelve nations, the Nile runs through nine, and the Amazon runs through seven. (2003, 18)

Needs will exceed carrying capacity. As hungry populations redraw political alliances and state borders in the competition over basic resources, the U.S. Department of Defense is presented with a new universe of state-based security threats. Megadroughts in northern Europe produce huge waves of emigration; North America is hit by high-intensity storms, producing soil loss and reducing agricultural production; Asia is hit by massive famine, producing "chaos and internal struggles as a cold and hungry China peers jealously across the Russian and Western borders at energy resources" (Schwartz and Randall 2003, 13). Deaths from war, starvation, and disease increase globally, as growing seasons become shorter and weather more intense. The United States and Australia become defensive fortresses to protect their natural resources, while North and South Korea become a new combined nuclear power, and other nations pursue the bomb. In short, by 2020 there have been massive realignments of peoples and interests around the world, increased warfare, and chronic shortages. As Schwartz and Randall put it, "modern civilization has never experienced weather conditions as persistently disruptive as the ones outlined in this scenario" (2003, 14).

In *The Day after Tomorrow* the disastrous effects of climate change are attributed, in part, to the failure of the security state to listen to climate scientists about the dangers of global warming. Schwartz and Randall, however, demonstrate that climate change can still be appropriated by the national security state to promote a militarized response—a bunker society—rather than a fundamental rethinking of the terms of the industrial economy.[15] Working from a classic military perspective assuming competing nation-states as the limit of security, it becomes a category error for the futurologists to suggest that the Department of Defense needs to mobilize against the threat of global warming and attempt to prevent the wide range of violence they predict. In the end, Schwartz and Randall can argue only that more nuclear weapons will be circulating among states increasingly inclined to warfare, more desperate, with fewer nonmilitary resources. Rather than transforming the Environmental Protection Agency (EPA) into a chief agency for national defense (perhaps drawing on the Department of Agriculture's Cold War involvement in the trees of Operation Upshot-Knothole), the futurologists can offer only one possible outcome: increased militarization of the United States. A projected global threat is mobilized here to underscore the need for the U.S. nuclear arsenal, just as was the case throughout the Cold War. The U.S. military-industrial complex is positioned as the necessary answer to international instability, rather than recognized as a significant contributor to greenhouse gases in its own right. The global network of more than a thousand U.S. military instillations requires a vast logistical supply chain offering a distinct U.S. national security economy of carbon emissions.[16]

Indeed, climate change was treated within the Bush administration as a threat not to all life but to U.S. national security. Across a spectrum of government agencies devoted to studying the environment in the first decade of counterterror, news of industry's contribution to greenhouse gases and climate change was delayed and sometimes even repressed. Just as the security state initially refused to accept scientific studies of the health effects of fallout in the 1950s and of nuclear winter in the 1980s, so it has positioned climate change as a threat to U.S. military policy (see Badash 2001; Wang 1999; Kopp 1979). This is most powerfully revealed in the accusation of James Hansen, a pioneering earth scientist and the director of NASA's Goddard Institute for Space Studies, that the Bush administration was regulating his public speaking on climate change (Revkin 2006b; see also Piltz 2005). One of the most prominent U.S. scientists to advance the theory that global warming is an imminent threat (see, for example, J. Hansen, Sato, and Ruedy 2012), Hansen was subjected to handlers who listened to his phone interviews and tried to regulate his public speaking. This is the kind of treatment once reserved for nuclear weapons scientists whose every utterance was believed to affect the stability of what was once known as the "free world."[17] As counterterror emerged as the primary concern of the administration, government reports on climate change were edited by federal officials to downplay evidence of human contributions to global warming and to emphasize uncertainty in climate models.[18] Research by government scientists pursuing a link between climate change and intensifying hurricanes was restricted, and the nationwide system of technical research libraries run by the EPA was closed, allegedly due to federal budget cuts—an act that drew protests from 10,000 scientists in 2006 (see Daley 2006; Giles 2006; Heilprin 2006; Lee 2006; see also Bearden and Esworthy 2007). In 2008 a survey of EPA scientists found that the majority of them had felt pressure from political appointees in the Bush administration to distort or censor environmental assessments (Union of Concerned Scientists 2008). Thus, while climate scientists debated the tipping point in global warming—the point at which massive environmental changes become unstoppable due to greenhouse gases—the Bush administration largely portrayed climate change as just one theory among many, and worked to delay any serious regulatory action at home or abroad (Eilperin 2006a).[19] This struggle over the politics of planetary danger was about nothing less than the counterterror state's ability to monopolize definitions of both *threat* and *security*.

Despite the security state's efforts to designate terrorism as the ultimate existential threat, there has been an extraordinary consensus, and degree of scientific evidence, concerning climate change across disciplines, species, and ecosystems (Oreskes 2004). Recent scientific studies have attributed to global warming fundamental changes in habitats, ecologies, and weather: birds are changing their migratory patterns in North America (National Wildlife Federation 2013), bears have stopped hibernating in Spain (G. Roberts 2006), two-thirds of the harlequin frog species in Central and South America have gone extinct, polar bears are headed for the endangered species list due to loss of habitat,[20] and the warming of the ocean is both bleaching coral reefs and melting the polar ice caps.[21] The extinction rate for species is accelerating (Parmesan 2006), and the oceans are losing the biodiversity that maintains ecological resilience to disease (Stokstad 2006; Worm et al. 2006). If current melt rates continue, the polar ice caps could be gone in the summer of 2040.[22] The warming of the Atlantic Ocean and the Gulf of Mexico may be contributing to larger and more violent hurricanes (J. Schwartz 2006). Thus, a profound contradiction structures the first decade of the counterterror: the United States is the largest historical contributor to greenhouse gases (Marland, Boden, and Andres 2006), the country that has enabled and conducted much of the basic research on climate change, and remains the primary state resisting an international response to it. As a recent study from the British treasury department has argued, the long-term financial cost of this delay could be unprecedented:

> Climate change will affect the basic elements of life for people around the world—access to water, food production, health, and the environment. Hundreds of millions of people could suffer hunger, water shortages and coastal flooding as the world warms. Using the results from formal economic models, the Review estimates that if we don't act, the overall costs and risks of climate change will be equivalent to losing at least 5% of global GDP each year, now and forever. If a wider range of risks and impacts is taken into account, the estimates of damage could rise to 20% of GDP or more. In contrast, the costs of action—reducing greenhouse gas emissions to avoid the worst impact of climate change—can be limited to around 1% of global GDP each year. The investment that takes place in the next 10–20 years will have a profound effect on the climate in the second half of this century and in the next. Our actions now and over the coming decades could create risks of major disruption to economic and social activity, on a scale similar to those associated with the great wars and the economic depression of the first half of the 20th century. And it will be difficult or impossible to reverse these changes. (Stern 2007, vi)

Five to twenty percent of global GDP now and forever. Hidden in these numbers are some of the most profound security issues any state has ever faced—floods, famine, droughts, and violent storms—a September 2001 attack and a Hurricane Katrina every year in perpetuity.[23]

Conclusion: Katrina as Hiroshima

It's as if the entire Gulf Coast were obliterated by a—the worst kind of weapon you can imagine.
—President George Bush, commenting on the wreckage left by Hurricane Katrina in Alabama, September 2, 2005

I can only imagine this is what Hiroshima looked like 60 years ago.
—Governor Haley Barbour commenting on Hurricane Katrina damage in Mississippi, August 30, 2005

Surveying the wreckage left by Hurricane Katrina on his first visit to the storm-ravaged Gulf Coast in 2005, President George Bush invited Ameri-

FIGURE 2.14. Hurricane Katrina hitting the Gulf Coast, August 2005, the National Oceanic and Atmospheric Administration.

cans to think of the event *as if* it were a nuclear attack (Bush 2005). Mississippi Governor Haley Barbour was more specific, presenting the unprecedented wind and flood damage in his state as equivalent to the atomic bombing of Hiroshima (quoted in Martel 2005). For Barbour, Katrina produced "nuclear destruction" (quoted in Pettus 2005). He declared in a wide range of media interviews: "The coast is just the greatest devastation I've ever seen. It's as if they set off a nuclear weapon there" (Barbour 2005). Other officials, rescue workers, and victims similarly relied on nuclear imagery to transform a category-4 hurricane and failed levee system into a de facto act of nuclear warfare (see figure 2.14).[24] Thus, the destruction caused by Hurricane Katrina was initially understandable to America's political leadership, and many of its citizens, only in terms of nuclear catastrophe.

Indeed, for many commentators in the U.S. media, the first issue raised by Hurricane Katrina was not violent weather—and the potential linkage of increasing hurricane strength to climate change—but rather the national security state's ability to respond to a nuclear attack. Even as stranded residents of the Gulf Coast awaited rescue, talk on cable news stations focused on the failure of the Federal Emergency Management Agency (FEMA) response not to an unfolding natural emergency but to an imagined nuclear one. On MSNBC, Chris Matthews (2005) asked FEMA and Department of Homeland Security officials what Americans would have been facing if "it was a bomb that went off, rather than a thunderclap of God's will?" In addition to marking the failures in governmental responses to the emergency, cable television shows used Katrina to rehearse WMD preparedness, focusing not on floods, levee systems, and environmental change but on biological warfare, chemical weapons, and terrorists armed with nuclear weapons. Commentators from across the political spectrum asked what the disaster revealed about the state of U.S. civil defense, using the destruction left by Katrina to conjure images of future nuclear devastation in other cities. Not surprisingly, citizens of Gulf Coast states called on the government to respond as it had long promised it would in a state of nuclear emergency.

These responses to a devastating storm reveal how embedded nuclear concepts are in U.S. political culture and underscore the strange reliance Americans have on nuclear threat to organize politics and experience—both foreign and domestic. Informing each of these comments is something more than the immediate trauma of Hurricane Katrina; it is the powerful psychosocial effects of the atomic bomb on American security culture. For how is it that so many Americans, from so many different social positions, could understand a nonnuclear, nonmilitary event in decidedly nuclear terms? What does it mean that a natural catastrophe could so immediately be transformed into an act of nuclear warfare in the public imagination? And what other logics about nature and security are blocked by this nuclear discourse?

What I have outlined in this chapter are the multigenerational imbrications of nuclear weapons and climate change in the United States. I have argued that the advent of the atomic bomb enabled a new understanding of the global biosphere but also installed a specific set of ideas about catastrophic risk in American security culture. For after rehearsing for generations the loss of an American city to the atomic bomb (in civil defense programs, nuclear war planning, and Hollywood films), the United States all but lost a city in 2005. However, New Orleans was almost lost not to the atomic bomb but to violent weather, a storm perhaps energized by the cumulative effects of greenhouse gases. The nuclear discourse attached to Hurricane Katrina reveals that Americans have been conditioned to approach mass destruction in very specific ways. However, it also reveals that they have little actual understanding of the explosive power of the bomb: even the smallest atomic bombs in the current U.S. nuclear arsenal are thirty to forty times more powerful than the weapon that obliterated

Hiroshima. Nevertheless, the turn toward nuclear discourse to explain a natural catastrophe reveals the power of the nuclear project in America and the multigenerational linkages between nuclear weapons and climate. The Cold War policy of containment involved not only producing bombs but also more-detailed maps of the earth, global systems for monitoring the air for radioactive trace elements, seismic monitoring systems to detect the distinct signatures of a nuclear explosion, and ultimately supercomputing and satellite systems that provided increasing sophistication in weather modeling. This "closed world" of Cold War military planning—to use Paul Edwards's (1996) concept—encapsulated the earth in military, command, control, and surveillance systems. In doing so, it also created new understandings of the earth, sea, and sky, and of the biosphere itself as an integrated ecological space.

The Cold War nuclear arms race, however, also installed an idea of apocalyptic destruction, one that has been deployed by the national security state for generations to enable a variety of state projects. Indeed, the balance of terror during the Cold War—the minute-to-minute possibility of a global exchange of thermonuclear warheads—transformed a specific image of apocalyptic destruction into an intimate space of state and nation building. The Cold War arms race taught Americans that they could live on the knife's edge of total war, and could do so in perpetuity. The effects of this project on the national culture are evident in many domains of everyday life but are clearest in the contemplation of planetary risks that are not nuclear, and not subject to a policy of deterrence. To linguistically transform Hurricane Katrina into an atomic explosion is in part to evoke mass destruction in its ultimate form, but it is also a way of capturing the event on terms that are historically useful to the national security state. A week after the storm, President Bush promised a thorough review of the emergency response effort, stating: "We want to make sure that we can respond properly if there is a WMD attack or another major storm" (quoted in ABC News 2005). In doing so, he again inserted the nuclear terms of the War on Terror into the debate about responses to a natural disaster. Mass death and destruction has meaning when framed in a nuclear discourse in the United States precisely because the Cold War arms race turned the bomb into an organizing principle in American society.

In other words, the Katrina as Hiroshima discourse is an act of translation rather than of misrecognition. As we have seen, the 1950s, 1980s, and 2000s all included politically charged moments in the United States in which the dangers posed by climate change and nuclear weapons were transposed. The designation of the United States as a superpower largely depends on the ability of the state to monopolize a discourse of danger, and to this end the atomic bomb has been an extraordinary instrument of state power. In declaring war on *terror* in 2001, the Bush administration did not declare war on all terror but expressed a more specific fear of the WMD. Today, climate change directly competes with the WMD as the primary planetary threat and demands a radically different political response. The tools for fighting climate change are in fact diametrically opposed to those used in the War on Terror: a global response to carbon emissions requires a new kind of political cooperation, innovative economic and technological changes, a shared vision of ecological sustainability, and above all a willingness to substitute global concerns for national interests. Rather than sustaining a military-industrial economy, engaging climate change requires a new form of planetary governance.

Returning to the synthetic forest of 1953 (see figure 2.1) we can see in the fury of the nuclear blast a possible counternarrative to that of the national security state, one grounded not in weapons but in a relationship toward the biosphere. For the most basic lesson of these bent and broken trees is that if enough industrial force is applied to natural systems, they will break. The value of the 1953 synthetic forest is that it marks not only the power of the bomb, but also the fragility of even an artificially reinforced nature— not only a new global effort to mediate international relations via nuclear technologies, but also the effects of industry on the biosphere. The lesson mistakenly taken from Operation Upshot-Knothole is that only military operations and civil defense were at stake in these experiments. In fact, the nuclear blast that transformed 145 Ponderosa pines into blades of grass blowing in an unnatural wind is but the most explicit manifestation of the industrial transformation of the natural world. The power of the bomb has been not only to link science and the state in a way that recognizes this fact, but also to distort U.S. political culture so that only specific kinds of threats (state-based and terrorist) are capable of mobilizing collective social action.

In the early twenty-first century, the imbrications of nuclear weapons and planetary threat remain so profound as to block both thought and action, allowing the security implications of a warming planet to elude the national security state. However, the ties between the atomic bomb and climate change remain ever present: today, the same supercomputers that maintain the U.S. nuclear stockpile at the national laboratories are also modeling the climate, even as the cars traveling the interstate highway system (designed by the Eisenhower administration as part of nuclear civil defense) contribute to global warming every second of the day. Moreover, the increasing calls for a new Manhattan Project to deal with climate change still embed the biosphere in a purely militarized and nationalized logic, while presuming that a single state actor can remedy the global climate crisis.[25] But to attend to the shrinking polar ice caps or the intensifying weather patterns is to reject the idea of national security and replace it with a planetary vision of sustainability. The technoscientific questions of biospheric sustainability are profound, requiring the integration of state policies and an understanding of diverse environmental problems as matters of collective responsibility, a proposition that offers a new means of coordinating global order. Today, however, *security* remains embedded in an extremely narrow concept of threat and national advantage in U.S. political culture, both legacies of Cold War state and nation building. But the lessons of the synthetic forest from 1953—reiterated in the disappearing frogs, the melting ice caps, the intensifying hurricanes, and the dying coral reefs of today—are that more profound changes are at hand, and that securing the biosphere requires nothing less than a postnational vision of American power.

THREE

SENSITIVE BUT UNCLASSIFIED
Secrecy and the Counterterror State

The power of the secret in contemporary American society is difficult to overestimate. Since 2001 the logics and policy goals of the counterterror state—including the rationale for *preemptive war*, the administrative terms of *extraordinary rendition* and the *detainee*, and the unprecedented surveillance of U.S. citizens— have all been formally designated as secrets under a discourse of imminent threat. However, the "newness" of the War on Terror masks the deep structure of this national security logic and the profound mutation in the nature of the state produced by the advent of the atomic bomb and the accompanying expansion of state secrecy devoted to protecting it. Indeed, the invention of the national security state after World War II transformed the United States into a new kind of secret society, one in which state power rests to an unprecedented degree on the ability of offi- cials to manage the public-secret divide through the mobiliza- tion of threat. This *secrecy/threat matrix* marks all state secrets as equivalents of the atomic secret, making revelation a matter not just of politics but of the life or death of the nation-state. The Cold War arms race—founded on the minute-to-minute pos- sibility of nuclear war—installed the secrecy/threat matrix as a conceptual infrastructure, enabling a new species of politics in the United States. I argue in this chapter that the transformation of the United States from a countercommunist to a counterter- rorist state has reconstituted and amplified this secrecy/threat matrix, revealing some curious new deployments of the state secret as well as aspects of its essential form.

Locating the "Secret"

Consider, for example, the following exchange I had with the Department of Energy (DOE) about reproducing an image from the U.S. nuclear program archives. I was looking for a version of a photograph illustrating the casing and nonnuclear parts of a modern thermonuclear weapon. In public hearings I attended in Los Alamos and Washington several versions of the image I had in mind were used to illustrate the challenges of the DOE's Science-Based Stockpile Stewardship (SBSS) program, the vastly expensive effort to maintain the Cold War nuclear arsenal without conducting underground nuclear tests that was begun in 1995. Under the terms of SBSS, the U.S. weapons laboratories have built a variety of new experimental test facilities as well as a fleet of state-of-the-art supercomputers designed to maintain nuclear expertise well into the mid-twenty-first century, as part of the "critical infrastructure" of the security state. In its long-range plan for maintaining the industrial capabilities and expertise of the U.S. nuclear weapons program through the year 2030, the DOE described the project this way:

> As the stockpile ages, new challenges and unforeseen issues will continue to arise. In order to ensure timely and effective responses to these issues, the science, technology and engineering base—both people and facilities—must be robust. By 2031, a new generation of weapons designers, code developers, experimentalists, and engineers must be capable of demonstrating a fundamental understanding of nuclear weapons functionality using computer-aided design and assessment tools that are increasingly more predictive and more precisely calibrated. High-fidelity experimental capabilities will be fully operational and will produce quantitative data that will help preclude the technical need for resumption of underground nuclear testing. (U.S. Department of Energy 2011, 3)

By 2031 a new generation must be in place. The DOE signals here that U.S. nuclear weapons have a deep future. It is a little-known fact that, despite the U.S. focus on eliminating nuclear weapons programs in the Middle East and the constant figuration of the "terrorist with a WMD" as the nightmare vision of the future, the U.S. counterterror state remains deeply committed to the bomb: even as the George W. Bush administration waged preemptive war to eliminate the threat of weapons of mass destruction (WMD) in Iraq in 2003, it was directing Los Alamos and Livermore scientists to begin design work on the first new nuclear warhead in a generation.[1] Similarly, President Barack Obama (2009) has called for a world without nuclear weapons, while committing substantial new resources to a state-of-the-art U.S. nuclear arsenal via SBSS.[2]

The photograph in question—concerning a dismantled nuclear device known as the B61—was used by Los Alamos weapons scientists and DOE officials in the post–Cold War period to document the difficulty of dealing with aging weapons parts (Masco 2006, 79). Under the SBSS program, each of the roughly six thousand components of a U.S. nuclear weapon has a specific surveillance program devoted to it, and the photographic illustration of those vulnerable parts became a central means of articulating for a variety of audiences the difficulty of maintaining the bomb without underground nuclear detonations. The photograph in question was therefore a key aspect of the public campaign to produce a new nuclear complex and justify the expense of SBSS at the end of the Cold War. In fact, images of aging nuclear weapons, laboratories, and scientists have been used repeatedly to create a sense of affective urgency around the U.S. nuclear complex (replacing the arms race with a race against the corroding effects of time itself).

I asked a variety of agencies in the federal government for the photograph, forwarding to them a low-resolution copy that I had scanned from SBSS publicity materials. Usually quite helpful and forthcoming with media requests, their reactions this time were alternatively curious, funny, and ultimately revealing. A Los Alamos representative said that although the laboratory designed the nuclear device known as the B61, the image could not be found in its media archives. He speculated first that perhaps I was looking for an Air Force image, and then suggested that the photograph would be more likely in the purview of Sandia National Laboratory, which is involved in engineering the casing and nonnuclear components for U.S. nuclear weapons. Sandia, however, did not respond to my media requests. Pantex, which is charged with dismantling U.S. nuclear devices, could not locate the image either and referred me to the Lawrence Livermore National Laboratory, which produced a similar image of a Livermore-designed nuclear device, known as the B83. Representatives at Livermore referred me to the DOE in Washington, where my request for the image was gently but promptly refused. Pushing a bit further, I inquired why the image, or one like it, was not available for use in a scholarly project. I received the fol-

FIGURE 3.1. Cover of *Closing the Circle on the Splitting of the Atom*, U.S. Department of Energy (1994).

lowing e-mail message: "In regards to the B-61 picture, after September 11, 2001, a review was conducted of our visuals library. As a result some images are not being released due to security concerns."

For many readers, this undoubtedly would seem to be a logical outcome. After all, images of nuclear weapons are historically the quintessential state secret—the very reason for having an elaborate system of classification and information control in the United States (see Masco 2006, 263). But what is the actual status of this photograph? Here, we might consult one of the most widely distributed DOE publications of the post–Cold War period—*Closing the Circle on the Splitting of the Atom* (U.S. Department of Energy 1994, see figure 3.1)—a text that documents the national infrastructure of contamination and environmental ruin left by the Cold War nuclear complex. The image in question appears in this publication, with the following caption:

> An example of a completed nuclear weapon and its component parts. At top, an intact B-61 nuclear bomb. At bottom, the assemblies and subassemblies that comprise this weapon. Dozens of facilities across the country engage in different processes and contribute specific parts to the production of nuclear weapons. (U.S. Department of Energy 1994, 20)

116

FIGURE 3.2. "What's Inside a Nuclear Weapon?" exhibit at the Bradbury Science Museum, Los Alamos, photograph by the author.

Thus, as of 1994, this image was in the public domain, part of a government publication intended for mass circulation. One might then conclude that it is the September 2001 attacks and the declaration of a War on Terror that have provoked the transformation of this photograph from a public to a nonpublic state. After all, the War on Terror was founded on fear of the WMD and the need to prevent the flow of information that might help terrorists or members of Bush's "axis of evil" (2002a)—Iraq, Iran, and North Korea—in their nuclear ambitions. However, *Closing the Circle* remains available today for downloading from a wide range of DOE programmatic websites.[3]

One might think that the document's continued availability is simply an oversight, a bureaucratic failure to pull an old document from a government website after the post-2001 reconstitution of the national security state as a counterterror formation. But consider the following photographs (figures 3.2 and 3.3) that I took at the Bradbury Science Museum at Los Alamos National Laboratory in New Mexico (note the inset photograph in each figure of a dismantled nuclear device). Figure 3.2 documents the same B61 as shown in *Closing the Circle*, but it adds a great deal of detail. The exhibit describes the basic components of a modern thermonuclear bomb, emphasizing the complexity of the bomb as a machine (involving thousands of parts that need to be matched together "within thousandths of an inch" and timed to operate within "millionths of a second" while

117

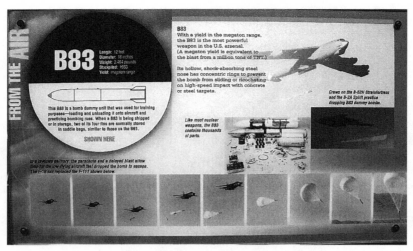

FIGURE 3.3. B83 exhibit at the Bradbury Science Museum, Los Alamos, photograph by the author.

experiencing extremes in temperature, humidity, and acceleration). Figure 3.3 presents a photograph of another dismantled weapon, the B83, as well as pictures of its delivery method, parachute, and airdrop. The exhibit text also offers a statistical portrait of the B83, in terms of length, weight, and age, while underscoring its explosive power as "the most powerful weapon in the U.S. arsenal." Thus, it is not the image itself or even a detailed description of a specific bomb that provoked official concern when I requested the photograph.

One might then conclude that it is an issue of proximity: that this image can be made visible only at the geographical center of U.S. nuclear science in Los Alamos, where information can be controlled via the surveillance of the security system itself. However, one can find another version of the B83 photograph (see figure 3.4) on display at the National Atomic Museum in Albuquerque, an institution devoted to telling the story of U.S. nuclear energy programs as well as the atomic bomb. The National Atomic Museum is affiliated with the Smithsonian Institution, and at the time I took this photograph it was located in the museum district of Albuquerque, adjacent to natural history and fine arts museums, a prime tourist destination. On display at the museum, in addition to images of the dismantled nuclear weapon and diagrams of its operation, is the casing of an actual B83 bomb, as well as a pictorial exhibit of how it would be delivered via

FIGURE 3.4. B83 nuclear weapon exhibit at the National Atomic Museum, Albuquerque, photograph by the author.

the U.S. Air Force. Thus, proximity to nuclear expertise, or to the security mechanisms of a U.S. national laboratory, is not a necessary criterion for the presentation of detailed nuclear weapons information: the National Atomic Museum is staffed by volunteers and is not overtly monitored by the security state.

Thus, the atomic bomb seems to be both a core concern of the security state—with official desire to protect the nuclear secret as the energizing core of the entire system of military-industrial compartmentalized knowledge in the United States—and subject to its own forms of intense publicity. Indeed, consider this final image from the Bradbury Science Museum (see figure 3.5), which asks not what is inside an atomic bomb but "What's in the U.S. Nuclear Stockpile?" Declaring this highly diversified, state-of-the-art arsenal to be a "defensive" project, the exhibit presents U.S. nuclear weapons as the core technology in a global military infrastructure of command and control, including redundant means of "delivery" to "enemy targets." The exhibit presents the designations of the bombs (capital B) and warheads (capital W) in the U.S. arsenal (B61, B83, W80-1, W78, W87, W62, W78, W88, and W80-0); the delivery methods (aircraft, cruise missiles, intercontinental ballistic missiles, and submarine-launched missiles); the design laboratories of each weapon (Los Alamos, Livermore, and Sandia);

SENSITIVE BUT UNCLASSIFIED

FIGURE 3.5. "What's in the U.S. Nuclear Stockpile?" exhibit at the Bradbury Science Museum, Los Alamos, photograph by the author.

and the strategic and tactical deployments on air, land, and sea that make up the nuclear triad (bombers, missiles, and submarines). Thus, the make, model, delivery method, and conceptual placement of each device in the U.S. nuclear arsenal are presented here as public knowledge—which again raises the question: what kind of information does the disassembled B61 bomb photograph now constitute?

The B61 photograph is both widely circulated—available to anybody interested enough in nuclear weapons policy and science to download a file from the DOE website or willing to visit museums devoted to the U.S. nuclear program—yet it is also restricted "due to security concerns." If it were a classified image, then the directors of the two museums could today be charged with espionage, as could the head of the DOE for posting materials online. And tourists, with snapshots such as the ones I present here, from either of the museum displays would be in immediate violation of federal law and subject to arrest. And you as the dear reader of this text would also be in possession of a nuclear secret, holding in your hands an object of potential espionage subject to legal or military action. But since the museum and Internet materials have not been pulled from circulation, my exchange with the DOE leads to the question: how can information be simultaneously in the "public domain" and a "state secret"?

The B61 photograph is an example of an expanding category of government information known as "sensitive but unclassified" (SBU). Information with this designation is not officially classified as a state secret, and thus subject to all the laws about handing such information; instead, it is simply withheld from public circulation.[4] I want to suggest that the evolving use of the SBU designation reveals an important aspect of the transformation of U.S. national security culture from a countercommunist to a counterterrorist state. It also marks a significant evolution in the power of the bomb—not as a military tool but as an administrative-legal-cultural form—to define contemporary domestic politics. The post–Cold War period (1991–2001) formally ended with the official turn to counterterror in September 2001, inaugurating a profound expansion of the security state but one based on the Cold War model. Indeed, a new concept of official secrecy was established in the immediate aftermath of World War II that increasingly positioned citizens as a potential threat to state security and that separated huge parts of government from either public scrutiny or democratic participation. The atomic bomb was mobilized in this moment to enable a new kind of security state, a "national security state" linking the official declaration of imminent threat to an expansive project of compartmentalized secrecy, creating the United States as a nuclear superpower. The U.S. War on Terror has sought to revitalize and extend this project through the secrecy/threat matrix, mobilizing fear not only of the atomic bomb but of the more ambiguous WMD to enable new agendas, both foreign and domestic. Before interrogating the logics of SBU knowledge, however, I want to explore how this secrecy/threat matrix has transformed the nature of the secret (and, in so doing, the relationship between citizens and the state). In the United States, the advent of the atomic bomb produced a radical reinvention of the democratic state form, one grounded in state secrecy, threat proliferation and countermobilization, and a permanent war posture.

The Power of the Secret

Recognition of the power and the complexity of the secret is a foundational moment in the social sciences. Emile Durkheim, for example, argues in *Elementary Forms of the Religious Life* that the secret provides a central means of organizing the distinction between the sacred and the profane. For him, that most sacred Aboriginal object, the *churinga*, is endowed with meaning by the taboos—specifically, the ritual secrecy—concerning access to it. Moreover, he notes that:

> In themselves, the churingas are merely objects of wood and stone like so many others; they are distinguished from profane things of the same kind by only one particularity: The totemic mark is drawn or engraved upon them. That mark, and only that mark, confers sacredness on them. (Durkheim 2005, 121)

The mark confers sacredness. Thus, Durkheim discovers not only that removing something from public view endows it with social power but also that the object of secrecy—its information—is often less important than the organizational approach to managing it. Meaning, in other words, is made in the social practice of secrecy, not in its informational content. Georg Simmel, following up on this insight, argues that secrecy is nothing less than constitutive of society—and therefore "one of the greatest achievements of humanity" (1906, 462). For Simmel, secrecy enables complexity in the social world, and "every relationship between two individuals or two groups will be characterized by the ratio of secrecy that is involved in it." The tension produced by withholding secrets is therefore productive in every sense, not only by defining insider and outsider status but also by energizing the social, allowing identifications and misidentifications, confessions, gossip, conspiracy theory, speculation, and belief. Sigmund Freud (1999, 1965) also understood the complexity of the hidden, and he may well be the greatest theorist of the secret: he argued that it is only by keeping secrets from ourselves that we are constituted as subjects. The core insight of psychoanalysis is not only that we are to a large degree unknowable to ourselves—as each mind constitutes a unique system of secrecy—but also that even a partial glimpse into our own hidden thoughts can be transformative.

From these perspectives, religion, social life, and the constitution of the self all depend on and are produced through the management of secrets. What each approach also suggests is that it is the systemic structure of the secret as much as its content that is productive; it is the rituals, the social restrictions, the individual repressions that mobilize affect, recognition, and misrecognition and that produce order. With the post–Cold War arrival of the information age and new technologies of mass communication, one might assume that the secret has less social power than it once had, as information now flows with an unprecedented speed and volume online. But I want to suggest here that in fact quite the opposite is true: U.S. society is today overdetermined not by the amount of information set free or constrained but rather by the political deployment of the secret *as an idea*. Theorizing how secrecy functions in the contemporary nation-state—specifically, in the United States as a nuclear superpower—consequently requires a radical expansion of our idea of the secret and its role in constituting social order.

I argue here that the rise of the national security state marks a transformation in both the nature of state power (in the form of the atomic bomb) and the constitution of the secret (a compartmentalized knowledge society). Instead of enabling a system in which knowledge is power, the national security state's system of compartmentalized secrecy produces a world in which knowledge is always rendered suspect. This is a profound shift in how secrecy functions socially. The great theorists of secrecy from the early twentieth century—Durkheim, Simmel, and Freud—all knew how to locate the secret and study its psychosocial effects. Indeed, studying secrecy became a way of unpacking social coherence, a means of understanding communication and miscommunication, power, order, and social accountability. It is precisely the secret as a *limit case* that functions to enable the public, which constitutes these theories of social order. With the formal constitution of the national security state in 1947, the United States becomes committed to the secret on a scale that ensures there is no coordinating center or logic organizing the secret, creating not a center of power but rather a highly structured, if ultimately uncoordinated, system. In such a nation-state, secrecy becomes an increasingly pathological administrative form, one that prevents anyone within the system from actually have confidence in knowledge, and where no one—citizen, solder, or official—is untainted by secrecy's distorting effects.

Consequently, the system of secrecy established to protect the atomic bomb in the mid-twentieth century constitutes what I believe is one of the most profound and understudied aspects of the nuclear revolution in the United States. Indeed, Simmel (1906, 492) today might laugh at the "greatest achievement of humanity" as it has not only enabled the development of unprecedented WMDs but also produced a social machinery so devoted to the secret that knowledge itself is drawn into question, and where the imagined hidden life of the government overpowers public collective thought.[5] The nuclear secret remains a fetish in the United States; it functions today as an engine of irrationality and power that colonizes governance and everyday life in the name of counterterror. As we shall see, the national security state is increasingly structured not by the value of knowledge or by the power of withholding knowledge, but rather by the theatrical performance of secrecy as a means to power: secrecy now functions as a form of antiknowledge in the United States, an empty signifier that stands in for governance, rationality, and evidence.

Instituting Secrecy

With the 1946 Atomic Energy Act and the 1947 National Security Act, the United States effectively removed huge areas of governmental affairs from citizens' purview. These acts formally installed a new security state in the United States, constituting a fundamental change in the nature of American democracy. The Atomic Energy Act created the first kind of information—nuclear weapons data—that did not need to be formally classified: it was "born" that way. The National Security Act then created a wide range of new governmental institutions—most prominently, the Central Intelligence Agency (CIA), the first of what would become seventeen intelligence agencies in the United States—that *by charter* would not be publicly accountable to citizens. Created in peacetime, the new laws and agencies marked the establishment of a permanent war economy as well as a fundamental commitment to state secrecy in the United States. Rationalized as an effort to protect military secrets about the atomic bomb in an uncertain world and to prevent a "nuclear Pearl Harbor" (see Dower 2010, 27), these acts inaugurated a split between national security and state security in the United States, with citizens implicitly recognized as a potential barrier to state security policies. After 1945 the U.S. security state apparatus increasingly used nuclear fear as an affective means of reconstituting the line between the foreign and the domestic, and to mobilize citizens as cold warriors.

Although the concept of a state secret was not invented during the Manhattan Project, the state structures that were established to build the atomic bomb have subsequently evolved into an unprecedentedly massive infrastructure in the United States—so massive, in fact, that its sheer scale is difficult to assess (see Burr, Blanton, and Schwartz 1998). Today there may well be more knowledge that is classified than is not, more knowledge that is produced and locked up in the military-industrial state than is offered by all nonmilitary academic literatures. Peter Galison has calculated the scale of secret versus public knowledge in the United States and offers this assessment:

> There are 500,000 college professors in the United States—including both two- and four-year institutions. Of course there are others—inventors, industrial scientists, computer programmers—responsible for generating and conveying knowledge, especially technical knowledge. But to fix ideas, four million people hold [security] clearances in the United States, plus some vast reservoir who did in the past but no longer do. Bottom line? Whether one figures by acquisition rate, by holding size, or by contributors, the classified universe is, as best I can estimate, on the order of five to ten times larger than the open literature that finds its way into our libraries. (2004, 231)

The classified archive is many times larger than the open library. Produced in the name of citizens who have no access to this knowledge except as employees of the security state, the classified universe is not simply a means of protecting the nation-state from the spread of dangerous military information; official secrecy is a social technology, a means of internally regulating and militarizing American society. The organizing principle for this system of secrecy is the atomic bomb, which is positioned in the universe of classification as the ideal type of state secret. Indeed, the system of secrecy that developed after World War II was premised on the idea that everything marked as *classified* had the potential to produce catastrophic results if made public. An important part of the cultural work accomplished by the state's recitation of nuclear danger in the first decades of the Cold War was to establish this linkage between the classified and the apocalyptic—merging a bureaucratic system for managing the military-industrial economy with images of imminent destruction of the nation-state at the slightest slippage or revelation. By discursively positioning every classified file as potentially an atomic secret, the state transformed a provisional system of wartime secrecy into a fully nationalized system of perception management and control.

In essence, a new social contract was formed in the first decade of the Cold War, enabled and structured by the affective power of atomic weapons. Simultaneously the ultimate weapon and the ultimate vulnerability, nuclear weapons presented a new set of contradictory resources and challenges to the state. For example, although declaring that the United States possesses "the greatest military potential of any single nation in the world," National Security Council Directive 68 (National Security Council 1993, 50)—the top-secret policy document that articulated the Cold War policy of Soviet containment—is nonetheless ultimately a text about U.S. nuclear vulnerability. The directive depicts the Soviet Union as an existential enemy in anticipation of its future nuclear potential and argues not only for a fourfold military buildup but also for a mobilization of all institutions of American society to fight a long Cold War. This reengineering of American society for a new kind of warfare required a widespread recalibration of everyday life, including political, economic, and military institutions as well as the urban landscape and ideas about the future (see Galison 2001). The early Cold War military planners Major General Walter E. Todd, commanding general of the Western Air Defense Force for the United Kingdom; Lieutenant General Willard S. Paul, an expert on economic mobilization in the U.S. Office of Defense Mobilization; and Val Peterson, head of the Federal Civil Defense Administration (1955) called in their *Scientific Monthly* article (titled "National Defense against Atomic Attack") for the construction of a perfect air defense involving the full accoutrements of now iconic "closed world" military technologies (see Edwards 1996), a dispersion of industrial sites away from urban centers, a relocation of housing stock to the periphery of cities, a constant war gaming of potential Soviet attack scenarios along with domestic civil defense exercises, a massive program to stockpile critical materials to feed and care for the entire national population, new building standards for construction designed to resist the effects of a nuclear blast, and a significant expansion of the U.S. capability to fight a nuclear war. Todd, Paul, and Peterson concluded:

> Mobilization is no longer to be undertaken upon declaration of war or after war starts. Either we stay ready at all times to absorb and survive the worst blow an enemy can strike, or we do not. If we do not, there probably will be no chance to mobilize afterward. If we do, there is a good chance that the blow will never be attempted, for we will have substituted many targets for a few. The enemy will no longer be able to destroy effectively the capacity to operate and, thus, to break

the national spirit by a massive attack on major metropolitan areas. (1955, 246)

We stay ready at all times. The immediate goal of the countercommunist state was to reengineer American society around and through the atomic bomb. Not only was nuclear fear integrated into military planning, but it also transformed the very nature of the nation-state.[6] Indeed, all the projects proposed by Todd, Paul, and Peterson were actually pursued, fusing the Cold War military project with a new kind of domestic economic strategy. But what was the actual nature of the nuclear threat? In 1950 the Soviet Union had no more than 5 nuclear devices, while the United States had more than 350; by 1961 the Soviet Union had amassed more than 2,400 weapons, but the United States had more than 24,000 warheads and bombs (Norris and Kristensen 2006). Few Americans at the time or today understand that the United States maintained at least a ten-to-one nuclear advantage throughout the first decades of the Cold War, the period of the most intense nuclear paranoia in the United States. So how do we reconcile the clear nuclear advantage the United States maintained through the early decades of the Cold War with the domestic nuclear discourse of absolute vulnerability and imminent surprise attack?

Nuclear fear was the central concept in a larger emotional management campaign designed and conducted by both the Truman and Eisenhower administrations to mobilize citizens for a new kind of war (see Oakes 1994). By concentrating public attention on specific images of nuclear threat and classifying all other aspects of the nuclear economy, the early Cold War state sought to calibrate the image of *crisis* to enable the Cold War project. The primary goal of what was called civil defense in the first decades of the nuclear age was not to protect citizens from the exploding bomb but rather to psychologically reprogram them as cold warriors. The calculated campaign of images—produced by the nuclear test program and delivered under the rubric of domestic defense—was an effort to access the emotions of U.S. citizens and thereby transform an emerging nuclear threat into a means of consolidating the power and importance of the security state. As a top-secret report to President Dwight Eisenhower put it in 1956:

Just as the Industrial Revolution of the early nineteenth century, with its far-reaching effects on war and peace, required vast social and psychological adjustments, so the present period faces extremely complex social and psychological changes. (Panel on the Human Effects of Nuclear Weapons Development 1956, 5)

Vast social and psychological adjustments are needed. Calling for a new state project to install "psychological defenses" in citizens and challenging each individual to experience an "emotional adaptation" to the thought and reality of nuclear warfare, the report concludes:

> The keystone of the program is knowledge—not merely information made available but information, both frightening and hopeful, so successfully conveyed as to become useful knowledge translated into plans, procedures, and the capability for constructive action. . . . In order to prepare the people, we believe that it will be necessary to involve them, and to involve them at deeper levels than mere factual information. (1956, 11; see also Vandercook 1986)

A deeper level than facts. Involving citizens meant teaching them about the effects of nuclear explosions—providing specific images of the bomb and censoring all others–while publicizing the emerging Soviet nuclear threat. Civil defense was an explicit program to teach citizens to fear the bomb, fuse that fear with anticommunism, and modulate its intensity so that a potentially terrified public did not become unwilling to support the larger Cold War program. The ultimate goal of civil defense was a citizen who was permanently mobilized as a cold warrior, restructured internally for constant readiness and hardened by nuclear fear. One of the most powerful attributes of the atomic bomb, in other words, is that it offered new access to the emotional life of the nation, producing a new kind of public constituted and militarized through a highly tailored vision of existential threat.

But if publicizing a specific concept and image of nuclear danger was the key to mobilizing citizens—to establishing an everyday life infused with the minute-to-minute possibility of nuclear war—the corollary project was an expanding use of state secrecy to manage the production of threat and control its public image. In the early Cold War period, the atomic bomb was the key to achieving global superpower status, as well as installing a concept of danger that was the exclusive domain of the security state. For the nuclear state, this secrecy/threat matrix became a concentrated means of managing domestic populations as well as pursuing the broader geopolitics of communist containment. Secrecy was not just about protecting technological secrets in a global competition with the Soviet Union; it was also a means of converting American society into a countercommunist state at the level of institutions, economies, politics, and emotions. The War on Terror is a contemporary effort to reproduce the success of this early Cold War project in population management, affective governance, and military-industrial expansion, while at the same time expanding existential danger itself through the phantasmatic figure of the "terrorist with a WMD."

The Counterterror State

Since 2001 secrecy has become a core tool in transforming the United States from a countercommunist to a counterterrorist state, and its official use is an ever-expanding practice.[7] In a variety of executive orders and formal directives in the aftermath of the 2001 terrorist attacks, the Bush administration required each federal agency to increase its control of information.[8] According to government audits, there were nine million formal classification decisions in 2001 but over sixteen million by 2004, an increase of 75 percent. Moreover, the rate at which records that are over twenty-five years old were declassified fell by over 75 percent in the same period. Thus, the official past and present have become newly politicized as well as highly censored domains (see Open The Government 2005a and 2005b). The cost of simply managing secret information in the United States is estimated to be over $7.2 billion a year, involving in one year alone over four thousand classification authorities and over 351,150 new classification decisions (U.S. Information Security Oversight Office 2004a and 2004b). Put differently, for every dollar spent on declassification during the first years of the War on Terror, $148 dollars were spent creating new secrets (Open The Government 2005a). The counterterror state has also evoked the *state secrets privilege* in court cases (to nullify the proceedings on the ground that trying the case would damage U.S. national security) thirty-three times more often than during the height of the Cold War.[9] However, these figures deal only with explicit classification or declassification decisions, the making of which is a formal regulatory process. Sensitive but unclassified information is a potentially larger and more influential category of knowledge. As I noted above, SBU information is not officially classified, it is information simply removed from public circulation and treated *as if* it were.

Officially justified as a means of protecting information about critical infrastructures following the terrorist attacks on New York and Washington in 2001, the SBU designation and its expanding use have radically changed the way information is handled in federal agencies. The 2002 Homeland Security Act charged federal employees to "identify and safeguard homeland security information that is sensitive but unclassified."[10]

However, the act defined none of its terms, leaving it up to each federal agency to draw the lines between public access and critical infrastructure protections. Concurrently, the Department of Justice advised all government agencies to limit the scope of Freedom of Information Act (FOIA) requests wherever possible—forcing litigation and thus contradicting the law's intent—while also pursuing an unprecedented application of the 1917 Espionage Act to target whistle-blowers within the government. In support of these new restrictions, the counterterror state has also embraced a *mosaic theory* of information threat. This theory assumes that disparate items of information (particularly those that appear innocuous and of no obvious use to an adversary) can nonetheless be assembled to create a whole that is more powerful than the sum of its parts. According to this theory, any piece of information is potentially a national security threat, as it is the creative linking together of bits of knowledge that is imagined to be dangerous. The extensive surveillance programs run by the National Security Agency after 2001—involving digital surveillance, archiving telecommunications across platforms, and data mining on a newly comprehensive global scale—rely on this concept. David Pozen has argued that an aggressive use of the mosaic theory of information synergy produces claims that are "unfalsifiable," leading inevitably to over-classification and threat proliferation (2005, 679).

The result of these new laws, practices, and interpretive strategies is obvious: information that flowed relatively freely a few years ago—for example, environmental impact studies of government projects—now fall into this SBU category and are often not available to citizens. A generalized state security concept trumps all other concerns (in this case, environmental protection) via the SBU approach. The images of prisoner abuse from Abu Ghraib prison fell in the SBU category and were released only after being leaked to *60 Minutes*, the *New Yorker*, *Salon.com*, and via litigation by the American Civil Liberties Union.[11] But less provocative information about government contracts, policy debates and initiatives, and anything that might be patentable also falls in the SBU category. Thus, the overall strategy of the counterterrorist state has been to replace a presumption of transparency in nonmilitary matters with wide-ranging restrictions that emphasizes noncirculation rather than, or in addition to, formal classification (see A. Roberts 2006, 36–41). It is via the SBU category that much of American society is being implicitly militarized—as keeping basic governmental information from citizens is increasingly equated with antiterrorism and normalized as an administrative practice.

The most important aspect of the SBU category of information is that it has never been defined by federal law; it is a strategically vague concept that is used differently by each federal agency. The U.S. Government Accountability Office (2006) found fifty-six different definitions of SBU in use, and could document few provisions to identify which (and how many) officials in an agency are authorized to mark information as SBU. The SBU designation is thus a largely unregulated category of information in the federal government. The first articulation of SBU as a category came from John Poindexter, while working as Ronald Reagan's national security advisor, before he gained notoriety for his role in the Iran-Contra scandal. At the start of the War on Terror, he also served as the head of the Defense Advanced Research Projects Agency until public revelation of his proposed Total Information Awareness data-mining project (devoted to capturing all digital communication) forced him to step down in 2002. In 1986, Poindexter defined SBU information this way:

> Sensitive, but unclassified information is information the disclosure, loss, misuse, alteration or destruction of which could adversely affect national security or other Federal Government interests. National security interests are those unclassified matters that relate to the national defense or the foreign relations of the U.S. government. Other government interests are those related, but not limited to the wide range of government or government-derived economic, human, financial, industrial, agricultural, technological and law enforcement information, as well as privacy or confidentiality of personal or commercial proprietary information provided to the U.S. government by its citizens. (quoted in Knezo 2003, 20)

National security or "other" interests. The "related but not limited to" concept here expands the SBU category to include most of governmental work: today, perhaps as much as 75 percent of nonclassified government information could be designated as SBU. When fully deployed, the SBU category effectively expands national security to include any kind of information whose release might be inconvenient to the execution of state policy. When combined with the mosaic theory of information risk, there is literally no aspect of governmental work that could not be conceptualized as an essential part of U.S. national security and thus seen as a threat if made public. Increasingly, anticipatory defense trumps democratic process across governmental activities.

Indeed, the SBU category was aggressively mobilized by federal agencies as an antiterrorism provision in October 2001, as a means of protecting critical infrastructures (also a strategically vague term) from terrorist attack (Knezo 2003, 25). From the perspective of the counterterror state, the value of SBU as a category is not only its ambiguity—as literally anything in the government can be separated from the public sphere, according to its logic—but also because there is no formal review process that citizens can use to challenge the designation of information as SBU. There is no federal agency charged with regulating the use of SBU or hearing appeals. It is therefore up to each federal agency, branch, office, and official to decide where to draw the line between public accountability and security, which allows near-infinite flexibility in standards and logics. If having basic information about governmental practices can be constituted as a threat, then SBU functions to blur the distinction between the citizen and the enemy. It also allows any kind of federal information to be marked for noncirculation, creating an expansive new category of withheld information located between the explicitly classified and the public.

Following the declassification campaigns of the immediate post–Cold War era, and the enormous democratization of access to information enabled by the Internet in the 1990s, the early twenty-first century has thus witnessed a fundamental shift in the idea and mechanisms of openness and transparency in the United States. Indeed, a central part of the conversion of the United States from a countercommunist to a counterterror state has been an information strategy of increased classification, noncirculation, and censoring of the existing public record. The U.S. National Archives have become a front line in the counterterror project, as historical records relating to presidential authority, war authorizations, intelligence on WMD issues, and other military matters going back to the start of the Cold War have been removed and either designated as SBU or reclassified (U.S. Information Security Oversight Office 2006).[12] At least a million pages of previously declassified materials have been pulled from the National Archives since October 2001 (see Bass and Herschaft 2007). Thus, the historical formation, as well as the current projects, of the security state have been subject to expanding forms of censorship. Official fear of the terrorist, and of the WMD, has enabled a formal reconstitution of the security state as secret entity, generating a wide range of covert actions within the United States and around the world. Secrecy in all its forms is a political tool, with the art of redaction an additional method for withholding information while complying with federal law (see figure 3.6).

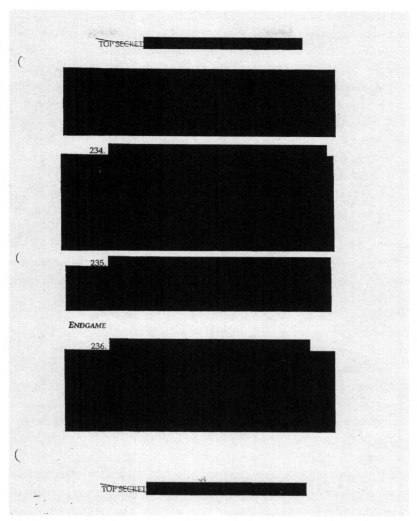

FIGURE 3.6. "Endgame" Redacted page from a Central Intelligence Agency report on interrogation techniques, U.S. Central Intelligence Agency (2004).

Agreeing with every major study of state secrecy in the past thirty years, William Arkin (2005, 12) argues that this level of secrecy is not only excessive but also profoundly damaging to a democracy, because it confuses the domestic politics of secrecy with efforts to protect military operations. Arkin notes, for example, that U.S. military activities that are easily recognized as such in the Middle East (from special operations to drone strikes) are nonetheless classified by the U.S. government, a state of affairs that serves only to keep U.S. citizens, not foreign nationals, military leaders, or adversaries, in the dark (see also Sagan and Suri 2003, 150). Chalmers Johnson (2000 and 2004) takes this insight a step further by pointing out that the CIA term *blowback* addresses not only the retaliatory consequences produced by U.S. covert actions at home and abroad, but also the damaging domestic effects of secrecy. Since U.S. covert operations are by definition unknown to U.S. citizens, actions taken around the world in response to them are literally unintelligible to U.S. citizens. Secrecy works here in a doubled fashion to enable state actions that might not be supported if they were subjected to public debate while at the same time denying citizens a means of understanding the long-term political effects of U.S. global activities. In a counterterror state, blowback has several additional perverse effects: since U.S. citizens have no insight into U.S. covert actions around the world, retaliatory acts appear to the American public as without context and thus irrational. And given that the premise of the War on Terror is that a "terrorist" is an irrational and inherently violent being who is dedicated to destroying the United States, blowback empowers yet another level of American misrecognition and fantasy: namely, that the United States is only a global military actor when provoked by irrationally violent attacks.

A similar observation was made by Daniel Moynihan (1998) in his post–Cold War review of official secrecy: he noted that the Cold War decision to keep the Venona intercepts of encrypted Soviet diplomatic communications classified to protect sources and methods in the 1950s actually worked primarily to keep U.S. citizens in the dark about the true scale of Soviet espionage in the United States, since the Soviets soon knew their code had been broken. Moynihan suggests that releasing the files before 1995 might have prevented or reduced the profound political divide in American society over the nature of Soviet infiltration—as the Venona intercepts documented that there were, in fact, Soviet spies in the United States but nowhere near the numbers imagined by Senator Joseph McCarthy (see also Shils 1996, 13). Thus, secrecy produces political fetishes that can fundamentally distort a democratic public sphere. For example, the CIA's increasing use of drones for targeted killings in Pakistan and Afghanistan has been the subject of widespread reporting (by nongovernmental agencies and media) and even confirmed by both President Obama and Secretary of Defense Leon Panetta, yet the CIA asserts in FOIA litigation that "the use (or non-use) of drones" is a "classified fact" and therefore not subject to any declassification claim.[13]

Jodi Dean (2002) argues that it is public recognition of state secrecy that enables a democracy to manage the split between what political life is supposed to be and what it is seen to be, between its ideal type and its lived experience. She argues that recognition of state secrecy—and the accompanying conspiratorial subtext to everyday life that it engenders—functions today to block political participation and curtail the possibility of truly democratic endeavors. Specifically, collective assumptions about the secret state (its capacities, interests, omnipotence) installs an ever ready alibi for failed or stalled politics in the public sphere, allowing the fantasy of democracy to coexist within its distorted reality. In Dean's view, citizens now work more passionately to locate and reveal the secret than to enact structural change through direct political action. The democratic state form, which formally claims to be both transparent and accountable, has been reduced, via the logic of the secret, to a fight over the terms of the visible and nonvisible rather than social progress. For Dean, engaging the secret therefore becomes an act of misrecognition for citizens, who assume that revealing the hidden, rather than mobilizing for collective action, is the way to organize democratic politics. She suggests that the evocation of the secret and the call to reveal it have therefore become surrogates for real politics in the United States—together constituting a fetish form that prevents the kind of collective mobilizations that enabled the social justice movements of past eras. Dean suggests, in short, that a belief in the secret constitutes the possibility of a democratic public—for *if only* citizens knew the state's secrets, they could correct the obvious failings of the current political system and create a more perfect society—but it also installs a public whose agency is therefore endlessly deferred in the act of chasing greater transparency. But if an informed, democratically energized citizenry is the first victim of the elaborate system of secrecy in the United States, policy makers also suffer.

There is a remarkable moment in Daniel Ellsberg's autobiography in which he describes a conversation with Henry Kissinger, who was then on the verge of becoming secretary of state. Ellsberg, the RAND analyst who eventually leaked the top-secret U.S. history of the Vietnam War known as the Pentagon Papers to the *New York Times* and the *Washington Post* (see Prados and Porter 2004), attempts to prepare Kissinger for the psychological effects of having access to above top-secret information. He informs Kissinger that, over the coming years, he will feel, in the following order: exhilarated (at the access), foolish (for what he once thought he knew), contempt (for those who do not have access), and increasing skepticism (about the quality of classified information). In the end, Ellsberg tells Kissinger:

> It will become hard for you to learn from anybody who doesn't have these clearances. Because you'll be thinking as you listen to them "What would this man be telling me if he knew what I know? Would he be giving me the same advice, or would it totally change his predictions and recommendations?" And that mental exercise is so torturous that after a while you give it up and just stop listening. I've seen this with my superiors, my colleagues . . . and with myself. . . . You will deal with a person who doesn't have those clearances only from the point of view of what you want him to believe and what impression you want him to go away with, since you'll have to lie carefully to him about what you know. In effect, you will have to manipulate him. You'll give up trying to assess what he has to say. The danger is, you'll become something like a moron. You'll become incapable of learning from most people in the world, no matter how much experience they may have in their particular areas that may be much greater than yours. (2003, 237–38)

You become something like a moron. Ellsberg reveals here a rarely commented-on aspect of compartmentalized secrecy: it relies not only on withholding information but also on lying. Individuals must lie in order to protect their own classification level in everyday interactions throughout the system, and thus they distort their social relations to protect the system of secrecy. Knowledge itself becomes doubly corrupted: first, because of the effect of compartmentalization on perceptions of expert knowledge as described by Ellsberg, and second, because perception control becomes as important as information management. Deception via classification becomes the internal structure of the security state, which over time works not to underscore the value of information—often the assumed goal of a system of compartmentalized classification—but rather to corrode the very terms of knowledge and expertise, making individual motivations and judgements also suspect.

The role of deception is crucial in the transformation of a democratic state into a security state, as the public good becomes absorbed into that of a security apparatus that by definition seeks to extend its power and reproducibility. This logic is made visible by even a cursory look into the state secrets privilege in the United States—the tool whereby the security state blocks a legal proceeding to protect national security interests.

The states secret privilege was formally established in the 1953 Supreme Court case *United States v. Reynolds*.[14] After an Air Force B-29 aircraft crashed near Marion, Georgia, in 1948, family members of the dead and injured sued the government for negligence and sought declassification of the accident report to support their claim. The families won in lower courts but lost on federal appeal in the Supreme Court. The Air Force argued that the B-29 mission involved research on "secret electronic equipment" and that to release any information about the crash would damage national security. This case set the precedent for a state secrets privilege in the United States, which has become a standard federal tool for nullifying legal challenges on national security grounds. The family members, however, continued to push for release of the accident report via the FOIA, receiving several copies during the 1990s that were heavily redacted. Then, in 2000, they found an uncensored copy of the once-classified, and by then highly litigated, accident report on the Internet. It had been inadvertently released by the Air Force as part of a larger declassification of fifty-year-old records. The report made no mention of the "secret electronic equipment" that was the basis for the initial Supreme Court state secrets ruling, but it did document negligence in the maintenance of the aircraft and the training of the crew. Thus, the Air Force appears to have classified the report in 1948 not for national security reasons but to avoid liability for the accident. The families sued again to have the 1953 ruling overturned as fraud, and the Justice Department successfully deployed the mosaic theory of secrecy to stop the legal proceedings: in essence, federal lawyers argued that it is impossible to understand today what seemingly innocuous bits of information might collectively have had national security implications in 1948, regardless of the initial Air Force arguments (Fisher 2006, 203). It is crucial here to recognize that the foundational legal case for the state secrets privilege in the United States is grounded in deception rather than a principled theory of national security—illustrating how secrecy functions not only to protect information but to create new realities as well as new forms of bureaucratic agency and protection. Since 2001 the state secrets privilege has been evoked to nullify judicial hearings in an exceptional number of high-profile cases, including the extraordinary rendition of a German citizen by the CIA, retaliatory suits against whistle-blowers in the Federal Bureau of Investigation and the Air Force, domestic data-mining operations in the United States, multiple cases involving the surveillance of U.S. citizens without a legal warrant, and accusations of targeted killing of foreign nationals and Americans abroad (Chesney 2006; Garvey and Liu 2011). The states secrets privilege is a central tool of the counterterrorist state in managing threat perception as well as legal standing. It is reveals the extraordinary power of the secrecy/threat matrix, which promises catastrophic consequences for a revelation of the secret while simultaneously classifying the considerations, evidence, and precedents supporting such an assessment.

The Affects of Secrecy

The nation state form is, in many respects, founded on the assumption of secrecy. Michel Foucault (1995 and 2003) has shown that the modern state maintains the right not only to keep secrets but also to subject its citizens to increasingly minute forms of surveillance. The eighteenth-century logic of the panopticon is of a sovereign who sees without being seen, a formulation built literally into the architectural infrastructure of the prison and ultimately the the mind of the prisoner. This logic is today replicated across U.S. digital surveillance activities on an unprecedented scale—creating a counterterror state that attempts to be completely hidden while rendering citizens completely transparent. Similarly, the modern project of population management involves a fine mesh of institutions devoted to measuring individuals and creating statistical portraits of citizens across a wide range of subjects, from health, to education, to the economy. Foucault charts a steady progression in the forms of knowledge, as well as the psychosocial intimacy of these state projects, from the overthrow of monarchal authority to the early twentieth-century nation-state, as the tools of surveillance and technologies of population management steadily increase in both power and resolution. Thus, there has always been a profound separation between citizens and the state, and the practice of democratic politics has always been highly mediated by practices of secrecy. Yet the kind of state produced in the aftermath of World War II in the United States—a nuclear-armed superpower—takes a core principle of the nation-state form, the use of secrecy in the name of collective security, and expands it into a totalizing structure that links all aspects of the state in a radical global counterformation. In this post–World War II system, secrecy becomes not just a technology of state power, a means of orchestrating policy and protecting state interests through the withholding of information, but also the basis for an entirely new kind of power: the ability to create new realities.

Specifically, in the nuclear age *the idea* of secret knowledge becomes deployable on its own. Evoking the secret thus becomes a means of claiming greater knowledge, expertise, and understanding than in fact is possible.

How else do we explain the fantastic collective failure of U.S. intelligence agencies to be attuned to the internal collapse of the Soviet Union in the late 1980s, even after generating nearly constant threat assessments of Soviet activities for four decades? How do we explain the constant tension in U.S. security culture over dissent in the United States and the frequent placing of nonviolent social activists into the category of the enemy? Secrecy has been enormously productive in terms of building and protecting a military-industrial economy, but it has also created new perceptions of state power that affect government officials as well as citizens. The linkage between the secret and the apocalyptic in the nuclear security state has transformed the citizen-state relationship both conceptually and in practice. The secrecy/threat matrix is, in this regard, ultimately a project of perception management that functions to create, protect, and project the idea of a "superpower state." Thus, the atomic bomb inaugurates a new kind of social contract in the United States, one that separates national security as a public discourse from state security as an institutional practice. It ultimately grounds the power of the state in the perceived ability to destroy or be destroyed, rather than in the strength of its democratic institutions (see, for example, D. Armstrong 2002).

The WMD as a technological form has always promised apocalyptic consequences if used in combat, but the idea of the WMD, its phantasmatic figuration, has been equally powerful in U.S. security culture. By defending all state secrets as the equivalent of the atomic secret, the U.S. security state has consolidated and defined its power via threat designation and inflation. The counterterror state's efforts to expand official secrecy alongside its amplification of the WMD as the single greatest threat to the United States (see U.S. White House 2002b) reveals one long-term effect of the Cold War secrecy/threat matrix: an official desire to close off citizens' access to the state altogether, in the name of protecting the public. Official secrecy can now effectively restrict even the most banal forms of government information using the SBU category and mosaic theory. These practices overturn the market logics of the information age, in which information made free was seen as a social good.[15] The effects of this information strategy are widespread in the United States, not only for systems of accountability but also for the sciences—in which self-censorship is increasingly sought for those working in fields of study that might have infrastructural, military, or patent applications. Thus, the broader effect of these policies is to define the public sphere not as an inherent aspect of democratic order but as a fundamental threat to that very order, identifying rights that citizens should willingly surrender for their personal safety. The extensive data collection of the National Security Agency after 2001, for example, has rendered every detail of American citizens' digital lives a security concern in the name of counterterror. Indeed, what does it mean when the free flow of information is the exception rather than the rule in a global superpower that is also a self-proclaimed democracy?

Finally, and importantly, the secret society that is the state is ultimately headless, an effect of both the systematic distortion in the believability of knowledge as it moves up the levels of a compartmentalized infrastructure and the demands on individuals to protect perceptions. Thus the secret is transformed over time in such a system: indeed, the idea of secret knowledge itself becomes deployable, corrupting public understandings of what is possible and what is not, and giving those with executive authority the ability to seem more knowing then they actually are. Instead of limiting agency via protected knowledge, the secrecy/threat matrix empowers a new kind of agency, unrestrained by facts. In the lead-up to the invasion of Iraq in March 2003, the Bush administration systematically deployed *the idea* that there were WMDs in Iraq as well as an imminent threat to the United States, to enable war. Vice President Dick Cheney, for example, stated in a speech to the Veterans of Foreign Wars National Convention on August 26, 2002, that there was absolute certainty about the Iraqi threat:

> Simply stated, there is no doubt that Saddam Hussein now has weapons of mass destruction. There is no doubt he is amassing them to use against our friends, against our allies, and against us. And there is no doubt that his aggressive regional ambitions will lead him into future confrontations with his neighbors—confrontations that will involve both the weapons he has today, and the ones he will continue to develop with his oil wealth. (Cheney 2002)[16]

There is no doubt. Here is the secrecy/threat matrix in action, for Cheney implies that the intelligence community has documented with perfect clarity not only the technical terms of the Iraqi biological, chemical, and nuclear programs but also the intent of the regime to use them "against our friends, against our allies, and against us." This is not a deployment of actual knowledge, as the lack of any evidence of weapons of mass destruction in Iraqi after the invasion demonstrates, but it is a political deployment of a claim to secret knowledge.[17]

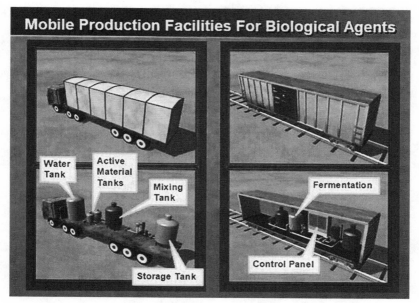

FIGURE 3.7. Iraqi mobile bioweapons labs, from Secretary of State Colin Powell's presentation to the United Nations, February 2003, U.S. State Department.

Secretary of State Colin Powell, in his historic presentation to the United Nations in February 2003, was even more exacting in his deployment of the secrecy/threat matrix.[18] He portrayed an Iraqi biological weapons program that was so advanced it was already capable of threatening the continental United States. Claiming to have sources in the Iraqi government, he presented diagrams of mobile weapons labs (see figure 3.7) and satellite imagery of "WMD" production facilities (see figure 3.8). Powell stated conclusively:

> We know that Iraq has at least seven of these mobile, biological agent factories. The truck-mounted ones have at least two or three trucks each. That means that the mobile production facilities are very few—perhaps 18 trucks that we know of. There may be more. But perhaps 18 that we know of. Just imagine trying to find 18 trucks among the thousands and thousands of trucks that travel the roads of Iraq every single day. (2003)

We know. This depiction of mobile "biological agent factories" effectively transforms every truck in Iraq into a potential WMD laboratory, illustrating the phantasmatic power of the concept of the WMD when used by officials

SENSITIVE BUT UNCLASSIFIED

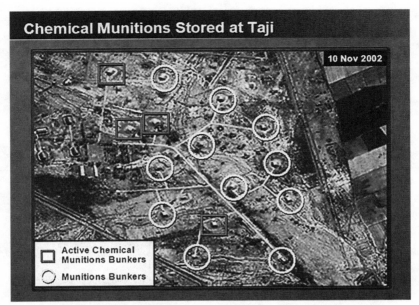

FIGURE 3.8. Iraq WMD sites, from Secretary of State Colin Powell's presentation to the United Nations, February 2003, U.S. State Department.

deploying a claim to secret knowledge. But the nature of the threat becomes increasingly specific in Powell's presentation, its very recitation of detail suggesting that even more exacting knowledge existed in the classified domain:

> We know from Iraq's past admissions that it has successfully weaponized not only anthrax, but also other biological agents, including botulinum toxin, aflatoxin, and ricin. But Iraq's research efforts did not stop there. Saddam Hussein has investigated dozens of biological agents causing diseases such as gas-gangrene, plague, typhus, tetanus, cholera, camelpox, and hemorrhagic fever. And he also has the wherewithal to develop smallpox. (2003)

We know. Powell claims that Iraq has the capability not only to weaponize biological weapons but also to deliver them via state-of-the-art technologies—including unmanned aerial vehicles or drones:

> The Iraqi regime has also developed ways to disperse lethal biological agents widely, indiscriminately into the water supply, into the air. For example, Iraq had a program to modify aerial fuel tanks for Mirage jets. This video of an Iraqi test flight obtained by UNSCOM [a United Nations Special Commission] some years ago shows an Iraqi

F-1 Mirage jet aircraft. Note the spray coming from beneath the Mirage. That is 2,000 liters of simulated anthrax that a jet is spraying. In 1995, an Iraqi military officer, Mujahid Salleh Abdul Latif, told inspectors that Iraq intended the spray tanks to be mounted onto a MiG-21 that had been converted into an unmanned aerial vehicle, or UAV. UAVs outfitted with spray tanks constitute an ideal method for launching a terrorist attack using biological weapons. (2003)

That is simulated anthrax. Iraqi jets as well as drones are presented here as a means of threatening not only Middle Eastern states but also the home territories of the United States and United Kingdom, a fantastic claim given the distances involved. After this expansive portrait of Iraqi military capabilities, Powell concludes that the weapons inspectors have failed to find the "WMDs" and that the threat from these secret weapons is immediate:

> There can be no doubt that Saddam Hussein has biological weapons and the capability to rapidly produce more, many more. And he has the ability to dispense these lethal poisons and diseases in ways that can cause massive death and destruction. (2003)

There can be no doubt. Powell's cartoons and fuzzy pictures of industrial sites appear today, years after the invasion, not simply as a fabrication of knowledge but rather as a tactical deployment of the idea of secret information, for his presentation was loaded with the promise that more detailed and exacting information existed, but that it could not be made public without putting U.S. interests at risk. Indeed, Powell began his presentation to the United Nations Security Council by stating: "I cannot tell you everything that we know, but what I can share with you, when combined with what all of us have learned over the years, is deeply troubling" (Powell 2003).

This deployment of "secret" knowledge relied on the mechanisms and techniques of government that were initially established after World War II to protect information about the atomic bomb—which linked existential threat and covert knowledge production in a new way. The campaign to invade Iraq also drew on culturally established forms of nuclear fear developed in the United States during the Cold War and cultivated for generations. We see here one result of a multigenerational system of state secrecy: a fundamental corruption in the terms of knowledge, where the *idea* of knowledge (imagined, projected, fantasized) replaces actual content as a means of engaging the world. The "will to believe" (in Iraqi WMDs and links between Saddam Hussein and Al Qaeda) by the Bush administration remains a staggering achievement of the counterterror state, but it was only enabled as official policy by the structural effects of compartmentalized secrecy, which worked to limit debate, discount all alternative sources of information, and discredit and politicize any course of action short of war. It was not a lack of good intelligence that led to the invasion of Iraq in 2003; rather, it was the long-term corrosive effects of a compartmentalized and politicized worldview on the very possibility of governance. The secrecy/threat matrix has been revealed to be a core tool in the War on Terror, but it has also been revealed to be a highly overdetermined form, one that functions to fundamentally distort both expertise and knowledge.[19] And in a counterterror state where knowledge itself is rendered either suspect or irrelevant, only fear, desire, and ideology remain as the basis for action in a world constituted as full of emergent and proliferating dangers.

FOUR

BIOSECURITY NOIR
WMDs in a World without Borders

The greater the threat, the greater is the risk of inaction—and the more compelling the case for taking anticipatory action to defend ourselves, even if uncertainty remains as to the time and place of the enemy's attack. To forestall or prevent such hostile acts by our adversaries, the United States will, if necessary, act preemptively. —**THE WHITE HOUSE "NATIONAL SECURITY STRATEGY OF THE UNITED STATES OF AMERICA" (2002)**

In the past, enemies of America required massed armies and great navies, powerful air forces to put our nation, our people, our friends and allies at risk. In the Cold War, Americans lived under the threat of weapons of mass destruction but believed that deterrents made those weapons a last resort. What has changed in the twenty-first century is that, in the hands of terrorists, weapons of mass destruction could be a first resort—the preferred means to further their ideology of suicide and random murder. These terrible weapons are becoming easier to acquire, build, hide, and transport. Armed with a single vial of a biological agent or a single nuclear weapon, small groups of fanatics, or failing states, could gain the power to threaten great nations, threaten the world peace. America, and the entire civilized world, will face this threat for decades to come. —**PRESIDENT GEORGE W. BUSH, "COUNTERING THE WMD THREAT"**

Noir—a crime genre marked by a mood of pessimism, fatalism, and menace. —*OXFORD ENGLISH DICTIONARY*

To anticipate the experience of terror and respond preemptively to it is the goal of the U.S. counterterror state in the twenty-first century. But future terror comes in an infinite number of potential guises and vectors, making a key domain of sovereign power the ability to decide which fears matter, which potentials require dramatic action in the here and now, which possible nightmares among the imagined multitude are to organize the future today. To see into the future and decide on malicious intent is also to deploy affective politics to create the militarized infrastructure of tomorrow. Counterterror, however, not only involves state actions to preempt feared potentialities; it also loads new potentialities—in the form of administrative capacities (new optics, logics, and institutions) and their unforeseeable effects (accidents, subversions, and blowbacks)—into a deep future. Crucially, every infrastructure installs its own future crisis.[1] It is important to consider how the state effort to proliferate objects of existential concern, and develop new administrative powers to engage them, installs as well as forestalls future disaster. Counterterror, in this way, is blinding as well as mobilizing, an act of scripting futures as well as of responding to contingent fears: it is a world-making project, but one structured at every level by apocalyptic intuitions and commitments.

This chapter investigates biosecurity as an emblematic project of the counterterror state, tracking the new material, imaginative, and affective infrastructures of an emerging U.S. effort to secure life on a planetary scale. This form of counterterror is an American phenomenon, a creation of hyperpower geopolitics, affectively driven governance, and a deep multi-generational commitment to militarization. It is also a world of noir sensibilities where nothing is quite what it seems and existential threat takes infinite forms, where the production of new capacities for action against imagined future dangers creates the conditions of possibility for those very dangers to emerge. As a biosecurity noir, this chapter considers how official efforts to anticipate and preempt future terrors can make those very terrors increasingly real, creating an infrastructure of future crisis in the name of warding off disaster today.

Crime Scene

In the days after the suicide-hijacker attacks on September 11, 2001, the United States was victim of a second wave of terrorism, one little remembered today but certainly as consequential to U.S. geopolitics as the suicide attacks on New York and Washington. From September 18 to October 9, at least five letters filled with anthrax were mailed from a New Jersey mailbox to news organizations (NBC, the *New York Post*, and American Media) and to elected officials (Tom Daschle, then majority leader of the Senate; and Patrick Leahy, then chair of the Senate Judiciary Committee; see Cole 2009). Two of the letters had "4th Grade at Greendale School, Franklin

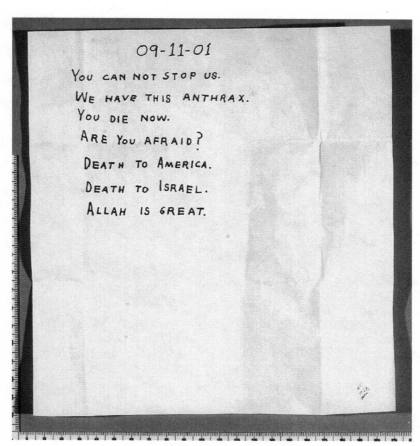

FIGURE 4.1. Anthrax letter mailed to Senator Patrick Leahy in September 2001, Federal Bureau of Investigation.

Park, New Jersey" as a return address and declared on an anthrax-saturated page "You Can Not Stop Us. We Have this Anthrax. You Die Now," before asking rhetorically "Are You Afraid?" (U.S. Department of Justice 2010; see figure 4.1).

Are you afraid? The answer to this bioterror question most decidedly was, and remains, yes. White House officials, who for weeks did not know how many deadly letters had been mailed, assumed they were targets of bioattack and at one point even believed they had been contaminated (Mayer 2008, 3). Anthrax spores were eventually found in the U.S. postal system as well as in the U.S. Supreme Court, the State Department, and Congress, which was forced to shut down and relocate in the midst of war planning and consideration of the U.S.A. Patriot Act. Medical authorities

FIGURE 4.2. Secretary of State Colin Powell presenting a vial of simulated anthrax to the United Nations, February 2003, U.S. Department of State.

advised some 30,000 federal employees to take antibiotics as a prophylactic response to possible anthrax contamination—spreading the experience of individualized vulnerability throughout the federal system. Twenty-three people were ultimately infected with anthrax, and five died of the illness, making the 2001 anthrax letters the single most deadly and disruptive bioterror event in modern U.S. history.

It is important to recognize the actual terror produced by the anthrax letters as well as the spectacular reaction of the emerging counterterror state to them. In his presentation to the United Nations in February 2003, for example, Secretary of State Colin Powell held up a vial of white powder (see figure 4.2) and declared:

> Less than a teaspoon of dry anthrax, a little bit, about this amount . . . less than a teaspoon full of dry anthrax in an envelope shut down the United States Senate in the fall of 2001. This forced several hundred people to undergo emergency medical treatment and killed two postal workers just from an amount, just about this quantity, that was inside of an envelope. Iraq declared [that it has] 8,500 liters of anthrax, but UNSCOM [a United Nations Special Commission] estimates that Saddam Hussein could have produced 25,000 liters. If concentrated into this dry form, this amount would be enough to fill

tens upon tens upon tens of thousands of teaspoons. And Saddam Hussein has not verifiably accounted for even one teaspoon-full of this deadly material. (2003)

If . . . could have . . . would be . . . not one teaspoon accounted for. This is the preemptive war machine at work, directing public fear and anger at a specific target, while conjuring existential threats to enable the most radical form of counterterror state action. The anthrax letters were hugely consequential, as they revealed the vulnerability of American institutions to mass disruption while providing a new affective intensity to official concerns about biological insecurity. The result was a national media campaign devoted to constituting and rehearsing a virulent and proliferating world of biological terrors needing to be secured—a key component in the remaking of U.S. national security as a form of counterterror.

By the end of October 2001, the Bush administration was already mobilizing the anthrax letters to enable a war to rid Iraq of weapons of mass destruction (WMDs), while the Federal Bureau of Investigation (FBI) opened what would become the largest investigation in its history to discover the source of the anthrax. The FBI named the case Amerithrax—a strange fusion of *America* and *anthrax* that was a portent of what was to come, as U.S. officials pursued the amplification of biothreat as a core project of the emerging counterterror state (see Hartmann, Subramanian, and Zerner 2005). Soon, the Bush administration would no longer evoke anthrax as the main object of fear but the larger, more ambiguous, WMD category—a strategic political shift that worked to endow a variety of objects, technologies, and potentials with the existential threat of the atomic bomb (see Vogel 2007). Official fear—of white powder, of biological warfare, of the unknown, and of surprise—created a paranoid state, one that relied on the affective intensities of biological insecurity to enable a wide range of unrelated foreign and domestic projects. By the end of 2001, the WMD, the terrorist, and the microbe would increasingly be fused in official language, creating a new concept of existential threat that was politically and culturally powerful precisely because it was both undefinable and unbounded. Thus, a free-floating anxiety was crafted that could be attached to any object, or potential, and amplified via the logic of anticipatory preemption into a kind of totalizing danger that seemed to demand urgent action in the present. As Melinda Cooper has pointed out, war and public health become "quite deliberately blurred" at this moment to enable a "strategic redefinition" of U.S. defense (2006, 114).

The 2001 anthrax letters, even more than the suicide-hijacker attacks, enabled the U.S. security apparatus to renew itself in the twenty-first century, replacing the nuclear weapons–centered vision of the twentieth-century national security state with the "terrorist with a WMD" fixation of the counterterror state. As we shall see, the emerging affective, imaginative, and material infrastructures of a new U.S. biosecurity project proliferate visions of catastrophic danger and eventually attempt to secure life on a global scale in the name of domestic defense. This is a new concept of American power, one founded on a radical and never-ending insecurity, whose objects multiply to the point where the only territorial limit to U.S. *defense* is the entire planet. Finally, by constituting shock, and even potential surprise, as existentially threatening, the counterterror state positions people, technologies, animals, and microbes as vectors of future danger, and thus makes them objects of anticipatory action in the now.

The Promise: Biosecurity in a "Threat-O-Genic" World

The global situation is not so much threatening as threat generating: threat-o-genic. It is the world's capacity to produce new threat at any and every moment that defines the situation.
—**Brian Massumi, "Potential Politics and the Primacy of Preemption"**

Biosecurity is an emerging concern in the United States, one that has dramatically expanded its logics, objects, and scope since the anthrax letters of 2001 to become a major new governmental infrastructure of the twenty-first century. The formal discourse of biosecurity first came to prominence in the early 1990s in the context of ranching operations in New Zealand, where industry concerns about protecting sheep from infectious disease led to new expert language and government protocols for protecting animal populations. The concept of biosecurity originally referred specifically to animal and agricultural safety, to protecting livestock and crops from disease; it is defined that way in most parts of the world to this day. The term was rarely found in the United States before the Bush administration's declaration of a War on Terror in 2001, a project that radically expanded the imagined threat of biological risk as a mode of governance.[2] If you asked for an American definition of *biosecurity* prior to 2001, you might have found something like this (adapted from the veterinary science program at the University of California, Davis):

Biosecurity is a practice designed to prevent the spread of disease onto your farm. It is accomplished by maintaining the facility in such a way that there is minimal traffic of biological organisms (viruses, bacteria, rodents, etc.) across its borders. Biosecurity is the cheapest, most effective means of disease control available. No disease prevention program will work without it.

What is biosecurity? Biosecurity has three major components: 1. isolation 2. traffic control 3. sanitation. Isolation refers to the confinement of animals within a controlled environment. A fence keeps your birds in, but it also keeps other animals out. Isolation also applies to the practice of separating birds by age group. In large poultry operations, all-in/all-out management styles allow simultaneous depopulation of facilities between flocks and allow time for periodic clean-up and disinfection to break the cycle of disease. Traffic control includes both the traffic onto your farm and the traffic patterns within the farm. Sanitation addresses the disinfection of materials, people and equipment entering the farm and the cleanliness of the personnel on the farm. (Jeffrey n.d.)

Isolation, traffic control, sanitation. What is notable here is the focus on a discrete population and its day-to-day isolation from disease: biosecurity has regional implications in this definition but is an extremely localized, farm-size practice based on logics of containment.

After 2001 biosecurity became a central priority of the counterterror state and an ever-expanding domain of interest, one that precisely because it could not locate, define, or limit its objects of concern proliferated spectacularly. Consider, for example, how President Bush presents the threat of the microbe only three years later in his programmatic declaration of a "biodefense for the twenty-first century":

Biological weapons in the possession of hostile states or terrorists pose unique and grave threats to the safety and security of the United States and our allies. Biological weapons attacks could cause catastrophic harm. They could inflict widespread injury and result in massive casualties and economic disruption. Bioterror attacks could mimic naturally-occurring disease, potentially delaying recognition of an attack and creating uncertainty about whether one has even occurred. An attacker may thus believe that he could escape identification and capture or retaliation. Biological weapons attacks could be mounted either inside or outside the United States and, because some biological weapons agents are contagious, the effects of an initial attack could spread widely. Disease outbreaks, whether natural or deliberate, respect no geographic or political borders. (U.S. White House 2004)

Bioterror mimics disease and respects no border. Here, engineered disease becomes an existential threat to the United States: it can traverse all boundaries, foreign and domestic, and transform unknown and unknowing individuals into disease vectors. There is no way to distinguish an intentional bioweapon attack from a naturally occurring disease at the moment of occurrence. This radical "uncertainty" about origins and intents allows the counterterror state to absorb a wide range of concerns into its militarized project of global preemption. Infectious disease is merged quite formally here with the logic of the WMD, activating the existential threat response once reserved for nuclear arsenals, which requires a total security state response. By merging and amplifying unpredictability and a worst-case vision of attack/epidemic, the counterterror state redefines infectious disease as a form of terrorism—creating a spectacular new affective logic of imminence. Biosecurity, for example, transforms the yearly flu—approached now as a potential biological weapon—into a form of terror, remaking a long-standing and relatively predictable public health issue into a possible concern of the security state.[3]

The breathtaking evolution of biosecurity in a few short years from a concern of the livestock industry into a multifaceted argument for preemptive war was achieved not at the level of facts and science but rather through the skillful deployment of threat identification and affective politics. The official whisper campaign linking Saddam Hussein to the anthrax letters of 2001, for example, was amplified by the Bush administration's effort in 2002 to vaccinate all Americans against smallpox (a disease that last killed an American in 1949 and is all but extinct today, stored only as samples in biological laboratories).[4] This logic of biological preemption, however, constituted a smallpox threat in the present even though no evidence existed of an actual smallpox vector—it was a "potential" mobilized as imminent threat. This kind of threat amplification relies on the mass media to redirect state resources and agendas, to affectively charge a not-yet-existing but potentially catastrophic danger to such a degree that it overwhelms all other concerns. Thus, the counterterror state can privilege a "potential" over existing forms of disease and violence via an imaginative campaign and affective recruitment. This is an illustration of how the affective economy of the War on Terror proliferates specific potentialities as imminent dangers while rejecting others, making the domain of biosecurity, in this case, more dependent on the imagination than physical evidence or statistical comparisons of risk. Since 2001 U.S. biosecurity has been the most radically evolving aspect of the War on Terror, addressing an ever-expanding spectrum of potential terrors—linking technologies, people, animals, and plants in a conceptual space of constantly expanding threat. Importantly, as the list of objects and organisms to secure expands, so does the territorial reach of U.S. biosecurity, folding into the global War on Terror an emerging planetary logic of American biodefense.

By 2006 the term *biosecurity* in the United States could refer to anything from food safety (mad cow disease) to infectious human diseases (seasonal flu) to new diseases (severe acute respiratory syndrome [SARS] and the H1N1 virus) to biological weapons (weaponized anthrax or smallpox) to the future creations of synthetic biology, ultimately positioning life itself as a new object of militarized concern.[5] Consider this 2006 definition of biosecurity from the National Academy of Sciences, which blurs the distinction between public health and arms control in a new way:

> The term "biosecurity" is used to refer to security against the inadvertent, inappropriate, or intentional malicious or malevolent use of potentially dangerous biological agents or biotechnology, including the development, production, stockpiling, or use of biological weapons as well as natural outbreaks of newly emergent and epidemic diseases. Although it is not used as often as it is in other settings, to refer to a situation where adequate food and basic health are assured, there may be significant overlap in measures that guarantee "biosecurity" in either sense. (2006, 32)

Biotechnology/biological weapons/disease/food/health. The central role of biosecurity in the early twenty-first century is to build capacities to respond to future potentials, but in doing so, it is first and foremost an affective domain of threat selection and amplification. In a short decade, it has grown into a distinctively American vision of planetary biological surveillance, merging infectious disease with the bioterrorist as desired objects of anticipatory preemption.

The counterterror state has generated a novel concept of security in the United States, a biosecurity that gains objects and scope as different experts and institutions claim it as their own. Like many of its chief objects of concern, biosecurity is emergent at both the conceptual and institutional level and cannot be reduced to a singular analytic form (see Lakoff and Collier 2008; Collier, Lakoff, and Rabinow 2004). Its ability to encompass new objects and potentials quickly and to be territorially bounded only at the planetary scale constitutes its chief virtue for the U.S. counterterror state, which relies on a constant proliferation of threatening potentials to reconstitute its affective governance and its geopolitical agenda. Biosecurity's incoherence is its virtue, in other words, as it merges distinct technological and health issues into a generic formulation that can gather resources through affective mobilization against selected threats, enabling a wide variety of projects to proceed under a logic of emergency defense. In summary, a chronology of U.S. biosecurity concerns since the end of the Cold War would be:

A. 1991–2001: food production, with a focus on the isolation and containment of livestock.
B. 2001 to 2005: terrorism, with a focus on intentional attacks on the American population and domestic territory.
C. 2005 to today: All of A and B plus infectious disease, with a focus on the global preemption of emerging dangers.

It is a remarkable fact that, in response to the five anthrax letters of 2001, biosecurity in the United States has grown from a limited domestic concern with livestock to a global ambition to secure life, positing a new kind of speculative, but nonetheless highly militarized, planetary politics. Although a biosecurity apparatus on this scale remains fanciful at the level of both technologies and institutions, it nonetheless presents a set of future-oriented goals and ambitions, offering up ideological resources for a new infrastructure of American power. The affective politics of the counterterror state—the ability to produce fear via the circulation of images and narratives of imminent danger—also remains highly productive in a broader cultural sense, regardless of the actual biomedical ability to secure life on scales ranging from the population to the militant to the microbe.

The Score: From Bug to Drug to Biowarfare

The consolidation of a new security discourse is always a highly consequential matter, since it not only installs a new social contract but also motivates the construction of a new infrastructure of state power. The Bush administration committed to funding biodefense in all its forms in an unprecedented manner in the fall of 2001, creating a wide-ranging set of national projects while directing governmental agencies from the federal to the county level to develop integrated biowarfare response plans. In 2004 President Bush claimed that there had already been an "extraordinary level of effort" in biodefense, including stockpiling enough smallpox vaccine for every American and immunizing 600,000 soldiers; increasing bioterrorism research in the Department of Health and Human Services thirtyfold; giving $4.4 billion to state preparedness programs for bioterror; establishing BioWatch, a network of environmental sensors to provide early warning of biological attack in major U.S. cities; and committing $5.6 billion to the BioShield program, an effort to create drugs and vaccines to counter "biological, chemical, radiological or nuclear weapons" (U.S. White House 2004). To this we could add the nearly $1 billion the U.S. Postal Service spent on its Biohazard Detection System, devoted to looking for anthrax in the nation's mail, and undisclosed sums spent on classified research in biodefense and global efforts to find WMDs in Iraq and elsewhere.[6] Most notable on this list is the BioWatch program, which has installed air sensors in thirty cities as a new kind of early warning and surveillance system for airborne biological threats. These sensors do not yet work quickly enough to counter biological weapons (the sensors currently need thirty-six hours to detect a threat) but promise, via a new "rolling deployment strategy" (a commitment to installing each new generation of the technology in anticipation of producing a working system), to deliver real-time surveillance of urban air in the United States at some point in the future.[7] Similarly, the BioShield program promises to develop a real-time biomedical response to all WMD emergencies for the entire U.S. population, a daunting task that fuses the production of counteragent drugs with U.S. national security in a new way. Together, BioWatch and BioShield are modeled on the long-promised Strategic Defense Initiative (SDI) of the Reagan era—a program to intercept nuclear-armed intercontinental ballistic missiles in flight, which three decades later is still a massive Department of Defense project that has yet to produce a viable defensive technology (although a single set of missile interceptors was installed in Alaska in 2004, as part of the department's new rolling deployment strategy). BioShield, like SDI before it, was intended to function as a demonstration of American technological and biomedical superiority, a utopian effort to eliminate biothreats by locking in military and biomedical industrial investments for the foreseeable future.[8]

Both BioWatch and BioShield promise a perfectible security through biomedicine, but to achieve that goal, their designers must first constitute the future as a field of multiplying catastrophic dangers that require urgent action in the present, illustrating how the production of terror and new military infrastructure are fully codependent. Although biosecurity's objects of concern remain ever elusive, this mode of governance is nevertheless enormously productive. First, it commits new resources to biodefense in all its forms—creating new alliances across health, drug, and defense institutions and producing a biosecurity complex as an expanding branch of the long-standing military-industrial complex. Second, precisely because these new projects are anticipatory, they require the constant remobilization of negative affect to achieve their goals. The counterterror state produces and proliferates fears as a means of mobilizing its own institutions, but also, because these are hypothetical projections, it maintains an unlimited set of potentials to mobilize. In this way, anticipatory preemption enables a permanent war modality, expanded here via the logics of biosecurity to include certain sectors of public health.

Biosecurity both relies on and generates terror about connectivity in the global economy, addressing twenty-first-century forms of communications, transportation, and commerce as an endless source of danger.[9] A core component of the War on Terror has been the establishment of a new set of discourses and institutions devoted to biothreat, creating new linkages across civilian health and military bureaucracies funded by new bioterrorism budgets. These projects rely on specific images of existential threat and a steady stream of expert discourse about catastrophic futures, imminent threats, and national unpreparedness to generate the affective conditions for their work. Biosecurity, in short, has quickly become a new expert domain in the United States—with its own professional languages, journals, institutes, and laboratories—and is an emerging form of scientific governance.

Consider figure 4.3, just one example of a vast new literature that increasingly combines "diseases, disasters, and bioterrorism" into a unified biosecurity problem.[10] This narrative project makes certain kinds of disaster—pandemics and WMD attacks—inevitable, a "not if, but when" calculation that focuses governmental and scientific energies on seeing a damaged future in the present (see Schoch-Spana 2004 and 2006). The temporal window before the inevitable catastrophic attack—of bioterror in each of its proliferating forms—becomes a call to expert action today. The horizon of crisis is thus extended from the future into the present and remade as the basis for official action, creating a new kind of counterterror state energized by the contradictory enterprise of imaginatively locating future threat in all its forms while simultaneously promising that each of these dangers can be preempted and removed from the world. U.S. biosecurity, in short, promises a world without terror via the constant production of terror, creating a potentially endless recursive loop of threat production and response, one that—because it begins with something that does not yet

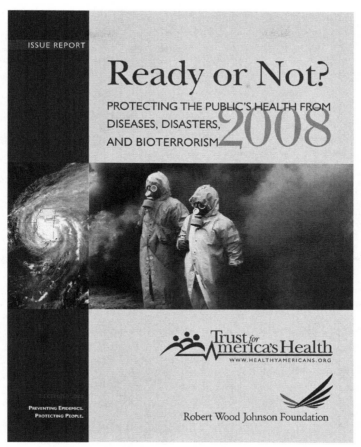

FIGURE 4.3. "Diseases, Disasters, and Bioterrorism," one example of the new biosecurity disaster literature, Robert Wood Johnson Foundation.

exist and may never exist—does not require physical evidence of danger. In this way, counterterror is an anticipatory projection that strives to generate emergency conditions to allow state action, and thus it is both a form of cultural reasoning drawing on historical forms of threat perception and is a new form of psychopolitics (Orr 2006).

This new conflation of terrorism and disease has produced an expanding infrastructure of laboratories devoted to research on the most dangerous known pathogens. Before 2001 the United States had five laboratories designated as biosafety level 4 (BSL-4)—devoted to research on the most lethal and virulent pathogens, smallpox, Lassa fever, and Ebola virus. By the end of the first decade of counterterror, the United States had fifteen

157

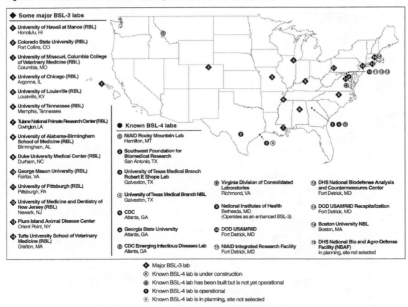

Figure 1: Known BSL-4 Labs and Some of the Major BSL-3 Labs in the United States

◆ Some major BSL-3 labs

◆ University of Hawaii at Manoa (RBL)
Honolulu, HI

◆ Colorado State University (RBL)
Fort Collins, CO

◆ University of Missouri, Columbia College
of Veterinary Medicine (RBL)
Columbia, MO

◆ University of Chicago (RBL)
Argonne, IL

◆ University of Louisville (RBL)
Louisville, KY

◆ University of Tennessee (RBL)
Memphis, Tennessee

◆ Tulane National Primate Research Center (RBL)
Covington, LA

◆ University of Alabama-Birmingham
School of Medicine (RBL)
Birmingham, AL

◆ Duke University Medical Center (RBL)
Durham, NC

◆ George Mason University (RBL)
Fairfax, VA

◆ University of Pittsburgh (RBL)
Pittsburgh, PA

◆ University of Medicine and Dentistry of
New Jersey (RBL)
Newark, NJ

◆ Plum Island Animal Disease Center
Orient Point, NY

◆ Tufts University School of Veterinary
Medicine (RBL)
Grafton, MA

● Known BSL-4 labs

① NIAID Rocky Mountain Lab
Hamilton, MT

② Southwest Foundation for
Biomedical Research
San Antonio, TX

③ University of Texas Medical Branch
Robert E Shope Lab
Galveston, TX

④ University of Texas Medical Branch NBL
Galveston, TX

⑤ CDC
Atlanta, GA

⑥ Georgia State University
Atlanta, GA

⑦ CDC Emerging Infectious Diseases Lab
Atlanta, GA

⑧ Virginia Division of Consolidated
Laboratories
Richmond, VA

⑨ National Institutes of Health
Bethesda, MD
(Operates as an enhanced BSL-3)

⑩ DOD USAMRIID
Fort Detrick, MD

⑪ NIAID Integrated Research Facility
Fort Detrick, MD

⑫ DHS National Biodefense Analysis
and Countermeasures Center
Fort Detrick, MD

⑬ DOD USAMRIID Recapitalization
Fort Detrick, MD

⑭ Boston University NBL
Boston, MA

⑮ DHS National Bio and Agro-Defense
Facility (NBAF)
In planning, site not selected

◆ Major BSL-3 lab
⊙ Known BSL-4 lab is under construction
⊛ Known BSL-4 lab has been built but is not yet operational
● Known BSL-4 lab is operational
⊚ Known BSL-4 lab is in planning, site not selected

FIGURE 4.4. Map of BSL-4 and BSL-3 Laboratories, from Rhodes (2007).

such laboratories and had multiplied the number of BSL-3 laboratories (where infectious diseases like SARS, West Nile virus, tuberculosis, and anthrax are studied) to such an extent that a 2007 congressional study found 1,356 registered sites scattered across the country but concluded that the actual "number and location of all BSL-3 and BSL-4 labs is not known" (Rhodes 2007, 14) (see figure 4.4).[11] Today there is no single agency in the federal government responsible for regulating BSL-3 and BSL-4 laboratories, the dangerous materials they contain, or the scientists that work in them. In their efforts to map the emerging field of biosecurity, Lynn Klotz and Edward Sylvester (2009, 96) located hundreds of laboratories working on countermeasures for bioweapons and noted that 219 laboratories have registered with the Centers for Disease Control and Prevention (CDC) to work on anthrax alone.[12]

The investment in civilian biodefense has thus been nothing short of remarkable, increasing sevenfold from 2001 to 2002 alone, and now averaging over $6 billion a year (see figure 4.5). The Congressional Research Service has estimated that the Manhattan Project cost $22 billion over five years and the Apollo program $98 billion over 14 years, in constant 2008 dollars (Stine 2009). Thus, the $67 billion spent in the first decade of U.S.

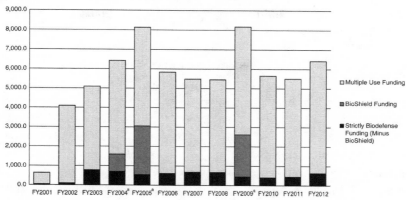

FIGURE 4.5. Nonmilitary biodefense funding since 2001, from Franco and Sell (2011).

biosecurity work represents multiple Manhattan Projects and is well on its way to the moon (see Franco and Sell 2011, 118). This is an enormous sum, but biosecurity does not address all health dangers—just those that can be imagined as, or mistaken for, weapons of mass destruction. U.S. biosecurity is a product of the War on Terror, and as a result it is framed by a militarized notion of threat, making only certain issues of public health a concern of the counterterror state. For example, the budget for the U.S. Department of Defense for 2012 alone was $553 billion, a figure that dwarfs the budget of the National Institutes of Health for the period 1938–2010.[13]

Put differently, the U.S. public health system, which has been under-funded for generations precisely because it was not considered a matter of national defense during the long Cold War, has been explicitly put on the front line of the War on Terror since 2001—as anthrax, SARS, avian flu, and the H1N1 virus have been mobilized alongside terrorists and WMDs as catastrophic events to be preempted via anticipatory state action. In each of these cases, the amplification of threat has been one of the key attributes of this new system, which relies on an affective atmosphere of imminent danger to unlock new forms of governmental agency. The linkage between the virus and the enemy is an old one, as a strategic confusion between the biological body and social body has enabled many political regimes to exclude designated groups, and may even be a formative logic of the nation-state form, with its historical connection of populations to territo-ries (Wald 2008; Foucault 2007; Martin 1990). Within the War on Terror administrative structure, this logic is taking on new forms and is no longer constrained by the territorial limits of the United States. Biosecurity has also opened a political space for public health advocates, well aware of Cold War military-industrial administrative and budgeting practices, to reposition public health as a U.S. national security matter.

Consider, for example, how Anthony Fauci, the director of the National Institute of Allergy and Infectious Diseases (NIAID) at the National Institutes of Health, responded to the violent events of September 2001. He quickly declared the new mission of his institute to be biosecurity, which he defined as a means not only of confronting terrorism in an age of anthrax attacks but also of curing a wide range of diseases. Fauci argued that by focusing on Category A biological agents—anthrax, smallpox, tularemia, plague, botulism, and hemorrhagic fever (that is, the kind of pathogens most useful to terrorists)—his institute would soon identify other kinds of pathogens and microbes and cure other diseases. He stated definitively: "When we develop antivirals against diseases like Lassa and Ebola, Marburg and Smallpox, we're going to fall upon antivirals for Hepatitis C" (2002, 2). This *dual-use* approach to biosecurity is modeled on Cold War military-industrial practices—in which building technologies for early warning of nuclear attack also produced revolutions in computers, telecommunications, satellite systems, and electronics, all of which eventually filtered into the commercial arena. A dual-use biodefense program promises breakthroughs in basic medicine even as it stockpiles vaccines and countermeasures against bioweapons. Fauci works here to transform counterterrorism into an opportunity for basic research, one that can address any form of biological threat through constant advances in the biosciences.

By 2011, the NIAID offered striking new language about WMDs on its website (see figure 4.6), claiming "allergies, infectious diseases, radiological, nuclear, and chemical threats" as part of its core mission, thereby absorbing an agency historically devoted to public health into the counterterror state apparatus. This is a strange new brew of interests and responsibilities, constituting a strategic effort to leverage the urgency of counterterror on behalf of a more general biomedicine. Fauci states that the goal of his institute over the next twenty years is nothing less than to produce a revolution in biomedical surveillance and response, constructing a new medical infrastructure that can go from "bug to drug in 24 hours" (2002, 2)—that is, meet the threat of bioterrorism by identifying any weaponized organism and deploying an exisiting drug to combat it within twenty-four hours of its identification. This goal of "bug to drug in 24 hours" potentially transforms biosecurity from a reactive form of counterterrorism into a positive form of public health—with viruses being contained and eliminated as fast as the

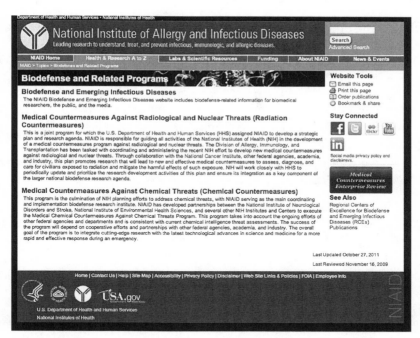

FIGURE 4.6. Biodefense homepage on the website of the National Institute of Allergy and Infectious Diseases (2011).

bioterrorist or nature can engineer them. It also recruits a long-term federal commitment to research in the biosciences and creates an array of new linkages across intelligence agencies, research laboratories, pharmaceutical companies, military departments, and emergency responders.[14] The result has been a dramatic increase in the budget of the NIAID, which gained over $1 billion from 2001 to 2002 alone via the new linkage to biodefense, enabling a major new institutional commitment to research on emerging diseases.

Fauci's goal of a system that can go from "bug to drug in 24 hours" is part of a larger strategic effort among health professionals to make biomedicine as central to the War on Terror as engineering was to the Cold War, and thus the engine of a twenty-first-century biomedical revolution. However, to link infectious disease to the national security state so powerfully, the threat first has to be located, conjured, or communicated, before it can be successfully countered. The threat, as we have already seen, also needs to be of a species that activates the security logics of the state, and not all threats do. So we might pause here to ask what is the documented nature of bioterrorism—its actual material form, not as an anticipated, imagined, or projected risk?

There have been two recorded incidences of bioterrorism in the United States in the past thirty years: in 1984 members of the Rajneeshee cult contaminated restaurants in Oregon with salmonella, causing over 700 people to become ill; and in 2001 the anthrax letters killed five people.[15] Although both events were malicious and frightening crimes, these cases of bioterrorism are so rare as to not register statistically as a cause of death in relation to disease or injury rates in the United States. According to the CDC, the foremost killers of U.S. citizens in 2010 were:

- Heart disease: 597,689
- Cancer: 574,743
- Chronic lower respiratory diseases: 138,080
- Stroke (cerebrovascular diseases): 129,476
- Accidents (unintentional injuries): 120,859
- Alzheimer's disease: 83,494
- Diabetes: 69,071
- Nephritis, nephrotic syndrome, and nephrosis: 50,476
- Influenza and pneumonia: 50,097
- Intentional self-harm (suicide): 38,364 (U.S. Centers for Disease Control and Prevention 2010)

This list of killers has been relatively stable for fifty years, while the discourse of *terror* has fluctuated widely, focusing on drug traffickers in the 1980s, so-called rogue states in the 1990s, and the profusion of concerns of today (see Xu et al. 2010, 9; see also Zulaika and Douglass 1996). But if heart disease and cancer together kill over a million Americans each year, why do they not constitute a terror threat? As S. Lochlann Jain (2013) has shown, the experience of cancer is filled with minute and existential terrors so powerful that they can fundamentally remake the survivor across physical, social, and psychological domains. So if the state wants to fight bioterror, we know exactly where it resides. Despite their high numbers in the United States, heart disease, accidents, and suicides are a normalized form of dying, not acknowledged by the counterterror state as objects of concern precisely because they cannot produce a military counterformation. Still, it is important to consider that—statistically speaking—bioterrorism does not register as a major cause of death in the United States over the past decade and is less than the number of Americans killed each year by accidentally drowning in their home pools and bathtubs, 1,100 people in 2009 alone (National Safety Council 2011, 156).[16] A crucial new aspect of the U.S. biosecurity project is that it relies on a post-statistical mode of thinking, one that makes strategic calculations about potential catastrophic threats and then mobilizes state resources against them *as if* they were confirmed events. Speculation mixes with fantasy, fear, and projection in the new world of counterterror, creating a national system that acts on its worst fears rather than on what it can actually locate and engage in the world.

What kind of state project is biosecurity? Michel Foucault argued that the arts of governance in the modern state form concern the linked projects of policing and welfare. His notion of biopower sought to underscore the increasing state attention to matters of the body—with the individual body as the subject of new forms of disciplinary attention in terms of schools, medical evaluation, and forms of self-mastery, and the population as a new object of study, expert administration, and improvement (Foucault 2003 and 2007). Infectious disease was one of the first arenas in which this notion of biopower was mobilized by the French state, becoming a laboratory for the management of populations and refinements in techniques of power (from acts of quarantine and hygiene campaigns to health care over the entire lifespan). The state's interest in combating disease links the projects of welfare (the improving of populations through positive acts) with the policing of populations (the prevention of injury) and defines the national community as a territorialized social body.

However, the current logics of U.S. biosecurity are also the direct products of a unique national security system formed after World War II. The newly constituted national security state established a novel linkage between external threat and the domestic economy at the start of the Cold War, producing a military-industrial complex that fundamentally transformed everyday American life and redefined *security* as deterring global nuclear war from one minute to the next in perpetuity (see Masco 2006). Nearly $6 trillion was spent on nuclear weapons in the second half of the twentieth century, making the bomb the third largest federal expenditure after the regular military and social security (S. Schwartz 1998). The Bush administration intended the War on Terror to mobilize a new security state for the twenty-first century, one modeled on the success of the Cold War nuclear state, but remade via a foundational commitment to preemptive counterterror. Terror—of the bomb, the bioterrorist, and the microbe—becomes a linking concern across different institutions of a government that is unified not by a positive vision of a constantly improving social order but rather, through the dual, if contradictory, fantasy of responding to constant imminent catastrophic threat while also assuming unlimited global power. A war on terror inevitably proliferates its objects of concern because its enemy has no specific location and no specific form, transforming the future of U.S. security from the minute-to-minute logic of nuclear deterrence to an open-ended commitment to threat identification and counterterror mobilization. The emerging infrastructures of the counterterror state thus rely on a constant expansion and inflation of threat to enable this form of governance.

But if bioterrorism is not historically a statistically significant cause of American death, how is it possible to create a political consensus, let alone a massive counterterror state, to combat it in perpetuity?[17] How is bioterror made visible and urgent in the year to year of bureaucratic statecraft if it is so rare that death by bee stings or being hit by lightning are greater risks to the average U.S. citizen over the past thirty years?[18] How is it that terror comes to *feel* ever present, even if terrorism itself is a spectacularly rare event in the United States?

Delirium: Simulating Terror

Written in plague time, events are projected according to the epidemiological traits of the pathogen released and possibly manipulated by the terrorists. The scenario is typically a worst case, where everything that can go wrong does go wrong: mass casualties that overwhelm society's ability to treat the sick and contain the spread of disease, delays in communications between health department and hospital, tensions and misunderstandings between public health and law enforcement officials that impede effective collaboration for the public good, scarcity of life-saving medical resources and the exacerbation of pre-existing social fault lines, jurisdictional tensions between local, state and federal governments, public panic, civil unrest, mob violence and the need for state force to contain disturbances.
—**Monica Schoch-Spana, "Bioterrorism, US Public Health and a Secular Apocalypse"**

Preemption as a security practice requires premediation, or a resonating fiction of a disastrous future about to unfold. What, then, are the narratives of contemporary security premediation? It becomes clear that current terrorism scenarios coalesce around the presupposition that terrorist attack is imminent in our midst and catastrophic.
—**Marieke De Goede, "Beyond Risk"**

The specific image of threat that energizes a security state matters to both the form and the content of its countermobilization—articulating radically different futures, publics, and social contracts. In a world of anticipatory dangers, the primary means of locating terror is to simulate it. The emerging scientific infrastructure for U.S. biosecurity is supported by preparedness exercises at all levels of government, an over $6 billion effort to coordinate local, state, and federal agencies via scenario-driven terror since 2001.[19] These exercises do more than reveal vulnerabilities and build new collaborations across different levels of government—they constitute terror as a spectrum of imminent threat. Since 2001 the biannual TOPOFF (Top Officials) exercises have involved tens of thousands of participants and increasingly complicated WMD attack scenarios: in 2003, a dirty bomb was imaginatively detonated in Seattle and a biological weapon used in Chicago; in 2005, a car bombing, a chemical attack, and an unknown biological warfare agent were acted out in New Jersey and Connecticut; and in 2007, nuclear materials were theatrically detonated in Portland, Phoenix, and Guam.[20] These preparedness exercises focus on WMD threats in increasingly complex configurations and rehearse expert rationality in anticipatory enactment. They also constantly rediscover a state that cannot possibly respond in real time to neutralize even well-planned, hypothetical attacks. Indeed, the crucial evolution in the concept of counterterror is the security state's commitment to anticipation and preemption rather than reaction, which refocuses defense on the radically contingent future and the need for ever greater capacities to engage it. In a world constituted as dangerously emergent—with multiplying vectors of vulnerability and attack—counterterror officials have produced a new temporal horizon for security itself, one focused on eliminating dangerous potentials before they become material.[21] In constituting a future of proliferating vulnerabilities and dangerous potentials to secure, the preparedness apparatus constantly fails in its anticipatory initiative. Thus, the result is not security but rather the production of a constant state of affective emergency among officials, which is required to drive the contingent (as yet unrealized future danger) into the realm of necessary governance. Drills, exercises, scenarios, and gaming, I suggest, are thus not only technical efforts to assess future danger, they are also the means of affectively elevating the merely contingent—the hypothetical—into a species of imminent and existential threat that demands official action over and above any other material concerns.

Despite this new focus on emerging dangers, contemporary biothreat is constituted in a very American way, one with a history that dates back to the foundation of the national security state as a means of managing nuclear threat. In addition to the logic of nuclear deterrence (a kind of anticipatory response to the danger of nuclear attack), one of the most important projects of the early Cold War nuclear state was to deploy the atomic bomb as a mechanism for accessing and controlling the emotions of citizens. A key to fighting the Cold War was producing the atomic bomb not only for military use but also in narrative and cinematic form for the American public as a means of social mobilization and psychological conditioning. Civil defense taught U.S. citizens to fear the near future in a specific way by involving them in increasingly detailed nuclear simulations, first via national exercises and then via highly scripted television and film depictions of nuclear threat. In the first decade of the Cold War, U.S. officials sought to mobilize the power of mass media to transform an imagined nuclear attack into a collective opportunity for psychological self-management, civic responsibility, and, ultimately, governance. Ideas about a collective imminent death were installed very deeply into American national culture at this moment, setting up ideological resources about existential threat that inform WMD politics to this day.

Before the arrival of biosecurity as a type of twenty-first-century governance, for example, there was a Cold War discourse about biological weapons and an effort to train national populations and constitute the security state through biothreat. The 1952 Federal Civil Defense Administration (FCDA) film *What You Should Know about Biological Warfare* follows the emotional management script developed for the atomic bomb: it presents a carefully modulated effort to mobilize citizens through depictions of biological threat while also assuring them of a functioning security state that is devoted at every level to public health and safety. The FCDA film (see figure 4.7) first describes the collective vulnerability of the American population, stating that citizens, factories, and crops are all likely targets of enemy attack since, "denied the products of our farms and factory, we could not wage war on any front." The narrator then establishes the existential danger of biowarfare (BW) by linking "germs, toxins, and plant growth regulators" to the atomic bomb, stating:

> We can be attacked, in spite of our excellent defenses. Attacks may be made in many ways—with bombs [an image of a nuclear mushroom cloud appears] or with biological weapons [a saboteur sprays an aerosol into a factory's fresh air intake]. . . . BW can be aimed at you in your home or at work, at your food crop, at your livestock.

Aimed at you. By extending the front line of the Cold War into the living room as well as the factory and farm, the FCDA prefigures what today is called biosecurity by linking animals, crops, and humans together in a

166

CHAPTER 4

unified biological universe of danger. But while acknowledging a vibrant public health regulatory system and attempting to dispel rumors, the FCDA is nonetheless equally committed to threat proliferation:

> Aerosols containing disease germs could be used. These aerosols could be sprayed over a large area. Submarines could release aerosols near coastal cities. Specially designed germ-carrying bombs could be dropped. Enemy agents could contaminate our water supplies. How do we protect ourselves from BW attack? Keep yourself and your family clean—don't help germs by making things easy for them. Germs have trouble living in clean places . . . [and if an announcement of biological attack is made] . . . don't give way to fear, just remember that scientists will already be working to control the outbreak.

Don't give way to fear—keep clean. After designating the crucial aspects of the human environment—air and drinking water—as vectors of biological attack, the FCDA advises citizens to perform sanitation procedures as a rudimentary form of anticipatory defense. It then traces the expert systems that are coordinated as biological defense. In a quick montage of public health nurses, family doctors, research scientists, and food safety inspectors, the FCDA shows how disease outbreaks will be identified, clusters mapped, treatments devised, and immunizations performed, concluding:

> Our health and medical systems are the foundations for our defense against biological weapons. Our food supply is guarded by a nation-wide network of federal, state, and local agencies and experts. If we are attacked with biological warfare health and medical authorities will tell you what to do, so that the disease can be brought under control. Cooperate with authorities and above all do not listen to scare talk, rumors, or myths.

Do not listen to scare talk. Here, fear is amplified to mobilize citizens to new levels of hygiene and vigilance, even as medical expertise is summoned to ward off the experience of terror. The FCDA links plants, animals, and humans as vulnerable life forms that need official protection from external attack. But unlike the proliferating logics of twenty-first-century biosecurity, this Cold War state of emergency is geographically bounded, and the state response is defined by traditional public health maneuvers—public hygiene, identification and containment of infection, and immunization. It is an emergency system that foments public fear in order to establish an expert medical system capable of responding to those fears and preventing terror from immobilizing citizens. Asking citizens to be fearful, docile, and trusting, this state project nonetheless attempts to calibrate fear against terror in order to generate a sustainable economy of Cold War attentiveness. The threat is localized and immediate, but state authority still depends on its ability to respond to and minimize the danger. This is a far cry from the contemporary logics of biosecurity, which emphasize the proliferation and uncontrollability of biodangers on a planetary scale.

In the end, the FCDA project of emotional management produced more terror and public resistance than officials anticipated, generating both antinuclear and peace movements. Consequently, by the 1960s civil defense had evolved into an *all-hazards* response to emergencies—placing nuclear and biological attacks alongside naturally occurring emergencies such as fires, floods, and earthquakes. As its focus shifted from WMDs to general disaster, the FCDA was serially renamed, eventually being subsumed into the Federal Emergency and Management Agency in 1979, which is currently part of the Department of Homeland Security. In the post–Cold War period, *preparedness* became the goal of emergency response, a concept that requires officials at all levels to create anticipatory protocols for crisis management—emergency scripts that allow local, state, and federal authorities to respond quickly to floods, fires, earthquakes, storms, and accidents. As Andrew Lakoff (2008b) has shown, the key lesson of such exercises is always that both citizens and the state are not prepared—thus, preparedness functions as an endless future horizon for governance, offering continuing and expanding opportunities for research and emergency planning, but also for emotional management and increasing militarization. As Melanie Armstrong argues, disaster exercises work to create "a community around the idea of crisis" (2012, 116). Simulations, concurrently, come to define what constitutes crisis itself.

After 2001, the War on Terror subsumed this focus on bureaucratic preparedness into a more general and aggressive form of anticipatory governance committed to preempting dangers, installing capacities into the future to extend the range and scope of state power, and using emotional management—specifically, terror—as a political resource at home and abroad. This counterterror state project amplifies public fear not to mobilize citizens with the goal of engineering a political consensus (as was the case in the early Cold War state) but to immobilize them, to suppress public participation in the realm of security politics by generating an atmosphere of constant imminent danger that is too large to individually engage.[22]

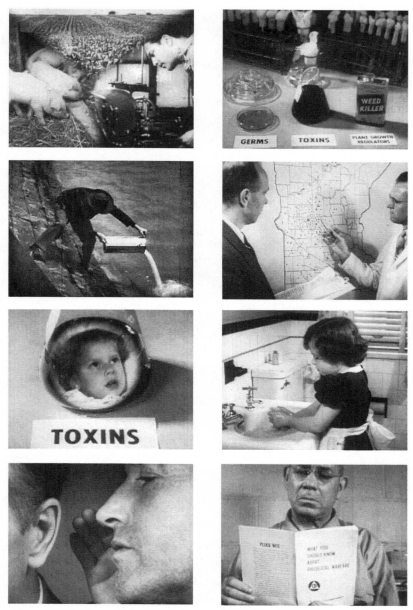

FIGURE 4.7. Image sequence from *What You Should Know about Biological Warfare* (1952), Federal Civil Defense Administration.

Compliance and docility become the primary obligations of the citizen in the world of counterterror. Infectious disease has played an increasingly important role in providing images of terrifying external threat since 2001, allowing the emerging logics of biosecurity to both fulfill and transcend Cold War security logics. Importantly, the new affective economy of counterterror focuses less on mobilizing citizens than on training experts and officials to believe in specific catastrophic futures. These existential visions of doom are constituted most immediately via exercises, scenarios, and gaming, becoming an imaginative infrastructure of the War on Terror.

To commit to preempting futures not yet realized is to engage the expert imagination in a new way and to move past factual evidence as the necessary orientation for policy. The imaginative, the hypothetical, the "what-if" gains coherence through rehearsal and repetition, and it is instantiated as a future that must be preempted through simulation and gaming. Scenario-based war gaming was an innovation of Cold War nuclear policy, pioneered at the RAND Corporation as a way to bring rationality to the escalating nuclear confrontation with the Soviet Union. In an effort to manage nuclear terror via rational choice theory, defense intellectuals at RAND sought to bring a mathematical clarity to nuclear policy. They approached nuclear war via scenario-driven games, involving technical assessments of Soviet military capabilities. RAND analysts also sought to understand the emotional make-up of Soviet leaders, their perceptions of strength and weakness, and specifically their risk tolerances across a wide range of nuclear policy actions (see Kahn 1960; see also Schelling 1966). War gaming was a key tool of Cold War policy and became an increasingly elaborate and formalized means of decision making (from training to strategy making to testing specific organizations and personalities) throughout the military. The assumption behind such gaming is that if one can model the kind of threats that are likely to occur (through imaginative practices and collective reasoning), then one can mobilize against them or at least come to appreciate the complexity of the task. Each exercise is constituted by a set of formal rules and concepts that sets the field of action, allowing officials and planners to experience emergency conditions in a hypothetical future. Cold War gaming assumed that Soviet leaders were rational (notably, devoted to their own political and biological survival), an assumption that enabled nuclear deterrence as a concept. Mutual assured destruction requires that all parties understand nuclear war is simultaneous suicide and thus work to control escalating risks out of self-interest.

The innovation of the War on Terror is that it focuses not on state military capabilities (a probable future based on observable technical capabilities) but rather on perceived terrorist desires (an improbable but hyperviolent future that need not be grounded in observed technological capacities).[23] Moreover, counterterror imagines an enemy (from terrorists to microbes) that cannot be reasoned with or deterred. These conceptual innovations move official threat evaluation more deeply into the imaginary than ever before, but they also produce a future that is understood to be ever more violent, ever more catastrophic.[24] Put differently, the complexity and unpredictability of the real world is always reduced in gaming, and certain futures become consolidated as more likely than others via consensus-driven scripts and conceptual repetition across games and agencies. In biosecurity gaming, anticipatory preemption is now linked to certain predetermined catastrophic scenarios (global contagions and engineered diseases), pulling expert thought across a vast range of disciplines and agencies relentlessly to specific worst-case scenarios that exceed current administrative capabilities.[25] This type of gaming is an expert exercise in the self-generation of terror, a psychosocial mobilization of certain catastrophic futures as the most vital ones for attempted governance. This expert process necessarily produces an ever-expanding counterterror state that privileges specific imaginary threats over existing forms of everyday violence.[26]

Consider the tabletop exercise known as Atlantic Storm, staged by the Center for Biosecurity at the University of Pittsburgh Medical Center on January 14, 2005.[27] A particularly elaborate biosecurity game, it engaged former American, Canadian, and European officials to play the leaders of their home countries, with former Secretary of State Madeleine Albright cast as the president of the United States (see figure 4.8). One of the largest and most publicized exercises of its kind, Atlantic Storm imagines a terrorist use of smallpox on multiple nations during a summit meeting in Washington, D.C. It challenges players to coordinate an official response of the transatlantic allies to a global epidemic in a world with limited supplies of smallpox vaccine. The exercise plays out in real time during the course of a day, with participants seated around a table, confronted by television screens and a large digital clock. Information is provided to the group via simulated newscasts from the "Global News Network" (GNN)— which announces the smallpox outbreaks, attributes the terrorist attacks to an Al Qaeda–related group calling itself the Al-Jihad Al-Jadid, and then tracks the escalating course of the global epidemic. Framed as a race against time—Bernard Kouchner (cofounder of Médecins Sans Frontières, who

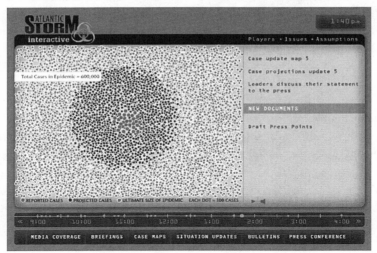

FIGURE 4.8. Image sequence from the Atlantic Storm bioterror scenario, Center for Biosecurity.

plays the president of France) declares early on: "This is the emergency period. We must not waste one hour"—the tabletop exercise is designed to terrify and to shock policy makers. The use of simulated mass media provides an impressive element of realism to the game, as GNN delivers breaking news to the assembled heads of state periodically throughout the day, allowing players and the audience of about a hundred official observers to feel the escalating health crisis and the terror of global contagion.[28]

The exercise is not intended to model a smallpox outbreak but rather to consider official responses to an international health emergency. Participants are asked to distribute a limited supply of smallpox vaccine, control the spread of the disease, live up to national and international obligations during the crisis, engage the World Health Organization, and maintain public confidence in their governments. In fact, none of these goals is achievable given the design of the exercise. The limited administrative resources (from vaccine to information to international health agreements) available, and the speed of the simulated outbreak, result in the spread of smallpox from local terrorist attacks to global contagion. The prerecorded GNN sequences give regular updates on the spread of the disease across Europe and the United States and can literally offer nothing but escalating projections of contagion. Moreover, given the incubation period for smallpox (at least a week), the attacks would have actually occurred long before the summit begins, and thus the simulated contamination—regardless of how the players respond in the game—is already widespread in Europe and North America. Rather than constituting effective governance, the exercise is designed to give players the feeling of helplessness in the midst of an escalating crisis. By fusing national security and public health on a global scale, the exercise also creates an affective context for immediately building a new biosecurity infrastructure.

The Atlantic Storm exercise materials state that all aspects of the scenario are grounded in "scientific fact" but also note that this is "one possible set of plausible events" (see UPMC Center for Health Security 2005). But the scenario presents a nearly perfect affective exercise in the production of terror: smallpox is described early in the exercise by GNN as the "most dreaded disease in history. It is painful. Kills one-third. Leaves some survivors blind and most disfigured." In the scenario, terrorists have gained possession of the virus from a former Soviet bioweapons facility (smallpox exists today only in small samples in the United States and Russia), built a laboratory disguised as a brewery in Austria, used publicly available microbiology equipment to weaponize the disease, and distributed it to their agents in the form of an aerosol spray for use in mass transit areas in Turkey, Germany, and Sweden. GNN turns for medical advice to D. A. Henderson (2009), the person who in real life led the World Health Organization's successful campaign to eliminate smallpox. But rather than exploring the public health measures that Henderson actually used to contain and eliminate the disease, GNN almost immediately cuts away from him to track news of the spreading contagion. Thus, the twentieth-century logics of public health are both recognized and silenced here by the twenty-first-century biosecurity logics of affective mobilization. Participants in the exercise do not learn how to manage smallpox but rather are asked to experience an existential force that cannot be stopped and to feel the helplessness of that situation. In the last act of the scenario, a smallpox outbreak occurs in the Washington, D.C., area, allowing summit participants to feel personally threatened by the disease in addition to being responsible for its global spread. The final GNN report, set six weeks in the future, drives the point home: the terrorist attacks have become a "cascading horror" involving millions of deaths around the world. A massive disruption of the global economy and transportation routes has occurred, leaving governments teetering on the brink of collapse under the threat of public uprisings and rising xenophobia. Global vaccine stockpiles have been consumed and there is no end in sight for this fast-moving, now planetary biocrisis.

The formal conclusions drawn from the Atlantic Storm exercise underscore the difficulty of building an emergency medical system in the midst of a global crisis, the strategic value of vaccine stockpiles, and the need for new administrative and legal understandings that can organize resources and communication across local, state and international agencies. Organizers of the exercise also sought to produce a consensus that homeland security actually begins overseas. Thus, the sense of urgency promoted by the exercise involved not only the logistical problem of countering bioterror attacks on two continents but also how to scale public health from the national to the global level. At the beginning of the exercise, for example, the United States has enough vaccine for all of its 300 million citizens, which could be the very definition of smallpox preparedness in a world with many competing security problems. But in this simulated catastrophe, the problem of epidemic disease is transformed into a collective transnational problem, merging domestic health concerns with a proliferating global economic, administrative, and military crisis. Atlantic Storm redefines public health in foreign countries as a strategic national security interest of the United States and thereby scales U.S. domestic security up to a planetary level. As Albright, playing the U.S. president, notes in a discussion of Turkey's request under Article 5 of the North Atlantic Treaty Organization (NATO) (which states that an attack on one member of NATO is an attack on all members) for large stocks of smallpox vaccine:

You all are talking about cooperation and I think that is very important. And I am a different president than the previous one [refer-
ring to George W. Bush] but it is still the same country. A lot of our
people are very knowledgeable about the fact that when we wanted
cooperation—at the time we were attacked and 3,000 people died
and Article 5 was invoked—but when we really needed help in Iraq,
many of you decided it was not useful.

We wanted cooperation. The relationship between security and health is
powerfully remade in this simulation, with the biopolitical stakes of an
imaginary smallpox epidemic rearticulating how war, alliance, and commerce are imbricated in a new global calculus of threat, one that finally col-
lapses the foreign into the domestic, as well as the terrorist into the microbe.

Crucially, there are no steps or escalations in this simulated health and
security crisis (see Kahn 1965)—the announcement of the terrorist event to
participants in the exercise was also the de facto announcement of global contagion. Atlantic Storm is an exercise in the affective production of urgency—
fomenting a state of global emergency for its players—not an effort to test
policy options. Unlike nuclear war gaming in the Cold War era, which tested
outcomes and modeled tactics in an effort to give leaders more options in a
time of nuclear crisis, Atlantic Storm can end only with the recognition of unpreparedness in the face of a proliferating global crisis.[29] Unlike the 1952 FCDA
film, the goal of this exercise is not to reestablish the authority of a caring state
over its citizens in the face of new technological dangers. Instead, Atlantic
Storm is designed to demonstrate the contemporary limits of federal governance and to create a productive panic among security professionals charged
with preempting collective dangers, now emanating both from the future
and the other side of the planet. Biosecurity is imaginatively constituted as
technologically achievable in Atlantic Storm (with the right stockpiles, global
governance structures, and surveillance techniques) and simultaneously
pushed off into a distant future, creating a new administrative horizon to be
engineered with biosecurity institution building on a global scale.[30]

Atlantic Storm remains a highly influential bit of insecurity theater, one
that biosecurity experts now cite as having "proven" the limits of contemporary global governance in the face of epidemic disease and the need for
a new biosecurity infrastructure to manage bioterrorism. Although the
exercise was made widely available to the public in online, digital, and textual versions, its primary audience was always U.S. policy makers. Indeed,
contemporary U.S. biosecurity might be said to have been born in crucial

ways through tabletop simulation: a June 2001 bioterrorism exercise known as Dark Winter, which modeled a smallpox attack on Oklahoma City by Iraqi agents, successfully launched a national campaign to stockpile enough smallpox vaccine for every American.[31] Mobilizing images of diseased children and simulated news coverage of the outbreak, the scenario also was staffed with former U.S. officials playing key roles. Dark Winter helped transform a small U.S. stockpile of vaccine for a disease eradicated during the Cold War into a national emergency in the United States. In the hours after the September 2001 anthrax attacks, Dark Winter also provided a powerful script for U.S. security professionals to use in thinking about the unfolding events. When a biological weapons alarm sounded in the White House on September 20, 2001, Vice President Dick Cheney screened a film of the Dark Winter exercise for the president and the National Security Council (Wald 2008, 176; Mayer 2008, 3). In other words, top-level U.S. national security officials turned to the Dark Winter simulation at a moment of actual crisis to understand their own immediate physical vulnerability. Biosecurity simulations were crucial to creating the imagined conditions of possibility for an emerging military focus on WMDs in Iraq as well as the necessary administrative enthusiasm for constructing a U.S. biosecurity apparatus. Thus, in the realm of anticipatory preemption, biosecurity simulations have proven to be wildly productive affective and political tools, producing in short order a new geopolitics and a new national biosecurity infrastructure.

The New "WMD"

We find ourselves at a moment when the perils to national security seem to come from many directions, when potential vulnerabilities seem countless. Biological weapons pose a strategic threat mirrored by no other form of attack other than nuclear weapons. There is no simple or immediate solution to the problem of biosecurity.
—Gigi Kwik et al., "Biosecurity"

To present biosecurity as simultaneously fundamental and nonexistent— as a not-yet-realized but critical future capacity—requires a careful calibration of threat perception.[32] Tara O'Toole, who moved from the Center for Biosecurity—which created the Dark Winter and Atlantic Storm exercises—to become the undersecretary for science and technology at the Department of Homeland Security in the Obama administration, has been a powerful expert voice arguing for bioterrorism as an immediate existential danger to the United States. Indeed, bioterrorism becomes an emblematic object of anticipatory preemption in her public policy work, as

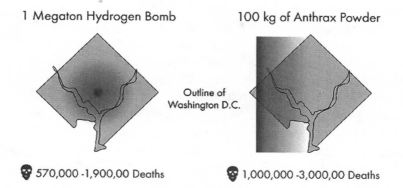

Lethality Mirroring Nuclear Weapons
Congressional Office of Technology Assessment, 1993

1 Megaton Hydrogen Bomb   100 kg of Anthrax Powder

Outline of
Washington D.C.

☠ 570,000 -1,900,00 Deaths   ☠ 1,000,000 -3,000,00 Deaths

Center for Biosecurity    UPMC | University of Pittsburgh Medical Center

FIGURE 4.9. "Anthrax Lethality Mirroring Nuclear Weapons," Tara O'Toole (2007) as adapted from the Office of Technology Assessment (1993).

she conceptualizes biothreat as the equivalent of the atomic bomb and emphasizes the potential for future radical revolutions in biomedicine to constitute new kinds of terrorist threat. In a 2007 presentation on strategic biodefense, O'Toole directly translates the existential threat of nuclear arsenals into that of bioterror, presenting an image of Washington, D.C., destroyed by a 1-megaton hydrogen bomb alongside a portrait of a 100-kilogram anthrax attack (see figure 4.9).[33] She argues:

> The lethality of biological weapons mirrors that of nuclear weapons. Nothing else—not large conventional explosions, not chemical weapons, and not radiation devices—is in the same class. In 1993, the Congressional Office of Technology Assessment determined that 100 kilograms of aerosolized anthrax released upwind of Washington, D.C., under favorable weather conditions would cause 1 to 3 million deaths—approximately the same number of casualties that would result from a one megaton hydrogen bomb dropped on the city. A subsequent analysis by the World Health Organization posited similar death tolls from a biological attack. (2007a, 2)

A lethality mirroring nuclear weapons. To produce weaponized anthrax on this scale today would require a significant bioweapons production facility, on the order of the one run by the Soviet Union (see Hoffman 2009), but in the near future, such a project might become more economical.[34] Indeed, the 1993 congressional study that this graphic is adapted from focused on state-based WMD programs and did not even mention terrorism (Office of Technology Assessment 1993). However, by demonstrating that the lethality of biological weapons could potentially mirror those of nuclear weapons, O'Toole argues not only that the threat is immediate but also, implicitly, that a federal response on a par with that of the U.S. nuclear complex is needed—mirroring the $6 trillion spent on the bomb (S. Schwartz 1998). Here, twentieth-century nuclear threat is translated into twenty-first-century biothreat via a new conceptulization of the WMD. What is spectacular about this emerging WMD concept is not only that it folds multiple technologies (nuclear, chemical, biological, and radiological weapons) into a singular existential threat category but also that it increasingly recognizes technologies that have not yet been invented. The promise of synthetic biology is evoked in biosecurity policy debates to craft a new kind of future terror, which is unbounded by anything except the imagination and deployed to enable administrative action today.[35]

O'Toole, in fact, argues that the twenty-first century will so revolutionize the biosciences that individuals will soon be able to manufacture designer diseases easily, without needing the resources of an industrial state to support their terroristic efforts. O'Toole offered this vision of the emerging biothreat problem to a group of biosecurity experts assembled at the 2010 BIO International Convention, challenging them to think seriously about the implications of future technological revolutions:

> About ten years ago, when I started to worry about the biothreat, I was in Boston. I was meeting with a group of about ten professors from Harvard and MIT, all of whom had been hired by biotech companies at the time, and they were very excited about their work. As I talked about bioterrorism—and this is pre-9/11, pre–anthrax attack—they were extremely skeptical. They thought, "you are crazy to worry about this"—which is basically what they told me. And I said, "well, all right, could any of you make and disperse a biological weapon that would kill thousands of people . . . could you?" There was a long pause, and then the whole nature of the conversation changed. They became much more serious and much more engaged. After talking about it for a few minutes, one professor (now very famous actu-

FIGURE 4.10. *Landscape with the Fall of Icarus*, c.1555 by Pieter Bruegel the Elder (Wikimedia commons image).

ally for his accomplishments) said, "but we can stay ahead of those guys." Those guys being the would-be terrorists. Well, maybe. Maybe we can.

This is a painting by Pieter Bruegel [see figure 4.10]. It's called "The Fall of Icarus." You remember that Icarus and his father invented wings held on by wax. And in the course of their adventures, Icarus ignored his father's advice and flew a little too close to the sun, which melted the wax on his wings and he fell into the sea. And what you see here in the painting is normal everyday life in the 1600s. You got a farmer plowing his field. You got a fisherman trying to put food on the table. You got a shepherd wasting time looking up at the sky, maybe he saw something, or thought he saw something. Some ship is sailing out to new harbors. Normal everyday life—but off in the corner is a man with wings falling into the ocean.

So here is my question to you: who is Icarus today? Is he some graduate student that is on the cusp of discovering something that will save millions of lives? Is he some kid in a garage tinkering with tools more powerful than he knows how to wield responsibly? Or is he one of our adversaries, one experiment away from succeeding in a bioattack? Can we stay ahead of these guys and what is your responsibility in all this? (2010)

A kid in a garage. Consider how O'Toole positions the promise of synthetic biology within the reality of contemporary threat, and crucially how she focuses on the unknown rather than the known (see also Smith, Inglesby, and O'Toole 2003). Here, every garage in the world is converted into a potential biosecurity problem, and the merger of experimental discoveries with accidents and attacks multiplies the potential dangers of a new biomedicine exponentially.[36] It is difficult to imagine the scale of the security apparatus that would be needed to manage, let alone preempt, this level of threat. But given the dystopian future anterior point of view—a world of proliferating, and entirely new, infectious dangers—anything less than a full national commitment to warding off this future would be calamitous. This alarmist vision relies on a complex fusion of temporalities to create its affective intensity: existing biomedical capacities meet as-yet-unrealized and unimaginable future ones in a race to keep ahead of the "bad guys." Disease becomes technology in the image of Icarus's fall, a shift to mythology at precisely the moment where one might expect a specific example from the biosciences to illustrate the emerging world of engineered biothreat. Anticipatory dangers, however, rely on the imagination to instantiate themselves as affectively real; thus, they allow experts to mobilize, in a radical new way, a lack of physical evidence of danger to enable substantial action in the here and now.

The current U.S. biosecurity discourse distorts what could be a robust public health concept in favor of global counterterrorism. After all, the dual-use biosecurity concept—the promise of a new biomedicine to both heal and hurt—works in a number of ways. By focusing on eliminating threats such as Ebola virus, anthrax, and smallpox, infectious disease specialists may indeed discover a means of treating common diseases, as many people hope. But to protect against the unknown or designer bioagent, U.S. scientists will have to locate and/or make these organisms in the laboratory so they can devise countermeasures (see Fauci and Collins 2012). Thus, in core domains, biosecurity today appears to be indistinguishable from biological weapons research: in fact, if any other country on the planet were building a new group of BSL-4 research laboratories that were not subject to international controls or inspections, U.S. defense experts might well accuse them of pursuing biological weapons and advocate preemptory action against them. Teaching a vast new cohort of individuals how to build biological weapons also has immediate implications for global nonproliferation efforts, which are sidestepped in the United States by calling these programs "defensive" or a form of "public health." Thus, the new generation of experts staffing the new biosecurity laboratories in the United States constitutes a threat as well as a resource (see Klotz and Sylvester 2009; Atlas and Reppy 2005).

Fantasies about perfect designer weapons built in U.S. biodefense laboratories abound today. For example, the Project for a New American Century, a neoconservative coalition that provided key personnel and ideas to President George W. Bush's administration, saw a new future for bioweapons before the War on Terror. Writing in its highly influential report, *Rebuilding America's Defenses*, the neoconservatives suggested:

> Although it may take several decades for the process of transformation to unfold, in time, the art of warfare on air, land, and sea will be vastly different than it is today, and "combat" likely will take place in new dimensions: in space, "cyber-space," and perhaps in the worlds of microbes. . . . Advanced forms of biological warfare that can "target" specific genotypes may transform biological warfare from the realm of terror to a politically useful tool. (2000, 60)

A politically useful tool. A militarized notion of biosecurity may provide a means of coordinating a global response to infectious disease, but it may also ignite a new kind of global arms race in the microbial laboratory.[37] In its first decade, U.S. biosecurity has participated in, and been informed by, a broader official effort to generate a purified category of existential threat, *the WMD*, which is no longer a specific technical or scientific term but rather a highly flexible means of maximizing affective mobilization. It also allows the pursuit of projects that permanently blur offensive and defensive capabilities, creating a militarized future open to entirely new configurations of both danger and power. Biosecurity, like counterterror, creates its own logics and coherence today, mobilizing past and future dangers as well as existing and imagined expertise in the attempt to constitute a highly flexible form of American power that, as we shall see, is increasingly planetary in its ambitions.

Securing Life Itself

An outbreak anywhere is a threat to populations everywhere.
—U.S. Homeland Security Council, *National Strategy for Pandemic Influenza*

The object of security has become a constantly emerging, transforming, mutating, contingent and infected life.
—Geoffrey Whitehall, "Preemptive Sovereignty and Avian Pandemics"

A biosecurity that merges technologies with microbes, existing bioweapons with naturally occurring diseases, not-yet-emerging diseases with engineered biothreats from the future has an immediate problem: how to define its theater of operation.[38] In its first decade, U.S. biosecurity has radically expanded its scope and reach, moving from a specific concern with food safety to a narrow defense against biological attack with known agents (anthrax), to infectious disease (SARS), to the potential dangers of bioscience (synthetic biology), and increasingly, to emerging multispecies diseases (zoonoses). This constant proliferation of biosecurity objects reveals that, under the contemporary logics of counterterror, biosecurity reaches its limit only when the category of life can no longer be expanded. Biosecurity not only accrues objects of concern—linking experts, disciplines, technologies, and species together in new ways—but it also continually rescales its problem, finding a limit only at the moment when life in its totality is the unit to be secured. In short, biosecurity has become an American ambition to monitor, manage, and preempt biological danger on a planetary scale.

The outbreaks of SARS (2003), avian flu (2005), and swine flu (2009) were not only demonstrations of the emerging global vectors of infectious diseases but also test cases for the emerging biosecurity apparatus, in its effort to monitor global outbreaks of disease in real time and to mobilize citizens and experts according to anticipated biological threats. In addition to new modes of global surveillance, restrictions on travel, and international quarantine procedures, the outbreaks produced new biosecurity directives to state and federal agencies: this kind of full-scale collective rehearsal allowed the epidemic to occur in the public imagination and to become affectively real, long before the disease actually became a domestic health issue. A rehearsal of global danger in the collective imagination has become synonymous with U.S. biosecurity, scaling effects from the global (travel, policing, and commerce) to the local (producing public antiseptic washing stations and even new sneezing techniques—into the elbow, not the hand). Thus, while infectious disease is not a new problem, biosecurity policies now anticipate foreign-born infections and mount national media campaigns amplifying worst-case outcomes for a global contagion, and thereby mobilizing experts and publics in advance of the disease. This anticipatory commitment to disease outbreaks is enabled by advances in the real-time surveillance of infectious disease and scenario-driven calculations of potential risks. The increasing expert pursuit of a global "situational awareness" for infectious disease and a broader threat projection for public health produces several ancillary effects in U.S. security culture: it naturalizes both crisis anticipation and threat inflation in the public sphere, calibrating everyday life to official declarations of danger, and it creates a universal global

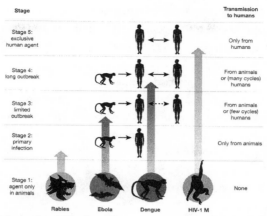

Figure 1 | Illustration of the five stages through which pathogens of animals evolve to cause diseases confined to humans. (See Box 1 for details.) The four agents depicted have reached different stages in the process, ranging from rabies (still acquired only from animals) to HIV-1 (now acquired only from humans).

FIGURE 4.11. Zoonotic pathogen transmission vectors, Wolfe, Dunavan, and Diamond (2007).

environment for U.S. surveillance and hypervigilance—one that mirrors, and easily collaborates with, explicitly militarized counterterror projects.

Put differently, if emerging diseases are a global phenomenon, then the U.S. logics of anticipatory preemption require an equally global surveillance and intervention capability, one that mirrors long-standing U.S. military interests in global force projection. In this regard, Nathan D. Wolfe, Claire Panosian Dunavan, and Jared Diamond (2007) have identified five pathways for emerging disease, focusing on the animal-human nexus (figure 4.11) as the likely source of the most virulent and deadly viruses. Emphasizing the moment of zoonotic emergence—when a disease jumps from an animal to human host—infectious disease experts now argue that the focus of U.S. biosecurity should be on identifying those individuals who interact with wildlife in forests and jungles and then travel to urban settings, becoming maximal vectors for contagion. Thus, biosecurity experts narrow their field of global anticipatory preemption significantly. They also align their project with the larger U.S. counterterror strategy of, as President Bush famously put it, "taking the fight to the terrorists abroad, so we don't have to face them here at home." Mirroring the logics of the War on Terror, which focuses on preempting attacks by overseas terrorists, this emerging biosecurity project seeks to identify those populations that interact with wildlife in zones of the world considered the likely sources of new diseases (see Keusch et al. 2009). Given a global population of seven billion people, anticipatory preemption here requires building an expert capacity to identify and track specific individuals (and, extending the logic, potentially specific animals and microbes), whether they are marked as terrorists or vectors.

There are two important conceptual effects of this focus on zoonotic diseases within the larger U.S. biodefense project: first, since infectious disease does not recognize borders, it creates a borderless world of threat (one in which state bureaucracies can slow down or prevent U.S. surveillance and preemptory response); second, U.S. domestic preparedness is now a global and potentially limitless future horizon, one of infinite and emerging complexity linking state actors, terrorists, and naturally occurring diseases as objects of preemption. Bioterror has no singular domain, but rather a galaxy of potentials requiring expert surveillance, assessment, preemptive response, and/or containment. The ever-flexible U.S. biosecurity apparatus is expanding once again to meet this mission, seeking to establish a future capacity to detect and preempt diseases on an emerging planetary scale.[39] The CDC, for example, is increasingly operating on U.S. military bases around the world, creating a network of new sites for the pursuit of threats from the forests and jungles of Latin America, Africa, and Southeast Asia that might jump species—and continents—to endanger the United States.[40] Similarly, there is a second tier of U.S. biosecurity facilities (on top of the BSL-4 laboratories) being built in the United States to look specifically at the animal-human nexus. Perhaps counterintuitively, Kansas, the cattle capital of the country, has won the bid to host the new National Bio and Agro-Defense Facility (figure 4.12) to study the most virulent infectious diseases in animals and has embarked on an ambitious new biotech initiative exploring the links between plant, animal, human, energy, and drug economies, called the Kansas Bioscience Authority.[41]

Both the National Bio and Agro-Defense Facility and the larger Kansas Bioscience Authority represent an effort to fuse biosecurity, biodefense, and biotechnology to produce a new midwestern regional economy grounded in biothreat, bioscience, and capitalist hype. At the Authority, animal health, bioenergy, biomaterials, plant biology, and drug discovery and delivery merge state-based biosecurity concerns with the long-term interest of biotechnology in acquiring basic patents and new markets. Biosecurity, as we have seen, accrues objects and logics. What might be considered its conceptual instability (a proliferating field of objects and interests) is actually its great strength, as the term *biosecurity* is imbued at every level with military-industrial, biomedical, and financial logics, meaning that each

FIGURE 4.12. Advertising materials for new biosecurity projects in Kansas.

new object of concern represents both a new logistical problem to solve and a new market.

The extraordinary power of biosecurity to link food, health, military, financial, pharmaceutical, and environmental interests was on full display at the first-ever biosecurity panels offered at the BIO International Convention in 2010. The meeting, which I attended, brought together a remarkably diverse set of experts, including top officials from the Food and Drug Administration; the CDC; the Departments of Health and Human Services, Homeland Security, Defense, and Agriculture; the National Security Council; the U.S. Army; the National Institute of Allergy and Infectious Diseases; the Kansas Bioscience Authority; and the Bill and Melinda Gates Foundation—as well as a host of specialists on emerging diseases and scientists from agricultural colleges, biotech companies (Novartis, Merke, PharmAthene, and Vertex), and biodefense firms. Key policy makers in government, military, research, and biotech all agreed that biosecurity was vitally important—an urgent concern—even while using substantially different operational definitions of the term. An argument emerged over whether the most deadly terrorist was "man" (necessitating a counterterrorism strategy focused on engineered biological weapons and located in the Department of Defense) or "Mother Nature" (requiring an orientation toward public health and emerging diseases located in the Department of Health and Human Services and the CDC). However, the terror of epidemic disease (whether naturally occurring or engineered) allowed the diverse experts to merge these distinct concerns, producing a new kind of "national health security" that was formally committed to the preemption of disease in all its forms. The word *biosecurity* has, thus, become the great institutional translator in U.S. national security and health debates, enabling new linkages across institutions with historically different interests, priorities, and forms of expertise, now unified in an expert confrontation with terror (of disease, of the WMD, of the unknown). In its first decade, biosecurity has expanded from a narrow set of concerns about the safety of the domestic food supply to an ever-emerging project of surveillance and preemption at the planetary level, linking individuals and microbes as objects of counterterror concern. Within such a rapidly expanding universe, one can expect extraterrestrial life to be folded into the mission at some point, as biosecurity has become an expert project that creates, encompasses, and enfolds external threat in all its living forms.

Because one cannot have too much health or too much security, biosecurity is today an emblematic project of the counterterror state. Indeed, under current biosecurity logics there is no space on planet earth that the United States does not potentially need to police nor any population (publics to experts to wildlife to microbes) immune to its anticipatory reach. Under this counterterror logic, U.S. personnel are deployed globally to protect the homeland, and seek the ability to move across international borders at will in pursuit of microbes or terrorists, creating a planetary scope for U.S. defense. The latest *Quadrennial Defense Review Report* (the Department of Defense's strategic plan) identifies the ability of U.S. personnel to move freely and quickly around the world as a paramount objective, referring to the need to defeat local "anti-access strategies aimed at impeding the deployment of U.S. forces" (U.S. Department of Defense 2010, 31). Public health, along with counterterrorism, development projects, and drug enforcement, becomes part of a larger geopolitical and diplomatic tool kit for U.S. interests, giving U.S. agencies interested in gaining access to specific regions of the world new codes to use in that pursuit.[42]

It is easiest to see this new focus and mode of global governance when comparing the current maps of emerging diseases with what the Pentagon calls the "arc of instability"—the regions of the world where poverty, lack of infrastructure, and scarcities of natural resources are believed likely to "breed" future terrorists (Barnett 2004; McDew 2010). Figure 4.13 is a map of international requests to the CDC for assistance with emerging diseases in the period 2007–11 (U.S. Centers for Disease Control and Prevention 2011; see also Jones et al. 2008). Compare the frequency of emerging diseases in parts of South America, Africa, and South Asia in this map to a map of U.S. military operations since the end of the Cold War (figure 4.14). In the name of combating emerging diseases, we have an emerging concept of U.S. governance, one that imagines building a global surveillance system capable of locating individuals anywhere in the arc of instability that might pose a potential threat, whether that threat is an emerging disease, a WMD, narcotics trafficking, or terrorism. Finally, attempting a global preemption of existential threats now presents U.S. officials with a roster of policy options—including counterterrorism, war, development, and public health—to allow the United States to intervene worldwide, making U.S. defense a concept that also has no borders: in its first decade, counterterror has transformed domestic defense into a planetary project.

Since September 2001, the emerging U.S. biosecurity project has been enormously productive at both the domestic and international level, enabling a powerful new merging of public health concerns with a militarized U.S. worldview. The assassination of Osama bin Laden, Al Qaeda's leader, in Pakistan in 2011 clearly illustrates this new fusion of health and counterterror. Prior to the nighttime commando raid that killed bin Laden, the Central Intelligence Agency (CIA) sent Pakistani medical professionals to offer free hepatitis B immunizations to neighborhood populations in Abbottabad, Pakistan, where bin Laden was believed to be living. Their real goal was not to fight infectious disease but to collect DNA samples from people living in bin Laden's household to test against tissue samples from bin Laden's family already in CIA possession (see Shah 2011). Armed with covert recording devices and syringes, these medical professionals were attempting to create a genetic database to be used in identifying the person of Osama bin Laden. How should we assess this act? Was it a medical program with an assassination team attached to it, or a military attack promoting preventive medicine? The killing of bin Laden presents the iconic fusion of war and health in the new U.S. vision of counterterror, merging covert operations, biosecurity, and biometric databases. In the end, the CIA vaccination team offered residents only one of the needed three shots, demonstrating that war trumped public health in this mission. This example also shows the rising global stakes for biosecurity in all its forms: in light of

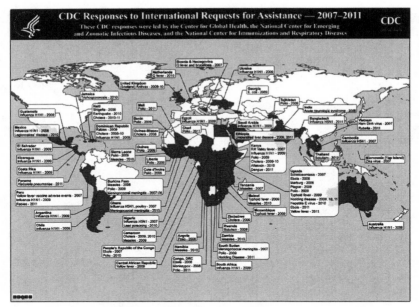

FIGURE 4.13. "CDC Responses to International Requests for Assistance, 2007–2011," Emerging and Zoonotic Diseases, Centers for Disease Control and Prevention.

FIGURE 4.14. Pentagon's "Arc of Instability" Map, U.S. Military Deployments since the End of the Cold War (Wikimedia commons image).

the CIA's operation—which transformed an international promise of future community health through preventive medicine into a targeted killing—organizations devoted to disease eradication have become increasingly politicized entities in the region (Walsh 2012a).[43] In reaction to the CIA vaccination ruse, at least one Pakistani leader has eliminated a polio vaccination program in his region, leaving roughly a hundred thousand Pakistanis at risk (Walsh 2012b) and hindering efforts to eradicate the disease. The killing of bin Laden reveals the potentially devastating global health consequences of a militarized approach to biosecurity, in which health becomes simply another vector of counterterror.

In the end, just as the Manhattan Project scientists could not have foreseen the effect that the atomic bomb would have on everyday American life, biosecurity experts are producing a future we cannot yet see, offering new institutions, metaphors, and practices to create a world full of threats and countermeasures while rendering other worlds and other notions of security unspeakable. Because its objects, techniques, and domains are all cast as emergent, biosecurity is both a highly flexible mode of governance and very likely to be a lasting contribution of the War on Terror. The ambition of the U.S. biosecurity apparatus today is to be nothing less than a planetary infrastructure, able to secure life in all its forms. Although the goal of securing all life remains the future-oriented fantasy of experts, it nevertheless creates a powerful vision and ideology of American power, one that will shape government agencies for decades to come, producing unpredictable effects. In practice, not all forms of life are valued equally or subject to the same situational awareness or modes of care by the security state, creating immediate gaps, hierarchies, and blind spots in biosecurity institutions. But biosecurity today is not a story about how experts ward off danger. Instead, it is a case study in how Americans build future capacities and what fears (of infections, of technologies, and of terror itself) give expert thought enough affective intensity to overwhelm all other immediate concerns.

The Revelation: The WMD Is All-American

The FBI's investigation into the anthrax letters of 2001 became the largest effort in its history, involving 600,000 investigator work hours and seventeen special agents on an Amerithrax Task Force, along with ten U.S. postal inspectors.[44] The investigation spanned six continents; involved over 10,000 witness interviews, eighty searches, 26,000 e-mail reviews, and analyses of four million megabytes of computer memory; and resulted in the issuance of 5,750 grand jury subpoenas. FBI investigators worked through the remains of Flight 93 that crashed in Pennsylvania on September 11, 2001, looking in vain for a connection between the anthrax and the suicide hijackers. They also sought to find a link to the government of Iraq, but they could not. By 2003 they were using bloodhounds to search the grounds around Fort Detrick, Maryland (home of the oldest U.S. bioweapons laboratory), eventually draining a small lake and finding a plastic container that some experts thought could have been used to create an underwater anthrax box—a devilishly clever way for the perpetrator to avoid detection or anthrax contamination—or perhaps it was simply a turtle trap. The quality of the anthrax used in the attack, which had been weaponized to be extremely light and thus maximally dangerous, ultimately focused the FBI on a source inside the U.S. biodefense world.

The first target of the investigation, Stephen Hatfill (who had once worked at Fort Detrick), was identified by Attorney General John Ashcroft as a person of interest and by the *New York Times* columnist Nicholas Kristof (2002) as the likely culprit. He was tried in the media without any actual evidence against him, and he eventually won a $5.8 million settlement for invasion of privacy. By the summer of 2008, the FBI's focus had shifted to Bruce Ivins, an anthrax specialist at Fort Detrick who had been a consultant on the Amerithrax investigation from the beginning of the case. Finding that Ivins had a previously unknown history of mental illness and access to the specific strain of anthrax used in the attacks, the FBI mounted an around-the-clock investigation of Ivins that lasted for over a year. As a grand jury was being called to indict Ivins for terrorist use of a WMD, he committed suicide. Friends attributed his suicide to the intense pressure of the investigation directed against him; the FBI declared the Amerithrax case closed.

Given the trajectory of U.S. biosecurity over the past decade, which evolved from a narrow concern with food safety to a global project of preempting emerging threats, supporting a massive new infrastructure of laboratories, national exercises, covert actions, and preventive wars, we might well ask how the FBI explains Ivins's motivation in the attacks. The agency concludes:

> The anthrax vaccine program to which he had devoted his entire career of more than 20 years was failing. The anthrax vaccines were receiving criticism in several scientific circles, because of both potency problems and allegations that the anthrax vaccine contributed to Gulf War Syndrome. Short of some major breakthrough or intervention, he feared that the vaccine research program was going to be discontinued. Following the anthrax attacks, however, his program was suddenly rejuvenated. (U.S. Department of Justice 2010, 8)

His program was rejuvenated. This is an astonishingly understated conclusion from officers of the counterterror state, for its implications are quite profound.[45] The FBI argues that to increase financial support for his anthrax research, Ivins initiated the attacks on key media sources and Democratic leaders in the Senate, with his letters designed to give the Bush administration a rationale for attributing the attack to foreigners, probably Muslim fundamentalists. The FBI concludes that Ivins manipulated the panic caused by the suicide-hijacker attacks in 2001 to his own personal ends, successfully leveraging the state of emergency to fund his biodefense work. This means that in the first decade of counterterror the only WMDs have been those produced literally, imaginatively, and rhetorically within the United States. And as a response to a homegrown terrorist attack from an expert inside the U.S. biodefense infrastructure, the counterterror state has proliferated the number of potential biothreat vectors (of laboratories, experts, and materials) to the point of literal incalculability.

Biosecurity is a *noir* in the United States today because to date its chief threats, though projected outward, are internal. Like any of the great film noirs of our time—including *Memento* (2000), with its brain-damaged insurance investigator who has no capacity to create new memories; *The Bourne Identity* (2002), whose amnesiac government assassin just wants out of the black ops world that co-opted and engineered his mind; or *Shutter Island* (2010), whose paranoid federal marshal realizes, while investigating a hospital for the criminally insane, that he is one of its patients and his investigation is, in fact, the largest therapeutic simulation ever attempted—the American biosecurity protagonist is actually looking most immediately for himself. This is not to say that there are no actual biological dangers (existing, emerging, or projected) or individuals and groups committed to attacking U.S. citizens and interests. Rather, it is to point out that the U.S. security apparatus builds itself under conditions of national panic, and to question what capacities, what potentials, what consequences are also being loaded into the collective future in the name of anticipatory defense.

FIVE

LIVING COUNTERTERROR

Because the terrorist threat continues, the national emergency declared on September 14, 2001, and the powers and authorities adopted to deal with that emergency must continue in effect beyond September 14, 2011. Therefore, I am continuing in effect for an additional year the national emergency. —PRESIDENT BARACK OBAMA, "NOTICE FROM THE PRESIDENT REGARDING THE CONTINUATION OF THE NATIONAL EMERGENCY WITH RESPECT TO CERTAIN TERRORIST ATTACKS"

The President is authorized to use all necessary and appropriate force against those nations, organizations, or persons he determines planned, authorized, committed, or aided the terrorist attack that occurred on September 11, 2001, or harbored such organizations or persons, in order to prevent any future acts of international terrorism against the United States by such nations, organizations or persons. —U.S. CONGRESS, "AUTHORIZATION FOR USE OF MILITARY FORCE," SEPTEMBER 12, 2001

In the first decade of its twenty-first-century emergency, the U.S. security state did nothing less than reinvent itself, imagining and pursuing a new planetary concept of American power organized around the anticipation and pursuit of terror. The endless futurity of terror (existing, imagined, emergent) transforms *defense* into a war that is boundless in both time and space and that is constantly evolving. The now annual presidential notice to Congress that the emergency provoked by the attacks on September 11, 2001, continues, endows the country's chief executive with wartime powers, creating a global theater of operations for the ever emerging U.S. counterterror state apparatus.[1] It is also a means of suspending democratic institutions to enable radical forms of state agency in the hope of eliminating terrors, both real and imagined. What began as an international response to the suicide-hijacker attacks on New York and Washington organized by a small group identified as Al Qaeda has evolved into an American vision of planetary engagement that is astonishingly productive and wide-ranging—constituting simultaneously a new geopolitics and a new domestic social contract. In the name of existential defense, security experts across a vast range of fields and agencies spend each day trying to anticipate and preempt dangers from the future—hoping to eliminate surprise and thereby engineer a world without events. Multidisciplinary, creative, hyperactive, gloomy—this counterterror state apparatus imagines a world without borders but filled with proliferating forms of terror (present, contingent, projected, imagined). It engages the future as a space of endless logistical need, where the spectrum of possible dangers requires ever new and expanding analytics, institutions, technologies, and forms of mobility. In this way, the counterterror state is not fighting a specific war that could be won or lost. Instead, it seeks to install technical capacities into the future to deal with terroristic threats both known and unknown, those expected and those not yet visible. As part of this expanding economy of counterterror, security experts are increasingly endowed with the power to imagine—and create—new forms of danger to engineer countermeasures to combat them. Thus, counterterror becomes terror becomes counterterror in a recursive system of anticipatory preemption, which focuses experts on engaging potential existential dangers—the *what ifs*—rather than on simply rebuilding and expanding nonmilitary American, and international, infrastructures.

In the proliferation of dangers and expert calls to build new capacities to meet them, it is easy to miss the fact that counterterror is naturalized as a permanent war (based on merging real, contingent, and imaginative practices). Indeed, war has become so deeply installed in everyday American life in the first decade of counterterror that it is no longer actually "war": the ongoing U.S. military actions (from troops, to special forces, to drone strikes) in Afghanistan, Pakistan, Yemen, and Iraq at the start of the second decade of counterterror are officially referred to as "overseas contingency operations."[2] By reframing the longest-running military actions in U.S. history as simply "overseas contingencies," the violence once known as war is remade as part of a larger species of planetary governance (merging military, humanitarian, drug enforcement, and disaster relief activities), becoming radically open-ended, multifronted, and politically diffuse. This reframing naturalizes U.S. military engagements across scales and types as simply another mode of international relations and announces that—since contingencies are, after all, contingent (articulating radically different possibilities of what might or might not happen)—the security state claims both near-term and deep future horizons for counterterror. For when can the contingent ever be truly defeated? How can one ever be fully prepared for the radically emergent? How does one dispel forever what *might* happen—let alone permanently and knowingly eliminate the worst-case scenarios of mushroom clouds, biological attacks, and terrorists armed with WMDs?

Counterterror is, in a key cultural sense, one logical multigenerational outcome of the contradictions installed in American society by the atomic bomb, a technology that remade the United States as a global superpower but did so only through the systematic application of nuclear terror—directly in Hiroshima and Nagasaki, geopolitically via the Cold War nuclear arms race, and affectively in the domestic form of U.S. civil defense. The national security state was empowered, organized, and psychosocially infused with nuclear terror from day one. Officials have relied on the existential threat of nuclear war for a wide range of projects since the destruction of Hiroshima and Nagasaki. Indeed, the national security state was formally established in 1947 to prevent a nuclear Pearl Harbor, and to advance the international power of the United States as a nuclear superpower. This new kind of security state used nuclear fear writ large to transform domestic U.S. security into a global project with far-reaching economic, military, and political consequences. As a mode of global governance, however, the resulting Cold War balance of terror was always unstable in one key domain, as it required two superpower states locked in perpetual competition and equally committed to avoiding nuclear war from one minute to the next via nuclear deterrence. The War on Terror solves the structural problem of an unstable bipolarity (and specifically the potential loss of a stabilizing enemy other) by bypassing contemporary politics altogether (i.e., reliance on a specific named other to combat in perpetuity) and claiming the future itself as the domain it needs to secure. The counterterror state draws its power from identifying a proliferating field of potential dangers on a planetary scale and then attempting to build a security state capable of responding to each contingency. Just note the proliferation of new securities in the past decade—homeland security, biosecurity, and cybersecurity—each of which is composed of a new universe of experts and objects that require a complex, global vision of American power combined with innovative modes of threat assessment and response. Each of these fields also enables new degrees and forms of militarism, merging new offensive and defensive capabilities through threat designation and affective governance. A concern about securing the U.S. homeland, for example, accompanies an expanding U.S. campaign of drone bombing in the homelands of Pakistanis, Yemenis, and Somalians (in countries with which the United States is not formally "at war"). The biosecurity apparatus, as I have argued, is not just preparing for infectious disease outbreaks within the United States but is researching future bioweapons and using disease eradication campaigns as a cover for covert operations on a global scale. The new official concern about domestic cybersecurity is tied directly to U.S. cyberwar campaigns (most publicly against Iranian nuclear facilities) as well as unprecedented forms of digital surveillance (as the National Security Agency now captures the bulk of all global digital communications in the name of counterterrorism, but also spies on government officials and conducts corporate espionage around the world). Importantly, the counterterror state pursues technical capacities for the sake of new forms of future agency and is, thus, itself radically emergent. This commitment to constant revolutionary change across experts, technologies, and administrative abilities is perhaps the chief accomplishment of the counterterror state and why it will likely have such a deep hold on the twenty-first century.

Moreover, counterterror is not only a highly flexible mode of security, based on an ever-expanding concept of terror and a highly elastic set of core concerns in the figuration of the WMD. It also addresses an unwinnable problem, for when can one say that terror—a basic emotional state—has been finally purged from American experience? Counterterror colonizes the American future by identifying an ever-shifting series of peoples, objects, technologies, hypotheticals, and contingencies to secure in the name of planetary defense. The fact that very few of these potentials (people, technologies, finances, microbes) can be perfectly secured on a global basis in practice is part of the recursive structure of counterterror, as both failure and surprise drive increasing calls for new capacities, increasing securitization, and more aggressive militarization. Counterterror, thus, thrives on a proliferating insecurity, using vulnerability (past, present, future) and imaginative creativity (scenarios, fears, nightmares) as its raison d'être. In this regard, counterterror is the perfect conceptual vehicle for a permanent mobilization of the security state. Infused with proliferating images of existential danger to be fought in perpetuity, counterterror is highly flexible in its core goals, objects, techniques, and future ambitions.

The transformations in American society during the first decade of terror politics could not be more profound: counterterror has produced a new social contract not through open political deliberation (there has been almost no formal debate about alternative notions of security and costs) but through the constant amplification of threats. Indeed, the War on Terror has fundamentally shifted American values, with the well-publicized illegal practices of the Bush administration (rendition, indefinite detention, torture, and domestic surveillance) enhanced by the Obama administration's imperial commitment to cyberwar, digital surveillance, and a global "targeted killing" (that is, assassination) program using both Special Forces and drones (see also Constitution Project 2013; Open Society Foundation 2013; Becker and Shane 2012; Sanger 2012). Counterterror has trumped human rights and law at every turn in the first decade of the War on Terror, raising very basic questions about U.S. support for international law, the rights of U.S. citizens, and the limits of war in the twenty-first century. The coherence of these policies across the Bush and Obama administrations and the absence of any substantial effort by Congress or the Department of Justice to adjudicate practices such as water boarding, indefinite detention, warrantless surveillance, and the killing of U.S. citizens and others with drone attacks are powerful indications of the new counterterror consensus in Washington.[3] As I have argued in this book, the United States has historically expanded its security apparatus not through careful deliberation but rather in times of national panic. The War on Terror, however, is unique, in that it is a conflict that cannot be bounded spatially or temporally, or won. For example, even if Al Qaeda were eliminated from the planet, that would not be the end of U.S. counterterror because the global future is now seen as the ultimate domain to secure. This notion of planetary security, as I have argued, is highly nationalist in orientation and thus remains at odds with collective emergencies like climate change that cannot be easily militarized for national advantage. Thus, counterterror, despite its proliferating objects of concern and expansive imaginative practices of threat designation, does not recognize all terrors, or even all of the most immediate and challenging ones. Anticipatory preemption works to relocate the domain of security from the material world of everyday precarity into the collective imaginary, as experts conjure up images of perfected terrors that overwhelm all lesser but lived experiences of insecurity, displacing governance from existing forms of violence, suffering, and crisis in favor of combating nightmarish, if largely speculative, *what ifs.*

As a result, counterterror has dominated the United States politically, socially, and financially in the early twenty-first century, a period of multiplying crises across capital, environment, and public institutions. Though the country is not confronted by a high-tech, nuclear-armed, global adversary like the Soviet Union, the Pentagon's current annual budget is over 50 percent higher than its average budget during the Cold War (Harrison 2011). The military campaigns in Afghanistan and Iraq are the longest wars in U.S. history and have so far cost at least $1.3 trillion; only World War II was a more expensive conflict (Belasco 2011; Daggett 2010, 2). By 2012 those who orchestrated the 2001 attacks (including Osama bin Laden and his chief lieutenants in Al Qaeda) were dead or in prison, but yearly U.S. national security expenditures remain at an all-time high (Hellman 2011), with no change in sight. The cost of the first decade of the War on Terror certainly exceeds $7.6 trillion (National Priorities Project 2011). This expenditure comes in the midst of recurring global economic crises (including a 2008 recession second in severity only to the Great Depression of the 1930s) that wiped out twenty years of accumulated wealth for the median U.S. household (Appelbaum 2012). Despite these startling economic facts, the national security system is not subject to calls for substantial economic reform and remains virtually immune to political criticism or review from elected officials of both major parties.

Indeed, counterterror has been the primary growth industry in the United States in the early twenty-first century. New national infrastructures of homeland security, biosecurity, and cybersecurity sit on top of the national security institutions built during the Cold War, already the largest national security apparatus in the world. The emerging counterterror infrastructure is staffed with experts and administrators leading lives that are classified secrets: in 2011, over 4.8 million Americans possessed a security clearance (U.S. Office of the Director of National Intelligence 2012, 3). The cost of maintaining government secrets is correspondingly at an all-time high, increasing 12 percent in 2011 alone, to reach a total of $11.3 billion (U.S. Information Security Oversight Office 2012, 3). The American commitment to militarization takes many forms, including maintaining a global system of over a thousand foreign military bases (Vine 2009, 42; see also Lutz 2009) and monopolizing two-thirds of the global arms trade (Shanker 2009). Increasingly, U.S. police departments have also been pulled into the national counterterror apparatus, participating in the yearly simulations of terrorist attacks while expanding capabilities via access to federal counterterror funds. Since 2001 rural as well as urban police departments have armed themselves with everything from military-grade weapons and bomb-detecting robots to drones in anticipation of WMD attacks but directed increasingly against everyday forms of crime and social protest.

To this spectrum of official counterterror agents, we could add the host of new experts in counterterrorism, WMD emergency response, homeland security, and biosecurity that are being produced in universities and colleges, with at least 350 new degree-granting programs in the United States alone.[4] These academic programs join the twelve "centers of excellence" funded by the 2002 Homeland Security Act, which link hundreds of educational institutions via counterterror, training new experts in terrorist risk assessment, microbial hazards, zoonotic disease defense, food safety, catastrophic event response, explosives, immigration, coastal security, transportation, and security visualization sciences.[5] These public counterterror training programs, of course, supplement the vast classified efforts in the Department of Defense and across the U.S. intelligence agencies—creating a new and highly redundant world of public, corporate, military, and classified counterterror expertise.[6] *Expertise*, as we have seen, is a crucial aspect of the *critical infrastructure* concept. Counterterror has produced a new competitive terrain across corporate, academic, military, intelligence, and scientific institutions for threat identification, anticipation, and response. Indeed, few contemporary social institutions or national infrastructures are not in some direct way now embedded within the larger U.S. counterterror state apparatus.[7]

In one sense this is a very American mode of security, a broad mobilization of social institutions to engage an emerging national danger as first happened during the Cold War. What is new is the radical open-endedness of the concept of terror, its claim on a deep future, and—precisely because anticipatory preemption is an imaginative enterprise—its self-colonizing nature. During the Cold War, one could debate what was the right balance of technological systems (missiles, warheads, bombers, submarines) to ensure global nuclear deterrence. In a counterterror state, there can never be enough security, as threat is a potentiality without limit, capable of producing endless new experiences of anticipated menace and danger. Counterterror, therefore, involves linking infrastructures of militarism, technoscience, surveillance, and affect in a constantly emerging fusion of imagination, anticipation, preemption, and violence. It constantly enfolds new domains—policing, border patrols, public health, transportation, computing, and finance—and reorients them toward specific feared outcomes by constituting a field of terror that is ever expanding and affectively overpowering. In this way, counterterror has quickly become the organizing principle for the U.S. security state, a vast set of institutions and experts who seek to address the problem of future violence by trying to engineer the global present.

However, not all forms of violence are recognized by the counterterror state, a reality that also allows and installs new crises. Of the 1.64 million soldiers deployed in Afghanistan and Iraq between 2001 and 2008, for example, over 300,000 now suffer from a brain injury or mental health problem (Tanielian and Jaycox 2008, xxi). This is but one immediate way the War on Terror loads new crises into the future, here in the form of vast medical and social problems, internal terrors of the most immediate kind for former War on Terror military personnel. The invisibility of these kinds of injuries is one key example of the new infrastructure of crisis inadvertently produced by the War on Terror, which includes direct forms of physical injury, the global blowback resulting from covert and acknowledged military operations, and slower violences not recognized at all by the security state and therefore left unaddressed. The vast investment in biosecurity laboratories, biosurveillance systems, and biowarfare research in the last decade, for example, has yet to produce any new antiviral medications or vaccines for use against any of the category four infectious diseases.[8] Meanwhile, the Centers for Disease Control and Prevention (2014) reports that one in six Americans get sick (with 128,000 hospitalizations and 3,000 deaths) each year from food-borne disease, a problem not of bioterrorism but of inadequate industrial regulatory systems. Similarly, the American Society of Civil Engineers reports that the U.S. water supply system is a "failing" infrastructure and a major disease vector, requiring a $60 billion investment to secure (American Society of Civil Engineers 2011)—about the amount invested in the militarized biosecurity infrastructure in the last decade to protect against WMD attack. In this way, the counterterror state enables forms of everyday violence that increase the day-to-day insecurity of American society in vital and immediate ways. Another defining feature of counterterror today involves its strange metrics: the U.S. National Counterterrorism Center compiles a global portrait of terror each year, providing a statistical account of this particular species of violence (constituting a new kind of planetary data bank mirroring the global portraits of emerging disease produced at the Centers for Disease Control and Prevention). In 2010 the center recorded 11,500 terrorist attacks in seventy-two countries and fifteen U.S. civilian casualties, all in Iraq, Afghanistan, or Uganda (U.S. National Counterterrorism Center 2011, 5). However, the center does not recognize U.S. drone attacks (a form of violence invented by the United

States) as terrorism, which raises the crucial unaddressed point that *U.S. defense* can be experienced by others as a form of terror. Terror produces terror, without exception.

It is always possible that in coming years the War on Terror could be scaled back, or that other security priorities could replace the formal language of counterterror (or more likely, that the defense budget will prove to be unsustainable). However, there is good reason to doubt that will happen, as counterterror has been embedded across American institutions. The problem confronting the counterterror apparatus is not that terrorist violence is fictitious—there are agents of destruction that would do great harm if they could. It is, rather, the more difficult question of scale, of how to evaluate degrees of danger and respond collectively without inflating a threat or politically exploiting potential danger. It is precisely within the political arena of calibrating a counterterror response that national security affect becomes so crucial for us to understand. Richard Clarke, the former national coordinator for Security, Infrastructure Protection, and Counter-Terrorism for the United States, has noted that former White House officials such as Dick Cheney, Donald Rumsfeld, and Condoleezza Rice have increasingly in their retirement offered a "trauma defense" to explain their immediate break with legal norms (related to detention, interrogation, and surveillance) after the September 2001 attacks (Clarke 2009). In doing so, he offers a portrait of the psychopolitics of terror inside the White House, noting that because these officials felt "shocked," "surprised," and/or "fearful" after the attacks, they chose to "break all the rules" in the name of national defense and now offer up that overwhelming fear as an alibi for failed and destructive counterterror policies. Similarly, the security state apparatus has, in the last decade, affectively codified the September 2001 attacks (in law, national security policy, expert cultures, and mass media) as a permanent rationale for the U.S. states of emergency and exception. The 2001 attacks now constitute a kind of ongoing injury that can never be healed and that can never be fully addressed despite an ongoing planetary counterterror campaign and wars on multiple fronts. Affect here becomes a kind of infrastructure for the security state, creating the collective intensities of feeling necessary to produce individual commitments, remake ethical standards, and energize modes of personal, and collective, sacrifice.

We could explore this kind of national security affect today in any number of sites. Consider, for example, the hull of the newly minted Navy assault ship the USS *New York*, emblazoned with the motto "strength forged through sacrifice—never forget." The hull was made from 7.5 tons of steel

A Versatile Laboratory
for a Changing World

"General Secretary Gorbachev, if you seek peace, if you seek prosperity for the Soviet Union and Eastern Europe, if you seek liberalization: Come here to this gate. Mr. Gorbachev, open this gate. Mr. Gorbachev — Mr. Gorbachev, tear down this wall!"

Ronald Reagan: Remarks at the Brandenburg Gate, June 12, 1987.

After the Berlin Wall fell in 1989, the Soviet Union breakup in 1991, and the unilateral test bans instituted by the Russian government in 1991 and the United States in 1992, the Cold War ended and a new era began. In the aftermath of September 11, 2001, and continuing with current events worldwide, the United States now contends with terrorists and extremists in a more uneasy balance. The new era, called the War on Terrorism by some and the post-Cold War World by others, is still in its infancy.

Just as during the Cold War, the Nevada Test Site stands ready to insure the safety and security of the American people.

FIGURE 5.1. Section of the Berlin Wall, Atomic Testing Museum, Las Vegas, photograph by the author.

taken from the ruins of the World Trade Center, a formal effort to code all future Navy missions as a counterstrike and response to the September 2001 attacks.[9] This kind of affectively laden material infrastructure is matched by the broader culture of military commemoration that infuses national security culture, and rehearses the events of September 11, 2001, as it once did Pearl Harbor—as an unending injury requiring a permanent mobilization and response (see Dower 2010). I attended one such event in February 2010 at the Atomic Testing Museum in Las Vegas, an institution then celebrating its fifth anniversary by installing a piece of twisted steel from the remains of the World Trade Center. The steel was to be placed in a room alongside a section of the Berlin Wall (see figure 5.1), suturing the end of the Cold War to the start of the War on Terror. As Troy Wade—a former director of nuclear weapons testing at the Nevada Test Site and the prime mover behind the development of the museum—put it in his introductory remarks:

> Artifacts from the World Trade Center are important not only as they serve to remind us of those events, and the heroes of those events, but also as the evidence of the bridge between the activities at the Nevada

FIGURE 5.2. Facing sections of the Berlin Wall and World Trade Center, final room, Atomic Testing Museum, Las Vegas, photograph by the author.

Test Site associated with the Cold War and the current activities of the Nevada Test Site associated with the War on Terrorism.

Bridging the Cold War/War on Terrorism. Here, the nuclear-oriented national security culture of the twentieth century is formally fused with the WMD-centered counterterror culture of the twenty-first century in Nevada via the installation of affectively charged relics that document both external threat and national vulnerability (see figure 5.2). This is a call for security experts in Nevada to see the War on Terror as they once did the Cold War—as an existential battle requiring a total commitment and mobilization, producing a constantly emerging security state.

Since its founding in 1952, the Nevada Test Site has been the center of experimental nuclear weapons science in the United States: 924 nuclear detonations (100 above ground) occurred at the site during the Cold War, and it remains a key site in the Department of Energy's Science-Based Stockpile Stewardship Program to maintain current U.S. nuclear weapons (Masco 2006). The Atomic Testing Museum opened in 2005 to tell the story of the site from the point of view of the multidisciplinary experts who built the bomb during the Cold War and who have maintained the nuclear arsenal since the moratorium on underground nuclear detonations began in 1992.

Created by former test site workers who felt their contribution to the Cold War was being forgotten, the museum was intended to describe the long service of nuclear cold warriors to the nation and to document the unique technical expertise developed in Nevada. Exhibits present a detailed history of U.S. nuclear weapons work from the point of view of experts, positioning U.S. national security as the skilled achievement of science, engineering, expertise, and craft. The museum first addresses the development of nuclear weapons science from World War II through the Cold War, and then devotes its final galleries to contemporary defense work at the test site. Thus, the museum presents visitors with a formal case for the continued national security contributions of nuclear/WMD experts at the test site, merging Cold War nuclear history with the expansive contemporary U.S. national security mission of counterterror.

With the exception of Las Vegas, the state of Nevada is largely U.S. military space and today is devoted to counterterror—a place where soldiers train for deployment in Afghanistan and Iraq, and where the U.S. drone war in Pakistan, Yemen, and Somalia is fought by pilots sitting in air-conditioned command centers who run global surveillance and assassination missions during the day and go home to Las Vegas at night. The test site has evolved into a major research center for the full spectrum of WMD production, detection, and emergency response capabilities—it is a unique expert space where first responders and administrators from state, federal, and military organizations come for training and disaster simulations. It has been a key site in developing the biosecurity apparatus, a place where the Department of Defense has studied how to build a variety of WMDs with commercially available equipment, including anthrax and radiological weapons. U.S. Special Operations forces have trained foreign agents for overseas covert actions at the test site, using the desert landscape to simulate that of the greater Middle East (Hersh 2012). A classified military space once devoted to nuclear weapons development has been converted to the full range of WMD research and response activities—with ongoing projects run by the Departments of Defense, Energy, and Homeland Security, as well as the Federal Bureau of Investigation and the Central Intelligence Agency as part of the War on Terror. To recognize these new priorities, the Nevada Test Site was formally renamed the Nevada National Security Site in late 2010, acknowledging that its primary mission is no longer limited to U.S. nuclear weapons development but involves managing the larger WMD category in all its recognized and emerging forms. The museum's anniversary event thus occurred in the midst of a formal conversion of *the* iconic Cold War nuclear site into the central WMD facility in the U.S. War on Terror.

The dedication of the World Trade Center artifacts was attended by a wide range of elected officials, including the mayor of Las Vegas and members of Congress; a host of Cold War veterans of the Nevada Test Site; representatives from the Department of Energy, U.S. Air Force, and Nevada Fire and Rescue; and the top leadership of the test site (see figure 5.3). The audience was filled with hundreds of security experts with top-secret clearances, who a generation earlier would have been part of the U.S. nuclear complex but who were now defined as homeland security, emergency response, and counterterrorism specialists, representing the galaxy of new state, federal, and private security organizations that have emerged since 2001 to fight terror. Wade opened the event by celebrating the accomplishments of the museum.[10] After noting the Cold War nuclear history presented in the museum, he focused on the fact that the Nevada Test Site is currently the "premier facility in the world" for WMD response, with "a thousand workers capable of responding in a moment's notice" to events anywhere in the world. The following speakers began by celebrating the museum but turned quickly to affective politics of September 11, 2001, rehearsing where they had been that day as well as the scale of personal loss.

Senator John Ensign (R-Nevada) took the opportunity to defend the Bush administration's use of water boarding and indefinite detention at Guantanamo Bay, Cuba:

Almost all Americans know that you are no longer allowed to bring liquids onto planes and if they do, they have to keep them a certain size and put them in a plastic bag. But the sad truth is how many Americans actually remember what caused this? Back in 2006, a group of British Muslims attempted to blow up eighteen transatlantic airliners using liquid explosives. Can you imagine eighteen jumbo jets going down one after another over the Atlantic? This is the type of highly motivated and highly deranged enemy we are still at war with. You are probably asking yourself: how did we discover this plot and why it never came to fruition? The simple answer is this: the capture and interrogation of Khalid Sheikh Mohammed, "KSM," the mastermind of 9/11. The capture of the mastermind of the attacks changed the landscape of the battlefield against Al Qaeda. While being interrogated by the Central Intelligence Agency, because of the enhanced interrogation techniques that were used, KSM eventually began talking

FIGURE 5.3. Flier for the dedication of the steel girder section from the World Trade Center, Atomic Testing Museum, Las Vegas.

about Al Qaeda's operations—its financial structure, its training camps, cell phone numbers, terror cell locations, and names of high-level operatives. It is because of the information that he and other senior Al Qaeda members gave to our intelligence agencies that countless American lives have been saved since 9/11. We have managed to keep our country safe by not allowing Al Qaeda to go on the offensive.

Can you imagine? Ensign conjures up a national public already forgetting the events of September 11, 2001, making them less attentive to and appreciative of the work of counterterror experts. He imagines an unnamed citizen who expects that a world without events is a naturally occurring condition, not the work of dedicated counterterror specialists who preempt dangerous outcomes at great personal risk. After his depiction of a counterterror state that successfully anticipates and preempts terrorist actions through previously illegal activities (such as water boarding, global kidnapping, and detention without charge) he offered a "never before told" story about an unnamed woman killed on the plane that hit the Pentagon. Her grieving and distraught husband, Ensign reports, received a phone call months later when her purse was found in the wreckage of the Pentagon. The purse contained a final note to him declaring her love, hastily written in the terrifying final moments of the flight. Here terror is both rendered sentimental and the basis for a new identity, as Ensign declared the pieces of the World Trade Center to be installed in the museum were nothing less than "the love letters of those Americans who were unable to write." American national identity is remade under the sign of permanent loss, requiring an unrestricted field for counterterror and an unending response.[11]

A Pentagon employee and two firemen from New York involved in recovery efforts after the attack on the World Trade Center then took the stage and performed the "9/11" attacks, presenting firsthand testimony and video clips, offering a minute-by-minute account of the planes hitting the building as well as the trauma of the event for those in the building and the emergency responders. Their presentations explored the viciousness of the attack, the loss of loved ones, the sacrifice of rescue workers, and the difficulty of recovering bodies from the rubble of the Pentagon and the World Trade Center. Amid the grisly details of body parts and flames and twisted steel and inexplicable loss, this two-hour performance of ur-violence was punctuated by calls to patriotic national culture—invitations to "love the flag" and to become a "warrior for freedom," but also to "strike back" against terror. The room became affectively charged, with the intensities of grief,

FIGURE 5.4. World Trade Center, September 11, 2001, exhibit, Atomic Testing Museum, Las Vegas, photograph by the author.

and rage, and fear, linking performers and audience in an amplifying sense of outrage. At one point, the Pentagon employee stopped to ask the crowd directly, "Are we going to let them get away with it?" (without specifying who "they" are). His question produced a negative roar from the assembled crowd of WMD and counterterror experts. At another moment, a New York fireman evoked the atomic bombing of Hiroshima to explain the scope of the World Trade Center trauma, playing on the language of Ground Zero used in New York and connecting the Peace Park at Hiroshima with the commemorative museum planned for New York (see Dower 2010; Kaplan 2003). A nonsensical comparison of radically different scales and technologies of violence, this was also a highly complicated moment for an audience of former nuclear, now WMD, specialists, confronting an unanticipated inversion in the image and source of (nuclear) terror. Asked to affectively identify themselves as nuclear victims (from a U.S. nuclear weapon), the multigenerational politics of terror were momentarily fused for the audience, constituting nuclear fear (decontextualized from history and fact) as a foundational American value and experience. The logic of the first responder as the person who heads into a crisis to help others was constituted as a linking motivation across military, intelligence, special forces, fire, and WMD experts, creating a collective image of responsibility and sacrifice for the national good in the face of ongoing terror (see figure 5.4). The trauma

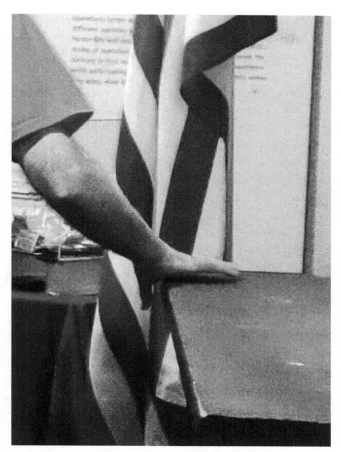

FIGURE 5.5. A visitor touching the World Trade Center fragment at the Atomic Testing Museum, Las Vegas, photograph by the author.

of the 2001 suicide-hijacker attacks was, in other words, actively cultivated as a form of permanent injury requiring a permanent mobilization, an affective space available to anyone able to imaginatively inhabit the World Trade Center or the Pentagon on a spectacularly violent day in 2001. Here are the figurations of a new expert emotional universe, one consolidated in a few affectively charged concepts—9/11, *terror*, WMDs—that are infinitely flexible in content, inexhaustible as resources, and always available, if highly overdetermined, calls to excitement.

The museum commemoration reveals the power of national security affect to connect people through feelings of anger and loss and to channel that energy into both personal and professional life. However, at no point in the proceedings was the invasion of Iraq in 2003 over nonexistent WMDs mentioned, or the foundational changes in U.S. civil liberties, or the larger actions of the counterterror state since 2001. Counterterror was constituted as a horizon not yet in sight, a movement waiting to happen rather than the ongoing revolution I have described in this book. It was *as if* the War on Terror had not yet begun, rather than already being the longest war in U.S. history. Museum personnel announced to applause that the section of the World Trade Center being dedicated would be the only piece in the country that the public would be able to touch, installed as an affectively charged relic and a permanent invitation for all to share in the national security affect informing the new world of WMDs and counterterror (see figure 5.5). In this universe of emerging dangers and capacities, affects and infrastructures, American identity is continually reconstituted through national trauma, generating desires for counterterror expertise, as well as for heroism, sacrifice, and revenge. But the theater of operations constituting everyday life is always much larger than the counterterror state can account for, raising vital questions about what kind of world is actually being built through the daily acts—the fantasies, anticipations, preemptions, and misrecognitions—of declaring a war on terror.

ACKNOWLEDGMENTS

The research and writing of this book was supported by a Charles A. Rys-kamp Research Fellowship from the American Council of Learned Society, a Grant for Research and Writing from the John D. and Catherine T. Mac-Arthur Foundation, and a National Endowment for the Humanities, Resi-dent Research Fellowship at the School for Advanced Research. Additional funding was provided by the Adolph and Marion Lichtstern Fund in the Department of Anthropology, and a Social Sciences Divisional Research Grant, from the University of Chicago. I am very grateful to each of these organizations for their support.

Earlier versions of chapter 2 appeared in *Cultural Anthropology*, of chap-ter 3 in *Social Studies of Science*, and chapter 4 in *Public Culture*. A section of chapter 5 appeared in *Bioinsecurity and Vulnerability*, edited by Leslie Sharp and Nancy Chen (Santa Fe: School of Advanced Research Press). My thanks to each of these venues, and their editors, for supporting this project both intellectually and in print.

I developed aspects of this book in a wide range of conference and lec-ture presentations over the past years. I would like to thank all the depart-ments, programs, workshops, and conferences that have intellectually en-gaged this work. For their critical engagements, invitations, and collegiality I am very grateful to: Nadia Abu El-Haj, Hussein Agrama, Hamdi Attia, Deborah Battaglia, Kennette Benedict, Lauren Berlant, Alex Blanchette, Yarimar Bonilla, John Borneman, Dominic Boyer, Donald Brennis, Elspeth Brown, Summerson Carr, Cathryn Carson, Steve Caton, Jessicca Cattelino, Nancy Chen, Nusrat Chowdhury, Tim Choy, Patricia Clough, John Coma-roff, Elizabeth Davis, Lynn Eden, Paul Edwards, Steven Epstein, James

Fabion, Catherine Fennell, James Ferguson, Kim Fortun, Peter Galison, Mike Fortun, Dilip Parameshwar Gaonkar, William Garriott, Deborah Gewertz, Faye Ginsburg, Bruce Grant, Hugh Gusterson, Susan Harding, Gabrielle Hecht, Stephen Helmreich, Stephen Hilgartner, Corrine Kratz, Marcel La Flamme, Premesh Lalu, Michael Lynch, Emily Martin, William Mazzarella, Marcos Mendoza, Kelly Moore, Rosalind Morris, Paul Nadasday, David Nugent, Omiko Ohnuke Tierney, Trevor Paglen, Nancy Peluso, Justin Richland, Lisa Rofel, Dan Rosenberg, Nathan Sayre, David Serlin, Lesley Sharp, Adam Smith, Amy Stambach, Ann Stoler, Anna Tsing, Andrew Mathews Michael Watts, Marina Welker, Kath Weston, Andrew Willford, Jessica Wineger, Alexei Yurchak, Caitlin Zaloom, and Charles Zerner.

I am especially indebted to Beth Povinelli, Danilyn Rutherford, and Jean Comaroff for their support and critical engagement over the life of this project. I would also like to thank Jim Siegel for conversations over the years that have informed this book.

Special thanks to Ken Wissoker and his team at Duke University Press for editorial support and care.

For readings, camaraderie, and the life-changing examples of their own critical work I am grateful to: Joe Dumit, Cori Hayden, Lochlann Jain, Jake Kosek, Jonathan Metzl, Michelle Murphy, Diane Nelson, Jackie Orr, Elizabeth Roberts, and Miriam Ticktin.

I would like to thank my colleagues at the University of Chicago, as well as students that have worked with me on issues of technoscience, insecurity, and national culture in seminars and workshops.

My thanks to family and friends in Chicago, Seattle, Tucson, Fort Bragg, San Francisco, Toluca, and New York for their love and support.

The very last words are, of course, for Shawn Smith, who has been central to this project from the very first one. I am deeply grateful for her critical engagement and generosity over the many years of this project.

NOTES

INTRODUCTION. THE "NEW" NORMAL

1. For example, New Orleans in 2005 and the New York City area in 2012 were both severely damaged by storm surges; after years of financial crisis, Detroit filed for bankruptcy in 2013; and in the summer of 2012, half of all counties in the continental United States (over 1,521 entities) were federally declared disaster areas due to the wide-ranging effects of drought (Suhr 2012).

2. The reclassification project was first discovered by the historian Matthew Aid (2006), who provides an extensive review of the case and litigation as well as key documents, including some of those discussed here.

3. At the height of the first Red Scare in the aftermath of World War I, Warren Harding (1921) argued for a "return to normalcy," creating a script that has been used to create a new standard of everyday expectation coterminous with an expansion of the security state.

4. For detailed historical assessments of the effects of Pearl Harbor on American political thought as well as the production of the security state apparatus, see Dower 2010; Gaddis 2004; Rudgers 2000; R. Wohlstetter 1962.

5. President Truman used this phrase on July 26, 1945, ten days after the first nuclear bomb was detonated secretly in New Mexico, in his Potsdam Declaration demanding Japanese surrender. Secretary of Defense Rumsfeld and military planners of the Iraq invasion used the phrase "shock and awe" repeatedly to describe their plan of attack on Iraq in 2003, installing a crypto-nuclear referent to the campaign and promising a new kind of war spectacle for mass media. On the military theory of "shock and awe" and its relationship to the atomic bombings of Hiroshima and Nagasaki, see Ullman and Wade 2006. See also Dower 2010 for an extensive discussion of the relationship of Pearl Harbor and Hiroshima to post-2001 militarism; and Freedman and Dockrill 2004, 73.

6. For a detailed history of the global antinuclear movement, see Wittner 1993, 1997, and 2003; on the concept of a counterpublic, see Warner 2002.

7. For an eyewitness account of the search for Iraqi WMDs as well as an insider assessment of the politics behind the U.S. invasion, see Duelfer 2009.

8. This logic is mirrored in the detainee policies adopted in secret after 2001, which redefined *torture* to focus on the *intent* of the interrogator rather than the act of using violence on a prisoner. It also informs the adoption of "Stand Your Ground" laws in the United States, which allow citizens to defend themselves with deadly force if they *feel* threatened.

9. In 2011 the Homeland Security Advisory System was replaced by the two-tiered National Terrorist Warning System, which dispensed with the color code in favor of just two conditions of threat: "imminent" and "elevated" (see U.S. Department of Homeland Security n.d.b).

10. The United States had 73 nuclear weapons for each Soviet nuclear weapon in 1950, 15 to 1 in 1955, and 12 to 1 in 1960, with the U.S. arsenal growing from 369 to 20,434 devices during that decade. The Soviet Union did not reach numerical parity with the United States in nuclear weapons until the late 1970s. For a detailed historical chart of global stockpiles of nuclear weapons, see Natural Resources Defense Council n.d.

11. Similarly, school shootings or attacks on abortion clinics in the United States are not official acts of terror unless they are motivated by specific political or religious logics that connect them to the currently idealized external enemy, radicalized Islam.

12. For history and analysis of U.S. military installations around the world, see Vine 2009; Lutz 2002 and 2009; C. Johnson 2000; for an assessment of the hidden costs of this global infrastructure of American power, see Costsofwar.org 2013.

13. As John Dower puts it, commenting on the expectation among many security professionals in the 1990s that a Pearl Harbor–like attack would enable a renewal of the military state, "like the cult of secrecy and the labyrinth of bureaucratic proliferation, the Pearl-Harbor-as-godsend mindset can become a trap. This, in part, helps explain the failure of the Bush administration's war on terror, which amounted to a mixture of acute paranoia on the one hand and, on the other hand, confidence that possessing the most sophisticated weapons of mass destruction imaginable would ensure success in deterring or defeating all enemies, real or imagined" (2010, 147). See also Rafael 2009; Weber 2004, 329; Sedgwick 2003, 131.

14. For theorizations of nuclear fetishism, see Hecht 2012; Masco 2006; Abraham 1998.

15. For a discussion of terrorism as a cultural concept and political form, see Asad 2007, 28; Zulaika and Douglass 1996. For an important discussion of nuclear terrorism, see Levi 2007.

16. For example, Seth Carus documents over fifty different definitions of a "weapon of mass destruction" used by U.S. governmental or international organizations (2006, 6). He also found that *WMD* was used on average once a year in the *New York Times* during the Cold War but over a thousand times in 2003 alone (3).

17. For an important theorization of nuclearity as a mobile categorization, one that constitutes a political and technical field rather than a discrete object, see Hecht

2012. WMD is a similarly flexible concept today—one that various technologies, techniques, and modes of attack slip into and out of depending on context and political intent.

1. "SURVIVAL IS YOUR BUSINESS"

1. The United States conducted 1,054 nuclear detonations (in addition to the bombings Hiroshima and Nagasaki) between 1945 and 1992, with 928 explosions conducted at the Nevada Test Site. On the global health effects of this program, see Masco 2006; Makhijani and Schwartz 1998; Advisory Committee on Human Radiation Experiments 1996; Makhijani, Hu, and Yih 1995; R. Miller 1986.

2. For damage assessments of a potential Soviet nuclear strike on the United States, see Keeney 2002; Office of Technology Assessment 1979.

3. My understanding of photographic afterimages has been developed in conversation with Shawn Michelle Smith (see Smith 1999).

4. For a detailed discussion of Benjamin's approach to the politics of visual culture, see Buck-Morss 1991; see also her important study of U.S. and Soviet art before the Cold War, 2000.

5. On the constitution of the Cold War state, see Friedberg 2000; S. Schwartz 1998; Leslie 1993; Gaddis 1982.

6. For NSC 68 as well as a detailed commentary on it, see Ernest May 1993. For a critical analysis of the nation security context of the early Cold War, see Brands 1989; and for a review of the concept of containment, see Gaddis 1982.

7. For historical and cultural analyses of the U.S. civil defense programs during the Cold War, see Garrison 2006; Krugler 2006; George 2003; Scheiback 2003; T. Davis 2002; Grossman 2001; McEnaney 2000; Oakes 1994.

8. The panel imagined a Soviet attack in 1959 in which ninety major cities were destroyed and fifty million people were killed. It concluded: "In the event of a massive nuclear attack on the United States, of the proportions assumed above, without drastically improved preparation of the people, support of the National Government and of the war effort would be in jeopardy, and national disintegration might well result" (Panel on the Human Effects of Nuclear Weapons Development 1956, 9). The panel then argued that the problem was how to incorporate the possibility of a Soviet sneak attack into the "feelings" of citizens (9) allowing atomic warfare to be naturalized as part of the everyday world (see Vandercook 1986). One could productively compare these early Cold War studies to recent counterterror studies of nuclear attack. For example, Charles Meade and Roger Molander (2006) modeled the effects of a ten-kiloton nuclear explosion in Los Angeles and concluded that the effects of the blast would overwhelm all services and cost the U.S. economy $1 trillion.

9. Val Peterson described the media campaign for atomic civil defense as "the greatest mass educational effort" in U.S. history (quoted in Garrison 2006, 36). In this regard, the civil defense program was also a laboratory for exploring how to mobilize and control a mass society.

10. This statement is based on a reading of two decades of FCDA annual reports; see, for example, Federal Civil Defense Administration 1956.
11. See Weller 2006; Braw 1997. See also *White Light, Black Rain* (2006), an important documentary that examines the history and status of film footage from the atomic bombings in Japan.
12. Grossman (2001, 47) has underscored how representatives of government, media, and industry explicitly sought to harmonize their civil defense messages, providing a reinforcing series of messages across the media spectrum. This worked both to reinforce the civil defense project and to reduce the opportunities for critique. See also Keever 2004; Scheiback 2003; Rojecki 1999.
13. For a history of the antinuclear movement, see Rojecki 1999; Katz 1986. See also Wittner 1993, 1997, and 2003.
14. Garrison (2006) argues that the civil defense programs of the Cold War should be judged a failure because no nationwide system of shelters was ever built. I would argue that the project of civil defense was building not a new urban infrastructure but a new emotional one. In this regard, the project was much more successful, installing a set of ideas and images about nuclear warfare that maintained public support for the nuclear state until the end of the Cold War and provided a set of ideological resources that President George W. Bush's administration relied on to initiate its War on Terror.
15. See Garrison (2006, 94–96) on the mother's movement against civil defense; McEnaney 2000 for an important analysis of the militarization of the home and gender roles; Elaine May 1990 on the domestic version of containment; Scheiback 2003 on the effects of civil defense on youth culture. For a discussion of gender in the language of Cold War defense intellectuals, see Cohn 1987. For a remarkable study of panic in Cold War psychology and nation building, see Orr 2006.
16. The J.C. Penney Company of Las Vegas, Nevada, created a variety of brochures to accompany its display of clothing using this language; for examples, see the civil defense exhibits at the Atomic Testing Museum in Las Vegas that recreate aspects of Operation Cue.
17. This project to test the cognitive effects on citizens of witnessing an exploding atomic bomb was a small part of a larger military effort, which involved thousands of troops at the Nevada Test Site. In a series of aboveground tests, soldiers were involved in atomic warfare exercises. They were also tested for the cognitive and psychological effects of being exposed to the visual image of the blast. In some cases, this involved simple cognitive drills administered minutes after the explosion or timing the soldiers in basic military activities, like dismantling and reassembling a rifle. Thus, across a wide spectrum of public and military projects, the national security state was testing the limits of participation and conditioning bodies, psyches, and emotions to the atomic bomb.
18. On the politics related to atmospheric fallout during aboveground nuclear testing, see Masco 2006; Wang 1999; Makhijani and Schwartz 1998; Hewlett and Holl 1989; R. Miller 1986; Kraus, Mehling, and El-Assal 1963; Bentz et al. 1957.

19. One of the most powerful voices in the renewed antinuclear movement of the 1980s was that of Physicians for Social Responsibility (PSR), which devoted its energies to publicizing the effects on health of nuclear war by offering detailed descriptions of probable attacks on American cities. For its public health campaign against nuclear war, PSR won the Nobel Peace Prize. Remarkably, PSR repurposed the U.S. civil defense campaign materials of the 1950s but provided more detailed figures about radiation injuries and casualties to mobilize resistance to the renewed nuclear project of the Reagan administration (see Forrow and Sidel 1998).

20. In response to the Nuclear Freeze Campaign, the Reagan administration pursued a new emotional management strategy in the form of the Strategic Defense Initiative (SDI), which promised an end to the arms race by installing a system of space-based lasers to shoot down ICBMs (see FitzGerald 2000). Though Reagan offered SDI to the public as a near-term technological fix to the nuclear standoff with the Soviet Union—a way out of the nuclear danger—it was never a realistic proposal. Over twenty-five years and $100 billion later, it has yet to hit a real-world target, but it has served the emotional needs of its constituency very well—allowing an aggressive pursuit of nuclear weapons technology and the militarization of space while also praising the ultimate goal of disarmament. *The Day After*, the Nuclear Freeze Campaign, and SDI all were, in various ways, emotional management campaigns that drew on the images of nuclear destruction produced during the aboveground testing regime to mobilize a response to the nuclear crisis of the 1980s. Rather than moving past Operation Cue, each of these projects redeployed the strategies of the early Cold War state to enable their political projects, whether they were activists working for disarmament or the state working to maintain support for the Cold War arms race.

21. The destruction of cities is a recurring theme in the nuclear cinema of Japan but is not mobilized as part of a militarized nation-building campaign as it is in the United States (see Broderick 1996). I would also note that there is a fundamental difference between disaster movies and nuclear cinema in the United States. The disaster movie uses destruction as a means of creating drama at the individual level, while nuclear cinema always nationalizes its content via a friend-enemy configuration. Thus, a disaster movie has heroic individuals, but the ultimate project of nuclear cinema is to establish and mobilize a national community through mass violence. For critical analyses of nuclear cinema, see Evans 1998; Sontag 1966. See also Page 2008 (for a history of New York's imaginative destruction); Taylor 1997 (on nuclear photography); Virilio 1989 (on war and perception).

22. On the American politics of regeneration through violence, see Slotkin 1996, as well as Rogin 1987 and 1998.

23. *Armageddon*, for example, was supported by the National Aeronautics and Space Administration as well as the Department of Defense, which allowed producer Jerry Bruckheimer and director Michael Bay to film on location in military installations in exchange for script changes that favored the armed services. For a discussion of the changes to the film's script made in exchange for support from the Pentagon, see Robb 2004 (94–95). For a study of Cold War cinema, see Rogin 1987;

see also his detailed reading (1998) of the militarized gender and race politics in the 1996 film *Independence Day*.

24. The Bush doctrine of preemptive war (see U.S. White House 2002a) formally ended the Cold War doctrines of containment and deterrence that had defined U.S. foreign policy since the 1950s (see Gaddis 1982).

25. In August 2006, after British authorities broke up a terrorist plot to smuggle explosive chemicals onto an airplane, the Department of Homeland Security raised the threat level to red, the highest level, and the Transportation Security Administration banned fluids from domestic U.S. flights for a period before setting new limits on carry-on items. The British plot was in its very early phases and not a viable threat to passenger safety, yet the U.S. response was total (see U.S. Department of Homeland Security 2006). This emergency response to a not-yet-viable threat does not make sense as a security strategy, but it is an excellent illustration of the official mobilization of affect, as well as the demand for public docility that supports the War on Terror. For an expert security analysis of British and American reactions to the liquid explosive plot, see N. Ahmed 2006. See also Schneier 2007.

26. In the fall of 2006, complying with directives from the Bush administration, the Los Alamos National Laboratory and Lawrence Livermore National Laboratory submitted to the Department of Energy their first new designs for nuclear weapons since the end of the Cold War. For an overview of new nuclear policy at the start of the War on Terror, see U.S. Department of Defense 2003. The Department of Energy has produced a detailed plan to rebuild the entire U.S. nuclear production complex, including designing new warheads and bombs, over the next twenty-five years (U.S. Department of Energy 2013).

2. BAD WEATHER

1. The nuclear sublime involves a cognitive confrontation with the power of a nuclear detonation. The result is a flooding of the senses with overwhelming information, which is followed by an effort to restore cognitive control through a naming of the thing. Thus, the nuclear sublime does not end in comprehension but rather in an intellectual compensation for the inability of the mind to fully comprehend the power of the exploding bomb (see Masco 2006).

2. For a detailed description of Shot Encore and the variety of experiments and personnel involved in the test, see U.S. Defense Nuclear Agency 1982; see also U.S. Department of Defense 1953.

3. From 1945 to 1992, in addition to the bombs at Hiroshima and Nagasaki the United States detonated 1,054 nuclear devices, the vast majority of them at the Nevada Test Site. See Masco 2006; Makhijani and Schwartz 1998; Advisory Committee on Human Radiation Experiments 1996; Makhijani, Hu, and Yih 1995.

4. See Kalckar 1958 for a scientific call to collect baby teeth to study radiation effects from atomic testing; see Egan 2007 for an assessment of Barry Commoner's pioneering work to study the effects of atmospheric fallout on children.

5. For example, see Hammond and Maugh 1974; Kroening 1965; Hare 1962; Bentz et al. 1957; Machta and Harris 1955. These fears were powerfully expressed in Nevil

Shute's 1957 novel *On the Beach*, in which postnuclear survivors gather in Australia to await the arrival of a deadly radioactive cloud (see also Stanley Kramer's award-winning 1959 film version).

6. For discussions of the foundational logics of the Cold War sciences, see Doel 2003; Edwards 1996; C. Miller and Edwards 2001; and also Leslie 1993. For a history of the discovery of global warming, see Weart 2003, and for a detailed study of the production of climate models see Edwards 2010.

7. See Harper 2003. Peter Sloterdijk has noted the essential linkage between modern war and the environment: "The true discovery of the environment was by gas warfare in the trenches of World War I. This type of war no longer kills by direct fire but by destroying the environment the enemy needs to survive. The art of killing with the environment is one of the big ideas of modern civilization. It contains the nucleus of contemporary terror: to attack not the isolated body of the adversary, but the body in its 'Umwelt'" (2005, 225; see also Sloterdijk 2009). From this perspective, what is unique about the radioactive fallout studies of the 1950s is the collective recognition of the global scope of the new weapon, the transformation of environmental injury into an experimental lens, and the consideration of its future-oriented genetic effects. See also Serres 2005 for an assessment of the relationship between war and nature in light of climate change.

8. The early Cold War sciences thus produced the first comprehensive efforts to build planetary data sets, engendering what Paul Edwards has called "global knowledge infrastructure" at the level of earth sciences information (2010, 8).

9. For a history of the widely circulated Apollo earthrise photograph (available at http://www.nasa.gov/images/content/54428main_MM_image_feature_102_jwlarge.jpg) and of the prior images produced by satellites, see Poole 2008. For detailed analyses of efforts to conceptualize the planet as a whole, as well as the important cognitive shift produced by the move from drawing earth to directly photographing it, see Cosgrove 2001; Jasanoff 2001. For the first color portrait of the global biosphere, see the NASA project page at http://grin.hq.nasa.gov/ABSTRACTS/GPN-2003-00027.html (accessed March 18, 2014).

10. For example, in addition to being a nuclear weapons design laboratory, Lawrence Livermore National Laboratory also maintains a real-time global system for monitoring atmospheric releases of radioactive and other hazardous materials at the National Atmospheric Release Advisory Center (see Sullivan et al. 1993). In 2002 scientists at Lawrence Livermore completed the first global climate simulation with a resolution of thirty miles; this was accomplished on the same supercomputers used to maintain the U.S. nuclear stockpile.

11. See Natural Resources Defense Council n.d.; in 2006 the United States had an arsenal of about 10,000 nuclear weapons, while Russia had close to 9,000.

12. See Turco et al. 1990; C. Sagan 1983–84. For assessments of the nuclear winter debate and the media response to it, see Badash 2001; Demeritt 2001; Rubin and Cummings 1989.

13. For critiques of nuclear winter studies, see Rueter and Kalil 1991; Thompson and Schneider 1986. For an assessment of the effects on the climate of smoke from oil

fires in Kuwait in 1991, see Hobbs and Radke 1992. For a detailed assessment of fire in nuclear warfare and a discussion of the politicization of U.S. nuclear warfare models, see Eden 2004 (see also Glasstone and Dolan 1977). Robock et al. 2007 and Toon et al. 2007 present updated nuclear winter studies focusing on regional conflict; each concludes that a hundred 13-kiloton bombs (the size used on Hiroshima) dropped on cities could produce climatic change. For an assessment of polar winter, the resulting ecosystem chaos that might be produced by either nuclear winter or global warming, see Cockell and Stokes 1999.

14. The SCOPE report was published in two volumes as *Environmental Consequences of Nuclear War* (Pittock, Harwell, and Hutchinson 1986). See also National Research Council 1985; J. Peterson 1983. For a study of the likely psychological effects of a nuclear winter on human populations, see Grinspoon 1986.

15. A recent report prepared by a group of retired generals and admirals, chaired by General Gordon R. Sullivan, identifies climate change as a "threat multiplier for instability in some of the most volatile regions of the world" and calls for a restructuring of military strategy, acquisitions, and logistics to be prepared to respond to the effects of climate change (CNA Corporation 2007, 6). Following Schwartz and Randall, the retired generals and admirals assume a primarily militarized response to climate change (including relocating military bases around the world that are vulnerable to rising sea levels), but they do also call for the United States to take a leadership role in the effort to reduce greenhouse gases around the world.

16. According to a recent Department of Defense report on energy security, in fiscal year 2005 "the United States consumed about 20 million barrels per day. Although the entire federal government consumed a mere 1.9 percent of the total U.S. demand, [the Department of Defense], the largest government user of oil in the world, consumed more than 90 percent of all the government's petroleum (liquid fuel) use" (Crowley et al. 2007, section 2, page 4). For an analysis of the geostrategic effects of the military oil consumption, see Klare 2007. For an analysis of U.S. global military bases, see C. Johnson 2006, 139.

17. In the first decade of counterterror, Bush administration statements on climate change have frequently worked not to mobilize a response to the problem but to control its image, to raise ambiguities about the scientific record, and challenge calls for immediate global control of greenhouse gases. For an illustration of the edits to the *Strategic Plan for the U.S. Climate Change Science Program*, see Grimaldi and Trescott 2007; "An Editor in the White House" 2005. For the most detailed accounts of the politicizing of climate change research by the Bush administration, see Donaghy et al. 2007; Maassarani 2007. A report by the U.S. House of Representatives Committee on Oversight and Government Reform (2007) on political interference with climate change science concludes there was a systematic effort by the Bush administration to limit the discussion of climate change by censoring the testimony of federal scientists and government officials, editing scientific and governmental reports on climate change, and resisting efforts to enforce environmental laws (see also Dickinson 2007).

18. See Macilwain and Brumfiel 2006; Thacker 2006; Revkin 2005. See also Eilperin 2008a.

19. For assessments of media coverage of climate change in the United States, see Antilla 2005; Demeritt 2001. For a study of the experts behind such environmental skepticism, see Jacques, Dunlap, and Freeman 2008.

20. See Eilperin 2006b. The Bush administration changed the regulatory process for the Endangered Species Act, adding dramatically fewer species to the list than was the case in any other administration in the thirty-five years since the act became law (Eilperin 2008b).

21. On frog extinctions, see Blaustein and Dobson 2006. On coral reefs, see Buddemeier, Kleypas, and Aronson 2004. On polar bears, see Roach 2006.

22. See National Center for Atmospheric Research 2006. See also Revkin 2006a. For a summary of the unprecedented weather in 2007, see Borenstein 2007.

23. The U.S. failure to consider climate a security state matter, despite its enormous investment in the military state, will be extraordinarily costly in the decades to come. From 2002 to 2007 the United States spent roughly $3.5 trillion on the military while allocating $37 billion to climate stabilization, a 97:1 ratio (see Pemberton 2008, 5).

24. Nina Russell, a clergywoman in Louisiana, completed this circuit of nuclear fantasy, telling the Baton Rouge *Advocate* a year after the storm: "Having just returned from hometown of Gulfport, Miss., I found out that Katrina did not do the damage. What really happened was that the Enola Gay went through a space warp and a 60-year time warp. Instead of dropping the bomb on Hiroshima, it dropped the bomb on Gulfport. The bomb was dropped in August 1945. Katrina happened in August 2005. And if you saw the destruction—you would believe that story!" See an article in the *Advocate* by Anders (2006). The *Advocate* also ran a headline "Katrina Deals Miss. an Atomic Blow" on August 31, 2005.

25. In 2008, Al Gore called on the U.S. to produce "100 percent zero carbon electricity in 10 years," explicitly evoking John F. Kennedy's challenge to land a man on the moon within a decade, and linking climate change to national security (Gore 2008). However, the costs of the Manhattan Project ($21 billion), or the Apollo Program ($96 billion), are likely to pale in comparison to the scale of investment needed to both understand and manage the global climate, as well as create a renewable energy regime; see Stine 2009.

3. SENSITIVE BUT UNCLASSIFIED

1. In 1992 the United States voluntarily began a moratorium on underground nuclear testing and stopped new nuclear weapons design work at the U.S. national laboratories. The Bush administration pulled out of the Antiballistic Missile Treaty in 2002 and then focused on expanding the role of U.S. nuclear weapons in its security policy, including new targets and new weapons systems. In fall 2006 the Lawrence Livermore and Los Alamos National Laboratories submitted their first new design for a nuclear weapon since the 1980s (see Medalia 2007, 17).

2. See U.S. Department of Energy 2011 and 2013 for detailed plans for building a twenty-first-century nuclear complex; see Wolfsthal, Lewis, and Quint 2014 for an assessment of the astronomical cost of the proposal to rejuvenate the nuclear production complex, arsenal, and delivery systems over the coming decades.

3. See, for example, "Closing the Circle on the Splitting of the Atom," Office of Environmental Management, http://www.energy.gov/em/downloads/closing-circle-splitting-atom (accessed March 18, 2014).

4. A version of the dismantled B61 appeared on the front page of the *Washington Post* in September 2012 as part of a series of articles by Dana Priest on the "aging and unreliable" U.S. nuclear arsenal (Priest 2012). Thus, the photograph was once again deployed, as it was in the immediate post–Cold War period, to argue for a massive new investment in the nuclear weapons complex.

5. See Melley 2012 for a brilliant analysis of the use of fiction by the national security state and the terms of a "covert sphere" of American life.

6. See S. Schwartz 1998 for a highly detailed assessment of the costs of the U.S. nuclear project in the twentieth century. A foundational relationship between military, governmental, industrial, and academic institutions was established through nuclear weapon science in the 1940s, creating a wide-ranging consensus in support of a U.S. security state that was founded on nuclear threat, anticommunism, and state secrecy. Indeed, the cultural, institutional, and environmental effects of the bomb have been installed very deeply in American society precisely because they are to a large degree constitutive of it after 1945 (Masco 2006; see also Priest and Arkin 2011; Wills 2010).

7. For a detailed chronology and assessment of post-9/11 changes in government secrecy and its impact on media coverage, see Reporters Committee for Freedom of the Press 2005; see also Stone 2006; Olmsted 1996. An invaluable resource is Steven Aftergood's blog, *Secrecy News* (www.fas.org/blog/secrecy). See also *Secrecy* (2008), a film by Peter Galison and Robb Moss.

8. President Bush signed Executive Order 13292 in 2003—which permitted classification of "scientific, technological, or economic matter related to the national security, which includes defense against transnational terrorism" (Bush 2003). For reviews of secrecy policy in the Bush administration, see Knezo 2003 and the detailed report prepared by Representative Henry Waxman (U.S. House of Representatives, Committee on Government Reform, Minority Staff Special Investigations Division 2004).

9. For an assessment of the Obama administration's record on secrecy and openness, see Aftergood 2013.

10. Homeland Security Act of 2002, Pub. L. 107-296, 116 Stat. 2135 (2002), sec. 896.

11. American Civil Liberties Union et al. v. Department of Defense et al., U.S. District Court for Southern District of New York, 04 Civ. 4151 (AKH), 2005. See also M. Benjamin 2006; A. Roberts 2006, 51–54; Hersh 2004.

12. For a detailed discussion and analysis of the reclassification program in the National Archives and Records Administration, see Aid 2006.

13. See ACLU v. CIA, No. 11-5320, 2013 WL 1003688 (D.C. Cir. 2013), Document #1377008, June 4, 2012, 6.

14. 345 U.S. 1 (1953). For a detailed history of the case, as well as an analysis of the state secrets privilege in the United States, see Fisher 2006.

15. One exception is the Wikipedia project, which uses a technology that allows anybody to edit web-based entries, creating a new kind of resource drawn from collective engagements. This technology's advantage is in valuing collective knowledge over compartmentalized knowledge. The power of the wiki concept has been recognized by the CIA, which has constructed its own wiki-project (see "Intellipedia" n.d.). The CIA's "Intellipedia" is secret (because it is not accessible to the public) but not compartmentalized, since anyone on the CIA network can upload data or correct existing entries. A more radical use of the wiki technology is the Wikileaks project (see https://wikileaks.org), which was founded in 2006 to offer "an uncensorable Wikipedia for untraceable mass document leaking and analysis. Our primary interests are oppressive regimes in Asia, the former Soviet bloc, Sub-Saharan Africa and the Middle East, but we also expect to be of assistance to those in the West who wish to reveal unethical behavior in their own governments and corporations" (see http://www.wikileaks.org/wiki/Media/Wikileaks_-_Uncovering_oppressive_regimes [accessed February 7, 2007]). Wikileaks, which has subsequently become a target of attack from security agencies around the world, is an effort to recover the idea of public accountability by deploying a global technology to counter official secrecy, offering a constantly updating repository of leaked materials. Reaction to high-profile posting by Wikileaks of State Department cables has produced a new wave of secrecy laws, as well as prosecutions of whistleblowers, leakers, and journalists in the United States to an unprecedented extent in the Obama administration.

16. Secretary of Defense Donald Rumsfeld reiterated these claims during the first weeks of the war in an interview on ABC News, stating that the United States knew exactly where the WMDs were in Iraq: "We know where they are. They're in the area around Tikrit and Baghdad and east, west, south and north somewhat. . . . I would also add, we saw from the air that there were dozens of trucks that went into that facility after the existence of it became public in the press and they moved things out. They dispersed them and took them away. So there may be nothing left. I don't know that. But it's way too soon to know. The exploitation is just starting" (U.S. Department of Defense 2003b). For a truly remarkable assessment of Cheney's use of secrecy and threat as bureaucratic tools, see Gellman 2008.

17. Cheney has long argued that a president should not be fully informed about covert actions to enable plausible deniability in public statements. As vice president, he found various ways of restricting briefing information (including reducing the daily national intelligence estimate to a single page) for President Bush (see Suskind 2006, 173–75).

18. For a transcript of his presentation to the United Nations, as well as images from his slide presentation, see Powell 2003. For a detailed assessment of the biological weapons claims in Powell's presentation, see Vogal 2008b.

19. The Obama administration, for example, while promising transparency in government, has prosecuted more individuals for leaking government information to the press than all prior administrations have (see Shane 2010). There is also evidence of increasing government secrecy: the U.S. Information Security Oversight Office (2011, 2) found a 40 percent increase in classification from 2009 to 2010 (see also German and Stanley 2011; Open the Government 2011; Priest and Arkin 2011). The categories "for official use only" and "sensitive but unclassified" have been replaced by the term "controlled unclassified information," an official effort to reduce the number of information management markings in the federal government that does not change the core logic of the SBU designation (Obama 2010).

4. BIOSECURITY NOIR

1. The always-on-alert nuclear apparatus of the Cold War was beset, for example, by internal malfunctions that repeatedly took the world unintentionally to the brink of nuclear war (see S. Sagan 1993; Hoffman 2009). We could also think here about the crisis built into the levee system in New Orleans that failed during Hurricane Katrina in 2005, or the nuclear reactors in Fukushima, Japan, that were overwhelmed by a tsunami and fire in 2011.

2. A search of the LexisNexis database for uses of *biosecurity* since 1990, for example, reveals the dominance of New Zealand in developing the concept, and almost no public discourse about biosecurity in the United States until 2001. Similarly, the term is used almost exclusively for concerns about food safety until the 2001 anthrax letters, when the term is predominantly used to refer to biological terrorism. By the mid-2000s, biosecurity appears as a global concept, but one that still is defined in various ways in different countries, with a strong emphasis globally on animal food and animal safety. See also Rappert and Gould 2009. I am grateful to Alex Blanchette for his research assistance in tracking the evolving global use of the term *biosecurity*.

3. For discussions of the militarization of public health in the twenty-first century, see Lowe 2010; Whitehall 2010; Cooper 2006; U.S. Homeland Security Council 2006; and King 2003.

4. The Bush administration was particularly concerned about Iraqi and former Soviet biological weapons programs (see Hoffman 2009; Guillemin 2005a and 2011). For historical context on the evolution of biodefense from the Cold War to the post–Cold War periods, see J. Miller, Engelberg, and Broad 2001; and Tucker 2000.

5. See Kwik et al. 2003. See also Lakoff and Collier 2008; Ryan and Glarum 2008. For a discussion of how the militarizing of life can cross the species barrier, see Kosek 2010.

6. In addition to the anthrax detection system, the U.S. Postal Service created a Mail Isolation Control and Tracking Program in 2001 that digitally records the exterior of every piece of mail in the United States (see Ron Nixon 2013).

7. For a critique of the BioWatch Program, see O'Toole 2007b. She notes that federal funding cuts to public health have limited the number of experts available to read

the data collected by the sensors; points out that the sensors have malfunctioned on occasion and could easily be circumvented by would-be terrorists; states that the program is not funded well enough to create a real-time and national system of biosurveillance; and finally, wonders if a national electronic health record system might provide a more systematic and useful means of achieving an early warning of a bioattack. BioWatch was also intended to detect only agents connected to potential biological attack, and not as a general system to monitor the air quality—which could provide data on, for example, the relationship between toxicity and urban rates of asthma. For an assessment of the false positive alarm rates within the current BioWatch system, which have led a number of local governments to disregard its warnings, see Willman 2012.

8. See Gotton 2005, and for a discussion of the ideological connections between the BioShield program and the SDI of the 1980s, see Guillemin 2005a, 183.

9. For discussions of how globalization has affected perceptions of disease, see King 2004; and also Ali and Keil 2008; Fidler and Gostin 2008; Lakoff and Collier 2008; National Academy of Sciences 2004 and 2006.

10. For another example, see Bipartisan WMD Terrorism Research Center 2011. The center rates the responses of state and federal agencies across different outbreak scenarios, giving most U.S. biosecurity programs in 2010 failing grades.

11. From 1945 to 1990, there were only two BSL-4 laboratories in the United States, both federal laboratories (the U.S. Army's Research Institute for Infectious Diseases, in Fort Detrick, Maryland, and the Centers for Disease Control and Prevention [CDC], in Atlanta, Georgia). From 1990 to 2000, three new laboratories were built, and since 2001 ten new BSL-4 laboratories have been built (see Rhodes 2007, 9; Klotz and Sylvester 2009).

12. This is an extraordinary investment of money and energy in a single danger. Cole (2009, 255) estimates that as much as $6 billion has been spent on anthrax research since 2001 and notes that that there were only eighteen recorded cases of anthrax from inhaled spores in the United States during the entire twentieth century (7).

13. For the defense budget, see CostsofWar.org 2013. For the historical budget data of the NIH, see National Institute of Health Office of the Budget 2013. The formal budget for the Department of Defense does not include the cost of the wars in Afghanistan and Iraq, the nuclear weapons budgets of the Department of Energy, the Department of Homeland Security, or future health care for veterans of the War on Terror—which raises the total cost of U.S. security to just shy of a $1 trillion a year (see Wheeler 2014). In 2005, 750 biologists signed a letter protesting the new emphasis on biodefense spending over public health (see Cole 2009, 250). See Franco and Sell 2011 for a study of civilian biodefense funding (over and above that in the classified realm) in the first decade of counterterror.

14. B. Smith, Inglesby, and O'Toole write: "The U.S. biodefense strategy must assume that the country may sustain large-scale bioterrorist attacks using unanticipated, engineered bioweapons. In such conditions, it would be necessary to design and produce new countermeasures very rapidly—ideally, in a matter of weeks or months.

Such a radical shortening of the 'bug-to-drug' timeline will not occur unless transformation of the drug development process itself becomes a central focus of U.S. biodefense strategy" (2003, 200). The authors call for an approach to biodefense funding resembling that of the Defense Advanced Research Projects Agency, with enticements to attract top scientists, a focus on the development of drug countermeasures, and long-term federal support for pharmaceutical companies that will produce those countermeasures on the necessary nationwide scale.

15. In the 1990s U.S. officials learned of an extensive covert Soviet bioweapons project (Hoffman 2009), and the Aum Shinrikyo cult in Japan released sarin gas in the Tokyo subway in 1995.

16. See also Mueller (2006, 2) on bathtub drowning rates and comparative risks. Alcabes (2009, 9) notes the 2001 anthrax attacks constitute an "epidemic" by epidemiological definitions because the twenty-two cases constituted an unusual number for an almost nonexistent disease, while in comparison tuberculosis kills millions each year globally.

17. See Zulaika and Douglass (1996, 6). See also Lipschutz and Turcotte, who note that because there is so little "data for terrorist attacks, statistics will not help in predicting events" (2005, 31).

18. For example, the National Safety Council recorded no domestic American deaths by terrorism from 2006 to 2009 but an average of 65 American deaths each year from bee stings and 49 from lightning strikes (National Safety Council 2011, 19).

19. Dausey et al. 2005. The U.S. Department of Homeland Security (2005) created a set of fifteen National Planning Scenarios focused on WMD terrorist attacks. These scenarios are used to coordinate state and federal response training.

20. For more on the TOPOFF exercises and the new National Exercise Program, see U.S. Department of Homeland Security n.d. For an assessment of the TOPOFF exercises and the larger ideological framing of disaster, see M. Armstrong 2012.

21. For an important assessment of the temporalities of crisis, see Samimian-Darash 2009. She argues that a "pre-event configuration" of concepts and narratives is achieved via this kind of expertise, one that becomes an interpretive platform for unfolding events. See also Anderson 2010a; De Goede 2008.

22. See Schoch-Spana for an important examination of how the public has been imagined—from "panic-stricken mob" to "community of resilience"—in U.S. national health security during the past decade (2012, 77). She underscores how ideas about public emotions and capabilities are at the center of emergency response planning.

23. For a discussion of the post-2001 White House policy of treating a 1 percent likelihood of a WMD attack as a certainty in terms of planning a response, fundamentally redefining the relationship between evidence and national security policy, see Suskind 2006.

24. Collier (2008, 244) argues that enactment is productive because it focuses on uncertainty and complexity rather than on measurable qualities. He shows how this emerging concept of governance constitutes a distinct break from older archival and statistical modalities.

25. Scenarios of contagion rely on what is now quite a conventional narrative script, as Wald writes: "The outbreak narrative—in its scientific, journalistic, and fictional incarnations—follows a formulaic plot that begins with the identification of an emerging infection, includes discussion of the global networks throughout which it travels, and chronicles the epidemiological work that ends with its containment. As epidemiologists trace the routes of the microbes, they catalog the spaces and interaction of global modernity. Microbes, spaces, and interactions blend together as they animate the landscape and motivate the plot of the outbreak narrative: a contradictory but compelling story of the perils of human interdependence and the triumph of human connection and cooperation, scientific authority and the evolutionary advantages of the microbe, ecological balance and impending disaster" (2008, 2). Biosecurity has folded terrorism into this well-established narrative form. For narratives of contagion as well as the history of the uses of fictional narratives to constitute the bioterror threat, see Briggs 2011; Alcabes 2009; Hartmann, Subramaniam, and Zerner 2005; Ostherr 2005; King 2004.

26. Schoch-Spana argues that these exercises also work to create an enemy, confuse disease with war, and direct anger at foreign sources to "create a geography of blame" (2006, 36). See also Petryna 2009 (on the global politics of clinical trials); Epstein 2007 and 1996 (on the politics of inclusion in medical research); and Orr 2005 (on the militarization of internal life).

27. The Center for Biosecurity was founded at the Johns Hopkins University in 1998 as the first academic research center devoted to major biological threats. In 2003 it became part of the University of Pittsburgh Medical Center, and in 2013 it changed its name to the Center for Health Security. It publishes a journal, *Biosecurity and Bioterrorism* and several newsletters and has extensive resources concerning the evolution of biosecurity across military and public health domains on its website.

28. The use of simulated newscasts has become a central mechanism for creating realism in biosecurity exercises, and it has had a dramatic psychological effect on participants in creating a feeling of emergency, see Schoch-Spana 2004. For a sensitive analysis of how communication is structured in biosecurity scenarios, see Briggs 2011.

29. See, for example, Smith et al., who argue that "Atlantic Storm showed that a set of highly accomplished political leaders were largely unfamiliar with the political and strategic stakes that might be associated with biological attack or national pandemics" (2005, 261). See also Hamilton and Smith, who invoke Atlantic Storm to call for the equivalent of a "moon mission" to expand biosecurity globally so as to eliminate the risk of epidemic disease (2006, 9).

30. The complexity of orchestrating any real-time response to global infectious disease is often overwhelming for experts. See MacPhail's (forthcoming) ethnography of the CDC's effort to manage the 2009 H1N1 influenza outbreak, which was a key moment in both the affective politics of disease threat projection and the generation of new infrastructures to identify and respond to emerging disease.

31. For overviews, scripts, and analysis of Dark Winter, see UPMC Center for Health Security n.d.

32. Guillemin writes: "To be relevant for city governments, bioterrorism scenarios had to reach catastrophic proportions but stay within the realm of practical response: that is, they could not be like nuclear holocausts or local preparation would lose its purpose" (2005b, 205).

33. See Office of Technology Assessment 1993 for a pre–War on Terror discussion of terrorism and WMDs, and Smith, Inglesby, and O'Toole 2003 on the politics of anticipating dangers and infrastructure building.

34. Germ weapons have often been called the "poor man's atomic bomb." For a history of biodefense research in the 1990s—including Operation Bacchus, a 1998 Defense Threat Reduction Agency experiment to build an anthrax factory with commercially available material at the Nevada Test Site—see J. Miller, Engelberg and Broad 2001, 297. For a detailed history of the 2001 anthrax attacks, see Guillemin 2011.

35. The underlying logics of biosecurity are contested within and across security institutions. The National Research Council, for example, criticized the Department of Homeland Security's process of assessing biological threats for not defining key terms and for using "subjectively assessed probabilities for terrorist decisions"; the council advocated the use of a model of the terrorist as an "intelligent, goal-oriented, and resourceful adversary" (2008, 3). The council also argues for a return to classic game theory as a means of modeling the terrorist threat and seeks a rigorous categorization process to limit the inflation of threats. For a discussion of the current capabilities as well as future promise of synthetic biology, see Presidential Commission for the Study of Bioethical Issues 2010.

36. Vogal (2008a) has argued explicitly against this "biotech revolution" model, marking it as a form of biotech hype that distracts from a more practical approach to biosecurity, one that focuses on tracking the experts, technologies, and materials needed to create a bioweapon.

37. J. Miller, Engelberg, and Broad note that the bioweapons research at Fort Detrick in the 1950s included the study of "ethnic weapons," or germs that targeted specific races (2001, 42). They also document the existence of extensive new biodefense research in the 1990s that blurred the distinction between defensive and offensive research. In early 2001, in one of its first official acts, the Bush administration pulled out of international negotiations to renew the Chemical and Biological Weapons Convention.

38. To this we could add the problem of genomic and biomedical information as a potential weapon; see Caduff 2012; see also Braun 2007; Dillon 2003.

39. On the concept of emergence in biosecurity, see Hinchliffe and Bingham 2008; and as a vital aspect of terror politics, see Dillon 2003 and 2007.

40. For example, in the most recent *Quadrennial Defense Review Report*, the Defense Department notes: "Countries that have the infrastructure and capability to report and track the spread of an outbreak of disease are able to save more lives. Detecting, diagnosing, and determining the origin of a pathogen will enable U.S. authorities to better respond to future disease outbreaks and identify whether they are natural or man-made. Accordingly, we are expanding the biological threat reduction program to countries outside the former Soviet Union in order to create a global network for

surveillance and response" (U.S. Department of Defense 2010, 36). Such a global network offers a wide range of potential uses and is not limited to public health. For a discussion of "capacity building," see Armed Forces Health Surveillance Center n.d. For a pre–War on Terror assessment of the Department of Defense's Global Emerging Infections Surveillance and Response System, see Brachman, O'Maonaigh, and Miller 2001.

41. For an insightful analysis of the politics of locating the National Bio and Agro-Defense Facility in Kansas, see LaFlamme 2011. On the Plum Island Animal Disease Center, which the Kansas facility will replace, see Carroll 2004.

42. U.S. military strategy assumes a planetary field of action, mobilizing access not just to the global commons but to any region where there are U.S. interests, creating a new logistical commitment to managing local forms of resistance. In strategic terms, this is considered the difference between "assured access," or unhindered movement on land and water and in air, space, and cyberspace; and "operational access," or "the ability to project military force into an operational area with sufficient freedom of action to accomplish the mission" (U.S. Department of Defense 2012, 1). The Defense Department's *Joint Operations Access Concept* identifies the "anti-access" strategies of local governments and parties as an evolving set of obstacles to the realization of U.S. military operations.

43. The CIA program has been widely condemned by global health experts. Samuel Worthington, the president of an international coalition of health and poverty groups, wrote the head of the CIA to protest the vaccination operation, stating: "The CIA's use of the cover of humanitarian activity for this purpose casts doubt on the intentions and integrity of all humanitarian actors in Pakistan, thereby undermining the international humanitarian community's efforts to eradicate polio, provide critical health services, and extend life-saving assistance during times of crisis like the floods seen in Pakistan over the last two years. Since reports of the CIA campaign first surfaced last summer we have seen a continued erosion of U.S. NGOs' ability to deliver critical humanitarian programs in Pakistan as well as an uptick in targeted violence against humanitarian workers. I fear the CIA's activities in Pakistan and the perception that U.S. NGOs have ties with intelligence efforts may have contributed to these alarming developments" (see http://www.mcclatchydc.com /2012/03/02/140644/letter-to-gen-petraeus-from-interaction.html, accessed June 1, 2012).

44. U.S. Department of Justice 2010, 4; see also National Academy of Sciences 2011. Even before the 2001 attacks, anthrax was a substantial security concern in the United States. Cole (2009, 168–69) documents anthrax hoaxes through the 1990s, most involving white powder mailed to abortion clinics. Guillemin (2005a, 103) documents U.S. anthrax experiments going back to 1953: specifically, Fort Detrick scientists studied anthrax by staging attacks on St. Louis, Minneapolis, and Winnipeg using generators mounted atop cars to disperse a simulated anthrax agent. In the Clinton administration, biodefense specialists made and tested a Soviet-style anthrax bomb and studied how to create a vaccine-resistant strain of anthrax

(J. Miller, Engelberg, and Broad 2001). Thus, anthrax attacks had been rehearsed in the expert imagination for decades before becoming a reality in 2001.

45. The National Academy of Sciences (2011), however, could not verify the genetic evidence the FBI used to identify Ivins as the perpetrator.

5. LIVING COUNTERTERROR

1. The day after the September 11, 2001, attack, President George W. Bush sent to Congress a request for authority to "deter and pre-empt any future act of terrorism or aggression against the United States"—a sentence rejected by congressional leaders precisely because it seemed to give the president unlimited powers to attack any individual, group, or state he designated as terrorist and to do so on a planetary scale, without any review or time limitation (quoted in Grimmett 2007, 2). Thus, the language of the congressional resolution was intended to specify the terrorist enemy—those directly involved in the domestic attacks on September 11, 2001—and therefore to both establish and limit presidential authority. But the key terms of the resolution—"appropriate force," "aided," and, above all, the "future" (U.S. Congress 2001) were not defined, allowing a White House interpretive strategy that proved to be spectacular in its wide-ranging claims for unlimited presidential authority. But perhaps the most powerful act of interpretation was based on the congressional mandate to "prevent future terrorist acts," which was quickly mobilized to eliminate the distinction between foreign and domestic territories. The Authorization to Use Military Force was passed with only one dissenting vote, that of Representative Barbara Lee (D-California) who argued against giving the president such an unlimited authorization for military action.

2. According to the U.S. Army in 2009, an "overseas contingency operation" includes major military combat, peace operations, humanitarian assistance, civilian evacuation, and international disaster relief (see U.S. Department of the Army 2009, 19). See Warnock 2000 for a history of the military use of the term from 1945 to 1997, when it tended to characterize extremely short-term deployments (lasting hours or days), not decade-long commitments. See U.S. Government Accountability Office 2009 for an assessment of the $888 billion spent on overseas contingency operations since 2001.

3. For a study of the 370 U.S. drone attacks in Pakistan from 2004 to 2013, see New America Foundation 2014. The Federal Bureau of Investigation has remade itself into a counterterror agency in significant ways: for example, in 2010 the bureau issued 24,287 national security letters—which are requests for information (from Internet providers, financial institutions, and libraries) about an individual that mandate secrecy about the request itself on the part of everyone involved—under counterterrorism provisions (see Bjelopera 2011, 7). Counterterror provisions have created significant changes in domestic spying as well as racial and religious profiling, sometimes with formal legal authority (for example, in the USA Patriot Act) and sometimes not (as in the New York City Police Department's program of covert surveillance of mosques).

4. For a list of degree-granting programs, see Naval Postgraduate School and the U.S. Department of Homeland Security n.d.

5. For a list of the centers of excellence, see U.S. Department of Homeland Security n.d.c.

6. This creates not only a high level of redundancy but also competition among agencies and departments at the local, state, and federal level, as well as among contractors. There is also a lack of agreement about basic terms and missions. For example, there is still no consensus on the definition of *homeland security* even ten years after the creation of the Department of Homeland Security, an agency with an annual budget of nearly $70 billion (see Reese 2012).

7. In an effort to produce synergies and information sharing across agencies, the Department of Homeland Security created seventy counterterror "fusion centers" that link local, state, and federal intelligence and policing organizations. Marketed as a centerpiece of the department's counterterror strategy and as a "force multiplier," this system of fusion centers has not uncovered a single terrorist threat in its first decade and cannot account for an expenditure of perhaps $1.2 billion (U.S. Senate 2012, 2–3).

8. The BioWatch sensor system installed in major U.S. cities to detect biological attacks using anthrax, smallpox, or plague has also been widely criticized for the number of false alarms and has been widely rejected by public health and emergency response authorities (Willman 2012). These not-yet-functioning national shields nevertheless work as affective tools, mobilizing expert commitments while allowing a constant public rehearsal of terror in the form of warnings of attack.

9. For a history of the USS *New York*, its logo, as well as a description of the use of steel from the World Trade Center ruins, see http://www.ussnewyork.com (accessed March 18, 2014) and http://www.new-york.navy.mil/ (accessed March 18, 2014).

10. The museum had had over 300,000 visitors by 2010, a remarkable accomplishment for the original group of scientists, engineers, and defense specialists who organized in the 1990s to build a museum devoted to telling the story of their once-classified Cold War nuclear science work (see Wray 2006).

11. For critical analysis of the contemporary public cultures of sentimentality and trauma in the United States, see Doss 2012; Sturken 2007.

REFERENCES

ABC News. 2005. "US to Dissect Katrina Response." *ABC News Online*. September 7. Accessed March 14, 2014. http://www.abc.net.au/news/newsitems/200509/s1454669 .htm.

Abraham, Itty. 1998. *The Making of the Indian Atomic Bomb: Science, Secrecy and the Postcolonial State*. London: Zed.

Adey, Peter, and Ben Anderson. 2012. "Anticipating Emergencies: Technologies of Preparedness and the Matter of Security." *Security Dialogue* 43 (2): 99–117.

Advisory Committee on Human Radiation Experiments. 1996. *The Human Radiation Experiments: Final Report of the President's Advisory Committee*. New York: Oxford University Press.

Aftergood, Steven. 2013. "An Inquiry into the Dynamics of Government Secrecy." *Harvard Civil Rights-Civil Liberties Law Review* 48 (2): 511–30.

Ahmed, Nafeez. 2006. "Sources: August Terror Plot Is a 'Fiction' Underscoring Police Failures." *Raw Story.com*. September 18.

Ahmed, Sara. 2004. "Affective Economies." *Social Text* 22 (2): 117–39.

Aid, Matthew M. 2006. "Declassification in Reverse." *National Security Archive*. February 21. http://www.gwu.edu/~nsarchiv/NSAEBB/NSAEBB179/.

Alcabes, Philip. 2009. *Dread: How Fear and Fantasy Have Fueled Epidemics from the Black Death to the Avian Flu*. New York: Public Affairs.

Ali, S. Harris, and Roger Keil, eds. 2008. *Networked Disease: Emerging Infections in the Global City*. Oxford: Wiley-Blackwell.

Alvarez, Luis, et al. 1980. "Extraterrestrial Cause for the Cretaceous-Tertiary Extinction: Experimental Results and Theoretical Interpretation." *Science* 208 (4448): 1095–108.

American Society of Civil Engineers. 2011. *Failure to Act: The Economic Impact of Current Investment Trends in Water and Wastewater Treatment Infrastructure*. Reston, VA: American Society of Civil Engineers.

American Society of Civil Engineers. 2012. "Report Card for America's Infrastructure." Accessed February 6. http://www.asce.org/reportcard/.

Anders, Smiley. 2006. "Devastation by Nature Rivals That of Man." *Advocate*. February 8.

Anderson, Ben. 2009. "Affective Atmospheres." *Emotion, Space and Society* 2: 77–81.

Anderson, Ben. 2010a. "Preemption, Precaution, Preparedness: Anticipatory Action and Future Geographies." *Progress in Human Geography* 34 (6): 777–98.

Anderson, Ben. 2010b. "Security and the Future: Anticipating the Event of Terror." *Geoforum* 41: 227–35.

Antilla, Liisa. 2005. "Climate of Scepticism: US Newspaper Coverage of the Science of Climate Change." *Global Environmental Change* 15: 338–52.

Appelbaum, Binyamin. 2012. "Family Net Worth Drops to Level of Early '90s, Fed Says." *New York Times*. June 12.

Arkin, William. 2005. *Code Names: Deciphering U.S. Military Plans, Programs and Operations in the 9/11 World*. Hanover, NH: Steerforth.

Armageddon. 1998. Directed by Michael Bay. Burbank, CA: Buena Vista Pictures.

Armed Forces Health Surveillance Center. n.d. "Capacity Building and Other Efforts." Accessed June 1, 2012. http://www.afhsc.mil/geisCapBuild.

Armstrong, David. 2002. "Dick Cheney's Song of America: Drafting a Plan for Global Dominance." *Harper's* 305 (1829): 76–83.

Armstrong, Melanie. 2012. "Rehearsing for the Plague: Citizens, Security, and Simulation." *Canadian Review of American Studies* 42 (1): 105–19.

Asad, Talal. 2007. *On Suicide Bombing*. New York: Columbia University Press.

Associated Universities. 1952. *Report of the Project East River*. New York: Associated Universities.

Atlas, Ronald, and Judith Reppy. 2005. "Globalizing Biosecurity." *Biosecurity and Bioterrorism* 3 (1): 51–59.

Badash, Lawrence. 2001. "Nuclear Winter: Scientists in the Political Arena." *Physics in Perspective* 3 (1): 76–105.

Badash, Lawrence. 2009. *A Nuclear Winter's Tale: Science and Politics in the 1980s*. Cambridge: MIT Press.

Barbour, Haley. 2005. "Interview on Hurricane Katrina's Aftermath." CNN *Larry King Live*. Accessed March 18, 2014. http://transcripts.cnn.com/TRANSCRIPTS/0508/31/lkl.01.html.

Barnett, Thomas P. M. 2004. *The Pentagon's New Map: War and Peace in the Twenty-first Century*. New York: Penguin Books.

Barth, Kai-Henrik. 1998. "Science and Politics in Early Nuclear Test Ban Negotiations." *Physics Today* 51(3): 34–39.

Barth, Kai-Henrik. 2003. "The Politics of Seismology, Nuclear Testing, Arms Control and the Transformation of a Discipline." *Social Studies of Science* 33 (5): 743–81.

Bass, Frank, and Randy Herschaft. 2007. "1M Archived Pages Removed Post-9/11." *Associated Press*. March 13.

Bearden, David M., and Robert Esworthy. 2007. *Restructuring EPA's Libraries: Background and Issues for Congress*. Washington: Congressional Research Service.

Beck, Ulrich. 2007. *World at Risk*. Cambridge: Polity.

Becker, Jo, and Scott Shane. 2012. "Secret 'Kill List' Proves a Test of Obama's Principles and Will." *New York Times*. May 29.

Belasco, Amy. 2011. *The Cost of Iraq, Afghanistan, and Other Global War on Terror Operations since 9/11*. Washington: Congressional Research Service.

Benjamin, Mark. 2006. "The Abu Ghraib Files." Salon.com. February 16. http://www .salon.com/news/feature/2006/02/16/abu_ghraib/.

Benjamin, Walter. 1969. "The Work of Art in the Age of Mechanical Reproduction." In Walter Benjamin, *Illuminations*, translated by Harry Zohn, 217–51. New York: Schocken.

Bentz, Richard, et al. 1957. "Some Civil Defense Problems in the Nation's Capital Following Widespread Thermonuclear Attack." *Operations Research* 5 (3): 319–50.

Berlant, Lauren. 2007. "Slow Death (Sovereignty, Obesity, Lateral Agency)." *Critical Inquiry* 33 (4): 754–80.

Bipartisan WMD Terrorism Research Center. 2011. "Bio-Response Report Card: 21st Century Biological Threats." Accessed February 4, 2014. http://www.wmdcenter.org /wp-content/uploads/2011/10/bio-response-report-card-2011.pdf.

Bjelopera, Jerome P. 2011. *The Federal Bureau of Investigation and Terrorism Investigations*. Washington: Congressional Research Service.

Blanchot, Maurice. 1995. *The Writing of the Disaster*. Translated by Ann Smock. Lincoln: University of Nebraska Press.

Blaustein, Andrew, and Andy Dobson. 2006. "A Message from the Frogs." *Nature* 439 (12): 143–44.

Borenstein, Seth. 2007. "2007 a Year of Weather Records in U.S." *Associated Press*. December 29.

Brachman, Philip S., Heather C. O'Maonaigh, and Richard N. Miller, eds. 2001. *Perspectives on the Department of Defense Global Emerging Infections Surveillance and Response System*. Washington: National Academies Press.

Brands, H. W. 1989. "The Age of Vulnerability: Eisenhower and the National Insecurity State." *American Historical Review* 94 (4): 963–89.

Braun, Bruce. 2007. "Biopolitics and the Molecularization of Life." *Cultural Geographies* 14: 6–28.

Braw, Monica. 1997. *The Atomic Bomb Suppressed: American Censorship in Occupied Japan*. Armonk, NY: M. E. Sharpe.

Brians, Paul. 2006. *Nuclear Holocausts: Atomic War in Fiction*. Accessed January 30, 2014. http://www.wsu.edu/~brians/nuclear/index.htm.

Briggs, Charles. 2011. "Communicating Biosecurity." *Medical Anthropology* 30 (1): 6–29.

Broderick, Mick, ed. 1996. *Hibakusha Cinema: Hiroshima, Nagasaki and the Nuclear Image in Japanese Film*. New York: Kegan Paul.

Buck-Morss, Susan. 1991. *The Dialectics of Seeing: Walter Benjamin and the Arcades Project*. Cambridge: MIT Press.

Buck-Morss, Susan. 2000. *Dreamworld and Catastrophe: The Passing of Mass Utopia in East and West*. Cambridge: MIT Press.

Buddemeier, Robert W., Joan A. Kleypas, and Richard B. Aronson. 2004. "Coral Reefs and Global Climate Change." Pew Center on Global Climate Change. Accessed December 30, 2006. http://www.pewclimate.org/docUploads/Coral%5FReefs%2Epdf.

Burr, William, Thomas S. Blanton, and Stephen I. Schwartz. 1998. "The Costs and Consequences of Nuclear Secrecy." In *Atomic Audit: The Costs and Consequences of U.S. Nuclear Weapons since 1940*, edited by Stephen I. Schwartz, 433–84. Washington: Brookings Institution.

Bush, George W. 2002a. "State of the Union Address." Accessed March 18, 2014. http://georgewbush-whitehouse.archives.gov/news/releases/2002/01/20020129-11.html.

Bush George W. 2002b. "President Bush Outlines Iraqi Threat." October 7. Accessed March 18, 2014. http://georgewbush-whitehouse.archives.gov/news/releases/2002/10/20021007-8.html.

Bush, George W. 2003. "Executive Order 13526—Classified National Security Information." Accessed March 18, 2014. http://www.fas.org/sgp/bush/eoamend.html.

Bush, George W. 2004. "President Announces New Measures to Counter the Threat of wmd." Accessed March 18, 2014. http://georgewbush-whitehouse.archives.gov/news/releases/2004/02/20040211-4.html.

Bush, George W. 2005. "President Arrives in Alabama, Briefed on Hurricane Katrina." Accessed March 18, 2014. http://georgewbush-whitehouse.archives.gov/news/releases/2005/09/20050902-2.html.

Caduff, Carlo. 2012. "The Semiotics of Security: Infectious Disease Research and the Biopolitics of Informational Bodies in the United States." *Cultural Anthropology* 27(2): 333–57.

Carroll, Michael Christopher. 2004. *Lab 257: The Disturbing Story of the Government's Secret Plum Island Germ Laboratory*. New York: Harper.

Carus, W. Seth. 2006. *Defining "Weapons of Mass Destruction."* Washington: National Defense University Press.

Cazdyn, Eric. 2007. "Disaster, Crisis, Revolution." *South Atlantic Quarterly* 106 (4): 647–62.

Cheney, Richard. 2001. "Vice President Cheney Delivers Remarks to the Republican Governors Association." Accessed March 18, 2014. http://georgewbush-whitehouse.archives.gov/vicepresident/news-speeches/speeches/vp20011025.html.

Cheney, Richard. 2002. "Vice President's Remarks to the Veterans of Foreign Wars." Accessed March 18, 2014. http://georgewbushwhitehouse.archives.gov/news/releases/2002/08/20020826.html.

Cheney, Richard. 2008. "Interview with Dick Cheney." *Fox News Sunday*. December 21. Accessed March 18, 2014. http://www.foxnews.com/story/2008/12/22/transcript-vice-president-cheney-on-fox-news-sunday/.

Chernus, Ira. 2002. *Eisenhower's Atoms for Peace*. College Station: Texas a&m University Press.

Chesney, Robert M. 2006. "State Secrets and the Limits of National Security Litigation." *Social Science Research Network*. Accessed March 25, 2010. http://ssrn.com/abstract=946676.

Clarke, Richard A. 2009. "Cheney and Rice Remember 9/11. I Do, Too." *Washington Post*. May 31.

Cloud, John. 2002. "American Cartographic Transformations during the Cold War." *Cartography and Geographic Information Science* 29 (3): 261–82.

Clough, Patricia Ticineto. 2007. "Introduction" in *The Affective Turn: Theorizing the Social*, edited by Patricia Ticeneto Clough with Jean Halley, 1–33. Durham, NC: Duke University Press.

CNA Corporation. 2007. "National Security and the Threat of Climate Change." Accessed March 19, 2014. https://www.cna.org/reports/climate.

Cockell, Charles S., and M. Dale Stokes. 1999. "Polar Winter: A Biological Model for Impact Events and Related Dark/Cold Climatic Changes." *Climactic Change* 41 (2): 151–73.

Cohn, Carol. 1987. "Sex and Death in the Rational World of Defense Intellectuals." *Signs* 12 (4): 687–718.

Cole, Leonard A. 2009. *The Anthrax Letters*. New York: Skyhorse.

Collier, Stephen J. 2008. "Enacting Catastrophe: Preparedness, Insurance, Budgetary Rationalization." *Economy and Society* 37 (2): 224–50.

Collier, Steven J., Andrew Lakoff, and Paul Rabinow. 2004. "Biosecurity: Towards an Anthropology of the Contemporary." *Anthropology Today* 20 (5): 3–7.

Comar, C. L., R. Scott Russell, and R. H. Wasserman. 1957. "Strontium-Calcium Movement from Soil to Man." *Science* 126 (3272): 485–92.

Committee on Meteorological Aspects of the Effects of Atomic Radiation. 1956. "Meteorological Aspects of Atomic Radiation." *Science* 124 (3212): 105–12.

Constitution Project. 2013. *Detainee Treatment*. Washington: Constitution Project.

Cooper, Melinda. 2006. "Pre-Empting Emergence: The Biological Turn in the War on Terror." *Theory, Culture & Society* 23 (4): 113–35.

Cosgrove, Denis. 2001. *Apollo's Eye: A Cartographic Genealogy of the Earth in the Western Imagination*. Baltimore, MD: Johns Hopkins University Press.

Costsofwar.org. 2013. "Economic Costs Summary." Providence, RI: Watson Institute. http://costsofwar.org/article/economic-cost-summary.

Craig, Campbell. 1998. *Destroying the Village: Eisenhower and Thermonuclear War*. New York: Columbia University Press.

Crowley, Thomas D., et al. 2007. *Transforming the Way DOD Looks at Energy*. Accessed March 18, 2014. http://www.dtic.mil/dtic/tr/fulltext/u2/a467003.pdf.

Crutzen, Paul J., and John W. Birks. 1982. "The Atmosphere after a Nuclear War: Twilight at Noon." *Ambio* 11 (2–3): 114–25.

Daggett, Stephen. 2010. *Costs of Major U.S. Wars*. Washington: Congressional Research Service.

Daley, Beth. 2006. "NASA Shelves Climate Satellites." *Boston Globe*. June 9.

Dausey, David J., et al. 2005. *Bioterrorism Preparedness Training and Assessment: Exercises for Local Public Health Agencies*. Santa Monica, CA: RAND Corporation.

Davis, Doug. 2001. "'A Hundred Million Hydrogen Bombs': Total War in the Fossil Record." *Configurations* 9 (3): 461–508.

Davis, Tracy D. 2002. "Between History and Event: Rehearsing Nuclear War Survival." *Drama Review* 46 (4): 11–45.

The Day After. 1983. Directed by Nicholas Meyer. Los Angeles: ABC Circle Films.

The Day after Tomorrow. 2004. Directed by Roland Emmerich. Los Angeles: Twentieth Century Fox.

De Goede, Marieke. 2008. "Beyond Risk: Premediation and the Post-9/11 Security Imagination." *Security Dialogue* 39 (2–3): 155–76.

Dean, Jodi. 2002. *Publicity's Secret: How Technoculture Capitalizes on Democracy.* Ithaca, NY: Cornell University Press.

Deep Impact. 1998. Directed by Mimi Leder. Hollywood, CA: Paramount Pictures.

Defense Advanced Research Project Agency. n.d. "Our Work." Accessed January 23, 2014. http://www.darpa.mil/our_work/.

Demeritt, David. 2001. "The Construction of Global Warming and the Politics of Science." *Annals of the Association of American Geographers* 91 (2): 307–37.

Der Derian, James. 2002. "The War of Networks." *Theory & Event* 5 (4): 1–11.

Derrida, Jacques. 1984. "No Apocalypse, Not Now (Full Speed Ahead, Seven Missiles, Seven Missives)." *Diacritics* 14 (2): 20–31.

Dickinson, Tim. 2007. "The Secret Campaign of President Bush's Administration to Deny Global Warming." *Rolling Stone.* June 29.

Dilanian, Ken. 2013. "Terror Database Too Vague to Flag Boston Suspect." *Los Angeles Times.* May 2.

Dillon, Michael. 2003. "Virtual Security: A Life Science of (Dis)order." *Millennium* 32 (3): 531–58.

Dillon, Michael. 2007. "Governing Terror: The State of Emergency of Biopolitical Emergence." *International Political Sociology* 1 (1): 7–28.

Doel, Ronald. 2003. "Constituting the Postwar Earth Sciences: The Military's Influence on the Environmental Sciences in the USA after 1945." *Social Studies of Science* 33 (5): 635–66.

Donaghy, Timothy, et al. 2007. *Atmosphere of Pressure: Political Interference in Federal Climate Science.* Washington: Union of Concerned Scientists and the Government Accountability Project.

Doss, Erica. 2012. *Memorial Mania: Public Feeling in America.* Chicago: University of Chicago Press.

Dower, John W. 2010. *Cultures of War: Pearl Harbor, Hiroshima, 9-11, Iraq.* New York: Norton.

Duelfer, Charles. 2009. *Hide and Seek: The Search for Truth in Iraq.* New York: Public Affairs.

Durkheim, Emile. 2005. *Elementary Forms of the Religious Life.* Translated by Karen E. Fields. New York: Free Press.

Eden, Lynn. 2004. *Whole World on Fire: Organization, Knowledge and Nuclear Weapons Devastation.* Ithaca, NY: Cornell University Press.

"An Editor in the White House." 2005. *New York Times.* June 7.

Edwards, Paul. 1996. *The Closed World: Computers and the Politics of Discourse in Cold War America.* Cambridge: MIT Press.

Edwards, Paul. 2000. "The World in a Machine: Origins and Impacts of Early Computerized Global Systems Models." In *Systems, Experts and Computers*, edited by Agatha Hughes and Thomas P. Hughes, 221–54. Cambridge: MIT Press.

Edwards, Paul. 2010. *A Vast Machine: Computer Models, Climate Data, and the Politics of Global Warming.* Cambridge: MIT Press.

Egan, Michael. 2007. *Barry Commoner and the Science of Survival.* Cambridge: MIT Press.

Ehrlich, Paul R., et al. 1983. "Long-Term Biological Consequences of Nuclear War." *Science* 222 (4630): 1293–1300.

Ehrlich, Paul R., et al. 1984. *The Cold and the Dark: The World after Nuclear War.* New York: W. W. Norton.

Eilperin, Juliet. 2006a. "Debate on Climate Shifts to Issue of Irreparable Change." *Washington Post.* January 29.

Eilperin, Juliet. 2006b. "U.S. Wants Polar Bears Listed as Threatened." *Washington Post.* December 27.

Eilperin, Juliet. 2008a. "Ozone Rules Weakened at Bush's Behest." *Washington Post.* March 14.

Eilperin, Juliet. 2008b. "Since '01, Guarding Species Is Harder." *Washington Post.* March 23.

Ellsberg, Daniel. 2003. *Secrets: A Memoir of Vietnam and the Pentagon Papers.* New York: Penguin.

Epstein, Steven. 1996. *Impure Science: AIDS, Activism, and the Politics of Knowledge.* Berkeley: University of California Press.

Epstein, Steven. 2007. *Inclusion: The Politics of Difference in Medical Research.* Chicago: University of Chicago Press.

Evans, Joyce A. 1998. *Celluloid Mushroom Clouds: Hollywood and the Atomic Bomb.* Boulder, CO: Westview.

Falkenrath, Richard A. 2001. "Problems of Preparedness: U.S. Readiness for a Domestic Terrorist Attack." *International Security* 25 (4): 147–86.

Farish, Matthew. 2010. *The Contours of America's Cold War.* Minneapolis: University of Minnesota Press.

Fauci, Anthony S. 2002. "An Expanded Biodefense Role for the National Institutes of Health." *Journal of Homeland Security* (April 20): 1–5.

Fauci, Anthony S., and Francis S. Collins. 2012. "Benefits and Risks of Influenza Research: Lessons Learned." *Science* 336 (6088): 1522–23.

Federal Bureau of Investigation. 2011. *The FBI: A Decade in Numbers, a Snapshot of How We've Changed since 9/11/2001.* Washington: Federal Bureau of Investigation.

Federal Civil Defense Administration. 1955a. *Operation Cue: The Atomic Test Program.* Washington: Government Printing Office.

Federal Civil Defense Administration. 1955b. *Cue for Survival.* Washington: Government Printing Office.

Federal Civil Defense Administration. 1956. *Annual Report for 1955.* Washington: Government Printing Office.

Fenrich, Lane. 1997. "Mass Death in Miniature: How Americans Became Victims of the Bomb." In *Living with the Bomb: American and Japanese Cultural Conflicts in the Nuclear Age*, edited by Laura Hein and Mark Selden, 122–33. Armonk, NY: East Gate.

Fidler, David P., and Laurence O. Gostin. 2008. *Biosecurity in the Global Age: Biological Weapons, Public Health, and the Rule of Law*. Palo Alto, CA: Stanford University Press.

Fisher, Louis. 2006. *In the Name of National Security: Unchecked Presidential Power and the Reynolds Case*. Lawrence: University of Kansas Press.

FitzGerald, Frances. 2000. *Way Out There in the Blue: Reagan, Star Wars, and the End of the Cold War*. New York: Simon and Schuster.

Fleming, James Rodger. 2010. *Fixing the Sky: The Checkered History of Weather and Climate Control*. New York: Columbia University Press.

Forrow, Lachlan, and Victor Sidel. 1998. "Medicine and Nuclear War." *Journal of the American Medical Association* 280 (5): 456–61.

Foucault, Michel. 1995. *Discipline and Punish: The Birth of the Prison*. Translated by Alan Sheridan. New York: Vintage.

Foucault, Michel. 2003. *"Society Must Be Defended": Lectures at the Collège de France, 1975–76*. Translated by David Macey. New York: Picador.

Foucault, Michel. 2007. *Security, Territory, Population: Lectures at the Collège de France 1977–78*. Translated by Graham Burchell. New York: Palgrave.

Franco, Crystal, and Tara Kirk Sell. 2011. "Federal Agency Biodefense Funding, FY2011–FY2012." *Biosecurity and Bioterrorism* 9 (2): 117–37.

Freedman, Lawrence, and Saki Dockrill. 2004. "Hiroshima: A Strategy of Shock." In *The World War Two Reader*, edited by Gordon Marel, 67–84. London: Routledge.

Freud, Sigmund. 1965. *The Psychopathology of Everyday Life*. Translated by James Strachey. New York: W. W. Norton.

Freud, Sigmund. 1999. *The Interpretation of Dreams*. Translated by Joyce Crick. Oxford: Oxford University Press.

Friedberg, Aaron L. 2000. *In the Shadow of the Garrison State: America's Anti-Statism and Its Cold War Grand Strategy*. Princeton, NJ: Princeton University Press.

Frontline. 2011. *The Anthrax Files*. Accessed February 15, 2012. Available at: http://www.pbs.org/wgbh/pages/frontline/anthrax-files/.

Furedi, Frank. 2006. *Culture of Fear Revisited*. London: Continuum.

Gaddis, John Lewis. 1982. *Strategies of Containment: A Critical Appraisal of Postwar American National Security Policy*. Oxford: Oxford University Press.

Gaddis, John Lewis. 2004. *Surprise, Security and the American Experience*. Cambridge, MA: Harvard University Press.

Galison, Peter. 2001. "War against the Center." *Grey Room* 4 (summer): 5–33.

Galison, Peter. 2004. "Removing Knowledge." *Critical Inquiry* 31 (autumn): 229–43.

Galli, Carlo. 2010. *Political Spaces and Global War*. Minneapolis: University of Minnesota Press.

Garrison, Dee. 2006. *Bracing for Armageddon: Why Civil Defense Never Worked*. Oxford: Oxford University Press.

Garvey, Todd, and Edward C. Liu. 2011. *The States Secrets Privilege: Preventing the Disclosure of Sensitive National Security Information during Civil Litigation*. Washington: Congressional Research Service.

Gellman, Barton. 2008. *Angler: The Cheney Vice Presidency*. New York: Penguin.

George, Alice. 2003. *Awaiting Armageddon: How Americans Faced the Cuban Missile Crisis*. Chapel Hill: University of North Carolina Press.

German, Mike, and Jay Stanley. 2011. *Drastic Measures Required*. New York: American Civil Liberties Union.

Ghamari-Tabrizi, Sharon. 2005. *The Worlds of Herman Kahn: The Intuitive Science of Thermonuclear War*. Cambridge, MA: Harvard University Press.

Giles, Jim. 2006. "Is US Hurricane Report Being Quashed?" *Nature* 443 (28): 378.

Glasstone, Samuel, and Philip J. Dolan, eds. 1977. *The Effects of Nuclear Weapons*. 3rd edition. Washington: U.S. Department of Defense and U.S. Department of Energy.

Gore, Al. 2008. "A Generational Challenge to Repower America." *Huffingtonpost.com*. July 17.

Gotton, Frank. 2005. *Project BioShield*. Washington: Congressional Research Service.

Grimaldi, James V., and Jacqueline Trescott. 2007. "Scientists Fault Climate Exhibit Changes." *Washington Post*. November 16.

Grimmett, Richard F. 2007. *Authorization for Use of Military Force in Response to the 9/11 Attacks (P.L. 107–40): Legislative History*. Washington: Congressional Research Service.

Grinspoon, Lester, ed. 1986. *The Long Darkness: Psychological and Moral Perspectives on Nuclear Winter*. New Haven, CT: Yale University Press.

Grossman, Andrew. 2001. *Neither Dead nor Red: Civilian Defense and American Political Development during the Early Cold War*. New York: Routledge.

Guillemin, Jeanne. 2005a. *Biological Weapons*. New York: Columbia University Press.

Guillemin, Jeanne. 2005b. "Inventing Bioterrorism: The Political Construction of Civilian Risk." In *Making Threats: Biofears and Environmental Anxieties*, edited by Betsy Hartmann, Banu Subramaniam, and Charles Zerner, 197–216. Landham, MD: Rowman and Littlefield.

Guillemin, Jeanne. 2011. *American Anthrax: Fear, Crime, and the Investigation of the Nation's Deadliest Bioterror Attack*. New York: Times Books.

Gusterson, Hugh. 1998. *Nuclear Rites: A Weapons Laboratory at the End of the Cold War*. Berkeley: University of California Press.

Gusterson, Hugh. 2004. *People of the Bomb: Portraits of America's Nuclear Complex*. Minneapolis: University of Minnesota Press.

Gusterson, Hugh. 2008. "Nuclear Futures: Anticipatory Knowledge, Expert Judgment, and the Lack That Cannot Be Filled." *Science and Public Policy* 35 (8): 551–60.

Gusterson, Hugh, and Catherine Besteman, eds. 2009. *The Insecure American: How We Got Here and What We Should Do about It*. Berkekey: University of California Press.

Hall, R. Cargill. 2002. "A History of the Military Polar Orbiting Meteorological Satellite Program." *Qwest* 9 (2): 4–25.

Hamblin, Jacob Darwin. 2005. *Oceanographers and the Cold War: Disciples of Marine Science*. Seattle: University of Washington Press.

Hamblin, Jacob Darwin. 2007. "A Dispassionate and Objective Effort: Negotiating the First Study on the Biological Effects of Atomic Radiation." *Journal of the History of Biology* 40 (1): 147–77.

Hamilton, Daniel S., and Bradley T. Smith. 2006. "Atlantic Storm." *EMBO Reports* 7 (1): 4–9.

Hammond, Allen L., and Thomas H. Maugh II. 1974. "Stratospheric Pollution: Multiple Threats to Earth's Ozone." *Science* 186 (4161): 335–38.

Hansen, James, Makiko Sato, and Reto Ruedy. 2012. "Perception of Climate Change." *Proceedings of the National Academy of Sciences* 109 (37): 2415–23.

Hansen, Miriam. 2004. "Why Media Aesthetics?" *Critical Inquiry* 30 (2): 391–95.

Harding, Warren. 1921. "Presidential Inauguration Address." Accessed March 18, 2014. http://www.inaugural.senate.gov/swearing-in/address/address-by-warren-g-harding-1921.

Hare, F. Kenneth. 1962. "The Stratosphere." *Geographical Review* 52 (4): 525–47.

Harper, Kristine C. 2003. "Research from the Boundary Layer: Civilian Leadership, Military Funding and the Development of Numerical Weather Prediction (1946–55)." *Social Studies of Science* 33 (5): 667–96.

Harrison, Todd. 2011. *Analysis of the FY 2011 Defense Budget*. Washington: Center for Strategic and Budgetary Assessments.

Hartmann, Betsy, Banu Subramaniam, and Charles Zerner, eds. 2005. *Making Threats: Biofears and Environmental Anxieties*. Lanham, MD: Rowman and Littlefield.

Hecht, Gabrielle. 2012. *Being Nuclear: Africans and the Global Uranium Trade*. Cambridge: MIT Press.

Heilprin, John. 2006. "New Publishing Rules Restrict Scientists." *Associated Press*. December 13.

Hellman, Chris. 2011. "$1.2 Trillion for National Security." *TomDispatch.com*. March 1.

Henderson, D. A. 2009. *Smallpox: The Death of a Disease*. Amherst, NY: Prometheus.

Hersh, Seymour. 2004. "Torture at Abu Ghraib." *New Yorker*. May 10.

Hersh, Seymour. 2012. "Our Men in Iran." *New Yorker*. April 6.

Hewlett, Richard G., and Jack M. Holl. 1989. *Atoms for Peace and War, 1953–1961: Eisenhower and the Atomic Energy Commission*. Berkeley: University of California Press.

Hinchliffe, Steve, and Nick Bingham. 2008. "Securing Life: The Emerging Practices of Biosecurity." *Environment and Planning A* 40: 1534–51.

Hobbs, Peter V., and Lawrence F. Radke. 1992. "Airborne Studies of the Smoke from the Kuwait Oil Fires." *Science* 256 (5059): 987–91.

Hoerlin, Herman. 1976. *United States High-Altitude Test Experiences: A Review Emphasizing the Impact on the Environment*. Los Alamos, NM: Los Alamos Scientific Laboratory.

Hoffman, David E. 2009. *The Dead Hand: The Untold Story of the Cold War Arms Race and Its Dangerous Legacy*. New York: Doubleday.

House, Tamzy J., et al. 1996. "Weather as a Force Multiplier: Owning the Weather in 2025." Accessed March 18, 2014. http://csat.au.af.mil/2025/volume3/vol3ch15.pdf.

"Intellipedia." n.d. Wikipedia. Accessed February 2, 2014. http://en.wikipedia.org/wiki /Intellipedia.

Jacques, Peter J., Riley E. Dunlap, and Mark Freeman. 2008. "The Organization of Denial: Conservative Think Tanks and Environmental Skepticism." *Environmental Politics* 17 (3): 349–85.

Jain, S. Lochlann. 2013. *Malignant: How Cancer Becomes Us*. Berkeley: University of California Press.

Janis, Irving L. 1951. *Air War and Emotional Stress: Psychological Studies of Bombing and Civilian Defense*. New York: McGraw-Hill.

Jasanoff, Sheila. 2001. "Image and Imagination: The Formation of Global Environmental Consciousness." In *Changing the Atmosphere: Expert Knowledge and Environmental Governance*, edited by Clark A. Miller and Paul N. Edwards, 309–37. Cambridge: MIT Press.

Jeffrey, Joan S. n.d. "Biosecurity for Poultry Flocks." University of California, Davis, Veterinary Medicine website. Accessed February 15, 2012. http://www.vetmed .ucdavis.edu/vetext/INF-PO_Biosecurity.html.

Jervis, Robert. 1989. *The Meaning of the Nuclear Revolution*. Ithaca, NY: Cornell University Press.

Johnson, Chalmers. 2000. *Blowback: The Costs and Consequences of American Empire*. New York: Metropolitan.

Johnson, Chalmers. 2004. *The Sorrows of Empire: Militarism, Secrecy, and the End of the Republic*. New York: Metropolitan.

Johnson, Chalmers. 2006. *Nemesis: The Last Days of the American Republic*. New York: Metropolitan.

Johnson, William Gray, Barbara A. Holz, and Robert Jones. 2000. *A Cold War Battlefield: Frenchman Flat Historical District, Nevada Test Site, Nye County, Nevada*. Las Vegas, NV: Desert Research Institute.

Jones, Kate E., et al. 2008. "Global Trends in Emerging Infectious Diseases." *Nature* 451 (7181): 990–94.

Kahn, Herman. 1960. *On Thermonuclear War*. Princeton, NJ: Princeton University Press.

Kahn, Herman. 1962. *Thinking about the Unthinkable*. New York: Horizon Press.

Kahn, Herman. 1965. *On Escalation: Metaphors and Scenarios*. New York: Praeger.

Kalckar, Herman. 1958. "An International Milk Teeth Radiation Census." *Nature* 182 (4631): 283–84.

Kaplan, Amy. 2003. "Homeland Insecurities: Reflections on Language and Space." *Radical History Review* 85 (winter): 82–93.

Katz, Milton. 1986. *Ban the Bomb: A History of SANE, the Committee for a Sane Nuclear Policy, 1957–1985*. New York: Greenwood.

Keeney, L. Douglas. 2002. *The Doomsday Scenario*. St. Paul, MN: MBI Publishing.

Keever, Beverly Ann Deepe. 2004. *News Zero: The New York Times and the Bomb*. Monroe, ME: Common Courage.

Keusch, Gerald T., et al., eds. 2009. *Sustaining Global Surveillance and Response to Emerging Zoonotic Diseases*. Washington: National Academies Press.

King, Nicholas B. 2003. "The Influence of Anxiety: September 11, Bioterrorism and American Public Health." *Journal of the History of Medicine* 58: 433–41.

King, Nicholas B. 2004. "The Scale of Politics of Emerging Diseases." *Osiris* 19: 62–76.

Klare, Michael T. 2007. "The Pentagon vs. Peak Oil." *TomDispatch.com*. June 14.

Klotz, Lynn C., and Edward J. Sylvester. 2009. *Breeding Bioinsecurity*. Chicago: University of Chicago Press.

Knezo, Genevieve J. 2003. *"Sensitive but Unclassified" and Other Federal Security Controls of Scientific and Technical Information: History and Current Controversy*. Washington: Congressional Research Service.

Kopp, Carolyn. 1979. "The Origins of the American Scientific Debate over Fallout Hazards." *Social Studies of Science* 9 (4): 403–22.

Kosek, Jake. 2010. "Ecologies of Empire: On the New Uses of the Honeybee." *Cultural Anthropology* 25 (4): 650–78.

Kraus, Sidney, Reuben Mehling, and Elaine El-Assal. 1963. "Mass Media and the Fallout Controversy." *Public Opinion Quarterly* 27 (2): 191–205.

Kristof, Nicholas. 2002. "The Anthrax Files." *New York Times*. August 13.

Kroening, John L. 1965. "Stratosphere and Troposphere: Transport of Material between Them." *Science* 147 (3660): 862–64.

Krugler, David F. 2006. *This Is Only a Test: How Washington D.C. Prepared for Nuclear War*. New York: Palgrave.

Kwik, Gigi, et al. 2003. "Biosecurity: Responsible Stewardship of Bioscience in the Age of Catastrophic Terrorism." *Biosecurity and Bioterrorism* 1 (1): 27–60.

LaFlamme, Marcel. 2011. "Locating NBAF: The Imperial (Bio)politics of Site Selection." Paper presented at the Annual Conference of the Association of American Geographers. Seattle, Washington.

Lakoff, Andrew. 2008a. "From Population to Vital System: National Security and the Changing Object of Public Health." In *Biosecurity Interventions: Global Health and Security in Question*, edited by Andrew Lakoff and Stephen J. Collier, 33–60. New York: Columbia University Press.

Lakoff, Andrew. 2008b. "The Generic Biothreat, or, How We Became Unprepared." *Cultural Anthropology* 23 (3): 399–428.

Lakoff, Andrew, and Stephen J. Collier, eds. 2008. *Biosecurity Interventions: Global Health and Security in Question*. New York: Columbia University Press.

Larkin, Brian. 2013. "The Politics and Poetics of Infrastructure." *Annual Review of Anthropology* 42: 327–43.

Lee, Christopher. 2006. "Budget Cut Would Shutter EPA Libraries." *Washington Post*. May 15.

Leiserowitz, Anthony A. 2004. "Before and after *The Day after Tomorrow*: A Study of Climate Change Risk Perception." *Environment* 46(9): 22–37.

Leslie, Stuart W. 1993. *The Cold War and American Science: The Military-Industrial Academic Complex at MIT and Stanford*. New York: Columbia University Press.

Let's Face It. 1954. Washington: Federal Civil Defense Agency.

Levi, Michael. 2007. *On Nuclear Terrorism.* Cambridge, MA: Harvard University Press.

Light, Jennifer. 2003. *From Warfare to Welfare: Defense Intellectual and Urban Problems in Cold War America.* Baltimore, MD: Johns Hopkins University Press.

Lipschutz, Ronnie D., and Heather Turcotte. 2005. "Duct Tape or Plastic? The Political Economy of Threat and the Production of Fear." In *Making Threats: Biofears and Environmental Anxieties,* edited by Betsey Hartmann, Banu Subramaniam, and Charles Zerner, 25–46. Lanham, MD: Rowman and Littlefield.

Lowe, Celia. 2010. "Viral Clouds: Becoming H5N1 in Indonesia." *Cultural Anthropology* 25 (4): 625–49.

Lutz, Catherine. 1997. "Epistemology of the Bunker: The Brainwashed and Other New Subjects of Permanent War." In *Inventing the Psychological: Toward a Cultural History of Emotional Life in America,* edited by Joel Pfister and Nancy Schnog, 245–67. New Haven, CT: Yale University Press.

Lutz, Catherine. 2002. *Homefront: A Military City and the American Twentieth Century.* Boston: Beacon.

Lutz, Catherine, ed. 2009. *The Bases of Empire: The Global Struggle against U.S. Military Posts.* New York: New York University Press.

Maassarani, Tarek. 2007. *Redacting the Science of Climate Change: An Investigative and Synthesis Report.* Washington: Government Accountability Project.

Machta, L., and D. L. Harris. 1955. "Effects of Atomic Explosions on Weather." *Science* 121 (3134): 75–81.

Machta, L., R. J. List, and L. F. Hubert. 1956. "World-Wide Travel of Atomic Debris." *Science* 124 (3220): 474–77.

Macilwain, Colin, and Geoff Brumfiel. 2006. "US Scientists Fight Political Meddling." *Nature* 439 (7079): 896–97.

MacKenzie, Donald. 1990. *Inventing Accuracy: An Historical Sociology of Nuclear Missile Guidance.* Cambridge: MIT Press.

MacPhail, Theresa. Forthcoming. *Siren Song: A Pathography of Influenza and Global Public Health.* Ithaca, NY: Cornell University Press.

Makhijani, Arjun, Howard Hu, and Katherine Yih, eds. 1995. *Nuclear Wastelands: A Global Guide to Nuclear Weapons Production and Its Health and Environmental Effects.* Cambridge: MIT Press.

Makhijani, Arjun, and Stephen I. Schwartz. 1998. "Victims of the Bomb." In *Atomic Audit: The Costs and Consequences of U.S. Nuclear Weapons since 1940,* edited by Stephen I. Schwartz, 395–431. Washington: Brookings Institution.

Marland, G., T. A. Boden, and R. J. Andres. 2006. "Global, Regional, and National CO2 Emissions." In *Trends: A Compendium of Data on Global Change.* Oak Ridge, TN: Oak Ridge National Laboratory, Carbon Dioxide Information Analysis Center.

Martel, Brett. 2005. "What Hiroshima Looked Like: Katrina's Full Wrath Still Being Felt, Death Toll Soars." *Associated Press.* August 30.

Martin, Emily. 1990. "Toward an Anthropology of Immunology: The Body as Nation-State." *Medical Anthropology Quarterly* 4 (4): 410–26.

Martin, Thomas J., and Donald C. Latham. 1963. *Strategy for Survival.* Tucson: University of Arizona Press.

Masco, Joseph. 2006. *The Nuclear Borderlands: The Manhattan Project in Post–Cold War New Mexico.* Princeton, NJ: Princeton University Press.

Mason, B. J., Harrie Massey, and L. H. Bedford. 1968. "The Role of Satellites in Observing and Forecasting the Global Behavior of the Atmosphere." *Proceedings of the Royal Society of London (Series A: Mathematical and Physical Sciences)* 308 (1493): 157–72.

Massumi, Brian. 2007. "Potential Politics and the Primacy of Preemption." *Theory & Event* 10 (2).

Massumi, Brian. 2010. "The Future Birth of the Affective Fact: The Political Ontology of Threat." In *The Affect Theory Reader*, edited by Melissa Gregg and Gregory J. Seigworth, 52–70. Durham, NC: Duke University Press.

Massumi, Brian. 2011. "The Half-Life of Disaster." *Guardian.* April 15.

Matthews, Chris. 2005. "Transcript." *Hardball with Chris Matthews, MSNBC.* August 31. Accessed March 18, 2014. http://www.nbcnews.com/id/9160108/.

May, Elaine. 1990. *Homeward Bound: American Families in the Cold War Era.* New York: Basic.

May, Ernest R., ed. 1993. *American Cold War Strategy: Interpreting NSC 68.* New York: Bedford.

Mayer, Jane. 2008. *The Dark Side: The Inside Story of How the War on Terror Turned into a War on American Ideals.* New York: Doubleday.

Mazzarella, William. 2010. "Affect: What Is It Good For?" In *Enchantments of Modernity: Empire, Nation, Globalization*, edited by Saurabh Dube, 291–309. London: Routledge.

McClintock, Anne. 2009. "Paranoid Empire: Specters from Guantanamo and Abu Ghraib." *Small Axe* 13 (1): 50–74.

McDew, Darren W. 2010. "Finding the Appropriate Force Mix: Balancing Capabilities with Priorities." Accessed June 1, 2012. http://www.ifpafletcherconference.com/oldspeaklists/2010speakersNtranscripts.htm.

McEnaney, Laura. 2000. *Civil Defense Begins at Home: Militarization Meets Everyday Life in the Fifties.* Princeton, NJ: Princeton University Press.

Meade, Charles, and Roger C. Molander. 2006. *Considering the Effects of a Catastrophic Terrorist Attack.* Santa Monica, CA: RAND Corporation.

Medalia, Jonathan. 2007. *The Reliable Replacement Warhead Program: Background and Current Developments.* Washington: Congressional Research Service.

Melley, Timothy. 2012. *The Covert Sphere: Secrecy, Fiction, and the National Security State.* Ithaca: Cornell University Press.

Mellor, Felicity. 2007. "Colliding Worlds: Asteroid Research and the Legitimization of War in Space." *Social Studies of Science* 37 (4): 499–531.

Miller, Clark A. 2001. "Scientific Internationalism in American Foreign Policy: The Case of Meteorology, 1947–1958." In *Changing the Atmosphere: Expert Knowledge* and *Environmental Governance*, edited by Clark A. Miller and Paul N. Edwards, 167–218. Cambridge: MIT Press.

Miller, Clark A., and Paul N. Edwards, eds. 2001. *Changing the Atmosphere: Expert Knowledge and Environmental Governance.* Cambridge: MIT Press.

Miller, Judith, Stephen Engelberg, and William Broad. 2001. *Germs: Biological Weapons and America's Secret War.* New York: Simon and Schuster.

Miller, Richard L. 1986. *Under the Cloud: The Decades of Nuclear Testing.* New York: Free Press.

Mintz, John. 2003. "U.S. Threat Level Rises to Orange." *Washington Post.* December 22.

Moynihan, Daniel Patrick. 1998. *Secrecy: The American Experience.* New Haven, CT: Yale University Press.

Mueller, John. 2006. *Overblown: How Politicians and the Terrorism Industry Inflate Threats and Why We Believe Them.* New York: Free Press.

Musharraf, Pervez. 2006. *In the Line of Fire: A Memoir.* New York: Simon and Schuster.

National Academy of Sciences. 2004. *Biotechnology Research in an Age of Terrorism.* Washington: National Academies Press.

National Academy of Sciences. 2006. *Globalization, Biosecurity, and the Future of the Life Sciences.* Washington: National Academies Press.

National Academy of Sciences. 2011. *Review of the Scientific Approaches Used during the FBI's Investigation of the Anthrax Letters.* Washington: National Academies Press.

National Center for Atmospheric Research. 2006. "Abrupt Ice Retreat Could Produce Ice-Free Arctic Summers by 2040." University Corporation for Academic Research, December 11. Accessed March 18, 2014. http://www.ucar.edu/news/releases/2006/arctic.shtml.

National Institutes of Health, Office of the Budget. 2013. *Appropriations History by Institute/Center (1938 to the Present).* Accessed March 18, 2014. http://officeofbudget.od.nih.gov/approp_hist.html.

National Priorities Project. 2011. *U.S. Security Spending since 9/11.* Accessed December 1, 2013. http://nationalpriorities.org/analysis/2011/us-security-spending-since-911/.

National Research Council. 1985. *Effects on the Atmosphere of a Major Nuclear Exchange.* Washington: National Academies Press.

National Research Council. 2008. *Department of Homeland Security Bioterrorism Risk Assessment: A Call for Change.* Washington: National Academies Press.

National Research Council. 2012. *Terrorism and the Electric Power Delivery System.* Washington: National Academies Press.

National Safety Council. 2011. *Injury Facts, 2011 Edition.* Itasca, IL: National Safety Council.

National Security Council. 1993 [1950]. "National Security Council Directive 68." Republished in *American Cold War Strategy: Interpreting NSC 68*, edited by Ernest R. May, 21–82. New York: Bedford.

National Wildlife Federation. 2013. *Shifting Skies: Migratory Birds in a Warming World.* Merrifield, VA: National Wildlife Federation.

Natural Resources Defense Council. n.d. "Table of Global Nuclear Weapons Stockpiles, 1945–2002." Accessed January 27, 2014. http://www.nrdc.org/nuclear/nudb/datab19.asp.

Naval Postgraduate School and the U.S. Department of Homeland Security. n.d. "Colleges and Universities Offering Homeland Security Programs." Accessed February 8, 2014. http://www.chds.us/?partners/institutions.

New America Foundation. 2014. *Drone Wars: Pakistan.* Accessed March 18, 2014. http://natsec.newamerica.net/drones/pakistan/analysis.

Nixon, Rob. 2011. *Slow Violence and the Environmentalism of the Poor.* Cambridge, MA: Harvard University Press.

Nixon, Ron. 2013. "U.S. Postal Service Logging All Mail for Law Enforcement." *New York Times.* July 3.

Norris, Robert S., and Hans M. Kristensen. 2006. "Nuclear Notebook: Global Nuclear Stockpiles, 1945–2006." *Bulletin of the Atomic Scientists* 62 (4): 64–67.

Oakes, Guy. 1994. *The Imaginary War: Civil Defense and American Cold War Culture.* New York: Oxford University Press.

Obama, Barack. 2009. "Remarks by President Barack Obama." April 5. Accessed March 18, 2014. http://www.whitehouse.gov/the_press_office/Remarks-By-President -Barack-Obama-In-Prague-As-Delivered/.

Obama, Barack. 2010. "Executive Order 13556 of November 4, 2010: Controlled Unclassified Information." *Federal Register* 75 (2160): 68675–77.

Obama, Barack. 2011. *Notice from the President Regarding the Continuation of the National Emergency with Respect to Certain Terrorist Attacks.* Washington: Office of the President of the United States.

Odum, Howard T., and Eugene P. Odum. 1955. "Trophic Structure and Productivity of a Windward Coral Reef Community on Eniwetok Atoll." *Ecological Monographs* 25 (3): 291–320.

Office of Technology Assessment. 1979. *The Effects of Nuclear War.* Washington: Government Printing Office.

Office of Technology Assessment. 1993. *Proliferation of Weapons of Mass Destruction: Assessing the Risk.* Washington: Government Printing Office.

Oliver, Jack, and Leonard Murphy. 1971. "WWNSS: Seismology's Global Network of Observing Stations." *Science* 174 (4006): 254–61.

Olmsted, Kathryn. 1996. *Challenging the Secret Government: The Post-Watergate Investigations of the CIA and FBI.* Chapel Hill: University of North Carolina Press.

Open Society Foundation. 2013. *Globalizing Torture: CIA Secret Detention and Extraordinary Rendition.* New York: Open Society Foundation.

Open the Government. 2005a. "Secrecy Report Card 2005." Accessed December 1, 2013. http://www.openthegovernment.org/sites/default/files/otg/SRC2005.pdf.

Open the Government. 2005b. "Secrecy Report Card 2005: An Update." Accessed March 18, 2014. http://www.openthegovernment.org/sites/default/files/otg/OTG _RC_update.pdf.

Open the Government. 2011. "Secrecy Report 2011." Accessed February 2, 2014. http:// www.openthegovernment.org/sites/default/files/SRC_2011.pdf.

Operation Cue. 1955. Washington: Federal Civil Defense Administration. Accessed March 18, 2014. https://archive.org/details/Operatio1955.

Operation Cue (1964 Revision). 1964. Washington: Department of Defense, Office of Civil Defense. Accessed March 18, 2014. https://archive.org/details/Operatio1964.

Operation Upshot-Knothole. 1953. Washington: Department of Defense.

Oreskes, Naomi. 2003. "A Context of Motivation: US Navy Oceanographic Research and the Discovery of Sea-Floor Hydrothermal Vents." *Social Studies of Science* 33 (5): 697–742.

Oreskes, Naomi. 2004. "The Scientific Consensus on Climate Change." *Science* 306 (5702): 1686.

Orr, Jackie. 2005. "Making Civilian-Soldiers: The Militarization of Inner Space." In *Making Threats: Biofears and Environmental Anxieties,* edited by Betsy Hartmann, Banu Subramaniam, and Charles Zerner, 47–69. Lanham, MD: Rowman and Littlefield.

Orr, Jackie. 2006. *Panic Diaries: A Genealogy of Panic Disorder.* Durham, NC: Duke University Press.

Osgood, Kenneth. 2006. *Total Cold War: Eisenhower's Secret Propaganda Battle at Home and Abroad.* Lawrence: University Press of Kansas.

Ostherr, Kirsten. 2005. *Cinematic Prophylaxis: Globalization and Contagion in the Discourse of World Health.* Durham, NC: Duke University Press.

O'Toole, Tara. 2007a. "Hearing on Bioterrorism Preparedness and the Role of DHS Chief Medical Officer." March 29. Text available at http://www.upmchealthsecurity .org/website/resources/To_USG/Testimony_Briefings/2007/20070329-btprepand dhscmo.html. Slides available at http://outerdnn.outer.jhuapl.edu/videos/012407 /otoole_slides.pdf.

O'Toole, Tara. 2007b. "Six Years after Anthrax: Are We Better Prepared to Respond to Bioterrorism?" Testimony to the U.S. Senate Committee on Homeland Security and Governmental Affairs, October 23. Accessed March 18, 2014. https://www.fas.org /irp/congress/2007_hr/bioterror.html.

O'Toole, Tara. 2010. "The Convergence of Emerging Technologies." Presentation at Advancing Bioscience and Global Security panel, BIO International Convention, Chicago, IL, May 5.

Page, Max. 2008. *The City's End: Two Centuries of Fantasies, Fears, and Premonitions of New York's Destruction.* New Haven, CT: Yale University Press.

Panel on the Human Effects of Nuclear Weapons Development. 1956. *The Human Effects of Nuclear Weapons Development: A Report to the President and National Security Council.* Washington: Atomic Energy Commission.

Parmesan, Camille. 2006. "Ecological and Evolutionary Responses to Recent Climate Change." *Annual Review of Ecology, Evolution, and Systematics* 37 (1): 637–69.

Pemberton, Miriam. 2008. *The Budgets Compared: Military versus Climate Security. Institute for Policy Studies and Foreign Policy in Focus.* Accessed March 18, 2014. http://www.ips-dc.org/reports/military_vs_climate_security.

Perkovich, George. 2004. *Deconflating "WMD."* Stockholm: Weapons of Mass Destruction Commission.

Peterson, Jeannie, ed. 1983. *The Aftermath: The Human and Ecological Consequences of Nuclear War*. New York: Pantheon.

Peterson, Val. 1953. "Panic: The Ultimate Weapon?" *Collier's*. August 21: 99–109.

Petryna, Adriana. 2009. *When Experiments Travel: Clinical Trials and the Global Search for Human Subjects*. Princeton, NJ: Princeton University Press.

Pettus, Emily Wagster. 2005. "Katrina a Tough Political Test for Barbour." *Associated Press*. September 3.

Piltz, Rick. 2005. "Censorship and Secrecy: Politicizing the Climate Change Science Program." *Climate Science Watch*. June 8. Accessed March 18, 2014. http://www.climatesciencewatch.org/index.php/csw/details/censorship-and-secrecy/.

Pittock, A. Barrie, Mark A. Harwell, and Thomas C. Hutchinson, eds. 1986. *Environmental Consequences of Nuclear War*. New York: John Wiley.

Planet of the Apes. 1968. Directed by Franklin J. Schaffner. Los Angeles: Twentieth Century Fox.

Poole, Robert. 2008. *Earthrise: How Man First Saw the Earth*. New Haven, CT: Yale University Press.

Povinelli, Elizabeth. 2011. *Economies of Abandonment: Social Belonging and Endurance in Late Liberalism*. Durham, NC: Duke University Press.

Powell, Colin. 2003. "Remarks to the United Nations Security Council." GlobalSecurity.org. Accessed March 18, 2014. www.globalsecurity.org/wmd/library/news/iraq/2003/iraq-030205-powell-un-17300pf.htm.

Pozen, David. 2005. "The Mosaic Theory, National Security, and the Freedom of Information Act." *Yale Law Journal* 115 (3): 628–79.

Prados, John. 2004. *Hoodwinked: The Documents That Reveal How Bush Sold Us a War*. New York: New Press.

Prados, John, and Margaret Pratt Porter, eds. 2004. *Inside the Pentagon Papers*. Lawrence: University Press of Kansas.

Presidential Commission for the Study of Bioethical Issues. 2010. *New Directions: The Ethics of Synthetic Biology and Emerging Technologies*. Accessed March 18, 2014. http://bioethics.gov/sites/default/files/PCSBI-Synthetic-Biology-Report-12.16.10.pdf.

Priest, Dana. 2012. "The B61 Bomb: A Case Study in Costs and Needs." *Washington Post*. September 16.

Priest, Dana, and William M. Arkin. 2010. "A Hidden World, Growing beyond Control." *Washington Post*. July 19.

Priest, Dana, and William M. Arkin. 2011. *Top Secret America: The Rise of the New American Security State*. New York: Little, Brown.

Project for the New American Century. 2000. *Rebuilding America's Defenses: Strategy, Forces, and Resources for a New Century*. Washington: Project for the New American Century.

Rafael, Vicente. 2009. "Translation, American English, and the National Insecurities of Empire." *Social Text* 27 (4): 1–23.

Rancière, Jacques. 2009. "The Aesthetic Dimension: Aesthetics, Politics, Knowledge." *Critical Inquiry* 36 (1): 1–19.

RAND Corporation. 1953. *Project Sunshine: Worldwide Effects of Atomic Weapons.* Santa Monica, CA: RAND Corporation.

Rappert, Brian, and Chandre Gould, eds. 2009. *Biosecurity: Origins, Transformations and Practices.* New York: Palgrave.

Reese, Shawn. 2012. *Defining Homeland Security: Analysis and Congressional Consider-ations.* Washington: Congressional Research Service.

Reporters Committee for Freedom of the Press. 2005. *Homefront Confidential: How the War on Terrorism Affects Access to Information and the Public's Right to Know.* 6th edition. Arlington, VA: Reporters Committee for Freedom of the Press. Ac-cessed February 2, 2014. www.rcfp.org/homefrontconfidential.

RETORT [Iain Boal, T. J. Clark, Joseph Matthews, and Michael Watts]. 2005. *Afflicted Powers: Capital and Spectacle in a New Age of War.* New York: Verso.

Revkin, Andrew. 2005. "Bush Aide Softened Greenhouse Gas Links to Global Warm-ing." *New York Times.* June 8.

Revkin, Andrew. 2006a. "Arctic Ice Shelf Broke Off Canadian Island." *New York Times.* December 30.

Revkin, Andrew. 2006b. "Climate Expert Says NASA Tried to Silence Him." *New York Times.* January 29.

Rhodes, Keith. 2007. *High Containment Biosafety Laboratories.* Washington: Govern-ment Accountability Office.

Roach, John. 2006. "Polar Bears Being Considered for U.S. Endangered List." *National Geographic News.* February 10.

Robb, David L. 2004. *Operation Hollywood: How the Pentagon Shapes and Censors the Movies.* Amherst, MA: Prometheus.

Roberts, Alasdair. 2006. *Blacked Out: Government Secrecy in the Information Age.* Cambridge: Cambridge University Press.

Roberts, Geneviève. 2006. "Climate Change vs. Mother Nature: Scientists Reveal That Bears Have Stopped Hibernating." *Independent.* December 21.

Robock, A., et al. 2007. "Climatic Consequences of Regional Nuclear Conflicts." *Atmo-spheric Chemistry and Physics Discussions* 7: 2003–12.

Rogin, Michael. 1987. *Ronald Reagan, the Movie, and Other Episodes in Political De-monology.* Berkeley: University of California Press.

Rogin, Michael. 1998. *Independence Day.* London: British Film Institute.

Rojecki, Andrew. 1999. *Silencing the Opposition: Antinuclear Movements and the Media in the Cold War.* Champaign: University of Illinois Press.

Roucek, Joseph S. 1983. "The Geopolitics of the Arctic." *American Journal of Econom-ics and Sociology* 42 (4): 463–71.

Rubin, David M., and Constance Cummings. 1989. "Nuclear War and Its Conse-quences on Television News." *Journal of Communication* 39 (1): 39–58.

Rudgers, David F. 2000. *Creating the Secret State: The Origins of the Central Intelli-gence Agency, 1943–1947.* Lawrence: University Press of Kansas.

Rueter, Theodore, and Thomas Kalil. 1991. "Nuclear Strategy and Nuclear Winter." *World Politics* 43 (4): 587–607.

Rumsfeld, Donald. 2002. "DoD News Briefing." February 12. Accessed March 18, 2014. http://www.defense.gov/transcripts/transcript.aspx?transcriptid=2636.

Ryan, Jeffrey R., and Jan F. Glarum. 2008. *Biosecurity and Bioterrorism: Containing and Preventing Biological Threats.* Oxford: Butterworth-Heinemann.

Sagan, Carl. 1983. "The Nuclear Winter." *Parade.* October 30, 4–7.

Sagan, Carl. 1983–84. "Nuclear War and Climatic Catastrophe: Some Policy Implications." *Foreign Affairs* 62 (2): 257–92.

Sagan, Carl, and Richard P. Turco. 1990. *A Path Where No Man Thought: Nuclear Winter and the End of the Arms Race.* New York: Random House.

Sagan, Carl, and Richard P. Turco. 1993. "Nuclear Winter in the Post–Cold War Era." *Journal of Peace Research* 30 (4): 369–73.

Sagan, Scott D. 1993. *The Limits of Safety: Organization, Accidents, and Nuclear Weapons.* Princeton, NJ: Princeton University Press.

Sagan, Scott D., and Jeremi Suri. 2003. "The Madman Nuclear Alert: Secrecy, Signaling, and Safety in October 1969." *International Security* 27 (4): 150–83.

Samimian-Darash, Limore. 2009. "A Pre-Event Configuration for Biological Threats: Preparedness and the Constitution of Biosecurity Events." *American Ethnologist* 36 (3): 478–91.

Sanger, David E. 2012. *Confront and Conceal: Obama's Secret Wars and Surprising Use of American Power.* New York: Crown.

Scheiback, Michael. 2003. *Atomic Narratives and American Youth: Coming of Age with the Atom, 1945–1955.* Jefferson, NC: McFarland.

Schelling, Thomas C. 1966. *Arms and Influence.* New Haven, CT: Yale University Press.

Schmitt, H. P. 1956. *Effects of Nuclear Explosions on Frozen Foods.* Washington: Government Printing Office.

Schneier, Bruce. 2007. "Details on the UK Liquid Terrorist Plot." *Schneier on Security.* August 6. Accessed March 18, 2014. https://www.schneier.com/blog/archives/2007/08/details_on_the_1.html.

Schoch-Spana, Monica. 2004. "Bioterrorism, US Public Health and a Secular Apocalypse." *Anthropology Today* 20 (5): 8–13.

Schoch-Spana, Monica. 2006. "Post-Katrina, Pre-Pandemic America." *Anthropology News* 47 (1): 32–36.

Schoch-Spana, Monica. 2012. "The People's Role in U.S. National Health Security: Past, Present, and Future." *Biosecurity and Bioterrorism* 10 (11): 77–88.

Schwartz, John. 2006. "Studies Link Global Warming to Great Power of Hurricanes." *New York Times.* May 31.

Schwartz, Peter, and Doug Randall. 2003. *An Abrupt Climate Change Scenario and Its Implications for United States National Security.* Accessed March 18, 2014. www.dtic.mil/cgi-bin/GetTRDoc?AD=ada469325.

Schwartz, Stephen I., ed. 1998. *Atomic Audit: The Costs and Consequences of U.S. Nuclear Weapons since 1940.* Washington: Brookings Institution.

Sebald, W. G. 2004. *On the Natural History of Destruction.* Translated by Anthea Bell. New York: Modern Library.

Secrecy. 2008. Directed by Peter Galison and Robb Moss. Oley, PA: Bullfrog Films.

Sedgwick, Eve Kosofsky. 2003. *Touching Feeling: Affect, Pedagogy, Performativity.* Durham, NC: Duke University Press.

Serres, Michel. 2005. *The Natural Contract.* Translated by Elizabeth MacArthur. Ann Arbor: University of Michigan Press.

Shah, Saeed. 2011. "CIA Organised Fake Vaccination Drive to Get Osama bin Laden's Family DNA." *Guardian.* July 11.

Shane, Scott. 2010. "Obama Takes a Hard Line against Leaks to Press." *New York Times.* June 11.

Shanker, Thom. 2009. "U.S. Increases Its Share of Worldwide Arms Market." *New York Times.* September 7.

Sheer, Robert. 1982. *With Enough Shovels: Reagan, Bush, and Nuclear War.* New York: Random House.

Shils, Edward. 1996. *The Torment of Secrecy.* Chicago: Elephant Paperback.

Siegel, James T. 1998. *A New Criminal Type in Jakarta: Counter-Revolution Today.* Durham, NC: Duke University Press.

Simmel, Georg. 1906. "The Sociology of Secrecy and of Secret Societies." *American Journal of Sociology* 11 (4): 441–98.

Simon, Stephanie. 2012. "Suspicious Encounters: Ordinary Preemption and the Securitization of Photography." *Security Dialogue* 43 (2): 157–73.

Sloterdijk, Peter. 2005. "Forward to a Theory of Spheres." In *Cosmograms*, edited by M. O'Hanian and Jean-Christophe Royoux, 223–41. New York: Lukas and Sternberg.

Sloterdijk, Peter. 2009. *Terror from the Air.* Los Angeles: Semiotext(e).

Sloterdijk, Peter, and Jans-Jurgen Henrichs. 2001. *Neither Sun nor Death.* Los Angeles: Semiotext(e).

Slotkin, Louis. 1996. *Regeneration through Violence: The Mythology of the American Frontier, 1600–1860.* New York: Harper Perennial.

Smith, Bradley, et al. 2005. "After-Action Report: Navigating the Storm." *Biosecurity and Bioterrorism* 3 (3): 256–67.

Smith, Bradley T., Thomas V. Inglesby, and Tara O'Toole. 2003. "Biodefense R & D: Anticipating Future Threat, Establishing a Strategic Environment." *Biosecurity and Bioterrorism* 1 (3): 193–202.

Smith, Shawn Michelle. 1999. *American Archives: Gender, Race and Class in Visual Culture.* Princeton, NJ: Princeton University Press.

Sontag, Susan. 1966. "The Imagination of Disaster." In Susan Sontag, *Against Interpretation, and Other Essays*, 209–25. New York: Farrar, Straus, and Giroux.

Star, Susan Leigh. 1999. "The Ethnography of Infrastructure." *American Behavioral Scientist* 43 (3): 377–91.

Stern, Nicholas. 2007. *The Economics of Climate Change: The Stern Review.* Cambridge: Cambridge University Press.

Stewart, Kathleen. 2007. *Ordinary Affects.* Durham, NC: Duke University Press.

Stewart, Kathleen. 2011. "Atmospheric Attunements." *Environment and Planning D* 29: 445–53.

Stine, Deborah D. 2009. *The Manhattan Project, the Apollo Program, and Federal Energy Technology R&D Programs: A Comparative Analysis.* Washington: Congressional Research Service.

Stockholm International Peace Research Institute. 2011. *Background Paper on SIPRI Military Expenditure Data, 2010.* Stockholm: Stockholm International Peace Research Institute.

Stokstad, Erik. 2006. "Global Loss of Biodiversity Harming Ocean Bounty." *Science* 314 (5800): 745.

Stoler, Ann Laura. 2009. *Along the Archival Grain: Epistemic Anxieties and Colonial Common Sense.* Princeton, NJ: Princeton University Press.

Stoler, Ann Laura, with David Bond. 2006. "Refractions off Empire: Untimely Comparisons in Harsh Times." *Radical History Review* 95 (spring): 93–107.

Stone, Geoffrey R. 2006. "Government Secrecy vs. Freedom of the Press." *First Reports* 7 (1): 1–34.

Sturken, Marita. 2007. *Tourist of History: Memory, Kitsch, and Consumerism from Oklahoma City to Ground Zero.* Durham, NC: Duke University Press.

Suhr, Jim. 2012. "Half of U.S. Counties Declared Disaster Areas." *Associated Press.* August 1.

Sullivan, Thomas J., et al. 1993. "Atmospheric Release Advisory Capability: Real-Time Modeling of Airborne Hazardous Materials." *Bulletin of the American Meteorological Society* 74 (12): 2341–61.

Suskind, Ron. 2006. *The One Percent Doctrine.* New York: Simon and Schuster.

Tanielian, Terri, and Lisa H. Jaycox. 2008. *Invisible Wounds of War.* Santa Monica, CA: RAND Corporation.

Taussig, Michael. 1987. *Shamanism, Colonialism, and the Wild Man: A Study in Terror and Healing.* Chicago: University of Chicago Press.

Taussig, Michael. 1992. *The Nervous System.* New York: Routledge.

Taylor, Bryan C. 1997. "Nuclear Pictures and Metapictures." *American Literary History* 9 (3): 567–97.

Thacker, Paul D. 2006. "Climate-Controlled White House." *Salon.* September 19.

Thompson, Stanley L., and Stephen Schneider. 1986. "Nuclear Winter Reappraised." *Foreign Affairs* 64 (5): 981–1005.

Todd, Walter E., Willard S. Paul, and Val Peterson. 1955. "National Defense against Atomic Attack." *Scientific Monthly* 80 (4): 240–49.

Toon, O. B., et al. 2007. "Atmospheric Effects and Societal Consequences of Regional Scale Nuclear Conflicts and Acts of Individual Terrorism." *Atmospheric Chemistry and Physics* 7: 1973–2002.

Tucker, Jonathan B., ed. 2000. *Toxic Terror: Assessing Terrorist Use of Chemical and Biological Weapons.* Cambridge: MIT Press.

Turco, R. P., O. B. Toon, T. P. Ackerman, J. B. Pollack, and Carl Sagan. 1983. "Nuclear Winter: Global Consequences of Multiple Nuclear Explosions." *Science* 222 (4630): 1286–92.

Turco, R. P., O. B. Toon, T. P. Ackerman, J. B. Pollack, and Carl Sagan. 1990. "Climate and Smoke: An Appraisal of Nuclear Winter." *Science* 247 (4939): 166–76.

Ullman, Harlan, and James Wade Jr. 1996. *Shock and Awe: Achieving Rapid Dominance*. Washington: National Defense University.

UN Commission for Conventional Armaments. 1948. "Resolution of the Commission for Conventional Armaments, August 12, 1948." In *Department of State Bulletin*, August 29.

Union of Concerned Scientists. 2008. *Interference at the EPA: Science and Politics at the U.S. Environmental Protection Agency*. Accessed March 18, 2014. http://www .ucsusa.org/assets/documents/scientific_integrity/interference-at-the-epa.pdf.

UPMC Center for Health Security. n.d. "Dark Winter." Accessed February 5, 2014. http://www.upmchealthsecurity.org/website/events/2001_darkwinter.

UPMC Center for Health Security. 2005. "Atlantic Storm Interactive." Accessed March 18, 2014. http://www.atlantic-storm.org.

U.S. Centers for Disease Control and Prevention. 2010. "Deaths and Mortality." Accessed March 18, 2014. http://www.cdc.gov/nchs/fastats/deaths.htm.

U.S. Centers for Disease Control and Prevention. 2011. "Map of International Requests for Assistance, 2007–2011." Accessed June 1, 2011. http://www.cdc.gov/24–7/CDC FastFacts/worldwide.html.

U.S. Centers for Disease Control and Prevention. 2014. "Estimates of Foodborne Illness in the United States." Accessed March 18, 2014. http://www.cdc.gov/foodbor neburden/index.html.

U.S. Central Intelligence Agency. 1949. Memorandum, Hillenkoetter to Executive Secretary, NSC, "Atomic Energy Program of the USSR." Accessed March 18, 2014. http://www2.gwu.edu/~nsarchiv/NSAEBB/NSAEBB179/.

U.S. Central Intelligence Agency. 1951. "Intelligence Estimates on Chinese Communist Intentions to Intervene in Korea." Accessed March 18, 2014. http://www2.gwu.edu /~nsarchiv/NSAEBB/NSAEBB179/.

U.S. Central Intelligence Agency. 2004. *Central Intelligence Agency Inspector General Special Review: Counterterrorism Detention and Interrogation Activities (September 2001–October 2003)*. U.S. Central Intelligence Agency. Accessed February 2, 2014. http://luxmedia.com.edgesuite.net/aclu/IG_Report.pdf.

U.S. Congress. 2001. "Authorization for Use of Military Force." Public Law 107-40, Joint Resolution of 107th Congress, September 18. Washington: Government Printing Office. Accessed March 18, 2014. http://www.gpo.gov/fdsys/pkg/BILLS -107sjres23enr/pdf/BILLS-107sjres23enr.pdf.

U.S. Defense Nuclear Agency. 1982. *Shots Encore to Climax: The Final Four Tests of the Upshot-Knothole Series, 8 May–4 June 1953*. Washington: Defense Nuclear Agency.

U.S. Department of Defense. 1953. *Operation Upshot-Knothole: Summary Report of the Technical Director, Program 1–9*. Washington: Department of Defense.

U.S. Department of Defense. 2003a. *Nuclear Posture Review: Implementation Plan*. Washington: Government Printing Office.

U.S. Department of Defense. 2003b. "Secretary Rumsfeld Remarks on ABC *This Week with George Stephanopoulos*. March 30. Accessed March 18, 2014. www.defense.gov /transcripts/transcript.aspx?transcriptID=2185.

U.S. Department of Defense. 2010. *Quadrennial Defense Review Report*. Washington: Government Printing Office.

U.S. Department of Defense. 2012. *Joint Operations Access Concept*. Washington: Government Printing Office.

U.S. Department of Energy. 1994. *Closing the Circle on the Splitting of the Atom*. Washington: U.S. Department of Energy, Office of Environmental Management.

U.S. Department of Energy. 2011. *FY 2012 Stockpile Stewardship and Management Plan: Report to Congress*. Washington: U.S. Department of Energy.

U.S. Department of Energy. 2013. *FY 2014 Stockpile Stewardship and Management Plan: Report to Congress*. Washington: U.S. Department of Energy.

U.S. Department of Homeland Security. 2003. *National Strategy for the Physical Protection of Critical Infrastructures and Key Assets*. Washington: Government Printing Office.

U.S. Department of Homeland Security. 2004. *National Response Plan*. Washington: Government Printing Office.

U.S. Department of Homeland Security. 2005. *National Planning Scenarios*. Washington: Government Printing Office.

U.S. Department of Homeland Security. 2006. "Remarks by Homeland Security Secretary Michael Chertoff, United States Attorney General Alberto Gonzales, FBI Director Robert Mueller and Assistant Secretary for TSA Kip Hawley." August 10. Accessed March 18, 2014. https://www.hsdl.org/?view&did=476386.

U.S. Department of Homeland Security. n.d.a. "National Exercise Program." Accessed February 4, 2014. http://www.dhs.gov/national-exercise-program.

U.S. Department of Homeland Security. n.d.b. "National Terrorism Advisory System." Accessed February 15, 2012. http://www.dhs.gov/files/programs/ntas.shtm.

U.S. Department of Homeland Security. n.d.c. "Science and Technology Directorate: Centers of Excellence." Accessed February 8, 2014. http://www.dhs.gov/st-centers -excellence.

U.S. Department of Justice. 2010. *Amerithrax Investigation Summary*. Washington: Government Printing Office.

U.S. Department of the Army. 2009. "Department of the Army Personnel Policy Guidance for Overseas Contingency Operations." Accessed February 7, 2014. http:// www.armyg1.army.mil/militarypersonnel/ppg/PPG.pdf.

U.S. Government Accountability Office. 2006. *Information Sharing: The Federal Government Needs to Establish Policies and Processes for Sharing Terrorism-Related and Sensitive but Unclassified Information*. Washington: U.S. Government Accountability Office.

U.S. Government Accountability Office. 2009. *Overseas Contingency Operations: Reported Obligations for the Department of Defense*. Washington: U.S. Government Accountability Office.

U.S. Homeland Security Council. 2006. *National Strategy for Pandemic Influenza: Implementation Plan*. Washington: Government Printing Office.

U.S. House of Representatives, Committee on Government Reform, Minority Staff Special Investigations Division. 2004. *Secrecy in the Bush Administration*. Prepared

by Henry A. Waxman. Accessed March 18, 2014. https://www.fas.org/sgp/library
/waxman.pdf .

U.S. House of Representatives, Committee on Oversight and Government Reform.
2007. *Political Interference with Climate Change Science under the Bush Administration.* Accessed March 9, 2014. http://permanent.access.gpo.gov/lps94771
/20071210101633.pdf.

U.S. Information Security Oversight Office. 2004a. *2004 Report on Cost Estimates for
Security Classification Activities.* Accessed February 2, 2014. http://www.archives
.gov/isoo/reports/2004-cost-report.html.

U.S. Information Security Oversight Office. 2004b. *Report to the President 2004.* Accessed February 2, 2014. www.fas.org/sgp/isoo/2004rpt.pdf.

U.S. Information Security Oversight Office. 2006. "Audit of the Withdrawal of Records from Public Access at the National Archives and Records Administration for
Classification Purposes." April 26. Accessed March 18, 2014. http://www.archives
.gov/isoo/reports/2006-audit-report.html.

U.S. Information Security Oversight Office. 2011. *2010 Report to the President.* Accessed
February 2, 2014. http://www.archives.gov/isoo/reports/2010-annual-report.pdf.

U.S. Information Security Oversight Office. 2012. *2011 Cost Report.* Washington: National Archives and Records Administration.

U.S. National Counterterrorism Center. 2011. *2010 Report on Terrorism.* Washington:
Office of the Director of National Intelligence.

U.S. Office of the Director of National Intelligence. 2012. *Annual Intelligence Authorization Act Report on Security Clearance Determinations for Fiscal Year 2011.*
Washington: Government Printing Office.

U.S. Senate, Committee on Homeland Security and Governmental Affairs, Permanent
Subcommittee on Investigations. 2012. *Federal Support for Involvement in State and
Local Fusion Centers.* Washington: Government Printing Office.

U.S. White House. 2002a. *The National Security Strategy of the United States of
America.* Washington: Government Printing Office.

U.S. White House. 2002b. *National Strategy to Combat Weapons of Mass Destruction.*
Washington: Government Printing Office.

U.S. White House. 2004. "Biodefense for the 21st Century." April 28. Accessed March
9, 2014. http://www.fas.org/irp/offdocs/nspd/hspd-10.html.

Vanderbilt, Tom. 2002. *Survival City: Adventures among the Ruins of Atomic America.*
New York: Princeton Architectural.

Vandercook, William F. 1986. "Making the Very Best of the Very Worst: The
'Human Effects of Nuclear Weapons' Report of 1956." *International Security* 11 (1):
184–95.

Vine, David. 2009. *Island of Shame: The Secret History of the U.S. Military Base on
Diego Garcia.* Princeton, NJ: Princeton University Press.

Virilio, Paul. 1989. *War and Cinema: The Logistics of Perception.* London: Verso.

Vogal, Kathleen M. 2008a. "Framing Biosecurity: An Alternative to the Biotech Revolution Model?" *Science and Public Policy* 35 (1): 45–54.

Vogal, Kathleen M. 2008b. " 'Iraqi Winnebagos of Death': Imagined and Realized Futures of US Bioweapons Threat Assessments." *Science and Public Policy* 35 (8): 561–73.

Vogel, H. 2007. "Weapons of Mass Destruction, WMD." *European Journal of Radiology* 63: 205–13.

Wald, Priscilla. 2008. *Contagious: Cultures, Carriers, and the Outbreak Narrative.* Durham, NC: Duke University Press.

Walsh, Declan. 2012a. "Fallout of Bin Laden Raid: Aid Groups In Pakistan Are Suspect." *New York Times.* May 2.

Walsh, Declan. 2012b. "Taliban Block Vaccinations in Pakistan." *New York Times.* June 18.

Wang, Jessica. 1999. *Science in an Age of Anxiety: Scientists, Anti-Communism, and the Cold War.* Chapel Hill: University of North Carolina Press.

Warner, Michael. 2002. *Publics and Counterpublics.* New York: Zone.

Warnock, A. Timothy, ed. 2000. *Short of War: Major USAF Contingency Operations, 1947–1997.* Washington: Air Force History and Museums Program.

Weart, Spencer R. 2003. *The Discovery of Global Warming.* Cambridge, MA: Harvard University Press.

Weber, Samuel. 2004. *Theatricality as Medium.* New York: Fordham University Press.

Weller, George. 2006. *First into Nagasaki.* New York: Crown.

Weston, Kath. 2012. "Political Ecologies of the Precarious." *Anthropological Quarterly* 85 (2): 429–56.

What You Should Know about Biological Warfare. 1952. Washington: Federal Civil Defense Administration. Accessed June 1, 2012. http://archive.org/details/What YouS1952.

Wheeler, Winslow T. 2014. "America's $1 Trillion National Security Budget." *Counterpunch.org.* March 14.

White Light, Black Rain: The Destruction of Hiroshima and Nagasaki. 2006. Directed by Steven Okazaki. Los Angeles: Home Box Office.

Whitehall, Geoffrey. 2010. "Preemptive Sovereignty and Avian Pandemics." *Theory & Event* 31 (2): 1–13.

Williams, Raymond. 1978. *Marxism and Literature.* Oxford: Oxford University Press.

Willman, David. 2012. "BioWatch: The Biological Defense Program That Cries Wolf." *Chicago Tribune.* July 7.

Wills, Garry. 2010. *Bomb Power: The Modern Presidency and the National Security State.* New York: Penguin.

Wittner, Lawrence S. 1993. *One World of None: A History of the World Nuclear Disarmament Movement through 1953.* Stanford, CA: Stanford University Press.

Wittner, Lawrence S. 1997. *Resisting the Bomb: A History of the World Nuclear Disarmament Movement, 1954–1970.* Stanford, CA: Stanford University Press.

Wittner, Lawrence S. 2003. *Toward Abolition: A History of the World Nuclear Disarmament Movement, 1971 to the Present.* Stanford, CA: Stanford University Press.

Wohlstetter, Albert. 1958. *The Delicate Balance of Terror.* Santa Monica, CA: RAND Corporation.

Wohlstetter, Roberta. 1962. *Pearl Harbor Warning and Decision*. Stanford, CA: Stanford University Press.

Wolfe, Nathan D., Claire Panosian Dunavan, and Jared Diamond. 2007. "Origins of Major Human Infectious Disease." *Nature* 447 (7142): 279–83.

Wolfsthal, Jon B., Jeffrey Lewis, and Marc Quint. 2014. *The Trillion Dollar Nuclear Triad*. Monterey, CA: James Martin Center for Nonproliferation Studies.

Woodward, Bob. 2003. *Bush at War*. New York: Simon and Schuster.

Worm, Boris, et al. 2006. "Impact of Biodiversity Loss on Ocean Ecosystem Services." *Science* 314 (5800): 787–90.

Wray, Matt. 2006. "A Blast from the Past: Preserving and Interpreting the Atomic Age." *American Quarterly* 58 (2): 467–83.

Xu, Jiaquan, et al. 2010. "Deaths: Final Data for 2007." *National Vital Statistics Reports* 58 (19): 1–136.

Ziegler, Charles A., and David Jacobson. 1995. *Spying without Spies: Origins of America's Secret Nuclear Surveillance System*. Westport, CT: Praeger.

Zulaika, Joseba, and William A. Douglass. 1996. *Terror and Taboo: The Follies, Fables, and Faces of Terrorism*. New York: Routledge.

INDEX

Page references in italics indicate illustrations.

global-economy connectivity generated by, 156; and terrorism scenarios, 164, 170–71, 226n19, 228n32; virus–enemy link, 159; *What You Should Know about Biological Warfare*, 166–68, *169*. *See also* anthrax letters

Biosecurity and Bioterrorism, 227n27

BioShield, 155

biosphere. *See* earth sciences/environmentalism

BioWatch, 155, 224–25n7, 231n8

Bipartisan WMD Terrorism Research Center, 225n10

Birks, John, 93

Blanchot, Maurice, 47

blowback, 134, 200

botulism, 160

The Bourne Identity, 191

Bradbury Science Museum (Los Alamos National Laboratory), 117, *117–18*, 119–20, *120*

Broad, William, 228n37

Bruckheimer, Jerry, 217n23

Bruegel, Pieter: *Landscape with the Fall of Icarus*, 179, *179*

BSL-3 and BSL-4 laboratories, 157–58, *158*, 180–81, 225n11

Bush, George W.: on biodefense, 154–55; biological weapons, 224n4; on biological weapons, 151–52; on Hurricane Katrina, 106–7, 109; on invading Iraq, 24, 72; on preemptive war, 72, 218n24; after September 11 attacks, 10, 230n1; on WMDS, 27, 145

Bush (George W.) administration: on classified information, 129, 222n8; on climate change, 104–5, 220n17; counterterror commitment of, 29–30; on endangered species, 221n20; illegal practices of, 197; Iraq policy of, 75; nuclear weapons policy of, 221n1; Pakistan policy of, 75; on smallpox vaccination, 152, 154–55; War on Terror, 5, 110, 163–64, 216n14; on WMDS, 38, 140, 149, 223n16

Cambodia, 75

cancer, 162

carbon emissions, 104, 110, 221n25

cartography, 89

Carus, Seth, 214n16

CDC (Centers for Disease Control and Prevention), 225n11; at the BIO International Convention, 185; on causes of death in the United States, 162; on foodborne disease, 200; global mandate of, 33; and the H1N1 influenza outbreak, 227n30; international requests for help from, 187, *188*; and zoonotic diseases, 184

Center for Biosecurity (later Center for Health Security; University of Pittsburgh Medical Center), 171–72, *172*, 176, *177*, 227n27

Central Intelligence Agency. *See* CIA

Chemical and Biological Weapons Convention, 228n37

Chemical Warfare Service, 3

Cheney, Dick, 8, 11, 40, 140, 176, 201, 223n17

China, Communist revolution in, 6

CIA (Central Intelligence Agency): on Chinese invasion of Korea, 5; creation of, 9, 124; document reclassification in, 3; Intellipedia project of, 223n15; on Soviet nuclear weapons science, 5–6; vaccination ruse/search for bin Laden, 187–89, 229n43; worldwide attack matrix of, 33–34. *See also* drone attacks

cinema, 51, 65–67, 69–71, 79, 99–101, 166–69, 217nn21–22

civil defense program, 42, 45, 47–53, *53*, *55*, 215nn8–9, 216n12, 216n14. *See also under* Cold War

Clarke, Richard, 201

climate change, 107–11; from atomic tests, 87, 218–19n5; carbon emissions, 104, 110, 221n25; and cartography, 89; global climate simulation, 219n10; global warming, 79, 99–106, 110–11; greenhouse

climate change (*continued*)
    gases, 104–6, 220n15, 220n17; militarized response to, 220n15; modeling of, 89, 95, 109; nuclear winter, 92–99, *97–99*; overview of, 79–80; political interference with science of, 104–5, 220n17; research on, 88–89, 106; U.S. neglect of, 105–6, 221n23

Clinton administration, 229–30n44

Closing the Circle on the Splitting of the Atom, *116*, 116–17

The Cold and the Dark (Ehrlich), 96, *97–99*

Cold War: arms race during, 15, 45, 47, 79, 217n20; civil defense campaign during, 25, 42, 73, 128; emotional management used in, 20–21, 26, 42, 49–50, 56–57, 63, 127–28, 215n8; end of, 72, 121, 218n24; existential threat fostered by, 2, 5–7, 20–21; infrastructures of, 26, 28; malfunctions of nuclear apparatus during, 224n1; mutual assured destruction during, 9, 15, 170; national security during, 4–5, 48; nation building during, 33; nuclear cinema during, 70; nuclear panics during, 7; proposed warning system during, 25; public support for, 52; speculative expert imaginary of, 15–16. *See also* atomic bomb; nuclear ruins and survival

Cole, Leonard A., 225n12, 229n44

Collier, Stephen J., 226n24

Collins, Joan, 58–59

color-coded warning system, 22–23, 25, 218n25

Comar, C. L., 86

Congress, 193, 197, 230n1

Congressional Research Service, 12

containment policy (NSC 68), 48, 126

Cooper, Melinda, 149

Corona satellite system, 89

counterterror, 193–210; agents of, 198–99; apocalyptic imaginary of, 14–17; Authorization to Use Military Force, 193, 230n1; beginning of, 121; Bush (George W.) administration's commit-

ment to, 29–30; commitment to total security, 18, 195–96; and complexity and unpredictability, 171, 226n24; costs of, 2–3; vs. democratic governance, 2–3; embeddedness of, 201; everyday violence enabled by, 200; executive power maximized via, 40; experts in, 199; by the FBI, 230n3; fusion centers, 231n7; and human rights/law, 197; infrastructure of, 198–99; insecurities generated by, 13–14, 196; intelligence apparatus for, 13; metrics used in, 200–201; negative vision of, 2–3, 7; and new normalcy (of threat), 4–5, 7–8; nuclear-attack studies, 215n8; overseas contingency operations, 195, 230n2; overview of, 193; and perceptions of the future, 14; as a permanent war, 194–95; police departments' role in, 198–99; and privacy, 35; public training in, 199; scope of, 194–97, 199; security state resulting from, 1–2, 199–200; and the "terrorist with a WMD," 27, 37–38, 41, 114–15, 128–29, 150; theater of operations of, 35–36; and threat assessment, 20. *See also* secrecy; War on Terror

Crutzen, Paul, 93

Cuban Missile Crisis, 91

cyberwar, 196–97

Dark Winter exercise, 176

DARPA (Defense Advanced Research Project Agency), 12, 131, 226n14

Daschle, Tom, anthrax mailed to. *See* anthrax letters

The Day After, 63–68, *66*, 217n20

The Day after Tomorrow (Emmerich), 99–101, *100*, 103

The Day the Earth Caught Fire, 101

Dean, Jodi, 135

death, 14–15, 46–54, 74–75, 94, 109, 113, 162–64, 177

Deep Impact (Leder), 69, *70*, 71

Defense Advanced Research Project Agency (DARPA), 12, 131, 226n14

mosaic theory of information, 130–31, 137, 139

"mothers against the bomb" movement, 62

Moynihan, Daniel, 134

Musharraf, Pervez, 72, 75

mutual assured destruction (MAD), 9, 15, 170

Nagasaki bombing, 9, 14–16, 39, 52, 73, 75, 195, 216n11

NASA (National Aeronautics and Space Administration), 91, 93, 217n23

National Academy of Sciences, 153, 230n45

National Archives and Records Administration, 3, 4, 132

National Atmospheric Release Advisory Center, 219n10

National Atomic Museum, 118–19, 119

National Bio and Agro-Defense Facility, 184, 185

National Counterterrorism Center, 200–201

"National Defense against Atomic Attack" (Todd, Paul, and Peterson), 126–27

National Institute of Allergy and Infectious Diseases, 160–61, 161, 185

National Institutes of Health (NIH), 159–60

National Planning Scenarios, 226n19

National Research Council, 228n35

National Safety Council, 226n17

National Security Act (1947), 9, 124

National Security Agency, 130, 140, 196

National Security Council, 3, 9, 48, 176, 185

National Security Council Directive 68, 126

national security state: affects, feelings, and emotions in, 17–22, 24–25, 201–2, 214n8; establishment/goals of, 195; expansions of, 6; and failure to predict global events, 6; infrastructures of, 26–35, 29, 32, 34, 42; intelligence apparatus of, 13; modeling nation-ending danger, 14–17; and normalization/naturalization, 8–9;

and politics of shock, 6; public fears shaped by, 21–26, 23; and secrecy, 121; and the social contract, 9; surprise/anticipation as fundamental to, 9, 11–12; threat matrix in, 9–14, 21, 213n5; worst-case scenarios in, 11, 13. *See also* counterterror; secrecy; War on Terror

"National Security Strategy of the United States of America," 145

National Strategy for the Physical Protection of Critical Infrastructures and Key Assets, 29–30

National Strategy to Combat Weapons of Mass Destruction, 38

National Terrorist Warning System, 214n9

NATO (North Atlantic Treaty Organization), 174–75

NBC, anthrax mailed to. *See* anthrax letters

neoliberal economics, 2

nephritis, nephrotic syndrome, and nephrosis, 162

nervous system, 9–10, 19–21, 24

Nevada as military space, 204

Nevada Test Site (later Nevada National Security Site), 56, 61, 202–5, 215n1, 216n17, 218n3. *See also* Atomic Testing Museum; Operation Upshot-Knothole

New Orleans, 108, 213n1, 224n1. *See also* Hurricane Katrina

New York (ship), 201–2

New York City, 73, 75, 75, 213n1

New York Post, anthrax mailed to. *See* anthrax letters

New York Times, 135, 190, 214n16

New Zealand, 150, 224n2

NIH (National Institutes of Health), 159–60

normalization, 6–9, 19–20, 23, 25, 49–50, 130, 162, 179; new normal, 5, 8

North Atlantic Treaty Organization (NATO), 174–75

nuclear cinema, 69–71, 101, 217n21

nuclear energy, benefits of, 50

Nuclear Freeze Campaign, 67–68, 217n20
nuclear ruins and survival, 45–76; and
activist groups against nuclear war, 62,
67–68, 217nn19–20; and aestheticized
politics, 47; *Armageddon* and *Deep
Impact*, 69–71, *70*; atomic warfare military exercises, 61, 216n17; and bombing campaigns, 75–76; civil defense
program, 42, 45, 47–53, *53*, *55*, 215nn8–9,
216n12, 216n14; *The Day After*, 63–68,
66, 217n20; first hydrogen bomb explosion, *74–75*; health effects of nuclear
war, 217n19; imagined Soviet nuclear
targets, 52–53, *53*; *Let's Face It*, 55–56;
"mothers against the bomb" movement,
62; and mushroom cloud imagery, 72;
and nation building, 46; New York City/
Pentagon imagery, 73, *74–75*, *75*; Operation Alert, 54, *55*, 62; Operation Cue,
57–63, *58*, *64*, 65–67, 216n16, 217n20;
overview of, 42, 45–47, 72, 75–76; and
panic, 49–57, *51*, *53*, *55*; survival images,
57–63, *58*, *64–65*; and thermonuclear
weapons, 62; visual image campaigns,
42. *See also* Cold War
nuclear sublime, 67, 77, 218n1
nuclear weapons. *See* atomic bomb; WMDs
nuclear winter, 92–99, *97–99*, 220n13
"Nuclear Winter" (Turco, Toon, Ackerman, Pollack, and Sagan), 92–94

Oakes, Guy, 49
Obama, Barack, 115, 134, 193
Obama administration, 176, 197, 223n15,
224n19
oceanography, 88
On the Beach (Shute), 218–19n5
Operation Alert, 54, *55*, 62
Operation Bacchus, 228n34
Operation Cue (film), 58, 62, 66, 71
Operation Cue (test program), 57–63, *58*,
64, 65–67, 216n16, 217n20
Operation Upshot-Knothole (atomic test),
77–78, *78*, 80–81, *83*, 90, 110

Operation Upshot-Knothole (film), *78*,
80–81
Orr, Jackie, 19, 50
O'Toole, Tara, 176–80, *177*, *180*, 224–25n7,
225–26n14

Pakistan, 75, 103, 134, 187–89, 194, 196, 204,
229n43
Panetta, Leon, 134
panic, 49–57, *51*, *53*, *55*. *See also* excitement
Pantex, 115
A Path Where No Man Thought (Turco and
Sagan), 96–97
Paul, Willard S.: "National Defense against
Atomic Attack," 126–27
peace movement, 168
Pentagon: "arc of instability" map by, 186–87,
188; budget of, 198; in nuclear-attack
imagery, 73, *74*, *75*; scale models of, 73,
74; tourist photographs of, 31. *See also*
Department of Defense; September 11
attacks
Pentagon Papers, 135
Peterson, Val, 49, *51*, 215n9; "National Defense against Atomic Attack," 126–27
Physicians for Social Responsibility (PSR),
67–68, 217n19
plague, 160
planetary crisis, 77–111; Bravo nuclear
detonation (1954), 83, *84–85*; definition of,
43; and earth sciences/environmentalism,
42–43, 79, 82–83, 86–91, *92–93*, 219nn7–8;
global warming, 79, 99–106, 110–11;
Hurricane Katrina as Hiroshima, 106–9,
107, 221n24; Mike nuclear detonation
(1952), 83, *84–85*; and national security,
89–92; and the nuclear sublime, 77, 218n1;
nuclear winter, 92–99, *97–99*, 220n13;
Operation Upshot-Knothole, 77–78, *78*,
80–81, *83*, 90, 110; overview of, 42–43,
77–80, 109–11; Project Sunshine, 86, 90;
radioactive fallout from testing, 82–83, *85*,
86–87, 90–91, 218–19n5, 219n7; Shot Teak,
87–88, 90; worst-case scenarios, 90–91

secrecy, 113–44; affects of, 138–44, *141–42*; and censorship, 132; compartmental-ized, 43, 121, 123, 135–36, 143–44; in the counterror state, 129–38; damaging effects of, 133–34; about drones, 134; in the information age, 123, 139; instituting, 124–29; lying necessitated by, 136; and mosaic theory of information, 130–31, 137, 139; and the national security state, 121; nuclear, 114–24, *117–20*; overview of, 43, 113–14; power of secrets, 113, 122–24; redaction, 132, *133*; secrecy/threat matrix, 113–14, 121–22, 128, 139–41, *141–42*, 144, 223n16; sensitive but unclassified (sbu) information, 121, 129–32, 139, 224n19; state secrets/classified knowledge, 124–29, 134–36, 222n6, 222n8, 224n19; state secrets privilege, 129, 136–38; and surveillance, 130, 138; about U.S. covert operations, 134, 223n17; about Venona intercepts, 134; and Wikileaks, 223n15
security clearance, 198
seismology, 88
sensitive but unclassified (sbu) informa-tion, 121, 129–32, 139, 224n19
September 11 attacks (2001): alleged link to Hussein, 71; American vulnerability displayed by, 10, 21; and the anthrax let-ters, 189; counterterror following, 1–2, 6, 72–73; as existential threat, 40–41; Navy missions as counterstrike to, 201–2; as nuclear discourse, 73, 75; as a perma-nent injury, 44, 201–2, 208–9; persons responsible for, 198, 205, 207; presi-dential powers following, 193, 230n1; reenactment of, 207–8; World Trade Center artifacts/exhibit, 201–3, *203*, 205, *206*, 207–10, *208–9*
shock, 1, 9–10, 17–20, 41, 158, 172, 201; shock and awe, politics of, 6, 9, 213n5
shock and awe, politics of, 18
Shot Teak test, 87–88, 90
Shute, Nevil: *On the Beach*, 218–19n5
Shutter Island, 191

Simmel, Georg, 122–24
simulation, 56, 95, 97, 166–68, 170, 175–76, 198, 219n10. *See also* Atlantic Storm exercise
Sloterdijk, Peter, 20, 219n7
smallpox: elimination of, 173–74; research on, 157, 160; vaccine for, 152, 154–55, 176. *See also* Atlantic Storm exercise
Smith, Bradley T., 225–26n14, 227n29
Smithsonian Institution, 118
social contract, 9, 26, 45, 126, 139, 154, 194, 197
Soviet Union: bioweapons project of, 177–78, 226n15; collapse of, 139; containment policy toward, 126; first nuclear test in, 6, 48; nuclear arsenal of, 50, 95, 127, 214n10, 219n11. *See also* Cold War
space sciences, 88
Special Operations forces, 204
spying, domestic, 230n3
"Stand Your Ground" laws, 214n8
State Department, 3
Statue of Liberty, 31, 100
Stewart, Kathleen, 18
Strategic Defense Initiative (sdi), 155, 217n20
Strategy for Survival (Martin and Latham), 53–54
stroke (cerebrovascular diseases), 162
strontium-90, 86, 95
suicide, 162. *See also* mutual assured destruction
Sullivan, Gordon R., 220n15
supercomputing, 89, 109, 114, 219n10
surprise, 6, 9–10, 12, 90, 194, 201
surveillance: digital, 130, 138, 196–97; of infectious diseases, 182–84, 187, 228–29n40; satellite, 89, 109; of urban air, 155, 224–25n7
swine flu, 182
Sylvester, Edward, 158

Taussig, Michael, 13
Tenet, George, 33

271

theatricality, definition of, 35

thermonuclear weapons, 62, 83, 86, 114–15. *See also* B61; B83

threat (as opposed to risk), 20–21, 31, 153, 162

Todd, Walter E.: "National Defense against Atomic Attack," 126–27

Toon, O. B., 95–96, 220n13; "Nuclear Winter," 92–94

torture, 197, 214n8

Total Information Awareness, 131

Transportation Security Administration, 25, 218n25

Truman, Harry, 9, 48, 127, 213n5

TTAPS (Turco, Toon, Ackerman, Pollack, and Sagan), 92–96

tuberculosis, 226n16

tularemia, 160

Turco, R. P., 95–96; "Nuclear Winter," 92–94; *A Path Where No Man Thought*, 96–97

Turcotte, Heather, 226n17

U-2 spy planes, 89

United States: covert operations by, 134, 196, 204, 223n17; hegemony of, 36; military budget of, 12; nonmilitary infrastructure of, 28; nuclear arsenal of, 95, 115, 119–20, *120*, 127, 203, 214n10, 219n11; nuclear expenditures of, 10, 163; as nuclear superpower, 121; nuclear weapons program of, 76, 114, 218n26, 221n1; security expenditures of, 13; Soviet espionage in, 134. *See also* Cold War

United States v. Reynolds, 137

unknown unknowns, 16–17

USA Patriot Act (2001), 3–4, 147

U.S. Army, 185, 230n2

Venona intercepts, 134

Vietnam, 75

Vietnam War, 135

vital systems security, 30

Vogal, Kathleen M., 228n36

Wade, Troy, 202–3, 205

Wald, Priscilla, 227n25

war gaming, 126, 170, 175

War on Terror: American values shifted by, 197; anticipatory preemption in, 36, 165, 214n13; vs. balance of terror, 8; biothreat, 156; color-coded warning system of, 22–23, 25, 73, 218n25; costs/scope of, 12–13, 28, 195, 198; and the counterterror state in 1947, 5; danger proliferated by, 26; emotional management used in, 73; and executive power's limits, 40; existential threat via, 40–41; failure of, 214n13; global security apparatus of, 10; goals of, 5; ideological resources for, 216n14; inauguration of, 3–5; infrastructures of, 28; injuries/mental health problems from, 200; national archives purged, 3, 4; overview of, 43–44; preemption favored over deterrence, 15, 218n24; reclassification of Cold War materials, 3–6, 132, 213n2; state-defined terror, 27, 214n11; state surveillance/data archiving in, 35; violence in everyday life normalized via, 78–79. *See also* biosecurity; Bush administration; counterterror; WMDs

Washington, D.C., 177, 197

Washington Post, 135, 222n4

Wasserman, R. H., 86

water supply system, 200

Watson Institute (Brown University), 12

weapons of mass destruction. *See* WMDs

weather prediction/modification, 88–89

Weber, Samuel, 35

What You Should Know about Biological Warfare, 166–68, *169*

Whitehall, Geoffrey, 181

White Light, Black Rain, 216n11

Wikileaks, 223n15

Wikipedia, 223n15

Williams, Raymond, 18

Praise for *Waiting for Wednesday*

"There's enough backstory for this third Frieda Klein mystery to stand alone, but the greatest pleasure is in following the series from the beginning to see the evolution of Klein, a detective of the mind. Another compelling entry in this complex, suspenseful series."

—*Booklist* (starred review)

"Demanding the reader's full attention, this richly detailed and intricate thriller weaves the story of Frieda's life, past and present, into a compelling and suspenseful story. Fans of Elizabeth George will appreciate French's attention to subtlety and detail."

—*Library Journal* (starred review)

"As a protagonist, Frieda Klein breaks all the rules. . . . Grounding Klein's complicated character is the authors' sublime prose. The Thames is so real we can smell its stink; the dark city streets so vividly evoked we can see steam rising off the pavement after a rain. This is top-notch writing, sensual, deep, and wise."

—*Mystery Scene*

"Not only is the plot of this story intricately woven by this husband and wife team of writers, but the ending is one that will leave you gasping for breath!"

—*Suspense Magazine*

Praise for *Tuesday's Gone*

"A fiercely intelligent, multilayered thriller."

—*Kirkus Reviews*

"Seamlessly mixes a foreboding tone and deliberate pacing with deft plot twists that should leave readers pleasantly chilled to the bone."

—*Publishers Weekly*

"Starts as a grim psychological thriller in the vein of Dennis Lehane's darker novels and turns into a fascinating puzzle in which character analysis holds sway. Highly recommended for fans of psychological suspense who enjoy a complex protagonist."

—*Library Journal* (starred review)

"The plotting is fast-paced with surprises galore, and characters literally come to life on the pages. . . . When readers are through, they will find themselves waiting impatiently for Wednesday to arrive!" —*Suspense Magazine*

"If you are looking for wickedly inventive crime fiction, you need look no further than the writing team of Nicci Gerrard and Sean French. . . . Unless you are into tension, paranoia, and burning the midnight oil to finish a book, don't embark on reading *Tuesday's Gone* after suppertime!"　　—*BookPage*

"*Tuesday's Gone* is one of those great, great books in the mystery genre wherein the more you know, the less you know—peel back one stratum and you cannot shovel fast enough to get into the next, which reveals anything but what you expected. French takes the novel on a number of unexpected twists and turns, not the least of which relates back to *Blue Monday*, which, as it turns out, didn't quite end on its last page."　　—Bookreporter.com

Praise for *Blue Monday*

"Fast-paced and spooky . . . it leaves readers with the promise of intriguing tales to come."　　—*People* (four stars)

"A neat puzzle with a satisfying resolution and a terrific twist at the end."
　　—*The New York Times Book Review*

"A superb psychological thriller . . . With its brooding atmosphere, sustained suspense, last-minute plot twist, and memorable cast of characters, this series debut will leave readers eager to discover what color Tuesday will be."
　　—*Publishers Weekly* (starred review)

"With its smart plot, crisp prose, and a stunning final twist, this is psychological suspense at its best. Absolutely riveting."　　—*Booklist* (starred review)

"This is psychological suspense done right. The authors pace themselves and build the tension slowly while carefully developing each of the players. For fans of Tana French's and Lisa Gardner's moody, dark, twisty thrillers."
　　—*Library Journal*

"Complex and flawed, Frieda Klein is a refreshingly human protagonist, an intriguing debut for a truly unique character."
　　—Tami Hoag, bestselling author of *Cold Cold Heart*

ABOUT THE AUTHOR

Nicci French is the pseudonym of the internationally best-selling writing partnership of suspense writers Nicci Gerrard and Sean French. They are married and live in Suffolk and London, England.

NICCI FRENCH

WAITING FOR WEDNESDAY

A FRIEDA KLEIN MYSTERY

PENGUIN BOOKS

To Pat and John, once more with feeling

PENGUIN BOOKS
Published by the Penguin Group
Penguin Group (USA) LLC
375 Hudson Street
New York, New York 10014

USA I Canada I UK I Ireland I Australia I New Zealand I India I South Africa I China
penguin.com
A Penguin Random House Company

A Pamela Dorman/Penguin Book

First published in Great Britain by Michael Joseph, an imprint of Penguin Books Ltd, 2013
First published in the United States of America by Viking Penguin,
a member of Penguin Group (USA) LLC, 2014
Published in Penguin Books 2015

THE LIBRARY OF CONGRESS HAS CATALOGED THE HARDCOVER EDITION AS FOLLOWS:
French, Nicci
Waiting for Wednesday / Nicci French.
pages cm
ISBN 978-0-670-01577-1 (hc.)
ISBN 978-0-14-312717-8 (pbk.)
1. Women psychotherapists—Fiction.   2. Murder—Investigation—Fiction.
3. Psychological fiction.   I. Title
PR6056.R456W25 2013
823'.914—dc23   2013016793

Printed in the United States of America
10 9 8 7 6 5 4 3 2 1

WAITING FOR WEDNESDAY

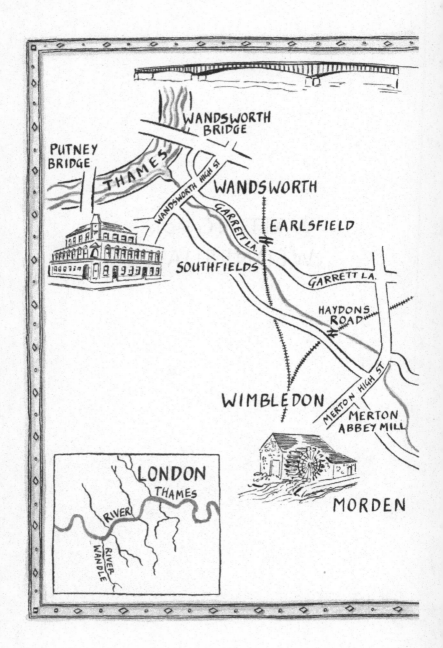

RIVER WANDLE

0   1   2   3
Miles

MITCHAM

CROYDON

WANDLE
PARK

MITCHAM
COMMON

MORDEN
HALL PARK

CROYDON RD

WADDON
PONDS

LONDON RD

BEDDINGTON
PARK

CROYDON RD

CAREW
MANOR

CARSHALTON

CARSHALTON
PONDS

ONE

There was no sign that anything was wrong. It was just an ordinary row house on an ordinary Wednesday afternoon in April. It had a long, narrow garden, like all the other houses in the road. The one to its left had been neglected for many years. It was overgrown with nettles and brambles; at the far end there was a plastic sandbox full of sludgy water and a child-sized goal that had been tipped over. The garden on the other side was paved and graveled, with plants in terra-cotta pots, chairs that the owners folded up in winter to store in their shed, and a barbecue under a black tarpaulin that would be wheeled into the center of the patio for the summer months.

But this particular garden had a lawn, just cut for the first time this year. White blossom shone on an old, twisted apple. The roses and shrubs in the borders had been pruned back so hard that they were like sticks. There were ranks of orange tulips near the kitchen door. There was a single sneaker with its laces still done up under the window, empty flower pots, a bird table, with a few seeds scattered on its flat surface, a couple of empty beer bottles by the boot scraper.

The cat walked up the garden, taking its time and pausing by the door, head lifted as if waiting for something. Then it deftly inserted itself through the cat flap and entered the kitchen, with its tiled floor, its table—big enough for six or more people—and its Welsh dresser, which was really too large for the room and was cluttered with china and odds and ends: tubes of dried-out glue, bills in their envelopes, a cookery book opened at a recipe for monkfish with preserved lemon, a balled pair of socks, a five-pound note, a small hairbrush. Pans hung from a steel rail above the cooktop. There was a basket of vegetables near the sink, a dozen more cookery books on a small shelf, a vase of flowers that were beginning to droop on the windowsill, a school textbook open spine down on the table. On the wall was a whiteboard with a "to-do" list in red felt pen. There was a half-eaten piece of toast, cold, on a plate on one of the surfaces, and a cup of tea beside it.

The cat dipped its head delicately into its bowl on the floor and ate one or two granules of dried cat food, wiped its paw over the side of its face, then continued through the house, out of the kitchen, whose door was always open, past the little lavatory to the left, up the two steps. It sidestepped a broken glass bowl and walked around the leather shoulder bag lying in the hallway. The bag was upended, its contents scattered over the oak floorboards. Lipstick and face powder, an opened pack of tissues, car keys, a small blue diary with a pen attached to it, a packet of paracetamol, a spiral-bound notebook. A bit farther on, a black wallet splayed open, a few membership cards dotted around it (Automobile Association, British Museum). A framed print from an old Van Gogh exhibition was tipped to one side on the cream wall, and on the floor, its frame cracked, lay a large family portrait: a man, a woman, three children with broad smiles.

The cat picked its way through the debris and walked into the living room at the front of the house. An arm lay outstretched in the doorway; the hand was plump and firm with nails cut short and a gold band on the fourth finger. The cat sniffed at it, then gave the wrist a cursory lick. It half climbed onto the body, in its sky-blue blouse and its black work trousers, digging its claws purringly into the soft stomach. Wanting attention, it nuzzled against the head of warm brown hair that was graying now and tied back in a loose knot. There were small gold studs in the earlobes. There was a thin chain and locket round the neck. The skin smelled of roses and something else. The cat rubbed its body against the face and arched its back.

After a while, it gave up and went to sit on the armchair to wash itself, for its coat was matted now and sticky.

Dora Lennox walked slowly back from school. She was tired. It was Wednesday, and she had double science last lesson, then swing band in the after- school club. She played the saxophone—badly, splitting notes, but the music teacher didn't seem fussy. She had only agreed to go because her friend Cam had persuaded her, but now Cam didn't seem to be her friend anymore, and whispered and giggled with other girls who didn't have braces, weren't skinny and shy but bold and curvy, with black lacy bras and shiny lips and bright eyes.

Dora's rucksack, heavy with books, bumped on her back; her music case swung against her shin; and the plastic carrier bag—bulging with cooking utensils and a tin of scorched scones that she'd made in food tech that morning—was ripped. She was glad to see their car parked near the house. It meant her mother was home. She didn't like coming back to an empty house, with all the lights off and a gray hush to every room. Her mother put life into things: the dishwasher rumbling, maybe a cake in the oven or at least a tin of biscuits laid out ready for her, the kettle boiling for tea, a sense of ordered bustle that Dora found comforting.

As she opened the gate and walked up the short, tiled garden path, she saw that the front door was open. Had she arrived just after her mother? Or her brother, Ted? She could hear a sound as well, a pulsing electronic sound. As she got closer, she saw that the small frosted-glass window, just to the side of the door, was broken. There was a hole in the glass and it bulged inward. As she stood looking at the strange sight, she felt something on her leg and looked down. The cat was rubbing against her, and Dora noticed that she had left a rusty stain on her new jeans. She stepped into the house, letting her bags slide to the floor. There were shards of glass from the window on the mat. That would need to be fixed. At least it hadn't been her. It was probably Ted. He broke things all the time: mugs, glasses, windows. Anything fragile. She could smell something as well. Something burning.

"Mum, I'm home!" she called.

There was more mess on the floor—the big family photograph, her mother's bag, bits and pieces strewn around. It was as if a storm had blown through the house, dislodging objects and tossing them about. Dora briefly saw her reflection in the mirror that hung above the table: small white face, thin brown plaits. She walked through to the kitchen where the smell was strongest. She opened the door of the oven and smoke poured out like a hot breath, making her cough. She took an oven glove, lifted the baking tray from the top shelf, and put it on top of the stove. There were six charred shrunken black disks on the tray. Utterly ruined. Her mother sometimes made biscuits for her after school. Dora closed the door and switched off the gas. Yes, that was it. The oven had been left on and the biscuits had burned. The alarm and the smoke had scared the cat, and she had run around breaking things. But why had the biscuits burned?

She called out again. She saw the fist on the floor in the doorway, fingers curled, but still she went on calling, not moving. "Mum, I'm home!"

She walked back out into the hall, still calling. The door to the front room was slightly open. She saw something inside, pushed against the door and stepped into the room.

"Mum?"

At first, stupidly, she saw splashes of red paint on the far wall and the sofa and great daubs of it on the floor. Then her hand flew to her mouth, and she heard a small moan coming up her throat, then widening out in the terrible room, becoming a shriek that went on and on and wouldn't stop. She put her hands against her ears to block out the sound, but now it was inside her. Not paint, but blood, streams of blood and then a dark, dark lake near the thing lying at her feet. An arm outflung, a watch on the wrist that still told the time, a comfortable body in a blue shirt and black trousers, one shoe half off. All that she knew. But the face wasn't a face any longer, because one of its eyes was gone and its mouth was shattered and shouted noiselessly at her through a spit of broken teeth. One entire side of the head was caved in and blistered with blood and gristle and bone, as if someone had tried to destroy it.

TWO

The house was in Chalk Farm, a couple of streets away from the noise of Camden Lock. There was an ambulance outside and several police cars. A tape had already been put up, and a few passersby had stopped to stare.

Detective Constable Yvette Long ducked under the tape and looked at the house, a late-Victorian semidetached, with a small front garden and a bay window. She was about to go inside when she saw Detective Chief Inspector Malcolm Karlsson stepping out of a car and waited for him. He seemed serious, preoccupied, until he noticed her and gave a nod.

"Have you been inside yet?"

"I just arrived," said Yvette. She paused for a moment, then blurted out, "It's funny seeing you without Frieda."

Karlsson's expression turned harsh. "So you're pleased she's not helping us out."

"I . . . I didn't mean that."

"I know you had problems with her being around," said Karlsson, "but that's been sorted. The chief decided that she was out, and she almost got killed in the process. Is that the bit that seemed funny?"

Yvette blushed and didn't reply.

"Have you been to see her?" Karlsson asked.

"I went to the hospital."

"That's not enough. You should talk to her. But meanwhile . . ."

He gestured toward the house, and they walked in. It was full of people in plastic overshoes, wearing overalls and gloves. They spoke in hushed voices or were silent. Karlsson and Yvette pulled on their shoes and gloves and walked down the hall, past a handbag lying on the boards, past a photograph in a smashed frame, past a man dusting for fingerprints, into the living room, where spotlights had been rigged up.

The dead woman lay under the lights as if she were onstage. She was on her back. One arm was flung out, the other lay by her side, the hand in a half fist. Her hair was brown, going gray. Her mouth was smashed open so it looked like an animal's demented snarl, but from where he stood, gazing down at her, Karlsson could see a filling glinting among the splintered teeth. On one side of her face, the skin was quite smooth, but sometimes death uncreases wrinkles, takes away the marks that life has made and adds its own. Her neck had the wrinkles of middle age.

Her right eye was open, staring. The left side of the woman's head had been caved in, sticky with liquid and bits of bone. Blood soaked into the beige carpet around her, had dried in splashes all over the floor, and sprayed the nearest wall, turning the middle-class living room into an abattoir.

"Someone hit her hard," murmured Karlsson, straightening up.

"Burglary," said a voice behind him. Karlsson looked round. A detective was standing at his back, slightly too close. He was very young, pimply, with a slightly uneasy smile on his face.

"What?" said Karlsson. "Who are you?"

"Riley," said the officer.

"You said something."

"Burglary," said Riley. "He was caught in the act and he lashed out."

Riley noticed Karlsson's expression and his smile melted away. "I was thinking aloud," he said. "I was trying to be positive. And proactive."

"Proactive," said Karlsson. "I thought we might examine the crime scene, search for prints, hair, and fibers, take some statements before deciding what happened. If that's all right with you."

"Yes, sir."

"Good."

"Boss." Chris Munster had come into the room. He stood for a moment, gazing at the body.

"What do we know, Chris?"

It took an effort for Munster to shift his attention back to Karlsson. "You don't get used to it," he said.

"Try to," said Karlsson. "The family don't need you to do their suffering for them."

"Right," said Munster, consulting his notebook. "Her name is Ruth Lennox. She was a health visitor for the local authority. You know, old people, new mothers, that sort of thing. Forty-four years old, married, three kids. The younger daughter discovered her when she came back from school at about half past five."

"Is she here?"

"Upstairs, with the father and the other two kids."

"Any estimate of time of death?"

"After midday, before six o'clock."

"That's not much use."

"I'm just repeating what Dr. Heath told me. He was saying that it was a heated house, warm day, sun through the window. It's not an exact science."

"Fine. Murder weapon?"

Munster shrugged. "Something heavy, Dr. Heath said. With a sharp edge but not a blade."

"All right," said Karlsson. "Is someone getting the family's prints?"

"I'll check."

"Anything stolen?" asked Yvette.

Karlsson glanced at her. It was the first time she'd spoken in the house. Her tone still sounded shaky. He'd probably been too hard on her.

"The husband's in a state of shock," said Munster. "But it looks like her wallet's been emptied."

"I'd better talk to them. In his study, you say?"

"First room you come to up the stairs, next to the bathroom. Melanie Hackett's with them."

"All right," said Karlsson. "There was a detective used to work round here, Harry Curzon. I think he retired. Could you get his number for me? The local police will know him."

"What do you want him for?"

"He knows the area. He might save us some trouble."

"I'll do my best."

"And have a word with young Riley here. He already knows what happened." Karlsson turned to Yvette and signaled her to follow him up the stairs. At the door, he paused and listened. He could hear no sound at all. He hated this bit. Often people blamed him because he was the bearer of bad news and at the same time clung to him because he promised some kind of solution. And this was a whole family. Three kids, Munster had said. Poor sods. She looked like she'd been a nice woman, he thought.

"Ready?"

Yvette nodded, and he knocked on the door, three times, then pushed it open.

The father was sitting in a swivel chair, rotating this way and that. He still wore his outdoor jacket and a cotton scarf tied round his neck. He was thin, and his face was white with mottled red patches on his cheeks, as if he'd just come in from the cold, and he kept blinking, as if he had dust in his eyes, licking his lips, pulling the lobe of one ear. On the floor at his feet the younger daughter—the one who'd found Ruth Lennox—was curled in a fetal ball. She was hiccuping and retching and snuffling and gulping. Karlsson thought she sounded like a wounded animal. He couldn't see what she looked like, only that she was skinny and had brown hair in unraveling plaits. The father put a helpless hand on her shoulder, then drew it back.

The other daughter, who looked fifteen or sixteen, sat across from them, her legs folded under her and her arms clasped around her body, as though she wanted to make herself as warm and as small as possible. She had chestnut curls and her father's round face, with full red lips and freckles over the bridge of her nose. She had mascara smeared around one of her blue eyes but not the other, which gave her an artificial look, clownlike, and yet Karlsson could see at once that she had a sultry attractiveness that even the ruined makeup and her chalky pallor couldn't mask. She was wearing maroon shorts over black tights, a T-shirt with a logo he didn't recognize. She stared at Karlsson when he entered, chewing her lower lip furiously.

The boy sat in the corner, his knees pulled sharply up to his chin, his face hidden by a mop of dark blond hair. Every so often he gave a violent shiver but didn't lift his head, even when Karlsson introduced himself.

"I'm so sorry," Karlsson said. "But I'm here to help, and I'll need to ask some questions."

"Why?" whispered the father. "Why would anyone kill Ruth?"

At this, a sound broke from the older girl, a sob.

"Your younger daughter found her," said Karlsson, gently. "Is that right?"

"Dora. Yes." He wiped the back of his hand across his mouth. "What's that going to do to her?"

"Mr. Lennox," said Yvette, "there are people who can help you with that . . ."

"Russell. Nobody calls me Mr. Lennox."

"We need to talk to Dora about what she saw."

The wailing from the small shape on the floor continued. Yvette looked helplessly at Karlsson.

"You can be with your father," said Karlsson, leaning down toward Dora. "Or if you'd prefer to speak to a woman, not a man, then . . ."

"She doesn't want to," said the elder sister. "Didn't you hear?"

"What's your name?" asked Karlsson.

"Judith."

"And how old are you?"

"Fifteen. Does that help?" She glared at Karlsson out of her unnerving blue eyes.

"It's a terrible thing," said Karlsson. "But we need to know everything. Then we can find the person who did this."

The boy suddenly jerked up his head. He struggled to his feet and stood by the door, tall and gangly. He had his mother's gray eyes. "Is she still there?"

"Sorry?"

"Ted," said Russell Lennox, in a soothing tone, moving toward him and holding out his hand. "Ted, it's OK."

"My mother." The boy kept his eyes fixed on Karlsson. "Is she still there?"

"Yes."

The boy tugged the door open and ran down the stairs. Karlsson raced after him but didn't get there in time. The roar ripped through the house.

"No, no, no," Ted was shouting. He was on his knees beside his mother's body. Karlsson put his arm round the boy and lifted him up, back, and out of the room.

"It's all right, Ted."

Karlsson turned. A woman had come in through the front door. She was solid, in her late thirties, with short dark brown hair in an old-fashioned bob and wearing a knee-length tweed skirt; she also had something in a yellow sling around her chest. Karlsson saw that it was a very small baby, its bald head poking out of the top and two tiny feet sticking out at the bottom. The woman looked at Russell, her eyes bright. "I came at once," she said. "What a terrible, terrible thing."

She walked across to Russell, who had followed his son down the stairs, and gave him a long hug, made awkward and arms' length by the baby wedged in between them. Russell's face stared out over her shoulder, helpless. She looked round at Karlsson.

"I'm Ruth's sister," she said. The bundle at her chest shifted and gave a whimper; she patted it with a clucking sound.

She had that excited calm that some people get in an emergency. Karlsson had seen it before. Disasters attracted people. Relatives, friends, neighbors gathered to help or give sympathy or just to be part of it in some way, to warm themselves in its terrible glow.

"This is Louise," said Russell. "Louise Weller. I rang people in the family. Before they heard it from someone else."

"We're conducting an interview," said Karlsson. "I'm sorry, but I don't think it's appropriate you should be here. This is a crime scene."

"Nonsense. I'm here to help," said Louise, firmly. "This is about my sister." Her face was pale, except for spots of red on her cheekbones. "My other two are in the car. I'll get them in a minute and put them somewhere out of the way. But tell me first, what happened?"

Karlsson hesitated a moment, then shrugged. "I'll give you all a few minutes together. Then, when you're ready, we can talk."

He guided them up the stairs and gestured to Yvette to follow him out of the room. "On top of everything else," he said, "they'll need to move out for a few days. Can you mention it to them? Tactfully? Maybe there's a neighbor or friends nearby." He saw Riley coming up the stairs.

"There's someone to see you, sir," he said. "He says you know him."

"Who is he?" asked Karlsson.

"Dr. Bradshaw," said Riley. "He doesn't look like a policeman."

"He's not," said Karlsson. "He's a sort of consultant. Anyway, what does it matter what he looks like? We'd better let him in, give him a chance to earn his money."

As Karlsson walked down the stairs and saw Hal Bradshaw waiting in the hall, he saw what Riley meant. He didn't look like a detective. He wore a gray suit, with just a speckle of yellowish color to it, and an open-necked white shirt. Karlsson particularly noticed his fawn suede shoes and his large heavy-framed spectacles. He gave Karlsson a nod of recognition.

"How did you even hear about this?" Karlsson asked.

"It's a new arrangement. I like to get here when the scene is still fresh. The quicker I get here, the more useful I can be."

"Nobody told me that," said Karlsson.

Bradshaw didn't seem to be paying attention. He was looking around thoughtfully. "Is your friend here?"

"Which friend?"

"Dr. Klein," he said. "Frieda Klein. I expected to find her here, sniffing around."

Hal Bradshaw and Frieda had worked on the same case, in which Frieda had very nearly been killed. A man had been found naked and decomposing in the flat of a disturbed woman, Michelle Doyce. Bradshaw had been convinced that she had killed the man; Frieda had heard in the woman's meandering words some kind of sense, a distracted straining toward the truth. Gradually, she and Karlsson had pieced together the man's identity: he was a con man who had left behind him many victims, each with motives for revenge. Frieda's methods—unorthodox and instinctive—and her actions, which could be obsessive and self-destructive, had led to her dismissal during the last round of cuts. But clearly this wasn't enough for Bradshaw. She had made him look stupid, and now he wanted to destroy her. Karlsson thought of all this. Then he thought of a dead woman lying a few feet away and a family grieving, and swallowed his angry words.

"Dr. Klein's not working for us anymore."

"Oh, yes," said Bradshaw, cheerfully. "That's right. Things didn't go very well at the end of that last case."

"It depends on what you mean by 'well,'" Karlsson said. "Three murderers were caught."

Bradshaw pulled a face. "If the consultant ends up in a knife fight and then spends a month in intensive care, that's not exactly an example of success. In my book, at least."

Karlsson was on the point of saying something, but again he remembered where he was.

"This is hardly the place," he said, coolly. "A mother has been murdered. Her family is upstairs."

Bradshaw held up a hand. "Shall we stop talking and go through?"

"I wasn't the one talking."

Bradshaw stepped inside and took a deep breath, as if he were appraising the aroma of the room. He moved toward the body of Ruth Lennox, treading delicately to avoid the pool of blood. He looked toward Karlsson. "You know, blundering into a crime scene and being attacked doesn't count as solving a crime."

"Are we talking about Frieda again?" said Karlsson.

"Her mistake is to get emotionally involved," he said. "I heard she slept with the man who was arrested."

"She didn't sleep with him," said Karlsson, coldly. "She met him socially. Because she was suspicious of him."

Bradshaw looked at Karlsson with a half smile. "Does that trouble you?"

"I'll tell you what troubles me," said Karlsson. "It troubles me that you seem to feel competitive with Frieda Klein."

"Me? No, no, no. Simply concerned for a colleague who seems to have lost her bearings." He gave a sympathetic grimace. "I feel very sorry for her. I hear she's depressed."

"I thought you'd come to look at a murder scene. If you want to discuss an earlier case, we should go somewhere else."

Bradshaw shook his head. "Don't you think this is like a work of art?"

"No, I don't."

"We need to think, What is he trying to express? What is he telling the world?"

"Maybe I should just leave you to it," said Karlsson.

"I imagine that you think this is a simple burglary gone wrong."

"I'm trying to avoid quick conclusions," said Karlsson. "We're gathering evidence. Theories can come later."

Bradshaw shook his head again. "That's the wrong way round. Without a theory, data is just chaos. You should always be open to your first impressions."

"So what's your first impression?"

"I'll be delivering a written report," said Bradshaw, "but I'll give you a free preview. A burglary isn't just a burglary."

"You'll have to explain that to me."

Bradshaw made an expansive gesture. "Look around you. A burglary is an invasion of a home, a violation, a rape. This man was expressing anger against a whole area of life that was closed to him, an area of property and family ties and social status. And when he encountered this woman, she personified everything that he couldn't have—she was at the same time a well-off woman, a desirable woman, a mother, a wife. He could have run away, he could have struck her a simple blow, but he's left us a message, just as he left *her* a message. The injuries were directed to her face, rather than to her body. Look at the splashes of blood on the wall, so out of proportion to anything that was needed. He was trying to literally wipe an expression off her face, an expression of superiority. He was redecorating the room with her blood. It was almost a kind of love."

"A strange kind of love," said Karlsson.

"That's why it had to be so savage," said Bradshaw. "If he didn't care, he wouldn't have to do something so extreme. It wouldn't matter. This has an emotional intensity."

"So who are we looking for?"

Bradshaw closed his eyes before he spoke, as if he were seeing something nobody else could see.

"White," he said. "Early to mid-thirties. Strongly built. Unmarried. Of no fixed abode. No steady job, no steady relationship. No family connections." He took out his phone and pointed it in various directions around the room.

"You need to be careful with those images," said Karlsson. "Things have a way of ending up online."

"I'm cleared for this," said Bradshaw. "You should take a look at my contract. I'm a criminal psychologist. This is what I do."

"All right," said Karlsson. "But I think we should leave. The scene-of-crime team needs to take over."

Bradshaw slipped his phone into his jacket pocket. "That's fine. I'm done. Oh, by the way, give Dr. Klein my best. Tell her I've been thinking of her."

As they left, they met Louise Weller coming back into the house. The baby was still slung round her, but now she was towing a tiny boy by the hand. At her heels stomped a slightly older girl, stocky like her mother. Even though she was wearing a pink nightgown and pushing a toy buggy in which a doll was swaddled, she reminded Karlsson of Yvette.

Louise Weller gave him a brisk nod. "Families should rally round," she said and, like a general leading a reluctant army, she marched her children into the house.

THREE

At twenty-five past three in the morning, when it was no longer night but not yet day, Frieda Klein woke up. Her heart was racing and her mouth was dry, her forehead beaded with sweat. It was hard to swallow or even to breathe. Everything hurt: her legs, her shoulder, her ribs, her face. Old bruises flowered and throbbed. For a few moments she did not open her eyes, and when she did, the darkness pressed down on her and spread out in all directions. She turned her head toward the window. Waiting for Wednesday to end, for the light to come and the dreams to fade.

The waves came, one after another, each worse than the one before, rising up and crashing over her, pulling her under, then spitting her out ready for the next. They were inside her, thrashing through her body and her mind, and they were outside. As she lay there, grayly awake, memories mixed with fading dreams. Faces gleamed in the darkness, hands reached out to her. Frieda tried to hold on to what Sandy had said, night after night, and to haul herself out of the tumult that had invaded her: *It's over. You're safe. I'm here.*

She stretched her hand out to where he should have been lying. But he had gone back to America. She had accompanied him to the airport, dry eyed and apparently composed even when he gathered her to him with anguish on his face to say good-bye; had watched him go through into Departures until his tall figure was no longer visible; had never told him how close she had come to asking him to stay or agreeing to go with him. The intimacy of their last few weeks, when she had let herself be cared for and felt her own weakness, had stirred up feelings in her that she had never before experienced. It would be too easy to let them sink back into the depths. It wasn't the pain of missing that she dreaded but the gradual easing of that pain, busy life filling up the spaces he had left. Sometimes she would sit in her garret-study and sketch his face with a soft-leaded pencil, making herself remember the exact shape of his mouth; the little grooves that time had worn into his skin; the expression in his eyes. Then she would lay down the pencil and let the memory of him wash through her, a slow, deep river inside her.

For a moment, she let herself imagine him beside her—how it would feel to turn her head and see him there. But he was gone, and she was alone in a house that had once felt like a cozy refuge yet, for the last few weeks—since the attack that had nearly killed her—had creaked and whispered. She listened: the pulse of her heart and then, yes, there was a rustle by her door, a faint sound. But it was only the cat, prowling the room. Sometimes, in this predawn limbo, Frieda found it a sinister creature—its two previous owners were dead.

Had something woken her? She had a muffled sense of a sound entering her sleep. Not the distant rumble of traffic that in London never ceases. Something else. Inside the house.

Frieda sat up and listened but heard nothing except the soft wind outside. She swung her feet to the floor, feeling the cat wind its body round her legs, purring, then stood, still weak and nauseated from the night terrors. There had been something, she was certain, something downstairs. She made her way onto the landing, then, step by step, gripping the banisters, down the stairs, stopping halfway. The house she knew so well had become unfamiliar, full of shadows and secrets. In the hall, she stood and strained to hear, but there was nothing, nobody. She turned on the lights, blinking in the sudden dazzle, and then she saw it: a large brown envelope lying on the doormat. She stooped and picked it up. It had her name written in bold letters across it: Frieda Klein. A line slashed underneath diagonally, cutting into the final *n*.

She stared at the handwriting. She recognized it, and now she knew that he was near—in the street outside, close to her home, to her place of refuge.

In a fever, she pulled on tracksuit bottoms, a T-shirt, and a trench coat. She pushed her bare feet into the boots by the front door. She took the door key from the hook and then was out into the darkness, a cool April breeze in her face, the hint of rain. Frieda stared around the unlit little cobbled mews, but there was no one there, and as fast as her sore body would go, she half hobbled and half ran out on the street, where the lamps threw long shadows. She looked up and down it. Which way would he have gone: east or west, north or south, toward the river or up into the maze of streets? Or was he standing in a doorway? She turned left and hurried along the damp pavement, swearing under her breath, cursing her inability to move quickly.

Coming out onto a wider road, Frieda saw something in the distance—a bulky shape moving toward her, surely human but larger and stranger than any human could possibly be. It was like a figure from her nightmares, and she pressed her hand against her heart and waited as it came closer and closer, and then at last resolved into a man slowly pedaling a bike, with dozens, hundreds, of plastic bags tied to its frame. She knew him, saw him most days. He had a wild beard and glaring eyes and cycled with slow determination. He wavered past, staring blindly through her, like Father Christmas in a bad dream.

It was no use. Dean Reeve, her stalker and her quarry, could be anywhere by now. Sixteen months ago, she had helped unmask him as a child-abductor and murderer, but he had escaped capture and killed himself. Two months ago, she had discovered that he had never died: the man found hanging from a bridge on the canal was in fact his twin, Alan, who had once been Frieda's patient. Dean was still in the world somewhere, watching over her, protective and deadly. It was he who had saved her life when she had been attacked by a disturbed young woman with a knife, though Mary Orton, the old woman Frieda had come to rescue, had died. He had slid out of the shadows, like a creature from her own worst dreams, and hauled her back from the darkness. Now he was telling her that he was still watching over her, a loathed protector. She could feel his eyes on her, from hidden corners, in the twitch of a curtain or the chink in a door. Was this how it would always be?

She made her way back to her house, unlocked the door, and stepped inside. She picked up the envelope once more and went with it into the kitchen. She knew she wouldn't get back to sleep, so she made herself tea, and only when it was brewed did she sit at the kitchen table and run her finger under the gummed flap. She drew out the stiff paper inside and laid it on the table. It was a pencil drawing or, rather, a pattern. It looked a bit like the mathematical rendering of an intricate rose, eight-sided and perfectly symmetrical. The straight lines had obviously been done with a ruler and, examining it more closely, Frieda could see marks where mistakes had been rubbed out.

She sat for some time, staring down at the image that lay in front of her, her expression stern, then she carefully slid the paper back inside the envelope. Rage crackled through her like fire, and she welcomed it. Better to be burned by anger than drowned by fear. So she sat in its flames, unmoving, until morning came.

Many miles away, Jim Fearby poured himself a glass of whisky. The bottle was less than a third full. Time to buy another. It was like petrol. Never let the tank get less than a quarter full. You might run out. He took the old newspaper clipping from his wallet and flattened it on the desk. It was yellowing and almost disintegrating after all the foldings and unfoldings. He knew it by heart. It was like a talisman. He could see it when he closed his eyes.

MONSTER "MAY NEVER BE RELEASED"

James Fearby
March 23, 2005

There were dramatic scenes at Hattonbrook Crown Court yesterday as convicted murderer George Conley was sentenced to life imprisonment for killing Hazel Barton. Justice Lawson told Conley, 31: "This was an atrocious crime. Despite pleading guilty, you have shown no remorse, and it is my belief that you remain a danger to women and may never be safe to be released."

As Justice Lawson ordered Conley to be taken down, there were shouts from the victim's family in the public gallery. Outside the court, Clive Barton, Hazel's uncle, told reporters: "Hazel was our beautiful young treasure. She had her whole life in front of her and he took that away from her. I hope he rots in hell."

Hazel Barton, a blonde eighteen-year-old schoolgirl, was found strangled in May of last year near her home in the village of Dorlbrook. Her body was found by the roadside. George Conley was arrested near the scene. He had left traces on her body and he confessed within days.

Speaking afterward, Detective Inspector Geoffrey Whitlam offered his condolences to the Barton family: "We can only guess the living hell they have gone through. I hope that the speedy resolution of this thorough investigation can bring them a measure of closure." He also paid tribute to his colleagues: "It is my belief that George Conley is a dangerous sexual predator. He belongs behind bars, and I want to thank my team for putting him there."

It is alleged that Hazel Barton was walking alone because her bus had failed to arrive. A spokeswoman for FastCoach, the local bus operator, commented: "We offer all condolences to Hazel Barton's family. We are fully committed to maintaining an effective service for our customers."

Under the headline were two photographs. The first was the mug shot of Conley, released by the police. His large face was blotchy; there was a bruise on his forehead; one eye was askew. The other was a family photo of Hazel Barton. It must have been taken on holiday because she was wearing a T-shirt and the sea was visible behind her. She was laughing as if the photographer had just made a joke.

Fearby carefully read through his seven-year-old report, running his forefinger along the lines. He sipped his whisky. Almost every word in the report was untrue. FastCoach did not provide an effective service for their customers. And, anyway, they were passengers, not customers. Whitlam's investigation had not been thorough. Even his own byline looked wrong. Only his mother had ever called him James. And the headline—which he hadn't written and wouldn't have written, even at the time—was the most wrong of all. Poor old Georgie Conley was many things, but he wasn't a monster, and now it looked like he was going to be released.

Fearby carefully folded the clipping and replaced it in his wallet, behind his press card. A precious relic.

FOUR

When Sasha arrived at a quarter to nine on Thursday morning, Frieda had just finished watering the plants on her small patio. She was wearing jeans and an oatmeal-colored pullover, and there were rings under her eyes, which looked darker and fiercer than usual.

"Bad night?" asked Sasha.

"No."

"I'm not sure I believe you."

"Would you like a cup of coffee?"

"Do we have time? My car's on a meter for another quarter of an hour, but we need to get to the hospital for half past nine. The traffic's dreadful."

Sasha had insisted on taking the day off work to bring Frieda to her follow-up appointment with the consultant and then with the physiotherapist.

"We're not going to the hospital."

"Why? Have they canceled?"

"No. I have."

"What made you do that?"

"There's something else I need to do."

"You have to see your doctor, Frieda. And the physiotherapist. You've been very ill. You nearly died. You can't just walk away from all the follow-up care."

"I know what the doctor will say: that I'm making progress but that I mustn't think about going back to work yet, because for the time being, making a good recovery is my work. You know the sort of things we doctors tell our patients."

"That sounds a bit negative."

"Anyway, there's something more important I have to do."

"What could be more important than getting better?"

"I thought I'd show you rather than tell you. Unless you want to go to work after all."

Sasha sighed. "I've taken the day off. I'd like to spend it with you. Let's have that coffee."

· · ·

The road narrowed into a lane lined with trees that were freshly in bud.
Frieda noticed the blackthorn. She stared fixedly: Some things change and
some things remain the same. But you never remain the same—you look at
everything through different eyes so that even the most familiar object takes
on a strange and ghostly cast. That small thatched cottage with a muddy
pond full of ducks in front of it, that sudden stretch of road winding down
over a patchwork of fields, or the farmhouse with its silos and its muddy
enclosure of cows, and the line of spindly poplars ahead. Even the way the
light falls on this flattened landscape, and the faint tang of the sea.

The graveyard was crowded. Most of the stones were old, green with
moss, and it was no longer possible to make out the inscriptions carved there,
but some were new and shiny and had flowers on them, with dates of the
dearly beloved and the sorely missed.

"Crowds of the dead," said Frieda, more to herself than to Sasha.

"Why are we here?"

"I'll show you."

She stopped in front of a carved stone and pointed. Sasha, leaning forward, made out the name:

JACOB KLEIN 1943–1988, MUCH MISSED HUSBAND AND FATHER.

"Is this your father?" she asked, thinking about Frieda as a teenager, finding him dead, trying to imagine the history of pain that lay behind the simple stone.

Frieda nodded, not taking her eyes off it. "Yes. That's my father." She took
a small step backward and said, "Look at the carving there, above his name."

"It's very nice," said Sasha, lamely, after examining the symmetrical pattern. "Did you choose it?"

"No." She reached into her bag and pulled out a piece of thick paper,
holding it in front of her, gazing from drawing to engraving and back again.
"What do you see?"

"It's the same," said Sasha.

"It is, isn't it? Exactly the same."

"Did you do it?"

"No."

"Then?"

"Someone sent it to me. Yesterday morning."

"I don't understand."

"They pushed it through my door in the early hours."

"Why?"

"That's the question." Frieda was talking to herself now, rather than Sasha.

"Are you going to tell me what's going on?"

"Dean did it."

"Dean? Dean Reeve?"

Sasha knew about Dean Reeve, the man who had abducted a little boy and dragged Frieda unwillingly into the outside world, away from the safety of her consulting room and the strange secrets of the mind. She had even helped Frieda by doing a DNA test that established Dean's wife, Terry, was, in fact, the little girl Joanna, who had disappeared into thin air more than two decades previously. Frieda had become convinced that Dean Reeve, whom the police accepted as dead, was still alive. He had become Frieda's invisible stalker, the dead man who watched over her and would never let her go.

"Yes, Dean Reeve. I recognize his handwriting—I saw it once on a statement he made at the police station. But even if I hadn't, I'd know it was his. He wants me to understand that he has found out about my family. He knows about the death of my father. He was here, where we are now, where my father is."

"Your father is buried in a churchyard, but I thought you were Jewish," Sasha said.

They were in a small café overlooking the sea. The tide was low, and long-legged seabirds picked their delicate way over the shining mudflats. Far out, a containership, as big as a town, was moving across the horizon. There was no one else in the café and no one out on the shingle. Sasha felt as though she'd been taken to the edge of the world.

"Did you?"

"Yes. Aren't you?"

"No." Frieda hesitated, then, making an obvious effort, said, "My grandfather was Jewish, but not my grandmother, so his children were no longer Jewish and neither, of course, am I. My mother," she added drily, "is most definitely not Jewish."

"Is she still alive?"

"Unless my brothers forgot to tell me, yes."

Sasha blinked and leaned forward.

"Brothers?"

"Yes."

"You've got more than one?"

"I've got two."

"You've only ever mentioned David. I never knew there was another."

"It wasn't relevant," Frieda said.

"Relevant? A brother?"

"You know about David because he's Olivia's ex and Chloë's father."

"I see," murmured Sasha, knowing better than to press her and thinking that in the last few hours she had learned more about Frieda than in the whole course of their friendship.

She pierced her poached egg and watched the yolk well up, then ooze onto the plate. "What are you going to do?" she asked.

"I haven't decided. Anyway, haven't you heard? He's dead."

Frieda hardly spoke on the way back. When Sasha asked her what she was thinking about, she couldn't answer. "I don't know," Frieda said. "Nothing really."

"You wouldn't take that as an answer from one of your patients."

"I've never been a very good patient."

After Sasha had driven away, Frieda let herself into her house. Inside, she fastened the chain and slid the bolt across the front door. She walked upstairs to her bedroom. She took off her jacket and tossed it onto the bed. She would have a long, hot bath and then she would go up to her little study in the garret room and do a drawing: concentrate, yet think of nothing. She thought of the graveyard, the desolate coastline. She pulled her sweater over her head. She started to undo the buttons of her shirt, but she stopped. She had heard something. She wasn't sure whether the noise was inside or a much louder noise outside and far away. She stayed completely still. She didn't even breathe. She heard the noise again, a small scraping sound. It was inside the house and close by, on the same floor. She could feel its vibration. She thought of the front door downstairs, with its bolt and chain. She tried to time it in her head, the scrambling downstairs, the fumbling with the chain. No, she couldn't make it work. She thought of the mobile phone in her pocket. Even if she could whisper a message into it, what good would that do? It would take ten minutes, fifteen minutes, to get here, and then there was the locked, bolted door.

Frieda felt her pulse race. She made herself breathe slowly, one breath after another. She counted slowly to ten. She looked around the room for a hiding place but it was no good. She had made too much noise as she came in. She picked up a hairbrush from her dressing table. It was hopelessly flimsy. She felt in the pocket of her jacket and found a pen. She held it tightly in her fist. At least it was sharp. It seemed like the worst thing in the world, but she edged out of her bedroom onto the landing. It would take just a few seconds. If she could get down the stairs without their creaking . . .

There was another scraping sound, louder now, and something else, a sort of whistle. It came from across the landing, in the bathroom. The whistling continued. Frieda listened for a few seconds, then stepped closer and pushed at the door of the bathroom so that it swung open. At first, she had a sudden sensation of being in the wrong room or the wrong house. Nothing was where it was supposed to be. There was exposed plaster and pipes and a huge space. The room seemed larger than she'd remembered. And in the corner a figure was bent over, pulling at something to get it loose.

"Josef," she said weakly. "What's going on?"

Josef was her friend—a builder from Ukraine who had entered her life in an unlikely way, falling through her ceiling when she was with a patient. But he had not taken no for an answer, and had a fanatical devotion to her. Now he started, then smiled a bit warily. "Frieda," he said. "I did not hear."

"What are you doing here? How did you get in?"

"I have the key you give me."

"But that key was for feeding the cat when I was away, not for this." She gestured. "And what is this?"

Josef stood up. He was holding a huge wrench.

"Frieda. You have been not well. I look at you and see you being sad and in pain and it is difficult." Frieda started to speak but Josef interrupted her. "No, no, wait. It is difficult to help but I know about you. I know that when you are sad you lie in your very hot bath for hours."

"Well, not for *hours*," said Frieda. "But where is my bath? I was just about to get into it."

"Your bath is gone away," said Josef. "While you were with your friend, Sasha, me, and my friend Stefan, we take your bath away and we take it to the dump. It was a bad plastic bath, and it was small, not good for lying in."

"It was very good for lying in," said Frieda.

"No," said Josef, firmly. "It is gone. I have great luck. I work on a house in Islington. He spends much, much money. He cut everything out of the house and throw it in four Dumpsters and put new things in. He is throwing out many beautiful things but the most beautiful thing is a big iron bath. I see the bath and I think of you. It is perfect."

Frieda looked more carefully at the bathroom. Where the bathtub had once stood, the wall and floor were now exposed. There were cracked tiles, bare floorboards, a gaping pipe. Josef himself was covered in dust, his dark hair speckled with it. "Josef, you should have asked me."

Josef spread his arms helplessly. "If I had asked you, you would have said no."

"Which is why you should have asked me."

Josef made a gesture, palm upward. "Frieda, you protect all other people and sometimes you get hurt from that. What you must do is let other people help you." He looked at Frieda more closely. "Why are you holding your pen like that?"

Frieda glanced down. She was still holding the pen in her fist, like a dagger. "I thought there was a burglar," she said. Once more she made herself take a deep breath. It had been well meant, she told herself. "So, how long will it take to put my old bathtub back just the way it was?"

Josef looked thoughtful. "That is problem," he said. "When we took the bath from the wall and the pipe and the brackets, there were big cracks from that. That bath was just all crap. And, anyway, it is now at the dump."

"This is probably some sort of crime, what you've done, but anyway, what happens now?"

"The beautiful bath is now in the workshop of another friend called Klaus. That is no problem. But here . . ." He gestured with his wrench at the damage and gave a sigh. "That is problem."

"What do you mean a problem?" said Frieda. "*You* did it."

"No, no," said Josef. "This is . . ." He said something in his own language. It sounded contemptuous. "The pipe connecting here is very bad. Very bad."

"It always worked fine."

"It was just being lucky. One movement of the bath and . . ." He made an eloquent gesture signifying a chaotic and destructive flood. "I will put a proper pipe here and make the wall good and tiles on the floor. It will be my gift to you, and you will have a bath that will be your place to be happy."

"When?" asked Frieda.

"I will do what must be done," said Josef.

"Yes, but when will you do it?"

"It will be a few days. Only a very few."

"I was going to have a bath now. All the way home I had an idea in my head of having it and what it was going to be like and how much I needed it."

"It will be worth the waiting for."

My very dearest Frieda, I'm sitting in my office, thinking of you. I can hold a conversation, cut up an onion, walk across Brooklyn Bridge, and you're there. I was going to say I haven't felt like this since I was a teenager, but I never felt like this as a teenager! I ask myself why I'm here, when my life's work is to make you happy. I can hear you say that happiness isn't the point, that you don't know the meaning of the word—but I know the meaning of the word: happiness for me is being loved by Frieda Klein.

You sounded a bit distracted on the phone this evening. Please tell me why. Tell me everything. Remember our river walk. Remember me. Sandy xxxxxxx

FIVE

Commissioner Crawford frowned. "Make this quick," he said. "I've got a meeting."

"Is it a problem?" said Karlsson. "I rang ahead before I came over."

"We're all doing more with less at the moment."

"Which is why I wanted to talk to you about Bradshaw."

The commissioner's frown darkened still further. He got up, walked to the window, and looked out over St. James's Park. He turned to Karlsson. "What do you think of the view?"

"Very striking," said Karlsson.

"It's one of the rewards of the job," said the commissioner. He brushed a few specks of dust off the sleeve of his uniform. "You should come here more often. It might clarify your mind."

"About what?"

"About running a tight ship," said the commissioner. "About being a team player."

"I thought it was about solving crimes."

The commissioner took a step away from the window toward Karlsson, who was still standing beside the large wooden desk. "Don't try that with me," he said. "A police force is about political influence, and it always has been. If I can't get up the home secretary's arse and get you the funding that you're pissing away, you won't be in a position to solve your crimes, any of you. I know things are tough, Mal, but these are tough times and we all have to make sacrifices."

"In that case, I'm willing to sacrifice Dr. Hal Bradshaw."

The commissioner looked at him sharply. "You mentioned him on the phone. Has he done something wrong?"

"I met him at the Chalk Farm murder scene. He just turned up."

"That's the arrangement," said the commissioner. "I know the way he works. The quicker he can get on the scene, the more use he can be to us."

"I think he's a distraction," said Karlsson.

"Does this have anything to do with that Dr. Klein?"

"Why should it?"

"Dr. Klein and Dr. Bradshaw were treading on each other's toes. One of them had to go. We went through a full consultation process. The fact is that your Dr. Klein is not trained in the forensic field."

Karlsson paused for a few seconds. "In my opinion," he said, "Dr. Bradshaw does not represent good value for money."

"Wait," said the commissioner. He strode across to his desk and pressed a button. He leaned down. "Send him in."

"What is this?" said Karlsson.

"I don't believe in being underhand," said the commissioner. "Things like this should be dealt with face-to-face."

Karlsson turned as a young uniformed officer opened the door and Hal Bradshaw walked in. Karlsson felt his cheeks flush with anger and hoped it didn't show. When he saw the hint of a smile on Bradshaw's face, he had to look away.

"Mal," said the commissioner. "I don't believe in going behind people's backs. Tell Dr. Bradshaw what you've just told me."

The three men were now standing in an awkward triangle in the middle of the commissioner's office. Karlsson had the feeling that he'd walked into a trap.

"I didn't realize that talking to my boss was going behind people's backs," he said, "but I'm happy to be clear about things." He turned to Bradshaw. "I don't believe that your presence is helpful to the inquiry."

"Based on what?"

"Based on the fact that I'm running it."

"That's not enough," said the commissioner. "Dr. Bradshaw's got a track record. He appears on the *Today* program."

"I don't think he represents a proper use of public money."

Bradshaw turned to the commissioner and gave a sigh. "I think this is a problem that you need to sort out between yourselves," he said.

"No," said the commissioner. "I want it sorted out here and now."

"I think my track record speaks for itself," said Bradshaw. "The real problem seems to be Mr. Karlsson's belief that a psychotherapist he happened to run into could be effective doing profiling work as a sort of hobby."

"Shall we stick to your track record?" said Karlsson.

"Absolutely," said Bradshaw. "I'm here because Commissioner Crawford knew my work and appointed me personally. If you have any objection to that, then now is the time to say it."

"All right," said Karlsson. "I experienced your profiling skills on the Michelle Doyce case. Your analysis of the crime scene was misleading. Your identification of the murderer was completely mistaken and would have derailed the entire course of the investigation if it hadn't been for Frieda Klein."

"It's not an exact science," said Bradshaw.

"Not the way you do it," said Karlsson. "Frieda Klein didn't just get it right, she almost got killed doing it. And that was after being effectively fired from the investigation."

Bradshaw give a sniff. "From what I heard, Klein's mishap came from the failings of your own officers. I may have my failings, but I've never stabbed a mental patient to death." He stepped back quickly when he saw that Karlsson had raised his right hand.

"Steady, Mal," said the commissioner.

"Frieda was fighting for her life," said Karlsson. "And she showed you up for the idiot you are." He turned to Crawford. "He talks about his track record. Just check it out. From what I've seen, Bradshaw is terrific at profiling criminals after they've been caught. Frieda Klein was more useful when we were still searching for them."

Crawford looked at the two of them.

"I'm sorry, Mal, but I want Dr. Bradshaw to stay on the case. Just find a way to work together. That's all."

Karlsson and Bradshaw walked out of the commissioner's office together. Without speaking they reached the lift, waited for it, got in, and rode to the ground floor. As they stepped out, Bradshaw spoke. "Was it Frieda who put you up to this?" he said.

"What are you talking about?"

"If she's going to damage me," he said, "she'll need to be better at it than that."

They could all see that Karlsson was in a thoroughly bad mood. It didn't help that the principal operations room in the police station was being painted. The desks were covered with sheets. Karlsson glanced into the various conference rooms, but they were already being used by other officers or had been filled with displaced furniture and computers. In the end, he led Yvette, Munster, and Riley down some stairs and into the canteen. Riley dumped a pile of files on a table, then they all queued for coffees and teas. Munster and Riley bought a bun each, covered with white icing. Karlsson looked disapproving.

"While we're here," said Munster.

"I missed breakfast," added Riley.

"As long as you don't get the files sticky," said Karlsson.

"We'd better get used to this," said Yvette, as they settled at their table in a corner of the canteen by a window. "When the cuts take effect, those of us who're left will be fighting for office space."

"Hot desking," said Riley.

"What?" Karlsson frowned.

"It's the modern kind of office. Nobody has their own desk. The idea is that you only occupy space when you need it."

"What about your stuff?" said Munster. "Your paper clips and coffee mug."

"You keep them all in a locker. It's a bit like school."

"Not like my school," said Munster. "If you left anything in your locker there, it got broken into and nicked."

"If you're quite ready," Karlsson interrupted.

"Hang on," said Munster. "Is Bradshaw coming?"

"He's busy today," said Karlsson.

"Probably appearing on TV," said Yvette, and Karlsson gave her a look.

"You go first," he said.

"The situation is pretty much what you saw at the scene. We've had officers taking statements up and down the road. Plus we sent a couple of them to spend time there for the next two or three afternoons, just in case there were people who walked there at that time of day. There's nothing that leaps out."

"Fingerprints?" said Karlsson.

"They've got dozens of them," said Yvette. "But this was a family house, people in and out all the time. They've started to eliminate family prints, but it's hopeless until we can narrow it down."

"Weapon?" said Karlsson.

"We haven't found one."

"Have you searched?"

"Within reason."

"There was a bin collection the next morning," said Munster. "A few officers had made a preliminary search the previous afternoon. But we didn't have the men."

"I don't even know why I'm bothering," said Karlsson. "But I'll say it anyway: CCTV?"

"Nothing in the road itself," said Yvette. "It's residential. It doesn't have them. We've got the footage from a couple of cameras on Chalk Farm Road. But we haven't been through it yet."

"Why not?"

"We've got a window of three or four hours and crowds of people wandering down to Camden Lock and we don't know what we're looking for."

There was a pause. Karlsson noticed a smile on Riley's face. "Is something funny?" he asked.

"Not really," Riley said. "It's different from what I expected."

"Is this your first?"

"You mean murder? I dealt with a death near the Elephant and Castle. But they caught the guy at the scene."

"Where's the fun in that?" said Karlsson. He turned back to Yvette. "The woman, Ruth Lennox. Why was she at home?"

"It was her afternoon off. Her husband said it's a day she normally goes shopping or does things around the house."

"Meets friends?"

"Sometimes."

"That day?"

Yvette shook her head. "He showed us her diary. There was nothing in it for that day."

"How are the family?" asked Karlsson.

"In shock. When I interviewed them they seemed stunned. They're staying with friends a few doors up from their house."

"What about the husband?"

"He's not the demonstrative type," said Yvette, "but he seems devastated."

"Have you asked him where he was at the time of his wife's murder?"

"He told us he had a four o'clock meeting with a Ms. Lorraine Crawley, an accountant for the company where he works. I rang her and she confirmed it. It lasted about half an hour, forty minutes. Which makes it very unlikely that he could have got back to his house in time to kill his wife and leave before the daughter came home from school."

"Unlikely?" said Karlsson. "That's not good enough. I'll talk to him again myself."

"You suspect him?" said Riley.

"If a woman is killed and there's a husband or a boyfriend around, then that's something to be taken into consideration."

"But look," said Munster. "As you saw yourself, the little girl found broken glass next to the front door and the door open."

"Was the door usually double locked?" asked Karlsson.

"Not when they were at home," said Yvette. "According to the husband."

"And?"

"Also according to the husband, when he'd calmed down and looked around, a set of silver cutlery had been stolen from a drawer in the kitchen sideboard. Also a Georgian silver teapot that was on a shelf in the cupboard. Plus the money from her wallet, of course."

"Anything else taken?"

"Not that we know of," said Yvette. "She had jewelry upstairs, but it wasn't touched."

"And—" Riley began, then stopped.

"What?" said Karlsson.

"Nothing."

Karlsson forced himself to adopt a gentler tone. "Go on," he said. "If you've got an idea, just say it. I want to hear everything."

"I was going to say that when I saw the body, she had nice earrings on and a necklace."

"That's right," said Karlsson. "Good." He looked back at Yvette. "So? What are we thinking?"

"I'm not saying you shouldn't talk to the husband," said Yvette, "but the state of the scene seems consistent with a burglary that was interrupted. The burglar goes to the kitchen, takes the silver. Then he encounters Mrs. Lennox in the living room. There's a scuffle. She receives a fatal blow. He flees in panic."

"Or," said Karlsson, "someone who knows Mrs. Lennox kills her and stages the burglary."

"That's possible," said Yvette, woodenly.

"But not very likely. You're right. So there we are: an apparent burglary, a dead woman, no witnesses, no fingerprints as yet, no forensics."

"What about your old detective?" said Munster.

"I think we need him," said Karlsson.

Standing on the pavement outside the Lennoxes' house, Harry Curzon looked like a golfer who'd taken a wrong turning. He was dressed in a red windbreaker over a checked sweater, light gray chinos, and brown suede shoes. He was overweight and wore thick, heavy-framed spectacles.

"So, how's retirement?" asked Karlsson.

"I don't know what kept me," said Curzon. "How far away are you? Seven, eight years?"

"A bit more than that!"

"You need to see the writing on the wall. It's all productivity and pen pushing now. Look at me. Fifty-six years old and a full pension. When you called me, I was heading up to the Lee River for a day's fishing."

"Sounds good."

"It is good. So, before I head off and you go back to your office, what can I do for you?"

"There's been a murder," said Karlsson. "But there's also been a burglary. You worked here."

"Eighteen years," said Curzon.

"I thought you could give me some advice."

As Karlsson showed Curzon around the house, the older man talked and talked and talked. Karlsson wondered whether he was really enjoying his days of fishing and golf as much as he'd said he was.

"It's gone out of fashion," said Curzon.

"What?"

"Burglary."

"Back in the seventies it was TV sets and cameras and watches and clocks. In the eighties it was video players and stereos, and in the nineties it was DVD players and computers. It took them a few years, but then the burglars suddenly woke up. A DVD player costs about the same as a DVD, and people are walking around in the streets with a phone and an iPod and probably a laptop that's worth more than anything they've got at home. What's the point of breaking in and getting a couple of extra years inside when you can mug them in the street and get something you can sell?"

"What indeed?" said Karlsson.

"Try going to a dodgy secondhand dealer and offering them a DVD player, and they'll laugh in your face. Garden equipment, though, that's salable. There's always a market for a hedge trimmer."

"Not really relevant in this case," said Karlsson. "So, you don't think this was a burglary?"

"Looks like a burglary to me," said Curzon.

"But couldn't it have been staged?"

"You could say that about anything. But if you were doing that, I reckon you'd break a window at the back. You're less likely to be spotted by a nosy neighbor. And you'd take some stuff from the room where the body was."

"That's basically what we've been thinking," said Karlsson. "So we're looking for a burglar and you know about burglars."

Curzon grimaced. "I'll give you some names. But these burglaries are mainly about drugs, and the junkies come and go. It's not like the old days."

"When you had your trusty local burglar?" Karlsson smiled.

"Don't knock it. We all knew our place."

"What I hoped," said Karlsson, "is that you'd be able to look at this crime scene and identify the burglar by his style. Doesn't every burglar have his own trademark?"

Curzon pulled another face. "There's no trademark to this. He broke the window, opened the door, and let himself in. You can't get more basic than that. The only trademark in this scene was the trademark of a basic idiot. They're the worst kind, except when you catch them in the act." He paused. "But I've had a thought. There's a couple of local shops—trinkets, cheap stuff mostly but not always. There's Tandy's up on the corner of Rubens Road and there's Burgess and Son over on the Crescent. Let's say that if someone goes in there and offers them some silverware, they don't ask too many questions. Get someone to look in the window over the next few days. They might see something. You could take it from there."

Karlsson was doubtful. "If you've killed someone, you're not exactly going to take your swag to the local jeweler, are you?"

Curzon shrugged. "These clowns are addicts, not bank managers. Burgess and Son is a bit farther away. That might be his idea of being a bit clever. It's worth a try, anyway."

"Thanks," said Karlsson.

On the way out of the house Curzon put his hand on Karlsson's sleeve. "Can I get you out on the course? Show you what you're missing out on?"

"I'm not really a golfer. In fact, not a golfer at all."

"Or come and get a little fishing in. You wouldn't believe how peaceful it is."

"Yes." Karlsson nodded. He didn't like fishing either. "Yes, that would be good. Maybe when the case is over. We can celebrate."

"I almost feel guilty," said Curzon. "Showing you what you're missing."

"Go there with Russell Lennox, if he feels up to it," said Karlsson to Yvette. "See if he recognizes anything."

"All right."

"Take young Riley with you."

"Fine." Yvette hesitated, then, as Karlsson turned to go, blurted out, "Can I ask you something?"

"Sure."

"Do you blame me?"

"Blame you? For what?" He knew what, of course—ever since Frieda had been found lying on the floor of Mary Orton's house, in that scene of carnage, Yvette had wanted his forgiveness, his reassurance that it wasn't really her fault.

"For not taking her concerns seriously. All that." Yvette gulped. Her face had turned very red.

"This isn't really the right time, Yvette."

"But . . ."

"It isn't appropriate," he said. His gentleness was worse than anger. She felt like a small child facing a kind, stern adult.

"No. Sorry. Tandy's and Burgess and Son."

"That's right."

Frieda took the phone out of its holster and considered it. Her eyes itched with tiredness, and her body felt hollow yet enormously heavy. The grave in Suffolk seemed like a dream now—a neglected patch of soil where the bones of a sad man lay. She thought of him, the father she had not been able to rescue. If she let herself go back, she could remember the way his hand had felt, holding hers, or breathe in his smell of tobacco and the cloves from his aftershave. His hopelessness. His heavy posture. And Dean Reeve had sat over him, with that smile.

The cat slid through the cat flap and she looked down at it, the two of them staring at each other. Still holding the phone, she walked slowly up the stairs—stairs were still hard for her—and sat on her bed, gazing out of the window at the soft gray evening that was settling over the city, making it mysterious again. At last she lifted the phone and keyed in the numbers.

"Hello," she said.

"Frieda!" There was no mistaking the warmth of his voice.

"Hello."

"I've been thinking of you."

"Where are you now?"

"In my office. Five hours behind you."

"What are you wearing?"

"A gray suit. A white shirt. You?"

Frieda looked down at her clothes. "Jeans and a creamy brown jumper."

"Where are you?"

"Sitting on my bed."

"I wish I was sitting on your bed too."

"Did you sleep well?"

"Yes. I dreamed I was ice-skating. Did you?"

"Dream I was ice-skating?"

"No! Sleep well?"

"All right."

"So you didn't."

"Sandy?" She wanted to tell him about her day, but the words wouldn't come. He was too far away.

"Yes, my very darling Frieda."

"I hate this."

"This?"

"All of it."

"Feeling weak, you mean?"

"That too."

"Me being here?" There was a pause. "What's that noise? Is there a thunderstorm going on?"

"What?" Frieda looked around. She'd almost stopped hearing the sound herself. "There's a new bath being put in."

"A new bath?"

"It wasn't exactly my idea. In fact, it wasn't my idea at all. It's a present from Josef."

"That sounds good."

"The bath hasn't arrived yet. So far, there's just lots of banging and drilling going on. There's dust everywhere. Including on several shirts—you left them here."

"I know."

"And some kitchen stuff, and a few books by the bed."

"That's because I'm coming back."

"Right."

"Frieda, I'm coming back."

SIX

s that Detective Chief Inspector Karlsson?"

"Speaking."

"Constable Fogle from Camden. I have a Mr. Russell Lennox with me."

"Russell Lennox?" Karlsson blinked. "Why on earth?"

"He's been involved in an affray."

"I don't understand. Why would he be involved in an affray? The poor man's wife's just been murdered."

"He seems to have caused some criminal damage. At a Burgess and Son."

"Ah."

"He broke a window, not to mention several pieces of china that the owner seems to think might be worth a good deal, and was also somewhat threatening."

"I'm on my way. Treat him gently, will you?"

Russell Lennox was in a small interview room, sitting with his hands plaited together on the table and staring ahead, blinking every so often as if to clear his vision. When Karlsson came in with the uniformed officer who had called him, Lennox turned his head. For a few moments it seemed that he didn't recognize the detective.

"I've come to take you home," said Karlsson, lowering himself into the chair opposite. "You know that you could be prosecuted for affray, assault, whatever?"

"I don't care."

"Would that help your children?"

Lennox just stared at the table surface and didn't reply.

"So you went back to Burgess and Son?"

Lennox gave a faint nod. "I couldn't get it out of my head. Anyway, what else am I supposed to do with my time? Ruth's sister Louise is with the children, and they don't want to see me upset on top of everything else. So, I walked over there, just to check. I saw this fork."

"One fork?" said Karlsson, doubtfully.

"Ruth's godmother gave them to us when we got married. I didn't care about them or notice them, really, but this one had a bent spike. That's how I recognized it. Judith used to get angry if she was given it at meals. She said it stabbed her gums. I went inside and asked to see it. Then things got out of hand." He looked up at Karlsson. "I'm not a violent man."

"I think there might be some argument about that," said Karlsson.

Jeremy Burgess, the owner of Burgess and Son, was small, skinny, with the wariness of someone who had spent years never quite getting anything pinned on him. Karlsson was leaning over a glass counter crammed with medals, old necklaces, cigarette cases, dented snuff boxes, thimbles, small silver boxes, glittery clip-on earrings, and oversized cuff links. He took the fork with its crooked tine and laid it on the glass.

"Where did this come from?" he asked.

Burgess gestured helplessly. "I just pay in cash for little things like that."

"I need to know, Mr. Burgess."

"I'm the one who was attacked. What's happening about that? I'm just trying to run a business."

"Shut up," said Karlsson. "I know about your business. If the local police aren't bothered, that's their affair. But this is evidence in a murder inquiry, and if you don't cooperate, then I will make your life very difficult indeed."

Burgess glanced uneasily at two women on the other side of the shop who were poring over a tray of rings. He leaned forward and spoke in a lower tone. "I'm just a businessman," he said.

"Give me a name and I'll go away. Otherwise I'll send some officers round here to go through this piece by piece."

"Billy."

"Billy who?"

"Billy. Young, dark-haired, thin. That's all I know."

Curzon's voice kept coming and going. He explained that the reception was bad out there on the river. "Hunt," he said. "Billy Hunt."

"You know him?"

"We all know Billy."

"Does he have a record?"

"Robbery, possession, this and that."

"Violence?"

"He's a bit of a wimp, our Billy," said Curzon, "but he may have gone downhill. I mean even farther downhill."

Karlsson put Riley onto it. Curzon didn't have an address or a number for Billy Hunt, but there were a couple of officers who'd been dealing with the local drug scene. They'd probably know, said Curzon. They hadn't seen Hunt for some time, but one of them remembered he'd once worked at a stall in Camden Lock. Selling implements made out of wire. Candlesticks. Little dogs for the mantelpiece. The stall was gone, but a woman who'd worked on it was now at the other end of the market, near the canal, selling hot soup. She didn't know Billy, but the guy who used to run the wire stall lived in a flat in Summertown. He was out at night mostly and slept during the day. It took repeated banging at the front door (the knocker was missing and the bell didn't seem to make a sound) before a woman appeared and, at their request, went to wake him up. He hadn't seen Billy for a couple of weeks, but he used to drop by a café in the high street or the pub next to it when he had any money.

Nobody seemed to know him in the café, but when Riley showed his badge to the pale young woman behind the bar in the pub, she pointed him to two men sitting drinking at a table. Yes, they knew Billy Hunt. Yes, one of them had seen him today. What had they talked about? Nothing much. Just to say hello. Where was he? That other pub. Which other one? The one up Kentish Town Road, the Goth one, the one with the skulls.

Riley walked up Camden High Street and found Munster parked outside Camden Town tube station. He got into the car beside him.

"What's the plan?" he said.

"Plan?" said Munster. "Find him. And then talk to him."

"Are we bringing him in?"

"We'll talk to him first."

The car pulled up before reaching the pub. Munster gazed up at the black façade and shook his head with distaste.

"I used to like heavy metal when I was a kid," said Riley. "I'd have loved this place."

"When you were a kid?" said Munster. "Right. Do we know what he looks like?"

Two young women, dressed from head to foot in black leather, both with shaved heads and multiple piercings, were seated at a table outside.

"Well, they're not Billy Hunt," said Riley, cheerfully. "Unless Billy's a girl's name."

At the other table a man was sitting alone, with a half-drunk pint of beer and a cigarette. He was thin and pale, with tufted dark hair, wearing black jeans and a rumpled gray jacket.

"That might be him," said Munster.

They got out of the car and approached him. He didn't notice them until they were a few feet away.

"We're looking for a William Hunt," said Munster.

"Only my mum calls me William," the man replied. "And then only when she's angry with me."

The two detectives sat at the table.

"Billy, then," Munster said. "We've been talking to a man named Jeremy Burgess. He runs a jewelry store just up the road from here."

Hunt stubbed his cigarette out on the table, took another from a packet and lit it with almost feverish concentration. "I don't know him."

"William," said Munster. "Now *I'm* getting angry with you." He took a printout from his pocket and spread it on the table. "He told us that you came in with this and he bought it from you."

Hunt turned the paper around and looked at it. Munster saw that even his hands, even his long fingers, were thin and pale. The nails were bitten short, but even so they were dirty and stained. "I don't know," he said.

"What do you mean, you don't know?" said Munster. "Is all this Georgian silver becoming a bit of a blur?"

"Are you going to buy me a drink?"

"No, I'm not going to buy you a drink. What do you think this is?"

"If you're looking for information, there should be something in it for me."

Munster turned to Riley, then back to Hunt. Riley was smiling. Munster wasn't. "You're not a potential informant. You're a suspect. If you don't answer questions, we can take you straight into custody."

Hunt ruffled his hair so that it stood up even more than before. "Every time there's some bit of property goes missing," he said, in a whine, "people like you come and hassle me about it. Have you ever heard the expression about giving a dog a bad name?"

Munster looked at him in disbelief. "Is this the dog that keeps being put in prison for hitting people and selling things that other people have stolen? And while we're on the subject, these bits of property don't just go missing on their own. People like you nick them. Don't mess us around,

Billy. We've heard about you. You've got a drug habit and you steal to pay for it."

Hunt took a gulp of beer, followed by a deep drag on his cigarette. He looked at Riley, who was grinning. "I don't know what's so funny," he said. "I only got started when I was inside. There's more cocaine inside than there is on the streets. And that wanker, Burgess. Everyone comes round and bothers me, and there's Burgess with his fucking shop. Why does everyone let him carry on?"

"Billy," said Munster. "Shut up. Where did you get the silver?"

Hunt paused. "There was a guy. He had some bits and pieces, bits of silver. He was desperate for cash, so I gave him some and passed it on to Burgess. End of story."

"Did you ask him where he got it?"

"No, I didn't. I'm not the *Antiques* fucking *Roadshow*."

"What's his name?"

"I don't know. Dave, I think."

"Dave," said Munster. "Dave what?"

"I don't know. I don't really know him."

"Where does he live?"

"South of the river, I think. But I'm not sure."

"Dave. South London," said Munster. "Possibly. Do you know how to get in touch with him?"

"It doesn't really work like that. You run into people. See them around. You know how it is."

"Yeah, I know," said Munster. "And while we're at it, could you tell me where you were on Wednesday?"

"When? The one just gone?"

"Yes. The sixth."

"I was out of London. I was down in Brighton. Had a few days away."

"Is there anyone who can confirm that?"

"I was down with a friend."

"What's his name?"

"His name?" said Hunt. Quite slowly, he stubbed his cigarette out and lit another. "Ian."

"Second name?"

"He was always just Ian."

"But you can tell us his address?"

Hunt looked doubtful. "I've got it written down somewhere. Or I did have. It was at a friend of Ian's. Ian won't be there. He moves around a lot."

"Arranging work for people," said Munster.

"For his friends."

"I can't believe I'm actually bothering to say this out loud," said Munster, "but have you got Ian's phone number?"

"It was on my phone. I'm not completely sure where my phone is."

"You realize what we're asking?" said Munster. "You've been here before. We want you to point us in the direction of someone who will say to us, 'Yes, Billy Hunt was with me in Brighton on Wednesday.' Is there such a person?"

"This isn't right," said Hunt. "This is a matter of . . . What this is about is . . . is . . . that I'm not like you. Or you," he added, looking at Riley, who seemed bemused. "You've got your nice homes and all your insurance and your water bills with your names on them."

"My water bill?" said Munster.

"And you've got all your nice friends and you go out to dinner with them. You all look out for each other and—and you can just prove where you were all the time and you've got a job and a pension and paid holidays."

"What the fuck are you talking about?"

"We're not all like you. Don't you read the papers? Some of us are having to struggle to get by."

"Will you shut up?" said Munster. "I don't care about any of this. But I'm finding it a bit difficult to pin anything down. Do you have an address?"

"You see, that's just what I'm talking about. People like you, you always have an address." Hunt drew imaginary quotation marks with his fingers around the word *address*.

"All right. Let's make it simple. Where did you sleep last night?"

"Last night?" said Hunt, thoughtfully. "I don't know. I stay with different people, with friends. I'm looking for somewhere permanent."

"Like you're looking for a job?" said Munster.

"Like that."

"One more thing," said Munster. "And this is just a formality, so that my colleague can write it in his notebook."

"What?"

"It wasn't by any chance you who stole the silver from sixty-three Margaretting Street?"

"No, it wasn't."

"All right," said Munster.

"So we're done?" said Hunt.

"No, we're not. I've had enough of this. You're coming with us."

"What for?"

"Well, just for a start, you've already admitted receiving and selling stolen goods."

"I didn't know they were stolen."

"Which, if you read the terms of the Act, is not relevant."

"I've told you everything I know." Hunt's voice rose in indignation. "If you need any more information, just get in touch with me."

"Except that we've established you don't have an address and you've mislaid your phone."

"Just give me your card," said Hunt. "I'll get in touch with you."

"I would," said Munster. "It's just that I've got a feeling that you might go the way of your friends Dave and Ian and be a bit difficult to track down. So are you willing to come, or do we have to arrest you?"

"I'll come. Haven't I been cooperating? Haven't I answered all your questions? I just want to finish my drink. And then go to the toilet."

"We'll come with you."

"I can go later," said Hunt. He sipped his beer. "Don't you like sitting outside? It's global warming, isn't it? We can sit out on the pavement in London drinking. It's like being by the Med."

"With skulls," said Riley.

Hunt peered up at them. "I don't like the skulls. They're depressing."

SEVEN

No drugs," said Olivia. "Obviously no drugs."

"Mum," said Chloë.

"And no spirits. You've told everybody no spirits? If anyone brings spirits, they'll be confiscated and their parents can collect them."

"You've said this about a million times."

"Have you got a list of everyone who's coming?" asked Olivia. "Then Frieda's friend can cross them off as they arrive."

"I haven't got a list."

"How do you know who's coming, then?"

"It's not like that, Mum," said Chloë. "For God's sake."

"But you must know how many people are coming." There was a pause. "Well?"

"Sort of."

"Well, sort of how many? Ten? Fifty? A thousand?"

"We've talked about this. We've talked about it a million times."

"This isn't a joke, Chloë. Did you hear about the teenage party in Hart Street last year? The father tried to deal with some gate-crashers and one of them pulled a knife. He lost a kidney, Chloë."

"What's all this about? You said I could have the party. If I can't have it, then just say so and we'll cancel it. Will that make you happy?"

"I want you to have a party," said Olivia. "It's your birthday. But I want you to enjoy it. You won't enjoy it if people are being sick and there are fights and the house is being vandalized."

"It won't be like that."

"And no sex."

"Mum!"

"What?"

"This is just embarrassing."

Olivia reached forward and touched Chloë's cheek. "You look lovely, by the way."

Chloë blushed and mumbled something.

"There are crisps and nuts and cartons and cartons of juice," said Olivia. "What I'm trying to get across to you, Chloë, is that you'll all have a better time if you don't get falling-over drunk. You can talk to each other and—and dance and things . . ."

"Oh, Mum . . ."

"But nobody enjoys being really drunk and falling over and being sick. That's not a good time. I mean, Frieda, back me up over this. Am I being a wet blanket?"

Frieda was standing by the window, gazing out into the garden. There were unlit candles in jam jars along the gravel path. There was a ring at the door.

"Oh, God," said Olivia. "Already?"

"I'll get it," said Frieda.

She went to the front door and opened it. "Josef! You're just in time."

Josef wasn't alone. Next to him was a man who was even taller and bulkier. He was wearing jeans and a leather jacket. He had long curly hair, tied at the back of his head in a ponytail.

"This is Stefan," said Josef. "And he is from Russia, but we will be pleasant to him in any case."

Frieda shook Stefan's hand, and he gave her a slow smile. "You are Frieda? I have heard. You are going to have a beautiful bath. It is big and made of iron, like in an old film."

"Yes, I've heard of you too," said Frieda. "You helped Josef take my nice old bath away."

"It was a bad bath," said Stefan. "Cheap rubbish. It cracked like that"—he snapped his fingers—"when we took it."

"Well, thank you both for doing this. Although I'm worried that while you're doing it, my bathroom still doesn't have a bath."

Josef looked concerned. "Yes, Frieda, I must talk with you. There is a small problem."

"What problem?"

"More problem with the pipes. But we talk later. I sort it."

"You know, I had to have a shower here," said Frieda. "While they were preparing for the party. I have to carry a towel round with me." She stopped herself. "But it's good of you to do this. You'd better come in. Can I get you something to drink?"

"Now we will have juice." Josef tapped the pocket of his coat. Evidently there was a bottle in there. "At the end of the night we will celebrate together."

Olivia gave Josef and Stefan a variety of instructions, constantly adjusted and added to. Meanwhile, the doorbell rang intermittently and young people began to drift in. Frieda stood to one side and watched the scene as if it were a piece of theater or an exotic tribe. Suddenly she saw a face she recognized and gave a start. "Jack! What are you doing here?"

Jack was training to be a psychotherapist, and Frieda was his supervisor. She knew him well, but seeing him in this context was a surprise. He, too, seemed taken aback and blushed a deep, unbecoming red. Even by his own standards, he was wearing bizarre and mismatched clothes—a pink and green hooped rugby shirt, with an ancient, moth-eaten tuxedo over the top, and baggy brown cords.

"Chloë invited me," he said. "I thought it might be fun. I didn't expect to see you, though."

"I'm on my way out."

"Is that Josef I can see?"

"He's the bouncer for the evening."

After a minute or two, Josef looked at her over Olivia's shoulder, with a faint smile that was a plea for help. Frieda walked across the room and tapped Olivia on the arm. "Let's go and get our meal."

"I just need to check on a few things."

"No, you don't."

Frieda led Olivia, still protesting, into the hallway, put her coat on for her, and pulled her out of the front door. As they went down the steps, Olivia stared around anxiously. "I can't help feeling that I'm locking *in* the people I ought to be locking *out*."

"No," said Olivia, to the waiter. "I don't need to taste it. Just pour it most of the way up. Thanks, and leave the bottle." She picked up the glass. "Cheers." She took a gulp. "Christ, I needed that. Did you see them all hugging each other as they arrived? It was as if they'd returned from a round-the-world trip. And as soon as they've finished hugging and shrieking, they're on their mobile phones. They're at a party, but somehow they instantly need to talk to the people who're not at the party or who're on their way to the party, or maybe they're checking whether there's a better party somewhere else." She took another gulp. "They're probably sending out a general call to the youth of north London to trash the house." She prodded Frieda. "At this point you're supposed to say, 'No, no, it'll be fine.'"

"It'll be fine," said Frieda.

Olivia gesticulated toward the waiter. "Why don't we order lots of little dishes?" she said. "Then we can just pick at them."

"You choose."

Olivia ordered enough for three or four hearty eaters and another bottle of wine. "I'm a big hypocrite, really," she said, when the waiter had gone. "My real worry about a party like this is that Chloë will do half of what I did when I was her age. Younger than her age. She's seventeen. When I think of parties when I was fifteen, fourteen . . . It was technically illegal. People could have gone to prison. I'm sure it was the same with you. David told me one or two things."

Frieda's expression became fixed. She took a sip of wine but didn't speak.

"When I think of some of the things I got up to . . ." Olivia continued. "At least people weren't filming me on their mobile phones and putting it on the Internet. That's the difference. When we were teenagers, you could do things and they were done, gone, in the past. Now they get filmed and sent by phone and put on Facebook. People don't realize they're stuck with their actions forever. It wasn't like that with us."

"That's not true," said Frieda. "People got hurt. People got pregnant."

"I wasn't going to get pregnant," said Olivia. "Mummy put me on the Pill at about the time I learned to walk. I'm not saying I was a complete wild child, it's just that . . . When I look at some of the decisions I made, well, I'd like to see Chloë choose better than that." She topped up her wineglass. Frieda held her hand over her own glass. "But in some ways, I think Chloë is more mature than I was at her age. Now, I know what you're going to say."

"What am I going to say?"

"You're going to say that if I was less mature than Chloë, I must have been a truly epic fuckup."

"That's not what I was going to say," said Frieda.

"Then what?"

"I was going to say that it was a good thing to say about your daughter."

"We'll see," snorted Olivia. "Meanwhile, the house is probably being reduced to its constituent parts."

"I'm sure you don't need to worry."

"I don't know what parties you went to," said Olivia. "I was once at this party. I was up in the parents' bedroom with Nick Yates, and by the time we were finished for the second time, the people downstairs had carried the upright piano out into the garden and started to play it, then forgotten about it, and it had started to rain. God. Nick Yates." A faraway expression came to Olivia's face. Then the food arrived.

"I'm so sorry." Olivia filled her plate from the different dishes. "Try this shrimp, by the way. It's to die for. I've been talking solidly about myself and my problems and my wicked past. I haven't even asked about how you're feeling. I know it's all been so terrible. How are you feeling? Does it still hurt?"

"It's not too bad."

"Are you still being treated?"

"Just checkups," said Frieda. "From time to time."

"It was the most terrible, terrible thing," said Olivia. "At first I thought we were going to lose you. You know, a couple of days ago I had a nightmare about it. I woke up and I was crying. Literally crying."

"I think it was worse for other people than it was for me."

"I bet it wasn't," said Olivia. "But they say that when really terrible things happen, it stops feeling real, like it's happening to someone else."

"No," said Frieda, slowly. "It felt like it was happening to me."

On the way back to the house, Olivia was walking unsteadily and Frieda took her arm.

"I'm looking for smoke," Olivia said. "Can you see smoke?"

"What?"

"If the house was literally on fire," said Olivia, "we'd be seeing smoke by now, wouldn't we? Over the roofs. And there'd be fire engines and sirens."

As they turned the corner into Olivia's road, they saw the front door open, people milling around. There was a loud electronic beat, a low throb. There were flashing lights. As they got closer, Frieda saw a group sitting on the front steps smoking. One of them looked up and smiled.

"It is Frieda, no?"

"Stefan, right?"

"Yes," he said, as if the idea amused him. "Frieda, you like a cigarette?"

Olivia gave an indistinct yell, brushed through the crowd on the steps and ran into the house.

"No, thanks," said Frieda. "How has it been?"

Stefan gave a shrug. "Okay, I think. A quiet party."

One of the boys sitting next to him laughed. "They were great, him and Josef."

"Like how?" Frieda sat on the step beside them.

"This gang of kids came. Chloë didn't know them. They started jostling people. But Josef and Stefan made them go away."

Frieda glanced at Stefan, who was lighting a new cigarette from the old one. "You made them go away?"

"It was no big thing," said Stefan.

"It was a big thing," said one of the other boys. "It was a very big thing."

They laughed, and one said something to Stefan in a language she couldn't understand, and he said something back, then looked at her.

"He is learning a funny Russian in his school," he said. "I am teaching him."

"Where's Josef?"

"He is with a boy," said Stefan. "A boy is not well."

"What do you mean 'not well'? Where are they?"

"The toilet on the upstairs," said Stefan. "He was sick. Very sick."

Frieda ran into the house. The hall was sticky under her feet and there was a smell of smoke and beer. She pushed her way past some girls. There was a group outside the closed door of the bathroom.

"Is he in there?" Frieda asked them in general.

Suddenly Chloë was there. She had been crying. Mascara was running down her face. Jack was hovering behind her, his hair sticking up in peaks and his face blotchy.

"They couldn't wake him," she said.

Frieda tried the door. It was locked. She knocked at it.

"Josef, it's me," said Frieda. "Let me in."

There was a click and the door opened. He was with a boy who was leaning over the lavatory. Josef turned around with an apologetic smile. "He was like this when he come almost," he said.

"Is he responsive?" said Frieda. Josef looked puzzled. "I mean, can he speak? Can he see you?"

"Yes, yes, fine. Just sick. Very, very sick. Teenage sick."

Frieda turned to Chloë. "He's all right," she said.

Chloë shook her head. "Ted's not all right," she said. "He's not. His mother's dead. She was murdered."

. . .

I tell you what, let's go away somewhere this summer—somewhere neither of us has ever been. Though I can't really imagine you anywhere except London. That's where I met you and that's the only place I've known you. Do you ever go anywhere else? The farthest afield I've seen you is Heathrow, which must be your idea of a kind of man-made hell. You hate planes, and you don't like beaches. But we could get a train to Paris or go walking in Scotland. You love walking the streets at night—but do you like other kinds of walking, where you have a map and a picnic? I know you—but there are so many things I don't know about you. That's what I've been thinking. Call me soon—Sandy xxxxxx

EIGHT

"Can I have a cup of tea?" said Billy Hunt. "I want a cup of tea and I want a lawyer. Tea with milk and two sugars, and a lawyer sitting next to me for every moment that you're interviewing me."

Munster turned to Riley. "Hear that?" he said.

Riley left the interview room.

"And a lawyer," said Hunt.

"Wait."

They sat in silence until Riley returned. He placed the polystyrene cup on the table in front of Hunt, with two sachets of sugar and a plastic stirrer. Slowly, and with great concentration, Hunt tore the sachets open, tipped their contents into the tea, and stirred. He sipped the tea.

"And a lawyer," he repeated.

There was a digital recorder on the table. Munster leaned forward to switch it on. As he spoke the day's date and identified the people in the room, he looked at the device to check that the light was flashing. There was always the worry that it wasn't working properly. Cases collapsed because of details like that.

"We're interviewing you on suspicion of handling stolen property. I'm going to caution you that you don't have to say anything, but that anything you say can be used in evidence. Also, if you remain silent, that fact can be presented to the court."

"Are you sure?" said Hunt.

"Yes, I'm sure," said Munster. "And I probably do this sort of thing even more often than you do."

Hunt drummed his fingers on the table. "I guess I can't smoke."

"No, you can't."

"I can't think when I don't smoke."

"You don't need to think. You just need to answer some questions."

"And what about my lawyer?"

"I was about to inform you that you are entitled to legal representation, and that if you don't have representation of your own, we can arrange it for you."

"Of course I don't have fucking legal representation of my own. So, yeah, get me one. I want a lawyer sitting here beside me."

"It doesn't work like that anymore," said Munster. "Money's tight. That's what they're telling us. We can bring you a phone and a phone number."

"Is that it?" Hunt seemed baffled. "No cigs and no lawyers?"

"You can talk to one on the phone."

"All right," said Hunt. "Get a phone."

It was twenty minutes before Billy Hunt had finished on the phone. Munster and Riley were back in the room and the recorder was on again.

"So," Munster began. "You've talked to your lawyer."

"It was a bad line," said Hunt. "I couldn't make out most of what she was saying. She had an accent as well. I don't reckon English is her first language."

"But she gave you legal advice?"

"Is that what you call legal advice? Why can't I get a real lawyer?"

"If you've got a problem, you can take it up with your MP. But that's the way the system works now."

"Why is that window all boarded up?"

"Because someone threw a brick at it."

"Can't you get it mended?"

"I don't really think that's your problem."

"And the room at the front—it's like a building site. You'll be next," he said. "You'll be out looking for a real job like the rest of us."

"You've now officially got legal representation," said Munster. "Take a look at this." He slid a piece of paper across the table.

Hunt examined it with a puzzled expression. "What's this?" he said.

"An inventory."

"What's that?"

"A list of what was stolen. Including, as you'll see, the silver forks you sold. Is there anything else there you remember?"

He shook his head. "Sorry," he said. "Those forks were all I got."

"From Dave," said Munster.

"That's right."

"So," Munster went on, "the items we retrieved were part of a larger haul, but you never saw the rest."

"That's right."

"And your link to this theft was Dave, whose second name you don't know, who you think lives south of the river, and who you have no means of contacting."

Hunt shifted awkwardly in his seat. "You know the way things are," he said.

"And your only alibi for the day of the burglary would be provided by a man called Ian, also with no second name, now currently on his travels. And uncontactable."

"Sorry about that," said Hunt.

"In other words," said Munster, "you can't tell us anything we can check, apart from what we already know."

"You're police," said Hunt. "I don't know what you can check and what you can't check."

"Of course, if you were to put us in touch with whoever passed that silver to you, we'd seriously consider dropping the charge against you."

"Then I wish I could put you in touch with him."

"Dave?"

"Yeah. But I can't."

"Is there anything at all you can tell us?"

"I don't know," said Hunt. "Just ask."

"Where did you spend last night? At least you can tell us that."

"I've been moving around," said Hunt. "I haven't got anywhere regular."

"You can only sleep in one place at a time. Where did you sleep last night?"

"It's in these flats, down near Chalk Farm. There's this friend of mine, friend of a friend. He's away. He lets me bed down there."

"What's the address?"

"I can't remember."

"Then take us there."

It was a short drive, then the three of them—Munster, Riley, and Hunt—walked into the courtyard of the battered, littered estate and up a staircase. On the third floor, Munster stopped and leaned on the balcony railing, looking across at the William Morris building. They were in the John Ruskin building. Beyond were houses that, even now, were worth more than a million pounds, but here one in every three or four flats was boarded up, waiting for a renovation that had probably been put on hold until someone was ready to pay for it. Hunt walked along the balcony and stopped. He took out a key from his jacket pocket and unlocked a front door.

"Stop," Munster said. "Don't go in. You wait out here with DC Riley."

He stepped inside and immediately was reminded of his early days in the force when he had spent much of his time in places like this. It was a smell of mustiness, damp, some food going off somewhere. It was the smell of not bothering, of giving up. The grubby linoleum, the dirty sofas and chairs in the living room, everything stained and old, except the large new flat-screen TV. In the kitchen, the sink was full of dishes; there was a greasy frying pan on the stove. He was seeking something that didn't fit, something different from the usual crap. It didn't seem as if he were going to find it. But then he went into the bathroom and there, finally, was something. He pulled on his plastic gloves. It was too big for an evidence bag. He called Riley and Hunt inside.

"What's that doing here?"

"It's a cog," said Riley. "It looks like it should be in some big old machine." There was a pause.

"Why shouldn't it be in a bathroom?" said Hunt. "It looks nice. Shiny. It's a decoration."

"You weren't admiring its shininess," said Munster. "You were washing it. Where did you get a thing like this from? It's hardly usual."

"It was from that guy."

"Dave?"

"That's right."

"Why didn't you mention it?"

"It wasn't on your list."

"Why were you washing it?"

"So that it would be nice and shiny when I sold it."

"We'll see," said Munster.

Karlsson, when Munster returned with the cog, held it for a moment, turning it over, feeling its heft and weight. Then he went to see Russell Lennox, who was sitting slack and passive in an armchair, staring ahead with bloodshot eyes.

"Mr. Lennox," he said, holding the cog, which was cold in his gloved hands. "Do you recognize this object?"

Russell Lennox gazed at the cog for several seconds without speaking. His lips were bloodless.

"Is that—" He stopped and pressed the bridge of his nose between forefinger and thumb. "Is that what she was killed with?"

"We believe so. Yes. But you didn't mention it among the items that were stolen."

"No. I didn't notice it was gone. It was just a thing we had on our mantelpiece. Ruth picked it up from some Dumpster a couple of years ago. She said it would scrub up nicely, unlike me and Ted." His face worked and he made a visible effort to control his emotions. "You're sure?"

"Your wife's blood was on it."

"I see." Russell Lennox turned away. "I don't want to look at it anymore."

Munster restarted the recorder. "We've been busy," he said. "Things have changed. Now, this is your last chance to cooperate. Where did you get the cog?"

Hunt's eyes flickered between him and Riley. "I said. From Dave."

"All right. That's enough of this crap." Munster stood up and left the room.

Hunt looked at Riley. "What did I say?"

"He's cross," said Riley. "You don't want to make him cross."

"Fucking shut up," said Hunt. "So is this some trick so I suddenly think you're my friend?"

"I was just saying."

A few moments later Munster came back into the room with Karlsson. He pulled a chair across and the two of them sat down. Munster placed a closed brown cardboard file on the table and looked across at Hunt. "Let it be noted that DCI Karlsson has joined the interview," he said. "William Hunt, the next time you want to wash blood off a murder weapon, I'd pop it in the dishwasher. If you rinse it under the tap, you always leave a bit. As you did."

"I don't know what you're talking about."

"Russell Lennox has identified it. They kept it on their mantelpiece as a sort of work of art. A dense and heavy work of art. Three days ago it was used to fatally assault one Ruth Lennox. You've been identified disposing of articles that were taken from the murder scene. The murder weapon has been found at a flat where you were staying. You've admitted attempting to clean it. It has your fingerprints on it. We are about to charge you with the murder of Ruth Lennox and with the burglary. Now, Mr. Hunt, have you got anything to say? It'll make it a great deal easier for all of us if you just admit what you did, write out a statement, and the judge will regard you with some degree of sympathy."

There was a long pause.

"There wasn't anyone called Dave," said Hunt.

"Of course there wasn't anyone called Dave," said Munster. "And?"

"All right," he said. "I did the burglary."

Another pause.

"And? What about Ruth Lennox?"

"You won't believe me," said Hunt.

"Believe you?" said Munster. "You've been lying solidly ever since we met you. Just own up."

There was another, even longer pause. To Riley it appeared that Hunt was doing a complicated mental calculation.

"I did the burglary," he said finally. "But I didn't kill her. I admit, I broke in, I took the stuff from the kitchen. But I was only there for a minute. The alarm was going, so I was in a rush. I went into the other room and she was on the floor. I just ran."

"You didn't just run," said Munster. "We found you with the object that was used to kill her."

"I picked it up. On the way out."

Karlsson stood up. "We've got you at the scene. And you've been lying all the way along the line. You're going away for this one." He nodded at Munster. "Just get the paperwork ready."

NINE

The drilling had stopped, but it was replaced by a hammering that wasn't just loud but shook the house. Frieda made tea for Josef so the noise would stop for a few minutes. Josef sat on the stairs and cradled his mug in his large, dirty hands.

"Under everything, this is a good house," he said. "The walls are good, fine bricks. Give me six months to rip away all the rubbish, all the plasterboard, and—"

"No, no, don't even say that!"

"What?"

"Six months. Those words are very frightening to me."

"I was talking. Just talking."

"All right, and while we're just talking, I thought you said you were going to put a new bath in. I hear lots of banging and the bathroom looks like it's been demolished and there's no sign of a bath."

"It is all fine. I do everything, I sort everything perfectly. Then, at the end, put the bath in. Click, click. Just like that."

Suddenly there was a jangling electronic tone of an old pop song that Frieda couldn't quite place. Josef's phone was on the table beside her. She picked it up. There was a name—Nina—flashing on the screen. She handed it to him but he saw the name and shook his head.

"Is she someone you're avoiding?" said Frieda.

Josef was flustered. "Someone I see a bit. But she ring and ring."

"It's usually best to tell people what you feel," said Frieda. "But I'm not going to give you advice on anything except finishing this bathroom."

"All right, all right," said Josef. He handed his mug to Frieda and went back upstairs.

When she was alone, Frieda swallowed two paracetamol with water. Then she turned to her work e-mail. Most messages she deleted or simply ignored. But there was one from Paz at the clinic she regularly worked for. She asked if Frieda could call her. And there was another she hesitated over. It was from a woman called Marta, who was writing on behalf of her old friend and Frieda's patient, Joe Franklin. She was apologetic: Joe didn't know she was writing and she felt bad about doing so—but did Frieda have any idea when she would be returning to work? Joe wouldn't see the therapist she had recommended, and he was in a bad way. He hadn't got out of bed for several days.

Frieda thought of her doctor and her friends, who were all insistent that she shouldn't return to work for several weeks yet. She thought of Joe Franklin sitting in her consulting room with his head in his hands, tears seeping through his fingers. She frowned and wrote an e-mail: "Dear Joe, I can see you at the usual time tomorrow, Tuesday, if that would suit you. Let me know and best wishes, Frieda Klein."

Then she picked up the phone and called the Warehouse, as the clinic was called. Paz answered and immediately questioned her about how things were going and her health, the way everyone did nowadays. It was like an obstacle she had to get past over and over again.

"Reuben is worried about you," said Paz. "We all are."

Reuben was the man who had founded the Warehouse. As a young man, he had been a charismatic spokesperson for a new kind of therapy and had been Frieda's supervisor. These days he was rather battered and disillusioned.

"And?"

"I wanted to see how you were. Someone contacted us. He wanted to see you. I mean as a patient. I said you weren't well."

"For God's sake, Paz, could you stop handing out my medical details?"

"But he pleaded. He sounded desperate."

"I'll call him."

"You're sure about this, Frieda?"

"It's not working that's the problem."

He was called Seamus Dunne. When Frieda dialed his number, he answered instantly. She introduced herself. "Is it a good time to talk?"

"Yes. It's fine." He sounded suddenly tense.

"You want to come and see me?"

"Yes. I do. I think—I feel it's urgent. I would like it to be as soon as possible."

"How did you find my name?"

"A friend of a friend recommended you," said Seamus. "Very highly."

"We can meet for an assessment session," said Frieda. Then you can decide if I'm the right person for you, and I can decide if I think I can help you. All right?"

"Good."

"Can you make eleven o'clock tomorrow morning?"

"Yes." There was a pause. "I think you'll find me a very interesting person."

A nasty little headache screwed its way up Frieda's temple. Cockiness. It wasn't a good start.

Seamus Dunne was a young man, slim and neat, with even features and shiny brown hair, slicked back. He was wearing a dark, tailored jacket, black cords, and a purple shirt that shimmered under the light. Frieda wondered how long he had taken to get ready for their meeting. He had a firm though slightly damp handshake and a clipped, emphatic way of speaking. His smile, when he produced it, seemed disconnected from what he was saying. He used her name slightly too often.

"So, Frieda, how do we do this?" he asked, after he had taken a seat opposite her and put his hands, palms down, on his knees.

"I'd like to know a few details about you and then I'd like you to tell me why you're here."

"Details. Right. Age, occupation, things you put on a form?"

"All right."

"I'm twenty-seven. I'm in sales and marketing, and very good at it. I get people to buy things they didn't even know they wanted. Perhaps you disapprove of that, Frieda, but, really, it's how the world works. You don't find out what people need and give it to them. You create the need in them and then you fulfill it."

"Do you live in London?"

"Yes. Harrow."

"Tell me something about your family."

"My father died when I was seventeen. I didn't mind. He was useless anyway, and he always had it in for me. I was glad when he went. My mum, she's another story. She adores me. I'm the baby of the family. I've got two older sisters and then there's a gap and there's me. She still does my washing for me, would you believe? And I go there every Sunday for lunch. Just me and her."

"Do you live alone?"

"On and off. I like living by myself. I don't get lonely, and I have lots of friends." He paused, looked up, flashed her a smile, and then looked down at his hands again. "And girlfriends. Women seem to like me. I know how to make them happy."

"And do you?"

"What?" He was momentarily startled.

"Make them happy."

"Yes. I was saying. For a while, but I don't want to be tied down, you see. I'm not a faithful sort of man. I want variety, excitement. I like feeling my heart pound. I used to steal when I was a kid for the thrill of it. Are you shocked by that?"

"Should I be shocked?"

"I don't know. Anyway, it's the same with women. I like the beginning of things, the chase. That's why I'm good at my job too. I get a kick out of persuading people to buy things they don't need. I get a kick out of making women want me. It's only with my mum that I'm calm and ordinary."

Frieda scrutinized him. There were beads of sweat on his forehead although the room was quite cool. "If you like your life so much, why are you here, with me?"

Seamus sat up straighter and took a breath. "I like having power over people." She could see him swallow, and when he spoke it was more slowly, as if he were considering every word. "I remember, when I was a boy, I used to cut my father's hair. My father was a big man, much bigger than I am, and solid. He had a thick neck and broad shoulders, and beside him I felt very small. But every so often I would be holding these sharp scissors and he would shut his eyes and let me snip his hair off." He paused for a moment, as if recollecting something. "I can remember the dampness of the hair and the smell of it. Pushing my fingers into it, feeling the skin underneath. It smelled of him. When he let me touch his hair, I knew he was giving me power over him. I can still hear the sound of the blades. I could have killed him with those scissors. I had power over him, and that made me feel strong and tender at the same time. Looking after him with something that could wound him."

He forced his eyes up and met Frieda's gaze. He faltered slightly. "I'm sorry, is something wrong?"

"Why do you say that?"

"You look, I don't know, puzzled?"

"Go on," she said. "What were you going to say?"

"I used to hurt animals," he said. "That gave me the same feeling. Mostly little things, birds and insects. But sometimes cats, a dog once. And now women."

"You like hurting women?"

"They like it too. Mostly."

"You mean, hurting them sexually?"

"Of course. It's all part of sex, isn't it—hurting, pleasing, causing pain and pleasure, showing who's master? But now—well, now there's this woman I've met. Danielle. She says I've gone too far. I frightened her with what I did. She says she won't see me anymore unless I get help."

"You mean you're here because Danielle told you to come?"

"Yes."

"Really?"

"Don't you believe me?"

"I'm interested in the way you describe yourself as someone who likes to have power over people. But you've listened to Danielle, you've responded to her concern, and you've acted on it."

"She thinks I could do something—well, something that could get me into trouble. Not just killing a cat. And she's right. I think so too."

"You're telling me that you're worried you could seriously hurt someone?"

"Yes."

"And is that all you have to tell me?"

"*All?* Isn't that enough?"

"Apart from Danielle's worries, which you share, are there other things that are troubling you?"

"Well." He shifted in his chair, glanced away and then back again. "I'm not great at sleeping."

"Go on."

"I go to sleep all right, but then I wake, and sometimes that's fine and sometimes I just know I won't go back to sleep. I lie there and think about stuff."

"Stuff?"

"You know. Little things seem big at three in the morning. But everyone goes through patches of not sleeping. And I've lost my appetite a bit."

"You don't eat properly?"

"That's not why I'm here." He seemed suddenly angry. "I'm here because of my violent feelings. I want you to help me."

Frieda sat quite straight in her red armchair. The sun poured through the window, ran like a river through the room where she told patients who made their way to her that they could tell her anything, anything at all. Her ribs hurt and her leg ached.

"No," she said at last.

"I'm sorry?"

"I can't help you."

"I don't understand. I come here telling you I might seriously harm someone, and you tell me you can't help me."

"That's right. I'm not the proper person."

"Why? You specialize in things like this—I've heard about you. You know about people like me."

Frieda thought about Dean Reeve, the man who had stolen a little girl and turned her into his submissive wife, who had stolen a little boy and tried to make him into his son, who through Frieda's carelessness had snatched a young woman and murdered her just because she got in his way, who was still alive somewhere with his soft smile and his watching eyes. She thought of the knife slashing at her.

"What are people like you like?" she said.

"You know—people who do bad things."

"Have you done bad things?"

"Not yet. But I can feel them inside me. I don't want to let them out."

"There is a paradox here," said Frieda.

"What?"

"The fact of asking me for help might suggest that you don't really need it."

"I don't know what you mean."

"You're worried about being violent, about a lack of empathy. But you listened to Danielle. And you're asking for help. That shows insight."

"But what about torturing animals?"

"You shouldn't do that. But you said it was a long time ago. So: don't do it again."

There was a pause. He looked confused. "I don't know what to say."

"What about 'good-bye'?" said Frieda.

Seamus left and Frieda went and stood by her window, her eyes resting on the site across the street. Once there had been houses there, before a wrecking ball had swung through their walls, smashing them into dust, and diggers and cranes had moved in among the rubble. For a while, it had been a construction site, with Portakabins and men in hard hats drinking tea. Boards had gone up round the perimeter, announcing the imminent arrival of a brand-new office block. But then work had stopped: this was a recession after all. The men had left with their diggers, though one stumpy crane still stood in the middle of the space. Weeds and shrubs had grown up where the rubble had been. Now it was a wild place. Children played there; homeless people sometimes slept there. Frieda occasionally saw foxes roaming through the brambles.

No. She couldn't help Seamus Dunne, although the image of him cutting his father's hair remained with her, the bright blades opening and closing in her mind.

Dearest Frieda, I do understand that you can't make any plans just now. Just don't make plans without me, OK? I went to see some very purple paintings today. And I bought some pots of herbs for the balcony—though I don't know if they will survive the cold wind that cuts through this city like a knife. I think you could grow to love it here. I'm glad I decided to move here, not go to Cornell after all. You could certainly lose yourself in the crowds and the strangeness. There are days when I fancy I glimpse your face. A certain lift of your chin. A red scarf. I am lonely here without you. My love, Sandy xxxxx

TEN

Jim Fearby never gave up: his doggedness was his gift and his curse. He couldn't help it, he was made that way.

When he was ten and on a school trip, he had seen a demonstration of how to light a fire without a match. It looked simple the way the man in the combat jacket did it—a board with a notch cut into it, a long stick, a handful of dry grass and bark, a minute or so of rolling the spindle between his two palms, and there was an ember catching at the tinder nest, which he gently blew into a flame. One by one the class tried to do the same, and one by one they failed. When Fearby got back home, he spent hours rolling a stick between his palms until they were sore and blistered. Day after day he squatted in their small garden, his neck aching and his hands throbbing, and one day an ember glowed beneath the tip of his stick.

Fearby's mother, who was now long dead, had always declared rather proudly that her son was more stubborn than anyone she had ever met. His wife called it bloody-mindedness. "You're like a dog with a bone," she would say. "You can never let go." Fellow journalists said the same, sometimes admiringly, sometimes with incredulity or even contempt, and recently with that shake of the head: old Jim Fearby and his notions. Fearby didn't care what they thought. He just rolled his spindle, waited for the ember to catch and grow into a flame.

It had been like that with George Conley. No one else had cared about Conley, barely thought of him as a fellow human being, but he had struck a spark in Fearby, who had sat through every single day of his trial. It was his passivity that touched him: Conley was like a beaten dog just waiting for the next blow. He didn't understand what was happening to him but neither was he surprised by it. He'd probably been bullied and jeered at all his life; he no longer had the hope in him to fight back. Fearby never used words like *justice*—they were too grandiose for an old hack like him—but it didn't seem fair that this sad lump of a man should have no one to fight his corner.

The first time Jim Fearby had visited George Conley in prison, way back in 2005, the experience had given him nightmares. HMP Mortlemere, down in Kent on the Thames Estuary, wasn't such a bad place and Fearby wasn't sure what it was that had particularly got to him. There were the resigned, tired faces of the women and children in the waiting room. He had listened to their accents. Some of them had come from across the country. There was the smell of damp and disinfectant, and he had kept wondering about the smells the disinfectant was covering up. But, almost embarrassingly, it was mainly the locks and the bars and the high walls and the barbed wire. He had felt like a child who had never properly understood what a prison was. The real punishment is that the doors are locked and you can't go out when you want to.

During the trial, pathetic Conley had been bemused, almost numb, in the face of so much attention. When Fearby had met him for the first time in prison, he was pale and utterly defeated. "This is just the beginning," Fearby had told him but he seemed barely to be paying attention.

Fearby had seen on his road map that Mortlemere was next to a bird sanctuary. Afterward he had parked his car and walked along a path by the water, mainly so that the cold northerly wind could blow the rank prison smell off him. But even so, he couldn't seem to shake away the stench, and that night and for many nights afterward, he had dreamed of doors and steel bars and locks and lost keys, of being shut in, of trying to look out at the world through glass so thick that nothing was visible except blurry shapes.

In the years since, in the course of writing articles and finally his book, *Blind Justice*, he had visited Conley in prisons all over England, up in Sunderland, down in Devon, off the M25. Now, visiting him at HMP Haston, in the Midlands, Fearby hardly noticed his surroundings. The parking, the registration, the entrance through multiple doors had become routine, irritating rather than traumatic. The prison officers knew him, they knew why he was there, and mainly they were sympathetic to him—to Fearby and to Conley.

Over the years, Fearby had heard of inmates who had used prison as a sort of school. They had learned to read; they had studied for A levels and degrees. But Conley had only got fatter, paler, sadder, more defeated. His dark hair was greasy and lank. He had a long ragged scar down from the corner of one eye, the result of an attack while he was queuing for lunch one day. That had been early in his sentence, when he was the subject of constant threats and abuse. He was jostled in the corridor; his food was interfered with. Finally he was confined to solitary for his own protection. But gradually things changed, as questions were raised, as the campaign began, largely inspired and then sustained by Jim Fearby. Fellow prisoners started to leave him alone and then became positively friendly. In recent years, even the prison officers had softened.

Fearby sat opposite Conley as he had so many times before. Conley had become so fat that his bloodshot eyes almost disappeared in the fleshy slits in his face. He compulsively scratched at the top of his left hand. Fearby made himself smile. Everything was good. They were winning. They should both be happy.

"Did Diana come to see you?" he asked.

Diana McKerrow was the solicitor who had taken over Conley's case for the latest appeal. At first, Fearby had worked closely with her. After all, he had known more about the case than anyone else in the world. He knew the weak links, all the people involved. But as the case had proceeded, she had stopped phoning him. She had been harder to reach. Fearby tried not to mind. What mattered was the result, wasn't it? That was what he told himself.

"She phoned," said Conley, never quite looking Fearby in the face.

"Did she tell you about the appeal?" Fearby spoke slowly, separating each word, as if he was talking to a small child.

"Yeah, I think so."

"It's all good news," said Fearby. "They've got the details of the illegal interview." Conley's expression didn't change. "When the police picked you up, they didn't interview you properly. They didn't warn you. They didn't explain things the way they should have done. They didn't pay attention to your . . ." Fearby paused. At the next table a man and a woman were facing each other, not speaking. "Your special needs," said Fearby. "That's enough on its own to quash the conviction. But added to the details of your alibi that the prosecution suppressed . . ."

Fearby stopped. He could see from the blank look in Conley's eyes that he had lost his attention.

"You don't need to get bogged down in the details," said Fearby. "I just wanted to come and say to you that I know what you've gone through all these years. All that stuff, all that shit. I don't know how you did it. But you just need to hang on a bit longer, be strong, and it'll all come right. You hear what I'm saying?"

"Coming right," said Conley.

"There's something else," said Fearby. "I wanted to say that it's good, but it'll be hard as well. When someone gets paroled, they prepare them for months. They take you out on visits, you know, walks in the park, trips to the seaside. Then, when you're on the outside, you get to stay in a halfway house and they check up on you. You've heard that, haven't you?" Conley nodded. Fearby couldn't make out if he was really following what he was saying. "But it won't be like that for you. If the appeal court quashes your conviction, you'll just walk free that minute, straight out the door. It'll be difficult. You should be prepared for that."

Fearby waited for a reaction, but Conley just seemed puzzled. "I just came up here today to tell you that I'm your friend. Like I've always been. When you're out, you might want to tell your story. A lot of people would be interested in what you've been through. It's an old-fashioned tragedy-and-triumph story. I know about these things, and you'll want to put out your own side of the story, because if you don't, people will do it for you. I can help you with that. I've been telling your story right from the beginning, when no one else would believe you. I'm your friend, George. If you want help telling your story, I can do that for you." Fearby paused, but the reaction still didn't come. "Are you all right for things at the moment? Anything I can get you?"

Conley shrugged. Fearby said good-bye and that he'd be in touch. In the old days he would have driven home however late it was, but since his wife had left him and the children had gone, he usually made a day of it. People joked about the hotels at motorway service stations, but they suited him. He'd got a cheap deal at this one. Thirty-two pounds fifty. Free parking. Coffee and tea in the room. A color TV. Clean. Except for the paper flap across the toilet bowl, there was no sign that anyone else had ever been in there.

He had the usual luggage. His little suitcase. His laptop. And the bag with the files. The real files were back at home. They filled most of his office. These were the ones he needed for reference: the basic names and numbers and facts, a few photos and statements. As always, his first action was to take the purple pending file from the bag and open it on the little desk next to the color TV. While the miniature white plastic kettle was starting to heat up, he took a new sheet of lined paper, wrote the date and time of the meeting at the top and noted everything that had been said.

When he had finished, he made himself a cup of instant coffee and removed a biscuit from its plastic wrapping. It was then that he remembered his first visit to Conley at Mortlemere. "This is the beginning," he'd said, "not the end." He looked at the file. He thought of the room full of files at home. He thought of his marriage, the squabbles, the silences, and then the

ending. It had seemed sudden, but it turned out that Sandra had been planning it for months, finding a new flat, talking to a solicitor. "What will you
do when it ends?" she had said—referring not to their marriage but to this
case, in the days when they still talked of such things. It was more like an
accusation than a question. Because there never really were endings. He'd
been thinking he could produce a new edition of his book if Conley was
released. But it felt wrong now. The book was just negatives: why this hadn't
happened, why that wasn't true, why this was misleading.

The question now was different and new: if George Conley hadn't killed
Hazel Barton, who had?

ELEVEN

N orthern countries," said Josef. "They all drink the same."

"What do you mean, drink the same?"

Josef was driving Frieda in his old van. They were on the way to Islington because Olivia had rung in a near-hysterical state to say that the washbasin in the upstairs bathroom had been ripped off the wall during the party and she needed it repaired. Urgently. And she was never, ever going to have teenagers in her house again. Josef had agreed to abandon the bathroom briefly to help Olivia. Frieda felt strangely torn in her emotional reaction. There was Josef taking a break from doing up her bathroom for nothing in order to help her sister-in-law. Not for nothing: Frieda would insist on that, if she had to pay for it herself. At the same time he was constantly in her house, which had stopped being her own. And each time she looked at what once had been her bathroom, its state seemed to be getting worse rather than better.

"In the south, they drink wine and stay upright. In the north they drink clear liquid and fall down."

"You mean they drink to get drunk."

"Forget cares, lose sorrow, escape darkness."

Josef swerved to avoid a man who stepped blithely out into the road, his ears encased in giant yellow headphones.

"So, at this party, were there lots of people drinking clear liquid and falling down?"

"They learn too young." Josef gave a huge, sentimental sigh. "The recovery position."

"That sounds ominous."

"No, no. This is just life. People fight, people dance, people kiss and hold, people talk about dreams, people break things, people are sick."

"All in a few hours."

"Chloë, she did not have such a good time."

"Really?"

"She kept trying to clear the mess. No one should clear the mess before the party is over. Except for broken glass."

Josef drew up outside Olivia's house, and they got out of the van. Olivia opened the door before Frieda rang. She was wearing a man's dressing gown and her face was tragic.

"I just had to go to bed," she said. "Everything's such a mess."

"It was quite a mess before," said Frieda. "You said you wouldn't notice a bit extra."

"I was wrong. It's not only the washbasin. My blue lamp is broken. My wheelbarrow is broken because they tried to see how many people could fit in it and still be moved—that, apparently, was your friend Jack's idea. How old is he? I thought he was an adult, not a toddler. And my nice coat has disappeared. Kieran's favorite hat he left before he went away has a cigarette burn in the crown." Kieran was her mild and patient boyfriend—or perhaps her ex. "The neighbors have complained about all the bottles dumped in their gardens and the noise, and someone has peed into my ornamental orange tree in the hall."

"I will fix the washbasin anyway," said Josef. "And perhaps the wheelbarrow too."

"Thank you," said Olivia, fervently.

"Don't let him take the washbasin away," said Frieda.

"What?"

"Is a joke," said Josef. "Is a joke against me by Frieda."

"I'm sorry, Josef, I didn't mean that." She looked at the wheelbarrow. "How many did it hold?"

Olivia gave a shaky giggle. "Something ludicrous, like seven. Standing up. It's lucky nobody got themselves killed."

Although it was days later, the floor was still sticky underfoot. Pictures hung lopsidedly on the wall. There was the sweet smell of alcohol in the air, and Frieda saw dirty smudges on the paintwork and grime on the stair carpets.

"It's like one of those children's picture books: spot the hidden object," said Olivia, pointing at a glass inside a shoe. "I keep finding unspeakable things."

"You mean condoms?" asked Josef.

"No! Oh, God, what happened that I don't know about?"

"No, no, is all right. I go on up." He bounded up the stairs, carrying his bag.

"Let's have something to drink," said Olivia, leading the way into the kitchen. "Sorry! I didn't know you were back from school."

Chloë was sitting at the table, and opposite her was a gangly, disheveled figure: a mop of greasy dark blond hair, feet in trainers with the laces undone, jeans sliding down his skinny frame. He turned his head and Frieda saw a thin, pallid face, hollow eyes. He looked bruised and wrung out. Ted: the boy she had last seen retching over the toilet bowl. The boy who had just lost his mother. He met her gaze, and a blush mottled his cheeks. He mumbled a few incoherent words and slumped farther over the table with his face half hidden by one hand. Nails bitten to the quick. A little tattoo—or probably an ink drawing—on his thin wrist.

"Hello, Frieda," said Chloë. "I wasn't expecting you. It's not chemistry today, you know."

"I'm here with Josef."

"The washbasin."

"Yes."

"It must have been loose anyway. It just came away."

"Because two people sat on it!" Olivia lowered her voice. "Aren't you going to introduce me to your friend?"

Chloë looked embarrassed. "This is Ted. Ted, my mum."

Ted squinted up at Olivia and managed a hello. Olivia marched up to him, grabbed his limp, unwilling hand and shook it firmly. "I'm so pleased to meet you," she said. "I keep telling Chloë she should bring friends home. Especially handsome young men like you."

"Mum! That's why I don't."

"Ted doesn't mind. Do you, Ted?"

"And this is Frieda," said Chloë, hastily. "She's my aunt." She cast a beseeching glance at Frieda.

"Hello." Frieda nodded at him. If it were possible, he turned even more crimson and stuttered something incoherent. She could see that he wanted to run and hide from the woman who'd seen him vomiting—weeping too.

"Shall we go to my room?" Chloë asked Ted, and he slid off the chair, a raw-boned, awkward, self-conscious young man, all angles and sharp edges.

"I heard about your mother," Frieda said. "I'm very sorry for your loss."

She felt Olivia stiffen. Ted stared at her, his pupils enormous. Chloë picked up one of his hands and held it between her own to comfort him. For a moment he seemed stranded in his emotions, unable to move or speak.

"Thank you," he said at last. "It's just . . . Thanks."

"I hope you're all receiving proper help."

"What?" hissed Olivia, as Chloë led Ted from the room, glancing back over her shoulder with bright eyes. "Is that—"

"Her friend whose mother was killed. Yes."

Olivia's hand flew to her mouth. "I didn't make the connection. Poor boy. Poor, poor boy. What a dreadful thing. He's quite attractive, isn't he, in a grungy kind of way? Do you think Chloë's in love with him? What a calamity. I mean what happened to him. At such an age, too. Just think of it! Let's have that drink."

Billy Hunt stared up at Karlsson. His eyes were bloodshot, and he was twitchier and thinner than ever, but he wasn't budging.

Karlsson sighed. "You're making life hard for us and hard for yourself. You've admitted breaking and entering; the stolen items have been traced back to you; the murder weapon with your prints all over it, and Mrs. Lennox's blood, has been found. Just admit what you did."

"Unless I didn't do it."

"The jury won't believe you." Karlsson stood up. His head felt tight with weariness and irritation. Now his team would have to trawl through the evidence to put a watertight case together. The time he wanted to be spending with his children, Bella and Mikey, would be spent instead examining statements, going through the house with a fine-tooth comb, talking to expert witnesses, making sure the correct procedures had been followed.

"Wait."

"What now?"

"I wanted to say—there is somewhere I went just before."

"Before?"

"Before . . . you know."

"Tell me anyway."

"Before I went to the house, where she was."

"Mrs. Lennox."

"Right. I went to another place first."

"Which you haven't told us about?"

"Right." Billy bobbed his head up and down. "You'll see why."

"Hang on, Billy. If you're going to change your statement, we need to do this officially. I'll come back."

In the corridor, he met Riley.

"Hey," said Riley.

"What?"

"I've just come from Margaretting Street," said Riley. "We found something. Under the mat. In fact, I found it. Munster thought you'd want to know."

"What is it?"

Riley held up a transparent evidence sachet. Inside was a used envelope on which was scrawled a message, written with a blunt pencil.

Karlsson took it and held it up: "Hello, Ruth, I'm here but where are you? Maybe in the bath. Give us a call when you read this, and we can have our tea." At the end there was what looked like two interlocking initials or perhaps a signature. "What's this?"

"Munster thinks it's a *D* and an *M*, but I think it's *O* and *N*."

"It might have been there for months. Who's following it up?"

"DC Long, sir, and Munster. But I'm going back there later. It's probably not so important, though, is it, even if it is recent? I mean, if Billy killed her, it doesn't really matter what time exactly she died, right?"

"No, it could be important," said Karlsson, thoughtfully.

"You're welcome, then," said Riley, with a cheerful smile.

Karlsson raised his eyebrows. "Just get back to Margaretting Street," he said.

Yvette Long showed the note to Russell Lennox, who stared at it, then shook his head. "I don't recognize the writing."

"What about the initials?"

"Are those initials? Is that a *G*?"

"A*G*?"

"Or maybe it says Gail."

"Do you know a Gail?"

"I don't think so. Or it could be Delia, or even Dell. I don't know a Delia either, or a Dell. Or it could just be a squiggle."

"Which of your wife's friends used to pop round during the day?"

"Oh." Russell Lennox frowned. "Lots. I don't know. She knew almost everyone in our neighborhood. There were her friends and then people she was friendly with—and she helped organize the street party every year, which means people were always coming in and out. And then there were her friends who aren't so local. She was very popular, my wife. I was always amazed at how many people she kept in contact with. You should see her

Christmas card list." He stared at Yvette and shook his head slowly from side to side. "I can't believe I'm already using the past tense," he said. "Was. She was. As if it happened years ago."

"We've got her address book on her computer," said Yvette. "We can look through that. But if you think of anyone in the meantime—"

"I thought you'd got the guy who did it?"

"We're just crossing the t's," said Yvette.

"I've been trying to remember the last thing we said to each other. I think I said I'd be back a bit later than usual, and then she reminded me not to forget my cousin's birthday."

"Well," Yvette said, awkwardly.

"At first, I thought that was too prosaic. But it's typical of her. She always remembered birthdays and anniversaries and stuff like that."

"Mr. Lennox—"

"I did forget my cousin's birthday, of course. It was yesterday, and I didn't remember until now."

"That's understandable."

"I suppose so." His tone was dull.

Jennifer Wall said that Ruth had been the perfect neighbor, friendly without being nosy, always ready to lend eggs or sugar or milk, even nice when one of her boys had kicked a football through the Lennoxes' kitchen window.

Sue Leadbetter remembered the time, not long ago, when Ruth had taken care of her while she'd had flu—bringing Lemsip and loo paper to the house, even getting papers and magazines for her.

Gaby Ford said she used to meet Ruth almost every morning when they both left for work. They would greet each other and sometimes exchange a few words. Ruth had a way, she said, of putting one arm on her shoulder for a few minutes, which she had always appreciated. She was often in a bit of a rush, but she was always cheerful, and it was no different during the days leading to her death. She'd never known her down in the dumps or hung-over. They were such a nice family. A close family. You didn't come across that so much nowadays.

Jodie Daniels, one of her oldest friends, had seen her at the weekend. They had gone to the garden center together and then had coffee. Ruth was just normal—unaffected, interested in other people, a bit concerned that Judith wasn't working properly for her GCSEs. They had talked about whether or not she should dye her hair, now that it was rapidly turning gray, and Ruth had decided she wouldn't. She had said she wanted to grow old gracefully. Oh, God.

Graham Walters had bumped into Ruth's car, two days before she died, and scraped it. She had been incredibly understanding, which was typical. That was the last time he had seen her.

She had bent down and stroked Elspeth Weaver's dog the morning of her death, then got into her car.

She had reversed down the road to make way for Robert Morgan, driving in the opposite direction.

She had phoned that morning from work and told Juliet Melchett that she and Russell would love to come to the Melchetts' party.

At eleven a.m., also from work, she had ordered a bunch of flowers from John Lewis to be sent to Russell's aunt, who had broken her hip.

But none of those people had gone round there and pushed a note through the door.

However, with Dawn Wilmer, who lived two streets away and whose eldest son was in the same class as Ruth's younger daughter, they finally struck lucky. She recognized the note as hers.

"You pushed this through her door?"

"Yes."

"On the day she died."

"Wednesday. Yes. Should I have said? I mean, I spoke to an officer and said I hadn't seen anything suspicious, and I thought I said I was round by her house earlier, but perhaps I didn't. I mean, I didn't go in or anything. I didn't see anything strange or suspicious."

"What time would this have been?"

"I don't know, just after four. Before four thirty, anyway. I'm sure of that because Danny—that's my son—comes home late that day, and I knew Dora did as well. That was why Ruth suggested I go round for tea—we didn't know each other that well. I'm quite new in the neighborhood, and my son's only just started at the school. It was nice of her."

"So—you went round for tea, as arranged, and she wasn't there."

"She was there. She just didn't come to the door."

"Why do you say that?"

"Her car was there. All the lights were on."

"Did you wait for a long time?"

"A minute or so, no more. I knocked and rang the bell—I even shouted through the letter box. I didn't have my phone with me, so I couldn't call her, and that was why I pushed the note through."

"Between four and half past four, you say?"

"After four and before four thirty." The woman's face wrinkled anxiously. "Do you think—is it possible—that she was in there dead?"

"We're just trying to establish timings," said Yvette, neutrally. "You're sure you didn't see anything unusual?"

"Nothing."

"And you stood at the door for about a minute?"

"Yes."

"You saw no broken window? Next to the front door."

"No. I'm sure I would have noticed that."

"All right. Thank you very much for your help."

Billy Hunt dragged the back of his hand against his nose. "I was somewhere else. I just want to say that this sounds worse than it was. There weren't any kids there."

"Where?"

"There's this nursery school. But it was empty. It's not finished yet."

"What did you take?"

"Nothing," said Hunt, holding out his palms as if to prove it. "It was empty. I broke one pane of glass and that was all it took. They need to tighten their security before they open. Cut my hand, though."

"What was the name of this nursery?"

"Busy Bees. Over in Islington, just up from the Caledonian Road."

"What time?"

"I don't know. About four maybe."

"So you claim at about four o'clock last Wednesday, you were breaking into a children's nursery in Islington. What did you do then?"

"I was going to walk back home along the canal, but it started to rain. I saw a bus and jumped on it. The one five three. It took me to Camden. I was having a smoke, so they threw me off, and I walked up from there. I was just going along the road and ringing on a few doorbells until I found one where they didn't answer."

"What then?"

"I broke the window, opened the door. The alarm was going, so I was in a rush. There were alarms everywhere. There was one in the hallway and one in the room where . . . you know, she was. I just grabbed a few things and headed off." He shook his head. "It's not my fault. If it hadn't been rain-ing, I wouldn't have caught the bus, and I wouldn't have been there."

Karlsson switched off the recorder. "And Mrs. Lennox would still have been alive."

"No," said Hunt. "That's not what I said. Put the tape back on."

"Forget about the bloody tape."

TWELVE

A s Frieda approached her front door, key in hand, she saw that it was already open. She couldn't see at first what was happening but then saw there was a man at one end of a large, undeniably impressive bathtub, and then she saw that the man was Josef's friend, Stefan, and that Josef was at the other end. The second thing Frieda noticed was that the bath was almost too wide for the doorway. She could see that by the gray scraping marks on the doorpost. The third thing she noticed was that they were carrying the bath outward rather than inward.

"Frieda," said Stefan, panting slightly. "I can't shake hands."

"Are you having trouble getting it in?"

"No," said Josef, from the other end. "We take in fine and upstairs. But problem. Now we take it out and back."

"What do you mean 'back'?" said Frieda.

"Wait."

With much groaning and a suppressed scream when Josef got his fingers trapped between the bath and the doorway, they got it outside and laid it down on the cobblestones.

"That bath is fucking heavy," said Stefan, then looked at Frieda guiltily. "Sorry. It is big, though."

"But why are you taking it out?"

"Is heavy," said Josef. "Hard for floor, I think. We check it now. Probably need joist."

Frieda heard the phone ringing inside. "You mean a steel girder?" she said.

"So you don't fall through floor in bath."

"Well, you'd know about that," said Frieda. "Are you sure?"

Stefan smiled. "We are sure."

"What do you mean?" said Frieda. The phone was still ringing. "Hang on." She pushed past them, but before she could reach the phone, it had stopped. It was almost a relief, something that didn't have to be dealt with, someone who didn't have to be talked to. She stood still for a moment,

watching Josef and Stefan pushing the bath back into Josef's van. It seemed
to sag under the weight of it. And then the phone rang again, insistently, like
a person jabbing at her. She picked it up and heard a woman's voice.

"Can I speak to Dr. Frieda Klein, please?"

"Who is this?"

"My name's Jilly Freeman. I'm calling from the *Sunday Sketch*." There
was a pause. "I'm sorry. Are you still there?"

"Yes," said Frieda.

"We're running a story in tomorrow's paper, and we'd like to hear your
comments on it."

"Why?"

"Because it concerns you."

Frieda felt a stab of dread and at the same time a numbness, as if she were
receiving a blow on a part of her body that had been hit before and then had
partially healed. She felt an impulse to smash the phone rather than continue
the conversation. Was it something to do with the attack? Were the police
reconsidering it? Were the press trying to sniff something out?

"What is it?" she said.

"You've seen a patient called Seamus Dunne."

This was so unexpected that Frieda had to think, just to recall the name.
At the same time, Josef stepped into her line of sight and gestured that they
were leaving.

"We need to talk," she said to him.

"Soon." Josef backed away.

"What?" said the woman on the phone.

"I was talking to someone else. How do you know about Seamus Dunne?"

"Dr. Klein, it might be better if I could come round to your house and
conduct a proper interview in person."

Frieda took a deep breath and, as she did so, caught a glimpse of her reflection in the glass of a picture on the wall. Was that person really her? The
thought of someone else, anyone else, coming round to her house made her
feel sick. "Just tell me what this is about."

"All we're doing is reporting on some new psychological research which
we think is really important. As you know, some people think that psychoanalysts aren't sufficiently accountable to the public." Jilly Freeman left a silence that Frieda didn't break. "Well, anyway, there's this academic called
Hal Bradshaw who has been conducting research. Do you know him?"

"Yes," said Frieda. "I do."

"Well, what he's done is to select some prominent analysts—and you're one of them. And then he sent people to see these analysts with instructions to show the identical classic symptoms of a person who was an imminent danger to the public, to see how the analyst responded." There was another pause and Frieda didn't speak. "So I was ringing to ask if you had any comment."

"You haven't asked me a question."

"From what I understand," said Jilly Freeman, "this patient, Seamus Dunne . . ."

"You said he was pretending to be a patient."

"Yes, as part of this research project, and he displayed what are the clear, accepted signs of being a violent psychopath."

"Which are?" said Frieda.

"Um . . ." said Jilly Freeman. There was a pause, and Frieda heard pages being turned. "Yes, here it is. Each of the supposed patients were to talk of having been violent toward animals in their childhood and then to having vivid fantasies of attacking women and to talk about putting these into practice. Did Seamus Dunne talk about that?"

"I don't discuss what my patients say in their sessions."

"But he wasn't a real patient. And he's talked about it. He gave me an interview."

"As part of the research project?" said Frieda.

She looked around for a chair and sat down. Suddenly she felt utterly exhausted, as if she might go to sleep even while she was talking. It was as if she had locked the door and blocked the windows and they'd still managed to get in through a gap she'd missed.

"What we want to know for our piece on the research is whether you reported any concerns to the authorities."

There was a ring at the door.

"Wait a minute," said Frieda. "I've got to let someone in."

She opened the door. It was Reuben.

"Frieda, I just—" he began, but she held up her hand to silence him and waved him inside. She noticed that he seemed disheveled and distracted. He walked past her and disappeared into the kitchen.

"What were you saying?" said Frieda.

"I wanted to ask you if you'd reported any concerns to the authorities."

Frieda was distracted by the sound of clinking from the kitchen. Reuben reappeared with a can of beer.

"No," said Frieda. "I didn't."

Reuben mouthed something at her, then took a large gulp of beer from the can.

"From what we've been informed," continued Jilly Freeman, "this experiment was designed to present various therapists with a patient who was a clear, present danger to the community. The patient was a psychopath, and it was your duty—in fact, it was your legal responsibility—to report him to the police. Could you comment on that?"

"But he wasn't a psychopath," said Frieda.

"Is it her?" said Reuben. "Is it fucking her?"

"What are you talking about?" Frieda hissed.

"What?" said Jilly Freeman.

"I'm not talking to you." Frieda angrily waved Reuben away. "You've said yourself that he wasn't a psychopath. There was no need to report him. I may have had some concerns about this particular man, but I wouldn't discuss that with anyone but him."

"I'm sorry," said Jilly Freeman, "but this experiment was to test how therapists respond when they are confronted with a patient who shows the classic signs, established by research over the years, of being a psychopath. The public will want to know whether they are being protected."

"I'm going to talk to you for one more minute," said Frieda, "and then I'm putting the phone down. You've told me that he wasn't actually a psychopath. He was just saying psychopathic things."

"Don't psychopaths say psychopathic things? What else do you have to go on, apart from what patients say to you?"

"And second, as I said to Seamus Dunne himself, psychopaths don't ask for help. He was talking about lack of empathy, but he wasn't displaying it. That's my answer."

"And you trusted yourself to ignore the classic signs of a psychopath?"

"Your minute's up," said Frieda, and ended the call.

She looked at Reuben. "What are you doing here?" she said.

"I just saw Josef driving away."

"He's working on my bathroom."

"I guess that's why I can't track him down." His expression hardened. "It was her, wasn't it? It was that journalist, what's her name?"

"It was a woman called Jilly Freeman," said Frieda.

"That's it, that's the one."

"How do you know?"

Reuben emptied his glass. "Because they've done it to me as well," he said. "They've fucked me the way they've fucked you. Jilly rang me up and broke the news to me, and in the middle of our conversation she mentioned your name as well. I tried to ring you, but there was no answer."

"I've been out," said Frieda.

"I thought I'd better come straight round. Jesus, I need a cigarette. Can we go outside?"

He fetched another can of beer from the kitchen, then opened the door and stepped outside onto the street. Frieda followed him. He handed her the beer while he lit his cigarette. He took a succession of deep drags on it. "This young man," said Reuben. "He said he wanted to talk to me. He'd heard such good things about me. He was worried about himself. He'd been cruel to animals as a child, he had fantasies of hurting women. Blah, blah, you know the rest."

"What did you say to him?"

"I said I'd see him for a bit. And then Ms. Jilly rings me up and tells me that I'm going to be on the front page for letting a psychopath loose on the streets."

"What did you say to her?"

He took another deep drag on his cigarette. "I should have said what you said. That sounded good. I lost it. I just shouted at her and slammed the phone down." He jabbed a finger at Frieda. "We're going to sue them. That fucker Hal Bradshaw and that fucking journalist and her paper. We're going to take them down."

"What for?" said Frieda.

Reuben banged his fist against the wall of the house. "For deception," he said. "And violating our privacy. And for libel."

"We're not going to sue them," said Frieda.

"I was going to say that it's all right for you," said Reuben. "But you're in a state of distress. You're recovering from injury. They can't do this to us."

Frieda put a hand on his shoulder. "We should just leave it," she said.

Reuben turned to Frieda and something in his look alarmed her, fierce and defeated at the same time. "I know, I know," he said. "I should just shrug it off. Ten years ago I would have laughed it off. I would almost have welcomed it. But I feel I've had it. That journalist. I'll show her fantasies about hurting women."

. . .

People had been gathering since midday, but there had been minor delays, the last spasms of a clogged bureaucratic system that had kept George Conley in prison for months after it had become clear he would have to be released. It was nearly three o'clock in the afternoon when he eventually emerged from Haston Prison into watery sunlight, clutching one plastic bag and wearing an overcoat that was too tight and much too thick for a spring day. There were beads of sweat on his pale, fleshy face.

Most of the people waiting for him were journalists and photographers. His local MP was there as well, although Fearby knew how little he had done for Conley, only joining the campaign when it was clear it would be successful. A small group from a revolutionary organization had come with banners proclaiming the bigotry of the police force in general. But there were no relatives waiting for Conley. His mother had died while he was in prison, and his sister hadn't been to see him since he was arrested. She had told Fearby that she was glad she was married and had taken the name of her husband, because his name made her feel sick. She wanted nothing to do with him. And there were no friends either: he had always been a lonely figure in the small town where he had lived, someone who stood on the edge, looking in baffled wistfulness at life going on. After he was arrested, neighbors said that they had always known he was odd, creepy. It hadn't surprised them at all. Apart from Fearby, he had had no visitors in prison until the last few weeks.

Diana McKerrow, Conley's solicitor, stood near the gates holding a bottle of sparkling wine in readiness. She spoke to the press on behalf of her client, reading from a piece of paper that she pulled out of her jacket pocket: words about the scandal of the police investigation, the lost years that Conley would never recover, the faith of a few good souls who had never ceased to believe in his innocence. She didn't mention Fearby by name, and Fearby himself stood apart from the small crowd. He didn't know what he'd been expecting. After so many years of working toward this moment, it felt thin and dreary. One overweight man shuffling anxiously out of the gates, wincing as the cameras flashed.

The journalists surged forward. Microphones were held out to him.

"How does it feel to be free?"

"Are you going to sue?"

"What are your plans now, Mr. Conley?"

"Where will you go?"

"What's the first thing you'll do?"

"Are you angry?"

"What have you missed?"

"Can you tell us your thoughts about the police?"

Fearby was certain that some of them had checkbooks ready. They wanted his story now. All these years he'd been vilified and then forgotten; now he was a hero—except he didn't fit the role of hero. His replies came out in mumbles, half sentences: "I dunno," he said. "What d'you mean?" He glanced from side to side anxiously. Diana McKerrow put one arm under his elbow. His MP arranged himself on the other side, smiling for the cameras.

Fearby knew that they would all soon forget about Conley again. He would be left in peace, in his little room in a house full of other misfits and loners, passive and defeated. He felt a pang of simultaneous guilt followed at once by resentment: was he going to have to be Conley's only friend even now? Visit him and take him out for a drink, try to find him an occupation? Was this his reward for freeing him into the world?

He inched his way through the crush and touched Conley on the arm. "Hello, George," he said. "Congratulations."

"Hello," said Conley. He smelled unwashed; his skin had a gray, prison pallor, and his hair was thinning.

"You're going to be busy for the rest of the day. I just wanted to say hello and give you my phone number. When you want, give me a call and I'll come and see you." He forced enthusiasm into his voice. "We can have a meal, go for a drink, a walk." He hesitated. "You might find all this attention hard, but it'll die down soon. You'll need to think about what you're going to do next."

"Next?"

"I'll come and see you."

Conley stared at him, his lower lip hanging loose. He was like a small, fat child, thought Fearby. It didn't feel like a happy ending.

Later, at the press conference, the officer in charge of the investigation read out a statement. He wished to be candid about the fact that mistakes had been made. George Conley's confession to the murder of Hazel Barton had been obtained—here he coughed, grimaced—without following the proper procedures.

"You mean illegally," someone shouted from the back.

Steps had been taken, the officer continued. Reprimands delivered. Procedures tightened. The same mistakes would not be made again.

"What about Mr. Conley?" asked a young woman in the front row.

"I'm sorry?"

"He's been in prison since 2005."

"And we're sorry for the mistakes that were made."

"Has anyone been fired?" called a voice.

The inspector's face tightened. "As I say, we have looked very carefully at the way the investigation was conducted. Individual officers have been reprimanded. But it would not be in anyone's interest to make a scapegoat out of . . ."

Fearby thought that the message was very clear. The police believed that Conley was the killer but had got off on a technicality. What was more, they were making sure that everyone else in the room understood that. He felt anger rise in him.

"Excuse me," he called out, in a loud voice. "I have a question for you."

Heads turned. There he was, Jim Fearby, the one who'd been obsessed with the case for years. A journalist who'd been around for decades, one of the old breed who got hold of a story and wouldn't let go. He was in his sixties now, stooped and silver-haired. He looked a bit like a bird of prey with his beaked nose and pale eyes, windblown, and weather blasted.

"Mr. Fearby," said the inspector, smiling with no warmth. "Yes?"

"Now that George Conley has been released, an innocent man . . ."—he paused to let the words fill the room—"can you tell us what steps you will be taking to find out the real perpetrator? After all, a young woman was brutally murdered."

The inspector coughed again, a hard and hacking sound to give him time to prepare his answer. "At present, there are no new leads," he said eventually.

"At present?"

"As I said. Any more questions?"

Fearby drove home through the gathering dusk. Conley's last prison, unlike his previous ones, had been quite close to where he lived—in a small town just outside Birmingham. When Sandra had left him, he'd thought he would perhaps go somewhere different—the Lake District, perhaps, or even farther north, where cold, clean winds blew off the hills. He could begin again. But in the end he'd stayed, surrounded by his files, his books, his pictures, his DVDs of old films. It didn't matter so much where he lived; it was just a place to sleep, to think.

He went into his study and gazed at the piles of notebooks and folders that were filled with the evidence of his obsession: police reports, legal reports, letters sent and received, petitions . . . He poured himself a large slug of gin because he'd run out of whisky and added water because he'd run out of tonic. What sailors used to drink, he thought—a sad, solitary drink to get you through the hours. He must have fallen asleep in his chair, because when the phone rang it felt at first like part of a dream.

"Is that Jim Fearby?"

"Who is it?"

"I saw you at the press conference. Are you still writing about the case?"

"What's it matter?" Fearby still felt only half awake.

"I want to meet you."

"Why?"

"You know a pub called the Sir Philip Sidney?"

"No."

"You can find it. I'll be there at five tomorrow evening."

I tried to call you. When we see each other, I'm going to give you a short lesson in how to use your mobile! (Mainly, leave it turned on and have it with you.) Now it's probably too late to try again. You'll be asleep. Speak soon and until then, take care. S xxxxx

THIRTEEN

Karlsson sat opposite Billy Hunt. "You must be the world's worst burglar," he said.

"So you saw I was telling the truth?"

"On the bright side," said Karlsson, "it was a building site, which meant there were plenty of CCTV cameras, and I saw the best images I've ever seen. You could have used some of them for your passport photo."

"I told you I was there."

"But, as we know, you were also at the murder scene. Why didn't you call an ambulance or the police?" said Karlsson.

"Because I was being a burglar," said Hunt. "I mean, I'm not a burglar, but at that moment I was in the middle of taking things. Anyway, I wasn't thinking straight."

"So what did you do?"

"I got out. Ran away."

"And then?"

"I had this stuff to sell. I told you, I needed cash."

"So you sold all the silver?"

"Right."

"Except the cog?"

"It needed, you know . . ."

"The blood cleaning off it?"

"I felt bad about it," said Hunt. "Seeing her there. What was I meant to do?"

Karlsson stood up. "I don't know, Billy. I wouldn't know where to begin."

FOURTEEN

Frieda?"

"Hello, Chloë." Frieda walked through to the living room with the phone and eased her sore body into the armchair by the hearth, where in the winter she lit a fire every day. Now that it was spring and the weather was balmy, the sky a delicate washed blue, it stood empty. "Are you OK?"

"I need to see you."

"Before Friday?" Friday was the day that Frieda taught her chemistry, which Chloë loathed with a scowling intensity.

"Now."

"Why?"

"I wouldn't ask if it wasn't important."

It was nearly six o'clock. Frieda thought of the pot of tea, the slice of quiche she'd bought from Number 9 for her supper, the quiet evening in the dimly lit cocoon of her house that she'd planned, sitting in her study with her soft-leaded pencils and her thick-grained paper, the answering machine turned on and no demands on her, then the softness of her pillows and the sealing darkness. Maybe no dreams, just oblivion. She could say no.

"I'll be there in half an hour."

"I'm not at home. I'm in a café near the Roundhouse. You can't miss it. It's got this giant upside-down airplane hanging outside, and it's an alternative art gallery as well."

"Hang on, Chloë—"

"Thanks, Frieda!" Chloë interrupted enthusiastically, then ended the call before Frieda could change her mind.

The café was named, for no obvious reason, Joe's Malt House, and there was indeed a large upside-down plane nose-diving down its outside wall. Frieda pushed open the door and went into a long, dark room cluttered with tables and mismatched chairs, the walls hung with paintings she could barely make out in the gloom. People were sitting at tables and milling about at the bar that cut across the middle of the room. Music played, throbbing and insistent; the air was thick with the smell of beer, coffee, and incense.

"Do you need a table?" asked a young woman, dressed in shredded black, with a lightning streak tattooed down her cheek. Her accent was upper-class Estuary. Her boots were like the Terminator's.

Frieda heard her name and squinted up the room. She made out Chloë at the far end, waving her arms in the air to attract her attention. "No, thank you," she said to the woman. Then she approached her niece.

"This had better be important."

"Beer?"

"No, thank you."

"Or tea. They do herbal teas here."

"What's this about?"

"I had to get you here. It's Ted."

"Ted? You mean the young man?"

"He needs help."

"I'm sure he does."

"But the thing is, he won't do anything about it. He just gets angry when people tell him, so I thought I'd have to do it for him."

"I can give you names, Chloë, but he's got to want to—"

"I don't need names, Frieda. I've got you."

"Oh no you don't."

"You have to help."

"I don't. This is not the way to do it."

"Please. You don't understand. I really like him and he's so messed up." She grabbed Frieda's hand. "Oh, fuck, he's here already. He's just come in."

"You haven't done what I think you've done?"

"I had to," hissed Chloë, leaning forward. "You wouldn't have come if I'd told you and neither would Ted."

"Exactly."

"You can make him better."

"His mother's been killed, Chloë. How can I make him better?"

Frieda stood up, and as she did, Ted stumbled past the bar and saw them both. He stopped and stared. He was in the same disheveled, undone state as before—clothes flapping, trousers slipping down, laces trailing, hair falling over his pale face, the hectic blotches on his cheeks. He stared from Chloë to Frieda, then back again.

"You?" he said. "What's going on?"

Chloë scrambled to her feet and went over to him. "Ted," she said. "Listen."

"What's she doing here? You *tricked* me."

"I wanted to help you," said Chloë, desperately. For a moment Frieda felt very sorry for her niece. "I thought if you two could just talk a bit . . ."

"I don't need help. You should see my sisters. They're the ones who need help. I'm not a little kid anymore." He looked at Chloë. "I thought you were my friend."

"That's not fair," said Frieda, sharply. He turned his wretched, sneering face toward her. "I agree Chloë acted wrongly. But she did it because she *is* your friend and she cares. Don't lash out at her. You need your friends."

"I'm not going to lie on your fucking couch."

"Of course you're not."

"And I'm not going to cry and say my life is over now that I don't have a mother." But his voice rose dangerously high as he stared at her defiantly.

"No. And it isn't. Maybe we can just get out of here, the three of us, and have some tea or a mug of hot chocolate or something in the little place across the road, which is quiet and doesn't have dreadful paintings on the wall, and then we can all go back to our separate homes, and no real harm done."

Chloë sniffed and gazed pleadingly at him.

"All right," he said. "I haven't had hot chocolate for years. Not since I was a kid." As if he were a middle-aged man.

"Sorry." Chloë's voice was small.

"It's all right, I guess."

"Good," said Frieda. "Now can we get out of here?"

Chloë and Ted had a mug of hot chocolate each, and Frieda had a glass of water.

"I don't think it makes things better," said Ted, "just because you talk about them."

"It depends," said Frieda.

"I think it makes things worse, like jabbing a wound to keep it bleeding. *Wanting* it to bleed."

"I'm not here to make you see someone you don't want to see. I just think you should drink your hot chocolate."

"Don't you get sick of spending your days with rich, narcissistic wankers going on about childhood traumas, endlessly fascinated by all their noble, manufactured suffering?"

"Your suffering isn't manufactured, though, is it?"

Ted glared at her. His face had a peeled look, as if even the air would sting him. "It'll pass," he said. "That's what my mum would have said. One fucking day at a time."

"That's one of the sad things about people dying," said Frieda. "We talk about them in the past tense. We say what they would have done. But if that's what she would have said, it's not stupid. Time does pass. Things change." She stood up. "And now I think we're done," she said.

Chloë drained her mug. "We're finished as well," she said.

When they were outside, Frieda was ready to say good-bye, but Chloë seemed reluctant to let her go. "Which way are you going?"

"I'll walk back through the park."

"You're going in the same direction as us. Past Ted's house. Except he's not staying there. They're staying with neighbors."

"I can speak for myself," said Ted.

"All right," said Frieda, and they started walking, an uneasy trio, with Chloë in the middle.

"I'm sorry," Chloë said. "This is all my fault. I shouldn't have done this. I've embarrassed you both."

"You can't force help on people," said Frieda. "But that's all right."

"Frieda walks everywhere. She's like a taxi driver. You could name any two places in London and she could walk between them." Chloë was talking as if she were frightened by the idea of a moment's silence. "And she's really critical of it as well. She thinks it all went wrong after the Elizabethan age or the Great Fire of London. This is Ted's road. This is where it all happened. I'm sorry, I don't want to start it up all over again. I've done enough damage. This is actually his house, I mean his parents' house, but I'm going along the road with him to say good-bye and sorry and then . . ." She turned to Frieda, who had suddenly stopped. "Frieda, are you all right?"

Frieda had been about to make way for a group of people—two men and a woman—getting out of a car, but she had recognized them at the very moment they recognized her.

"Frieda . . ." Karlsson seemed too surprised to say anything else.

The other man appeared more contemptuously amused than surprised. "You can't stay away, can you?" said Hal Bradshaw. "Is that some sort of syndrome?"

"I don't know what you mean," said Frieda.

"I was going to ask how you are," Bradshaw continued. "But I think I already know."

"Yes. Your journalist rang me up."

Bradshaw smiled. He had very white teeth. "Perhaps I should have warned you. But it would have spoiled things."

"What's this?" asked Karlsson. He seemed both uncomfortable and distressed.

"You don't need to know." Frieda didn't want anyone to know, and particularly not Karlsson, but she supposed that soon enough they all would, and the gossip, the glee, the happy, whispering pity would begin all over again.

The woman was Yvette Long.

"Frieda. What are you doing here?"

"I've been having cocoa with my niece, Chloë. And this is Ted."

"Yes," said Bradshaw, still smiling. "We do know Ted Lennox. Are you coming inside? I assume that's what you want."

"No." Frieda was about to deny any connection, when she looked at the clenched, haunted figure of Ted standing with Chloë. It would have sounded like a betrayal. "I was on my way home."

"She can go where she pleases, can't she?" said Yvette, fiercely, turning her brown-eyed glare on Hal Bradshaw, who seemed unperturbed.

Frieda had to stop herself from smiling at the novelty of Yvette's defending her. And defending her from what?

Yvette and Bradshaw walked up the steps to the house, but Karlsson stayed on the pavement, hovering awkwardly.

"Are you involved in this somehow?" he asked.

"Chloë knows Ted," Frieda said. "She wanted me to have a word with him. That's all."

Karlsson nodded to himself. "I'm glad to see you anyway," he said. "You look all right."

"Good," said Frieda.

"I've been meaning to talk to you. To see you. But now I've got to . . ." He gestured at the house.

"That's fine," said Frieda. She nodded good-bye to Chloë, turned, and walked away in the direction of Primrose Hill.

Karlsson watched Frieda's progress, then went with the others into the house. Munster and Riley were already inside. They followed Munster through into the kitchen. Yvette was taking folders from her bag and arranging them on the table. They all sat down. Karlsson thought of the Lennoxes sitting there, rowdy Sunday lunches, then tried not to. He looked at Bradshaw. "What was it that Frieda was saying to you?"

"Just shop talk," said Bradshaw.

"Right," said Karlsson. "Let's sort out where we are."

"Are we really not charging Billy Hunt?" said Munster.

"It should be him," said Yvette. "It really should. But the CCTV puts him in Islington just after four. The neighbor knocked on the door at four thirty and she didn't answer."

"She might have been in the bath," said Munster. "She might have had headphones on."

"What do the forensics say about the time of death?" said Karlsson, his eyes on Riley, whose expression was blank.

Yvette picked up a file and thumbed through the papers. "It's not much use," she said. "She could have died any time between half an hour and three hours before she was found. But, look, we're not taking the word of someone like Billy Hunt, are we? I mean, nothing about his statement makes sense. For example, he says he set off the alarm. If he didn't kill her, then why didn't the person who did kill her set it off?"

"Because she let him in," said Bradshaw. "Psychopaths are plausible, convincing."

"You said before that he was expressing rage against women."

"I stand by that."

"Why was the alarm on?" said Yvette.

"What do you mean?" said Karlsson.

"Why would the burglar alarm be switched on if she was home?"

"That's a good question." Karlsson stood up and walked to the front door. He opened it and stepped outside. Then he returned to the kitchen. "This house doesn't have a fucking burglar alarm," he said. "We're being idiots."

"There we are," said Yvette. "So Billy Hunt was lying. Again."

Karlsson drummed his fingers on the table. "Why would he lie about that?"

"Because he's a psychopath," said Bradshaw.

"He's a thieving layabout," said Karlsson, "but he wasn't lying."

"What do you mean?" said Yvette.

"Look," said Karlsson, pointing at the ceiling. "There's a smoke alarm."

"How could Hunt set off a smoke alarm?"

"He didn't," said Karlsson. "Look at the scene-of-crime file. Riley, what will I find in the file?"

Riley's eyes flickered nervously. "Do you mean, like, one thing in particular?" he said.

"Yes, one thing in particular. Oh, never mind. As far as I remember, there was a tray of burned something or other on the cooktop. That's what set off the alarm."

Yvette flicked through the file. "That's right," she said.

"Are you saying Billy Hunt broke into the house and took some burned cakes out of the oven?" Munster asked dubiously.

Karlsson shook his head. "You should talk to the little girl again, but I know what she'll say. She came home, smelled burning, took the tray out of the oven. Then she found her mother. Check the smoke alarm in the living room, Chris. Hunt said there was an alarm in there as well."

Munster left the room.

"All right," said Yvette. "So that explains the alarm. It doesn't help us with the time."

"Hang on," said Karlsson.

Munster came back into the kitchen. "There isn't one," he said.

"What?" said Karlsson. "Are you sure?"

"There's one in the hallway. That must be the other one he heard."

Karlsson thought hard. "No," he said at last. "Anyway, if smoke sets off the smoke alarm, you don't talk about alarms. You think of them as one alarm."

"Really?" said Yvette.

"Are Ruth Lennox's effects here or at the station?"

"At the station."

"All right," said Karlsson. "Give me a moment. I need to make a call."

He stepped outside. After a long pause, Yvette spoke to Bradshaw. "Is something up with you and Frieda?"

"Have you talked about it with her?" he said.

"What do you mean 'it'?"

"Your involvement with her incident, accident, whatever you call it."

"Sorry, I don't understand what you mean."

"It's just that I hope you don't feel guilty about it."

"Look—" Yvette began fiercely, and was interrupted by Karlsson coming back into the kitchen.

"I just talked to the woman in Storage," he said. "And I found what I expected to find. What Hunt heard in the living room was Ruth Lennox's phone. It had an alarm on it. It was set to go off at ten past four in the afternoon. That was the other alarm that Billy Hunt heard."

"It may have been," said Yvette.

"It was," said Karlsson. "Put everything together. Look what we've got. Biscuits or cakes burning in the oven. A smoke sensor. And a phone alarm set for ten past four. It's reasonable to suggest that the alarm was to remind her that they were ready."

"Possible."

"It's also reasonable to suggest that when the alarm went off, Mrs. Lennox was no longer able to respond to it. So she was dead by ten past four, at the very latest."

There was a silence around the table.

"Fuck," said Yvette.

FIFTEEN

She was expecting him. She glanced at herself in the mirror to make sure she was looking in control and reasonably healthy—she couldn't stand the thought of anyone's pity, and certainly not his—then ate the slice of quiche standing by the kitchen window, with the cat at her feet, rubbing its flank against her calves. The house was quiet now after a day of terrible bangs and tearing sounds and drilling. Stefan had been there again as he and Josef had carried two industrial-looking beams into the house. But they were gone now. Frieda didn't know what she actually wanted, but she did know that she felt suddenly more alert and less jangled, as if a knob had been turned very slightly and her world had come into clearer focus.

The doorbell rang at ten minutes past nine.

"Hello, Frieda," said Karlsson. He held out a bunch of red tulips, wrapped in damp paper. "I should have brought these to you weeks ago."

"Weeks ago I had far too many flowers. They all died at the same time. This is better."

"Can I come in?"

In the living room, he took one of the chairs by the empty grate. "I always think of you sitting by a fire," he said.

"You've only really known me in the winter."

There was a silence: they were both remembering the work they'd done together and the way it had ended so violently.

"Frieda . . ." he began.

"You don't need to."

"I do. I really do. I haven't been to see you since you left the hospital because I felt so bad about what had happened that I went into a kind of lockdown about it. You helped us—more than that, you rescued us. And in return we got rid of you, and then we nearly got you killed."

"*You* didn't get rid of me, and *you* didn't nearly get me killed."

"Me. My team. Us. That's how it works. I was responsible and I let you down."

"But I wasn't killed. Look at me." She lifted her chin, squared her shoulders, smiled. "I'm fine."

Karlsson shut his eyes for a moment. "In this job you have to develop a thick skin or you'd go mad. But you can't have a thick skin when it involves a friend."

Silence settled around the word. Images of Karlsson flitted through Frieda's mind: Karlsson at his desk, calm and in control; Karlsson striding along a road with a tight face; Karlsson sitting by the bed of a little boy who, they thought, was perhaps dying; Karlsson standing up to the commissioner for her; Karlsson with his daughter wrapped around his body like a frightened koala; Karlsson sitting beside her fire and smiling at her.

"It's good to see you," said Frieda.

"That means a lot."

"Have your children left yet?" she asked.

"No. They go very soon, though. I was supposed to be spending lots of time with them. Then this case came up."

"Hard."

"Like a toothache that won't go away. Are you really OK?"

"I'm fine. I need a bit of time."

"I don't mean just physically." Karlsson flushed, and Frieda was almost amused.

"You mean am I in a state of trauma?"

"You *were* attacked with a knife."

"I dream about it sometimes." Frieda considered. "And I need to tell you that I also think about Dean Reeve. Something happened a few days ago that you should know. Don't look anxious, I don't want to talk about it now."

There was a silence. Karlsson seemed to be weighing something in his mind. To speak or not to speak.

"Listen," he said finally. "That boy Ted."

"I'm sorry about that."

"That's not what I wanted to say. You know about the case?"

"I know his mother was killed."

"She was a nice woman, with a decent husband, close family, good friends, neighbors who liked her. We thought we'd got the man who did it, all simple and straightforward. It turns out that he couldn't have, and we're back where we started. Except that it makes even less sense."

"I'm sorry," Frieda said neutrally.

"Dr. Bradshaw has a theory."

"I don't want to hear it," Frieda said quickly. "That's one of the perks of being pushed out."

Karlsson looked suspicious. "Is there some problem with Bradshaw?"

"Does it matter?" Frieda didn't say anything further, just waited.

"You wouldn't come to the house with me, would you? Just once? I'd like to discuss it with someone I trust."

"What about Yvette?" asked Frieda, although she already knew she was going to say yes.

"Yvette's terrific—apart from the fact that she let you get nearly murdered, of course. She's my trusted colleague, as well as my attack dog. But if I want someone to look at a house, just to get the smell of it, have a thought or two, I'd ask you—I *am* asking you."

"As a friend."

"Yes. As a friend."

"When?"

"Tomorrow morning, when the house is empty?"

"That would suit me fine."

"Are you serious? I mean, that's great. Shall I send a car?"

"I'll make my own way."

It's a beautiful evening, with a full moon shining on the river. I wonder what it's like in London—but, of course, it's nearly morning for you now. You're asleep. At least I hope you are. Sandy xxxx

SIXTEEN

S o it was that the very next day Frieda once more walked past the Roundhouse, past the little café where Ted and Chloë had drunk hot chocolate the evening before and the larger one where an airplane nose-dived down the wall and music throbbed, into Margaretting Street. Karlsson was already outside, drinking coffee from a paper mug that he raised in salute as she came toward him. He noticed that she walked more slowly than she used to, and with a slight limp.

"You came."

"I said I would."

"I'm glad."

"As long as you're sure no one's in?"

"I'm certain. The family has been staying with neighbors. The house is still officially a crime scene. Although there's a cat that keeps coming in and out through the cat flap."

"And Hal Bradshaw?"

"Fuck him." The vehemence of Karlsson's response surprised her.

Frieda followed Karlsson through the front door. Although the window was still broken, the barriers had been cleared away, and the forensic team had gone. But the house had the special emptiness of an abandoned place, already neglected and musty from disuse—and, of course, it was the place where a woman (a wife, a mother, a good neighbor, Karlsson had said) had recently been murdered. As Frieda stood in the silent hallway, she felt that the house somehow knew it and felt abandoned.

A large photograph, the frame cracked and the glass smashed, was propped against the wall and she bent down to look at it.

"The happy family," said Karlsson. "But it's usually the husband, you know."

Official family photographs that are framed and hung in the hall are always happy. Everyone has to stand close together and smile: there was Ted, not as gangly and disheveled as she'd seen him, with the smooth face of youth; there was the elder of the girls, her arresting pale eyes and nimbus of coppery curls; the younger daughter, skinny and anxious, but grinning despite her train-track braces, her head tipped slightly toward her mother's shoulder. There was the husband and father, as proud and protective as a husband and father is meant to look when he's standing with his family grouped around him for the picture that will represent them—he had a scrawny look, with graying brown hair, thin cheeks, his elder daughter's eyes, eyebrows that tilted at a comic angle.

And there she was, standing in the center with her husband—in a flecked sweater, her soft hair tied back loosely, her candid face smiling out of the picture. One hand on the shoulder of her elder daughter, who sat in front of her, and one against her husband's hip. It was a touching gesture for the official portrait, thought Frieda, casual and intimate. She bent closer and stared into the dead woman's eyes. Gray. No makeup that she could see. Small signs of age drawing down her mouth and creasing her brow. Smile marks and frown marks, the map of our days.

"Tell me about her. Describe her," she said to Karlsson.

"Her name is Ruth Lennox. Forty-four years old. A health visitor, and has been since her younger daughter started school; she had several years out when the children were small. Married to Russell Lennox," Karlsson pointed to the man in the photo, "happily, from all accounts, for twenty-three years. He's an executive in a small charity for children with learning difficulties. Three kids, as you see—your Ted, Judith, who's fifteen, and Dora, thirteen. All at the local high school. Has a dragon of a sister who lives in London. Both her parents are dead. On the PTA. Good citizen. Not rich, but comfortable: two modest but stable incomes and no big outgoings. Three thousand pounds in her current account, thirteen thousand in her savings account. Healthy enough pension pot. Donates to various charities by standing order. No criminal record. Clean driving license. I'm using the present tense but, of course, last Wednesday she sustained a catastrophic injury to the head and would have died instantly."

"Who did you think it was, before you discovered it couldn't be?"

"A local druggie with a record, but it turns out that he has a rock-solid alibi. He was caught on CCTV somewhere else at the time of her death. He admitted to breaking in, stealing some stuff, finding her body and fleeing the scene. We didn't believe him, but for once in his life he was telling the truth."

"So the broken window was his?"

"And the burglary. There was no sign of a break-in when a neighbor came round earlier—we know Ruth Lennox must have been already dead. Obviously, the implication is that she let the killer in herself."

"Someone she knew."

"Or someone who seemed safe."

"Where did she die?"

"In here." Karlsson led her into the living room, where everything was tidy and in its proper place (cushions on the sofa, newspapers and magazines in the rack, books lining the walls, tulips in a vase on the mantelpiece), but a dark bloodstain still flowered on the beige carpet and daubs of blood decorated the near wall.

"Violent," said Frieda.

"Hal Bradshaw believes it was the work of an extremely angry sociopath with a record of violence."

"And you think it's more likely to be the husband."

"That's not a matter of evidence, just the way of the world. The most likely person to kill a wife is her husband. The husband, however, has a reasonably satisfactory alibi."

Frieda looked round at him. "We're taught to beware of strangers," she said. "It's our friends most of us should worry about."

"I wouldn't go that far," said Karlsson.

They went through to the kitchen and Frieda stood in the middle of the room, looking from the tidily cluttered sideboard to the drawings and photos stuck to the fridge with magnets, the book splayed open on the table. Then, upstairs, the bedroom: a king-sized bed covered with a striped duvet; a gilt-framed photo of Ruth and Russell on their wedding day twenty-three years ago; several smaller framed photos of her children at different ages; a wardrobe in which hung dresses, skirts, and shirts—nothing flamboyant, Frieda noticed—some things obviously old but well looked after. Shoes, flat or with small heels; one pair of black leather boots, slightly scuffed. Drawers in which T-shirts were neatly rolled, not folded; underwear drawer with sensible knickers and bras, 34C. A small amount of makeup on the dressing table, and one bottle of perfume, Chanel. A novel by her side of the bed, *Wives and Daughters* by Elizabeth Gaskell, with a bookmark sticking out, and under it a book about small gardens. A pair of reading glasses, folded, to one side.

In the bathroom: a bar of unscented soap, apple handwash, electric toothbrush—his and hers—and dental floss, shaving cream, razors, tweezers, a canister of deodorant, face wipes, moisturizing face cream, two large towels and one hand towel, two matching washcloths hung on the side of the bath, with the tap in the middle, a set of scales pushed against the wall, a medicine cabinet containing paracetamol, aspirin, Band-Aids of various sizes, cough medicine, Monistat, a tube of eyedrops, anti-indigestion tablets . . . Frieda shut the cabinet.

"No contraceptives?"

"That's what Yvette asked. She had an IUD—the Mirena coil, apparently."

In the filing cabinet set aside for her use in her husband's small study, there were three folders for work, and most of the others related to her children: academic qualifications; child benefit slips; medical records; reports, on single pieces of paper or in small books, dating back to their first years at primary school; certificates commemorating their ability to swim a hundred meters, their participation in the egg-and-spoon race, or the cycling proficiency course.

In the shabby trunk beside the filing cabinet: hundreds and hundreds of pieces of creativity the children had brought back from school over the years. Splashy paintings in bright colors of figures with legs attached to the wobbly circle of the head and hair sprouting like exclamation marks, scraps of material puckered with running stitch and cross stitch and chain stitch, a tiny homemade clock without a battery, a small box studded with over-glued sea shells, a blue-painted clay pot, and you could still see the finger marks pressed into its asymmetrical rim.

"There are also several bin bags full of old baby clothes in the loft," said Karlsson, as she closed the lid. "We haven't got to them yet. It takes a long time to go through a house like this. Nothing was thrown away."

"Photo albums?"

"A whole shelf given over to them. She wrote the date and occasion under each. She didn't do motherhood by halves."

"No."

Frieda went to stand by the window that overlooked the garden. There were drifts of blossom around the fruit tree, and a cat sat in a patch of sunlight. "There's nothing here she wouldn't want to be seen," she said.

"What do you mean?"

"I always think that nobody's life can tolerate a spotlight shone into its corners."

"But?"

"But from everything you tell me and everything I've seen, hers seems entirely ready for the spotlight, don't you think? As if this house were a stage."

"A stage for what?"

"For a play about being good."

"I'm supposed to be the cynical one. Do you mean you think nobody can be that good?"

"I'm a therapist, Karlsson. Of course that's what I think. Where are Ruth Lennox's secrets?"

But of course, she thought, several hours later and sitting at Number 9—her friends' café near where she lived—real secrets aren't found in objects, in schedules, in the words we speak or the expressions we put on our faces, in underwear drawers and filing cabinets, deleted texts, and diaries pushed to the bottom of the bag. They are lodged far deeper, unguessable even to ourselves. She was thinking about this as she faced Jack Dargan, whom she supervised and even during her convalescence, met at least once a week to track his progress and listen to his doubts. And Jack was a thorny ball of doubt. But he never doubted Frieda: she was the constant in his life, his single point of faith.

"I have a favor to ask," Jack was saying animatedly. "Don't look anxious—I'm not going to let down my patients or anything. Especially not Carrie." Since discovering that her husband Alan had not left her but had been murdered by his twin, Dean Reeve, Carrie had been seeing Jack twice a week and he seemed to have done better than even Frieda, who believed in him, had expected. He laid aside his self-conscious pessimism and his awkwardness and concentrated on the woman in distress.

"What is this favor?"

"I've written a paper on trauma, and before I send it out, I wanted you to look at it."

Frieda hesitated. Trauma felt too close for her to review it dispassionately. She looked at Jack's flushed face, his tufty hair, and ridiculous clothes (today he was wearing brown, balding jeans, a secondhand yellow and orange shirt that clashed with his coloring and his hair, and a green waterproof, even though the sky was cloudless). In his confusion, he reminded her of Ted Lennox, of so many other raw and self-conscious young men.

"All right," she said reluctantly.

"Really?"

"Yes."

"Can I ask you something?"

"You can always ask."

"But you won't always answer. I know." Jack avoided her eyes. "I'm only asking because the others won't and—"

"What others?" Frieda interrupted.

"Oh, you know. The usual suspects."

"Am I that scary? Go on, then."

"Are you all right?"

"That's what you—they—wanted to ask?"

"Yes."

"The paper you've written was just an excuse?"

"Well, yes. Kind of—though I have written it. And I would like you to look at it if you have time."

"And I'm assuming that you're asking me because you're worried that I'm not."

"No—well, yes. You seem—" He stopped.

"Go on."

"Brittle. Like an eggshell. More unpredictable than you usually are. Sorry. I don't mean to offend you. But maybe you aren't taking your recovery seriously enough."

"Is that what you think?"

"Yes."

"All of you?"

"Well—yes."

"Tell everyone—whoever takes it upon themselves to be worried for me—that I'm fine."

"You're angry."

"I don't like the thought that you've been discussing me behind my back."

"Only because we're concerned."

"Thank you for your concern, but I'm fine."

Later that afternoon, Frieda had a visitor she wasn't expecting, who brought the recent past flooding back. She opened her door to find Lorna Kersey standing on the doorstep, and before Frieda had time to say anything, she had stepped inside and closed the door behind her with a bang.

"This won't take long," she said, in a voice high and cracked with rage.

"I won't pretend I don't know why you're here."

"Good."

"I'm very sorry for your loss, Mrs. Kersey."

"You killed my daughter, and now you say you're sorry for my loss."

Lorna Kersey's daughter, Beth, had been an unhappy and dysfunctional young woman who suffered from paranoid delusions and who had killed Mary Orton. Frieda had got to the house too late to stop her. The vividness of the flashbacks in which she remembered Beth standing over her with a knife, and reexperienced the blade slicing through her, still woke her in the night, drenched in sweat. She had known that she was dying, felt herself sliding into darkness and oblivion—yet she had survived and Beth Kersey had not. The police had called it self-defense, and even Karlsson hadn't believed Frieda when she insisted that it was Dean Reeve who had killed Beth and saved her life.

"Yes, I'm sorry," said Frieda, steadily. It would do no good to tell Lorna Kersey she hadn't killed her daughter. She wouldn't believe her, and even if she did, what did that matter? Beth, poor lonely Beth, was dead, and a mother's anguish was etched into Lorna Kersey's face.

"You came to me, and you got me to tell you things about Beth we never told anyone. I trusted you. You said you would help find her. You made me a promise. And then you killed her. Do you know what it feels like to bury a child?"

"No."

"No. Of course you don't. How can you bear to get up in the morning?"

Frieda thought of saying that Beth had been very ill, that in her frantic sickness of the mind she had slaughtered an old woman and would have killed her, Frieda, as well. But of course Lorna Kersey knew all of that. She wanted someone to blame, and who more obvious than Frieda?

"I wish there was something I could say or do that would—"

"But there isn't. There's nothing. My child's dead, and now she'll never be all right. And you did that. In the name of helping people, you destroy them. I'll never forgive you. Never."

Frieda—you sounded a bit distracted today. I know that something is up but in spite of everything that's passed between us, you're not very good at confiding in me, are you? Why? I think you feel you have to deal with things by yourself, as if it's some kind of moral obligation. Or maybe you don't trust other people to help you. I guess what I'm saying is that you should— can—trust me, Sandy xxx

SEVENTEEN

The Sir Philip Sidney was a pub on the side of a busy road. It looked lost and abandoned between a gas station and a furniture store. When Fearby walked in, he recognized his man immediately, and he knew at the same moment that he was a policeman or an ex-policeman. Gray suit, white shirt, striped tie, black shoes. Slightly overweight. Fearby sat down beside him.

"Drink?" he said.

"I was just leaving," said the man.

"What's your name?"

"You don't need to know," said the man, "because we're never going to meet again. You know, we all got pretty sick of you. On the force."

"They got pretty sick of me on my paper as well," said Fearby.

"So you must be feeling chuffed with yourself."

"Is that what you've dragged me out here to tell me?"

"Are you finished with the story?"

"I don't know," said Fearby. "Conley didn't kill Hazel Barton. Which means someone else did."

"The police are not currently pursuing other leads. As you know."

"Yes," said Fearby. "Is that it?"

"I was wondering if you had any avenues of inquiry?"

"Avenues of inquiry?" said Fearby. "I've got a roomful of files."

"I was having a drink once," said the man, in a casual tone, "and someone told me that on the morning of the Hazel Barton murder, a few miles away in Cottingham, another girl was approached. But she got away. That's all. It was just something I heard."

"Why wasn't this given to the defense?"

"It wasn't thought relevant. It didn't fit the pattern. Something like that."

"So why are you telling me now?"

"I wanted to know if you were interested."

"That's no good to me," said Fearby. "That's just pub chat. I need a name. I need a number."

The man got up. "It's one of those things that irritate you, that won't let you go," he said. "You know, like a little stone in your shoe. I'll see what I can do. But that will be it. One call, and then you won't hear from me again."

"You were the one who called me."

"Don't make me regret it."

Frieda ordered a black coffee for herself, a latte and a Danish for Sasha. She sat at the table and opened the newspaper. She turned page after page until she reached the article she was looking for. Just a few minutes earlier, Reuben had been shouting down the phone at her about it, so she was prepared. She skimmed it quickly.

"Oh," she said, suddenly, as if she'd been jabbed. There was a detail she hadn't expected.

"What's happening with your home improvement?" Sasha asked. "I knew that Josef was giving you a new bathtub. I didn't realize it would take so long."

"I've almost forgotten what my old bathroom was like," said Frieda. "Or what it was like to *have* a bathroom."

"He probably thought of it as a kind of therapy for you," Sasha said. "Maybe a hot bath is the one experience you allow yourself that's a complete indulgence with no redeeming moral features. So he thought you'd better have a good one."

"You make me sound . . . bleak."

"I think it was also therapy for Josef."

Frieda was puzzled. "Why would it be therapy for Josef?"

"I know that you were there when Mary Orton was killed. I know how terrible it was for you. But Josef knew her as well. He looked after her, repaired her house. And she looked after him. Her Ukrainian son. Better than her English sons."

"That's true," said Frieda.

"When that happened to her and to you, it hit him hard. I have the feeling that when something bad happens to him, he doesn't talk about it. He gets drunk or he makes something for someone."

"Maybe," said Frieda. "I just wish his therapy wasn't so messy. And so loud."

"And now you're getting written about in the papers again. Do you ever get sick of being picked on?"

Frieda let a few moments go by. "It's not that," she said. "I didn't know about this, but there's something you should know."

"What do you mean?"

"These researchers targeted four psychotherapists. I'm one, of course. Reuben's another. One of them is Geraldine Fliess. They probably chose her because she's written about extreme mental disorders. And the other is James Rundell."

Neither of the women spoke immediately, and they didn't need to.

"Who brought us together, I suppose," said Sasha.

"And got me arrested."

Rundell had been Sasha's therapist. When Frieda had discovered that he had slept with Sasha while she was his patient, she had not only confronted Rundell but attacked him in a restaurant and been taken to a police cell, from which Karlsson had rescued her.

"Does the article mention me?" said Sasha. "Sorry. I know that sounds selfish. I didn't mean that."

"It doesn't mention you," said Frieda. "So far as I can see."

"You don't need to worry, you know. I am better. That's all in the past. It doesn't have power over me anymore."

"I'm glad."

"In fact . . ." Sasha paused, and Frieda looked at her inquiringly. "In fact, I've been meaning to tell you, but there didn't seem to be a right time. I've met someone."

"Really? Who is he?"

"His name's Frank Manning." Her face took on a soft and dreamy expression.

"You have to tell me more than that! What does he do?"

"He's a barrister—a criminal barrister. I met him only a few weeks ago. It all happened so quickly."

"And is it . . ." She hesitated. She wanted to ask Sasha if this Frank was single and free or, like several of Sasha's previous relationships, there were complications. She feared for her beautiful young friend.

"You want to know if he's married? No. He's divorced and he has a young son. Don't look at me like that, Frieda! I trust him. If you met him, you'd know what I mean. He's honorable."

"I want to meet him." Frieda took Sasha's hand in hers and pressed it. "I'm very glad. I should have guessed—you're looking very radiant."

"I'm just happy—I wake up in the morning and I feel alive! I haven't felt like this for so long. I'd almost forgotten how lovely it is."

"And he feels the same."

"Yes. He does. I know he does."

"I have to meet him. See if he's good enough for you."

"I'll arrange it. But, Frieda, you, Reuben, Rundell, all in the article. Is that just a coincidence?"

"The man running the research project is a psychologist called Hal Bradshaw. He works with the police, and we were both on the case that nearly got me killed. "

"And you didn't get on?"

"We disagreed about various aspects."

"Do you mind if I have a look at the article?"

Frieda pushed the newspaper across the table. Sasha leaned over and peered at it, not reading it through but seeing it in flashes. She took in the headline:

SILENT WITNESSES

She saw a row of photographs. A picture of Frieda that had been in another press report, a photograph of her taken in the street, caught unawares. There was a picture of James Rundell, more youthful than when she'd been involved with him, and a much older picture of Reuben. He looked like a psychoanalyst in a French New Wave movie.

She read the intro: "A disturbing new report suggests that therapists are failing to protect the public from potential rapists and murderers."

She moved her finger down the page, searching for Frieda's name.

> When confronted with a patient showing the classic signs of a murderous psychopath, Dr. Frieda Klein offered no treatment and made no attempt to report him to the authorities. When questioned about why she had failed to report a psychopath to the police, Dr. Klein responded that she had "had some concerns" about the patient but that she "wouldn't discuss them with anyone but him." In fact, Dr. Klein had refused to treat the patient.
>
> Frieda Klein, a 38-year-old brunette, hit the headlines earlier this year when she was involved in a shocking incident in which two women were knifed to death and Klein herself was

hospitalized. An eighty-year-old woman, Mary Orton, was killed in a crazed attack by a knife-wielding schizophrenic, Beth Kersey. Police accepted Klein's explanation that she killed Kersey in self-defense.

The leader of the research project, Dr. Hal Bradshaw, commented: "While it is understandable to feel sympathy for what Dr. Klein has gone through . . ."

"That's nice of him," said Sasha.

"Of who?" said Frieda.

"Bloody Hal Bradshaw." She turned back to the paper.

"While it is understandable to feel sympathy for what Dr. Klein has gone through, I think there is a serious question of whether she is a risk both to her patients and to the public at large."

Dr. Bradshaw spoke of the urgent issues that his research has raised. "It brings me no pleasure to expose the failings in the analytic community. We tested the responses of four psychoanalysts, and of those four, only one acted responsibly and called the authorities. The other three failed in their responsibilities both as healers and as protectors of the public.

"When he talked to me, one of the patients in the study, Seamus Dunne, was still angry about his experience: 'I was told that Dr. Klein was a top expert, but when I gave her the story that showed I was a psychopath, she didn't react at all. She just asked irrelevant questions about food and sleeping and things like that. She seemed like her mind was on other things.'"

Sasha threw down the paper. "I know I'm supposed to say something comforting to you, but I literally don't know how you can bear this. You've become this object out in the world that people kick around and throw things at and tell lies about. The idea of this guy coming to you and saying he was in need and asking for your help and it was all a trick—don't you feel violated?"

Frieda took a sip of her coffee. "Sasha, if it weren't you, I'd say it wasn't a problem and that it comes with the territory. And I'd say it was all quite interesting, if it weren't happening to me."

"But it is me, and it is happening to you."

Frieda smiled at her friend. "You know, sometimes I wish I weren't doing this job at all. I'd like to be a potter, that's what I'd like. I'd have a lump of clay on my wheel, and it wouldn't matter what I was feeling or what anybody was feeling. At the end of it, I'd have a pot. Or a cup. Or a bowl."

"If you were a potter," said Sasha, "I'd be lost or worse. And you don't want to be a potter anyway."

"That's nice of you to say, but you would have got better on your own. People usually do, you know."

Frieda pulled the newspaper back to her side of the table and glanced at it again.

"Are you going to do anything about it?" Sasha asked.

Frieda took a notebook from her bag and flipped through it until she found the page she wanted. "You know people who are good with technical things, don't you? Finding things on the Internet."

"Yes," said Sasha, warily.

"I want to see Seamus Dunne. I've got his phone number, but I don't know where he lives. There must be ways of finding out."

"I'm not sure that's a good idea," said Sasha. "If you're going to get into a fight again and get arrested, Karlsson may not be able to get you out this time."

"It's nothing like that," said Frieda. "I just need to talk to him. In person. Can that be done?"

Sasha looked at the notebook. "I suppose so," she said. She took her phone from the table and punched the number into it.

"What are you doing?" Frieda asked, but Sasha just held up her hand.

"Hello," she said, speaking into the phone in a nasal tone quite different from her own. "Is that Mr. Seamus Dunne? Yes? We're actually trying to make a delivery to you, and our driver seems to have the wrong address. Can you confirm it for me?" She picked up a pen and started writing in Frieda's notebook. "Yes . . . Yes . . . Yes . . . Thank you so much, we'll be right with you." She pushed the notebook across to Frieda.

"That wasn't quite what I meant when I said I needed technical help."

"No violence, please."

"I'll do my best."

EIGHTEEN

N o," said Seamus Dunne, when he saw Frieda. "No way. And how do you even know where I live?"

She peered over his shoulder. Student house. Bare boards. Bikes in the hall. Still-packed boxes.

"I just want to talk to you."

"Talk to the newspaper. Or Bradshaw. It wasn't my responsibility."

"I'm not interested in any of that," said Frieda. "Or the article. It was just something you said."

Dunne's eyes narrowed in suspicion. "Is this a trick?"

Frieda almost laughed at that. "You mean, am I coming to see you under false pretenses?"

Dunne shook his head nervously. "Bradshaw said we were all in the clear. It was completely legal."

"I told you," said Frieda. "I don't care. I'm here to say two things. Let me in and I'll say them. Then I'll go."

Dunne seemed in an agony of indecision. Finally he opened the door and let her in. She walked through the hall to the kitchen. It looked as if a rugby team had ordered takeout and not cleared up, then had a party and not cleared up, then had got up the next morning and had breakfast and not cleared up. And then left. Seamus Dunne was a bit old for this.

He noticed her expression. "You look shocked," he said. "If I'd known you were coming, I'd have cleared up."

"No," she said. "It reminds me of being a student."

"Well, I'm still a student," he said. "It may not look like much, but it's better than the alternative. So, I guess you've come to shout at me."

"Do you think you deserve to be shouted at?"

Dunne leaned back on the counter, almost dislodging a pile of plates topped by a saucepan containing two mugs. "Dr. Bradshaw told us about an experiment in which a researcher sent some students to different psychiatrists, and they just had to say they had heard a thud inside their heads.

Every single one of them was diagnosed with schizophrenia and admitted to a psychiatric hospital."

"Yes, I know the experiment," said Frieda. "It wouldn't be allowed today."

"Maybe that's a pity," said Dunne, "because it was pretty revealing, don't you think? But you don't want to hear that."

"The way I see it," said Frieda, "people who weren't really psychopaths were sent to therapists, and only one of them made the mistake of taking them seriously."

"So what were the two things you wanted to say?"

"I was interested in what you said in the article."

"I thought so."

"No, not the way you think. You said I asked you about irrelevant things, food, sleeping. By the way, how is your sleeping?"

"Fine."

"No, really. Do you sleep through the night? Or do you still wake up?"

"I wake up a bit. Like most people."

"And what do you think about?"

"Stuff, you know. I go over things."

"And your appetite?"

He shrugged and there was a pause. "Why are you looking at me like that?"

"Do you know what I think?"

"You're probably about to tell me."

"When you came to see me, pretending to be looking for help, I think you subconsciously used that as an excuse to really ask for help."

"That's just Freudian rubbish. You're trying to catch me out."

"You're not sleeping properly; you're not eating properly. There's this." She gestured at the kitchen.

"That's just a student kitchen."

"I've seen student kitchens," said Frieda. "I've lived in student kitchens. This is a bit different. And, anyway, you're—what? Twenty-five, twenty-six? I think you're slightly depressed and finding it difficult to admit to anyone or even yourself."

Dunne went very red. "If it's subconscious, and you think I don't want to admit it even to myself, then how do I disprove it?"

"Just think about it," said Frieda. "And you might want to talk to someone about it. Not to me."

There was another pause. Dunne picked up a dirty spoon and tapped it against a stained mug. "What was the other thing?" he said.

"That story you told me."

"Which? The whole thing was a story."

"No. About cutting your father's hair and feeling a mixture of tenderness and power."

"Oh, that."

"It felt distinct from everything else, like an authentic memory."

"Sorry to disappoint you. It was just something I said."

"It wasn't your memory?"

"I learned it."

"Who told you to say it?"

"It was in my pack—I don't know. Dr. Bradshaw, maybe, or whoever made up our characters."

"Who actually gave you your instructions?"

"One of the other researchers. Oh—you want his name?"

"Yes, please."

"Why? So you can go and make him feel guilty as well?"

"Is that what I made you feel?"

"If you want to know, I felt really nervous, coming to you like that. A bit sick. It wasn't easy." He glared at Frieda. "His name's Duncan Bailey."

"Where does he live?"

"You want his address as well?"

"If you have it."

Seamus Dunne muttered something but then tore off the top of an empty cereal box that was lying on the floor and scribbled on it before handing it to Frieda.

"Thank you," she said. "And remember what I said about talking to someone."

"Are you going now?" Seamus Dunne seemed taken aback.

"Yes."

"You mean that's the end of it?"

"I'm not quite sure it's the end, Seamus."

Jim Fearby had gone back through his files to make sure he had all the facts in his head. He always made notes first in the shorthand he had learned when he'd joined the local newspaper in Coventry as a junior reporter, more than forty years ago. Nobody learned shorthand now, but he liked the hieroglyphic squiggles, like a secret code. Then, on the same day if possible, he would copy them into his notebook. Only later would he put it all onto his computer.

Hazel Barton had been strangled in July 2004; her body had been found lying by a roadside not many miles from where she lived. Apparently, she had been walking home from the bus stop, after the bus had failed to arrive. She was eighteen years old, fresh-faced and pretty, with three older brothers, and parents who had indulged and adored her. She had planned to become a physiotherapist. Her face smiled radiantly from the newspapers and TV screens for weeks after her death. George Conley had been seen standing over her body. He had been arrested at once and charged soon after. He was the local weirdo, the blubbery, unemployed, slow-witted loner who lurked in parks and outside playgrounds: of course he did it. And then he confessed and everyone was happy, except Jim Fearby, who was a stickler for detail and never took anyone else's word for things that happened. He had to read the police reports, had to rake through the files, thumb through law books.

He was sitting in front of the TV, not really watching it, when the phone rang.

"Have you got a pen?"

"Who is this?"

"Philip Sidney."

Fearby fumbled for a pen.

"Yes?"

"Vanessa Dale," said the voice, then gave a phone number and made Fearby read it back to him. Fearby started to ask something, but the line was already dead.

Frieda poured two whiskies and handed one to Josef. "How's it going?" she said.

"The joist is good. It is strong. But now after I take the floor up, I think it is better to do tiles. Tiles on the floor. Then new floor make wall look old and bad. So maybe tiles for the wall as well. You should choose."

Josef seemed to have forgotten about his glass, so Frieda clinked hers against his to remind him. They both drank.

"When I asked, 'How's it going?' I was asking about you, not just the bathroom. But I want to say that I'm going to start paying for all of this. You can't afford it."

"Is fine."

"It's not fine. I've been thinking about myself too much. I know that you were close to Mary Orton. It was very sad for you, I know, what happened."

"I dream of her," said Josef. "Two times maybe four times. It's funny."

"What do you dream?"

Josef smiled. "She was living in Ukraine. In my old home. I tell her I'm surprised to see her living. She talk to me in my own language. Stupid, no?"

"Yes. Very stupid. But not stupid at all."

Darling Frieda—It's too late to phone you. I've just checked out the link you sent me. Who is this fucking Hal Bradshaw anyway? Can we do something about this? One of my oldest friends is a lawyer. Should I have a word with her?

But I hope you know how highly you're regarded by all the people who matter—your friends, your colleagues, your patients. This story is just a vicious charade that makes no difference to that.

I've had an idea for the summer—we can hire a longboat on the Canal du Midi. You'd like that. I went on one before and they're very cozy (some people would find them oppressive; not you. They are a bit like your house, except they move). We could drift along the waterways and stop for picnics and in the evenings go to little brasseries. Say yes! xxxx

NINETEEN

W e were all so shocked," said the woman sitting opposite Munster and Riley. "I can't quite believe it. I mean, Ruth was so . . ." She stopped and searched for a word. Her face screwed up. "Down to earth," she supplied eventually. "Cheerful. Practical. I don't know—not someone who things like this happen to. I realize how stupid that sounds."

They were in the low-rise modern building from which Ruth Lennox had worked as a health visitor, sitting in a small room off the open-plan office with her line manager, Nadine Salter.

"It doesn't sound stupid, said Chris Munster, after Riley had failed to respond. He looked a bit dazed this morning: his face was creased, as if he had only just woken up. "It's what most people say about her. That she was a friendly, straightforward woman. How long had she worked here?"

"About ten years. Mostly she was out, seeing people, not here in the office."

"Can you show us her desk?"

"Of course."

They went into the large room, past desks of avidly curious people pretending to work. Ruth Lennox's desk was scrupulously tidy, which was what Munster and Riley had come to expect—her folders, her notebooks, her work diary, her correspondence, and her stationery had been put away in the drawers. Apart from the rather old computer, the only things on the surface were a small jug of pens, a little pot of paper clips and staples, and a framed photo of her three children.

"We're going to have to remove her computer and her correspondence," said Munster. "For now, we're just interested in the Wednesday she died. April the sixth. Was she here?"

"Yes. But just for the half-day. She always had Wednesday afternoon off. We have a general staff meeting in the morning, at about eleven, and then she leaves after that."

"So she was in the office that day, not out on visits?"

"That's right. She came in at about nine, and left again at midday."

"Was there anything different about her that day?"

"We've been talking about that. She was just her normal self."

"She didn't mention anything that was troubling her?"

"Not at all. We talked about how awful it is for young people trying to find jobs, but just in a general way—her kids are too young for that to worry her. Poor things. And she gave me a recipe."

"Did you see her go?"

"No. But Vicky, over there, was having a cigarette outside. She saw her getting into a cab."

"A black taxi?"

"No. As I said, a cab."

"Do you know which firm?"

"No, I don't."

"Hang on," said Riley.

He walked over to Ruth Lennox's desk and came back with a small card, which he handed to Munster. "This was pinned to her board," he said.

Munster looked at the card. C & R Taxis. He showed it to Nadine Salter. "Would she travel by cab on her visits?" he asked.

Her face took on a disapproving expression. "Not on our budget."

C & R Taxis was based in a tiny room with smeary windows next to a betting shop on Camden High Street. An old man was sitting asleep on a sofa. A portly man was sitting at a desk with three phones in front of him and a laptop. He looked up at the two detectives when Munster asked about Ruth Lennox.

"Ruth Lennox? Last Wednesday?" He scrolled down his computer screen with a deft, stubby finger. "Yeah, we took her last Wednesday. Ahmed drove her."

"Where to?"

They waited for him to say that Ahmed had driven Ruth Lennox home to Margaretting Street. He didn't.

"Shawcross Street, SE17, number thirty-seven. No, we didn't collect her." One of the phones rang loudly. "I should get that."

Out in the street, Munster and Riley looked at each other.

"Shawcross Street," Munster said.

The road they needed was one-way, so they parked beside an enormous block of flats, built in the thirties. It was being prepared for demolition and the windows and doors were sealed with sheet metal.

"I wonder what Ruth Lennox was doing round here," said Munster, climbing out of the car.

"Isn't that what a health visitor does?" said Riley. "Visit people?"

"This isn't her patch."

They walked round the corner into Shawcross Street. At one end, there was a row of large, semidetached Victorian houses, but thirty-seven wasn't one of these. It was a fifties-style, flat-fronted, dilapidated building with metal-framed windows that had been divided into three flats, although the top flat looked empty. One of its windows was smashed, and a tatty red curtain blew out of it.

Munster rang the bottom bell and waited. Then he rang the middle one. Just as they were turning to go, the entrance door opened and a small, dark-skinned woman peered out suspiciously. "What is it?" she asked.

Chris Munster held up his ID. "Could we come in?"

She stood aside and let them into the communal hallway.

"We want to check on the residents of this building. Do you live here?"

"Yes."

"Alone?"

"No. With my husband, who's in bed, and my two sons, who are at school, if that's what you were going to ask. What is this?"

"Is your husband ill?" asked Riley.

"He lost his job." The woman glared, her face tight. "He's on disability. I've got all the forms."

"We don't care about that," said Munster. "Do you know a woman called Ruth Lennox?"

"I've never heard of her. Why?"

"She came to this address last Wednesday."

He took the photograph of Ruth out of his pocket and held it out. "Do you recognize her?"

She examined the picture, wrinkling her face. "I don't take much notice of people who come and go," she said.

"She's been the victim of a crime. We think she came here on the day she died."

"Died? What are you suggesting?"

"Nothing. Really nothing. We just want to find out if she was here that day, and why."

"Well, she wasn't in our place at any rate. I don't know any Ruth Lennox. I don't know this woman." She jabbed the photo. "And we're law-abiding citizens, which can be hard enough these days."

"Do you know who lives in the other flats?"

"There's nobody above. They moved out months ago. And I don't know about downstairs."

"But somebody lives there?"

"I wouldn't say *lives*. Somebody rents it, but I don't see them."

"Them?"

"Them. Him. Her. I don't know." She relented. "I hear a radio sometimes. During the day."

"Thank you. And last Wednesday, did you see anyone there?"

"No. But I wasn't looking."

"Perhaps your husband might have seen something, if he's here during the day?"

She looked from one face to the other, then gave a small, weary shrug. "He sleeps a lot, or sort of sleeps, because of his pills."

"No. That's all right. Can you tell me who your landlord is?"

"You don't see him round here."

"What's his name?"

"Mr. Reader. Michael Reader. Maybe you've heard of him. You see his boards up everywhere. His grandfather bought up loads of these houses after the war. He's the real criminal."

TWENTY

Duncan Bailey—a psychology graduate student at Cardinal College, where Hal Bradshaw was a visiting lecturer—lived in Romford, in a concrete, Brutalist apartment block. It was built on a grand scale, with chilly corridors and high ceilings, large windows that overlooked a tumble of buildings and tangled ribbons of roads. He was an unusually small young man. He seemed out of place and almost comical in the cavernous living room. He had light brown hair and a neat goatee, lively blue eyes, a thin and mobile face. His manner was genial and mischievous.

"No hard feelings, I hope," he said, with a smile.

"Why would there be?"

"Some people might feel they'd been humiliated. But it's all in the cause of science. Anyway, Dr. Bradshaw said you might not see it that way."

"He should know," said Frieda. "But, as I understand it, you all had to pretend to be the same case study, describe the same symptoms, is that right?"

"Dr. Bradshaw said we could go off script as much as we wanted as long as we smuggled in the vital ingredients."

"So, things like the story about cutting the father's hair: that was in your story too?"

"Yes. Did you like it?"

"Did Dr. Bradshaw create the case study himself?"

"He signed off on it, but it was put together by one of the other researchers. We never met as a group. I came into it rather late, as a favor."

"Who were they?"

"So you can visit them too?"

"Maybe."

"Don't you want to know which one I went to see?"

"Not particularly."

"It was your friend."

Poor Reuben, thought Frieda.

"James Rundell." He looked at her inquiringly, head cocked to one side. "I can see why someone would want to punch him."

Frieda suppressed a smile at the thought of James Rundell meeting this sharp, cynical, bright-eyed young man.

"But you can't just go around thinking you can control people," Duncan Bailey continued. "I mean, it's very nice to meet you, of course, but someone more sensitive than I might be intimidated by your visit, Dr. Klein. Do you see what I mean?"

"I just want the names."

Bailey thought for a moment. "Why not? They'll be in the psychology journal soon enough. Shall I write them down for you? I can give you their addresses if that would help. Save you going to any trouble. But don't you have anything better to do with your weekend?"

Sandy's face came into Frieda's mind. She smiled at Bailey.

"Why, yes. As a matter of fact, I think I'll go to New York."

Five and a half hours later, Frieda was on a plane. The last-minute flight had been eye-wateringly expensive; she was going for a ridiculously short time; above all, she was scared of flying and for nearly a decade had avoided it. She sat in an aisle seat and ordered a tomato juice. The woman next to her snored gently. Frieda sat upright, burning with fear: because she was flying, because Dean Reeve was still alive, because she knew what it felt like to die, because she was so glad she would be seeing Sandy, and because caring so much was dangerous. It was safer to be alone.

When Fearby phoned Vanessa Dale, she said she'd moved away years earlier. Now she lived in Leeds. She worked in a chemist's. Fearby said that was fine. He could come and see her. Did she have a break? Oh, and one other thing. Did she have a photograph of herself? From that time? Could she bring it with her?

He met her outside on the pavement and walked with her to a coffee shop a few doors along. He ordered tea for himself and for her a kind of coffee with an exotic name. Although it was the smallest size, the foamy concoction looked enough for four people. Vanessa Dale was dressed in a dark red skirt over thick tights, ankle boots, and a brightly patterned shirt. He noticed she had a badge with her name on just above her left breast. He took out his pen and his notebook. You think you'll remember things, but you don't. That was why he wrote everything down, transcribed it, put the date beside each entry.

"Thank you for taking the time," he said.

"That's all right," she said.

"Did you manage to find an old picture?"

She opened her purse and took out two passport pictures, snipped from a set of four. He looked at it, then at her. The older Vanessa was plumper in the face, the hair long and dark. "Can I keep this?" he said.

"I'm not bothered," she said.

"Someone rang me," said Fearby. "Someone from the police. He said that you contacted them on the thirteenth of July 2004. Is that right?"

"I did contact the police once, years ago. I don't remember the date."

"Why did you ring them?"

"Someone gave me a fright. I called the police about it."

"Could you tell me what happened?"

Vanessa looked suspicious. "What's this about?"

"I told you, I'm writing a story. But your name won't come into it."

"It seems stupid now," said Vanessa, "but it was really creepy. I was walking back from the shops near where my parents lived. There was a bit of scrubland. There's a Tesco's there now. And a car pulled up. A man asked for directions. He got out of the car, and then he made a grab at me. He got me round the throat. I hit out and screamed at him, then ran away. My mum made me phone the police. A couple of them came round and talked to me about it. That was it."

"And it didn't feature in the trial."

"What trial?"

"The trial of George Conley."

She looked blank.

"Do you remember the murder of Hazel Barton?"

"No."

Fearby thought for a moment. Was this just another wrong turn? "What do you remember about your attack?"

"It was years ago."

"But a man tried to kidnap you," said Fearby. "It must have been a memorable experience."

"It was really weird," said Vanessa. "When it happened it was like a dream. You know when you have a really scary dream and then you wake up and you can hardly remember anything about it? I remember a man in a suit."

"Was he old? Young?"

"I don't know. He wasn't a teenager. And he wasn't an old man. He was quite strong."

"Big? Little?"

"Sort of average. Maybe a bit bigger than me. But I'm not sure."

"What about his car? Do you remember its color, its make?"

She screwed up her face in concentration. "Silver, I think. But I might be saying that because most cars are silver. Honestly, I can't remember anything, really. I'm sorry."

"Nothing?"

"I'm sorry, it was just a blur even then, and now it's seven years ago. I remember the man and the feeling of his hand on my throat and the car revving and revving, and that's all."

Fearby wrote everything—such as it was—in his notebook.

"And he didn't say anything?"

"He asked for directions, like I said. He may have said things when he was grabbing me. I don't remember."

"And you never heard back from the police?"

"I didn't expect to."

Fearby closed his notebook. "Well done," he said.

She looked puzzled. "What do you mean?"

"You fought him off."

"It wasn't like that," she said. "It didn't feel like me. It was like watching myself on TV." She picked up her phone. "I've got to get back."

TWENTY-ONE

Frieda didn't know New York: it was an abstract to her, a city of shadows and symbols, of steam rising from drains; a place of arrivals and scatterings.

She liked flying in when it was still dark, though dawn showed in a ribbon of light, so that everything was partially hidden from her, just a shifting pattern of massed buildings and pulsing lights, life glimpsed through windows. Soon she would see it laid out clear before her, its mystery resolving into plainness.

She hadn't told Sandy she was coming because she hadn't known that she was. It was early morning and he would still be in bed, so she did what she always did when she felt uncertain: she walked, following the map she had bought, until at last she was looking back at the skyline of Manhattan, which was at once familiar and alien. Frieda thought of her own narrow little house, surrounded by a network of small streets. There, she knew when a shop's shutters had been newly painted or a plane tree had been pruned. She thought she could have found her way blind to her front door. Suddenly, she felt almost homesick and could barely comprehend the instinct that had brought her here.

By seven o'clock she was in Sandy's neighborhood, but she hesitated to wake him yet. The day was cool and cloudy, with a blustery wind that threatened rain. Even the air smelled different here. She made her way up the street to a small café, where she ordered a coffee, taking it to one of the metal tables by the window that looked out onto the street. She was cold, tired, and full of a thick and mysterious trouble. She couldn't work out if this came from the events of the past weeks, or from being here, of being about to see Sandy again. She had missed him so, yet now she couldn't imagine seeing him. What would they say to each other, and what could possibly match the intensity of their separation? It occurred to her, with a force that made her flinch, as if she'd been hit hard in the stomach and winded, that perhaps she had come to end things with Sandy. Once the thought had occurred to her, it settled like lead in her stomach. Was that it, then?

The little room filled up with people. Outside, it began to drizzle, spat-
tering the window so the shapes in the street wavered and blurred. She felt
far from herself—here but not here, alone in a teeming city, invisible. The
gray sky made her feel as if she were underwater; the journey made time into
a kaleidoscope. Maybe she should leave before anything happened, pretend
she had never been here.

Sandy, walking past the deli on his way to the bakery on the corner where
he always bought freshly baked rolls for breakfast, glanced briefly at the
window of the café, then away again. But with a corner of his vision he had
caught sight of a face that reminded him of someone—and he looked back
again, and through the raindrops on the glass he saw her. She was sitting
with her chin resting in one hand, gazing straight ahead. For a moment, he
wondered if he was dreaming. Then, as if she could feel his eyes on her, she
turned her head. Their eyes met. She gave the smallest smile, drained her
coffee, stood up and left the café, emerging onto the street. He saw how she
still limped; how tired she looked. His heart turned over. She had a leather
satchel slung over her shoulder, but no other luggage.

"Christ. What are you doing here?"

"I've come to see you, obviously."

"Christ," he repeated.

"I was about to call you. I didn't want to wake you."

"You know me." He rubbed his unshaven cheek and stared at her. "Early
riser. What time is it for you?"

"I don't know. No time. Now."

"So you've just been sitting here, waiting?"

"Yes. What's in the bag?"

"Breakfast. Do you want some?"

"That would be nice."

"But, Frieda—"

"What? Is there some other woman in your flat?"

Sandy gave a shaky laugh. "No. No other woman in my flat just now."

He untied the belt of her raincoat and took it off her, hanging it on the hook
beside his own coat. She liked the way he took such care. He unzipped her
boots and took them off, pairing them against the wall. He led her to his
bedroom and closed the thin brown curtains, so the light became dim and
murky. The window was slightly open and she could hear the sounds of the

street; the day beginning. Her body felt soft and slack—desire and fatigue and dread plaited loosely together until she couldn't tell them apart. He peeled off her clothes and folded them, putting them on the wooden chair, then unclasped the thin necklace she was wearing and trickled it onto the windowsill. He ran his fingers over her scars, over her tired, stale, jet-lagged body. All the while she looked at him steadily, almost curiously, as if she were making up her mind about something. He wanted to close his eyes to her scrutiny, but couldn't.

Later, she had a shower while he made her coffee, strong and hot, and she drank it in bed with the thin sheet pulled over her.
    "Why did you suddenly decide to come?"
    "I don't know."
    "When are you here until?"
    "Tomorrow afternoon."
    "Tomorrow!"
    "Yes."
    "Then we have to make the most of the time we have."

Frieda slept, but shallowly, so that she heard Sandy make calls in the other room canceling arrangements while the sounds of the street entered her dreams. They walked through the neighborhood and bought cooking utensils for Sandy's flat and ate a late lunch in a deli. Sandy talked about work, people he'd met, Brooklyn, their summer plans. He mimicked colleagues, acted out scenarios, and she remembered the first time they'd met. She had thought him another of those doctors—maybe a surgeon, he had a surgeon's hands—self-possessed, amiable, charming when he wanted to be, with maybe a touch of the ladies' man about him. Not of interest to her. But then she'd heard his buoyant gust of laughter and seen how his smile could be wolfish, sardonic. He could be detached sometimes, anger made him mild and aloof, but at others he was almost womanly. He cooked meals for her with a delicate attention to detail; had a relish for gossip; tucked the sheet under the mattress with a hospital corner, the way his mother must have taught him while he was still little and, by his own account, fiercely shy.
    Only when Frieda was more relaxed did he ask her any questions. Frieda told him about the Lennox family, gave him news of her friends. They were both conscious that something lay ahead of them, some subject to be broached, and now they circled it cautiously, waiting.

"And that news story?" he asked.

"I don't want to talk about it."

"But I do. You're here for twenty-four hours. We have to talk about things like that."

"Have to?"

"You can't intimidate me with that voice, Dr. Frieda Klein."

"I didn't like it. Is that what you want to hear?"

"Did you feel humiliated?"

"I felt exposed."

"When you want always to be invisible. Were you angry?"

"Not like Reuben." She smiled at the memory. "Now he *was* angry. Still is."

"And did you feel that you acted improperly at all?"

Frieda scowled at him and he waited patiently.

"I don't think so," she said eventually. "But maybe I have to feel justified, or it would be too painful. But I really don't believe so. The man who came to me was a charlatan. He wasn't a psychopath, just acting out the part. Why should I have taken him seriously?"

"Did you know that at the time?"

"In a way. But that isn't really the point."

"What is the point?"

"The point is that what happened has set me off on something."

"What does that mean, set you off?"

"The man who came to me told me a story."

"I know that."

"No," Frieda said impatiently. "There was a story within the story, and I felt . . ." She stopped, considered. "I felt summoned."

"That's an odd word."

"I know."

"You have to explain."

"I can't."

"What was the story?"

"About cutting someone's hair. A feeling of power and tenderness. Something sinister and sexual. Everything else was sham, phony, but this felt authentic."

"And it summoned you?" Sandy was staring at her with a worried expression on his face that Frieda found infuriating. She looked away.

"That's right."

Nicci French

"But to *what?*"

"You wouldn't understand."

"Try me."

"Not now, Sandy."

They ate in a small fish restaurant a short walk from the flat. The wind had died down and the air smelled fresher. Frieda wore a shirt of Sandy's over her linen trousers. There was a candle between them, a bottle of dry white wine, hunks of bread, and olive oil. Sandy told Frieda about his first marriage—how it had become an aridly competent affair by the end. How they had wanted different things.

"Which were?"

"We imagined the future differently," said Sandy. He looked to one side. Frieda examined him. "You wanted children?"

"Yes."

A small, weighty silence wedged itself between them.

"And now?" she asked.

"Now I want you. Now I imagine a future with you."

At three in the morning, when it was as dark and as quiet as a great city ever gets, Frieda put a hand on Sandy's shoulder.

"What?" he murmured, turning toward her.

"There's something I should say."

"Shall I turn the light on?"

"No. It's better in the dark. I've asked myself if we should end this."

There was a moment of silence. Then he said, almost angrily, "So at the moment of most love and trust between us, you think of leaving?"

She didn't say anything.

"I never had you down for a coward," he said.

Still Frieda lay against him in silence. Words seemed futile.

"And what have you answered yourself?" he asked, after a while.

"I haven't."

"Why, Frieda?"

"Because I'm no good for anyone."

"Let me decide that."

"I am chock full of unease."

"Yes." His voice was soft again in the darkness, his hand warm on her hip. She could feel his breath in her hair.

"Dean's still out there. He's been to my father's grave—"

"What? How do you know?"

"Never mind that now. I know. He wants me to know."

"You're sure that—" She made an impatient movement, and he stopped.

"Yes, I'm certain."

"That's horrible and incredibly disturbing. But Dean can't get between the two of us. Why should you want to end things with us because of a psychopath?"

"When I said I felt summoned—"

"Yes."

"It feels a bit like going into the underworld."

"Whose underworld? Yours?"

"I don't know."

"Then, Frieda, don't go there. It was just a stupid story. It's your mood talking, the trauma you've been through. It's not rational. You're mistaking depression for reality."

"That's too easy to say."

"Can I ask you something without you closing down on me?"

"Go on."

"When your father killed himself and you found him"—he felt her stiffen—"you were fifteen. Did you ever talk to anyone about it?"

"No."

"And since then?"

"Not as such."

"Not as such. Don't you think that all this," he made an invisible gesture, "all this about Dean, about your work with the police, this new idea you've got about some story summoning you—all of this is just about you as a teenage girl finding your father hanging from a beam? Not saving him? And that's what you should be thinking of, rather than charging off on another rescue mission?"

"Thank you, Doctor. But Dean is real. Ruth Lennox was real. And this other thing . . ." She turned her body so that now she was lying on her back, gazing up at the ceiling. "I don't know what it is," she admitted.

"Stop all that you're doing. Stay here. Stay with me."

"You should be with someone who's happy." She added: "And who you can have children with."

"I've made my choice."

"But—"

"I've made my choice. If you want to leave me because you no longer love me, then I have to accept that. But if you want to leave me because you love me and it scares you, I won't accept it."

"Listen to me."

"No."

"Sandy—"

"No." He propped himself up on one arm and leaned over her. "Trust me. Let me trust you. I'll come into the underworld with you if you want. I'll wait for you at its entrance. But I won't be sent away."

"You're a very stubborn man."

Limb against limb; mouth against mouth; bodies losing their boundaries. Light spilling into darkness and dawn returning.

A few hours later, Frieda packed her toothbrush, checked her passport, said good-bye as if she were going round the corner to the newsagent. She'd always hated farewells.

TWENTY-TWO

t was the weekend, and Karlsson had canceled all arrangements so that he could spend two clear days with Mikey and Bella. His chest ached with the knowledge that in a few days they would be gone, far away from him, just photographs on his desk that he would stare at, tinny voices at the end of the phone, jerky images on Skype. Every minute with them felt precious. He had to stop himself holding Bella too close, stroking Mikey's hair until he squirmed away from him. They mustn't know how much he minded them going or feel anxious and guilty for him.

He took them to the pool at Archway, where there was a twisting slide into the deep end and wave machines that made them shriek with gleeful fear. He threw them up into the air, let them duck him, ride on his shoulders. He dived under the turquoise water, his eyes open, and saw their white legs thrashing around among all the other legs. He watched them as they raced into the shallow end, two squealing figures, their eyes pink from the chlorine.

They went to the playground, and he pushed them on the swings, spun the roundabout until he was dizzy, crawled through a long plastic tube behind them, and climbed up a pile of rubber tires. My children, he thought, my boy and girl. He held their smiles in his mind for later. They ate ice cream and went to lunch at a Pizza Express. Everywhere he looked, he seemed to see single fathers. He had made mistakes, he had always put work first, thinking he had no choice, and he had missed the bedtime rituals and the morning chaos. There had often been several days in a row when he hadn't seen his children at all, out before they woke and home after they slept, and had once flown home from holiday early. He had let his wife take up the slack, and he hadn't understood the consequences until it was far too late and there was no way back. Was this the price he had to pay?

They played a board game that he made sure he lost, and he showed them a very simple magic trick he'd learned with cards, and they shouted at him as if he were a wizard. Then he put on a video and the three of them sat on the sofa together, he in the middle, warm and full of sadness.

When the phone rang, he ignored it and at last it stopped. Then it rang again. Mikey and Bella looked at him expectantly and moved away, so he reluctantly stood up, went over to it, and picked it up from its holster.

"Yes?"

"It's Yvette."

"It's Sunday."

"I know, but . . ."

"I'm with my kids." He hadn't told her they were leaving. He didn't want anyone at work to know and pity him. They'd start inviting him out for drinks after work, stop thinking of him as the boss and think of him as a poor sap instead.

"Yes." She sounded flustered. "I just wanted to keep you in the loop. You told me I should."

"Go on."

"Ruth Lennox went somewhere before she went home: a flat near Elephant and Castle. We've managed to trace the landlord; he was away, so it took a bit of time. He seemed relieved to find that we were only contacting him about a murder," she added drily. "He confirmed that the flat was rented to a Mr. Paul Kerrigan, a building surveyor."

"And?"

"I talked to Mr. Kerrigan. And there's something up. I don't know what. He didn't want to talk over the phone. We're meeting him tomorrow morning."

There was a silence. Yvette waited, then said forlornly: "I thought you'd like to know."

"What time?"

"Half past eight, at the building site he's currently working on. The Crossrail development, down on Tottenham Court Road."

"I'll be there."

"Do you think—"

"I said I'll be there."

Karlsson put the phone back in its holster, already regretting his sharpness. It wasn't Yvette's fault.

Later, after Mikey and Bella had been collected by their mother and he'd gone for a run, he paced the garden with one of his illicit cigarettes. Birds were singing in the dusk, but that just made him feel sourer and more defeated. He went indoors and picked up the phone, then sat on the sofa where his children had been just a couple of hours previously. He held the phone and stared at it as if it could tell him something. At last, before he could change his mind, he called Frieda's number. He had to talk to someone, and she was the only person he could bear to unburden himself to. The phone rang and rang; he could almost hear it echoing in her tidy, empty house. She wasn't there. He called her mobile, although he knew that she almost never turned it on or even listened to messages left there—sure enough, it went straight to voice mail.

He closed his tired, sore eyes and waited for the feeling to recede. The thought of work was a relief from the thought of life.

"What was it like?" said Sasha, later that evening.

"When I got out of the tube," said Frieda, "on the way back from the airport, it was quite strange. For just a moment, London seemed different. It looked grubby and stunted and quite poor. It was like moving to the third world."

"I was really asking you about New York."

"You've seen the movies," said Frieda. "You've probably been there several times. You know what it's like."

"When I was asking you about New York, I was really asking you about Sandy."

"He thinks I should move there," said Frieda. "He says I should be somewhere that's less dangerous."

"And be with him."

"Yes. That too."

"Are you tempted?"

"I said no before," said Frieda. "Now—I don't know. I miss him. But I've got things to do here. Things that need finishing. Now, when am I going to meet this new man of yours?"

Frieda, are you safely home? Thank you for being here xxxx

TWENTY-THREE

At twenty past eight, Karlsson was standing on the edge of a vast crater in the heart of the city, looking at the activity in front of him: small diggers trundled across mashed earth, cranes lowered huge pipes into trenches, men in yellow jackets and hard hats gathered in groups or sat on top of machines, operating their articulated metal arms. Around the site were several Portakabins, some of them seeming almost as permanent as the buildings they were next to.

He saw Yvette walking toward him. She looked solid and competent to him, with her robust shoes and her brown hair tied tightly back. He wondered what he looked like to her: he felt fragile, incomplete. His head banged from the three whiskies he'd drunk last night, and his stomach felt hollow.

"Morning," she said cheerfully.

"Hi."

"He said he'd meet us in the office." Yvette jerked her head toward the main Portakabin, a few yards away, with wooden steps leading up to the door.

They made their way over the rutted ground and up the steps, then Yvette knocked at the door, which was opened almost at once. The man in front of them was also wearing a yellow jacket, although his was over a pair of brown corduroy trousers and a red cable-knit sweater that had a hole on the shoulder and appeared homemade. He was solidly built, with a creased face and brown eyes, and looked rather like a cuddly teddy bear, Yvette thought. Although he could only have been in his mid-forties, his thick hair was silver gray and stood up in comical tufts.

"Paul Kerrigan?"

"That's me." He had a soft Irish accent.

Yvette held up her ID. "I'm DC Yvette Long," she said. "We spoke on the phone. And this is DCI Malcolm Karlsson."

Karlsson looked into the man's brown eyes and felt a tremor of anticipation. He nodded at him.

"You'd better come in."

They entered the Portakabin, which smelled of wood and coffee. There was a desk in there, a trestle table, and several chairs. Karlsson sat to one side and let Yvette ask the questions. He already knew that they had reached a watershed: he could feel the inquiry shifting under their feet, turning into something altogether different and unexpected.

"We were given your name by Michael Reader."

"Yes." It wasn't a question.

"He said you rented thirty-seven A Shawcross Street from him and had done for almost ten years."

Kerrigan's eyes flickered. Karlsson looked at him closely.

"That's right. Since June 2001." He looked down at his large, calloused hands.

"The reason we're asking you is because we want to trace the last movements of Ruth Lennox, who was murdered twelve days ago. A taxi driver delivered her to that address on the day she died."

"Yes," he said again. He seemed passive and defenseless. He was simply waiting for the truth to emerge, lie in front of the three of them.

"Were you there?"

"Yes."

"You knew Ruth Lennox?"

There was a silence in the room. Karlsson listened to the sounds coming from the building site: the roar of engines and the shouts of the men.

"Yes," said Paul Kerrigan, very softly. They could hear the sound he made when he swallowed. "I'm sorry I didn't come before. I should have done. But I didn't see the point. She was dead. It was finished. I thought I could stop the hurt spreading."

"Were you having a relationship?"

He glanced from Yvette to Karlsson, then put both hands on the table in front of him. "I have a wife," he said. "I have two sons who are proud of me."

"You understand this is a murder inquiry," said Yvette. Her eyes were bright.

"Yes, we were having a relationship." He blinked, folded his hands together. "I find it hard to say that out loud."

"And you saw her on the day she was killed?"

"Yes."

Karlsson spoke at last. "I think perhaps you'd better tell us the whole story."

Paul nodded slowly. "Yes," he said. "But I . . ." He stopped.

"What?"

"I don't want anyone to know." He paused. "I don't know how to do this."

"Perhaps you can just tell us in chronological order what happened. Begin at the beginning."

He stared out of the window, as if he couldn't start while looking at them. His face, made for happiness, was sad and crumpled. "I met Ruth ten years ago. We live quite near each other. We met at fund-raising events for the mothers and toddlers." He smiled. "She was selling falafels, and I was helping with the lottery tickets in the next-door stall. We got on. She was very easy to get on with—everyone liked her. She was kind and practical and made you feel everything was going to be all right. I didn't know that at the time, of course. I just thought she was nice. You probably think that *nice* isn't a very romantic word. It wasn't that kind of affair." He made a visible effort and went on with the story: "We met after, for coffee. It just felt natural."

"Are you saying," interrupted Yvette, "that you and Ruth Lennox were lovers for ten years?"

"Yes. We got the flat after a few months. We chose that area because it wasn't somewhere we'd bump into anyone we knew. We never went to each other's houses. We met on Wednesday afternoons."

Yvette leaned forward. "You're saying that every Wednesday afternoon, for ten years, you and Ruth Lennox met at this flat?"

"Except when we were on holiday. Sometimes we couldn't make it."

"And no one knew?"

"Well, as a matter of fact my partner knows. I mean, my work partner. At least, he knows that every Wednesday I'm not available. He turns a blind eye. He probably thinks it's funny—" He stopped abruptly. "Nobody else knew anything. We were careful. Once or twice we'd see each other on a street near our homes and we'd ignore each other. Not even a smile. Nothing. We never phoned each other or sent each other messages."

"What if one of you had to cancel?"

"We'd tell each other the week before, if we could. If one of us went to the flat and the other hadn't turned up after fifteen minutes, we'd know something had happened."

"That all sounds very neat," Yvette said. "A bit cold-blooded."

He unplaited his hands. "I don't expect you to understand, but I love my wife, and Ruth loved her husband. We wouldn't have hurt them for the world. Or our kids. This was separate. Nobody would be affected. We never even talked about our families when we were together." He turned back to the window. "I can't believe I'll never see her again," he said. "I can't believe I won't go to the door and open it and she'll be standing there with her smiling face. I dream about her, and when I wake I feel so calm, and then I remember."

"We need you to tell us about that last Wednesday," said Yvette.

"It was the same as always. She came about half past twelve. I was already there. I always get there before her. I'd bought some bread and cheese for lunch and some flowers, which I'd put in a vase she'd bought the year before, and I'd put the heating on, because although it was a warm day, the flat felt a bit chilly."

"Go on."

"So." He seemed to find it hard to speak now. "She came and—do you need to know everything?"

"Just the bare facts for now. You had sex, I take it." Yvette sounded harsh, even to herself.

"We made love. Yes. Then we had a bath together before we ate the food. Then she left and I locked up and left about half an hour after her."

"What time would this be?"

"She left at about three, maybe a touch earlier, ten to three or something. Like she always did. So I left at three thirty or a quarter to four."

"Did anyone see you?"

"I don't think so. We never met the other people in the building."

"Do you know where she was going?"

"She always went home straight away."

"And you?"

"Sometimes I went back to work. That day I went home."

"Was your wife there?"

"No. She arrived at about six, I think."

"So you saw no one between leaving Shawcross Street and your wife arriving home two hours or so later?"

"Not that I remember."

"When did you hear about Ruth Lennox's death?" asked Karlsson.

"It was in the papers the next day. Elaine—my wife—showed me. Her photo was there, and she was smiling. At first I had this stupid idea that it was about us—that someone had discovered and put it in the papers. I couldn't speak. She said, 'Isn't this terrible? Did we ever meet her?'"

"And what did you say?"

"I don't know. Elaine said, 'Doesn't she have a nice face? Poor children.'

Things like that. I don't know what I said. It's all a blur now. I don't know how I got through the evening. The boys were there, and there was a general noise and bustle and they had their homework, and Elaine made a meal. Shepherd's pie. And I put it in my mouth and swallowed it. And I had a shower and just stood there for ages and nothing seemed real."

"Did you feel guilty?"

"What about?"

"About having an affair for ten years."

"No."

"Although you're married."

"I never felt guilty," he repeated. "I knew Elaine and the boys would never know. It wasn't hurting anyone."

"Did Ruth feel guilty?"

"I don't know. She never said she did."

"You are certain your wife didn't know?"

"I'd know if she knew."

"And Ruth's husband, Russell Lennox? Did he know anything or have suspicions?"

"No."

"Did Ruth Lennox tell you that?"

"She would have told me if he'd suspected, I'm sure." He sounded uncertain, though.

"And that day, did she seem any different?"

"No. She was the same as always."

"And how was that?"

"Calm. Cheerful. Nice."

"She was always calm and always cheerful and nice? For ten years?"

"She had ups and downs, like anyone."

"And was she up or down on that Wednesday?"

"Neither."

"Just in the middle, you mean?"

"I mean she was fine."

Yvette looked at Karlsson to see if he had any further questions. "Mr. Kerrigan," said Karlsson. "Your relationship with Ruth Lennox sounds oddly like a marriage to me, rather than an affair. Domestic, calm, safe." Placid, he thought, almost dull.

"What are you saying?" Now he looked angry. His hands curled into fists.

"I don't know." Karlsson thought of Frieda: what would she ask this man who was sitting passively in front of them, his shoulders slumped and his big hands restless? "You do understand this alters everything?"

"What do you mean?"

"You aren't stupid. Ruth Lennox had a secret. A great big secret."

"But nobody knew."

"You knew."

"Yes. But I didn't kill her! If you think that—look, I swear to you, I didn't kill her. I loved her. We loved each other."

"Secrets are difficult to keep," said Karlsson.

"We were careful. Nobody knew."

Karlsson took in Kerrigan's sad, uneasy face. "Is it possible that she was going to end it?"

"No. It's not possible."

"So nothing had changed."

"No." His face was swollen with misery. "Will they have to know?"

"You mean her husband? Your wife? We'll see. But it may be difficult."

"How long?"

"For what?"

"How long do I have before I have to tell her?"

Karlsson didn't answer. He looked at Paul Kerrigan's round, sweet-natured face for a few moments, then said, musingly, "Everything has a consequence."

TWENTY-FOUR

When Rajit Singh opened the door, he was wearing a heavy black jacket. "It's the heating," he said. "Someone was meant to come today to fix it."

"I'll only be a minute," said Frieda. "I won't even need to take my coat off."

He led her through to a sitting room in which every piece of furniture, the chairs, a sofa, a table, seemed to jar with everything else. On the wall was a picture of the Eiffel Tower in brightly colored velvet.

"Which therapist did you see?" asked Frieda.

Singh's face tightened. "Are you going to sue us?"

"No," said Frieda. "This is all for my benefit. Let's just say I'm curious."

"Look," said Singh, "we didn't have anything to do with that stuff in the newspaper. I thought it would appear in a psychology journal that no one would read and that would be the end of it. I don't know how that happened."

"It doesn't matter," said Frieda. "I'm not bothered with that. Just tell me about your part in it."

"I ended up with the therapist who passed the test. She's a woman called Geraldine Fliess. Apparently, she wrote some book about how we're all really psychopaths or something like that. Anyway, I went and saw her, gave the spiel about having been cruel to animals and that I had fantasies of hurting women. Later, she got back in touch with me, asking me who my doctor was and other things like that."

"I'm interested in the story you all told. Where did all the bits that had nothing to do with the checklist come from? Things like that story about cutting hair. What was that about?"

"What does it matter?"

Frieda thought for a moment and looked around her. The room wasn't just cold. There was a smell of damp. There didn't seem to be a single object that hadn't been left there by the landlord and that was the sort of stuff— abandoned, unloved—you'd pick up in car-trunk sales, house clearances.

"I think it's difficult to pretend to be a patient," Frieda said. "For most people, the difficult bit is to ask for help in the first place. Once they're sitting in a room with me, they've already made a painful decision. I think it's just as difficult to pretend to ask for help."

"I don't know what you're talking about."

"You probably don't want to hear this from me . . ."

"You know, I've got a feeling you're about to say something about me that isn't complimentary."

"Not at all. But I wonder if when you volunteered for this experiment, the chance to go to a therapist but not *really* go to a therapist, it gave you an opportunity to express something. A kind of sadness, a feeling of not being cared for."

"That is absolute crap. That's exactly what therapists like you do. You read things into what people say in order to give you power over them. And then if they deny it, it makes them look weak. What you're objecting to is the fact that you got involved in an experiment that showed you up. From what I've heard, you and Dr. Bradshaw have some kind of history, and if I've played some part in that, then I'm sorry. But don't suck me into your mind games."

"It doesn't look as if you live here," said Frieda. "You haven't hung up a picture, or put a rug down, or even left a book lying around. You're even dressed like you're outside."

"As you can feel for yourself, it's cold in here. When the man fixes the boiler, I promise you I'll take my jacket off."

Frieda took a notebook from her pocket, scribbled on a page, tore it out, and handed it to Singh. "If you want to tell me anything about what you said—I mean anything apart from the stupid Hare Psychopathy Checklist—you can reach me at that number."

"I don't know what you want from me," said Singh, angrily, as Frieda left the house.

Ian Yardley's flat was in a little alley just off a street market. Frieda pressed a buzzer and heard an unintelligible noise from a speaker, then a rattling sound. She walked up some carpeted stairs to a landing with two separate doors, labeled one and two. Door one opened, and a dark-haired woman peered out.

"I'm here to see—"

"I know," said the woman. "I don't know what this is about. You'd better come in. Just for a minute, though."

Frieda followed her inside. Yardley was sitting at a table, reading the evening paper and drinking beer. He had long curly hair and glasses with square, transparent frames. He was dressed in a college sweatshirt and dark trousers. His feet were bare. He turned and smiled at her.

"I hear you've been hassling people," he said.

"I think you called on my old friend Reuben."

"The famous Reuben McGill," he said. "I must say I was a bit disappointed by him. When I met him, he looked like someone who'd lost his mojo. He didn't seem to respond to what I was saying at all."

"How did you want him to respond?" said Frieda.

"What rubbish," said the woman, from behind her.

"Oh, sorry," said Ian. "I'm not being a proper host. This is my friend Polly. She thinks I shouldn't have let you in. She's more suspicious than I am. Can I offer you a drink? A beer? There's some white wine open in the fridge."

"No, thanks."

"Not while you're on duty?"

Frieda began to ask some of the same questions she'd asked Rajit Singh, but she didn't get very far because Polly kept interrupting her, asking what the point of all this was, while Ian just continued to smile, as if he were enjoying the spectacle. Suddenly he stopped smiling.

"Shall I make things clear?" he said. "If you're here out of some faintly pathetic attempt at revenge, then you're wasting your time. This was all cleared by the ethics committee in advance, and we were indemnified. I can show you the small print, if you're interested in reading it. I know it's embarrassing when it's demonstrated that the emperor has no clothes. If you're the emperor. Or the empress."

"As I've tried to explain," said Frieda, "I'm not here to argue about the experiment, I'm—"

"Oh, give us a fucking break," said Polly.

"If you'll just let me finish a sentence, I'll ask a couple of questions and then I'll leave."

"What do you mean, and then you'll leave? As if you had any right to be here in the first place! I've got another idea." Polly prodded Frieda on the shoulder. It was close to where she was still bandaged and made her flinch slightly. "You've been made a fool of. So deal with it. And just leave, because Ian has nothing to say, and you're starting to harass him and to get on my nerves." She started shoving Frieda as if she wanted to push her out of the flat.

"Stop that," said Frieda, raising her hands in defense.

"Time for you to go," shouted Polly, and pushed even harder.

Frieda put her hand on the woman's chest and pressed her back against the wall and held her there. She leaned close, so that their faces were only inches apart, and she spoke in a quiet, slow tone. "I said, 'Stop.'"

Yardley stood up. "What the hell's going on?"

Frieda turned, and as she turned, she took her hand away, then stepped back. She wasn't clear what happened next. She felt a flurry to the side of her. She sensed Polly flying at her, then stumbling over a low stool, and falling heavily across it.

"I can't believe this," said Yardley to Frieda. "You come here and you start a fight."

Polly started to struggle to her feet, but Frieda stood over her. "Don't you even think about it," she said. "Just stay where you are." Then she turned to Yardley. "I think Reuben understood you pretty well."

"You're threatening me," he said. "You've come here to attack me and to threaten me."

"That hair story had nothing to do with you, did it?" said Frieda.

"What hair story?"

"You're too much of a narcissist," said Frieda. "You wanted to impress Reuben, and he didn't go for it."

"What the fuck are you talking about?"

"It's all right," said Frieda. "I've got what I came for."

And she left.

Jim Fearby brought out a large map of Great Britain. There wasn't room for it on the wall, so he laid it out on the floor of the living room, with objects (a mug, a tin of beans, a book, and a can of beer) on each corner. He took off his shoes and walked across the map, staring down at it and frowning. Then he stuck a flagged pin-tack to the spot where Hazel Barton's body had been found, another where Vanessa Dale had been approached by the man in a car that had perhaps been silver.

He skewered her photograph onto the big cork noticeboard, next to Hazel Barton's picture. Two doesn't make a pattern—but it's a start.

TWENTY-FIVE

The only patient Frieda still saw was Joe Franklin. Many of the rest were waiting for her to return, sending her e-mails asking when she thought she would be well enough. Some she worried about. They jostled at the edge of her consciousness, with their pain and their problems. A few she thought perhaps she would never see again. She had said that in two weeks, at the start of May, she would resume her old duties whatever her doctor might advise, but in the meantime, twice a week and often more, she went to her rooms in the mansion block in Bloomsbury. Today, she had been grateful for the opportunity to leave her house because at a quarter to eight that morning, Josef had arrived. Frieda had left him trudging back and forth from the van, his face beaming at her behind piles of boxes.

After her session with Joe, Frieda stood with her back to the neat room, staring into the tangled space outside. She was thinking or at least letting thoughts run through her mind. Her old life seemed far away, a ghost of itself. The woman who had sat in the armchair hour after hour and day after day receded as she pictured her. She had always thought that the center of her life was in this room, but now it seemed to have shifted: Hal Bradshaw and his four researchers, Karlsson and his cases of death and disappearance, Dean Reeve somewhere out there watching her—all these had pulled her out of it.

She didn't know why she couldn't lay Bradshaw's stunt to one side. It prickled in her mind, shifted and changed in its meaning. There was something that wouldn't let her go, like a piece of string twitching in her hands. Sometimes at night, lying awake with the darkness pressing down on her, she would think of the four of them and what they had said to her. The blades opening and closing: the image of tenderness and dangerous power.

Her mobile rang in her pocket, and she took it out.

"Frieda."

"Karlsson."

"You turned your phone on."

"I can see why you became a detective."

He laughed, then said, "You were right."

"Oh, good. What about?"

"Ruth Lennox. She was too good to be true."

"I don't think I said that. I said she was like an actress performing her life."

"Exactly. We've found out that she was having an affair. For ten years. Every Wednesday. What do you say to that?"

"That it's a long time."

"There's more, but I can't talk about that now. I've got to go and see the husband."

"Did he know?"

"He must have done."

"Why are you telling me?"

"I thought you'd like to know. Was I wrong?"

"I don't know."

"Can I come round for a drink later? I can fill you in. It can help to talk things through with someone on the outside."

Something in his voice, the nearest he had ever come to pleading, stopped Frieda refusing.

"Maybe," she said cautiously.

"I'll be there at seven."

"Karlsson—"

"I'll call if I'm running late."

The Lennox family had moved back into their home. The carpet had been removed; the walls had been washed, though the bloodstains were still visible; the broken glass and scattered objects had been taken away.

When Karlsson and Yvette arrived, the door was opened for them by a woman wearing an apron. He could smell baking.

"We've met before," said the woman, noticing Karlsson's expression, "but you've forgotten who I am, haven't you?"

"No, I remember you." He recalled the baby in a sling, the little boy at her side, ashen with exhaustion, the girl pushing her buggy, as if she were trying to copy her mother.

"I'm Louise Weller. Ruth's sister. I was here on the day it all happened." She ushered them inside.

"Are you staying here?" said Karlsson.

"I'm looking after the family, as much as I can," she said. "Someone's got to. It won't get done by itself."

"But you have children of your own."

"Well, of course Baby's always here. My sister-in-law is helping out with the other two when they're not at their nursery. This is an emergency," she added reprovingly, as if he had forgotten that. She regarded him critically. "I suppose you're here to see Russell."

"You must have been close to your sister," said Karlsson.

"Why do you say that?"

"You're here helping her family even though you have small children of your own. Not everyone would do that."

"It's my duty," she said. "It's not hard to do one's duty."

Karlsson gave her a closer look. He felt she was telling him who was in charge. "Did you see much of your sister?"

"We live over in Fulham. My hands are full with my family, and we have very different lives. We saw each other when we could. And Christmas, of course. Easter."

"Did she seem happy?"

"What does that have to do with anything? She was killed by a burglar, wasn't she?"

"We're just trying to build up a picture of your sister's life. I was interested in her frame of mind. As you saw it."

"She was fine," said Louise, shortly. "There was nothing wrong with my sister."

"And she was happy in her family life?"

"Haven't we suffered enough?" she said, looking at Yvette and then back at Karlsson. "Are you digging around trying to find something nasty?"

Yvette opened her mouth to say something, but Karlsson flashed her an urgent look, and she stopped herself. Somewhere out of sight, the baby began to cry.

"I'd just got him to sleep." Louise gave a long-suffering sigh. "You'll find my brother-in-law upstairs. He has his own room at the top."

Russell Lennox's room was a little den at the back of the house that looked over the back garden. Karlsson and Yvette could barely squeeze inside. Yvette leaned on the wall to one side, next to a poster of Steve McQueen clutching a baseball glove. Lennox was sitting at a small pinewood desk, on which was a computer. The screensaver was a family group. They were posing by a blue sea, all wearing sunglasses. Karlsson reckoned it must have been taken a few years earlier. The children were smaller than he remembered.

Before speaking, he examined Lennox, assessing his condition. He seemed in control, clean-shaven, in an ironed blue shirt, evidently the work of his sister-in-law.

"How are you doing?" said Karlsson.

"Haven't you heard?" said Lennox. "My wife's been murdered."

"And I was expressing concern. I want to know how you are. I want to know how your children are."

Lennox replied in an angry tone but without meeting Karlsson's eyes. He just stared down at the carpet. "If you really want to know, Dora is scared to go to school, Judith cries all the time, and I can't talk to Ted at all. He just won't communicate with me. But I don't want your concern. I want all this brought to an end." Now he looked up at Karlsson. "Have you come to tell me about the progress of the investigation?"

"In a way," said Karlsson. "But I also need to ask you a few questions as well." He waited for a moment. He wanted to do this gradually, but Lennox didn't speak. "We're trying to build up a fuller picture of your wife's world." He glanced at Yvette. "Some of it may feel intrusive."

Lennox rubbed his eyes, like someone trying to wake himself up. "I'm beyond all that," he said. "Ask me anything you want. Do anything you want."

"Good," said Karlsson. "Good. So. Well, one question: would you describe your relationship with your wife as happy?"

Lennox started slightly, narrowing his eyes. "Why would you even ask that?" he said. "You were here when it happened. On the same day. You saw us all. You saw what it did to us. Are you making some kind of insane accusation?"

"I'm asking a question."

"Then I'll give you a simple answer, which is, yes, we were happy. Satisfied? And now I'll ask you a simple question. What's going on?"

"We've had an unexpected development in the inquiry," said Karlsson. As he spoke, he was aware of listening to himself and being repelled by what he heard. He was talking like a machine because he was nervous about what was going to happen.

Frieda handed him a mug of tea, and he took several sips before putting the mug on the table.

"Christ, I needed that," he said. "Just before I told him, I felt as though I was in a dream. It was as if I were standing in front of a large plate-glass window, holding a stone in my hand, round and solid like a cricket ball. I was about to throw it at the window, and I was looking at the glass, smooth and straight, knowing that in a few seconds it would be lying on the ground in jagged pieces." He stopped. Frieda was sitting down again with her own mug of tea, still untouched. "You can see that I'm getting better. I didn't tell you not to analyze the image, not to read hidden meaning into it. Except that I have now. But you know what I mean."

"How did he react?" said Frieda.

"You mean what happened when the stone hit the glass? It shattered, that's what. He was devastated. He'd lost his wife and it was as if I were taking her away from him all over again. At least he'd had the memory of her, and there I was contaminating it."

"You're sounding too much like a therapist," said Frieda.

"That's rich, coming from you. How can anyone be too much like a therapist?" He took another sip of tea. "The more like a therapist everyone is, the more they're in touch with their feelings, the better."

"The only people who should be like therapists are therapists," said Frieda. "And then only when they're at work. Policemen should be like policemen. So, to get back to my question, did he react in any way that was relevant to the investigation?"

Karlsson put his mug down.

"At first, he denied it absolutely and said how much he trusted her and that we'd made a mistake. Then Yvette spelled out in detail what we'd learned about Paul Kerrigan, about the flat, about the days when they met, about how long it had been going on. In the end, he saw reason. He didn't cry, he didn't shout. He just looked almost empty."

"But did you get the impression that he knew?"

"I don't know. I just don't know. How could it be possible? Ten years, eleven years. She was seeing this man, having sex with him. How did he not smell him on her? How did he not see it in her eyes?"

"You think he must have suspected, at least?"

"Frieda, you sit there day after day with people telling you their dark secrets. Do you ever just think that the clichés about relationships turn out to be true? What it's like to fall in love, what it's like to have a child, and then what it's like to break up. The old cliché, you can live with someone for years and then realize you don't know them."

"Who are we talking about now?" Frieda asked.

"Well, that was a bit of me, but it's mainly about Russell Lennox. What I hoped for, obviously, is that we'd tell him about the affair, he'd break down, confess everything, case closed."

"But he didn't."

"I should have brought you."

"You make me sound like a dog."

"I should have invited you to come. As a favor. I'd like you to have been there to see his face at the moment I told him. You notice these things."

"But Yvette was there."

"She's worse than I am, and I'm bloody awful. You should ask my ex-wife. She'd say that I didn't know what she was feeling, and I'd say that if she wanted me to know what she was feeling, she ought to tell me and . . . Well, you get the idea."

"If he could sit with you on the day of the murder," Frieda said, "and not break down, then today would be no problem for him. And I wouldn't have been any help to you."

"Do you miss it?" asked Karlsson. "Be honest."

Frieda was silent for a long time.

"I don't know," she said. "Maybe. Sometimes I catch myself, like when I heard about Ruth Lennox's secret life. But I tried to stop myself."

"Oh, God," said Karlsson, with a stab of alarm. "You're meant to be recovering and here I am, trying to drag you back into what nearly killed you."

"No! It's not like that at all. It's good to see you. It feels like a visit from the outside world. Some of the visits I have from the outside world are bad, but this is one of the good ones."

"Yes," said Karlsson. "Listen, Frieda. I've only just discovered about that bloody scam. I'd like to wring Hal Bradshaw's pompous neck."

"That probably wouldn't help my cause."

"He's got it in for you, hasn't he? You made him look bad, and he can't bear that, and he won't ever forget it. No wonder he's had such a smirk on his face recently."

"Are you saying he set the whole thing up just to get at me?"

"He's capable of it. If I had my way, I'd never have to listen to his drivel about the art of crime again. Unfortunately, the commissioner is a fan." He hesitated, then added, "Perhaps I shouldn't tell you this, but I'm going to anyway. At the beginning of the Lennox inquiry, I told the commissioner that I didn't want us to use Bradshaw anymore. I thought I was making an informal suggestion, but Crawford hauled Bradshaw in and made me repeat what I'd said in front of him. There's nothing he loves more than playing one person off against another."

"What's this got to do with me?"

"Bradshaw started slagging you off, so I defended you and said he was jealous of you because you'd made him look stupid. It's probably my fault for taunting him. I wish there was something I could do."

"There isn't. And if you think of something, please don't do it."

"I'm not going to have him getting his hands on the Lennox children, though."

"Are you going to tell them?"

"Yes. Although perhaps their dad will do it for me. Poor kids. First their mother gets murdered, and then their whole past gets demolished. You know the son already, don't you?"

"I've met him. Why are you looking at me like that?"

"I've got a proposition."

"The answer's no."

It was Riley who discovered all the bottles. They were in the small shed in the garden, which was full of the tiny lawnmower, spades, rakes, pruning shears, a large ripped tarpaulin, a wheelbarrow, a stack of empty plastic flowerpots, old jam jars, a box of bathroom tiles. Somebody had wanted them to remain hidden, for they were pushed into a corner behind the half-used tins of paint and had been carefully covered with a dust sheet. He looked at them for a while, then went to get Yvette.

Yvette pulled them out one by one and inspected them. Vodka, white cider, cheap whisky: alcohol to get drunk on, not to give pleasure. Were they the children's or the parents'? Old bottles or recent? They looked new. They looked secret.

TWENTY-SIX

Karlsson needed to find an appropriate adult. Often an appropriate adult for a juvenile is a parent, but in the case of the Lennox children, one of their parents was dead and the other was not at all appropriate in the circumstances. He thought about asking Louise Weller, Ruth's sister, to be present instead—but Judith Lennox said that she would prefer to *die* than talk about her mother in front of her aunt, and Ted had muttered about Louise getting off on the whole thing.

"She can't keep away," he said. "We don't want her or her cakes or her religion. Or her bloody baby."

So the appropriate adult was a woman nominated by Social Services, who turned up at the police station prompt and eager. She was in her early sixties, thin as a bird, bright-eyed, and glittering with nervous excitement. It turned out that this was her first interview ever. She'd done the training, of course, she'd read everything she could lay her hands on and, what was more, she prided herself on her gift for getting on well with young people. Teenagers were so frequently misunderstood, weren't they? Often, all they needed was someone to listen to them and be on their side, which was why she was here. She smiled, her cheeks slightly flushed.

"Very well," said Karlsson, doubtfully. "You understand that we will conduct three interviews, one after the other, with each of the Lennox children. The eldest, Ted, isn't strictly juvenile—he's just eighteen. As you know, you're simply there to make sure they're properly treated, and if you feel they need anything, you should say so."

"Such a painful and difficult age," said Amanda Thorne. "Half child and half adult."

"I'll conduct the interviews, and my colleague, Dr. Frieda Klein, will also be present."

When he had told Yvette that he was taking Frieda to talk to Ted, Judith, and Dora, not her, she had stared at him with such a reproachful expression that he had almost changed his mind. He could deal with her anger, not her distress. Her cheeks burned, and she mumbled that it was fine, perfectly all right, it was up to him and she understood.

Ted was first. He shuffled into the room, laces trailing, hair straggling, hems fraying, all rips and loose ends. His cheeks were unshaven and there was a rash on his neck; he looked unwashed and malnourished. He refused to sit, and stood by the window instead. Spring had come to the garden. There were daffodils in the borders and blossom on the fruit tree.

"Remember me?" said Frieda.

"I didn't know you were with them," he said.

"Thanks for agreeing to see us like this," said Karlsson. "Before we begin, this is Amanda Thorne. She's what is known as an appropriate adult. It means—"

"I know what it means. And I'm not a child. I don't need her here."

"No, dear," said Amanda, rising to her feet and crossing the room to him. "You're not a child. You're a young man who's been through a terrible, terrible event."

Ted gazed at her with contempt. She didn't seem to notice.

"I'm here to support you," she continued. "If there's anything you don't understand, you must tell me, and I can explain. If you feel upset or confused, you can tell me."

Ted looked down at her tilted, smiling face. "Shut up."

"What?"

"Shall we start?" Karlsson interrupted.

Ted folded his arms, stared jeeringly out of the window, and wouldn't meet their eyes. "Go on, then. Are you going to ask me if I know about my mum and her other life?"

"Do you?"

"I do now. My dad told me. Well, he started to tell me and then he was crying and then he told me the rest."

"So you know your mother was seeing someone else?"

"No. I just know that's what you think."

"You don't believe it?"

Ted unfolded his arms and turned toward them. "You know what I think? I think you'll get your hands on every bit of her life and make it ugly, dirty."

"Ted, I'm very sorry, but this is about a murder," said Karlsson. "You must see that we have to conduct a full investigation."

"Ten years!" The words were a shout, his face contorted with fury. "Since I was eight, and Dora was three. Did I know? No. How does it make me feel that it's all been a lie, a charade? How do you think?" He turned wildly to Amanda Thorne. "Come on, Appropriate Adult. Tell me what I must be feeling. Or you." He waved a dirty-nailed hand at Frieda. "You're a therapist. Tell me about it."

"Ted," said Frieda. "You need to answer the questions."

"You know what? Some of my friends used to say that they wished she was *their* mother. They won't say that now."

"Are you saying you had absolutely no idea?"

"Do you want to take a break?" Amanda Thorne asked.

"No, he doesn't," Karlsson said sharply.

"Of course I had no idea. She was the good mother, the good wife, the good neighbor. Mrs. fucking Perfect."

"But does it make sense to you now?"

Ted turned to Frieda. He seemed bony and brittle, as if he might crumble into a pile of sharp fragments if anyone touched him, tried to hold him. "What d'you mean?"

"You're suddenly and painfully having to see your mother in a new way—not the person everyone seems to describe as safe and calm and unselfish. Someone with another, radically different, side to her, with needs and desires of her own and a whole life she was leading in secret, separate from all of you—and I'm asking if in retrospect that makes any sense to you."

"No. I don't know. I don't want to think about it. She was my mum. She was . . ."—he closed his eyes for a moment—"comfy."

"Exactly. Not a sexual being."

"I don't want to think about it," he repeated. "I don't want the pictures in my head. Everything's poisoned."

He wrenched his body sharply away from them once more. Frieda sensed he was on the verge of tears.

"So," Karlsson's voice broke into the silence, "you're saying you never suspected anything."

"She was a terrible actor, useless at things like charades. And she couldn't lie to save her life. She'd go red and we'd all laugh at her. It was a family joke. But it turns out she was a pretty fantastic actor and liar after all, doesn't it?"

"Can you tell us about the day she was killed, Wednesday, the sixth of April?"

"Tell you what?"

"When you left home, what you did during the day, what time you returned. That kind of thing."

Ted gave Frieda a wild stare, then said: "OK. My alibi, you mean. I left home at the usual kind of time. Half eight, something like that. I had to be early at school, which is only a few minutes away, because I had my mock art exam. For which I just heard I got an A star, by the way." He gave a savage grin. "Brilliant, wasn't it? Then I was at school for the rest of the day. Then I met Judith, we hung about for a bit and came home together. And found police everywhere. Good enough for you?"

"Good enough."

Judith Lennox was next. She came through the door quietly as a ghost, staring at each of them in turn with her pale blue eyes. She had coppery curls and freckles over the bridge of her nose. Although her hair needed washing and she was dressed in old jogging pants with a baggy green jersey, which probably belonged to her father, down almost to her knees and with long sleeves covering her hands, she was obviously lovely, with the peachy bloom of youth that days of crying couldn't entirely conceal.

"I've nothing to say," she announced.

"That's quite all right, dear," murmured Amanda Thorne. "You don't need to say anything at all."

"If you think it was Dad, you're just stupid."

"What makes you say that?"

"It's obvious. Mum was cheating on him, so you think he must have found out and killed her. But Dad adored her, and anyway, he didn't know a thing, not a thing. You can't make something true just by thinking it."

"Of course not," said Karlsson.

Frieda considered the girl. She was fifteen, on the edge of womanhood. She had lost her mother and lost the meaning of her mother; now, she must fear that she could lose her father as well. "When you found out about your mother—" she began.

"I came home with Ted," said Judith. "We held hands when we found out." She gave a small sob. "Poor Ted. He thought Mum was perfect."

"And you didn't?"

"It's different for daughters."

"What do you mean?"

"He was her darling boy. Dora was her sweet baby. I stole her lipstick—well, I didn't, really. She didn't go in much for makeup or stuff. But you know what I mean. Anyway, I'm the middle child."

"But you're sure that no one knew?"

"That she was cheating on Dad all that time? No. I still don't really believe it." She rubbed her face hard. "It's like a film or something, not like real life. It's not the kind of thing she would do. It's just stupid. She's a middle-aged woman, and she's not even that attractive—" She broke off, her face twisting. "I don't mean it like that, but you know what I'm saying. Her hair's going gray and she has sensible underwear and she doesn't bother with what she looks like." She seemed suddenly to realize that she was talking about her mother in the present tense. She wiped her eyes. "Dad didn't know anything, I promise," she said urgently. "I swear Dad didn't suspect a thing. He's gutted. Leave him alone. Leave us alone."

The interview with Dora Lennox wasn't really an interview. She was scrawny and limp and exhausted, smudged from all her weeping. Her father had grown years older in the days since his wife had died, but Dora had become like a tiny child again. She needed her mother. She needed someone to gather her up and cradle her in loving arms, make all the horror go away. Frieda laid a hand on her damp, hot head. Amanda Thorne cooed and told her everything was going to be all right, seeming not to grasp the idiocy of her words. Karlsson stared at the girl, his brow furrowed. He didn't know where to start. The house was too full of pain. You could feel it prickling against your skin. Outside, the daffodils glowed in the warm brightness of spring.

When Yvette asked Russell Lennox about the bottles, he just stared at her as if he hadn't understood a word.

"Do you know who put them there?"

He shrugged. "What's that got to do with anything?"

"Perhaps nothing, but I need to ask. There were dozens of bottles hidden in the shed. There might be a harmless explanation, but it suggests that someone was drinking secretly."

"I don't see why. The shed's full of junk."

"Who uses the shed?"

"What do you mean?"

"Who goes into it? Did your wife?"

"It wasn't Ruth."

"Or perhaps your son and his friends—"

"No. Not Ted."

"Did you put the bottles there?"

The room filled with silence.

"Mr. Lennox?"

"Yes." His voice rose, and he looked away from her, as though he couldn't bear to meet her gaze.

"Would you say—" Yvette stopped. She was no good at this. She asked questions too harshly. She didn't know how to sound clear yet nonjudgmental. She tried to imagine Karlsson asking the questions. "Do you have a drink problem?" she asked abruptly.

Russell Lennox jerked his head up. "No, I don't."

"But those bottles . . ." She thought about the white cider: nobody would drink that if they didn't have a problem.

"People think that because you drink, you have a drink problem, and they think if you have a drink problem you have a larger problem underneath." He spoke rapidly, his words running together. "It was just a stupid phase. To help me through. I put them in the shed because I knew everyone would say what you're saying now. Make it shameful. It was simpler to hide it. That's all. I was going to throw them away when I got the chance."

Yvette tried to separate out his sentences. "To help you through what?" she asked.

"It. Stuff." He sounded like his son.

"When did you go through this phase?"

"Why?"

"Recently?"

Russell Lennox put his hand to his face, half covering his mouth. He made an indistinct sound through his fingers.

"Are you still drinking?"

"Are you my GP now?" His words were muffled. "Do you want to tell me it's not good for me? Do you think I don't know that? Perhaps you want to tell me about liver damage, addiction, the need to acknowledge what I'm doing and seek help."

"Were you drinking because of problems in your marriage?"

He stood up. "Everything is evidence to you, isn't it? My wife's private life, my drinking too much."

"A murder victim doesn't have a private life," said Yvette. "They both seem relevant to me."

"What do you want me to say? I drank too much for a bit. It was stupid. I didn't want my kids to know, so I hid it. I'm not proud of it."

"And you say it wasn't for any particular reason?"

Russell Lennox was gray with weariness. He looked malnourished, older and younger than his real age. He sat down again opposite Yvette, slumping in his chair. "You're asking me to make everything neat. It wasn't like that. I'm getting older, my life felt stale. Sex—well, there wasn't much of that, and I—" He suddenly started to stammer, his face growing red. "It's a problem lots of middle-aged men have."

"You were impotent?" Yvette wasn't good at asking intimate questions. Her face flushed as red as his.

"Not impotent, no! Just it wasn't so easy anymore. Maybe that's what started me drinking in the first place, and then, well—nothing changing. No excitement. Maybe Ruth was feeling the same thing."

"Perhaps," said Yvette. "But did your wife know you were drinking?"

"What's that got to do with her being dead? Do you think I killed her because she found out my guilty secret?"

"Did she?"

"She suspected. She had a nose for people's weaknesses."

"So she knew."

"She smelled it on me. She was pretty contemptuous—that's a bit rich, isn't it, with what she was doing at the same time?"

"Which you still claim you had no knowledge of."

"I don't *claim*. I had no knowledge."

"And you still say you had a good marriage?"

"Are you married?"

Yvette felt a violent blush heat her neck and face. She saw herself through his eyes—a solid, brown-haired, clumsy, lonely woman with big feet and large ringless hands. "No," she replied shortly.

"No marriage looks good when you start searching for the fault lines. Until now, I would have said that, although we sometimes wrangled and sometimes took each other for granted, we had a good solid marriage."

"And now?"

"Now it doesn't make sense. It's been smashed apart, and I can't even ask her why."

. . .

Frieda had only just arrived home when there was a ring at the door. She opened it to find two police officers, a man and a woman.

"Are you Dr. Frieda Klein?" asked the man.

"Did Karlsson send you?"

The two officers looked at each other.

"I'm sorry," said the man. "I don't know what you mean."

"Well, what are you here for?"

"Can you confirm that you are Dr. Frieda Klein?"

"Yes, I can. Is something wrong?"

The officer frowned. "I have to inform you that we need to interview you in connection with an alleged case of assault causing actual bodily harm."

"What case? Is this something I'm supposed to have witnessed?"

He shook his head. "We're responding to a complaint that names you as the perpetrator."

"What on earth are you talking about?"

The female officer looked down at her notebook. "Were you present at flat four, number two Marsh Side on the seventeenth of April?"

"What?"

"It is currently occupied by Mr. Ian Yardley."

"Oh, for God's sake," said Frieda.

"You admit you were present?"

"Yes, I admit I was present but—"

"We need to talk to you about this," said the man. "But we can't do it on the doorstep. If you wish, we can take you to an interview room."

"Can't you just come in so that we can sort it out?"

"We can come in and put a few questions to you," said the man.

In their bulky uniforms, the two of them made Frieda's house seem smaller. They sat down awkwardly, as if they were unused to being inside. The man took off his hat and laid it on the arm of the chair. He had curly red hair and pale skin.

"It's been reported that there was an incident," he said. He took a notebook from the side pocket of his jacket, slowly opened it and inspected it, as if he were seeing it for the first time. "I need to inform you from the outset that we are investigating a case of common assault and also a case of assault causing actual bodily harm."

"What actual bodily harm?" said Frieda, trying to remain calm. The officer looked back down at his notebook.

"A complaint has been made by Mr. Ian Yardley, the owner of the flat, and by Polly Welsh. Now, at this point I need to warn you that you are not under arrest and that you are free to stop the interview at any time. And I also need to tell you that you do not have to say anything but it may harm your defense if you do not mention when questioned something that you later rely on in court. Anything you do say may be given in evidence." When he had finished this small speech, the officer's pale skin reddened. Frieda was reminded of a small boy reciting a speech at a school assembly. "We always have to say that."

"And that I'm entitled to a lawyer."

"You've not been arrested, Dr. Klein."

"What was the 'actual bodily harm'?" asked Frieda. "Was she injured?"

"I believe there was bruising and some medical attention was needed."

"Does that count as actual bodily harm?" said Frieda.

"It is alleged," said the woman, "that psychological harm was caused. Sleep problems. Distress."

"Psychological harm," said Frieda. "Is it possible that Dr. Hal Bradshaw was connected with the assessment?"

"I can't comment on that," said the man. "But you admit that you were present at the incident."

"Yes," said Frieda. "Haven't they waited rather a long time to report it?"

"From what I've heard," said the man, "Miss Welsh was at first too traumatized to talk about it. She needed reassurance and treatment before she was able to come forward. We're trying to be more sensitive in our response to women who suffer violence."

"Well, that's a good thing," said Frieda. "Do you want to know what happened?"

"We would be interested in your version of events, yes," said the man.

"I arranged to see Ian Yardley to ask him some questions," said Frieda.

"You were angry with him, I understand. You felt humiliated by him."

"Is that what he said?"

"That's what our inquiries suggest."

"I wasn't angry with him. But his friend . . ."

"Miss Welsh."

"She was aggressive as soon as I arrived. She jabbed at me and tried to push me out of the flat. I pushed back. When she tried to retaliate, I think she fell over a chair. It all happened very quickly. And then I left. End of story."

The man looked down at his notebook.

"One report claims that you pushed Miss Welsh against a wall and held her there. Is that accurate?"

"Yes, that's right. She started pushing me. I told her to stop, and when she wouldn't, I pushed her against the wall. But not roughly. Just to make her stop. Then I let her go and she came at me and fell over. I wasn't even touching her."

"She just fell," said the woman.

"That's right."

The man looked back at his notes. "Do you have a history of fighting in public?"

"What do you mean?"

He turned a page. "You know a man called James Rundell?" he said. "We've heard something about a fight in a restaurant, significant damage done. And it ended with your being arrested."

"Where did you hear about that?"

"It's information we've received."

"What's the relevance?"

"We're just trying to establish a pattern. And isn't James Rundell involved in this case as well?"

"The two cases have nothing in common," said Frieda. "And there was no fight in Ian Yardley's flat."

Suddenly the man glanced round, like a dog that had caught a scent. "What's that?" he said.

It was the banging from upstairs in the bathroom. It had become so much a part of Frieda's life that she had almost stopped hearing it. "Do you really need to know?" she said. "After all, I've got an alibi. I'm down here with you."

The female officer frowned at her. "There's nothing funny about violence against women," she said.

"That's it," said Frieda. "I'm done. If you want to charge me, then go ahead. Otherwise, we have nothing left to talk about."

With a grimace of concentration, the man wrote several lines of notes, then closed his book and stood up. "Between ourselves," he said, "if I were you, I would talk to a solicitor. We've put weaker cases than this one in front of a jury. But even if we don't, you might well be facing a civil case."

When they were gone, Frieda sat for several minutes staring in front of her. Then she looked through her address book and dialed a number. "Yvette," she said. "Sorry, it's Frieda. Have you got a moment?"

. . .

Thank you for your letter. I carry it around with me. It's so like you to write a real letter—on good-quality paper, in ink, with proper grammar and no abbreviations. I can't remember the last time anyone sent me a letter. My mother, maybe, years ago. She used to write to me on very thin airmail paper, gummed down. I could never read her tiny, cramped handwriting.

My mother, yours. All the things we've never told each other yet. I think we need to spend a month in a lighthouse, with rough seas all round us. Make up for all the lost time. Sandy xxxx

TWENTY-SEVEN

Yvette and Karlsson walked together from the Lennoxes' house to the Kerrigans'. It took less than ten minutes. Yvette struggled to keep pace with his long stride. She had a bad cold: her throat was sore, her glands ached, and her head throbbed. Her clothes felt tight and itchy.

The house was smaller than Ruth and Russell's, a redbrick terraced building up a narrow side street, with a tiny front garden that had been graveled over. Elaine Kerrigan opened the door before the chime had died away. She stood before them, a tall woman with a long pale face and fading hair caught up in a loose bun; glasses hung round her neck on a chain. She was wearing an oversized checked shirt over loose cotton trousers. The sun caught her as she gazed at them, and she raised her hand—wedding ring and engagement ring on the fourth finger—to shield her from its dazzle.

She knows, Yvette thought. Her husband must have sat her down and told her.

She led them into the living room. Sun streamed through the large window and lay across the green carpet and the striped sofa. There were daffodils on the mantelpiece, doubled by the mirror. Yvette caught a glimpse of her own face there—flushed and heavy, with dry lips. She licked them. Elaine Kerrigan took a seat and gestured for them to do the same. She laid her long, delicate hands in her lap and sat up straight.

"I've been thinking about how to behave," she said, in a voice that was low and pleasant, with a faint burr of an accent that Yvette couldn't place. "It all seems unreal. I know I'm the wronged wife, but I can't feel that yet. It's just so . . ." She looked down at her hands, lifted her eyes again. "Paul doesn't seem the sort of man someone would choose to have an affair with."

"When did he tell you?" asked Yvette.

"When he came back yesterday. He waited till his tea was on the table and blurted it out. I thought he was joking at first." She grimaced. "It's mad, isn't it? It can't be happening to me. And this woman's dead. Did he say that I was the one who told him about it? I saw the story in the paper. I thought she had a nice face. I wonder if she thought about me when it was all happening."

"We know it must be a shock," said Yvette. "Obviously we need to establish people's movements on the day that Ruth Lennox died."

"You mean my husband's? I can't remember. I've looked in the diary but the page is blank. It was just another Wednesday. Paul says he was definitely here at the time, but I don't remember if I came home from work first or if he did. I can't remember if he was later than usual. If something unusual had happened, I suppose it would have stuck in my mind."

"What about your sons?"

She turned her head. Following her gaze, Karlsson and Yvette saw the photograph next to the daffodils of two boys, young men even, both with dark hair and their father's broad face. One had a scar above his lip that pulled his smile slightly awry.

"Josh is at university in Cardiff. He hadn't come back for Easter by then. The other, Ben, he's eighteen and he takes his A levels this year. He lives at home. He's a bit vague about dates. And everything else. I haven't told them yet about the affair. After that, I can tell them about the murder. That'll be fun. How long was it for?'

"Sorry?"

"How long had the affair been going on?"

"Your husband didn't tell you?"

"He said it was more than a fling, but he still loved me and he hoped I would forgive him."

"Ten years," said Yvette, calmly. "They met on Wednesday afternoons. They rented a flat."

Elaine Kerrigan sat up even straighter. Her face seemed to loosen, the skin grow slack. "Ten years." They could hear her swallow.

"And you didn't know?"

"Ten years, with a flat."

"And we will also need to conduct a search here," said Yvette.

"I understand." Elaine Kerrigan's voice was still polite, but it had become faint.

"Have you noticed nothing unusual in his behavior?"

"Over the last ten years?"

"Over the last few weeks, perhaps."

"No."

"He hasn't been upset or distracted?"

"I don't think so."

"You didn't know that several hundreds of pounds have been

disappearing monthly from your husband's bank account to pay for the rooms he rented?"

"No."

"You never met her?"

"The other woman?" She gave them a tired half smile. "I don't think so. But she lived near here, didn't she? Maybe I did."

"We would be grateful if you could try to find out exactly what time you and your husband came home on the Wednesday—ask colleagues at work, perhaps."

"I'll do my best."

"We'll see ourselves out."

"Yes. Thank you."

She didn't stand up as they left, but stayed sitting upright on the sofa, her long face blank.

"Do you want a drink?" Yvette asked Karlsson, trying to sound casual—as if she didn't care one way or the other. She heard her voice grate.

"I'm taking the rest of the day off, and I won't be in tomorrow, so I . . ."

"Fine. Just a suggestion. There was something I wanted to mention. Frieda rang me."

"What about?"

As Yvette described the details of Frieda's police interview, Karlsson started to smile, but finally he just looked weary.

"I said she should talk to you about it, but she said you'd probably had enough of her. You know, after that last time with Rundell."

"What is it with her?" said Karlsson. "There are nightclub bouncers who get into fewer fights than she does."

"She doesn't always choose them."

"Yes, but they seem to happen wherever she goes. Anyway, she rang you. You'd better make a couple of calls."

"I'm sorry. I didn't mean to bother you with it."

Karlsson hesitated, looking at her flushed face. "I didn't mean to snap. I'm spending the time with my kids," he said gently. "They're going away soon."

"I didn't know—how long for?"

He found he couldn't tell her. "Quite a long time" was all he could manage. "So I want to make the most of this."

"Of course."

. . .

Mikey had had his hair cut very short; it was like soft bristle; his scalp showed through and his ears stuck out. Bella's hair had been cut as well, so it was a mass of loose curls around her face. It made them seem younger and more defenseless. Karlsson felt too tall and solid beside them. His heart swelled in his chest and he stooped down and held them against him. But they squirmed free. They were excited; their bodies throbbed with impatience. They wanted to tell him about the flat they were going to live in, which had balconies on both sides and an orange tree in the courtyard. A fan in every room, because it was very hot in the summer. They'd got new summer clothes, shorts and dresses and flip-flops. It hardly ever rained there—the rain in Spain falls mainly on the plain. There was an outdoor pool a few streets away, and at the weekends they could get a train to the coast. They would have to wear a uniform to their new school. They already knew some words. They could say, *"¿Puedo tomar un helado por favor?"* and *"Gracias"* and *"Mi nombre es Mikey, mi nombre es Bella."*

Karlsson smiled and smiled. He wanted them never to leave and he wanted them to be gone already, because waiting to say good-bye was the worst thing of all.

TWENTY-EIGHT

The following morning when Frieda received Rajit Singh's call, she arranged to meet him in her rooms, which stood empty for so many hours of the week now, the red armchair abandoned. Later in the day she had to see Joe Franklin, so she could stay on for that, stand for a while at the window that overlooked the deserted and overgrown building site, sifting through the rubble of her thoughts. She walked as swiftly as her injured leg would allow through the narrow streets, the familiar clutter of shops. She had the sensation of following a thread, as thin as a spider's, through a dark and twisting labyrinth. She didn't know why she couldn't let go of the story: it had been a fake tale, crudely obvious, designed to trip her up and make her look foolish and incompetent. She should feel enraged, humiliated, exposed; instead, she felt troubled and compelled. She woke in the night, and her thoughts, drifting up from the mud of her dreams, snagged on the story. There was a faint but insistent tug on the thread.

Singh arrived promptly. He was still wearing his thick black jacket—in fact, he seemed to be wearing the same clothes that Frieda had last seen him in. His face sagged with weariness, and he sat heavily in the chair opposite her, as if this were indeed a therapy session.

"Thank you," he said.

"What for?"

"For seeing me."

"I think I was the one who asked you to contact me."

"Yeah, but we fucked you over, didn't we?"

"Is that how it feels?"

"I don't know about the others, but I felt a bit crap about all the coverage."

"Because you felt what you did was wrong?"

"It seemed a good idea at the time. I mean, how can therapists be checked? Teachers have inspectors, but therapists can do whatever damage they want in the privacy of their little rooms and no one's to know. And if patients don't like it, then the therapist can just turn it back on them: if you don't like it, it's because there's something wrong with you, not me. It's a self-justifying system."

"That doesn't sound like you. It sounds like Hal Bradshaw speaking. Which doesn't mean it's wrong. There is a problem about checking up on therapists."

"Yeah, well, but when it got all that attention, it felt wrong. Everyone found it funny, and then when I met you . . ." He stopped.

"I didn't seem quite as crazy as Bradshaw said I was?"

Singh shifted in his seat uncomfortably. "He said you were a loose cannon. He said you—and people like you—could do a lot of damage."

"So he set out to check us?"

"I suppose that's how he sees it. But that's not why I'm here. There's nothing I can do about that. You said I should get in touch if there was anything I wanted to say."

"And there is?"

"Yeah. I guess. I'm, um, how do I put it? Not in the best place right now. As you noticed. I don't like my work as much as I thought I would—I thought it would be more seminars and discussions and research in groups and stuff, but mostly it's just me on my own, grubbing away in the library."

"Alone."

"Yeah."

"And you're alone in your personal life as well?"

"You're probably wondering why this has anything to do with the story," he said.

"Tell me."

Singh looked down at the floor. He seemed to be pondering something.

"I was in a relationship," he said at last. "For a long time—well, a long time for me, anyway. I haven't had so much—well, anyway, that's irrelevant. We were together a year and a half, pretty much. Agnes, she was called. *Is* called. She hasn't died. But it didn't go well or end well or whatever. But that's not what I came here to say. The thing is, it was Agnes who gave me the detail about cutting the hair. I don't know why you're so interested in it. The whole thing was just a story. But I was writing up the notes for everybody and thought it needed a touch of color, and it came into my mind. I've no idea why. So I put it in."

"So your ex-girlfriend gave you the story about cutting her father's hair?"

"I wanted to tell you so that you'd see it's not a big deal. It was just a stupid story. And random—it just occurred to me and I used it. I could have used anything—or nothing."

"Did you change any of the details?"

"I can't really remember." He winced. "We were lying in bed, and she was stroking my hair and saying it had got really long and could do with a cut. And did I want her to cut it for me. Then she said this thing about her father—or I think it was about her father. I don't remember that bit. It could have been someone else. But she talked about holding the scissors and how that gave a feeling of power and tenderness at the same time. I suppose it stuck in my mind because it all felt so intimate. Though she never did cut my hair."

"So the story was your ex-girlfriend's memory?"

"Yes."

"Agnes."

"Agnes Flint—why? Do you want to talk to *her* now?"

"I think so."

"I don't get it. Why's it so important? We made a fool of you. I'm sorry. But why does any of this matter?"

"Can I have her number?"

"She'll just tell you the same as I have."

"Or an e-mail address would do."

"Maybe Hal was right about you after all."

Frieda opened her notebook and unscrewed the cap of her pen.

"I'll tell you, if you tell her she's got to answer my calls."

"She won't answer your calls just because someone else tells her to."

Singh sighed heavily, took the notebook, and scribbled down a mobile number and an e-mail address. "Satisfied?"

"Thanks. Do you want my advice?"

"No."

"You should go for a run—I saw some running shoes in your living room—then have a shower and shave and put on different clothes and leave your cold little flat."

"Is that it?"

"For a start."

"I thought you were a psychotherapist."

"I'm grateful to you, Rajit."

"Will you tell Agnes I said—?"

"No."

Jim Fearby had breakfast in the service station next to the hotel he had stayed in the night before: a minipack of corn flakes, a glass of orange juice from the tall plastic container in which a plastic orange bobbed unconvincingly, a mug of coffee. He returned to his room to collect his overnight bag and brush his teeth, watching breakfast TV as he did so. He left the room, as always, looking as if nobody had stayed there.

His car felt like home. After he had filled up with gas, he made sure he had everything he needed: his notebook and several pens, his list of names, with numbers and addresses written neatly next to some of them, the folder of relevant information he had prepared the day before, the questions. He wound down the window and smoked a cigarette, his first of the day, then set the satnav. He was just nineteen minutes away.

Sarah Ingatestone lived in a village a few miles from Stafford. He had rung her two days ago and arranged to meet her at half past nine in the morning, after she had taken her two dogs for their walk. They were terriers—small, sharp, unfriendly yapping creatures that tried to bite his ankles as he stepped from the car. He was tempted to knock them on their snouts with his briefcase, but Sarah Ingatestone was watching him from the front door, so he forced a smile and made enthusiastic noises.

"They won't do any harm," she called. "Coffee?"

"Lovely." He sidestepped a terrier and went toward her. "Thanks for agreeing to see me."

"I'm having second thoughts. I Googled you. You're the one who got that man George Conley out of prison."

"I wouldn't say it was all me."

"So he can go and do it again."

"There's no evidence that—"

"Never mind. Come in and take a seat."

They sat in the kitchen. Sarah Ingatestone made instant coffee while Fearby arranged his props in front of him: his spiral-bound notebook, which was identical to the one he'd had all those years ago as a junior reporter, his sheaf of papers in the pink folder, the three pens side by side, although he always used his pencil for shorthand. They didn't speak until she'd put the two mugs on the table and taken the chair opposite him. He looked at her properly for the first time: graying hair, cut mannishly short, gray-blue eyes in a face that wasn't old, but yet had sharp creases and furrows in it. Worry lines, not laugh lines, thought Fearby. Her clothes were old and shabby, covered with dog hair. She was called Mrs. Ingatestone, but there was no sign of a Mr. in this house.

"You said this was about Roxanne."

"Yes."

"Why? It's been over nine years, nearly ten. No one asks about her any more."

"I'm a journalist." Best keep it vague. "I'm following up some queries for a story I'm involved in."

She folded her arms, not defensively but protectively, as if she were waiting for a series of blows to fall upon her. "Ask away," she said. "I don't mind what it's for, really. I like saying her name out loud. It makes her feel alive."

So it began, down the list of questions, pencil moving swiftly, making its hieroglyphic marks.

How old was Roxanne when she disappeared?

"Seventeen. Seventeen and three months. Her birthday was in March—a Pisces. Not that I believe in that. She would be—she is—twenty-seven years old now."

When did you last see your daughter?

"The second of June 2001."

What time?

"It would have been around half past six in the evening. She was going out to see a friend for a quick drink. She never came back."

Did she go by car?

"No. It was just down the road, no more than ten or fifteen minutes' walk."

By road?

"Yes. A quiet lane most of the way."

So she wouldn't have taken a shortcut—over fields or anything?

"Not a chance. She was all dressed up—in a little skirt and high heels. That's what we argued about actually—I said she wouldn't be able to walk five yards, let alone a mile or so, in that garb."

Did she ever arrive at the friend's?

"No."

How long did the friend wait before alerting anyone?

"Apparently she tried phoning Roxanne's mobile after about forty-five minutes. I didn't know anything about it until the next morning. We—my husband and I—went to bed at about half past ten. We didn't wait up." Her voice was flat. She laid down the answers like cards, face up on the table.

Were you living here when Roxanne disappeared?

"No. But nearby. We moved when—after—well, my husband and I separated three years after. We just couldn't— It wasn't his fault, more mine if anything. And Roxanne's sister, Marianne, went too, to university, but she doesn't come home much, and I don't blame her. And, of course, Roxanne never came back. I waited as long as I could in a house that everyone else had left, and at last I couldn't stand it any longer. I used to put hot water bottles in her bed when it was cold, just in case. So I came here and got my dogs."

Can you please show me where you used to live on this map?

Fearby pulled it out from the folder and spread it on the table. Sarah Ingatestone put on her reading glasses, peered at it, then put her finger on a spot. Fearby took one of his pens and made a small ink cross.

You say you had argued?

"No. Yes. Not seriously. She was seventeen. She had a mind of her own. When I told them, the police thought—but that's not true. I know." She pressed her hands tightly together, stared at him fiercely. "She wasn't one to bear a grudge."

Do the police believe she's dead?

"Everyone believes she's dead."

Do you believe she's dead?

"I can't. I have to know she's coming home." The face quivered, tightened again. "Do you think I shouldn't have moved? Should I have stayed where we'd all lived together?"

Can you describe Roxanne? Do you have a photo?

"Here." Glossy shoulder-length brown hair; dark eyebrows; her mother's gray-blue eyes but set wider in her narrow face, giving her a slightly startled look; a mole on her cheek; a large, slightly crooked smile—there was something asymmetrical and frail about her appearance. "But it doesn't do her proper justice. She was little and skinny but so pretty and full of life."

Boyfriend?

"No. Not that I knew of. She'd had boyfriends before but nothing serious. There was someone she liked."

And her character? Was she shy or outgoing, for instance?

"Shy, Roxanne? She was ever so friendly—bold, you could even say. She always said what was on her mind and could have a bit of a temper—but she'd go out of her way to help people. She was a good girl, really. A bit wild, but she had a good heart."

Would she have talked to a stranger?

"Yes."

"Would she have got into a car with a stranger?

"No."

When Fearby got up to go, she clutched his arm. "Do you think she's alive?"

"Mrs. Ingatestone, I couldn't possibly—"

"No. But do you? If you were me, would you think she was alive?"

"I don't know."

"Not knowing is like being buried alive myself."

Jim Fearby pulled over in a lay-by and took out his list of names. One was already crossed out. Next to Roxanne Ingatestone's name, however, he put a tick. No, he didn't think she was alive.

TWENTY-NINE

Joe Franklin had been more cheerful than for a long time, but Frieda knew that he moved through repeating cycles of depression. For months he would be heavy, gray, and defeated, barely able to go through the motions of living, often incapable of making it to her rooms or of uttering a word when he got there. The deathly numbness would lift and, for a while, he would emerge into a brighter world, exhausted and relieved. But he always got sucked back into the black hole of himself. Coming to see her was his way of holding on to a corner of life, but it was also his comfort blanket.

Frieda had often felt during her own therapy that she was standing in the desert, under the blowtorch of the sun, parched and bleached and unforgiven, with nowhere to hide. Joe, however, crept into her room like an animal into a lair. He hid from himself, and perhaps she allowed him to do that in a way that wasn't necessarily helpful. Solace, not self-knowledge. Yet how much should we face ourselves full on?

As she was thinking these things, making her notes after the session, with the spring sun slanting through the window and lying in a blade across the floor, her mobile vibrated in her pocket. She took it out: Sasha.

"I'm about to leave work. Are you free?"

"Yes."

"Can I come and see you?"

"All right. I'll be home in about half an hour—is that good?"

"Perfect. I'll bring a bottle of wine. And Frank."

"Frank?"

"Is that OK?"

"Of course."

"I feel a bit nervous—as if I'm about to introduce him to my family. I want you to like him."

Frieda walked to her house in the soft dying day. Petals of blossom lay on the pavement. She thought about Rajit Singh and the story he had told that was someone else's story; tonight, she would send a message to Agnes Flint. And she thought about Joe and then about the happiness she had heard in Sasha's voice. As she unlocked her front door, she wondered how long it would be before she could have a hot bath again, with no dust swirling through her rooms.

The door stuck against something and she frowned, then squeezed through the narrow opening into her hall. There were two large bags there, blocking the entrance. There was a jacket lying on the floor beside them. There were voices and laughter coming from her kitchen. She could smell cigarette smoke. She pressed the light switch, but no light came on.

"Hello?" she called, and the voices ceased.

"Frieda!" Josef appeared in the kitchen doorway. He was in his work clothes, but held a brimming glass of vodka, and he seemed to have trouble walking in a straight line. "Come in and join."

"What's going on? Whose are these bags?"

"Hello, Frieda." Chloë appeared beside Josef. She was wearing what looked to Frieda like a jersey, but presumably was meant to be a dress, because there was no skirt underneath it. Her face was smeary with smudged makeup and she, too, was holding a glass of vodka. "I'm so grateful to you. So, so grateful."

"What do you mean, you're grateful? What have I done? Jack!" Jack was coming unsteadily down the stairs. "What's going on? Is this a party?"

"A gathering," Jack said, looking sheepish. "Chloë told me to come over."

"Did she now? And why don't the lights work?"

"Ah." Josef took a hasty swig of his vodka. "Electrical problems."

"What does that mean? Are these your bags, Chloë?"

"Frieda," a voice roared cheerfully.

"Reuben? What's Reuben doing here?"

Frieda strode past Josef and Chloë into the kitchen. Lit candles had been placed on the windowsills and surfaces, and smoke hung in blue clouds. There was an open vodka bottle and an ashtray with several butts stubbed out in it. The cat clattered through the cat flap and wound itself around Frieda's legs, mewing piteously for attention. Reuben, his shirt half unbuttoned and his feet up on the chair, raised his glass to her.

"I came to see my good friend Josef," he said. "And my good friend Frieda, of course."

Frieda yanked open the back door to let the smoke out. "Will someone tell me what's going on? First of all, why don't the lights work? What have you done?"

Josef looked at her with a wounded expression and put both palms upward. "The wires have been cut by a mistake."

"You mean, 'I cut the wires.'"

"Complicated."

"Why are your bags in the hall, Chloë? Are you going somewhere?"

Chloë gave a scared giggle, then a hiccup. "It's more like I've arrived," she said.

"What?"

"I've come to stay with you."

"No, you have not."

"Mum's on a rampage. She's booted poor Kieran out, too, and she hit me with a hairbrush. I can't live with her, Frieda. You can't make me."

"You can't live here."

"Why not? I've nowhere else to go."

"No."

"I can sleep in your study."

"I'll ring Olivia."

"I'm not going back there. I'd prefer to be on the streets."

"You can stay with us," said Reuben, magnanimously. "It'd be fun."

"Or with me," put in Jack. "I've got a double bed."

Frieda looked from Reuben to Josef to Jack, then back at Chloë. "One night," she said.

"I won't get in your way. I'll cook for us."

"One night, so you won't need to cook. And there's no bath and no light anyway."

The doorbell rang.

"That'll be Sasha," said Frieda. "Pour three large vodkas."

Frank was quite short, solid, with his hair cut close to his scalp and dark melancholy eyes, with a slight cast in one so that he seemed to be both looking at Frieda and past her. His handshake was firm, his manner almost shy. He was wearing a beautifully cut suit and carrying a briefcase because he'd come straight from work.

"Come in," said Frieda. "But be warned—it's mayhem."

THIRTY

think I should be present," said Elaine Kerrigan.

"He's eighteen years old," said Yvette, firmly. "He counts as an adult."

"That's ridiculous. You should see his bedroom." There was a pause. "You wait here. I'll get him."

Yvette and Munster sat in the living room and waited. "Do you ever think," she asked, "that we just go around and make things worse? In the great scheme of things. That in the end, when we're done, the general level of happiness is a bit less than it was before?"

"No, I don't," said Munster.

"Well, I do."

The door opened and Ben Kerrigan came in. Yvette first saw his stockinged feet, with odd socks, one red, one with green and amber stripes, a big toe poking through the end. Then she saw faded gray corduroy trousers, a flowery blue shirt, long floppy dark brown hair. He sank onto the sofa, one leg pulled up beside him. He pushed his hair back off his face.

"You've heard about your father and this woman," said Yvette, after they'd introduced themselves.

"A bit."

"How did it make you feel?"

"What do you think?"

"You tell me."

"I wasn't exactly happy about it. Does that surprise you?"

"No, it doesn't. Were you angry?"

"Why should I be?"

"Because your father was being unfaithful to your mother."

"It doesn't matter what I feel."

"Could you tell us where you were on Wednesday, the sixth of April?"

Ben looked puzzled, then grimly amused. "Are you serious?"

"Yes."

"All right, then. I'm a schoolboy. I was at school."

"And you can prove that?"

He gave a shrug. "I'm in the sixth form. We go out sometimes, if we've got a free period. We might go for a coffee or, you know, a walk."

"But not for the whole day," said Yvette. "And when you have coffee, you have it with someone. You have a walk with someone. And they can vouch for you?"

"I don't know. Maybe. Maybe not."

"Hang on," said Munster. "What you need to do first is take this seriously. A woman has been killed. Some children have lost their mother. We don't want to waste our time chasing up false leads. So, what we want you to do is, first, to show us some respect, and second, pull your finger out, look through your diary or your phone, talk to your friends, and put together a convincing story of what you were doing for every minute of that Wednesday. Because if we have to do it ourselves, we won't be very happy about it. Do you understand?"

"Whatever," said Ben. "So is it just me? Are you going to hassle Josh as well?"

"Your brother was a hundred and fifty miles away, so far as we know, but we'll check up with him."

"Can I go now?" said Ben. "I've got homework to do."

When they were back in the car, Yvette asked if they could make a diversion via Warren Street.

"Is this about Frieda?" said Munster.

"Why shouldn't it be about Frieda?"

"I was just saying."

When Frieda opened the door, Yvette noticed over her shoulder that there were people there. She recognized Josef but no one else. For a few seconds, the two women stared at each other, then Frieda stepped back and invited Yvette in. She shook her head.

"Why did you call me about the charge?" she asked.

"If it's a problem," said Frieda, "just say."

"I didn't mean that." Yvette glanced round to see if Munster was listening, but he was oblivious in the front seat of the car with his headphones on. "Since your injury, we hadn't talked properly."

"We hadn't talked at all."

"Yes, well." Yvette bit her lip. "Anyway, I hadn't said things I meant to say. So when you rang, I didn't know how to interpret it."

"You don't need to interpret it," said Frieda. "I told you about it on the phone. I thought Karlsson was sick of clearing up my messes."

"And now it's my turn?"

"As I said, if it's a problem . . ."

"I called the police down at Waterloo. Look, Frieda, what you did wasn't sensible. All right, that bastard Bradshaw set out to humiliate you. If it were me, I'd want to go and sort him out. But you can't do things like that. If you do, you leave yourself open to all kinds of trouble."

"So you think I'm in trouble?"

"I talked to the officer you saw. I explained about our relationship with you, things you've done for us. So I think this will go away."

"Yvette, this was all rubbish."

"I'll take your word for it. But if these things get into court, you just never know which way they'll go. And another thing: you don't want to put yourself into the power of someone like Bradshaw."

"Thank you," said Frieda. "Really. I hope you haven't gone out on a limb for me. But I just want you to know that when I went to see Ian Yardley, it wasn't anything to do with Bradshaw."

"Then what was it about?"

"I don't know," said Frieda. "Just a feeling."

"I get worried about your feelings."

Frieda began to close the door, then hesitated. "What was it you wanted to say to me? I mean, apart from my so-called fight."

Yvette looked at the people behind Frieda. "Some other time," she said.

THIRTY-ONE

osh Kerrigan was making rolled cigarettes, adding thick tufts of tobacco to the Rizla paper, rolling it deftly between thumb and forefinger, licking the edge, and laying the thin, straight tube beside the others he'd already assembled. He had six so far and was on to his seventh. Yvette was finding it hard to concentrate on what he was saying. Perhaps that was the point: he was making it quite clear that she was simply an interruption. She was getting a bit tired of these Kerrigan boys.

"Josh," she said, "I can understand why you might be upset—"

"Do I seem upset?" He passed the Rizla over the tip of his tongue.

"But I'm afraid I'm not going until you've answered my questions."

"No. You're fine." He laid the seventh cigarette beside the others and tapped it into line with a finger, tipping his head on one side to examine them. He had a small vertical scar just above his lip that pulled it up slightly, giving him the suggestion of a perpetual smile.

"Where were you on Wednesday, the sixth of April?"

"Cardiff. Is that a good enough alibi?"

"It's not an alibi at all yet. How can you prove you were in Cardiff then?"

"Wednesday, the sixth of April?"

"Yes."

"I have lectures on Wednesdays, until five. I don't think I could have got back to London in time to murder my father's lover, do you?"

"You didn't have lectures that Wednesday. Your term had ended."

"Then I was probably out somewhere."

"You need to take this more seriously."

"What makes you think I'm not?"

He started on the next cigarette. At least there wasn't much tobacco left in the tin, only enough for one or two more.

"I want you to give proper thought to where you were on that Wednesday and who you were with."

He lifted his head and Yvette saw the glint of his brown eyes. "I was probably with my girlfriend, Shari. We got together at the end of term, so it was pretty intense. The things you're finding out about the sex life of the Kerrigan family."

"You think or you know?"

"I'm a bit hazy on dates."

"Don't you have a diary?"

"A diary?" He grinned as if she had said something unintentionally funny. "No, I don't have a diary."

"When did you return to London for the holidays?"

"When? At the end of that week, I think. Friday? Saturday? You'll have to ask Mum. I know I was back by the Saturday because there was a party. So it was probably the Friday."

"Did you come back by train?"

"Yes."

"So you can look at the ticket or your bank statement to confirm the date."

"If I paid by card. Which I'm not sure about."

He had finished the tobacco at last. One by one he delicately lifted the cigarettes and put them into the empty tin. Yvette thought his hands were trembling, but perhaps she was imagining things: his expression gave nothing away.

"Did you have any idea about your father's affair?"

"No."

"What do you feel about it?"

"Do you mean, am I angry?" he asked mildly, one dark eyebrow lifting. "Yes. Especially after all Mum's gone through. Am I angry enough to kill someone? I think if I was going to kill anyone, it'd be my dad."

"I really don't think I can help you."

Louise Weller was still wearing an apron. Maybe she lived in it, he thought. She must always be clearing up messes or cooking meals, scrubbing floors, helping her children splash paint onto sheets of paper. He saw that her shirt sleeves were rolled up.

"How old are your children?" he asked, following his train of thought.

"Benjy's thirteen weeks old." She looked down at the baby asleep on the bouncy chair beside her, eyes twitching in dreams. "Then Jackson is just two, and Carmen is three and a bit."

"You do have your hands full." Karlsson felt tired just thinking of it and at the same time dizzy with a kind of nostalgia for those days of mess and tiredness. For one brief moment, he let himself think of Mikey and Bella in Madrid, then blinked the image away. "Does your husband help?"

"My husband is not a healthy man."

"I'm sorry to hear that."

"But they're good children," said Louise Weller. "They're brought up to behave well."

"I'd like to ask you a few general questions about your sister."

Louise Weller raised her eyebrows. "I don't see why. Someone broke in and killed her. Now you have to find out who. You seem to be taking your time about it."

"It might not be as simple as that."

"Oh?"

Karlsson had spent years in the Met. He'd told mothers about children dying; he'd told wives about their husbands being murdered; he'd stood on countless doorsteps to deliver bad news, watching faces go blank with the first shock, then change, crumple. Yet he still felt queasy about telling Louise Weller that her sister had lived a double life. Ridiculous as it was, he felt that he was betraying the dead woman to the prim-mouthed living one.

"Your sister," he said. "It turns out that she had a complicated life."

Louise Weller didn't move or speak. She just waited.

"You don't know about it?"

"I don't know what you're talking about."

"Has Mr. Lennox not said anything?"

"No, he hasn't."

"So you had no idea that Ruth might have had a secret she was keeping from her family?"

"You're going to have to tell me what you're referring to."

"She was having an affair."

She made no response. Karlsson wondered if she'd even heard. Finally she spoke. "Thank goodness our mother never lived to find out."

"You didn't know anything about it?"

"Of course I didn't. She would have known how I would feel about it."

"How would you have felt about it?"

"She's a married woman. She has three children. Look at this nice house. She never did know how lucky she was."

"What do you mean by that?"

"People are very selfish nowadays. They put freedom before responsibility."

"She's dead," Karlsson said mildly. He suddenly felt the need to defend Ruth Lennox, though he wasn't sure why.

The baby woke, his face crinkled, and he gave a piteous yelp. Louise Weller lifted him up and calmly unbuttoned her shirt, placing him at her breast and casting Karlsson a bright look, as if she wanted him to object.

"Can we talk about the specifics?" Karlsson said, trying neither to look at the naked breast nor away from it. "Your sister, Ruth, who has been killed and who was having an affair. You say you had no idea?"

"No."

"She never said anything to you that, now you think about it, might have suggested there was something going on?"

"No."

"Does the name Paul Kerrigan mean anything to you?"

"Is that his name? No. I've never heard it."

"Did you ever see any sign that there was a strain in her marriage?"

"Ruth and Russell were devoted to each other."

"You never got the impression that there was any problem?"

"No."

"Did you notice that he was drinking heavily?"

"What? Russell? Drinking?"

"Yes. You didn't see that?"

"No, I did not. I have never seen him drunk. But they say that it's the secret drinkers who are the problem."

"And you had no sense at all, looking back, that he knew?"

"No." Her eyes glittered. She wiped her hands down her apron. "But I wonder why he didn't tell me when he discovered."

"It's not something that's easy to say," said Karlsson.

"Do his children know?"

"Yes."

"And yet they haven't shared it with me. Poor things. To find that out about your mother." She looked at Karlsson with distaste. "Your job must be like lifting up a stone. I don't know how you have the stomach for it."

"Someone's got to do it."

"There are things it's better not to know about."

"Like your sister's affair, you mean?"

"I suppose everyone will find out now."

"I suppose they will."

Back in his flat, Karlsson tidied away the last of the mess his children had made. He found it hard to believe he had ever been irritated by it. Now it simply filled him with tenderness—the miniature plastic figures embedded in the sofa, the wet swimming things on the bathroom floor, the pastel crayons that had been trodden into the carpet. He stripped both their beds and pushed the sheets into the washing machine, and then, before he had time to stop himself, called Frieda's number. He didn't recognize the person who answered.

"Hello. Who's this?"

"Chloë." There was a terrific banging going on in the background. He could barely make out her words. "Who are you?" she asked.

"Malcolm Karlsson," he said formally.

"The detective."

"Yes."

"Do you want me to call Frieda?"

"It's all right. It can wait."

He put the phone down, feeling foolish, then called another number.

"Hello, Sadie here."

"It's Mal."

Sadie was the cousin of a friend of Karlsson's whom he had met a few times over the years, with his wife, or with Sadie's current boyfriend. Their last meeting had been at a lunch a few weeks ago, both on their own, when, leaving at the same time, she had said that they ought to meet up, have a drink.

"Can I offer you that drink?" he said now.

"How lovely," she said, and he was reminded of what he had always liked about her: her straightforward enthusiasm, her undisguised liking for him. "When?"

"How about now?"

"Now?"

"But you're probably busy."

"As it happens, I'm not. I was just worrying that my hair needs washing."

He laughed, his spirits lifting. "It's not a job interview."

They met in a wine bar in Stoke Newington and drank a bottle of white wine between them. Everything was easy. Her hair looked fine to him, and so did the way she smiled at him, nodded in agreement. She wore bright, flimsy layers of clothes and had put lipstick on. He caught a whiff of her perfume. She put her hand on his arm when she spoke, leaned in close. Her breath was on his cheek and her pupils were large in the dimly lit room.

They went back to her flat because he didn't want to be in his, even though it was closer. She apologized for the mess, but he didn't mind that. He was a bit fuzzy from the wine and he was tired and all he wanted to do was to lose himself for a while.

She took an opened bottle of white wine from the fridge door and poured them each a glass. She looked up at him, expectant, and he leaned down and kissed her. As they undressed, he couldn't stop thinking what a long time it had been since he had done this. He closed his eyes and felt her against him, her soft skin, took in the smell of her. Could it really be this easy?

Paul Kerrigan wasn't exactly drunk, but after three pints and no food since the cheese sandwich he hadn't finished at lunch, he was blurry, hazy, a bit adrift. Theoretically, he was on his way home, but he really didn't want to go there, to see his wife's thin, sad face, his sons' hostile, derisive stares. He was like a stranger in his own house, a hated impostor. So now he walked slowly, feeling the weight of his heavy body with each step he took, the thump of blood in his aching head. He needed to make sense of all that had happened, but this evening everything felt like an effort and thoughts were sludge in his brain.

One month ago, Ruth had been alive and Elaine had known nothing, and his boys had been full of teasing affection for him. Each morning when he woke, he had to realize all over again that the old life was over.

He reached the corner of his road and stopped. The pub was disgorging its drinkers onto the pavement in a burst of noise. He didn't hear the footsteps behind him, or turn in time to see who it was who brought something heavy down on the back of his head, so that he reeled, stumbled, fell in an ungainly heap onto the road. The blow came again, this time on his back. He thought how that would hurt later. And so would his cheek, which had scraped along the tarmac when he fell. He could taste blood, and there was also grit in his mouth. Through the roar in his head, he could hear the pub-goers, like distant static. He wanted to call out for help but his tongue was swollen and it was easier to close his eyes and wait for the footsteps to recede.

At last, he struggled to his feet and blundered along the street to his front door. He couldn't make his fingers hold the key, so he knocked and knocked until Elaine opened it. For a moment she stared at him, as if he were a monster standing in front of her, or a madman. Then her hand flew to her mouth in a cartoonish gesture of horror that he would have found funny in his safe old life.

. . .

"I didn't do it." Russell Lennox's eyes were bloodshot. He had the sweet, stale smell of alcohol on him. Since the bottles had been found hidden in the garden shed, he seemed to have taken to drink in earnest—almost as if, now the secret was out, he had given himself permission.

"It would be understandable if . . ."

"I didn't do anything. I was here. Alone."

"Can anyone confirm that?"

"I told you I was."

"You seem to have had a fair bit to drink."

"Is that illegal?"

"The man who was having an affair with your wife has been badly beaten up, not ten minutes from your house."

"He had it coming to him. But I didn't do it."

That was all he'd say, over and over, while Dora peered through the banisters at him, her face small and pale in the darkness.

Frieda lay in bed and tried to sleep. She lay quite straight, staring at the ceiling, and then she turned onto her side, rearranging the pillow, closing her eyes. The cat lay at her feet. She put an image in her mind, of a shallow river running over pebbles, but the water bubbled and the faces rose from the bottom. Thoughts stirred in the mud of her mind. Her body was sore.

It was no good. She could hear Chloë downstairs. She was talking to someone on Skype and had been for what seemed like hours, sometimes loudly and emphatically, with occasional bursts of laughter. Or was she crying? Frieda looked at the time. It was nearly one o'clock, and tomorrow Chloë had school and she herself had a whole day to get through. She sighed and got out of bed, tweaking her curtains back to see the half-moon and then going down the stairs.

Chloë looked up from her computer guiltily. Frieda saw the image of Ted Lennox there, his peaky adolescent face staring out at her. She stepped back, out of range. "I didn't know you were still awake."

"I don't want to be."

"I need to talk to Ted."

"You were talking rather loudly. And I think it's time for you to go to bed."

"I'm not sleepy."

"Go to bed, Chloë. You have classes tomorrow." Frieda stepped forward so that she could see Ted and Ted could see her. He looked dreadful. "You, too, Ted."

"Can I have some tea first? With just a small amount of milk," Chloë asked.

"This isn't a hotel."

"Sorry." Chloë didn't sound sorry. She grimaced into her computer screen and raised her eyebrows dramatically at Ted.

"Take your things up with you. And don't touch anything in my study."

She returned to her room, but for a long while she didn't get into her bed. Instead she stood at the window, gazing out at the night.

THIRTY-TWO

When Karlsson woke, he wasn't sure where he was. He shifted in the bed and felt the warmth, saw the edge of a shoulder and thought, she's come back. And then he remembered and felt a lurch, and it was as if the color had leached out of the world. He fumbled for his watch and found it still on his wrist. It was twenty to six. He lay back in the bed. There was a murmur of something he couldn't make out from Sadie beside him. Wasn't this what he had been wanting? Something uncomplicated, easy, affectionate, pleasurable? An ache started in his head and spread through his body. He felt an immense, disabling tiredness. Very cautiously, he edged himself out of the bed and started to dress.

"You don't have to run away," said Sadie, from behind him.

She had pulled herself up and was leaning on one elbow. Her face was puffy from sleep. "I could make you some breakfast," she said. She looked kind and concerned.

"I've really got to go," said Karlsson. "I need to get back and get changed and go into work. I've really got to rush."

"I can get you a tea or a coffee."

"That's all right."

Karlsson felt a sudden sense of panic, so that he was almost choking. He pulled his trousers on and fastened them. It all seemed to be taking a long time and he sensed Sadie watching him, a character in an unfunny farce. He pushed his shoes on. They felt too small for his feet. He picked up his jacket and turned to her. She was lying in the same position.

"Sadie, I'm sorry, I . . ." He couldn't think what else to say.

"Yes, all right." She turned away from him and twisted the duvet around her so that he could see only the back of her head. He saw her bra draped over the end of the bed. He thought of her putting it on yesterday morning and then taking it off last night. He had an impulse to sit down, pull the duvet back and tell Sadie everything, explain what he was feeling, why this was all wrong, why they were wrong for each other and why he was wrong for anyone. But that wouldn't be fair to her. He'd already done enough.

He came out onto the quiet street. There was a hum of traffic, but the main sound was birdsong all around him, with a blue sky and early morning sunshine. It felt wrong. It should have been raining and gray and cold.

Frieda sat at her kitchen table while Josef boiled the kettle, ground coffee, washed up the remains of Chloë's breakfast. A good thing about Josef—and she had to hang on to the good things, in the middle of everything else—was that she didn't have to make conversation. So she could just sit at the table and stare in front of her. Finally, he put the mug of coffee in front of her and sat down with his own mug.

"Is difficult to help," he began. "There is a Ukrainian joke about three people helping old lady across the road. And a person say, Why take three people? And they say, Because the old lady not want to cross the road." He took a sip from his coffee. "Is funny in Ukrainian."

"So where are we?" said Frieda.

"It is finished today, even if I kill myself to finish it. This evening you will have a bath in your own beautiful bath."

"Good," said Frieda.

"And Chloë? She is staying here?"

"I don't know," said Frieda. "I need to find out what's going on. We'll see."

Josef looked at Frieda with a concerned expression. "You are not angry," he said. "You should be angry."

"What do you mean?"

Josef gestured around him. "I tried to make you better with your new bath, but it is difficult to help. And I make things worse for you."

"It wasn't your fault—"

"Stop. The bath didn't come, then came and went away again. And the electricity stopped."

"Now that *was* irritating."

"You need help and I make it worse for you and now Chloë is here. I saw upstairs and there is her things everywhere in your study."

"Is there? Oh, God, I haven't been up there. Is it bad?"

"Is bad. There is girl things and clothes all over your things. Apple cores too. Wet towels. Mugs growing things inside. But I am saying, you should be angry. You should be hitting out. Fighting, no?"

"I'm not angry, Josef. Or maybe I'm too tired to be angry." She relapsed into silence. "But that bath had better be done by this evening or else—"

A ringtone went off, and it took Frieda a moment to realize it was her own. It came from her jacket, which was draped over a chair. She fumbled through the pockets until she found it. She heard a woman's voice: "Is that Frieda Klein?"

"Yes."

"This is Agnes Flint. You left a message."

As soon as Jim Fearby saw the photograph, he sensed he could cross her off his list. Claire Boyle was—had been—a plump, round-faced girl, with frizzy blond hair. Her mother had sat him down and brought him tea and cake, then had produced a handful of photographs from a drawer. Valerie Boyle settled down in the armchair opposite and talked about how her daughter had always been difficult.

"Did she ever run away?" Fearby asked.

"She got in with the wrong crowd," Valerie said. "Sometimes she'd stay out all night. Sometimes even for a few days. When I got upset she just flared up. There was nothing I could do."

Fearby put his notebook down. Really, he could leave now, but he had to stay long enough to be polite. He looked at Valerie Boyle. He felt he could classify these mothers by now. Some of them had grief like a chronic illness. They were gray with it, had fine lines scratched in their faces, a deadness in the eyes, as if there were nothing worth looking at. Then there were women like this one. Valerie Boyle had a quavering quality, a sense of flinching from a blow that might come at any moment, as if she were in the middle of an embarrassing scene that might turn nasty.

"Was there trouble at home?" Fearby asked.

"No, no," she said quickly. "She had some problems with her dad. He could turn a bit violent. But, like I said, she was difficult. Then she just disappeared. The police never did that much."

Fearby wondered if it had just been violence, or whether it had been sex as well. And the woman in front of him: had she stood by and watched it happen? In the end, there would have been nothing for the girl to do but escape. She was probably somewhere in London, one of the thousands of young people who'd had to escape, one way or another. Perhaps she was with one of the "wrong crowd" her mother had talked about. Fearby silently wished her luck.

But when Fearby drove up to the little estate just outside Stafford, he knew he was onto something. The group of houses was just a few minutes' drive, but the area was semirural, surrounded by scrubby open spaces, playing fields, some woods. He saw signs for footpaths. This was more like it. Daisy Crewe's mother was unwilling to let him in; she talked through the barely open door with the chain still attached. Fearby explained that he was a journalist, that he wanted to find out what had happened to her daughter, that he would only be a minute, but she was immovable. She said she didn't want to talk about it. The police had given up. They'd put it behind them.

"Just a couple of minutes," said Fearby. "One minute."

"What is it you want?"

Fearby got a glimpse of haunted dark eyes. He was used to it by now, but sometimes he felt the odd pang, that he was hunting people down and opening up their old wounds. But what else could he do?

"I read about your daughter," he said. "It was a tragic case. I wanted to know whether you'd had any warning. Was she unhappy? Did she have trouble at school?"

"She loved school," said the woman. "She had just started the sixth form. She wanted to be a vet."

"What was her mood like?"

"Are you asking me whether Daisy ran away from home? The week after she . . . well, she was going on a school trip. She'd done a part-time job for six months to pay for it. You know, my husband's at home here. He's on disability. It broke him. We keep going over that evening. She was walking over to see her best friend. She always took a shortcut across the common. If only we'd driven her. We just go over and over it."

"You can't blame yourself," said Fearby.

"Yes, you can."

"I'm so sorry," said Fearby. "But have you got a photograph?"

"I can't give you one," said the woman. "We gave some to journalists at the time. And the police. We never got them back."

"Just to look at."

"Wait," said the woman.

He stood on the doorstep and waited. After a few minutes, there was the sound of the chain being unfastened. The woman handed him a photograph. He looked at the girl, a young and eager face. He thought, as he always did, of what was to come, what that face would witness. He noted the dark hair, something about the eyes. Perhaps no one else would see it, but to him, the girls he was interested in were like a family, like a gang. He took out his phone.

"Is that all right?" he said.

The woman shrugged. He took a picture with his phone and handed the photograph back.

"So what are you going to do?" said the woman. "What are you going to do about our Daisy?"

"I'm going to find out what I can," said Fearby. "If I find out anything, anything at all, I'll let you know."

"Will you find Daisy?"

Fearby paused. "No. No, I don't think so."

"Then don't bother," said the woman, and closed the door.

Frieda had been interested to meet the woman who had broken Rajit Singh's heart, but when Agnes Flint opened the door of her flat, she thought she must have come to the wrong door. The young woman had a smooth, round face and coarse brown hair swept messily back. She wore a black sweater and jeans. But she was saved from being nondescript by her large dark eyes and a slightly ironic expression. Frieda had a sense of being appraised.

"I don't know what this is about," she said.

"Just give me a minute," said Frieda.

"You'd better come in. I'm on the top floor."

Frieda followed her up the stairs.

"It looks a bit boring from the outside," Agnes said, over her shoulder. "But wait till you get inside."

She opened the door and Frieda followed her in. They were in a living room with large windows on the far side.

"I see what you mean," she said.

The flat looked over a network of railway tracks. On the other side was a warehouse and beyond that were some apartment buildings that marked the south bank of the Thames.

"Some people hate the idea of living by the railway," said Agnes, "but I like it. It's like living next to a river, with strange things flowing past. And the trains are far enough away. I don't get commuters staring in at me while I'm in bed."

"I like it," said Frieda. "It's interesting."

"Well, that makes two of us." There was a pause. "So you've been talking to poor old Rajit."

"Why do you call him that?"

"You've met him. He wasn't much fun when we were together."

"He was a bit depressed."

"I'll say. Has he sent you to try to plead for him?"

"Didn't it end well?"

"Does it ever end well?" There was a rumble from outside and a train passed. "They'll be in Brighton in an hour," Agnes said. "Do you mind if I ask you a question? I mean, since you've come all the way to my flat."

"Go ahead."

"What are you doing here? When you rang up, I was curious. Rajit probably told you that he had difficulty taking no for an answer. He rang. He came round. He even wrote me letters."

"What did they say?"

"I threw them away without opening them. So when you rang, I was kind of curious. I wondered whether he was sending women on his behalf. Like some kind of carrier pigeon. Are you a friend of his?"

"No. I've met him only twice."

"So what are you?"

"I'm a psychotherapist."

"Did he come to see you as a patient?"

"Not exactly."

A smile of recognition spread across Agnes's face. "Oh, I know who you are. You're *her*, aren't you?"

"It depends on what you mean by 'her.'"

"What's this about? Is this some kind of complicated revenge?"

"No."

"Don't get me wrong. I'm not judging you. If someone made a fool of me like that, I'd fucking crucify them."

"But that's not why I'm here."

"No? Then why?"

"There was something Rajit said." Frieda saw herself from the outside, going from person to person, reciting a fragment of a story that seemed increasingly detached from its context—an image that she couldn't shake off but that glinted, sharp and bright, in the darkness of her mind. She should stop this, she told herself. Return to the life she'd been in before. She felt Agnes Flint waiting for her reply.

"Rajit wasn't actually the student who was sent to me; that was someone else. But all the four researchers told the same story, one that supposedly demonstrated they posed a clear threat."

"Yeah, I read about it."

"In this story, there was an arresting detail, which Rajit said actually came from you."

"I don't understand."

"About cutting his father's hair—well, I guess your father's hair, if it came from you originally and he changed it for his purpose."

"Cutting my father's hair."

"Yes. The feeling of power and tenderness you got from that."

"This is freaking me out a bit."

"He said you told him the story when you were lying in bed together, and you were stroking his hair and telling him it needed cutting."

"Oh. Yes. Now what?"

Now what? Frieda didn't know the answer to that. She said wearily, "So it was just a memory you had, a simple memory?"

"It wasn't my memory."

"What do you mean?"

"It was something a friend once said to me. She told me this story about cutting hair. I don't think she said it was her father's, actually. Maybe it was her boyfriend's or her brother's or a friend's. I can't remember. I don't know why I even remember her saying it. It was just a little thing and it was ages ago. It just kind of stayed with me. Weird to think of Rajit writing it into his spiel. Passing it on."

"Yes," said Frieda, slowly. "So your friend told you and you told Rajit."

"A version of it."

"Yes."

Agnes looked quizzically at Frieda. "Why on earth does it matter?"

"What's your friend's name?"

"I'm not going to tell you until you've answered my question. Why does it matter?"

"I don't know. It probably doesn't." Frieda gazed into Agnes's bright, shrewd eyes: she liked her. "The truth is, it bothers me, and I don't know why, but I feel I have to follow the thread."

"The thread?"

"Yes."

"Lila Dawes. Her real name is Lily, but no one calls her that."

"Thank you. How do you know her?"

"I don't. I knew her. We were at school together. Best friends." Again that ironic smile. "She was a bit wild but never malicious. We kept in touch after she dropped out, when she was just sixteen, but not for long. Our lives were so different. I was on one road and she—well, she wasn't on a road at all."

"So you have no idea where she is now?"

"No."

"Where were you at school?"

"Down near Croydon. John Hardy School."

"Is Croydon where you both grew up?"

"Do you know the area?"

"No, not at all."

"It's near Croydon. Next to it."

"Do you remember her address?"

"It's funny. I can't remember what happened last week, but I can remember everything about when I was young. Ledbury Close. Number eight. Are you going to try to find her?"

"I think so."

Agnes nodded slowly. "I should have tried myself," she said. "I often wonder about her—if she's OK."

"You think she might not be?"

"She was in a bad way when I last saw her." Frieda waited for Agnes to continue. "She'd left home, and she had a habit." She gave a shiver. "She looked pretty bad, thin, with spots on her forehead. I don't know how she was getting the money to pay for it. She didn't have a real job. I should have done more, don't you think?"

"I don't know."

"She was in trouble, I could see that, and I just wanted to run a mile, as if it were contagious. I tried to put her out of my mind. Every so often I think of her, and then I push her down again. Some friend."

"Except you remembered that story and passed it on."

"Yeah. I can see her now, telling me. Grinning."

"What did she look like when you knew her?"

"Little and thin, with long dark hair that was always falling over her eyes, and a huge smile. It used to take over her whole face. Gorgeous, in an odd kind of way. Like a monkey. Like a waif. She wore eccentric clothes she picked up from vintage shops. Boys loved her."

"Does she have family?"

"Her mum died when she was little. Maybe things would have turned out differently if she'd had a mother. Her dad, Lawrence, was lovely—he doted on her, but he couldn't keep her in order, not even when she was small. And she has two brothers, Ricky and Steve, who are several years older than her."

"Thank you, Agnes. I'll tell you if I find her."

"I wonder what she's like now. Maybe she's settled down, become respectable. Kids, a husband, a job. It's hard to imagine. What would I say to her?"

"Say what's in your heart."

"That I let her down. So odd, though, how it's all come back like this— just because of a silly story I told to poor Rajit."

Frieda—you haven't answered my last phone calls or my e-mails. Please let me know that everything's all right. Sandy xxxxx

THIRTY-THREE

Frieda walked home slowly. She could feel the warmth seeping into her body, hear her feet softly tapping on the pavement. People moved toward her and then flowed past, their faces blurred and indistinct. She saw herself from the outside; the thoughts that streamed through her brain seemed to belong to someone else. She knew that she was tired after all the nights of wakefulness and disordered dreams.

She did not go straight to her house but turned aside to sit awhile in Lincoln's Inn Fields. It was a small, green square, bright with blossom and new tulips. In the middle of the day it was often full of lawyers in their smart suits, eating their lunch, but now it was quiet, except for a pair of young women playing tennis on the court at the far side. Frieda sat down with her back against one of the great old plane trees. Its girth was tremendous and its bark dappled. She closed her eyes and tipped her face to the sun that fell through its leaves. Perhaps she should do as Sandy said and go to New York, where she would be safe and with the man she loved, who loved her and who knew her in a way that no one else in the world ever had. But then she would no longer be able to sit in the shade of this beautiful old tree and let the day settle around her.

When she got up again, the sun was sinking lower and the air was beginning to feel cool. She thought wistfully of her bath. And she thought of Chloë, took out her mobile, and made the call.

Olivia's voice was ragged. Frieda wondered if she'd been drinking. "I suppose Chloë's been telling you all sorts of horrible lies about me."

"No."

"Bad mother. Fucked up. Wash our hands of her."

"Listen, Olivia, stop!" Frieda heard her own voice, harsh and stern. "I'm ringing up to talk about Chloë."

"She hates me."

"She doesn't hate you. But it's probably a good thing if she stays with me for a few days while you sort things out."

"You make me sound like a sock drawer."

"Say, one week," said Frieda. She thought of her tidy, secure house invaded by Chloë's mess and drama and experienced a feeling of near panic. "I'll come over tomorrow evening. Half past six."

She turned off her phone and put it into her pocket. Her own plan was that she was going to go home, have a very long, very hot bath in her new and beautiful bathroom and climb into bed, pulling the duvet over her head, shutting out her thoughts. And hope that she wouldn't dream, or at least that she wouldn't remember her dreams.

She opened her front door. Several pairs of muddy shoes lay on the mat. A leather satchel. A jacket she didn't recognize. There was a nasty smell coming from the kitchen. Something was burning, and an alarm was making a piercing sound that felt to Frieda as though it was coming from inside her head. For a moment she considered leaving her own house and simply walking away from everything that was going on in there. Instead, she went up to the alarm in the hall ceiling and pressed the button to turn it off, then called out for Chloë. There was no reply, but the cat dashed past her and up the stairs.

The kitchen was full of fumes. Frieda saw that the handle of her frying pan was blistered and twisted. That must be the nasty smell. There were beer bottles, empty glasses, a lovely bowl had been used as an ashtray, and two dirty plates lay on the table, which was sticky and stained. She cursed under her breath and threw open the back door. Chloë was in the middle of the yard, and she saw that Ted was there as well, sitting with his back against the far wall and his knees drawn up to his chin. There were several cigarette butts scattered round him and a beer bottle at his feet.

"Chloë."

"I didn't hear you come in."

"There's quite a mess in there."

"We were going to clear it up."

"I've been speaking to Olivia. You can stay here for one week."

"Great."

"But there are rules. This is my house and you have to respect it and me. You clear things up, for a start. Properly. You don't smoke inside. Hello, Ted."

He raised his face and stared at her. His eyes were red rimmed, and his lips were bloodless. "Hi," he managed.

"How long have you been here?"

"I was just going."

"When did you last eat?"

"We were going to have pancakes," said Chloë, "but they went wrong."

"I'll make you some toast."

"I don't want to talk to you about stuff, if that's what you're thinking."

"It wasn't."

"That's all everyone seems to want. For me to talk about my feelings and weep and then you can hug me and tell me everything will be OK in the end."

"I'm just going to make toast."

There was a knocking at the door, hard and insistent, although Frieda wasn't expecting anyone.

"Come inside now," she said, to the two of them. "I'll see who's here."

Judith stood on the doorstep. She was wearing a man's shirt over baggy jeans held up by a rope and broken flip-flops. There was a colorful bandanna wrapped round her chestnut curls. Her eyes, set wide in her face, seemed bluer than when Frieda had seen her at that awful interview, and there was vivid orange lipstick on her full mouth, which was turned down sullenly. "I'm here for Ted. Is he here?"

"I'm making toast for him. Do you want some?"

"OK."

"This way."

Frieda led the girl into the kitchen. She gave a nod to Ted, who nodded back, then raised her hand in half greeting to Chloë, whom she obviously knew.

"Louise is clearing out Mum's clothes."

"She can't do that!" Ted's voice was sharp.

"She is."

"Why can't she fuck off to her own house?"

"Will you come back with me?" his sister asked. "It's better if we're there together."

"Here's your toast," said Frieda. "Help yourself to the honey."

"Just butter."

"I'm very sorry about your mother."

Judith shrugged her thin shoulders. Her blue eyes glittered in her freckled face.

"At least you've got Ted," said Chloë, urgently. "At least you two can help each other. Think if you were alone."

"You were together when you found out, weren't you?" asked Frieda. "But since then, have you talked about it to each other?" Neither of them spoke. "Have you talked to anyone?"

"She's dead. Words don't change that. We're sad. Words won't change that."

"There's this woman the police sent," said Judith.

"Oh, yes." Ted's voice was raw with contempt. "Her. She nods all the time, as if she has some deep understanding of our pain. It's crap. It makes me want to throw up." He tipped himself back on his chair so he was balanced on only one of its legs and spun himself slowly.

"Mum hated it when he did that." Judith waved at her brother. "It was like a family thing."

"Now I can do it as much as I want, and no one will bother about it."

"No," said Frieda. "I agree with your mother about that. It is very irritating. And dangerous."

"Can we go home, please? I don't want to leave Dad on his own with Louise being all sad and disapproving." She faltered. There were tears in her eyes, and she blinked them away. "I think we should go home," she repeated.

Ted lowered his chair and stood up, a spindly, scruffy figure. "OK, then. Thanks for the toast."

"That's all right."

"Bye," said Judith.

"Good-bye."

"Can we come again?" Judith's voice was suddenly tremulous.

"Yes." Chloë's voice was loud and energetic. "Anytime, day or night. We're here for you—aren't we, Frieda?"

"Yes," said Frieda, a little wearily.

She trudged upstairs to the bathroom. The bath was there in all its glory. She turned on the taps and they worked. But there was no plug. She looked under the bath and in the cupboard, but it wasn't there. The plug in the washbasin was too small, and the one in the kitchen was an irritating metal kind that didn't have a chain but twisted down. She couldn't have a bath, after all.

Karlsson and Yvette arrived at the Lennox house shortly after Judith had left. The shouting was over, and in its place there was a curdled silence, an air of unease. Russell Lennox was in his study, sitting at his desk and staring blindly out of the window; Dora was in her room, no longer sobbing but lying curled into a ball, her face still wet and swollen from tears. Louise Weller had been clearing up. She had washed the kitchen floor, vacuumed the stairs, and was just about to make a start on some of her sister's clothes, when the doorbell rang.

"We need to look through Mrs. Lennox's things one more time," explained Yvette.

"I was making a start on her clothes."

"Perhaps not just yet," Karlsson told her. "We'll tell you when you can do that."

"Another thing. The family wants to know when the funeral can be."

"It won't be long. We should be able to tell you in the next day or so."

"It's not right."

Karlsson felt an impulse to say something rude back to her, but he replied blandly that it was difficult for everybody.

They made their way upstairs, into the bedroom that the Lennoxes had shared for more than twenty years. There were signs of Louise Weller's work: there were several plastic bags full of shoes, and she seemed to have emptied most of the small amount of makeup Ruth had owned into the wastepaper bin.

"What are we looking for?" asked Yvette. "They've been through all this."

"I don't know. There's probably nothing. But this is a family full of secrets. What else don't we know about?"

"The trouble is, there's so much," said Yvette. "She kept everything. Should we look through all those boxes in the loft with her children's reports in? And what about the various computers? We've been through theirs, of course, but each child has a laptop and there are a few old ones that obviously don't work anymore but haven't been thrown away."

"Here's a woman who for ten years met her lover in their flat. Did she have a key? Or any documents at all that would shed light on this? Did she really never send or receive e-mails or texts? I've taken it for granted that this affair must have something to do with her death, but perhaps there's something else."

Yvette gave a sarcastic smile. "As in, if she was capable of adultery, what else might she have done?"

"That's not exactly what I meant."

Standing in the bedroom, Karlsson thought about how they knew so much about Ruth Lennox and yet didn't know her at all. They knew what toothpaste she used and which deodorant. What her bra size was and her knickers and her shoes. What books she read and what magazines. They knew what face cream she used, what recipes she turned to, what she put in her shopping trolley week after week, what tea she favored, what wine she drank, what TV programs she watched, what box sets she owned. They were familiar with her handwriting, knew what ball points and pencils she wrote with, saw the doodles she made on the sides of pads; they had studied her face in the photographs around the house and in the albums. They had read the postcards she'd received from dozens of friends over dozens of years from dozens of countries, riffled through Mother's Day cards and birthday cards and Christmas cards. Checked and double-checked her e-mail and were sure she'd never used Facebook, LinkedIn, or Twitter.

But they didn't know why or how she had managed to conduct a ten-year affair under the nose of her family. They didn't know if she'd felt guilty. They didn't know why she had had to die.

On an impulse, he pushed open the door to Dora's bedroom. It was very neat and quiet in there. Everything was put away and in its proper place: clothes neatly folded into drawers, paper stacked on the desk, homework books on the shelves above it, her pajamas folded on the pillow. In the wardrobe, her clothes—the clothes of a girl who didn't want to become a teenager yet—hung above paired, sensible shoes. It made Karlsson feel sad just to look at the anxious order. A thin spindle of pink caught his eye on the top of the cupboard. He reached up his hand and pulled down a rag doll, then drew in his breath sharply. It had a flat pink face and droopy legs, red cotton hair in plaits, but its stomach had been cut away, and the area between its legs snipped open. He held it for several moments, his face grim.

"Oh!" Yvette had come into the room. "That's horrible."

"Yes, isn't it?"

"Do you think she did that herself? Because of what she found out about her mother?"

"Probably."

"Poor little thing."

"But I'll have to ask her."

"I think I've found something. Look." She opened her hand to show a little dial of tablets. Karlsson squinted at them. "This was in that long cupboard next to the bathroom—the one full of towels and flannels, body lotion, tampons, and all sorts of bits and pieces they didn't know what to do with."

"Well?"

"The Pill," said Yvette. "Inside a sock."

"Funny place to keep your contraceptives."

"Yes. Especially when Ruth Lennox had a coil."

Karlsson's mobile rang. He took it out of his pocket and frowned when he saw who was calling. He had had two brief texts and one message from Sadie, asking him to get in touch. He was about to let it go to voice mail again. But then he hesitated: she clearly wasn't going to give up and he supposed he might as well get it over with.

"I'm sorry I didn't call you back. I've been busy and—"

"No. You didn't call me back because you didn't want to see me again and you thought if you ignored my calls I might just go away."

"That's not fair."

"Isn't it? I think it is."

"I made a mistake, Sadie. I like you a lot and we had a nice evening, but it's the wrong time for me."

"I'm not calling to ask you out, if that's what you're worried about. I got the message. But you need to meet me."

"I don't think that's a good idea."

"It's a very good idea. You need to sit down opposite me, look me in the eyes, and explain yourself."

"Sadie, listen—"

"No. You listen. You're behaving like an awkward teenager. You asked me out, we had a nice evening, we made love—that's what it felt like to me, anyway. And then you crept away, as if you were embarrassed. I deserve more than that."

"I'm sorry."

"I deserve an explanation. Meet me at the same wine bar at eight o'clock tomorrow. It'll only take half an hour, less. You can tell me why you behaved like that, then you can go home, and I won't call you again."

And she ended the call. Karlsson looked down at the mobile in his hand and raised his eyebrows. She was rather impressive, that Sadie.

THIRTY-FOUR

F rieda always felt a little strange when she went south of the river. But going to Croydon was like going to another country. She'd had to look it up on a map. She'd had to go to Victoria and get on an overground train. It had been full of commuters coming into London, but going out, it was almost empty. London, this huge creature, sucked people in. It wouldn't be until late afternoon that it blew them out again. As the train crossed the river, Frieda recognized Battersea, the derelict power station. She even saw, or nearly saw, where Agnes Flint's flat must be, just near the huge market. After Clapham Junction and Wandsworth Common, it gradually became vague and nameless for her, a succession of glimpsed parks, a graveyard, the backs of houses, a shopping center, a junkyard, a flash of someone hanging out washing, a child bouncing on a blue trampoline. Even though the streets had become unfamiliar, she continued to stare out the window. She couldn't stop herself. Houses and buildings didn't hide from trains the way they did from cars. You didn't see their smart façades but the bits behind that the owners didn't bother about, that they didn't think anyone would really notice: the broken fences, the piles of rubbish, abandoned machinery.

When she got out of the station, she had to use the street map to find her way to Ledbury Close. Number eight was a pebble-dashed detached house, indistinguishable from its neighbors, except that it was somehow more cared for—there was more precise attention to detail. Frieda noticed the new windows, the frames freshly painted in glossy white. On each side of the front door a purple ceramic pot contained a miniature bush, trimmed into a spiral. They were so neat, they looked as if they had been done with scissors.

Frieda pressed the doorbell. It didn't seem to make a sound, so she pressed it again, and she heard a sound from somewhere inside and saw a blurred shape through the frosted glass of the door. It opened, revealing a large man, not fat but big, so that he seemed to fill the doorway. He was almost completely bald with messy gray hair around the fringes of his head. His face was flushed with the red of someone who spent time outside, and he was dressed in bulky gray work trousers, a blue and white checked shirt, and heavy dark leather boots that were yellow with dried mud.

"I wasn't sure if the bell was working," said Frieda.

"Everyone says that," said the man, his face crinkling around the eyes. "It rings at the back of the house. I have it like that because I spend a lot of time in the garden. I've been out there all morning." He gestured up at the blue sky. "On a day like this." He looked at Frieda questioningly.

"Are you Lawrence Dawes?"

"Yes, I am."

"My name is Frieda Klein. I'm here because . . ." What was she going to say? "I'm here because I'm trying to find your daughter, Lila."

Dawes's smile faded. He suddenly seemed older and more frail.

"Lila? You're looking for my Lila?"

"Yes."

"I don't know where she is," he said. "I lost touch with her."

He raised his hands helplessly. Frieda saw his fingernails, dirty from the garden. Was that it? Had she come all the way to Croydon just for that?

"Can I talk to you about her?"

"What for?"

"I met someone who used to know her," said Frieda. "An old friend of hers called Agnes Flint."

Dawes nodded slowly. "I remember Agnes. Lila used to go around with this little gang of girls. She was one of them. Before things went wrong."

"Can I come in?" asked Frieda.

Dawes seemed to be thinking it over, then gave a shrug. "Come through to the garden. I was just about to have some tea."

He led Frieda through the house. It was clearly the home of a man—a very organized man—living alone. Through a door she saw a large flat-screen TV and rows of DVDs on shelves. There was a computer. Underfoot was a thick cream-colored carpet, so that all the sounds were muffled.

Five minutes later they were standing on the back lawn, holding mugs of tea. The garden was much larger than Frieda had expected, going back thirty, maybe forty, meters from the house. There was a neat lawn with a curved gravel path snaking through it. There were bushes and flowerbeds and little flashes of color: crocuses, primroses, early tulips. The far end of the garden was wilder and beyond it was a large, high wall.

"I've been trying to tidy things up," said Dawes. "After the winter."

"It seems pretty tidy to me," said Frieda.

"It's a constant struggle. Look over there." He pointed to the garden next door. It was full of long grass, brambles, a ragged rhododendron, a couple of ancient fruit trees. "It's some kind of council house. There'll be a family of Iraqis or Somalians. Nice enough people. Keep themselves to themselves. But they stay a few months and move on. A garden like this takes years. Do you hear anything?"

Frieda moved her head. "Like what?"

"Follow me."

Dawes walked along the path away from the house. Now Frieda could hear a sound, a low murmuring that she couldn't make out, like a muttered conversation in another room. At the end of the garden, there was a fence, and Frieda stood next to Dawes and looked over it. With an improbability that almost made her laugh, she saw that there was a dip on the other side and in the dip a small stream trickled along the end of the garden with a path on the other side, then the high wall she had already seen. She saw Dawes smiling at her surprise.

"It makes me think of the children," he said. "When they were small, we used to make little paper boats and put them on the stream and watch them float away. I used to tell them that in three hours' time, those boats would reach the Thames and then, if the tide was right, they'd float out to sea."

"What is it?" asked Frieda.

"Don't you know?"

"I'm from north London. Most of our rivers were buried long ago."

"It's the Wandle," said Dawes. "You must know the Wandle."

"I know the name."

"It rises a mile or so back. From here it goes past old factories and rubbish dumps and under roads. I used to walk along the path beside it, years ago. The water was foamy and yellow and it stank back then. But we're all right here. I used to let the children paddle in it. That's the problem with a river, isn't it? You're at the mercy of everybody who's upstream from you. Whatever they do to their river, they do to your river. What people do downstream doesn't matter."

"Except to the people *farther* downstream," said Frieda.

"That's not my problem," said Dawes, and sipped his tea. "But I've always liked the idea of living by a river. You never know what's going to float by. I can see you like it too."

"I do," Frieda admitted.

"So what do you do, when you're not looking for lost girls?"

"I'm a psychotherapist."

"Is it your day off?"

"In a way." They turned and walked back down the garden. "What do you do?"

"I do this," said Dawes. "I do my garden. I do up the house. I do things with my hands. I find it restful."

"What did you do before that?"

He gave a slow smile. "I was the opposite, the complete opposite. I was a salesman for a company selling photocopiers. I spent my life on the road." He gestured to Frieda to sit down on a wrought iron bench. He sat on a chair close by. "You know, there's an expression I never understood. When people say something's boring, they say, "It's like watching grass grow." Or "It's like watching paint dry." That's exactly what I enjoy. Watching my grass grow."

"I'm really here," said Frieda, "because I'd like to find your daughter."

Dawes put his mug down very carefully on the grass next to his foot. When he turned to Frieda, it was with a new intensity. "I'd like to find her as well," he said.

"When did you last see her?"

There was a long pause.

"Do you have children?"

"No."

"It was all I wanted. All of that driving around, all that work, doing things I hated—what I wanted was to be a father, and I was a father. I had a lovely wife and I had the two boys and then there was Lila. I loved the boys, kicking a ball with them, taking them fishing, everything you're supposed to do. But when I saw Lila, the moment she was born, I thought, You're my little . . ." He stopped and sniffed, and Frieda saw that his eyes were glistening. He coughed. "She was the loveliest little girl, smart, funny, beautiful. And then, well, why do things happen? Her mum, my wife, she got ill and was ill for years and then she died. Lila was thirteen. Suddenly I couldn't get through to her. I'd thought we had a special bond, and then it was like I was talking a foreign language. Her friends changed, she started going out more and more and then staying away from home. I should have done more, but I was away so much."

"What about her brothers?"

"They'd left by then. Ricky's in the army. Steve lives in Canada."

"So what happened?"

Dawes spread his hands helplessly. "I got it wrong," he said. "Whatever I did, it wasn't enough or it wasn't what she needed. When I tried to put my foot down, it just drove her away. If I tried to be nice, it felt like it was too late. The more I wanted her to be there, the more she rejected me. I was just her boring old dad. When she was seventeen, she was mainly living with friends. I'd see her every few days, then every few weeks. She treated me a bit like a stranger. Then I didn't see her at all. I tried to find her, but I couldn't. After a while, I stopped trying, although I never stopped thinking of her, missing her. My girl."

"Do you know how she was supporting herself?"

Frieda saw his jaw flexing. His face had gone white.

"She was having problems. I think there may have been drugs. She hadn't been eating properly. Not for years."

"These friends. Do you know their names?"

Dawes shook his head. "I used to know her friends when they were younger. Like Agnes, the one you've met. They were lovely the way girls are together, laughing, going shopping, thinking they're more grown-up than they are. But she dropped them, took up with a new crowd. She never brought them back, never introduced me to them."

"When she moved out for good, have you any idea where she lived?"

He shook his head again. "It was somewhere in the area," he said. "But then I think she must have moved away."

"Did you report her missing?"

"She was almost eighteen. One time I got so worried, I went to the police station. But when I mentioned her age, the policeman at the desk wouldn't even write a report."

"When was this? I mean, the last time you saw her?"

He knitted his brow.

"Oh, God," he said at last. "It's more than a year now. It was November of the year before last. I can't believe it. But that's one of the things I think about when I'm working out here. That she'll walk through the door, the way she used to."

Frieda sat for a moment, thinking.

"Are you all right?" Dawes asked.

"Why do you say that?"

"Maybe it takes one to know one, but you look tired and pale."

"You don't know what I normally look like."

"You said it's your day off. Is that right?"

"Yes. Basically."

"You're an analyst. You talk to people."

Frieda stood up, ready to go. "That's right," she said.

Dawes stood up as well. "I should have found someone like you for Lila," he said. "It's not really my way. I'm not good at talking to people. What I do instead is to work at something, fix something. But you're easy to talk to." He looked around awkwardly. "Are you going to search for Lila?"

"I wouldn't know where to start."

"If you hear anything, you'll let me know?"

On the way out, Dawes found a piece of paper, wrote his phone number on it and gave it to Frieda. As she took it, an idea occurred to her.

"Did she ever cut your hair?" she asked.

He touched his bald pate. "I've never had much to cut."

"Or you hers?"

"No. She had beautiful hair. She was proud of it." He forced a smile. "She'd never have let me anywhere near it. Why do you ask that?"

"Something Agnes said."

Back on the street, Frieda looked at the map and set off, not back to the station she'd come from but the next one along. It was a couple of miles. That would be all right. She needed the walk, and she felt more alive now, alert to her surroundings in this part of the city she'd never seen. She found herself walking along a two-lane road, lorries rumbling by. On both sides there were housing projects, the sort that had been quickly knocked up after the war and now were crumbling. Some of the flats were boarded up, others had washing hanging from their little terraces. It didn't feel like a place for walking, but then she turned into a street of little Victorian terraced houses, and it suddenly became quiet. Still, she felt uncomfortable, miles from home.

As she approached the station, she passed a phone box and stopped. There wasn't even a phone in it. It had been ripped away. Then she looked more closely. On the glass walls there were dozens of little stickers: young model, language teacher, very strict teacher, escorts *de luxe*. Frieda took a notebook from her bag and wrote down the phone numbers. It took several minutes, and two teenage boys walking past giggled and shouted something, but she pretended not to hear.

Back in her house, she made a phone call.

"Agnes?"

"Yes?"

"Frieda Klein."

"Oh—did you find anything?"

"I didn't find Lila, if that's what you mean. She seems to have vanished. Her father can't find her. It's not good news, but I thought you'd want to know."

"Yes. Yes, I do. Thank you." There was a pause. "I'm going to the police to report her missing. I should have done it months ago."

"It probably won't do any good," Frieda said softly. "She's an adult."

"I have to do something. I can't just let it go."

"I understand that."

"I'll do it at once. Though now that I've waited all these years, I don't know what difference an hour will make."

Jim Fearby was nearly three fifths of the way through his list. There were twenty-three names on it, obtained from local newspapers and missing-person Web sites. He was beginning to see the pattern, and he had learned over the years to trust his instincts. Three he had already put a tick by; one he had put a query by; others he had crossed out. He had nine families left to visit—nine mothers who would look at him with stricken faces, haunted eyes. Nine more stories of missing and nine more sets of photos for him to add to the collection of young women's faces he had tacked up on his corkboard in his study.

They stared down at him now as he sat back in his chair with his tumbler of whisky, no added water, and his cigarette. He never used to smoke inside the house, but now there was no one to care. He looked from face to face: There was the first girl, Hazel Barton, with her radiant smile—he felt he knew her well by now. Then there was Vanessa Dale, the one who had got away. Roxanne Ingatestone, her asymmetrical face and gray-green eyes. Daisy Crewe, eager and a little dimple on one cheek. Vanessa Dale was safe, Hazel Barton was dead. What about the other two? He stubbed out his cigarette and lit another at once, sucking smoke down into his lungs, staring at the faces until it almost seemed that they were alive under his gaze and were looking back at him, asking him to find them.

That was a very enigmatic little e-mail. What's going on? I miss you. Sandy xxx

THIRTY-FIVE

rieda had arranged to meet Sasha at eight o'clock. Sasha had rung to say there was something she needed to tell her. Frieda hadn't known from her voice whether it was good or bad, but she did know it was important. Before then, as she had promised, she went to see Olivia.

She was taken aback by Olivia's appearance. She came to the door in a pair of striped drawstring trousers, a stained camisole, and plastic flip-flops. The varnish on her toenails was chipped, her hair was greasy, and her face, puffy and pale, was bare of any makeup. Without it, she looked vulnerable and defeated.

"Did you forget I was coming?"

"Not really. I didn't know what time it was."

"It's six thirty."

"God. Time flies when you're asleep." She made an attempt at a laugh.

"Shall I make us some tea?"

"I could do with a drink."

"Tea first. There are things we need to discuss."

They went into the kitchen together, which was as bad as Frieda had ever seen it. It was a bit like the disorder Chloë had created in Frieda's kitchen, with glasses and bottles everywhere, rubbish spilling out of bin bags onto the sticky tiles, puddles of wax over the table, a sour smell in the air. Frieda started stacking things into the sink to create a space.

"She ran away from me, you know," Olivia said, who seemed not to notice the state of the room. "She might have told you I threw her out, but I didn't. She said terrible things to me and then ran off."

"She says you hit her with a hairbrush."

"If I did, it was only a soft-bristled one. My mother used to hit me with a wooden spoon."

Frieda dropped tea bags into the pot and picked two mugs out of the sink to wash. "Things have got a bit out of control here," Frieda said. "You need to sort them out before Chloë comes back."

"We're not all like you. Everything in its proper place. That doesn't mean I'm not coping."

"You look ill. You've spent the afternoon in bed. The house is in a dreadful state. Chloë's left. I gather Kieran's left too."

"He's a fool. I told him to get out, but I didn't think he'd take me literally."

"How much are you drinking?"

"You can't tell me how to live my life, you know."

"Chloë's in my house, and we need to talk about how long she's going to be there, and when you'll be ready for her to come home. She can't come home at the moment, can she?"

"I don't see why not."

"Olivia, she's still a child. She needs boundaries and she needs order."

"I knew you were going to tell me I was a crap mother."

"I'm saying that Chloë needs to be woken in the morning, talked to in the evening. She needs a clean kitchen and food in the fridge, a room where she can do her schoolwork, a sense of stability."

"What about me? What about what I need?"

For a few minutes, there was silence. Olivia sipped her tea, and Frieda made piles of dishes and pans and put bin bags out into the hall. After a while, Oliva said in a small voice, "I didn't mean to hit her. I didn't mean to tell Kieran to get lost. I wasn't thinking straight. I just felt wretched."

Frieda attacked the pans with a scouring pad. She felt terribly tired, defeated by the disorder of Olivia's days. "You need to take control of your own life," she said.

"That's all very well to say. Where do I start?"

"Take one thing at a time. Clear up the house from top to bottom. Drink a little less. Or nothing at all. You might feel better just by doing that. Wash your hair, weed the garden."

"Is that what you tell your patients? Wash your hair and weed the bloody garden?"

"Sometimes."

"This wasn't how I imagined my life would turn out, you know."

"No, but I think—" Frieda began.

"It's like the man said, we all need to be loved."

"What man?"

"Oh, just a man." Olivia was beginning to cheer up. "It was a bit embarrassing, actually. I met him last night when I was a tiny bit the worse for wear. I was so upset by everything, and I went to that nice wine bar and had a few drinks, and it was when I was going home that I bumped into him." She gave a small yelp of laughter—a mixture of shame and exultation. "The kindness of strangers, you know what they say."

"What happened?"

"Happened? Nothing like that, Frieda. Don't give me one of your looks. I tripped over on the street and there he was. My Good Samaritan. He helped me up and dusted me down, then said he'd make sure I got home safely."

"That was kind of him," said Frieda, drily. "Did he want to come in?"

"I couldn't just turn him away. We had another glass together. And then after a bit he went."

"Good."

"He seemed to know you."

"Me?"

"Yes. I think he sent his regards. Or his love."

"What was his name?"

"I don't know. I asked him—and he said that names weren't important. He said he'd had several names, and it was easy to change them. He said you could change names the way you change clothes, and I should try it myself one day. I said I wanted to be called Jemima!" She gave one of her raucous bursts of laughter.

But the air had cooled around Frieda. She sat down opposite Olivia and leaned across the table toward her, speaking with quiet urgency. "What did this man look like, Olivia?"

"Look like? Well. I don't know. Nothing to write home about."

"No, really," said Frieda. "Tell me."

Olivia made the face of a sulky schoolgirl. "He had gray hair, cut very short. He was solid, I suppose. Not tall. Not short."

"What color were his eyes?"

"His eyes? You are strange, Frieda. I can't think. Brown. Yes, he had brown eyes. I told him he had eyes like a dog we once had, so they must have been, mustn't they?"

"Did he say what he did?"

"No, I don't think so. Why?"

"You are sure he said he knew me?"

"He said he'd helped you recently. He said you'd remember."

Frieda shut her eyes for a moment. She saw Mary Orton gazing at her as she lay dying. She saw a knife raised toward her—and then, like a flutter at the margins of her vision, she saw, or sensed, a shape, a figure in the shadows. Someone had saved her.

"What else did he say?"

"I think I talked more than he did," said Olivia.

"Tell me anything you remember."

"You're scaring me a bit."

"Please."

"He knew I had a daughter called Chloë and that she was staying with you."

"Go on."

"There's nothing else. You're giving me a headache."

"He didn't mention Terry or Joanna or Carrie."

"No."

"Or send any message."

"Just his regards or love. Oh, and something about daffodils."

"Daffodils—what about daffodils?"

"I think he said he'd once given you daffodils."

Yes. Dean had sent a little girl across the park to her, bearing a bunch of daffodils and a message. Four words that Frieda had carried with her: "It wasn't your time."

She stood up. "Did you leave him alone at all?"

"No! Well, I went to the loo, but apart from that—he didn't steal anything, if that's what you mean. He was just being kind to me."

"How many spare keys do you have?"

"What? This is stupid. Anyway, I don't know. I've got keys and so has Chloë and there are a few others knocking around, but I've no idea where they are."

"Listen, Olivia. I'm going to get Josef to come round and change all the locks in the house and fit proper safety devices on your windows."

"Have you gone mad?"

"I hope so. He'll come tomorrow first thing, so make sure you're up in good time."

"What's going on?"

"Nothing, I hope. It's just a precaution."

"Are you going?"

"I'm meeting Sasha. But, Olivia—don't go letting any more strange men into your house."

THIRTY-SIX

Before his appointment with Sadie, Karlsson spent twenty minutes with Dora Lennox. They sat in the kitchen together while Louise made loud clearing-up noises in the living room and hall. Karlsson thought that everything about Dora was pale—her thin white face, her bloodless lips, her small, delicate hands, which kept fiddling with the salt cellar. She seemed insubstantial. Her blue veins showed under her milky skin. He felt brutal as he took out the rag doll, hearing the suppressed whimper she gave on seeing it. "I'm sorry to distress you, Dora, but we found this in your room."

She stared at it, then away.

"Is it yours?"

"It's horrible."

"Did you do this, Dora?"

"No!"

"It doesn't matter if you did. No one's going to be angry with you. I just need to know if you did this yourself?"

"I just wanted to hide it."

"Who from?"

"I don't know. Anyone. I didn't want to see it."

"So you cut it up a bit and then wanted to hide it?" Karlsson asked. "That's OK."

"No. I didn't do it! It's not mine. I wanted to put it in the dustbin but then I thought someone would see it."

"If it's not yours, whose is it?"

"I don't know. Why are you asking?" Her voice rose hysterically.

"Dora. Listen. You haven't done anything wrong, but I just need to know how this came to be in your room, if it's not yours."

"I found it," she said, in a whisper.

"Found it where?"

"I was at home one day on my own, ill. I had a temperature and had the day off school. No one else was there. Mum said she'd come back from work early, and she left me a sandwich by my bed. I couldn't read because my head hurt, but I couldn't sleep either, and I just lay there listening to sounds in the street. Then there was a clatter and someone pushed something through the letter box, but I thought it would be junk mail or something. Then later, when I needed the bathroom, I saw it from the top of the stairs and I went down and picked it up and saw—" She gave a small shudder and came to a halt, staring up at Karlsson.

"You're saying that someone pushed this through the letter box?"

"Yes."

"Cut up like this?"

"Yes. It scared me. I don't know why, but I just had to hide it."

"And it was done during the day, when normally no one would have been there?"

"I had the flu," she said defensively. The cat came and curled itself around her legs and she picked it up and buried her face in its fur.

Karlsson nodded. He was thinking that on any ordinary day it would have been Ruth Lennox who found the mutilated doll. A message. A warning.

This time, Sadie had not put on any makeup or perfume. She had arrived early and ordered a tomato juice, and greeted Karlsson as if he were a business colleague. He bent down to kiss her cheek, which she turned away from him, so he kissed her ear instead.

"Get yourself a drink if you want. Then we can talk."

He went and bought himself half a pint of beer, then took the chair opposite her. "I don't know what there is to say," he began. "I behaved like an idiot. I've always liked you, Sadie, and I didn't want to mess you around."

"But you did mess me around. If I'd known you just wanted one quick fuck on your night off, I wouldn't have let you near me."

"I'm sorry." There was a silence, and she regarded him coolly. He found himself talking, to fill it and to bring some warmth back into her unyielding face. "The thing is," he said, "I've been a bit wretched."

"Lots of us are a bit wretched."

"I know. It's not an excuse. My children—Mikey and Bella, you met them when they were younger—they've gone away with their mother."

"Gone away—for a holiday, you mean?"

"No. She's got this new man—she's going to marry him, I guess, so he's really their stepfather—and he got a job in Madrid and they've gone there. The four of them, the happy family." He heard and hated the bitterness in his voice. "So they've gone away for two years. I'll see them, but it won't be the same. Well, it hasn't been the same since they moved out, of course. I kind of lost them then, but now I feel I've really lost them. And now that they've gone, I . . ."

He stopped dead. He suddenly found he couldn't continue, couldn't tell Sadie that he didn't really know what his life was about anymore. That he woke each morning and had to make an effort to face the world.

"I thought I could fill the gap a bit," he said lamely. "Just to get through."

"Fill the gap with me?"

"I suppose so. I feel detached from everything, as if everything is happening to someone else and I'm watching it, like in a film. So when I woke that morning and saw you lying next to me, I just—well, I knew I'd made a mistake, and I wasn't ready for you or anyone."

"So that's it?"

"Yes."

"You should have thought about it before."

"You're right."

"I'm a person, me. Someone you used to call a friend."

"I know."

"I'm sorry about the way you're feeling. It must be hard." She stood up, her tomato juice unfinished on the table. "Thank you for being honest with me, in the end. If you ever feel in need of comfort again, call someone else."

Frieda arrived back at her house just before Sasha. She called Josef, who said he would go round to Olivia's immediately, put bolts on the front and back door and change all the locks the next morning. Then she called Karlsson, but only got his voice mail. She didn't leave a message—what would she say? "I think Dean Reeve was in my sister-in-law's house last night?" He wouldn't believe her. She didn't even know if she believed herself, but dread washed through her.

Sasha arrived just after eight, bearing a takeaway, steam rising from the bag. She was wearing a loose orange dress, and her hair was soft around her face. Frieda saw that her cheeks were slightly flushed and her eyes bright. She pulled naan out of a damp brown paper bag and laid it on a plate. Frieda lit candles and pulled a bottle of wine out of the fridge. She thought how strange it was that even in front of Sasha she could so successfully conceal her distress and fear. Her voice sounded steady; her hands as she poured wine were steady.

"Is Chloë still here?"

"Yes. But she's seeing her father tonight, so I have the house to myself for once."

"Do you mind?"

"I don't think I had a choice."

"That wasn't the question."

"Sometimes I come in," Frieda said, "and she's made herself completely at home. Mess everywhere. School stuff slung every which way. Dirty dishes in the sink. Sometimes her friends are here as well. Not to mention Josef. There's noise and chaos and even the smell is different. And I feel like an intruder in my own home. Nothing belongs to me in the same way. It's all I can do not to run away."

"At least it'll soon be over. She's only here for a week, isn't she?"

"That was the agreement. This looks good. Wine?"

"Half a glass. So I can clink it against yours."

They sat at the table facing each other and Frieda lifted her glass. "So, tell me."

Sasha didn't lift hers, just smiled radiantly. "Do you know, Frieda, the world seems sharper and brighter. I can feel energy pumping through me. Every morning I wake up and the spring outside is inside my body as well. I know you're anxious that I'll let myself get hurt again—but you've met Frank. He's not like that. And, anyway, isn't that partly what falling in love is? Opening yourself up to the possibility of feeling joy and being hurt? Letting yourself trust? I know I've made mistakes in the past. But this feels different. I'm stronger than I used to be, less pliable."

"I'm very glad," said Frieda. "Really."

"Good! I know you'll like each other. He thinks you're terrific. But I'm not just here to gush about Frank, like a teenager. I've got something else I need to say. I haven't told anyone else but—"

The doorbell rang.

"Who can that be? It's too early for it to be Chloë and, anyway, she has a key."

The bell rang once more, and then someone knocked. Frieda wiped her mouth on the paper napkin, took a gulp of wine, and stood up. "Whoever it is, I'll send them away," she said.

Judith Lennox was standing at the door. She was wearing an oversized man's jacket and what looked to Frieda like jodhpurs. Dora was beside her, her long brown hair in a French plait, her face pinched and pale.

"Hello," Judith said, in a small voice. "You said I could come."

"Judith."

"I didn't want to leave Dora alone. I thought you wouldn't mind."

Frieda looked from one face to the other.

"My dad's gone out drinking," said Judith. "And I don't know where Ted is. I can't spend any more time in the house with Aunt Louise. There'll be a second murder."

Dora gave a strangled sob.

"You'd better come in," said Frieda. She didn't know which feeling was stronger—pity for the two girls on her doorstep or a stifling sense of anger that she had to look after them.

"Sasha, this is Judith and Dora." Sasha looked up, startled. "They are friends of Chloë's."

"Not really," put in Judith. "Ted's a friend of Chloë's. I know her a bit. Dora's never met her, have you, Dora?"

"No." Dora's voice was a whisper. She was almost translucent, thought Frieda—blue veins under pale skin, blue shadows under eyes, neck that seemed almost too thin to hold up her head, bony knees, skinny legs with a big bruise on one shin. She'd been the one who'd found her mother dead, she remembered.

"Sit down," she said. "Have you had anything to eat?"

"I'm not hungry," said Dora.

"Not since breakfast," said Judith. "And you didn't eat any breakfast, Dora."

"Here." Frieda got out two extra plates and pushed them in front of the girls. "We've got plenty to go round." She glanced at Sasha's bemused face. "Judith and Dora's mother died very recently."

Sasha leaned toward them, her face soft in the guttering candlelight. "I'm so sorry."

"Someone killed her," said Judith, harshly. "In our house."

"No! That's dreadful."

"Ted and I think it was her lover."

"Don't," said Dora, piteously.

Frieda noticed how in Ted's absence Judith took on his anger, his corrosive bitterness.

"Can I have some wine?"

"How old are you?"

"Fifteen. You're not going to tell me that I shouldn't drink wine because

I'm only fifteen?" She gave an ugly snort. Her blue eyes glittered and her voice scratched.

"This is a school night and I hardly know you. I'll give you some water." Judith shrugged. "Whatever. I don't really feel like it actually."

"Dora, have some rice," said Sasha. She had a cooing note to her voice. She's broody, thought Frieda. She's fallen in love and she wants babies.

Dora put a teaspoon of rice onto her plate and pushed listlessly at it. Sasha put her hand over the young girl's, at which she put her head on the table and started crying, her thin shoulders shaking, her whole starved body shuddering.

"Oh dear," said Sasha. "Oh, you poor thing." She knelt beside the girl and cradled her. After a few moments, Dora turned urgently toward her, pressing her wet face into Sasha's shoulder, holding on to her like a drowning person.

Judith stared at them, her expression blank.

"Can I speak to you?" she hissed to Frieda, above the hiccuping sobs.

"Of course."

"Out there." Judith jerked her head toward the yard.

Frieda rose and opened the back door. The air was still quite gentle after the warmth of the day, and she could smell the herbs she had planted in their tubs. "What is it?" she asked.

Judith looked at her, then away. She seemed both older than her years, and younger: an adult and a child at once. Frieda waited. Her curry would be a congealing oily mass.

"I'm not feeling well," said Judith. And then Frieda knew what she was going to say. This was the kind of thing she should be telling her mother.

"In what way?" she asked.

"I'm feeling a bit sick."

"In the morning?"

"Mostly."

"Are you pregnant, Judith?"

"I don't know. Maybe." Her voice was a sullen mumble.

"Have you done a test?"

"No."

"You ought to do one as soon as possible. They're very reliable." She tried to make out the expression on the girl's face. "You can buy them across the counter at a chemist's," she added.

"I know that."

"But you're scared because then you'd know for certain."

"I guess."

"If you were pregnant, do you know how far gone you are?"

Judith shrugged. "I'm just a few days late."

"Is it just from one sexual encounter?"

"No."

"You have a boyfriend?"

"If that's the right word."

"Have you told him?"

"No."

"Nor your father?"

She gave her laughing snort—derisive and unhappy. "No!"

"Listen. You must find out if you're pregnant first of all, and if you are, you have to decide what you want to do. There are people you can speak to. You won't have to deal with it alone. Are there other adults you could speak to? A family member, a teacher?"

"No."

Frieda half closed her eyes. She let the weight settle on her. "OK. You can do the test here, if you want, and then we'll talk about it."

"Really?"

"Really."

"And maybe you should think about talking to your father."

"You don't understand."

"He might not react the way you think."

"I'm his little girl. He doesn't want me to wear makeup! I know how he'll react. Mum dying, police everywhere, and now this. It'll *kill* him. As for Zach—" She stopped and grimaced. Her small face worked with her emotions.

"Is Zach your boyfriend?"

"He'll be furious with me."

"Why? It takes two, you know, and you're the one who has to deal with the consequences."

"I'm supposed to be on the Pill. I *am* on the Pill. I just forgot for a bit."

"Is Zach at your school?"

She pulled a face.

"What does that mean?"

"It means no."

Frieda stared at her and Judith stared back.

"How old is Zach?"

"What's that got to do with anything?"

"Judith?"

"Twenty-eight."

"I see. And you're fifteen. That's a big age gap."

"Thanks. I can do the math."

"You're underage."

"That's just a stupid rule old people make up to stop young people doing what they did when they were young themselves. I'm not a child."

"Tell me something, Judith. Did your mother know about Zach?"

"I never told her. I knew what she'd say."

"So she had no idea?"

"Why would she?" Judith gazed back into the lit kitchen. Dora was sitting with her head propped on her hand, talking; Sasha was listening intently. "Except," she added.

"Except?"

"I think she may have discovered I was on the Pill."

"What makes you think that?"

"I knew she'd find them if I put them anywhere obvious. She had a talent for it—sniffing out other people's secret things. If I'd put them in my underwear drawer or in my makeup bag or under the mattress, she'd have dug them out at once. Like Ted's weed. So I put them in a sock in the cupboard next to the bathroom, which nobody opens from one year to the next except to chuck stuff in. But I think she found them. Maybe I'm being paranoid, but I think she changed the dial so the arrow was pointing to the right day. I just used to take one and not bother about the day matching up, but someone changed it. Twice. I'm sure they did."

"Perhaps it was her way of telling you she knew."

"I dunno. It seems a bit stupid to me. Why wouldn't she just say?"

"Because she knew you'd be angry with her and clam up?"

"Maybe." Judith turned. "So you think she knew?"

"Perhaps."

"And she was waiting for me to confide in her?"

"It's a possibility."

"But I never did."

"No."

"I feel like she's someone I never knew. I can't remember her face properly."

"It's very hard." Frieda made up her mind. "Listen, Judith. There's a late-night chemist a couple of minutes away. If I can, I'm going to buy you an e.p.t. kit, and then you can do it here, at once."

"Now?"

"Yes."

"I don't think I can."

"At least you'll know. The worst thing is not knowing." Her old mantra. Wearing a bit thin now. The girl's strained face glimmered in the darkness. Frieda put a hand on her shoulder and steered her into the kitchen.

"Your curry's all cold," said Sasha, coming over to her and putting a comforting hand on her arm.

"Yes, well. We'll go to a restaurant next time. I've just got to go out for a few minutes."

"Where?"

"Just to the chemist's to get a few things."

"She thinks she's pregnant, doesn't she?" Sasha asked, in a low voice.

"How on earth do you know that?"

"Are you going to get an e.p.t.?"

"Yes. If it's open."

Sasha said, turning away and speaking in a casual voice, "I've got one in my bag she can use. I was going to double-check, but I don't need to. I already know."

"Oh, Sasha!" Images flashed through Frieda's mind—Sasha not lifting her glass, Sasha talking to Dora in a new voice of maternal tenderness, Sasha's hesitation earlier that evening, as if she were about to tell her something. "That's what you wanted to tell me!"

"Yes."

Judith wasn't pregnant. Her sickness and her lateness were, Frieda told her, probably to do with shock and grief. But she needed to think about this properly, she said, not simply continue as she had been doing. She was fifteen and in a relationship with a man who was more than thirteen years older than she. "You need to talk to someone," she said.

"I'm talking to you, aren't I?"

Frieda sighed. Tiredness was making her head pound. "Someone who's not me," she replied.

She made Judith a mug of tea, and Dora, who was limp from crying, some hot chocolate. "I'll order you a cab," she said. "Your father and aunt will be worried."

Judith snorted.

Then the doorbell rang again.

"That'll be Chloë," said Frieda.

"I'll go." Sasha rose and put a hand on Frieda's shoulder, then went to the door.

It wasn't Chloë, it was Ted. He was clearly stoned.

"Isn't Chloë back yet?" he asked.

"No. I'm just ordering a cab," Frieda told him, putting her hand over the receiver. "You can all go home together." She gave the taxi company her address and put the phone down.

"No way. No way in the world. Dad's drunk out of his head, and Aunt Louise is very, very angry in a stomping kind of way. I'm not staying there tonight."

"Well, then, I'm not either," said Judith. Her blue eyes blazed with a kind of scared excitement. "Nor will Dora. Will you, Dora?"

Dora stared at her. She looked stricken.

"The cab will be here in about five minutes. You're all going home."

"No," said Ted. "I can't go there."

"You can't make us," added Judith. Dora put her head on the kitchen table again and closed her eyes. Her lids seemed transparent.

"No. I can't. Where are you going, then?"

"Does it matter?"

"Yes. You're eighteen now, I think, and a boy, and you can look after yourself—theoretically, at least. Judith is fifteen and Dora thirteen. Look at her. Have you got a friend you can stay with?"

"Can't we stay here?" Dora said suddenly. "Can't we be in your house for a night? It feels safe here."

"No," said Frieda. She could feel Sasha's eyes on her.

She considered picking up a plate and throwing it against the wall; she imagined taking a chair and smashing it against the window so that clean air streamed into this hot kitchen, with its smell of curry and sweat and grief. Or better still, just running out of her house, shutting the door behind her— she'd be free, in the April night, with stars and a moon and the wind soft in her face, and they could deal with their own chaotic sadness without her.

"Please," said Dora. "We'll be very quiet and we won't make a mess."

Ted and Judith were silent, just gazing at her and waiting.

"Frieda," said Sasha, warningly. "No. This isn't fair on you."

"One night," said Frieda. "One night only. Do you hear? And you have to ring home and tell your aunt and your father, if he's in a state to understand."

"Yes!"

"And when the cab arrives, I'll send it away but tell them to come back first thing tomorrow to take you home. You are all going to school. Yes?"

"We promise."

"Where can we sleep?" asked Dora.

Frieda thought of her lovely calm study at the top of the house that was now strewn with Chloë's mess. She thought of her living room, with the books on the shelves, the sofa by the grate, the chess table by the window. Everything just so. Her refuge against the world and all its troubles.

"Through there," she said, pointing up the hall.

"Have you got sleeping bags?"

"No." She stood up. Her body felt so heavy it took an enormous effort of will to move at all. Her head thudded. "I'll get some duvets and sheets, and you can use the cushions from the sofa and chair."

"I'll sort all of that." Sasha sounded urgent. She looked at Frieda with an expression of concern, even alarm.

"Can I have a bath?" asked Ted.

Frieda stared at him. The new plug that she'd just bought was in her bag. "No! You can't. You mustn't! Just the washbasin."

The bell rang again and Sasha went to cancel the cab. Then, almost immediately, Chloë came in, in her usual high pitch of angry excitement after seeing her father. She threw her arms around Ted, around Frieda, around Sasha.

"Out of here," said Frieda. "I'm going to clean the kitchen, then go to bed."

"We'll tidy," Chloë shouted gaily. "Leave it to us."

"No. Go into the other room and I'll do it. You're all to go to sleep now—you're getting up at seven and leaving shortly after that. Don't make a noise. And if anyone uses my toothbrush, I'll throw them out, whatever time of night it is."

You seem to have gone off radar. Where are you? Talk to me!
Sandy xxxxx

THIRTY-SEVEN

t's fun, isn't it?" said Riley.

"In what way?" asked Yvette.

"We're looking through people's things, opening their drawers, reading through their diaries. It's all the stuff you want to do, but you're not meant to. I wish I could do this at my girlfriend's flat."

"No, it's not fun," said Yvette. "And don't say that aloud, even to me."

Riley was going through the filing cabinet in the Kerrigans' living room. They'd searched the main bedroom and the kitchen already. Paul Kerrigan had stayed in hospital only one night after he was beaten up and now he was out, but his wife had let them in, tight-lipped and silent. She hadn't offered them coffee or tea, and as they searched among the couple's possessions, lifting up underwear, turning on computers, reading private letters, noticing the tidemark in the bath and the moth holes in some of Paul Kerrigan's jumpers, they could hear her slamming doors, banging pans. When Yvette had last met her, she had been dazed and wearily sad. Now she seemed angry.

"Here," she said, coming into the room. "You might not have found these. They were in his bike pannier in the cupboard under the stairs."

She was holding a small square packet between forefinger and thumb, with an air of distaste. "Condoms," she said, and dropped them onto the table, as if they'd been used. "For his Wednesday dates, I assume."

Yvette tried to keep her expression neutral. She hoped Riley wouldn't say anything, wouldn't react. "Thank you." She picked up the packet to put in the evidence bag.

"He didn't use them with you?" said Riley, in a bright voice.

"I had cancer several years ago, and the chemotherapy meant that I'm now infertile," said Elaine Kerrigan. Briefly, her stiff expression changed to one of distress. "So, no, he didn't."

"So . . ." Yvette began.

"There's something else I should say. Paul didn't get home until quite late on that day."

"We're talking about the sixth of April."

"Yes. I was here a long time before him. I remember because I made a lemon meringue pie, and I was worried it would spoil. Funny the things you worry about, isn't it? Anyway, he was late. It must have been gone eight."

"Why didn't you tell us that before?"

"It's hard to remember everything at once."

"Yes, I can see that," said Yvette. "We'll need you to make a new statement."

She glanced at Riley. There was a gleam about him, almost as if he were suppressing a smile.

"He had a long shower when he came in," continued Elaine, "and put his clothes straight into the wash. He said he'd had a hard day on site and had to wash away the grime before supper."

"It's important you tell us everything you know," said Yvette. "I know how angry you must be, but I want to be clear that there is no connection between your finding this and your new account of events, which is quite damaging to your husband's situation."

"I'm angry with Paul, if that's what you mean," said Elaine. "I'm quite glad someone beat him up. It feels like they were doing it for me. But I'm just telling you what I remember. That's my duty, isn't it?"

As they were leaving, they met the two Kerrigan sons. They had their father's face and their mother's eyes, and they both stared at Yvette and Riley with what looked to Yvette like hatred.

Meanwhile, Chris Munster was searching the flat where Paul Kerrigan and Ruth Lennox had met every Wednesday afternoon for the past ten years, barring holidays. He was making an inventory. Dutifully, he wrote down everything he found: two pairs of slippers, his and hers; two toweling robes, ditto; a single shelf full of books in the bedroom—an anthology of poems about childhood, an anthology of writings about dogs, Winston Churchill's *History of the English-Speaking People*, a collection of humorous pieces, a volume of cartoons that Munster didn't find particularly amusing—all books that he supposed were meant to be read in snatches. The bed linen had been removed for traces of bodily fluids, but there was a brightly patterned quilt thrown over the small chair and a woven strip of rug running along the floor. The curtains were yellow checked, very cheery. The stripped-pine wardrobe was empty except for two shirts (his) and a sundress with a torn zipper.

In the clean, bare bathroom: two toothbrushes, two washcloths, two towels, shaving cream, deodorant (his and hers), dental floss, mouthwash. He imagined the two of them carefully washing, cleaning their teeth, gargling with mouthwash, examining themselves in the mirror above the sink for traces of their activities, before getting back into their sensible clothes and going back to their other lives.

In the kitchen-living room there were four recipe books, along with a set of basic cooking utensils (pots, pans, wooden spoons, a couple of baking trays) and a small number of plates, bowls, glass tumblers. Four mugs that looked to Munster much like the mugs he had seen in the Lennox house. She might well have bought them at the same time. There was a bottle of white wine in the little fridge and two bottles of red wine on the surface. There was a dead hyacinth tilting in its dried-up soil. Two onions shriveling on the windowsill. A striped tablecloth thrown over the wooden table in the center of the room. Jigsaws on the side, several, of different levels of difficulty. A pack of cards. A digital radio. A wall calendar with nothing written on it. A red sequined cushion on the two-seater sofa.

Ten years of lying, he thought. Just for this.

"Kerrigan no longer has an alibi," said Karlsson.

"Well, maybe he doesn't," said Yvette. "I'm not sure which of Mrs. Kerrigan's stories I believe."

"So you're taking his side." There was a sound to his left, a sort of cackle. It came from Riley.

"Yvette's definitely not taking Kerrigan's side. She can't stand him."

"And what did he need condoms for?" said Karlsson. "Not for his wife."

"And not for Mrs. Lennox," said Yvette. "We know she had an IUD fitted."

"He still could have worn a condom," said Riley.

"What for?" said Karlsson.

Riley looked uneasy now. Karlsson shouldn't need to be told this.

"You know," he said. "To stop him catching something from Ruth Lennox. You know what they say: when you sleep with someone, you're sleeping with all their partners and their partners' partners and their partners' partners . . ."

"Yes, we get the idea," said Yvette.

Karlsson suddenly thought of Sadie. It had been bad enough already. It wasn't possible, was it? He suppressed the idea. It was too terrible to think about. "Do you think so?" he asked.

"No," said Yvette, firmly. "If the condoms had been for Ruth Lennox, they would have been in the flat, and Munster didn't find any there. There must have been someone else."

"That sounds right," said Karlsson. "The question is, did Ruth Lennox know about that?"

"The other question is why she had that dial of pills in her cupboard."

"Also," said Yvette, "I've been thinking about the doll."

"Go on."

"We're assuming it was sent to Ruth Lennox, and it was a warning. Which would mean that someone was onto them."

"Yes?"

"What if it was meant for Dora all the time? We know she was being badly bullied at school in the months leading up to her mother's death. Maybe kids who knew she was ill and would be alone in the house did it."

"Why?" Riley sounded indignant.

"Because kids are cruel."

"But that's just horrible."

"They would think it was just a game," said Yvette. Everyone noticed the note of bitterness in her voice and her color rose.

"You may be right." Karlsson spoke quickly to cover the awkwardness. "We might be leaping to conclusions."

"Poor thing," said Riley. "Whichever it was."

"The pills belonged to Judith Lennox," said Frieda.

She had come to the police station first thing that morning. Karlsson noticed the rings around her eyes, the strain in her face. She wouldn't sit down, but stood by the window.

"That clears up one mystery."

"She's fifteen."

"It's not so unusual for a fifteen-year-old to be sexually active," said Karlsson. "At least she's being careful."

"Her boyfriend is much older, in his late twenties."

"That's a big gap."

"And Judith thinks perhaps her mother found out about them."

"I see."

"I thought you should know. I told Judith I would pass on the information."

"Thank you."

"His name is Zach Greene." She watched Karlsson scribble the name on the pad in front of him.

"Do you want some coffee?"

"No."

"Are you all right?"

She considered the question, wondering whether to tell him about Dean and her fear that he had been in Olivia's house. "It doesn't matter," she answered at last.

"I think it does. "

"I have to go now."

"You're not back at work yet, are you?"

"Barely."

"So please sit down for a few minutes and tell me what's up."

"I have to go. There are things I have to do."

"What things?"

"You wouldn't understand. I don't understand."

"Try me."

"No."

"I'm going to have it."

Sasha and Frieda were sitting in a small café beside Regent's Canal. Ducks leading flotillas of ducklings steered through the litter and twigs that bobbed in the brown waters.

"You've decided."

"*We*'ve decided."

"Are you sure about this? A month ago, you barely knew him."

"I know—but don't look so worried. I want you to be glad for me."

"I am glad. Well, glad and worried too. It's so very quick. Do you know each other well enough?"

"If it had been only a week, I'd still be certain. I'm going to move in with Frank, and I'm going to have a baby. My whole life is changing."

"You deserve your happiness," said Frieda. And she thought of Sandy in America. He seemed very far off now. Sometimes she could barely remember his face or the sound of his voice.

THIRTY-EIGHT

J osef took the cards from the café table and thumbed through them.

"And I've got some phone numbers," said Frieda, "from the stickers on the side of the phone box."

"So I phone the number," said Josef.

"I know it's a big thing to ask. But if I phoned, they'd be puzzled hearing a woman's voice and I'd have to explain things and it probably wouldn't work."

"Frieda, you say that already."

Frieda took a sip from her cup. The tea was cold. "I suppose I feel guilty asking you to phone up a prostitute. In fact, a number of prostitutes. I'm grateful to you for doing it. You've already done so much."

"Too much, maybe," said Josef, with a smile. "So I call now?" Frieda pushed her mobile across the table. He took the phone and selected a card. "We take the French teacher." He dialed the number and Frieda couldn't stop herself wondering whether he'd done this before. Over the years, several of her patients had talked of using prostitutes, or fantasizing about using prostitutes. At medical school, she had been at parties, once or twice, where a stripper had turned up. Was that the same thing or something completely different? "Get over it," she remembered a red-faced medical student shouting at her. "Lighten up." Josef was writing something on the card. The instructions sounded complicated. Finally he handed her the phone.

"Spenzer Court."

"Spenser," said Frieda.

"Yes. And it is by Carey Road."

Frieda looked at the index of her *A–Z*. "It's a few streets away," she said. "We can walk."

A gateway at the end of Carey Road led into the council estate. The first block was called Wordsworth Court, and they went along a ground floor level, consisting of lock-up garages and giant steel bins. Frieda stopped for a moment. There were split bin bags strewn about, a supermarket trolley lying on its side, a broken TV that had probably been thrown from an upper level. A woman in a full veil was pushing a pram along the far side.

"You know, I never understood places like this," she said, "until, one time, I was in a hill town in Sicily and I suddenly did. That was the idea about this sort of estate. It was going to be like the little Italian town that the architect had spent his holiday in, full of squares where children would play, and there would be markets and jugglers, and hidden passageways, where people could bump into each other and gossip and go for evening strolls. But it didn't quite work out."

"Is like Kiev," said Josef. "But these not so good when is twenty degrees cold."

They reached Spenser Court and walked up a staircase to the third floor, picking their way through old food cartons. They went along the balcony. Josef looked at his card and then at the flat in front of him. The window next to the door was barred, but also broken and blocked from the inside with plasterboard.

"Is here," he said. "Is difficult to be in mood for the sex."

"That's the way it's always been. In London anyway."

"In Kiev also."

"We need to be calm with her," said Frieda. "Reassuring."

She pressed the doorbell and glanced at Josef. Did he feel like she did? A strange nausea and guilt about what was going on in the city where she lived? Was she just being prim or naïve? She knew the ways of the world. Josef looked calmly expectant. There was a fumbling sound, then the door opened a few inches, and Frieda caught a glimpse of a face behind the taut chain: young, very small, lipstick, bleached hair. Frieda started to say something, but the door slammed shut. She waited for the chain to be unfastened, the door opened properly, but there was silence. She and Josef looked at each other. Frieda pressed the doorbell again, but there was no response. She leaned down, pushed the letter box open, and peered through. Something was blocking her view.

"We just want to talk," she said. There was no response. She handed her phone to Josef. "Try calling her. Say who you are."

He looked puzzled.

"Who I am really?"

"Say you're the man who made the appointment."

He called and waited.

"Leave message?" he said.

"No, don't bother. She probably thought we were from Immigration or the police or someone who meant trouble."

"Is you."

"What?"

"Is you. She see woman, she think we do something to her."

Frieda leaned on the balcony railing and looked down. "You're right," she said. "This was a stupid plan. I'm so sorry I dragged you out here for nothing."

"No. It's not nothing. I keep your phone. You give me the map. You go back to café, you sit have nice tea and a cake. I will come in one hour."

"I can't ask you to do that, Josef. It's not right. And it's not safe."

Josef smiled at that. "Not safe? With you not protecting me?"

"It feels wrong."

"You go now."

When they got back onto Carey Road, Frieda took some banknotes from her purse and gave them to him. "You should ask them if they know a girl called Lily Dawes. Lila. That's what she mainly called herself, I think. I wish I had a picture to show them but I don't know how to get one. Give them twenty pounds anyway, and another twenty if they tell you anything. Does that seem enough? I don't know about these things."

"Is OK, I think."

"And be careful."

"Always."

Frieda left him there. After a few moments, she glanced back and saw him talking on the phone. She went back into the café and ordered another cup of tea but didn't touch it. What she really wanted was just to rest her head on her hands and sleep. She felt she should read or think about something. She took the sketch pad out of her bag and spent twenty minutes making a sketch of the great plane trees in Lincoln's Inn Fields. She couldn't get them right and told herself that she would go back there soon and do it from life. She put the pad away and looked around the café. There was a couple sitting at a table by the door. She met the eye of the man, who gave her a hostile look, so from then on she just stared in front of her. When she felt a touch on her shoulder, she started as if she had been asleep, but she was sure she couldn't have been. It was Josef.

"Is it an hour already?" she said.

He looked down at the phone before handing it to her. "An hour and a half," he said.

"What happened? Did you find anything out?"

"Not here," said Josef. "We go to pub. You buy me drink."

They could see a pub as soon as they were back on the pavement, and they walked to it in silence. Inside, there was noise from a games machine, with several teenage boys clustered around it.

"What do you want?" said Frieda.

"Vodka. Big vodka. And cigarettes."

Frieda bought a double vodka, a packet of cigarettes, a box of matches, and a glass of tap water for herself. Josef looked at his drink disapprovingly.

"Is warm like the bathwater," he said. "But *budmo.*"

"What?"

"It means we shall live always."

"We won't, you know."

"I believe you will," he said sternly, and drank his vodka in a single gulp.

"Can I get you another?" she said.

"Now we go for the cigarette."

They stepped outside. Josef lit one and inhaled deeply. Frieda thought of long-ago days outside the school gates at lunchtime. He offered the packet to her and she shook her head. "So?" she said.

His expression was sad, as he answered: "I talk to four women. There is one from Africa, I think, maybe from Somalia. She speak English like me but much, much worse. I understand little. Man there also. He want more than twenty for her. Much more. Angry man."

"Oh, my God, Josef. What happened?"

"Is normal. I explain."

"He could have had a gun."

"Gun would be problem. But no gun. I explain to him and I go. But no use. And then I see a girl from Russia and then one girl I don't know where from. Romania, maybe. The last girl, the girl I just see, she say a few words, and I have a strong feeling and I talk to her in Ukrainian. She have big shock." He gave a smile but there was harshness in his eyes.

"Josef, I'm so sorry."

He stubbed out his cigarette on the pub wall and lit another. "Ah. It's not so big a thing. You expect me to say, 'Oh, it's little girl from my own village.' I'm not a child, Frieda. It's not just the plumbers and the haircutters who come here from my country."

"I don't know what to say."

"I do not say that it is a good job. I see her apartment. It is dirty and damp, and I see the signs of drugs. That is not good."

"Do you want us to do something to help?"

"Ah," he said again, dismissively. "You start there and you finish nowhere. I know this. It is bad to see, but I know it."

"I should have been the one doing all of this. It's my problem not yours."

Josef looked at her with concern. "Not good for you to do right now," he said. "You not well. We are both sad about her, about Mary. But you were damaged too. Not all better."

"I'm fine."

Josef gave a laugh. "That is what everybody says, and it means nothing. 'How are you?' 'I'm fine.'"

"It means you don't need to worry. And I also want to say that I'm sorry I wasted your time."

"Waste?"

"Yes. I'm sorry I dragged you all the way down here."

"No. Not wasted. The one woman, the Romanian. I think Romanian. She also have the drugs, I think. You see it in the eyes."

"Well, not always . . ."

"I see it. I talk to her of your Lily. I think she know her."

"What do you mean you think?"

"She know a Lila."

"What did she say about her?"

"She know her a bit. But this Lila, she was not completely . . . What do you say when someone is a bit part of it but not complete?"

"A hanger-on?"

"Hanger-on?" Josef considered the phrase. "Yes, maybe. This girl Maria knew Lila a bit. Lila also with the drugs, I think."

Frieda tried to digest what Josef had said. "Does she know where we can find her?"

Josef shrugged. "She not see her for a while. For two months or three months. Or less or more. They are not like us with the time."

"Did she know where Lila had gone?"

"She did not."

"She must have moved away," said Frieda. "I wouldn't even know where to start. That's fantastic, Josef. But I guess it's the end of the trail." Then she noticed a faint smile on his face. "What is it?"

"This Lila," he said. "She have a friend. Maybe a friend with the drugs or the sex."

"Who was it?"

"Shane. A man called Shane."

"Shane," said Frieda. "Does she have a number for him? Or an address?"

"No."

"Did she know his second name?"

"Shane, she said. Only Shane."

She thought hard and murmured something to herself.

"What you say?"

"Nothing, nothing much. That's good, Josef. It's amazing you found that out. I never thought we'd get anything. But what do we do with it?"

Josef gazed at her with his sad brown eyes. "Nothing."

"Nothing?"

"I know you need to rescue this girl. But you cannot do this. Is over."

"Is over," repeated Frieda, dully. "Yes. Perhaps you're right."

That evening, Frieda put the plug in her bath. She had bought oil to pour in and a candle that she would light. For a long time now, she had imagined lying in the hot foamy water in the dark, just the guttering candle and the moon through the window to give light. But now it came to it, she found she wasn't in the right mood. It would just be a bath. She pulled out the plug and stood under the shower instead, briefly washing away the day. The bath would have to wait. It would be her reward, her prize.

THIRTY-NINE

Before interviewing Paul Kerrigan, Karlsson Skyped Bella and Mikey, sitting in his office and looking at their photographs in frames on his desk and at their jerky images on the screen. They were excitable, distracted. They didn't really want to be talking to him, and their eyes kept wandering away to something out of sight. Bella told him about a new friend called Pia who had a dog. She had a large sweet bulging in her cheek, and it was hard to hear what she was saying. Mikey kept twisting his head to mouth something urgently at whoever was in the room. Karlsson couldn't think of anything to talk about. He felt strangely self-conscious. He told them about the weather and asked them about school, like some elderly uncle they'd barely ever met. He tried to make a funny face at them, but they didn't laugh. He ended the call early and went to the interview room.

Kerrigan's face was swollen from his attack. There was a purple and yellow bruise on one cheek, and his lip was cut. There were also pouches of fatigue under his eyes and deep grooves bracketing his mouth, like that of an old man. He was unshaven, the collar of his shirt grimy, and one of the buttons was undone so that his stomach showed through, shockingly white and soft. Karlsson asked him once more about his movements on Wednesday, April 6, when Ruth Lennox had been murdered. He had a large white handkerchief that he buried his entire battered face in.

"Sorry," he spluttered. "I don't understand why you're asking me this again. I've just been in the hospital, you know."

"I'm asking because I want to get things clear. Which they are not. What did you do when you left Ruth Lennox?"

"I've told you. I went back home."

"What time?"

"Late afternoon, early evening. I had dinner with Elaine." He wrinkled his jowly face. "She made a pudding," he said slowly and clearly, as if his meal were his alibi.

"You weren't there until quite late that evening, Mr. Kerrigan."

"What do you mean?"

"Your wife has told us that you didn't return home until nearly eight o'clock."

"Elaine said that?"

"Yes. And that you had a shower and put your clothes in the wash."

Paul Kerrigan shook his head slowly. "That's not right," he said.

"We just want to know what you did between the time that Ruth Lennox left the flat and the time that you returned home several hours later."

"She's angry with me. She wants to punish me. You must see that."

"Are you saying she's lying about the time you came back?"

"Everything's ruined," he said. "Ruth's dead and my wife hates me and my sons have contempt for me. And she wants to punish me."

"Do you know what contraceptive Ruth Lennox used?" Karlsson asked.

Paul Kerrigan blinked. "Contraceptive? What are you talking about?"

"You were sleeping with her for ten years. You must have known."

"Yes. She had the coil fitted."

"You're telling me you knew she was using contraception."

"That's what I just said."

"Yet your wife found condoms in your bicycle pannier." Karlsson looked closely at Kerrigan's swollen, flushed face. "If your wife is no longer fertile and Ruth Lennox had an IUD, why would you have condoms?"

Now there was a long silence. Karlsson waited patiently, impassively.

"It's complicated," said Kerrigan, finally.

"Then you'd better explain it to me."

"I love my wife. You won't believe that. And we've had a good marriage, until now. Ruth didn't alter that. I had two parallel lives, and they didn't touch. If Elaine hadn't found out, none of this would have mattered. I just wanted to keep my marriage safe from harm."

"You were going to explain about the condoms."

"I don't know how to say this out loud."

"But you're going to have to."

"I have needs that my wife can't meet."

Karlsson was starting to feel almost queasy, but he had to proceed.

"Which was what Ruth Lennox was for, I suppose."

Kerrigan made a hopeless gesture. "She was at first. But then it became like another marriage. I liked it, in a way. But I needed something else."

"And?"

"There's been someone else. For a while."

"Who?"

"Do you need to know?"

"Mr. Kerrigan, you don't need to worry about what I need to know. Just answer my questions."

"Her name's Sammie Kemp. Samantha. She's done some casual administrative work for my company. That's how we met. It was just fun."

"Did Ruth Lennox know of your relationship with Samantha Kemp?"

"It wasn't exactly a relationship."

"Did she know?"

"She may have suspected."

"You should have told us this before."

"It's got nothing to do with anything."

"Did she confront you about it?"

"What did she expect? She knew I was being unfaithful. She knew I was sleeping with my wife. So . . ."

Karlsson almost laughed at that. "That's really quite a clever way of almost convincing yourself. But Ruth Lennox didn't see it like that?"

"It's not as if she didn't know things had run their course."

"You were going to leave her?"

"Not according to her," Paul Kerrigan said bitterly, before he could stop himself. A flush spread over his face.

"Let me get this clear. You were having an affair with another woman, Samantha Kemp, and you wanted to end your relationship with Ruth Lennox, but she wouldn't accept that."

"I wanted it to be mutual. No recriminations. Ten good years. Not many people manage that."

"But Ruth Lennox didn't see it that way. Was she angry? Did she ever threaten to tell your wife?"

"She wouldn't have behaved like that."

"Shall we stick for the moment to what you actually did, rather than what you're claiming she wouldn't have done, if she hadn't been murdered?"

"I was with Sam that Wednesday."

"With Samantha Kemp?"

"Yes."

"It's a pity you didn't tell us this before."

"I'm telling you now."

"So you went from your Wednesday afternoon with Ruth Lennox to another assignation with Samantha Kemp."

"Yes."

"Where?"

"At her flat."

"I'll need her contact details."

"She's got nothing to do with any of this."

"She has now."

"She won't be pleased."

"You realize this changes everything? You had a secret that only one other person knew. You and Ruth Lennox had to trust each other. That was probably easy, as long as you both wanted to continue your affair. For ten years you protected each other from being discovered. The problem arose when one of you wanted to leave."

"That's not how it was."

"She had power over you."

"You're making a mistake. She didn't threaten to expose me, and I was with Samantha Kemp from the moment I left the flat until the time I came back home. Check it out, if you don't believe me."

"Don't worry, we will."

"If that's all, I have things to do."

He stood up from the chair, scraping it across the floor. Karlsson stared at him and waited, and eventually Kerrigan lowered himself into the chair once more.

"I haven't done anything except be stupid," he said.

"You've lied to us."

"Not because I killed Ruth. I loved her."

"But you were planning to leave?"

"Not planning in the way you mean. Just aware things were coming to an end."

"She could have wrecked your marriage."

"She has anyway, hasn't she? From beyond the grave."

"How was she going to make you stay with her?"

"I've already said that she wasn't. She was just angry. You're twisting words to suit your suspicions."

"I think you're still withholding information. We will find it out in the end."

"There's nothing to find out."

"We'll see."

"I tell you there's nothing. Under the mess is just more mess."

Farther along the corridor, Yvette was interviewing Zach Greene, Judith Lennox's boyfriend. He worked part time for a software firm based in a converted warehouse just off Shoreditch High Street. He was a tall, skinny man with small pupils in eyes that were almost yellow. He had bony wrists, long, nicotine-stained fingers, and his brown hair was shaved close to his skull in a soft bristle. Yvette could see a V-shaped scar running from his crown to just above his delicate left ear. He had rosebud lips and shapely eyebrows, like a woman's, a nose stud, and a tattoo just visible above his shirt. Everything about him contradicted everything else: he looked soft and rugged, feeble and aggressive, older than his years and much younger. He smelled of flowers and tobacco. His shirt was a pastel green, and on his feet were stout army boots. He was oddly attractive and a bit creepy, and he made Yvette feel dowdy and deeply unsure of herself.

"I know that theoretically it's against the law."

"No, it's definitely against the law."

"But why do you assume we were actually having sex?"

"Judith Lennox says you were. If she's lying, then say so."

"Why do you assume I knew her age?"

"How old are *you*?"

"I'm twenty-eight."

"Judith Lennox is fifteen."

"She looks older."

"That's a large age difference."

"Jude is a young woman. She knows her own mind."

"She's a girl."

He gave a tiny, almost invisible shrug with one shoulder. "Power is what matters, don't you think?" he said. "The law is there to prevent the abuse of power. In our case, it's irrelevant. As far as I'm concerned, we're both consenting adults."

"The fact remains that she's a minor. You're guilty of a criminal offense."

For a brief moment, anxiety broke the surface. His face puckered. "Is that why I'm here?"

"You're here because her mother was killed."

"Look. I'm really sorry about that, but I don't see the connection."

"Did you ever meet Mrs. Lennox?"

"I *saw* her. I didn't meet her."

"She didn't know about you?"

"Jude thought she wouldn't understand. And I wasn't going to argue."

"You're quite sure you never met?"

"I think I'd remember."

"And you think that Mrs. Lennox wasn't aware of your existence."

"Not that I know of."

"Did she suspect that Judith was involved with someone?"

"I never met the woman. Why don't you ask Jude?"

"I'm asking you," said Yvette, curtly. She saw him give his tiny smile.

"As far as I know, she didn't suspect. But mothers have a way of sensing things, don't they? So maybe she noticed something was up."

"Where were you on the evening she was murdered—Wednesday, the sixth of April?"

"What? Do you really think I would have killed someone because I didn't want them to find out about a relationship with their daughter?"

"It's a criminal offense. You could go to prison."

"This is all crap. She's nearly sixteen. She's not a little kid in pigtails with scabby knees. You've seen her. Drop-dead gorgeous. I met her at a club. Where you have to be eighteen to get in, by the way. And show your ID."

"How long have you been involved with her?"

"What do you mean by *involved*?"

"Oh, please, just give me an answer."

He closed his eyes. Yvette wondered if he could feel the pulse of her hostility from where he was sitting.

"I met her nine weeks ago," he said. "Not long, is it?"

"And she's on the Pill?"

"You'll have to ask Jude about things like that."

"Are you still with her?"

"I don't know."

"You don't know?"

"No. That's the truth." For a moment, his mask seemed to slip. "She couldn't bear to touch me. She wouldn't even let me hug her. I think she feels responsible for it all. Does that make sense?"

"Yes."

"Which somehow makes *me* responsible too."

"I see."

"Not really responsible," he added hastily.

"No."

"So, really, I think it's over. You should be pleased. I'm legal again."

"I wouldn't say that," said Yvette.

That evening, there was a ring at the doorbell of the Lennox house. Russell Lennox heard it from the top of the house and waited for someone else to answer it. But Ted was out, and he thought that Judith was too—that was something he ought to know, of course. Ruth would have known. Dora was in her room and already in bed. And, for once, Louise wasn't in the house, vacuuming with her bloody baby strapped round her or doing her endless baking. The doorbell rang once more and Russell sighed. He went heavily down the stairs.

He didn't recognize the woman on the doorstep, and she didn't immediately introduce herself, just stared at him as though she were searching for someone. She was tall and bony rather than thin, with long hair tied loosely back and glasses hanging round her neck on a cord. She was wearing a long patchwork skirt with a muddy hem.

"I thought I should come."

"I'm sorry—who are you?"

She didn't answer, just raised her eyebrows, almost as though she were amused. "You should recognize me," she said at last. "I'm your partner in humiliation."

"Oh! You mean . . ."

"Elaine Kerrigan," she said, and held out her long slim hand, which Russell took, then didn't know how to let it go.

"But why are you here?" he asked. "What do you want?"

"Want? To see you, I suppose. I mean, see what you look like."

"What do I look like?"

"You look done in," she said, and suddenly tears welled in Russell's eyes.

"I am."

"But really I came to thank you."

"What for?"

"For beating up my husband."

"I don't know what you're talking about."

"You gave him a lovely black eye."

"You're on the wrong track."

"And a swollen lip, so he can't talk properly. And I don't have to listen to his lies."

"Mrs. Kerrigan—"

"Elaine. You did what I wanted to. I'm grateful."

Russell was about to protest again, then his face softened in a smile. "It was my pleasure," he said. "You'd better come in. Maybe you're the only person in the world I want to talk to."

FORTY

This time Frieda didn't need to ring the doorbell. Lawrence Dawes was at the front of the house with another man. Dawes was up a stepladder, and the other man was holding it. When Frieda announced herself, he looked round, frowned, and descended the steps with care.

"I'm sorry," he said. "I've forgotten the name."

Frieda told him, and he nodded in recognition. "I'm terrible with names. I do apologize. I remember you very clearly. This is my friend Gerry. He helps me with my garden, I help him with his, and then we have a drink to celebrate. And this woman is a psychiatrist, so be careful what you say."

Gerry was a similar age to Dawes but looked entirely different. He was dressed in checked shorts that reached his knees and a short-sleeved shirt that was also checked, but of a different kind, so that he almost shimmered. His legs and arms were thin, wiry, and deeply tanned. He had a small gray mustache that was very slightly uneven.

"You're neighbors?" said Frieda.

"Almost," said Gerry. "We share the same river."

"Gerry's a few houses upstream from me," said Dawes. "He can pollute my stream, but I can't pollute his."

"Cheeky sod," said Gerry.

"We've been giving my roses some attention," said Dawes. "They've really started growing, and we're trying to train them. You know, roses round the door. Do you like roses?"

"Yes, I suppose so," said Frieda.

"We were about to have some tea," said Dawes.

"Were we?" said Gerry.

"We're always about to have tea. We've either just had it, or we're about to have it, or both. Would you like to join us?"

"Just for a few minutes," said Frieda. "I don't want to keep you from your work."

Dawes stowed his stepladder away—"Kids'll nick anything that moves," he said—and they went through the house to the back lawn. Frieda sat on the bench, and the two men came out, carrying mugs, a teapot, a jug of milk, and a plate of chocolate biscuits. They laid them out on a small wooden table. Dawes poured the tea and handed a mug to Frieda.

"I know what you're thinking," he said.

"What?" said Frieda.

"You're a psychiatrist."

"Well, a psychotherapist."

"Every time you come, I'm doing up the house. I'm digging the garden, I'm making the roses look nice. What you're thinking is that I have this feeling that if I make my house nice enough, my daughter will want to come back to it." He sipped his tea. "I suppose that's one of the problems, doing your job."

"What's that?"

"You can never just sit in a garden and have a nice cup of tea and a normal conversation. People think, Well, if I say this, she'll think that, and if I say that, she'll think this. It must be difficult for you to stop working."

"I wasn't thinking anything like that. I really was just drinking the tea and wasn't thinking about you at all."

"Oh, that's nice," said Dawes. So what were you thinking about?"

"I was thinking about the little river at the bottom of your garden. I was wondering if I could hear it, but I can't."

"When there's been more rain, then you can hear it, even inside the house. Have a biscuit."

He pushed the plate across to Frieda, who shook her head. "I'm fine."

"You don't look fine," said Dawes. "You look like you need feeding up. What do you think, Gerry?"

"Don't let him tease you," said Gerry. "He's like my old mother. Always wanting everyone to clear their plate."

They sat in silence for a few minutes. Frieda thought she could just hear the soft murmur of the stream.

"So what brings you here?" asked Dawes, eventually. He wasn't smiling at her anymore, but looked somber. "Have you got another day off?"

"I'm not exactly working at the moment. I'm taking some time off."

Dawes poured some more tea and milk into her mug. "You know what I think?" he said. "I think you've taken time off work because you're supposed to be resting. And instead you're chasing around. Chasing around after my Lila."

"I'm a bit worried about her," said Frieda. "Does that make sense to you?"

"I've been worried about her since she was born. I can remember the first time I saw her: she was lying in a cot next to my wife's bed in the ward. I looked down at her, and she had a little dimple in her chin, like me. Look." He touched the end of his chin. "And I said to her, or to myself, that I was going to protect her forever. I was going to make sure that no harm ever came to her. And I failed. I suppose you never can protect a child like that, not once they get older. But I failed as badly as it's possible to fail."

Frieda looked at the two men. Gerry was staring into his tea. Maybe he'd never heard his friend talk so openly and emotionally before.

"The reason I'm here," said Frieda, "is that I wanted to tell you what I've done. I'd hoped I could find your daughter, but I haven't got very far. I've heard from someone who knew her slightly."

"Who?"

"A girl called Maria. I didn't even meet her, so it's at second hand. But apparently she mentioned a man called Shane, who was some sort of friend of your daughter's. Or, at least, he had some kind of connection with her. I don't have a second name, and I don't know anything about him. I wondered if the name rang any bells with you."

"Shane?" said Dawes. "Was he a boyfriend?"

"I don't know. I have only the name. He might have been a friend or some sort of associate. Or it may all be a misunderstanding. This woman was quite vague, I think."

Dawes shook his head slowly. "I don't know anyone by that name. But as I told you when we met before, in the last years I didn't know anything about my daughter's friends. I think she lived in different worlds. The only names I have were of school friends, and she'd lost touch with all of them."

"Mr. Dawes . . ."

"Please, call me Larry."

"Larry, I was hoping you could give me the names of her friends. If I talked to them, I might be able to get some information."

Dawes glanced at his friend. "I'm sorry," he said. "I'm sure you're a good person, and I'm touched by anyone who cares about my daughter. God knows, most people have already forgotten her. But if you have suspicions, why don't you go to the police?"

"Because that's all I've got: suspicions, feelings. I know people in the police, and that won't be enough for them."

"Yet you've come all the way down here twice, just because of your feelings."

"I know," said Frieda. "It sounds stupid, but I can't stop myself."

"I'm sorry," said Dawes. "I can't help you."

"I'd just like some numbers."

"No. I've been through this too often. I spent months looking and worrying and getting my hopes up. If you get any real information, then just tell the police, or come and see me and I'll do what I can. But I can't stir it all up again—I just can't. And I don't want you to."

Frieda put her mug on the table and stood up. "I understand."

"Sometimes," said Dawes, "if someone really wants to get lost, then they can stay lost."

"You're right. Perhaps I was really coming to see you to say sorry."

Dawes seemed puzzled. "Sorry? What for?"

"Various things. I tried to look for your daughter, and I haven't succeeded. And I blundered into your personal grief. I've got a habit of doing that."

"Maybe that's your job, Frieda."

"Yes, but they're usually supposed to ask me before I do it."

Dawes's expression turned bleak. "You're just realizing what I realized some time ago. You think you can protect people, care for them, but sometimes they just get away from you."

Frieda looked at the two men, sitting there like a comfortable old couple. "And I interrupted your work as well," she said.

"He needs interrupting," said Gerry, with a smile. "Otherwise he never stops with his gardening and his building and his mending and his painting."

"Thank you for the tea. It's been nice, sitting in the garden with you both."

"Are you going to the station?" asked Gerry.

"Yes."

"I'm going that way, so I'll walk with you."

Together they left the house. Gerry insisted on carrying Frieda's bag, though she really didn't want him to. He strode along beside her, in his mismatching multicolored checks, with his lopsided mustache, a woman's leather bag slung incongruously from his shoulder, and for a few minutes they didn't speak.

"Do you have a garden?" asked Gerry, eventually.

"Not really. A bit of a yard."

"Soil's the thing—getting your hands dirty. The pleasure of eating your own produce. Do you like broad beans?"

"I do," said Frieda.

"From the plant to the pan. Nothing like it. Lawrence gardens so he doesn't have to brood."

"About his daughter, you mean?"

"He doted on her."

"I'm sorry if I've stirred up painful memories."

"No. It's not as if he ever forgets. He's always waiting for her, and always wondering where he went wrong. But it's better to be active. Digging and mending, sowing and picking."

"I understand."

"I suppose you do. But don't go bringing hope into his life if it comes to nothing."

"I don't mean to do that."

"Hope's the thing that will destroy him. Remember that, and be a bit careful."

On the train back, Frieda stared out the window but saw nothing. She felt an ache of incompletion, of failure and, above all, of tiredness.

She made one last phone call. Then she would have done everything she could, she told herself, to rescue a girl she'd never met and to whom she had no connection, yet whose story had sunk its hooks into her mind.

"Agnes?" she said, when the woman answered. "This is Frieda Klein."

"You've found something?"

"Nothing at all. I just wanted to ask you something."

"What?"

"Apparently Lila knew a man called Shane. Does that ring a bell?"

"Shane? No. I don't think so. I met several of her new friends. Mostly at this grotty pub, the Anchor. They used to hang out there. Maybe there was someone called Shane, but I don't remember him. I don't remember any of their names."

"Thanks."

"You're not going to find her, are you?"

"No. I don't think I am."

"Poor Lila. I don't know why you tried so hard. You tried harder than anyone who knew her. As if your life depended on it."

Frieda was painfully struck by those last words. For a moment, she was silent. Then she said, "Shall we give it one last try? Together?"

. . .

Perhaps Chloë told you that I rang your house and spoke to her. She said you were OK. But she seemed a bit distracted. There were lots of noises going on in the background. You may not know that I also rang Reuben and he said that you were NOT OK. That everyone's worried about you but that no one can really get through to you. What the fuck is going on, Frieda? Or shall I just fly over and hammer at your door until at last you have to answer me? Sandy don't get it."

Agnes, dressed in baggy jogging trousers and a gray hoodie with fraying sleeves, was sitting beside Frieda in a cab. She looked tired. It was raining, and through the dark, wet windows they could see only the glimmering lights of cars and the massed shapes of buildings. Frieda thought of how she could have been in her house now, empty after so many weeks of disruption. She could have been lying in her new bath, or playing chess, or sitting in her study, drawing and thinking and looking out into the wet night.

"Get what?" she asked mildly.

"I was in bed with a novel and a cup of tea, all cozy. And then you ring up out of the blue and all of a sudden I'm on my way to some dingy little pub full of girls off their heads on who-knows-what and men with tattoos and dead eyes, just because Lila used to hang out there. Why?"

"Why are you going?"

"No. I know why I'm going. Lila was my mate. If there's some chance I can find her, I have to. But why are *you* going? Why do you even care?"

Frieda was tired of asking herself the same question. She closed her eyes and pressed her cool fingertips against her hot, aching eyeballs. She could see Ted Lennox's white face, like a petal on dark water, and Chloë's fierce, accusing gaze.

"Anyway, here we are," said Agnes, with a sigh. "I certainly never thought I'd set foot in this place again."

Frieda told the cab driver to wait for them, and they both stepped out into the rain. They could hear the beat of music coming from the Anchor, and there was a huddle of smokers around the door. The tips of their cigarettes glowed, and a miasma of smoke hung around them.

"Let's get this over with. You want me to look for anyone I think I might have seen hanging out with Lila."

"Yes."

"Two years ago."

"Right."

"Because we need to find someone called Shane."

"Yes."

"Do you think you're quite right in the head?"

They shouldered their way through the smokers and into the pub, if that was what it was. Frieda rarely went to pubs: she hated the smell of beer and the jangling music, the lights of the jukebox. Now she felt dozens of eyes on them as they entered: it didn't feel like a place where outsiders came casually for a pint. It was a dark room that stretched back out of view, where crowds of people, mostly men, were sitting at tables or standing at the bar and in corners. A few women straggled on the outskirts of the groups; Frieda saw their short skirts and cold white thighs, their shoes with dagger heels and their makeup; she heard their high, frantic laughter. The long dim room was hot and smelled stale. A man stumbled and almost fell in front of them, short and squat with spittle shining on his cheek, the drink he was holding splashing onto the floor.

"Should we buy drinks?" asked Agnes.

"No."

Together they inched their way through the crowd, Agnes peering from face to face, her eyes flickering, a frown of concentration on her face.

"Well?" asked Frieda.

"I don't know. Maybe him."

She hunched her shoulder toward a small table at the end of a room. A woman was sitting on the man's lap, and they were kissing and unabashedly feeling each other, and beside them another man was watching them impassively, as if they were animals in a zoo. He was rail thin, with peroxide blond hair, pale skin, and a line of tiny red spots running like stitches along his forehead.

"Right."

Frieda stepped forward and tapped him on the shoulder. He looked at her. His pupils were enormous, giving him an otherworldly appearance.

"Can I have a word?" she asked.

"Who are you?"

"I'm looking for Shane."

"Shane." It wasn't a question, just an echo. "Shane who?"

The pair beside him stopped kissing and disentangled themselves. The woman leaned forward and took a swig from the glass on the table. Her face was empty of expression.

"Shane who knew Lila Dawes."

"I dunno about any Lila."

"But you know Shane?"

"I knew a Shane once, but I haven't seen him. He doesn't come here anymore."

"He went to prison," the woman beside him said, in a flat voice. She was buttoning her blouse—wrongly, Frieda saw. The man whose lap she was sitting on tried to pull her back into him, but she pushed him away.

"You know him?"

"Do you know Lila?" added Agnes, eagerly, almost imploringly.

"Was she one of the girls who hung around with Shane?"

"Why did Shane go to prison?"

"I think he hit someone," the blonde said. "With a bottle."

"Is he still there?"

"I don't know. You could ask Stevie. He knows Shane."

"Where can I find Stevie?"

"Right behind you," said a voice. Frieda and Agnes turned to find a thick-set man with a shaved head and an oddly soft, girlish face behind them. "What do you want with Shane?"

"Just to find him."

"Why?"

"He knew my friend," said Agnes, whose voice trembled slightly. Frieda put a hand on her arm in reassurance.

"Which friend was that?"

"Lila. Lila Dawes."

"Lila? Shane had so many friends."

"Was he a pimp?" asked Frieda, her voice cool and clear in the over-heated room.

"You should be careful what you call people," said Stevie.

"Is he still in prison?"

"No, he only did a couple of months. Good behavior."

"Do you know where I can find him now?"

Stevie smiled, not at Frieda but at the man sitting at the table. "You know what our Shane's doing now? He's working at a horse sanctuary in Essex. He's feeding ponies whose owners haven't treated them right. Lucky ponies."

"Where in Essex?"

"Why do you want to know? Got a horse you don't want?"

"I want to talk to him."

"Somewhere by a big road."

"Which big road?"

"The A12. It's got a stupid name. Daisy. Or Sunflower."

"Which?"

"Sunflower."

"Thank you," said Frieda.

"And fuck you too."

Sharon Gibbs from the south of London, nineteen years old, had last been seen approximately one month ago, perhaps five weeks. Her parents hadn't reported her missing immediately—according to the police report he had in front of him, she was something of a drifter, perhaps one of those who go intentionally missing. Even in the bureaucratic language, Fearby sensed indifference, hopelessness. She looked like another dead end.

But when he stood in front of his large map and peered again at the small flags he'd pinned to it, he felt the surge of excitement that had kept him going through this strange one-man investigation. For it seemed clear to him that there was a pattern before his eyes. But then—at the end of a day, when he sat in this room with his whisky, his fags fugging up the window, surrounded by crumpled balls of paper, overflowing ashtrays, cartons of take-aways, half-finished mugs of coffee, piles of books thumbed through and then discarded—it faded away.

He looked around him, for a moment seeing things as a stranger would see them. It was a mess, no doubt about it, but an obsessive mess. The walls were covered with maps, photographs of girls and young women, Post-it stickers with numbers scribbled on them. It made him seem like a stalker, a psychopath. If his wife walked in now, or his children . . . He could picture their expressions of dismay and disgust. He was wearing shabby clothes, his face needed shaving, his hair needed cutting, he reeked of tobacco and drink. But if he was right, if these faces that stared at him from his walls had all been killed by the same person, then all of that would be justified, and he would be a hero. Of course, if he was wrong, he would be a lonely fool and a pathetic failure.

It was no good thinking like that: he'd come too far and done too much. He just had to hold on to his original instinct and keep going, holding his doubts at bay. He sighed and picked up his overnight bag, his car keys, his cigarettes, and shut the door on his stale, untidy house with relief.

.   .   .

Brian and Tracey Gibbs lived in a first-floor flat in south London, at the point where the density of the city was petering out into suburbia. They were poor, Fearby could tell that at once. Their flat was small, and the living room they showed him into needed a fresh coat of paint. He knew from the cutting that they were in their forties, but they looked older—and he felt a surge of anger. The comfortable middle classes can cheat time, while people like the Gibbses are worn down by it, rubbed away. Brian Gibbs was thin and apologetic. Tracey Gibbs was larger and at first more aggressive. She wanted to tell Fearby that they'd done their best, been good parents, never done anything to deserve this. Their only child. It wasn't their fault. All the while, her husband sat mute and thin beside her.

"When did you last see her?" asked Fearby.

"Six weeks ago. Give or take a few days."

"And when did you report her missing?"

"Three and a half weeks ago. We didn't know," she added quickly, defensively. "She's an adult. She lives with us, but she comes and goes as she pleases. Days could go by . . ." She faltered. "You know how it is."

Fearby nodded. He did.

"Could I see a picture of her?"

"There." Tracey Gibbs pointed, and he saw a framed photograph of Sharon: a round, pale face; dark hair in a neat, glossy bob; small mouth smiling for the camera. Fearby had seen too many young women smiling for the camera recently.

"Is she going to be all right?" Brian Gibbs asked, as if Fearby were God.

"I hope so," he replied. "Do you think she went of her own accord?"

"The police think so." This, bitterly, from the mother.

"You don't?"

"She got into bad company."

"What company was that?"

"The worst was this Mick Doherty. I told her what I thought of him, but she wouldn't listen."

She plaited her hands tightly together; Fearby saw that the wedding ring was biting into her finger and that the varnish on her nails was chipped. She looked uncared for. There were moth holes in Brian Gibbs's ancient pullover. There was a hairline crack running up the mug of tea they had given him and a chip on its rim.

"I see," he said, trying to sound neutrally cheerful.

"I know where he works. The police weren't bothered, but I can tell you where to find him."

"All right."

He took the address. It wouldn't do any harm, he thought, and there was nothing else left for him to do, nowhere else to go.

FORTY-TWO

Karlsson opened the file. Yvette was writing in her notebook. Riley and Munster looked bored. Hal Bradshaw was sending a text. He noticed Karlsson's fierce glance and put the phone down on the table but continued to steal glances at it. Karlsson took his watch off and laid it next to the file.

"We're going to talk about this for five minutes," he said, "because that's about all I can stand, and then we should go our separate ways and try to solve this case. Do you know what I wish? I wish Billy Hunt had killed her and that he was safely in prison and that we hadn't lifted the rock and found out about all the adultery and drink and drugs and underage sex."

"Maybe Billy Hunt really did it after all," said Riley.

"Billy Hunt didn't do it."

"Maybe his alibi is flawed. Maybe the timing on the CCTV wasn't right."

"Fine," said Karlsson. "Check it out. If you can break his alibi, you'll be a hero. Now, back in the real world. Remember when we first saw the body, all those days ago? I wondered who would kill this nice mother of three. Now the queue goes out the door. Who shall we start with? There's Russell Lennox: betrayed husband, drink problem, tendency to violence."

"We don't know it was him who beat up Paul Kerrigan."

"No, but I'd lay a bet on it."

"And he didn't know about his wife's affair," said Munster.

"You mean he *said* he didn't."

"His print was on the cog along with Billy's," put in Yvette.

"Because he owned it. But, still, that sounds most likely. Confronts his wife, picks up that cog thing. There's the awkward matter of his alibi, of course. So let's keep leaning on him. Their children were at school and they're children. But now we've got Judith and her every-parent's-nightmare boyfriend. Ruth discovers about him. Arranges a meeting at their house. Threatens him with the law. He picks up the cog. I don't like Zach Greene. I don't like him at all. Which, unfortunately, isn't evidence. Any comments?"

He looked around. "Thought not. But we should lean on him some more. Where did he say he was that afternoon, Yvette?"

Yvette turned pink. "He didn't actually say," she muttered.

"What do you mean?"

"I asked him. But, now you mention it, he didn't give me an answer. He went on about them being consenting adults or something. He distracted me."

Karlsson stared at her. "Distracted you?" he repeated pleasantly, coldly.

"Sorry. It was stupid of me. I'll get back to him."

He stared down at his papers for a moment. He didn't want to shout at her in front of Riley and Bradshaw, but it took an effort.

"Moving on. We have Kerrigan. He wants to break off with Ruth. Or she discovers about his office affair. Confronts him. He picks up the cog."

"Would she do it at her house?" said Yvette. "Wouldn't the flat be more logical?"

"She might have threatened him at the flat," said Bradshaw. "She could have said she would inform his wife. For him to confront and kill her in her own home would be a tit for tat. Exposing her in her own family home."

Karlsson frowned at Bradshaw. "I thought your theory was that the murderer was a loner, of no fixed abode, that he had no family connections, that the murder was a kind of love."

"Ah, yes," said Bradshaw. "But in a real sense Kerrigan was a loner, estranged from his family, and because of this rented flat, he actually was of no fixed abode and the murder was, arguably, a last, desperate expression of love, the end of love."

What Karlsson really wanted to do was to lean across, take Bradshaw's smartphone, and hit him over the head with it repeatedly. But he said nothing.

"And then there's Kerrigan's wife, Elaine. Humiliated wife. Finds out about Ruth, confronts her, picks up cog."

"But she didn't know about the affair," said Yvette. "Or Ruth's name. Or where she lived."

"Maybe she did know," said Munster. "They always do."

"What do you mean, *they?*" Yvette glared at him.

"Women." Munster was wary of Yvette's sharp tone. "You know, when their husbands are unfaithful. They know. Deep down. At least, that's what some people say."

"Crap," said Yvette, derisively.

"Anyway, we suspect that someone knew," said Karlsson. "Someone might have pushed that cut-up doll through the Lennox letterbox as a warning."

"That could just be coincidence."

"In my world," announced Bradshaw with a modest smile, "coincidence is another word for—"

"You're right," cut in Karlsson, decisively. "It could be coincidence. It might have been Dora's charming school friends persecuting her. Did you talk to her again, Yvette?"

Yvette nodded. "She said she'd assumed it was for her. And she thinks it arrived around lunchtime. She got distressed. But she didn't want to talk about it really—apparently things are better at school since her mother was killed. Everyone wants to be her friend suddenly." She made a grimace of disgust.

"OK. So, the doll's either a clue or it isn't. Maybe we can talk to the head teacher and see if she can throw any light on it. Moving on, what about the sons?"

"Josh and Ben Kerrigan?" Yvette wrinkled up her face. "They're both pretty contemptuous and angry. But Josh seems to have been in Cardiff—although he hasn't been able to come up with any concrete alibi, apart from being in bed with his girlfriend, who confirms that was probably the case. No sign on his bank statements that he used his card for a train ticket or anything. But that doesn't mean much—as he himself pointed out, he could have used cash. His younger brother, Ben, was in a lesson. Apparently. His teacher can't remember his being there, but she can't remember his *not* being there, and she thinks she would have noticed."

"Brilliant."

"What about Louise Weller?" asked Yvette. "She was on the scene pretty quickly."

"On the scene?" Karlsson shook his head. "She came round to help."

"It's a common expression of guilt," Bradshaw explained comfortably. "Perpetrators like to involve themselves in the inquiry."

"What? Mother of three kills sister?"

"You can't rule it out," said Bradshaw.

"I'm the one who rules people in or out." Karlsson spoke quickly. "But you're right. We'll talk to her again. And the Kerrigan boys. Anything else?"

"Samantha Kemp," said Riley.

"What?"

"The woman Kerrigan had his affair with."

"Yes, I know who she is, but . . ." Karlsson paused. "You've got to talk to her anyway, to check Kerrigan's claim he was with her that afternoon. Maybe it'll turn out she has a jealous boyfriend." He slammed the file shut. "Right, that's it. Yvette, check that alibi. Chris, you talk to this Samantha Kemp. Now, for God's sake, one of you go out and get me something."

FORTY-THREE

Yvette was still smarting as she left the room. She could feel Chris Munster looking at her sympathetically, which made it worse. She snapped at him when he asked her if she wanted a coffee and slammed herself down at her desk.

First, she rang Zach at his workplace in Shoreditch, but the woman who answered the phone said he wasn't in that day—he didn't work full time and as a matter of fact he wasn't the most reliable of employees. So she rang his mobile and went straight to voice mail, then his landline, which rang and rang. She sighed and pulled on her jacket.

On her way out, she met Munster once more.

"Where are you going?" she asked.

"To see Samantha Kemp. You?"

"To see bloody Zach Greene."

"Would you like me to—"

"No, I would not."

Samantha Kemp was doing some work for a digital camera company just off Marble Arch. She met Munster in the small room set aside for visitors on the first floor; its window overlooked a sari shop.

When she came into the room, Munster was surprised by how young she was. Paul Kerrigan was a plump, graying, middle-aged man, but Samantha Kemp was in her twenties, neatly dressed in a black skirt and a crisply ironed white shirt. A ladder ran up her tights, from her ankle to her shapely knee. She had fluffy platinum blond hair that framed her round pale face.

"Thank you for seeing me. This won't take long."

"What's it about?"

Munster saw she was nervous: she kept sliding her palms down her skirt.

"Is it true that you know Paul Kerrigan?"

"Yes. I do work for his company sometimes. Why?" A flush spread over her fair skin, and even when the color receded it left faint blotches on her cheeks. "What's this about?"

"Can you remember what you were doing on Wednesday, the sixth of April?" She didn't answer. "Well?"

"I heard you. I just don't know what you're getting at. Why should I tell you anything about my private life?"

"Mr. Kerrigan says that you were with him on the afternoon and evening of Wednesday, the sixth of April."

"With him?"

"Yes."

"Is that a problem?"

"You tell me."

"He might be married, but that's his lookout, not mine."

"Wednesday, the sixth of April."

"He's not happy, you know."

"It doesn't matter."

"He's not." To his horror, Munster saw that she was about to start crying: tears stood in her gray-blue eyes. "And I comfort him. I'm not going to be made to feel bad about that."

"The point is, did you comfort him on Wednesday, the sixth of April?"

"Is he in trouble?"

"Do you have a diary?"

"Yes," she said. "Yes. I was with him on that Wednesday."

"You're sure?"

"Yes. It was the day after my birthday. He bought me a bottle of champagne."

"What time?"

"He arrived in the afternoon, about four. And we drank some champagne and then . . ." Her face was flaming again. "He left at about seven or eight. He said he had to go back for his dinner."

"Is there anyone who can confirm this?"

"My flatmate, Lynn. She came back at about six and had a bit of the champagne. I suppose you need her details as well."

"Please."

"Does she know about us? His wife, I mean? Is he in trouble?"

Munster looked at her. Surely she must know about Ruth Lennox. But it was impossible to tell, and he didn't want to be the one to break it to her. Paul Kerrigan should do his own dirty work.

. . .

Zach Greene lived near Waterloo, a few roads south of the station on a street that was clogged with midday traffic: cabs and cars and vans and buses. Cyclists wove in and out of the queues, heads down against a strengthening wind. An ambulance blared past.

Number 232 was a small terraced house set slightly back from the road, with steps leading up to a cracked green door. Yvette rang the bell, then knocked hard as well. She already knew he wouldn't be in, so she was surprised when she heard footsteps and the rattling of a chain. A woman stood in front of her, clutching a baby in a striped cloth diaper.

"Yes?"

"I'm looking for Zach Greene," said Yvette. "Does he live here?"

"He's our tenant. He lives in the flat. You have to go through the garden." She came out in her slippers and took Yvette down the steps, pointing. "His flat has its own entrance. Go round the back to the garden and you'll find it."

"Thank you." Yvette smiled at the baby, who stared at her in terror, then started to bawl. She'd never been good with babies.

"Tell him to keep the noise down, will you? He was making a hell of a racket last night, just after I'd got this one off to sleep at last."

Yvette went into the small garden, where a child's plastic tricycle lay tipped on its side. She found the door to the basement flat, rang the bell and waited. Then she knocked on the door, and it creaked open a few inches.

For a moment, Yvette stood quite still, listening intently. Outside, she could hear the clamor of traffic. From within, there was nothing.

"Hello," she called. "Zach? Mr. Greene? It's Detective Long here."

Nothing. The wind blew a flurry of white blossom down on her where she stood. For a moment she thought it was snow. Snow in April: but stranger things happen. She pushed the door wider and stepped inside, onto a balding doormat. Zach Greene was not a tidy man. There were shoes on the floor, piles of junk mail, a couple of empty pizza boxes, a tangle of phone chargers and computer cords, a cotton scarf with tassels.

She took a few more cautious steps.

"Zach? Are you here?" Her voice rang out in the small space. To her right, a tiny kitchen, a stove encrusted with ancient food, an army of mugs, granules of instant coffee. Two shirts hanging to dry on the radiator. A smell of something spoiling somewhere.

It's odd, she thought, how you know when there's something wrong. You get a feel for it. Not just the open door, the smell. Something about the silence, as if it hummed with the aftermath of violence. Her skin prickled.

Another shoe, a brown canvas one with yellow laces, on the floor, in the barely opened door that presumably led to Zach's bedroom. She pushed the door with the tips of her fingers. The shoe was on a foot. The beginnings of the leg could be seen, encased in dark trousers and riding up to expose a striped sock, but everything else was covered with a patterned quilt. She took in the pattern: birds and swirling flowers; it looked Oriental, brightening up the gray and brown pokiness of the dingy flat.

She looked at her watch and noted the time, then squatted down and very carefully drew off the quilt, feeling how damply sticky it was, seeing now that she was close up to it how its vivid pattern had obscured the stains.

It must be Zach lying in front of her at the foot of his bed, but the narrow face, the golden eyes, the rosebud lips that had given her the creeps were all gone—smashed into a pulp. Yvette made herself look properly, not squint in a reflex of horror. She could still make out the delicate earlobes in his wrecked face. There was blood everywhere. People didn't know how much blood they had flowing through them, warm and fast—only when you saw it pooled around a body did you realize. Puddles of dark, sweet-smelling blood, thickening now. She laid one finger against his back, under his purple shirt; the skin was white and hard and cold.

She stood up, hearing her knees creak, and thought of Karlsson when he arrived at a crime scene: she tried to make herself into a camera. The muddy streaks in the passageway, the tipped picture above the bed, the thickening blood, the rigid flesh, the way his arms were flung out as if he were falling through the air. She remembered the noise the woman upstairs had said she'd heard last night.

And then she took out her phone. She could make out the sounds of the baby, still howling. They arrived so quickly, the ambulances and the police cars. It seemed only minutes before the flat had been transformed into a makeshift laboratory, bright lights shining, with Zach's body at the center. Paper shoes, plastic gloves, brushes to dust for the fingerprints, bottles of chemicals, tweezers and evidence bags, tape measures, thermometers. Riley was talking to the woman upstairs. Munster, standing by the door and taking gulps of air, was talking into his phone. Zach was just an object now, a specimen.

Above the hubbub, Karlsson said to her, "Chris is speaking to Greene's parents. Do you think you could be the one to tell Judith Lennox?"

She felt beads of sweat on her forehead as she thought of the fierce, desolate daughter. "Sure."

"Thanks. As soon as possible, I think."

Yvette knew it would be bad and it was. She stood and listened to herself say the words and watched Judith Lennox's very young, very vulnerable face crumple. She spun round the small room, her slender figure twitching, all the separate parts of her apparently disconnected—hands fluttering, face tweaked in strange grimaces, head bobbing on thin neck, feet slipping in her frantic urge to move. They were in a room that the head teacher had put aside for them. There was a desk by the plate-glass window and shelves full of folders in different colors. Outside, two teenagers—a boy and a girl— walked past and glanced without obvious interest into the large window.

Yvette felt helpless. Should she go and wrap her arms round the girl's fragile bones, hold her still for an instant? This time it was a shriek that must surely fill the whole school, empty classrooms, and bring teachers running. She banged against the desk and was sent in another direction. Yvette was reminded of a moth bruising its soft powdery wings against harsh surfaces.

She put out a hand and caught Judith by the hem of her shirt, heard it rip slightly. The girl stopped and stared wildly at her. She was still wearing dark orange lipstick, but the rest of her face was like a small child's. Suddenly, she sat, not on the chair but in a heap on the uncarpeted floor.

"What happened?" she whispered.

"We're trying to find out exactly. All I can tell you at present is that he has been killed." She thought of the mashed face and swallowed hard. "In his flat."

"When? *When?*"

"We haven't established the time of his death." Stiff, pompous, she was embarrassed by her own awkwardness.

"Recently, though?"

"Yes. I'm sorry to have to ask, but I'm sure you'll understand. Can you tell me when you last saw him?"

"Go away." Judith covered her ears with her hands and rocked back and forward on the floor. "Just go away now."

"I know it's very painful."

"Go away. Go away. Go away. Leave me alone. Leave all of us alone. Get out. Why is this happening? Why? Please please please please."

Yvette had only once been to Frieda's house and never to her consulting rooms until now. She tried not to seem curious; she didn't want to look too intently at Frieda herself, partly because Frieda's steady gaze had always made her uncomfortable and partly because she was shocked by Frieda's appearance. Perhaps she was thinner, Yvette couldn't tell, but she was certainly tauter. She seemed stretched tight. There were dark smudges under her eyes, almost violet. Her skin was pale and her eyes very dark, with a smokiness to them that was different from their usual glitter. She didn't look well, Yvette decided.

She watched Frieda walk toward her red armchair with a limp that she tried to disguise but couldn't, and thought, *This is my fault*. For a moment, she let herself remember Frieda lying in Mary Orton's house, unmoving, the sight of the blood. Then she saw young Judith Lennox flying around the schoolroom, like a broken moth, shouting at her to get out, to leave. Perhaps the simple truth is that I'm a hopeless detective, she thought. She hadn't even been able to get an alibi from Zach Greene.

Frieda gestured to the chair opposite, and Yvette sat down. So this was where Frieda's patients sat. She imagined closing her eyes and saying, *Please help me. I don't know what's wrong with me. Please tell me what's wrong with me . . .*

"Thank you for agreeing to see me," she said.

"I owe you a favor." Frieda was smiling at her.

"Oh, no! It's me . . ."

"You made the complaint against me go away."

"That was nothing. Idiots."

"Still, I'm grateful."

"I didn't want to meet at the station. I thought this would be better. I don't know if you've heard. Zach Greene was murdered. He was Judith Lennox's boyfriend."

Frieda seemed to become even more still. She shook her head slightly. "No. I hadn't heard. I'm sorry," she said softly, as though to herself.

"She's in a dreadful state," Yvette continued. "I've just left her. The school councilor was there and the head. I'm worried for her."

"Why are you telling me this?"

"You've met her. I know about your behind-the-scenes dealings with the Lennox family." She held up a hand. "That sounded wrong. I didn't mean it grumpily."

"Go on."

"I wondered if you could go and see her. Call on her. Just to see how she is."

"She's not my patient."

"I understand that."

"I hardly know her. Her brother is a friend of my niece's. That's the only connection. I've met the poor girl a few times."

"I didn't know how to deal with her. There are things they don't teach you. I could call up one of our people, I suppose." She wrinkled her nose dubiously at the thought. "Hal fucking Bradshaw would be only too pleased to tell her what she was feeling and why. But I—well, I guess I thought you could help."

"For old times' sake?" Frieda asked, ironically.

"You mean you won't?"

"I didn't say that."

OK. I won't fly over and hammer at your door and I will trust
you. But you make it very hard, Frieda. Sandy

FORTY-FOUR

n the morning, Jim Fearby called on the family of Philippa Lewis. They lived in a new estate in a village a few miles south of Oxford. A middle-aged woman—she must have been Philippa's mother, Sue—slammed the door as soon as he identified himself. He had read about the case in the local paper, the usual story of walking home after staying late at school and not arriving; he had seen the blurry photo. She had seemed a plausible candidate. He put a tick after her name, followed by a question mark.

Up toward Warwick, Cathy Birkin's mother made him tea and cake, and before the first mouthful he knew that this was a name he'd be crossing off the list. She'd run away twice before. The cake was quite nice, though. Ginger. Slightly spicy. Fearby had started to notice another sort of pattern. The mothers of the runaway girls were the ones who would invite him in and give him tea and cake. He could almost remember the houses and the girls by the cake he'd been served. The one up near Crewe, Claire Boyle, had been carrot cake. High Wycombe, Maria Horsley: chocolate. Were they still trying to prove that they had done their best, that they weren't bad parents? The ginger cake was slightly dry and stuck to the roof of his mouth. He had to wash it down with his cooling tea. As he chewed, he felt his own pang of conscience. He'd been putting it off and putting it off. It was on the way and would only be a small diversion.

He almost hoped that George Conley would be out, but he wasn't. The small block where he had moved to was neat enough. When Conley opened the door, he gave only the smallest flicker of recognition, but Fearby was used to that. When Conley had talked to him over the years, he had never seemed comfortable looking at him directly. Even when he talked, it was as if he were addressing someone slightly to the side of Fearby and behind him. As soon as Fearby stepped inside he was hit by the warmth and the smell, which seemed part of each other. It wasn't really identifiable, and Fearby didn't want to identify it: there was sweat, dampness. He suddenly thought of the sour smell you get behind garbage vans in summer.

Fearby had lived alone for years, and he knew about life with surfaces that never got properly wiped, dishes that piled up, food that was left out, clothes on the floor, but this was something different. In the dark, hot living room, he had to step around dirty plates and glasses. He saw opened cans half filled with things he couldn't recognize, white and green with mold. Almost everything—plates, glasses, tins—had stubs of cigarettes on or in it. Fearby wondered whether there was someone he could call. Did someone somewhere have a legal responsibility to deal with this?

The television was on, and Conley sat down opposite it. He wasn't exactly watching the screen. It looked more like he was just sitting in front of it.

"How did you get this place?" said Fearby.

"The council," said Conley.

"Does anyone come round to help you? I know it must be difficult. You've been inside so long. It's hard to adjust." Conley just looked blank, so Fearby tried again. "Does anyone come to check up? Maybe do some cleaning?"

"A woman comes sometimes. To check on me."

"Is she helpful?"

"She's all right."

"What about your compensation? How's it going?"

"I don't know. I saw Diana."

"Your lawyer," said Fearby. He had to speak almost in a shout to be heard above the television. "What did she say?"

"She said it'd take time. A long time."

"I've heard that. You'll have to be patient." There was a pause. "Do you get out much?"

"I walk a bit. There's a park."

"That's nice."

"There's ducks. I take bread. And seeds."

"That's nice, George. Is there anyone you'd like me to call for you? If you give me a number, I could call the people at the council. They could come and help you clear up."

"There's just a woman. She comes sometimes."

Fearby had been sitting right on the edge of a sofa that looked as if it had been brought in from outside. His back was starting to ache. He stood up. "I've got to head off," he said.

"I was having tea."

Fearby looked at an open carton of milk on the table. The milk inside was yellow. "I had some earlier. But I'll pop back soon, and we can go out for a drink or a walk. How's that sound?"

"All right."

"I'm trying to find out who killed Hazel Barton. I've been busy."

Conley didn't respond.

"I know it's a terrible memory for you," said Fearby. "But when you found her, I know you bent down and tried to help her. You touched her. That was the evidence that was used against you. But did you see anything else? Did you see a person? Or a car? George. Did you hear what I said?"

Conley looked round, but he still didn't say anything.

"Right," said Fearby. "Well, it's been good to see you. We'll do this again." He picked his way carefully out of the room.

When Fearby got home, he went online to find the number of the Social Services department. He dialed it, but the office was closed for the day. He looked at his watch. He had thought of calling Diana McKerrow about Conley's situation, but her office would be closed as well by now. He knew about these compensation cases. They took years.

He went to the sink, found a glass, rinsed it, and poured himself some whisky. He took a sip and felt the warmth spreading down through his chest. He'd needed that. He felt the staleness of the day in his mouth, on his tongue, and the whisky scoured all that away. He walked through the rooms with his drink. It wasn't like Conley's flat, but it was a distant relation. Men adrift, living alone. Two men still trapped in their different ways by the Hazel Barton case. The police had no other suspects. That was what they'd said. Only George Conley and he knew different.

Suddenly the dirty glasses and bits of clothing, the piles of papers and envelopes scared him. People hardly ever came to the house, but the thought of anyone coming into this room and feeling some part of what he had felt in George Conley's flat made him flush with a sort of shame. For the next hour he picked clothes up, washed glasses and plates, wiped surfaces, vacuumed. At the end, he felt it was closer to some sort of normality. It needed more. He could see that. He would buy a picture. He could put flowers in a vase. Maybe he would even paint the walls.

He took a lasagna from the freezer and put it into the oven. The back of the packet said fifty minutes from frozen. That would give him time. He went to his study. This was the one part of the house that had always been tidy, clean, and organized. He took the map from the desk, unfolded it, and laid it out on the floor. He opened the top drawer of his desk and took out the card covered with red stickers. He peeled off one sticker and carefully

placed it on the village of Denham, just south of Oxford. He stood back.
There were seven of them now, and a pattern was clearly forming.

Fearby took another sip of whisky and asked himself the question he'd
asked himself many times before: was he fooling himself? He'd read about
murderers and their habits. How they were like predatory animals that oper-
ated in territories where they felt comfortable. But he'd also read about the
dangers of seeing patterns in random collections of data. You fire arbitrary
shots at a wall, then draw a target around the marks that are closest together
and it looks as if you were aiming at it. He examined the map. Five of them
were close to the M40 and three to the M1, no more than twenty minutes'
drive from a motorway exit. It seemed completely obvious and compelling.
But there was a problem. As he'd read through newspapers, checked online
for missing teenage girls, one of his main criteria in weeding them out was
looking for families near motorways, so maybe he was creating the pattern
himself. But he thought of the girls' faces, the stories. It felt right to him. It
smelled right. But what good was that?

FORTY-FIVE

arlsson sat down opposite Russell Lennox. Yvette started the recorder
and sat to one side.

"You know you're still under oath," Karlsson said, "and that you're
entitled to legal representation." Lennox gave a faint nod. He seemed dazed,
barely responsive. "You need to say it aloud. For the tape, or chip, or whatever it is."

"Yes," said Lennox. "I understand. I'm fine."

"You're quite a family," said Karlsson. Lennox looked blank. "You seem
to do damage to everyone you come into contact with."

"We're a family in which the wife and mother was killed," said Lennox,
hoarsely. "Is that what you mean?"

"And now your daughter's boyfriend."

"I didn't know about that, until I heard about the death."

"The murder. Zach Greene was hit with a blunt instrument. Like your
wife." There was a pause. "How did you feel about him?"

"What do you mean?"

"About your fifteen-year-old daughter's relationship with a twenty-eight-
year-old man."

"As I said, I didn't know about it. Now that I do, I feel concern for my
daughter. For her welfare."

"Mr. Greene died some time during the day yesterday. Can you tell us
where you were?"

"I was at home. I've been at home a lot lately."

"Was anyone with you?"

"The children were at school. I was there when Dora came home at about
ten past four."

"What did you do at home?"

Lennox seemed terribly tired, as if even talking was a great effort. "Why
don't you just ask me if I killed that man? That must be why you brought
me in here."

"Did you kill him?"

"No, I didn't."

"All right, so what did you do at home?"

"I pottered around. Sorted through some things."

"Maybe you can help us by coming up with something we can check. Did someone call round? Did you make any calls? Did you go online?"

"Nobody came round. I probably made some calls and went online."

"We can check that."

"I watched a bit of TV."

"What did you watch?"

"The usual rubbish. Probably something to do with antiques."

"'Probably something to do with antiques,'" said Karlsson, slowly, as if he were thinking about it as he repeated it. "I'm going to stop this now." He leaned forward and pressed a button on the recorder. "You're going to go away and have a think, maybe talk to a lawyer, and come up with something better than what you've said. And meanwhile, we'll make our own checks on who you were phoning and where you were." He stood up. "You need to think of your children, your family. How much more of this are they meant to take?"

Lennox rubbed his face, like a man checking whether he'd shaved. "I think about them every minute of every day," he said.

Chris Munster was waiting for Karlsson in his office. He had just returned from Cardiff, where he had been interviewing Josh Kerrigan's girlfriend, Shari Hollander.

"Well?"

"She just repeated what Josh Kerrigan said: that he'd probably been with her, they'd spent practically every minute of the day together since they'd started going out, she couldn't quite remember. But she was pretty sure that there wasn't a time when he was away for a large chunk of the day or night."

"It's a bit vague."

"He didn't use his credit card to buy any kind of transport to London on that day. But he did take a hundred pounds out in cash a couple of days before, so he could have used that."

"But he's not looking very likely, is he? Not that he ever was."

"I wouldn't say that."

Karlsson looked at Munster more attentively. "What do you mean?"

"There was something his girlfriend mentioned that I thought might interest you."

"Go on."

"She said Josh was furious with his father. Spitting mad, she said. She said he'd had a letter, telling him his dad was not the happy family man he set himself up as."

"So he knew."

"That's what she said."

"Good work, Chris. We need another talk with him. Right now. And his little brother while we're at it."

Josh Kerrigan had got himself a haircut—or maybe, thought Karlsson, looking at the uneven tufts, he'd done it himself with clippers. It made his face seem rounder and younger. He sat in the interview room and couldn't keep still, but drummed his fingers on the table, twisted in his chair, tapped his feet.

"What now?" he asked. "More questions about my whereabouts?"

"We spoke to Shari Hollander."

"Did she say I was with her, like I said?"

"She said you probably were."

"There you go, then."

"She also said that you knew about your father's affair."

"What?"

He suddenly looked scared.

"Is that true? Did you receive a letter telling you about the affair?"

Josh stared at Karlsson, then away. A heaviness settled on his young face, making him resemble his father. "Yes. I got a letter sent to me, care of my physics department."

"Anonymous?"

"That's right. So whoever sent it didn't even have the courage to admit who they were."

"Who do you think it was?"

Josh gazed darkly at Karlsson. "Her, of course. Who else?"

"You mean Ruth Lennox?"

"That's right. Though I didn't know that at the time."

"Do you still have the letter?"

"I tore it into little bits and threw it in the bin."

"What else did you do?"

"I tried to put it out of my mind."

"Nothing at all?"

"I didn't get on a train to London, if that's what you mean."

"Did you speak to your father about it?"

"No."

"Or your mother?"

"No."

"Are you close to your mother?"

"I'm her son." He looked down, as if he were embarrassed about meeting Karlsson's eye. "She's always put me and Ben before anything else—even when she had cancer, we were all she thought about. And Dad," he added viciously. "She put him first too."

"But you didn't tell her about this letter?"

"No."

"Did you tell your brother?"

"Ben's a kid doing his A levels in a few weeks' time. Why would I tell him?"

"Did you?"

Josh pulled at a tuft of newly cut hair. "No." But he sounded stiff and uneasy.

"Listen to me, Josh. We're going to talk to your brother, and if his account doesn't agree with yours, you're going to be in even more trouble than you are right now. It's better to tell us the truth at once. Better for Ben, as well."

"All right, I told him. I had to tell someone."

"Did you tell him over the phone?"

"Yes."

"How did he react?"

"Like me. Like anyone would. He was shocked, angry."

"Is that all?"

"He thought we should tell Mum. I didn't."

"How did it end?"

"We agreed we'd wait until I came back for Easter, that we'd talk about it then."

"And did you?"

He gave a wide, sarcastic smile. "We sort of got overtaken by events."

"And you didn't tell your mother?"

"Like I said."

"And Ben didn't either?"

"He wouldn't without telling me."

"And you're telling me that neither of you confronted your father, however angry you were with him."

"I said no."

"Why were you both so quick to believe what the letter said?"

Josh seemed taken aback. "I dunno," he said. "We just did. Why would anyone make up something like that?"

"And there's nothing else you want to tell me?"

"No."

"You're sticking to your story that you didn't know who the mystery writer was?"

"Yes."

Karlsson waited. Josh Kerrigan's eyes flickered toward him, then away again. There was a knock at the door, and Yvette put her head around it. "I need a word," she said.

"We were done here anyway. For now." Karlsson stood up. "We'll speak to your brother."

Josh shrugged. But his eyes were anxious.

'No," said Ben Kerrigan. "No, no, and no. I did not tell my mother. I wish I had. But we decided to wait till we were together. I had to look at her over the breakfast table and not say anything. And him." His face twisted.

"Yes?"

"I didn't say anything to him either. I wanted to. I wanted to punch him in his stupid fat face. I'm glad he's got beaten up. He's just a wanker. It's such a fucking cliché, isn't it? Except the other woman wasn't some bimbo. What did he think he was doing? Ten years. He was cheating on Mum for ten years."

"But you never confronted him or told your mother about the letter."

"Like I said."

"And you never got the impression that your father knew about the letter."

"He didn't know anything." Ben's voice rang with scorn. "He thought he could get away with it, and no price to pay."

"Or your mother?"

"No. She trusted him. I know Mum. She thinks that once you trust someone, it's unconditional."

"Why did you hide this information from us?"

"Why do you think? We're not stupid, you know—we do realize that you're all thinking this murder is some kind of revenge." His voice rose in distress.

"All right." Karlsson tried to hold his eyes. "Let's take it slowly, from the beginning. You were here, living with your parents, when Josh told you."

"Yes."

"What did you do when you found out?"

"Nothing."

"Nothing at all?"

"I keep telling you."

"You didn't talk to anyone apart from Josh?"

"No."

"But you believed it was true?"

"I *knew* it was true!"

"How?"

"I just did."

"How did you know, Ben? What made you so sure?" He waited, then asked, "Did you find out anything else?" He saw Ben flinch involuntarily before he shook his head. "Ben, I'm asking you one more time: did you try to find anything out?" He stopped and let silence fill the space between them. "Did you go through your father's things, looking for evidence? It would only be natural. Ben?"

"No."

"Alone in the house, with this new and horrible suspicion, and you didn't do anything?"

"Stop it."

"We will find out."

"OK. I may have."

"You may have?"

"I poked around a bit."

"Where?"

"You know. Pockets."

"Yes."

"And his phone. His papers."

"His computer?"

"That too."

"And what did you find?"

"Nothing much."

"You do understand how serious this is, Ben?"

The boy turned to him. Karlsson could hear his ragged breathing. "All right. I looked fucking everywhere. Of course I did. What would you have done? Me and Josh agreed that I would do a search, and then I went through all his grubby tissues and his receipts and his e-mails and nicked his mobile phone to look at texts and calls. We—me and Josh—rang a few numbers I didn't recognize, just to check. There wasn't anything. But I couldn't stop. If I hadn't found something, I could have gone on for the rest of my life, trying to find the evidence that he was cheating on my mum. How could I have ever found evidence to prove she wasn't cheating?"

"But you did find something?" Karlsson said gently.

"I went through his history."

"On his computer, you mean?"

"I don't really know what I was looking for. There was a search he'd done on Google Images for Ruth Lennox. And I just knew. It's the way you look up someone you know, just to see if there's a picture of them somewhere."

"So. You and Josh knew your father was having an affair with someone called Ruth Lennox."

"Yes. Then of course I did a search for her name. He thought he was being so clever. He doesn't understand computers."

"What did you find?"

"An e-mail from her. Hidden in a folder called something boring like Household Insurance. Just one e-mail." He snorted derisively.

"What did it say?"

"It didn't say, 'Darling Paul, I like fucking you,' if that's what you mean," Ben said savagely. "It said that yes, she would like to see him again and that he wasn't to worry, everything was going to be all right." He grimaced violently. "It was kind of tender and practical. I thought of Mum being so ill and weak and still looking after us, and then this other woman loving Dad as well, and it seemed so fucking unfair."

"When was it sent?"

"The twenty-ninth of April 2001."

"And you still insist you didn't tell your mother?"

"I didn't."

"But you did push a mutilated doll through the Lennoxes' letter box."

Ben turned a deep red. "Yeah. I didn't plan to. But I saw this stupid doll stuffed in a big basket of toys at a friend's house—it was his kid sister's. And I just took it on a whim and cut it up a bit to show her what we thought of her. I had to do something."

"She never got your little message, though. Her ill daughter picked it up and thought it was meant for her."

"Oh, shit."

"So you and Josh knew where she lived?"

"Yes."

"Did you go there at other times?"

"No. Not really."

"Not really?"

"I might have stood outside every so often. To see her."

"Did you see her?"

"No. I saw her kids, I think. It all made me feel a bit sick, if you want to know. Poisoned."

"Is there anything you haven't told me?"

Ben shook his head miserably. "Josh is going to be mad at me. He made me swear not to say anything."

"That's what happens when you start breaking the law. People get mad at you."

FORTY-SIX

rieda had got Judith's e-mail address from Chloë and sent her a short message saying she would be waiting for her at four o'clock the next afternoon at Primrose Hill, by the entrance, just minutes from Judith's school. The weather had changed: it was blustery and the clouds were low and gray, threatening rain.

She saw Judith long before Judith saw her. She was in a knot of friends, which loosened and dispersed as they went, and finally it was just the girl making her way slowly toward the gate. As she came into the park, she noticed Frieda sitting on the bench and her step quickened. A series of expressions flickered on her face: bewilderment, anger, fear. Then it hardened into a mask of hostility. The blue eyes glittered.

"Why is *she* here?"

"Because it's not me you need to speak to. It's DC Long. Yvette."

"I don't know what you're talking about. I don't need to talk to either of you. I don't want to. I want everyone to fuck off. Leave me alone, all of you." Her voice cracked. A hoarse sob forced its way out of her mouth and she lurched where she stood, as if she would fall.

Frieda stood up and gestured to the bench. "You've been under terrible pressure. You must feel as if you're about to explode with it."

"I don't know what you're going on about. I don't want to be here. I want to go home. Or somewhere," she added.

But she didn't move, and for a moment she looked so young and so full of uncertainty and terror that Frieda thought she would burst into tears. Then, as if her legs would no longer hold her, she crumpled onto the bench beside Yvette and pulled her knees up, wrapping her arms around them, hunching her body up protectively.

"Tell Yvette why you're so scared."

"What do you mean?" whispered Judith.

"You can't protect him."

"Who?"

"Your father."

Judith closed her eyes. Her face became slack, suddenly like that of a middle-aged woman, defeated by tiredness.

"I sometimes think I'm going to wake up and this will be just a dream. Mum will still be there and we'll be arguing about stupid stuff, like staying out late and makeup and homework, and all the horrible things won't have happened. I wish I'd never had a boyfriend. I wish I'd never met Zach. I feel sick when I think about him. I want to be like I was before all of this." She opened her eyes and looked at Frieda. "Is it because of me he's dead?"

"You tell me."

And then Judith did at last burst into tears. She leaned forward and covered her face with her hands and rocked her body to and fro and wept. Yvette stared at her, then tentatively put out one hand and touched her on the shoulder, but Judith lashed out and pushed her away. It was several minutes before the sobs got quieter, and at last they ceased. Frieda took a tissue from her bag and, without a word, handed it over. Judith dabbed at her sodden face, still making sniffling sounds.

"I told him about Zach," she said at last, in a whisper.

"Yes."

"Did he kill him?"

"I don't know that." Frieda handed her another tissue.

"But you did right to tell us," added Yvette, decisively. "We would have found out anyway. You're not to feel responsible."

"Why? Why shouldn't I? It's my fault. I had sex with him." Her face puckered. "And then I told my dad. He just wanted to protect me. What's going to happen to him? What's going to happen to us? Dora's just a little girl."

"Yvette's right, Judith: you're not responsible."

"He'll know it was me who told you."

"He should never have put you in this position," Yvette said.

"Why is this happening to us? I just want to go back to when it was all right."

"We should take you home," said Frieda.

"I can't see him, not now. I just can't. My poor darling dad. Oh, God." And she ended on a juddering sob.

Frieda made up her mind. "You'll come to my house," she said, thinking of how her calm, orderly home had become like a circus for other people's grief and chaos. "You and Ted and Dora. We'll call them now." She nodded at Yvette. "And you'll have to speak to Karlsson."

. . .

When Yvette told Karlsson what she'd learned from Judith, he just stared at her for a moment.

"Stupid, fucking idiot," he said finally. "Who's going to look after his family now? What a mess. Russell Lennox knew about Judith and Zach. Josh and Ben Kerrigan knew about their father and Ruth Lennox. Where's this going to end?" His phone rang and he snatched it up, listened, said, "We'll be there," then put it down again.

"That was Tate in forensics. He's invited us to a guided tour of Zach's flat."

"But—"

"Have you got anything better to do?"

James Tate was a small, stocky, dark-skinned and peppery-haired man with a peremptory manner and sarcastic sense of humor. Karlsson had known him for years. He was meticulous and dispassionate, very good at his job. He was waiting for them, and when they arrived he gave them a small nod and handed them both paper shoes and thin latex gloves to put on before they stepped into the scene of the crime.

"You couldn't have just told me on the phone?" Karlsson asked.

"I thought you'd like to see it for yourself. Like this, for example."

He pointed at the doorbell. "Nice clear prints."

"Do they match—"

"Don't be in such a hurry." He opened the door into the little entrance hall. "Exhibit number two." He pointed at the muddy footprints on the floor. "Size forty-one shoes. We've got a clear image. And three: signs of some kind of struggle. This picture has been dislodged."

Karlsson nodded. Yvette, following them past the disordered kitchenette into the bedroom, had the strange sensation that she would find the body all over again.

"Four. Blood splash. Here, here, and here. And substantially more there, of course, where the body was. Exhibit four, or should that be five: in that bin there," he pointed, "we found a very dirty kitchen towel covered with more blood. We took it away for DNA testing. Somebody had used it to clean himself up."

"And that would be . . ."

"Exhibit six: fingerprints, containing traces of the victim's blood, all against that wall. There. What do you think?"

"What do I think? What do you *know*?"

"We can construct a very plausible scenario. Someone—a man wearing size forty-one shoes—entered. Presumably he was let in by the victim, but we can't be sure. There was no sign of a forced entrance. They had some kind of a struggle in the hall, then went into the bedroom where the victim was bludgeoned to death with a weapon as yet unfound. The perpetrator must have got splashed with the victim's blood, and he wiped himself with the cloth and flung it into the bin. I take it he was feeling unsteady by then. He leaned against that wall, leaving several very satisfactory fingerprints. Then he left." Tate beamed at them. "There."

"And the fingerprints belonged to?"

"Russell Lennox." Tate's triumphant smile faded. "Aren't you impressed?"

"No, I'm sorry. I really am. But there's being careless and there's being really careless."

"You know all about that, Mal. Murderers are almost always in a near-psychotic state because of the stress. They suffer memory loss. I've found wallets, jackets at crime scenes."

"You're right," said Karlsson. "I'm not going to say no to a clear result."

"You're welcome," said Tate.

FORTY-SEVEN

Frieda and the Lennox children arrived at her house to find Josef, Reuben, and Chloe already there.

"It's all right," said Chloë. "Reuben's making supper. Oh, hi, Ted!" She blushed and smiled.

Then the door opened and Reuben peered round, his face flushed and beaming. Drunk, thought Frieda. Drunk as a lord.

"Hello, Frieda. I thought we all needed a bang-up meal and since you won't come to me, I thought—" He noticed the Lennoxes bunched in a corner, dazed and scared. "Sorry. I didn't realize. You must be the poor kids whose mother died."

"Yes," said Judith, faintly. Dora started to snivel.

"Very tough," said Reuben. "Very very very tough." He lurched a bit. "I'm so sorry."

"Thank you."

"But for now, I've made enough for an army. The more the merrier. And the food is ready." He gave a sweeping bow and winked at Judith.

"I don't think it's the right night," Frieda said firmly. "We need to have a bit of quiet here. I'm sorry."

His expression curdled. He glared at her and raised his eyebrows, ready to pick a fight.

"Don't be mean, Frieda!" Chloë was indignant. "He's been working for *hours* on this. You don't mind, do you, Ted?" She put a hand on his shoulder, and he stared at her with stupefied eyes.

"Nah. It's OK," he said listlessly. "It doesn't really matter one way or another."

"I don't think—" began Frieda.

"Great!"

Reuben drew a large blue casserole dish from the oven, his hands swathed in two tea towels. Frieda already knew what it was. Reuben's specialty, his fallback dish, his comfort food, ever since she had known him, was a particularly hot, spicy, and meaty chili con carne. When he triumphantly lifted the lid, the sight of the meat and the purple kidney beans almost made her gag. He ladled the chili onto the plates and passed them round, then he poured wine into the glasses. Judith prodded the greasy pile in front of her. "It's very nice, but I think I'm going to go and lie down," she said. "Can I lie on your bed for a bit?"

"Of course."

"I've been having revenge fantasies about that bastard Hal Bradshaw," said Reuben, loudly and cheerily, as Judith left the room.

"Who's he?" asked Chloë, looking anxiously at Ted.

"He's the bastard that conned me and Frieda and set us up to public ridicule. I keep imagining different scenarios. Like I'm walking past a lake and I see Bradshaw drowning and I just watch him as he sinks below the surface. Or I come across the scene of a car accident and Bradshaw is lying on the road and I just stand and watch him bleed out. I know what you're going to say, Frieda."

"I'm going to tell you to be quiet right now."

"You're going to tell me that fantasies like that aren't very healthy. They're not *therapeutic.*" He stressed the last word as if there were something disgusting about it. "So what do you think?"

"I think you've had too much wine and this is not the night."

"That's not much fun," said Reuben.

"No," chimed in Ted. His cheeks were blotchy and his eyes bright. "Not fun at all. Revenge should be bloody."

"I've been planning a real revenge with Josef," said Reuben.

Frieda looked at Josef, who had just taken a mouthful. He made an effort to chew and swallow it.

"Not the planning so much," Josef said. "The talking."

"There are things builders know how to do," Reuben continued, apparently unaware of the tangible air of distress in the room. "Josef can gain entry. You hide shrimps inside the curtain rails and behind the radiators. When they start to rot, the smell will be staggering. Bradshaw won't be able to live in his own house. Then there's more subtle things you can do. You can loosen a water pipe connector beneath the floorboards, just a little, just so there's a drip of water. That can cause some serious damage."

"That's awesome," said Ted, in a loud, harsh voice. His eyes glittered dangerously.

"This is just a fantasy you're talking about," said Frieda. "Right?"

"Or I could do worse than that," said Reuben. "I could tamper with the brakes on his car—with Josef's help, of course. Or torch his office. Or threaten his wife."

"You'd go to prison. Josef would be sent to prison and then deported."

Reuben opened another bottle of wine and started to fill the glasses again.

"I'm going to take Dora to her bed," said Frieda. "And when I come back, I think you should go. You and Josef are going home."

"I'm having a second helping," said Reuben. "More, Ted?

"Reuben, you've gone far enough."

But a few minutes later, when she came back into the room, Reuben began again. She knew him in this mood—petulant and dangerous, like a sore-headed bull.

"I think you're being pious about this, Frieda. I'm an advocate for revenge. I think it's healthy. I want to go round the table, and everyone has got to say the person that they would like to take revenge on. And what the revenge would be. I've already named Hal Bradshaw. I'd like him to be tied to a mountain top naked for all eternity, and then every day a vulture would come and eat his liver." He grinned wolfishly. "Or something."

"But what about when it had finished?" said Chloë.

"It would grow back every day. What about you, Josef?"

Josef gave a sad smile. "I don't say his name. The man with my wife. Him I want to punish."

"Excellent," said Reuben. "So what punishments would you like to devise for him? Something medieval?"

"I don't know," said Josef. "If my wife is with him—"

Ted interrupted. He was clearly a bit drunk. His eyes glittered. "If I could find my mother's killer, I'd—I'd—" He gazed around the table, his fist clenched around his wineglass. "I hate him," he said, softly. "What do you do to the people you hate? People you want to destroy?"

"It's OK, Ted," said Chloë. She was trying to hold the hand that was clasping his glass, but he shook her off furiously.

"Attaboy!" cried Reuben jubilantly. "Let it out. That's the way. Now you, Frieda. Who's going to be the object of your implacable revenge?"

Frieda felt a spasm of nausea in her stomach, rising in her chest. She felt as if she were standing on the edge of a chasm, with just her heels on the ground, her toes poking into the darkness and the temptation, always that temptation, to let herself fall forward into the deep darkness toward—well, toward what?

"No," she said. "I'm not good at these sorts of games."

"Oh, come on, Frieda, this isn't Monopoly."

But Frieda's expression hardened with a kind of anger, and Reuben let it go.

"The bath," said Josef, trying to make everything all right in his clumsy way. "Is OK?"

"It's very good, Josef. It was worth it." She didn't tell him she hadn't yet used it.

"Finally, I help," he said. He was swaying on his feet.

At last they had left. The soft spring dusk was darkening to real night. The clouds had blown away and the ghost of a moon was visible above the rooftops. Inside, an air of anticipation and dread filled the rooms. Even Chloë's animation had petered out. Judith, who had come downstairs when she heard the front door slam, sat in a chair in the living room, her knees drawn up, her head pressed down on them, her hair wild. If anyone spoke to her and tried to comfort her, she would simply shake her head vehemently. Dora lay on a cot in Frieda's study with a mug of cocoa beside her, which had cooled to form a wrinkled skin on its surface. She was playing a game of Snake on her phone. Her thin plaits lay across her face. Frieda sat beside her for a few moments, without speaking. She turned her head and said, in a voice that sounded almost querulous: "I knew about Judith and that older man."

"Did you?"

"A few days ago, when Dad was drunk, I heard him shouting at Aunt Louise about it. Is Judith going to be OK?"

"In time."

"Did Dad . . .?"

"I don't know."

Frieda went downstairs. Outside on the patio, Ted was smoking and pacing to and fro, his head enclosed in a giant pair of headphones. None of them could help the others, or be helped by them. They were just waiting, while Chloë barged around the house with cups of tea or firm, encouraging pats on a bowed shoulder.

Frieda had asked Ted if there was anyone she should call, and he had turned his sullen gaze on her. "Like who?"

"Like your aunt."

"You've got to be joking."

"Don't you have other relatives?"

"You mean like our uncle in the States? He's not much use, is he? No, it's us and it's Dad, and if he's not there, there's no one at all."

She sat with him for a while, relishing the cool night air. Nothing in her life felt rational or controlled anymore: not her house, which used to be her refuge from the violent mess of the world; not her relationship with these young people, who had turned to her, as if she knew answers that didn't exist; not her creeping involvement with the police again; not her unshakable preoccupation with the shadowy world of the missing girl Lila. Above all, not her sense that she was following a voice that only she could hear, an echo of an echo of an echo. And Dean Reeve, keeping watch. She thought of Sandy, only halfway through his day, and wished that this day were over.

FORTY-EIGHT

The following morning, Frieda woke everyone early and took them all to Number 9 for breakfast—a raggle-taggle crew of bleary-eyed, anxious teenagers, who seemed closer today to childhood than adulthood. Their mother had been murdered, their father was being held by police, and they were waiting for the sentence to fall.

She saw them all onto the bus, waiting till it drew away, then returned home. She felt drained and subdued, but she had things to do. Josef was building a garden wall in Primrose Hill; Sasha was at work. So Frieda took the train out from Liverpool Street, through the nearly completed stadiums and sports halls of the Olympic Park. They looked like toys abandoned by a giant child. Coming out of the station at Denham, she climbed into a taxi waiting at the rank.

A horse refuge named after a flower. Frieda had imagined rolling meadows and woodland. The taxi passed a large, semidemolished set of warehouses, then a housing estate. When the taxi stopped and the driver announced that they had arrived, Frieda thought she must have come to the wrong place, but then she saw the sign: The Sunflower Horse and Donkey Refuge. The driver asked if she wanted him to wait for her. Frieda said she might be some time, so he wrote his number on a card and gave it to her.

As the car drove away, she looked around. By the entrance, there was a pebbledashed house. There were deep cracks in the façade and an upper window was covered with cardboard. It seemed deserted. On the wall, to the side of the entrance, there was another sign, stenciled: Visitors Report to Reception. She walked into a yard lined with stable buildings made out of cinder blocks and concrete, but there was no reception that she could see. There were piles of horse manure and straw bales and off to the side, a rusting tractor with no tires on the front wheels. Frieda stepped delicately across the yard, making her way between muddy brown puddles.

"Is there anyone here?" she called out.

She heard a scraping sound, and a teenage girl carrying a spade emerged from one of the stable doorways. She was dressed in rubber boots and jeans and a bright red T-shirt. She wiped her nose with the back of her hand. "Yeah?"

"I'm looking for someone called Shane."

The girl just gave a shrug.

"I heard that a man called Shane works here."

The girl shook her head. "No."

"Maybe he used to work here."

"I don't know nobody called Shane."

"How long have you been working here?"

"A few years. On and off."

"And you know everyone who works here?"

The girl rolled her eyes. "Course I do," she said, and disappeared back into the stable. Frieda heard the spade scraping on the concrete floor. She walked out of the yard onto the road where she had come in, looked at her watch, and wondered what to do. There was no pavement, just a grass verge, and she felt vulnerable beside the cars that were passing her with a rush of air and noise. As she got beyond the buildings, she reached a rough wooden fence that separated the field from the road.

She leaned on the fence and looked across at the space that was bordered on the far side by the busy A12, cars and lorries rumbling along it. It was scrubby and abandoned, broken only by occasional clumps of gorse and in the middle, a large dead oak tree. And then there were horses and a few donkeys scattered around. They were old and mangy, but they seemed contented enough, heads down, nibbling at the grass, and Frieda found it relaxing just watching them. It was a strange scene, neither town nor country but something messily in between. It looked like land that had been neglected, unloved, half forgotten about. Maybe some buildings had been there, had been demolished, and the grass and the gorse had grown back. One day someone would notice it again, next to the motorway, close to London, and they'd build an industrial estate or a service station, but until then it would struggle on. Frieda rather liked it.

She rummaged in her pocket and found the card that the taxi driver had given her. She was just reaching for her phone when a car pulled up at the entrance to the refuge. A man got out. He was tall, slightly stooped, with unkempt hair that was nearly white and a beaked nose. They were thirty or more yards apart, too far to talk comfortably. Frieda stood back from the fence. She walked a few steps toward him, and he walked toward her. He had a watchful, unsmiling air, and as she took in the glare of his pale, hooded eyes, they stared at each other. The expression on his face didn't alter: it was as though he were looking not at but through her.

"Do you work here?" the man asked.

"No. I was trying to find someone, but he's not here." A thought occurred to her. "You aren't called Shane, are you?"

"No," said the man. "I'm not." And he walked past Frieda into the yard. Suddenly he stopped and turned. "Why do you want him?"

"It's difficult to explain."

The man came back toward her. "Tell me anyway."

"I'm searching for a girl," said Frieda, "and I thought that someone called Shane might help me. I was told he was here, but they haven't heard of him."

"Shane," said the man, reflectively. "I haven't heard of him. Still, you may as well come along."

Frieda raised her eyebrows in surprise. "Why should I do that?"

"I'm trying to find someone as well." He spoke slowly and somberly.

"I'm sorry, but I don't know you. You're a stranger to me, and I don't know who you're meeting or why you're here. I've finished, and I'm going home."

"It'll just take a minute." He scrutinized her. "My name's Fearby, by the way. Jim Fearby. I'm a journalist."

The sun passed behind a cloud, and the landscape in front of them darkened. Frieda had the feeling of being in a dream, where everything made sense but was senseless. "I'm Frieda Klein."

"And who *are* you?"

"I don't know." She stopped, hearing the words. "I'm just someone trying to help someone."

"Yes. What's the name of your missing girl?"

"Lila Dawes."

"Lila Dawes?" He frowned. "No, I haven't heard of her. But come with me."

They walked into the yard where the girl was now sweeping. She was obviously puzzled to see Frieda again.

"I'm looking for a man called Mick Doherty," said Fearby.

"He's over the other side," said the girl. "Doing the fence."

"Where?"

The girl sighed. She led them through the yard to the field and pointed across. They could see signs of someone moving on the far side, right by the main road.

"Is it safe to walk across?" asked Fearby.

"They don't bite."

A small gate opened into the field. Fearby and Frieda walked across it in silence. Two horses came up to them, and Fearby glanced at Frieda.

"They think we've got food," said Frieda.

"What will they do when they find we haven't?"

A small ragged horse nuzzled against Frieda. She stroked it between the eyes. How long was it since she had been that close to a horse? Twenty years? Longer? She felt the warmth of its breath on her. Comforting. It smelled sweet, musty, earthy. As they got closer to the far side, they saw a man fastening the fence to a new post, twisting wire with pliers. He looked at them. He was tall, with very long reddish brown hair tied back in a ponytail. He wore jeans and a black T-shirt. At first the T-shirt appeared to have long sleeves, but then Frieda saw his arms were covered with a network of tattoos. He had earrings in both ears.

"Are you Mick Doherty?" asked Fearby.

The man frowned at them. "Who are you?"

"We're not police. I'm looking for a young girl called Sharon Gibbs. She's missing. Your name came up as someone who knew her."

"I've never heard of her."

"I think you have. You are Mick Doherty?"

"That's right."

"We just want to find her." Frieda heard the *we* but didn't protest. This odd man spoke wearily but with a tone of authority. "However, if we don't find anything, we'll have to turn over what we know to the police. I'm sure that's not a problem, but . . ." Fearby paused and waited.

"I'm clean. You've got nothing on me."

Still Fearby waited.

"I don't know what you want." His eyes slid to Frieda. "You're wasting your time here."

"Sharon Gibbs."

"OK. I know her a bit. So what?"

"When did you last see her?"

"You say she's missing?"

"That's right."

"When did she go missing?"

"Several weeks ago now."

Doherty finished twisting a wire fastening on the fence. "I haven't seen her for months. Maybe more. I've been away."

"You've been away."

"That's right."

"Where?"

"In prison. Just for a bit. Bloody set up, I was. I went in in January. I got out last week. They let me out and they got me a job. Shoveling fucking dung for fucking donkeys."

"And have you seen Sharon since getting out?"

"Why would I have? She's not my girlfriend or anything, if that's what you're getting at. Just a squirmy little kid."

"A squirmy little kid who got into the wrong company, Mr. Doherty." Fearby fastened his unnerving eyes on the man. "And whose parents are very anxious about her."

"That's not my problem. You're talking to the wrong person."

A thought struck Frieda. "Do people call you Shane?"

"What do you mean?"

"Reddish hair, Irish name."

"I'm from Chelmsford."

"But they call you Shane."

Doherty gave a faint, sarcastic smile. "Sometimes they do. You know. Begorra."

"Tell me about Lila Dawes."

"What?"

"You knew a girl called Lila Dawes. Also missing." She felt Fearby stiffen beside her, as if a current of electricity had passed through him.

"Two missing girls," he said softly. "And you knew them both."

"Who says I knew Lila?"

"Lila. Crack addict. Spent time with you, Shane—Mr. Doherty—around the time she went missing. A little under two years ago."

"You say you're not the police, so I don't have to say anything to you. Except . . ." He put the wire down. Frieda could see the spittle on his mouth and the broken blood vessels on his skin. He clenched and unclenched his fists so that the tattoos on his arm rippled, and his eyes wandered round her, as if he were trying to see something behind her. "Except piss off back to where you came from."

"Hazel Barton, Roxanne Ingatestone, Daisy Crewe, Philippa Lewis, Maria Horsley, Lila Dawes, Sharon Gibbs."

It sounded like a chant, an incantation. Frieda felt the breath go out of her body. She stood absolutely still and quiet. For a moment, it was as if she'd entered a dark tunnel that was leading toward a still darker place.

"What the fuck are you talking about, old man?"

"Missing girls," Fearby said. "I'm talking about missing girls."

"OK. I knew Lila." He gave a smirk of recollection. "I don't know where she went."

"I think you do," said Frieda. "And if you do, you should tell me, because I'm going to find out."

"People come and go. She was always more trouble than she was worth."

"She was just a teenage girl who had the terrible bad luck of meeting you."

"My heart bleeds. And, yeah, I knew Sharon a bit. Not those others."

"Was this the first time you'd been in prison?" Fearby asked.

"I think I've had enough of your questions."

"Dates, Mr. Doherty."

Something in his voice made the man's expression waver for a moment, the sneer replaced by a kind of wariness. "Eighteen months ago I was in Maidstone prison."

"What for?"

"There was a thing with a girl."

"A thing." Fearby repeated the words as if tasting them. "What did you get?"

Doherty just shrugged.

"How long?"

"Four months, give or take."

Frieda could sense Fearby working something out. His face was raveled with concentration, deep furrows lining his forehead.

"OK," he said at last. "We're done."

Fearby and Frieda walked back across the field. Two horses followed them; Frieda could hear their hooves on the dried earth, like a drum.

"We need to talk," Fearby said, as they reached his car. She simply nodded. "Is there somewhere we can go? Do you live nearby?"

"No. Do you?"

"No. How did you get here?"

"I got a taxi from the station."

"We can find a café."

Frieda got in beside him; the seat belt didn't work; the car smelled of cigarettes. On the backseat there were several folders. Only when they were seated at a table by the window of a small, dingy café on Denham High Street, with mugs of too-milky tea in front of them untouched, did they exchange another word.

"You begin," said Fearby. He put a Dictaphone in front of him, then opened a spiral-bound notebook, and took a pen out of his jacket pocket.

"What are you doing?"

"Making notes. Is that OK?"

"I don't think so. And turn that off."

Fearby looked at her as if he were seeing her properly for the first time. Then a faint smile appeared on his weathered face. He turned off the machine and laid his pen down.

"Tell me why you're here."

So Frieda told her story. At first, she was conscious of its irrationality: just a paranoid instinct in the wake of her own trauma that had led her in a fruitless and inexplicable search for a girl she had never known. She heard herself talking about the tiny vivid anecdote that had sparked off her quest, of the dead ends, the sad encounters with Lila's father and with the woman from Josef's homeland, who had pointed her in the direction of Shane. But bit by bit she realized that Fearby wasn't responding with incredulity, as if she had gone slightly mad, the way that others had. He nodded in recognition, leaned forward; his eyes seemed to grow brighter and his granite face softer.

"There," she said, when she had finished. "What do you think?"

"It sounds like the same man."

"You're going to have to explain."

"Well. I suppose it all began with George Conley."

"Why does that name sound familiar?"

"He was found guilty of murdering a girl called Hazel Barton. You'll probably have heard of him because he was released a few weeks ago, after spending years in the nick for a crime he never committed. Poor sod, he'd almost have been better off staying inside. But that's a whole other story. Hazel was the first girl, and the only one whose body was found. I believe Conley interrupted the crime, whereas all the others—But I'm getting ahead of myself. And, in fact, Hazel wasn't really the first—there were others. Vanessa Dale, for a start, and I just didn't realize that at the time, because Vanessa was the one who got away. I tracked her down, though. I should have done it sooner, when she had a fresher memory, or any memory, but I didn't know. I didn't understand for many years what the story was really about, what a long, dark shadow it cast. Back in the day, I was just a hack, with a wife and kids, covering local news. Anyway—"

"Stop," said Frieda. Fearby looked up at her, blinking. "I'm sorry, but I don't understand a word you're saying."

"I'm trying to explain. Listen. It all links up, but you have to follow the connections."

"But you're not making any connections."

He sat back, rattled his teaspoon in his cooling tea. "I've lived with it too long, I guess."

"Are you trying to tell me that the girls whose names you gave Doherty are all connected, and that Lila Dawes may be too?"

"Yes."

"How?"

Fearby stood up abruptly. "I can't tell you. I need to show you."

"Show me?"

"Yes. It's all written down. I've got maps and charts and files. Everything's there."

"Where?"

"At my house. Will you come and have a look?"

Frieda paused. "All right," she said at last.

"Good. Let's go."

"Where do you live? London?"

"London? No. Birmingham."

"Birmingham!"

"Yes. Is that a problem?"

Frieda thought of her house waiting for her, of her friends who didn't know where she was, of her cat whose bowl would be empty. She thought of Ted, Judith, and Dora—but she couldn't resist the strangeness of the encounter, the pull of this strange old man. She would call Sasha and tell her to hold the fort.

"No," she said. "Not a problem."

FORTY-NINE

I n the warmth of the car, Frieda felt herself sliding toward sleep. She had had several nights of insomnia, worse than usual, tormented in between by scraping, violent dreams, and was ragged and scorched-eyed with tiredness. But she struggled against sleeping in front of Fearby, this shabby bird of prey; she couldn't let herself be defenseless in front of him. Yet it was no good, she couldn't stay awake. Even as she let herself go at last, her eyes closing and her body softening, she was thinking how odd it was that she should trust someone she didn't know at all.

Fearby turned off the M25 and onto the M1. This was a road he knew; it seemed fitting they should be driving it together. He slid some Irish folk music into the CD player, turned the volume down so it was only just audible, and glanced at her. He couldn't make her out. She must be in her mid- to late-thirties—from a distance, she looked younger, with her slim upright body and her supple movement, but up close her face was gaunt; there were hollows under her eyes and a strained, almost haunted expression on her pale face. He hadn't asked her what she did. Frieda Klein: it sounded German, Jewish. He looked at her hands, lying half folded in her lap, and saw they were ringless, with unvarnished nails cut short. She wasn't wearing any jewelry or makeup. Even in sleep, her face was stern and troubled.

Nevertheless—and his heart lifted—he had a companion, a fellow traveler, at least for a while. He was so used to working alone that it had become hard to tell where the outside world blurred with his private obsessions. She would be able to tell him: she had a good, clear gaze, and whatever motives she had for her own particular quest, he had felt her cool shrewdness. He smiled to himself: she didn't like being ordered around.

She murmured something and threw up one hand. Her eyes clicked open and, in a moment, she was sitting up straight, pushing her hair off her hot face.

"I fell asleep."

"That's OK."

"I never fall asleep."

"You must have needed it."

Then she sat back once more and gazed out of the windshield at the cars streaming past in the opposite direction.

"Is this Birmingham?"

"I don't actually live in the city. I live in a village, or small town, really, a few miles away."

"Why?"

"Sorry?"

"Why don't you live in the city?"

"It's where I lived with my wife and kids. When my wife left, I never got around to moving."

"Not from choice, then?"

"Probably not. Don't you like the countryside?"

"People should think about where they live, make a deliberate choice."

"I see," said Fearby. "I'm passive. And you've made a choice, I take it."

"I live in the middle of London."

"Because you want to?"

"It's somewhere I can be quiet and hidden. Life can carry on outside."

"Maybe that's what I feel about my little house. It's invisible to me. I don't notice it anymore. It's just a place to go. I'm an ex-journalist. What do you do?"

"I'm a psychotherapist."

Fearby looked bemused. "Now that I wouldn't have guessed."

He didn't seem to understand just how wretched he had let his house become. There was a graveled drive almost entirely grown over with ground elder, dandelions, and tufts of grass. The windowsills were rotting, and the panes were filthy. A general air of neglect lay over everything, dust and grease and grime. In the kitchen, piles of yellowing newspapers were stacked on the table, which clearly wasn't used for eating at. When Fearby opened the fridge door to look for milk that wasn't there, Frieda saw that, apart from beer cans, it was quite empty. It was a house for a man who lived alone and wasn't expecting company.

"No tea, then," he said. "How about whisky?"

"I don't drink in the day."

"Today is different."

He poured them both a couple of fingers into cloudy tumblers and handed one to Frieda.

"To our missing girls," he said, chinking his glass against hers.

Frieda took the smallest stinging sip, to keep him company. "You were going to show me what you've found."

"It's all in my study."

When he opened the door, she was speechless for a few seconds, her eyes trying to become accustomed to the combination of frenzy and order. Briefly, she was reminded of Michelle Doyce, the woman to whom Karlsson had introduced her, who had filled her rooms in Deptford with the debris of other people's lives, carefully categorizing litter.

Fearby's study was dimly lit because the window was half blocked with teetering piles of paper on its sill: newspapers and magazines and printouts. There were piles of papers on the floor as well: it was almost impossible to make a path through them to the long table that acted as his desk, also disappearing under scraps of paper, old notebooks, two computers, a printer, an old-fashioned photocopying machine, a large camera with its lens off, a cordless phone. Also, two chipped saucers overflowing with cigarette stubs, several glasses, and empty whisky bottles. On the rim of the table there were dozens of yellow and pink Post-it notes, with numbers or words scribbled on them.

When Fearby turned on the Anglepoise task lamp, it illuminated a paper copy of a photograph of a young woman's smiling face. One chipped tooth. It made Frieda think of Karlsson, who also had a chipped tooth and who was many miles away.

It wasn't the mess of the room that arrested her, however: it was the contrast of the mess to the meticulous order. On the corkboards, neatly pinned into place, were dozens of young women's faces. They were obviously separated into two categories. On the left, there were about twenty faces; on the right, six. Between them was a large map of Britain, covered with flags that went in a crooked line from London toward the northwest. On the opposite wall, Frieda saw a huge time line, with dates and names running along it in neat, copperplate writing. Fearby was watching her. He pulled open the drawers of a filing cabinet, and she saw racks of folders inside, marked with names. He started pulling them out, putting them on top of the dangerous heap of things on his table.

Frieda wanted to sit, but there was only one swivel chair, and that was occupied by several books.

"Are they the girls?" she asked, pointing.

"Hazel Barton." He touched her face gently, almost reverently. "Roxanne Ingatestone. Daisy Crewe. Philippa Lewis. Maria Horsley. Sharon Gibbs."

They smiled at Frieda, young faces smooth, eager.

"Do you think they're dead?"

"Yes."

"And maybe Lila is too."

"It can't be Doherty."

"Why?"

"Look." He directed her toward his time line. "This is when Daisy went, and Maria—he was in prison."

"Why are you so sure it's the same person?"

Fearby pulled open the first folder. "I'm going to show you everything," he said. "Then you can tell me what you think. It may take some time."

At seven o'clock, Frieda called Sasha, who agreed to go round to her house and stay there until she returned. She sounded concerned, a note of panic in her voice, but Frieda cut the conversation short. She also called Josef to ask him to feed the cat and perhaps water the plants in her yard.

"Where are you, Frieda?"

"Near Birmingham."

"What's this?"

"It's a place, Josef."

"What for?"

"It would take too long to explain."

"You have to come back, Frieda."

"Why?"

"We all worry."

"I'm not a child."

"We all worry," he repeated.

"Well, don't."

"You are not well. We all agree. I come to collect you."

"No."

"I come now."

"You can't."

"Why can't?"

"Because I'm not telling you where I am."

She ended the call, but her mobile rang again almost immediately. Now

Reuben was calling; presumably, Josef was standing beside him with his tragic eyes. She sighed, turned the phone off, and put it into her bag. She'd never wanted to have a mobile in the first place.

"Sharon Gibbs," said Fearby, as if nothing had interrupted them.

At half past ten, they were done. Fearby went outside for a cigarette and Frieda went to look in his cupboards for some food. She wasn't hungry, but she felt hollow and couldn't remember when she had last eaten. Not today; not last night.

The cupboards, like the fridge, were almost empty. She found some quick-boil rice and vegetable stock cubes long past their sell-by date: that would have to do. As she was boiling the rice in the stock, Fearby came back in and stood watching her.

"So, what do you think?" he asked.

"I think either we're two deluded people who happen to have bumped into each other at a donkey sanctuary—or that you're right."

He gave a grimace of relief.

"In which case, it's not Doherty or Shane or whatever he's called."

"No. But it's odd, isn't it, that he knew them both? I don't like coincidences."

"They lived the same kind of lifestyle—two young women who'd fallen off the track."

"Perhaps they knew each other?" Frieda suggested, lifting the rice off the stove, letting the steam rise into her face, which felt grimy with toil and weariness.

"That's a thought. Who would know?"

"I have one idea."

After they'd eaten the rice—Fearby had eaten most of it, Frieda had just picked at hers—Frieda said she should take the train back. But Fearby said it was too late. After some argument about hotels and trains, Fearby ended by getting an old sleeping bag out of a cupboard, and Frieda made a sort of bed for herself on a sofa in the living room. She spent a strange, feverish night, in which she didn't know when she was awake and when she was asleep, when her thoughts were like dreams and her dreams were like thoughts, all of them bad. She felt or she thought or she dreamed that she was on a journey that was also a kind of obstacle race, and only when she had got past the obstacles, solved all the problems, would she finally be allowed to sleep. She thought of the photographs of the girls on Fearby's wall, and their faces became mixed up with the faces of Ted, Judith, and Dora Lennox, all staring down at her.

From about half past three she was starkly, bleakly awake, staring at the ceiling. At half past four, she got up. She went to the bathroom and ran herself a bath. She lay there and watched the edges of the window blind grow light. She dried herself with the towel that looked like the least used and dressed herself in yesterday's dirty clothes. When she emerged from the bathroom, Fearby was there pouring coffee into two mugs.

"I can't offer you much of a breakfast," he said. "I can go out at seven and get some bread and eggs."

"Coffee will be fine," said Frieda. "And then we should go."

Fearby put a notebook, a folder, a little digital recorder into a shoulder bag, and within half an hour they were back on the motorway, heading south. For a long time, they drove in silence. Frieda looked out of the window, then at Fearby. "Why are you doing this?" she said.

"I told you," he said. "At first, for George Conley."

"But you got him out," said Frieda. "That's something most journalists wouldn't achieve in their whole career."

"It didn't feel enough. He only got out on a technicality. When he got out and everyone was cheering and celebrating and the media were there, it felt incomplete. I needed to tell the whole story, to show that Conley was innocent."

"Is that what Conley himself wants?"

"I've been to see him. He's a ruined man. I don't think he's capable of putting into words what he wants."

"Some people who looked at your house would say that you were a ruined man."

Frieda thought Fearby might flare up at that or say something defensive, but he smiled. "Would say? People have said it already. Starting with my wife and colleagues. My *ex*-colleagues."

"Is it worth it?" said Frieda.

"I'm not asking for thanks. I just need to know. Don't you agree? When you saw those photographs of the girls, didn't you want to know what happened to them?"

"Did it ever occur to you that there may not be any link between the pictures on your wall, except that they're just poor sad girls who went missing?"

Fearby glanced at her. "I thought you were supposed to be on my side."

"I'm not on anybody's side," Frieda said, with a frown, and then she re-laxed. "Sometimes I think I'm not even on my own side. Our brains are constructed so that we find patterns. That's why we see animal shapes in clouds. But really they're just clouds."

"Is that why you came all the way up to Birmingham? And why we're driving all the way back to London?"

"My job is listening to the patterns people make of their lives. Sometimes they're damaging patterns or self-serving or self-punishing, and sometimes they're just wrong. Do you ever worry what would happen if you discov-ered that you were wrong?"

"Maybe life isn't that complicated. George Conley was convicted of mur-dering Hazel Barton. But he didn't do it. Which means someone else did. So, where in London are we going?"

"I'll put the address into your satnav."

"You'll like it," said Fearby. "It's got the voice of Marilyn Monroe. Well, someone imitating Marilyn Monroe. Of course, that might not appeal to a woman as much as a man, I mean the idea of driving around with Marilyn Monroe. In fact, some women might find it quite annoying."

Frieda punched in the address, and for the next hour and a half, the car was guided down the M1, round the M25 by a voice that didn't really sound like Marilyn Monroe's at all. But he was right about the other bit. She did find it annoying.

Lawrence Dawes was at home. Frieda wondered if he ever wasn't at home. At first he seemed surprised. "I thought you'd given up," he said.

"I've got news for you," said Frieda. "*We*'ve got news for you."

Dawes invited the two of them through, and once more Frieda found herself sitting at the table in Dawes's back garden being served tea.

"We found Shane," she said.

"Who?"

"He was the man your daughter was associated with."

"Associated with? What does that mean?"

"You knew that your daughter was involved with drugs. He was involved with drugs too. In a more professional way." Dawes didn't react, but didn't seem like a man expecting good news. "Shane was just a nickname. His real name is Mick Doherty."

"Mick Doherty. Do you think he's connected with my daughter's disap-pearance?"

"It's possible. But I don't know how. It was when I went to see Doherty, out in Essex, that I met Jim. We were both looking for Doherty, but for different reasons."

"How do you mean?"

"I was investigating the case of a young woman called Sharon Gibbs," Fearby said. "She had gone missing, and I learned that she had known this man, Doherty. When I met Frieda, I discovered that we both wanted to talk to him about different missing women. It seemed an interesting coincidence."

Dawes looked thoughtful and pained in a way that Frieda had never seen him before. "Yes, yes, I can see that," he said, almost to himself.

"You'd never heard of Shane," said Frieda. "But now that we know his real name—Mick Doherty—do you recognize it?"

Dawes shook his head slowly. "I can't remember ever hearing that name."

"What about Sharon Gibbs?"

"No, I'm sorry. It doesn't mean anything to me. I can't help you. I wish I could." He looked in turn at Frieda and Fearby. "I must seem like a bad father to you. You know, I always thought of myself as the sort of man who would move heaven and earth to find his daughter, if anyone had tried to harm her. But it wasn't like a five-year-old girl going missing. It was more like someone growing up, moving away, and wanting to lead her own life. Bit by bit, she disappeared. Some days I think of her all the time and it hurts. It hurts here." He pressed his hand to his heart. "Others, I just get on with things. Gardening, mending. It stops me thinking, but perhaps I shouldn't stop thinking, because that's a way of not caring so much." He paused. "This man, what's his name?"

"Doherty," said Fearby.

"You think he's connected with Lila's disappearance?"

"We don't know," said Fearby, then glanced at Frieda.

"There's some kind of link," said Frieda. "But he can't be responsible for both. Doherty was in prison when Sharon Gibbs disappeared. I can't make it out. Jim's been looking at some girls who've gone missing, and Sharon Gibbs fits with that pattern. But the case of your daughter seems different. Yet she seems connected to them through Doherty. Somehow he's the hinge to all of this, but I don't know why."

"Why is she different?" asked Dawes.

Frieda stood up. "I'll take the tea things in and wash up, and Jim can tell you what he's been up to. Maybe something will ring a bell with you. Otherwise, we've got through one brick wall only to run up against another."

Dawes started to protest, but Frieda ignored him. She picked up the patterned plastic tray that he had leaned against the leg of the table and put the mugs, the milk jug, and the sugar bowl onto it. Then she walked into the house and turned right into the little kitchen. The window above the sink looked out onto the garden, and Frieda watched the two men as she did the washing up. She could see them talking but couldn't hear anything that was being said. Dawes was probably the sort of man who was more comfortable saying things to another man. They got up from the table and walked down the garden away from the house. She saw Dawes gesturing toward various plants and to the end of the garden, where the little river flowed. The Wandle, shallow and clear, trickling its way toward the Thames.

There were four other mugs in the sink and some dirty plates and glasses on the Formica worktop. Frieda washed those as well, then rinsed and stacked them on the draining board. She looked around the kitchen, wondering if men reacted to absence differently from women. The contrast with Fearby's house was sharp. Here, it was tidy, clean, and well organized, where Fearby's house was dirty and neglected. But there was something they had in common. Frieda thought that a woman would perhaps have turned the home into some sort of shrine to the missing person, but Fearby and Dawes were the opposite. Their very different spaces were both like highly organized ways of keeping all those terrible thoughts and feelings of loss at bay. Fearby had filled his house with other missing faces. And this house? It seemed like a house where a man lived alone and had always lived alone. Even doing the washing up, she felt like a female intruder.

She wiped her hands on a tea towel, neatly hanging on its own hook, then stepped outside to join the men. They turned at the same moment and gave a smile of recognition, as though in the few minutes she had been away, they had bonded.

"We've been comparing notes," said Fearby.

"It feels like we've been doing the same sort of godforsaken work," said Dawes.

"But you were a salesman, not a journalist," said Frieda.

Dawes smiled. "Still too much time on the road."

"I suppose you got out just in time?" said Fearby.

"What do you mean?"

"Do offices have photocopiers anymore?"

"They certainly do," said Dawes.

"I thought they'd gone paperless."

"That's a myth. They use more than ever. No, Copycon is going strong. At least my pension still arrives every month." He smiled but then seemed to correct himself. "Is there anything I can do for you?"

"No. I don't think so."

"Tell me something, do you think my daughter is alive?"

"We don't know," said Frieda, softly.

"It's the not knowing that's hard," said Dawes.

"I'm sorry. I keep coming around and stirring up old feelings, and it's not as if I've got much to report."

"No," said Dawes. "I'm grateful anyone's trying to do anything for my daughter. You're welcome here whenever you want to come."

After a few more exchanges, Frieda and Fearby were back out on the street.

"Poor man," said Frieda.

"You came back out just in time, though. Dawes was just explaining in unnecessary detail how he and his neighbor were building a new wall."

Frieda smiled. "Speak of the devil," she said, pointing. And there was Gerry, walking down the road, clasping two enormous bags of compost that almost obscured him. Frieda saw that one bag was leaking, leaving a thick brown trail in its wake.

"Hello, Gerry."

He stopped, put the bags down, wiped a grimy hand across his forehead. His mustache was still uneven. "I'm getting too old for this," he said. "Not to seem unfriendly, but why are you here again?"

"We came to ask Lawrence a couple of questions."

"I hope you had good reason."

"I thought so, but—"

"You mean well, I can see that. But he's had enough pain. You leave him be now." He bent to lift up his bags again and stumbled away, his trail of soil behind him.

"He's right," said Frieda, soberly.

Fearby unlocked his car. "Can I drop you home?"

"There's a station round the corner. I can walk and take the train back. It's easier for both of us."

"Tired of me already?"

"I'm thinking of your trip back. Look, Jim, I'm sorry for dragging you all the way down here. It didn't amount to much."

He laughed. "Don't be ridiculous. I've driven across the country for way less than this. And been glad to get it." He got into his car. "I'll be in touch."

"Aren't you baffled by the way these girls can just disappear?"

"Not baffled," he said. "Tormented."

He closed the door but opened it again.

"What?" asked Frieda.

"How will I get in touch? I don't have your phone number, your e-mail, your address."

They swapped numbers and he nodded to her. "We'll speak soon."

"Yes."

"It's not over."

FIFTY

Frieda walked to the station slowly. The day was gray but hot, almost oppressive, and she felt grimy in the clothes she'd worn yesterday. She allowed herself to think of her bath—Josef's gift to her—waiting in her clean, shaded house, empty at last of all people.

She turned on her mobile, and at once messages pinged onto the screen: missed calls, voice mail, texts. Reuben had called six times, Josef even more. Jack had written her a very long text full of abbreviations she couldn't understand. Sasha had left two texts. Judith Lennox had phoned. There were also several missed calls from Karlsson. When she rang voice mail, she heard his voice, grave and anxious, asking her to get in touch as soon as she got his message. She stared down at her phone, almost hearing a clamor of voices insisting she get in touch, scolding her, pleading with her, and worst of all, being in a state of distress about her. She didn't have the time for any of that now, or the energy or the will. Later.

When she eventually reached her house, letters lay on the doormat and as she stooped to pick them up, she saw that a couple had been pushed through the letter box rather than posted.

One was from Reuben; she recognized his writing at once. "Where the fuck are you, Frieda?" he wrote. "Ring me NOW." He didn't bother to sign it. The other was from Karlsson and was more formal: "Dear Frieda, I couldn't get you on your phone so came round on the off chance. I really would like to see you—as your friend and as someone who is worried about you."

Frieda grimaced and pushed both notes into her bag. She walked into her house. It felt cool and sheltered, almost as if she were walking into a church. It had been so long since she had spent time there alone, gathering her thoughts, sitting in her garret-study, looking out over the lights of London, at the center of the city but not trapped in its feverish rush, its mess and cruelty. She went from room to room, trying to feel at home again, waiting for a sense of calm to return to her. She felt that she had passed through a storm, and her mind was still full of the faces she had dreamed about last night, or lain awake thinking of. All those lost girls.

The flap rattled, and the tortoiseshell cat padded across to her and rubbed its body against her leg, purring. She scratched its chin and put some more food into its bowl, though Josef had obviously come in to feed it. She went upstairs to her gleaming new bathroom, put in the plug and turned on the taps. She saw her reflection briefly in the mirror: hair damp on her forehead, face pale and tense. Sometimes she was a stranger to herself. She turned the taps off and pulled out the plug. She wouldn't use the bath today. She stepped under the shower instead, washed her hair, scrubbed her body, clipped her nails, but it was no use. A thought hissed in her head. Abruptly, she stepped out of the shower, wrapped herself in a towel, and went into her bedroom. The window was slightly open and the thin curtains flapped in the breeze. She could hear voices outside, and the hum of traffic.

Her mobile buzzed in her pocket, and she fished it out, meaning to turn it off at once because she wasn't ready to deal with the world yet. But it was Karlsson, so she answered.

"Yes?"

"Frieda. Thank God. Where are you?"

"At home. I've just come in."

"You've got to get over here now."

"Is it the Lennox case?"

"No." His voice was grim. "I'll tell you when you come."

"But—"

"For once in your life, don't ask questions."

Karlsson met her outside. He was pacing up and down the pavement, openly smoking a cigarette. Not a good sign.

"What is it?"

"I wanted to get to you before bloody Crawford."

"The commissioner? What on earth—"

"Is there anything you need to tell me?"

"What?"

"Where were you last night?"

"I was in Birmingham. Why?"

"Do you have witnesses to that?"

"Yes. But I don't understand—"

"What about your friend, Dr. McGill?"

"Reuben? I have no idea. What's going on?"

"I'll tell you what's going on." He stubbed out his cigarette and lit another. "Hal Bradshaw's house burned down last night. Someone set it on fire."

"*What?* I don't know what to say. Was anyone inside?"

"He was at some conference. His wife and daughter were there, but they got out."

"I didn't know he had a family."

"Or you wouldn't have done it?" said Karlsson, with a faint smile.

"That's a terrible thing to say."

"It surprised me as well. I mean that someone would marry him, not that someone would burn his house down."

"Don't say that. Not even as a bad joke. But why have you come here to tell me this?"

"He's in a bad way, saying wild things, that it was you—or one of your friends."

"That's ridiculous."

"He claims that threats have been made against him."

"By me?"

"By people close to you."

Frieda remembered Reuben and Josef at that dreadful meal, Reuben's revenge fantasies and the look of hatred on his face, and her heart sank. "They wouldn't," she said firmly.

"It gets worse, Frieda. He's spoken to the press. He hasn't gone as far as naming names, but it doesn't take a genius to put two and two together."

"I see."

"They're inside, waiting for you." Briefly, he laid a hand on her arm. "But I'll be there as well. You're not on your own."

The commissioner—a stocky man with beetling brows and a pink scalp showing through his thinning hair—was a deep shade of red. His uniform looked far too hot for the day. Bradshaw was in jeans and a T-shirt and hadn't shaved. When Frieda entered the room, he stared at her, then slowly shook his head from side to side, as if he was too full of pity and anger to trust himself to speak.

"I'm very sorry indeed about what happened," said Frieda.

"Sit down," said the commissioner, pointing to a small chair.

"I'd prefer to stand."

"Suit yourself. I've been hearing your story from Dr. Bradshaw. I'm be-wildered, absolutely bewildered, as to why we ever had professional dealings with you." Here he turned toward Karlsson. "I must say I'm disappointed in you, Mal, turning a blind eye to your friend letting a possible psychopath loose."

"But he wasn't a psychopath," said Karlsson, mildly. "It was a setup."

The commissioner ignored him.

"Punching a colleague. Attacking a young woman she'd never met before and forcing her to the floor, just because she stood up for her boyfriend. Stalking poor Hal here. Not to mention killing this schizophrenic young woman, of course."

"In justified self-defense," said Karlsson. "Be careful what you say."

Crawford looked at Frieda. "What have you got to say in your defense?"

"What am I defending myself against? Arson?"

"Frieda, Frieda," murmured Bradshaw. "I think you need some profes-sional help. I really do."

"I had nothing to do with it."

"My wife was in that house," said Bradshaw. "And my daughter."

"Which makes it even worse," said Frieda.

"Where were you?" said Crawford.

"I was in Birmingham. And I can put you in touch with someone who can confirm that."

"What about your friends?" asked Bradshaw.

"What about them?"

"They've taken your side against me."

"It is true that I have several friends who think you acted unprofessionally and unethically—"

"That's rich," said the commissioner.

"But they wouldn't do anything like this."

Karlsson coughed loudly. "I think this is getting us nowhere," he said. "Frieda has an alibi. There's not a shred of evidence, just Dr. Bradshaw's claims, which some might believe to be motivated by malice. In the mean-time, I have an interview to conduct with Mr. Lennox, who is being charged with the murder of Zach Greene."

Bradshaw rose and came close to Frieda. "You won't get away with this," he said, in a low voice.

"Leave her alone," said Karlsson.

Frieda walked back home. She tried not to think, just putting one foot in front of the other, moving steadily through the thickening crowds, feeling the warmth of the day on her. She needed to steady herself before she was with the Lennox family again. Soon they would have neither mother nor father to turn to.

FIFTY-ONE

A re you ready?" said Karlsson. Yvette nodded. "We've let him stew
long enough and it looks cast-iron to me. You won't have to do much.
Just keep an eye on me and make sure I don't do anything stupid.
Even I couldn't fuck up this one, though."

He nodded at her, and they walked into the interview room. Russell Lennox was sitting at a table and next to him was his solicitor, a middle-aged
woman in a dark suit. She was called Anne Beste. Karlsson didn't know her,
but he didn't give her much consideration. What could she do? Yvette started
the recording machine, then stepped away from the table and stood to one
side, leaning back against the wall. Karlsson reminded Lennox that he was
still under oath, then opened the file and carefully went through the forensic
evidence from Zach Greene's flat. As he talked, he glanced from time to time
at Lennox and Anne Beste to see the effect he was having. Lennox's wearily
impassive expression was unchanged. Anne Beste listened intently with a
frown of concentration and occasionally looked sideways at her client. They
never spoke.

When he had finished, Karlsson closed the file quietly. "Can you give me
some innocent explanation for the traces you seem to have left at the scene of
the murder?" Russell Lennox shrugged. "Sorry, you have to say something.
For the benefit of the machine."

"Do I have to explain it?" said Lennox. "I thought you had to make the
case against me."

"I think we're doing that pretty well," said Karlsson. "One more question:
have you any evidence about your whereabouts on the day of the murder?"

"No," said Lennox. "I've told you already."

"Yes, you have." Karlsson paused for a moment. Then, when he spoke, it
was in a calm, almost soothing tone. "Look, Mr. Lennox, I know what
you've been through, but haven't you put your family through enough? Your
children need to put this behind them and move on."

Lennox didn't speak, just stared at the table.

"All right," said Karlsson. "Let me tell you—both of you—what is going to happen. We're going to leave the room now, Mr. Lennox, and give you five minutes to discuss various issues with your solicitor. Then I'm going to come back into this room and you will be charged with the murder of Zachary Greene. I need to caution you clearly that you don't have to say anything, but it may harm your defense if you do not mention now something that you later rely on in court. Anything you do say may be given in evidence. But what I'd really like to say to you is we all, but especially you, and even more especially your family, need to lay this to rest."

When they were outside, Karlsson looked at Yvette and smiled grimly.

"Does it matter what he says?" she asked.

"It'll go a bit more quickly if he confesses," said Karlsson. "But it's not that big a deal."

"Can I get you a coffee?"

"Let's just wait."

After a couple of awkward minutes, Karlsson looked at his watch, then knocked on the door and stepped inside. Anne Beste held up her hand.

"We need more time."

Karlsson stepped back outside and closed the door. "What the hell's that about?" Had something gone wrong? Could they have made some mistake?

It was more like ten minutes when they were both back in the room. Anne Beste was briskly tapping the surface of the table with the fingers of her left hand. She glanced at Lennox, and he gave the smallest of nods.

"Mr. Lennox is willing to admit to the manslaughter of Zachary Greene." Karlsson looked at Lennox. "What happened?" he asked.

"I went to see him," said Lennox. "After Judith told me. I had to. I was desperate. I was just going to talk to him, but we started arguing, and I lost control. And then he was dead."

Karlsson sighed. "You fucking idiot. Do you realize what you've done?"

Lennox barely seemed to hear him. "What about the children?" he said.

Yvette started to say something, but Karlsson stopped her with a look.

"Do you know where they are?" Karlsson asked.

Lennox leaned back in his chair. His face was dark with misery. "They're all staying in that therapist woman's house."

"With Frieda?" said Karlsson. "What are they doing there?"

"I don't know."

"Mr. Lennox," said Yvette. "You do understand, don't you, that this isn't over?"

"What do you mean?"

"There have been two murders—Zach Greene's, to which you've confessed."

"Manslaughter," put in Anne Beste.

"And your wife's."

Lennox lifted his eyes to her, then dropped them.

"My client has cooperated, and now he has nothing further to say," said Anne Beste.

Karlsson rose. "We'll talk again tomorrow. As my colleague here says, this isn't over, Mr. Lennox."

FIFTY-TWO

Frieda opened her door to find Karlsson, Yvette, and a woman she didn't recognize outside. The woman forced her way inside. Ted and Judith, Dora and Chloë were sitting around the table in the living room, with mugs and plates and phones and a laptop.

"Oh, my darlings, my poor, poor darlings," said Louise. The three Lennoxes shrank from her, but she didn't seem to notice. Chloë put a hand on Ted's shoulder.

"What's going on?" Frieda asked Karlsson, who murmured a quick explanation to her. When she heard, she looked round at the young people. Her face became stern.

"We want to stay here." Judith turned to Frieda. "Please? Please, Frieda."

"They're quite welcome," Frieda said to Karlsson. "If I can do anything to help."

Louise put her hands on her hips, as if willing to square up to her. "No. Absolutely not. They're coming home with me. That's what they need. Children, say thank you to this woman for everything she's done." She looked back at Frieda with a fierce expression. "They need to be with their family," she said, in a sort of stage whisper. Then she turned back to the children. "Now, we're going back to our house, I mean *my* house, and this policewoman is coming with us."

"No!" said Chloë. "Frieda, can't you stop this?"

"No. I can't."

"But it's horrible and—"

"Chloë, quiet now."

Karlsson turned to Yvette. "Are you going to be all right dealing with this? It'll be difficult."

"I'll be fine." Yvette had paled. "That's what female police officers are for, isn't it? To do the emotional stuff."

"Not exactly," said Karlsson.

There was a chaos of bags being picked up and jackets looked for and Chloë being hugged and the three Lennoxes making their way out to

Louise's car. They got inside. It was a tight fit, with Yvette sitting in the front seat. Ted's face stared out through the window.

"This doesn't feel right," said Frieda.

"It's the beginning of the rest of their lives," said Karlsson. "They'd better get used to it. Sorry. That came out wrong. But what can we do? They've lost their mother, and now they're losing their father, for the time being at least. They need a family. You can't be that for them."

"But it's important how they hear about their father," said Frieda. "And how they're listened to afterward."

"You don't think Yvette can handle it? All right. You don't need to answer that. You'd probably be the person to do it."

"I didn't say that."

"I can't ask you," said Karlsson. "I'm sorry. Yvette may fuck it up. She probably will. But she'll do her very best, and at least she's on the payroll." He frowned. "Can I have a word?"

Frieda glanced at Chloë.

"What?" Chloë's voice was high and harsh.

"I'm going to have to tell you something in a minute," said Frieda. "It's about Ted and Judith's father. But, first, Karlsson and I are going out for a few minutes. Is that all right?"

"No! It isn't all right. They're my friends and I have a right to—"

"Chloë." Frieda spoke in a quiet, warning tone that silenced her niece. She pulled on a jacket and stepped outside.

"You don't mind walking?" she said.

"I'm used to it," said Karlsson.

Frieda led the way out of the cobbled mews and turned right. When they reached Tottenham Court Road, they stood for a moment and watched the buses and cars careering past them.

"You know," said Frieda, "that if you move from the countryside to a big city like London, you increase your chance of developing schizophrenia by five or six times."

"Why?" said Karlsson.

"Nobody knows. But look at all this. It makes sense, doesn't it? If we abolished cities and went back to living in villages, we'd reduce the incidence of the disease by a third at a stroke."

"That sounds a bit drastic."

Frieda turned south, then took a small quiet road off to the right.

"I missed you today," said Karlsson.

"But you saw me today. Remember? With Hal Bradshaw and your commissioner."

"Oh, that," Karlsson said dismissively. "That was just a farce. No, when Lennox confessed, I actually expected to see you standing there with your beady-eyed expression."

"But I wasn't. And you seem to have done all right. So what happened?"

As they headed west, Karlsson gave Frieda a brief account of the day's events.

"Will you charge him with manslaughter?"

"Probably. He hears about the relationship. Rushes round in a rage. A father's anger. A jury would probably be sympathetic to that."

"I don't suppose it matters," said Frieda, "but he didn't find out just before he killed Zach. According to Dora, he'd known for some time."

Karlsson frowned. "Really? That's not what he said. I'm not sure I want to know that. Oh, well, it probably won't make much difference. He's still an angry father. And we've got the pattern of behavior. An argument escalates into violence. It's the same thing."

Frieda stopped. "Yes. It is the same."

"You've got a way of saying that that makes it sound suspicious."

"No. I was just echoing what you were saying."

"We know that Lennox has a habit of turning violent. Look at him with Paul Kerrigan; we're pretty sure that was him, and even that dealer in stolen goods. Why not his daughter's predatory boyfriend?"

The streetlight shone on Frieda's face, which seemed thin and sad.

"Poor kids," she said softly. "With that dreadful aunt."

"Yes."

"And what about their mother's murder?"

Karlsson shrugged. "I'm going to have another go at Lennox," he said. "Everything points to him. But it's all so tangled. There's so much rage and grief swilling around the whole affair, so many people who knew or might have known. It was a leaky secret, after all, even though they thought they were being so careful."

"Tell me."

"The Kerrigan boys knew," said Karlsson. "It turns out that Ruth Lennox—this cheerful, kind woman—turned a bit nasty when she discovered that Paul Kerrigan was going to leave her, and she must have sent them a poison-pen letter. Someone did, anyway."

"Oh," said Frieda. "So that changes everything."

"They knew about the relationship, and they knew who it was with. They tracked her down—the younger one even posted a nasty little message through the Lennox letter box."

"What did it say?"

"It wasn't in words. It was a rag doll, with its genitals cut out."

"So it was like a warning."

"Perhaps—though the wrong person picked it up, as it happens. Also, once a secret's out, it spreads. You can't stop it. Who else did they tell? They swear they didn't mention it to Mrs. Kerrigan—but I don't know if I believe them. Those boys adore their mother."

FIFTY-THREE

She turned on her mobile once more and scrolled down her contacts.

"Agnes?"

"Yes."

"Frieda here. Sorry to bother you."

"I'm in a meeting. Is this—"

"It won't take long. Did you know Sharon Gibbs?"

"Sharon Gibbs? Yes. Not very well. We weren't friends—but she lived near us, and she was a year below me at school. Lila knew her. I think they hung out with the same crowd after we'd lost touch."

"Thanks. That's what I wanted to know."

"But—"

"You go back to your meeting."

Frieda sat on the bed, looking at the blowing curtain, hearing the sound of life outside. She thought of Sharon Gibbs's face, which had smiled at her from Fearby's crowded wall. His voice came back to her: *Hazel Barton, Roxanne Ingatestone, Daisy Crewe, Philippa Lewis, Maria Horsley, Lila Dawes, Sharon Gibbs.*

When her mobile rang, she reached out to turn it off, then saw it was Fearby calling.

"Sharon knew Lila," she said.

There was a pause.

"That makes sense," he said.

"What do you mean?"

"You know that conversation I had with Lawrence Dawes?"

"Yes. You seemed to be getting on pretty well."

"About being in the same line of work."

"Selling photocopiers and finding news. I can see the similarity."

"Come on, Frieda. Don't you get it? Being on the road."

"Being on the road," Frieda repeated dully.

"Yes. Don't you see?"

"No."

"It suddenly made horrible sense. I'm a journalist. So what do I do? I go to Copycon—that's the company he worked for. Who'd call a company Copycon? I spoke to the area manager."

"Did you say who you were?"

"You need to feel your way with these things," he replied vaguely. "Make people want to tell you stuff. And he did."

"What?"

"He told me the area Lawrence Dawes covered until he retired a few months ago."

Frieda felt clammy and sick. She could feel beads of sweat breaking out on her forehead.

"His own daughter?" she said. "All those others? Is that possible?"

"Everything fits, Frieda."

"Why didn't I know?"

"Why would you?"

"Because—are you sure?"

"I'm not sure. But I *know*."

"Where are you?"

"Near Victoria."

"Good. We've got to get hold of Karlsson."

"Karlsson?"

"He's a police officer. Quite senior."

"I'm not sure we're ready to go to the police yet, Frieda."

"We can't wait. What if he does it again?"

"They'll need more than we've got. Believe me, I know them."

"So do I," said Frieda. "Karlsson will listen. I can't explain—but he owes me. Anyway." She remembered the note he'd pushed through her door. "He's a friend."

Fearby still sounded unsure. "Where do you want to meet?"

"At the police station." She looked at her clock radio. "In about forty-five minutes. Three o'clock. Is that good?"

"I'll get there as soon as I can."

She gave him the address and ended the call. Her tiredness had lifted. She felt glitteringly awake and alert. Only her eyes throbbed, as if the migraines she had had as a teenager had reappeared. Lawrence Dawes. She had sat in his lovely, well-tended garden. She had drunk tea with him. Shaken his hand and looked into his weathered face. Heard the pain in his voice. How had she not known? She put her head into her hands, feeling the relief of darkness.

Then she swiftly pulled on baggy linen trousers and a soft cotton shirt, tied her hair loosely back, dropped her keys into her bag, and left.

Fearby was waiting for her. Approaching him, Frieda was struck by how odd he looked, with his shabby white hair and those eyes that glared from his creviced face. He was more crumpled than ever, as if he'd been sleeping outside. He seemed to be talking to himself, and when he saw her he simply continued with the sentence.

"So I have a few of the folders in my car, but of course we can collect everything else later, and there are still some notes I haven't typed up—"

"Let's go in," said Frieda. She put her arm under his sharp elbow and pulled him through the revolving door.

Karlsson was in a meeting, but when he heard that Dr. Frieda Klein was downstairs, he left it and bounded into Reception to meet her. She was standing very upright in the center of the hall, and her face was set in an expression of determination that he recognized from the old days. Beside her was a man who resembled a moth-eaten bird of prey. He was carrying several plastic bags bulging with folders and holding a tape recorder. Karlsson didn't connect him to Frieda. He looked like one of the obsessive people who wandered into the station to disclose lunatic conspiracies to the indifferent duty officer behind the desk.

"Come into my office," he said.

"This is Jim Fearby. He's a journalist. Jim, this is DCI Malcolm Karlsson."

Karlsson put out a hand, but Fearby had none to spare. He simply nodded twice and stared fiercely into Karlsson's face.

"We need to speak to you," Frieda said to Karlsson.

"Is this about Hal Bradshaw?"

"That's not important right now."

"Actually, it is quite important."

Karlsson ushered them into his room and pulled up two chairs for them. Frieda sat, but Fearby put his bags on the chair, then stood behind it.

"Hal Bradshaw has made it quite clear that—"

"No," Fearby said harshly, the first word Karlsson had heard from him. "Listen to her."

"Mr. Fearby—"

"You'll understand in a minute," said Frieda. "At least I hope you will."

"Go on, then."

"We believe that a man called Lawrence Dawes, who lives down near Croydon, has abducted and murdered at least six young women, including his own daughter."

There was silence. Karlsson didn't move. His face was expressionless.

"Karlsson? Did you hear?"

When he finally responded it was in a tone of deep dismay. "Frieda. What have you been doing?"

"I've been trying to trace a missing girl," said Frieda, steadily.

"Why don't I know about this? Is there an ongoing murder inquiry that I've somehow missed?"

"I told you they wouldn't believe you," said Fearby.

"You have to listen to me." Frieda fixed Karlsson with her bright gaze. "There's no inquiry because no one has made the connection. Except Jim Fearby."

"But how did you get involved?"

"It was something that that fake patient of Hal Bradshaw's told me."

"The one who shafted you?"

"That's irrelevant. I don't care about it anymore. There was a detail that stood out, and I couldn't get it out of my mind. It was too specific; it had the ring of authenticity among all the clichés he was trotting out. It haunted me. I had to find out what it meant."

Karlsson looked at Frieda and the disheveled character with her. He felt a moment of pity.

"I know it sounds irrational," she continued. "At first, I thought I was going crazy and it was just a projection of my own feelings. But I traced where the story came from. I went from the man who'd been sent to me by Hal to the other three researchers. I met Rajit, who had got the story from his girlfriend. I found her, and she told me it had come from her old friend, Lila. And then I discovered that Lila had been missing."

Karlsson held up his hand. "Why didn't you say anything? Why didn't you come to me, Frieda?"

"I knew what everyone says: people are missing all the time, and they don't want to be found. But this felt different to me. I met Lila's friend and then this man Lila had spent time with just before she disappeared. Nasty character. Dodgy, violent, creepy. That was where I met Jim."

"Who was also looking for Lila?" asked Karlsson.

"I was looking for Sharon."

"Sharon?"

"Another missing girl."

"I see."

"And all the others, of course. But it was Sharon who led me there." He smiled suddenly. "And that was where I met Frieda."

Karlsson looked at Fearby. He reminded him of the drunks who sometimes slept the night in the police cells. He smelled a bit like them too: the thick reek of whisky and stale tobacco. Frieda saw his expression.

"You should have heard of Jim Fearby," she said. "He was the journalist who got George Conley's murder conviction overturned."

Karlsson turned to Fearby with new interest. "That was you?"

"So you can see why I've mixed feelings about the police."

"Why are you here now?"

"Frieda told me to come. She said you'd help."

"I said you'd listen," said Frieda.

"We think Lila's father is responsible." Fearby walked round the desk and stood beside Karlsson, who could hear him breathing heavily. "For his daughter and Sharon and the others."

"Lawrence Dawes," said Frieda.

"This is the man in Croydon?"

"Yes."

"You're asking me to believe that the two of you have discovered that a man is responsible for several murders that the police didn't even know had been committed?"

"Yes." Fearby stared at Karlsson.

"The girls went missing," Frieda said. She was trying to speak as clearly and as logically as she could. "And because they lived in different places and no bodies were found, there was no connection made between them."

Karlsson sighed. "Why do you think this Lawrence Dawes is the killer?"

Fearby went back to the other side of the desk and started rummaging in the bags for something. "The real maps are in my house, but I did this for you. So you'd see."

He brandished a sheet of paper on which he'd drawn, very messily, a map of the route between London and Manchester, with asterisks where the various missing women had disappeared.

"It's all right, Mr. Fearby."

"You don't believe us." Frieda spoke quietly.

"Look. Try to see it from my point of view. Or the commissioner's."

"No. It doesn't matter. You don't believe us, but I still want you to help me."

"How?"

"I want you to go and interview Lawrence Dawes. And search his house, every room. And the cellar. I think there's a cellar. And his garden too. You'll find something."

"I can't just send a team of police officers to take a house apart on your suspicions."

Frieda had been watching him attentively as he spoke. Now her expression closed; her face became a blank. "You owe me," she said.

"Sorry."

"You owe me." She heard her voice, cool and hard. It wasn't how she was feeling. "I nearly died because of you. So you owe me. I'm calling in a favor."

"I see."

Karlsson stood up. He was trying to hide his angry distress and turned his back on Frieda and Fearby as he put on his jacket and slid his mobile into his pocket.

"You'll do it?" Frieda asked.

"I do owe you, Frieda. And, also, you're my friend. So I trust you as well, in spite of the apparent wildness of this. But you understand this might backfire?"

"Yes."

"On me, I mean."

Frieda met his gaze. She could have wept at his expression. "Yes, I understand."

"All right."

"I can't come with—"

"No."

"Will you let me know?"

He let his eyes meet hers. "Yes, Frieda. I'll let you know."

As they left his room, a familiar figure approached them.

"Oh, shit," Karlsson hissed.

"Malcolm," said the commissioner. His face was red with anger. "A word."

"Yes? I'm on my way to see Mr. Lennox. Can this wait?"

"No, it cannot wait. There was a report." He pointed a quivering finger.

"Her contract was terminated. There's this scandal with Hal. You know what I think. What the flaming hell is she doing here?"

"She's been an important—"

"Do you realize what this looks like?"

Karlsson didn't reply.

"Have you paid her?" Crawford jabbed Karlsson and, for a terrible moment, Frieda thought there might be a fight between Karlsson and his boss. She winced with the fresh knowledge of how he had risked himself for her.

"Commissioner, as you must be aware, Dr. Klein has been very helpful to us and—"

"*Have you paid her?*"

"No, I haven't been paid." Frieda stepped forward. Her voice was cold. "I'm just here as a member of the public."

"What the hell are you doing, then?"

"I came to see DCI Karlsson on a purely private matter. As a friend."

Crawford raised his eyebrows. "Careful, Mal," he said. "I'm paying attention." And he noticed Fearby. "Who's *that?*"

"This is my colleague, Jim Fearby," said Frieda. "We were both leaving."

"Don't let me stop you."

At the entrance, Fearby turned to Frieda. "That went well, after all."

"It went terribly," Frieda said dully. "I abused my friendship with Karlsson and lied to the commissioner."

"If we achieve what we're after," said Fearby, "none of that matters."

"And if we don't?"

"Then it doesn't matter either."

As they left, they met a woman coming in—middle aged and tall, with long brown hair and wearing a long patchwork skirt. Frieda was struck by her expression of fierce purpose.

FIFTY-FOUR

'd like to see Malcolm Karlsson," said the woman, speaking loud and fast.

"I think DCI Karlsson is rather busy at the moment. Do you have—"

"Or Yvette Long. Or that other one."

"Can you tell me what it's about?"

"My name is Elaine Kerrigan. It's about the murder of Ruth Lennox. There is something I need to say."

Yvette sat opposite Elaine Kerrigan. She saw the palor of her face and the brightness of her eyes. Her glasses, hanging round her neck on a chain, were smudged, and her hair hadn't been brushed.

"You told the officer on the desk there was something you needed to say."

"Yes."

"About the murder of Ruth Lennox?"

"That's right. Can I have a glass of water first, please?"

Yvette left the room and bumped into Karlsson. He looked awful, and she touched him on the elbow. "Are you OK?"

"Why wouldn't I be?"

"No reason. I'm in there"—jerking her head in the direction of the room—"with Elaine Kerrigan."

"What for?"

"I don't know. I'm just going to get her some water. She seems agitated."

"Does she indeed?"

"Have you finished with Russell Lennox?"

"I'm taking a break for an hour or so. It won't do him any harm to wait and worry." His face grew grim. "There's something I have to do."

"What's that?"

"You wouldn't understand. You'd think I'd gone mad. Sometimes I think I've gone mad myself."

. . .

There was nothing to do but wait. Fearby said he had people he needed to see while he was in London and drove off once more, leaving Frieda unsure of what to do with herself. In the end, she did what she always did at times of uncertainty or distress, when dark thoughts filled her: she walked. She found herself going toward King's Cross, weaving along minor streets to avoid the roar of traffic, then took the road that led to Camden Town, which made her think again of the house where the Lennox family used to live, in clutter and a sort of happiness, but which now stood empty. Russell was in prison; Ted, Judith, and Dora were at their aunt's house, many miles away. At least it was neat.

She turned onto the canal. The houseboats moored by the path had pot plants and herbs on their decks. On a couple of them, dogs lay in the sunshine; on one, Frieda saw a parrot in a large cage, eyeing her. Some were open to the public, selling banana bread and tie-dyed scarves, herbal tea, and recycled jewelry. People passed her on bikes; runners pounded by. Summer was coming. She could feel it in the warm air, see it in the thin brightness of the light and the sappy greenness of unfolding leaves on the trees. Soon, Sandy would be back, and they would have weeks together, not days.

She thought these things but couldn't feel them. Indeed, the clear light and the happy people seemed unreal, far off, and she belonged to a different world— one in which young women had been dragged out of their lives by a man who had a smiling, sympathetic face. He had killed his daughter, Lila, Frieda was sure of it now—and yet he had seemed genuinely grief stricken by her absence. A piece of chalked graffiti on the wall showed a huge mouth full of sharp teeth, and she shuddered, suddenly cold in spite of the warmth of the afternoon.

She walked along the canal as far as Regent's Park. The houses on the other side were grand here, like small castles or mock châteaux. Who would live in such places? She walked through the park swiftly, scarcely noticing the gaggles of children, the courting couples, the young man with closed eyes doing some strange, slow exercises on a roll-out mattress by the ornamental gardens.

At last, making her way through side streets, she was at home. The phone was ringing as she opened the door and she half ran to get it, in case it was Karlsson.

"Frieda? Thank God. Where the fuck—"

"Reuben, I can't talk now. I'm waiting for a call. I promise I'll phone you as soon as I can, all right?"

"Wait, did you hear about Bradshaw?"

"Sorry."

She slammed the phone down. How long would it take for Karlsson to go to Lawrence Dawes's house? When would he call? Now? This evening? Tomorrow?

She made herself some toast and marmalade and ate it in the living room, listening to the phone ringing over and over and the answering machine playing messages: Chloë, plaintive; Sasha, anxious; Reuben, furious; Sandy—oh, God, Sandy. She hadn't even told him what she was up to. She'd gone into a different world, of terror and darkness, and hadn't even thought to confide in him. She didn't pick up but let him leave his message asking her, yet again, to contact him, *please*. Josef, drunk; Olivia, drunker.

The day darkened and still Karlsson hadn't called. Frieda went upstairs to her study and sat at the desk that looked out over the great sprawl of the city, now lit up and glittering under the clear sky. In the countryside, the sky tonight would be thick with stars. She picked up her pencil and opened her sketch pad, made a few indeterminate lines, like ripples. She thought of the stream at the bottom of Lawrence Dawes's garden.

Perhaps she should have that long-delayed bath now. She was as tired as she had ever been, but far from sleep. Indeed, it felt as though sleep would never come again and she was trapped forever in this dry, hissing wakefulness where thoughts were knives.

And then the phone rang again.

"Yes?"

"Frieda."

"Karlsson? What did you find?"

"Nothing."

"That's not possible."

"One very bewildered and distressed father, and a house in which there is no evidence of any kind whatsoever that he has ever done anything wrong."

"I don't understand."

"Don't you? I felt very sorry for him."

"Something's not right."

"Frieda, I think you need help."

"Are you sure there was nothing at all?"

"Listen to me. You have to walk away from all of this. And I need to placate the commissioner, who's not a happy man, I can tell you. He wants to drag me in front of some official hearing."

"I'm sorry about that but—"

"Draw a line under everything." His voice was horribly gentle. "No more following your instincts. No more trying to rescue people who don't want to be rescued. No more teaming up with some mad old hack. Go back to the life we dragged you out of. Try to recover."

He ended the call, and Frieda sat for a long time in her garret room, staring at the kaleidoscope of lights spread out before her.

> Dear Sandy, I think I am in trouble, in the world and in my head or my heart—

But she stared at the few words for a long time and then pressed the Delete button.

Karlsson and Yvette sat in front of Elaine Kerrigan. Her face was unyielding, and she repeated, in a wooden tone, "I killed her."

"Ruth Lennox?"

"Yes."

"Tell me how it happened," said Karlsson. "When did you discover your husband's affair?"

"Why does it matter? I killed her."

"Did your sons tell you?"

"Yes." She took a sip of water. "They told me, and I went there and killed her."

"With what?"

"An object," she said. "I can't remember. I can't remember anything except I killed her."

"Take us through it," said Yvette. "We have plenty of time. Start from the beginning."

"She's protecting her sons," said Karlsson.

"So you think one of them did it?"

"She does, anyway."

"And you?"

"Fuck knows. Maybe everyone joined up together to do it, like in that book."

"I thought you believed it was Russell Lennox."

"I'm sick of this case. It's too full of misery. Come on, let's get a coffee. Then you're going home. I don't know when you last had any sleep."

FIFTY-FIVE

Frieda phoned Fearby and told him what had happened—or hadn't happened. There was a pause, and then he said he was still in London and he was coming right over. Frieda gave him her address, then tried to tell him it wasn't necessary, that there was nothing more to say, but he had already rung off. In what seemed like a few minutes, there was a knock at the door, and Fearby was sitting opposite her with a glass of whisky. He asked her to tell him exactly what Karlsson had said. Frieda reacted impatiently.

"It doesn't matter," she said.

"What do you mean?"

"They went to Lawrence Dawes's house. They turned it upside down. They didn't find anything suspicious at all."

"How did Dawes react?"

"You know what? I didn't ask. The police appeared out of the blue and searched his house and all but accused him of killing his daughter. I imagine he was shocked and distressed." Frieda felt a tiredness that was actually painful. "I can't believe it. I sat in his garden with him, and he talked about what he'd been through, and I set the police on him. Karlsson is furious with me as well. And rightly so."

"So where do we go from here?" said Fearby.

"Where do we go? We go nowhere. I'm sorry, but are you incapable of seeing what's in front of your nose?"

"Have you stopped trusting your instincts?"

"It was my instinct that got us into this."

"Not just your instinct," said Fearby. "I'd been following a trail, and we found we were on the same trail. Doesn't that mean anything to you?"

Frieda sat back in her chair and sighed. "Have you ever been out in the countryside, and you were walking on a path, and then you realized it wasn't really a path at all, it just looked like one, and you were lost?"

Fearby smiled and shook his head. "I never was much for walking."

"For all we know, Sharon Gibbs is somewhere reasonably happy, not wanting to be found. But, whatever the truth, I think we're done."

Fearby shook his head again, but he didn't seem dismayed or angry. "I've been doing this too long to get put off by something like this. I just need to go over my files again, make some more inquiries. I'm not going to give up now, not after all I've done."

Frieda looked at him with a kind of horror. Was he a bit like her? Was this the way she appeared to other people? "What would it take for you to give up?"

"Nothing," said Fearby. "Not after all this, after what George Conley suffered, after Hazel Barton's murder."

"But what about what you've suffered? Your marriage, your career?"

"If I give up now, that won't bring my job back. Or my wife."

Suddenly Frieda felt as if she were trapped in a disastrous therapy session in which she couldn't find the right thing to say. Should she try to convince Fearby that everything he had sacrificed his life for had been an illusion? Did she even believe it? "You've already done so much," she said. "You got George Conley out of prison. That's enough."

Fearby's expression hardened. "I need to know the truth. Nothing else matters." He caught Frieda's eye and gave a slightly embarrassed smile. "Just think of it as my hobby. It's what I do instead of having a garden plot or playing golf."

When Fearby got up to go, Frieda felt as if she were someone he had sat next to on a train journey and struck up a conversation with, and now they were arriving at the station and would part and never meet again. They shook hands at the door.

"I'll let you know how things progress," he said. "Even if you don't want me to."

When Fearby was gone, Frieda leaned against her door for a few minutes. She felt as if she needed to catch her breath but couldn't, as if her lungs wouldn't work properly. She forced herself to concentrate and take long, slow breaths.

Then, at last, she went up to her bathroom. She'd been waiting for the right time, but there was never a right time. There was always something left to do. She thought of Josef, her shambolic and eager friend, all the work he'd put into this for her. It was his act of friendship. She had good friends, but she hadn't turned to them, not even to Sandy. She could listen, but she couldn't talk, give help but not ask for it. It was strange that in the last days she had felt closer to Fearby, with his neglected home, his huge filing system, and his wreck of a life, than she had to anyone else.

The doorbell rang and for a moment she thought she wouldn't answer. But then, with a sigh, she turned away from the bath and went to the front door.

"Delivery for you," said the man, half obscured by a tall cardboard box. "Frieda Klein?"

"Yes."

"Sign here, please."

Frieda signed and took the box into the living room, levering open its top. As she did so, she was hit by a smell whose powerful sweetness reminded her of funeral parlors and hotel lobbies. Carefully, she lifted out an enormous bouquet of white lilies, tied at the bottom with purple ribbon. She had always hated lilies: they were too opulent for her, and their fragrance seemed to clog her airways. But who had sent them?

There was a miniature envelope with the flowers, and she opened it and slid out the card.

We couldn't let him get away with it.

The world narrowed, the air cooled around her. *We couldn't let him get away with it.*

Him? Who? Bile rose in her throat and her forehead was clammy. She put out one hand to steady herself, made herself breathe deeply. She knew who had sent her these flowers. Dean Reeve. He had sent her daffodils before, telling her it wasn't her time, and now he had sent her these lush, pulpy lilies. He had set fire to Hal Bradshaw's house. For her. She pressed her hand hard against her furious heart. What could she do? Where could she turn? Who would believe her, and who would be able to help?

She had a sickening sense that she had to do something or talk to someone. That was what she believed in, wasn't it? Talking to people. But who? Once it would have been Reuben. But their relationship wasn't like that anymore. She couldn't talk to Sandy because he was in America, and these weren't things to be put into words on the phone. What about Sasha? Or even Josef? Wasn't that what friends were for? No. It wouldn't work. She couldn't find the proper explanation, but she felt it would be a betrayal of their friendship. She needed someone outside everything.

Then she remembered someone. She went to the bin outside her house and thrust the flowers into it. Back inside, she rummaged through her shoulder bag, but it wasn't there. She went upstairs to her study. She pulled open one of the drawers of her desk. When she cleared out her bag, she either threw things away or kept them here. She went through the old postcards, receipts, letters, photographs, invitations, and found it. A business card. When Frieda had faced a medical disciplinary panel, she had encountered one kindly face. Thelma Scott was a therapist herself, and she had immediately seen something in Frieda that Frieda hadn't wanted to be seen. She had invited Frieda to come and talk to her anytime she felt the need and given Frieda her card. Frieda had been sure that she would never take her up on the offer, almost angry at the suggestion, but still she had kept it. She dialed the number, her hands almost trembling.

"Hello? Yes? I'm sorry to call at this time. You probably won't remember me. My name is Frieda Klein."

"Of course I remember you." Her voice sounded firm, reassuring.

"This is really stupid, and you've probably forgotten this as well, but you once came to see me, and you said I could come and talk to you if I needed it. I was just wondering if at some point I could do that. But if that's not convenient, then it's completely all right. I can find someone else to talk to."

"Can you come tomorrow?"

"Yes, yes, that would be possible. But there's no hurry. I don't want to force myself on you."

"What about four o'clock, the day after tomorrow?"

"Four o'clock. Yes, that would be fine. Good. I'll see you then."

Frieda got into bed. She spent most of the night not sleeping, besieged by faces and images, by fears and dark, pounding dread. But she must have slept a bit, because she was woken by a sound that at first she didn't recognize, then gradually realized was her mobile phone. She fumbled for it and saw the name Jim Fearby on it. She let it ring. She couldn't bear to talk to him. She lay back in the bed and thought of Fearby and had a sudden vivid, sickening, flashing sense of what it would be like to be mad, really mad, finding your own hidden meanings in a chaotic world. She thought of the troubled, sad people who came to her for help, and then the even more troubled, sadder people who were beyond anything she could do, the people who had voices in their heads, telling them about conspiracies, how everything made horrible, terrifying sense.

Frieda looked at her clock. It was a couple of minutes after seven. Fearby must have waited for a permissible time to ring her. She got up and had a cold shower, so cold it made her ache. She pulled on some jeans and a shirt and made herself coffee. She couldn't face anything else. What if Fearby had left a message? She didn't even want to hear his voice, but now she'd thought of it, she couldn't stop herself. She retrieved the phone from upstairs and called her voice mail. He probably wouldn't have said anything. But he had.

The message began with a nervous cough, like someone starting a speech without knowing quite what to say.

"Erm. Frieda. It's me. Jim. Sorry about everything yesterday. I should have thanked you for all you've done. I know I come over as a bit of a nutter. And an obsessive. Anyway, I said I'd keep you in touch. Which is probably not what you want to hear. I'm in London. I've been going over things, the files on the girls. I've had a thought. We weren't thinking about them properly. We didn't hear the engine. I'm going out to have another look. Then I'll call round to see you and fill you in. I'll be there at two. Let me know if that's no good. Sorry to go on so long. Cheers."

Frieda almost wished she hadn't heard the message. She felt she was being sucked back in. It was clear that Fearby would never let go. Like those people obsessed with the Freemasons or the Kennedy assassination, he would never give up and nothing would change his mind. She was tempted to ring him back and tell him not to come but then she thought, No. He could come one last time, and she would hear what he had to say and respond rationally, and that would be that.

The day was almost as much of a blur as the night had been. Frieda thought she might read a book, but she knew she couldn't concentrate. Normally, at a time like this, she would have done a drawing of something simple, like a glass of water or a candle. She didn't even want to go out, not in the daytime, with the people and the traffic noise. She decided to clean her house. That would do. Something that required no thought. She filled bucket after bucket with hot water and cleaning fluid and took objects off shelves and wiped them down. She sprayed the windows. She mopped floors. She polished surfaces. The more she cleaned, the more she had a comforting sense that nobody lived in the house or had lived there or had ever been there.

The phone rang periodically, but she didn't answer. She didn't know whether it had been a surprisingly long time or a surprisingly short time, but she looked up at the clock and saw it was five to two. She sat in a chair and waited. There was going to be no coffee. Certainly no whisky. He could say what he had to say, she would respond, and he could go. Then it would be over, and she could go talk to Thelma Scott and start to deal with all of this, because it just couldn't go on.

One minute past two. Nothing. She actually went to the door and opened it and stepped out. As if that would help. She sat back down. Ten past, nothing. Quarter past, nothing. At twenty past, she called Fearby and went straight to his voice mail.

"I was wondering where you were. I need to go out soon. Well, not that soon. I'll be here until half past four."

She thought he might be one of the people who had called during the day. There were fourteen messages on her answering machine. They were the usual suspects: Reuben, Josef, Sasha, someone about a possible patient, Paz, Karlsson, Yvette. She tried her voice mail. Nothing. For the next half hour she answered the phone three times. One was a fake survey, one was Reuben, one was Karlsson. Each time she said she couldn't talk. By three o'clock she was genuinely puzzled. Had she got the time wrong? She'd deleted Fearby's message as soon as she'd heard it. Was it possible she had misheard? God knew, she hadn't been thinking all that clearly. Was it really two o'clock? Yes, she was sure about that. He'd even said that if she couldn't make that time, she should ring back. Could he just be late? Caught in traffic? Or maybe he had decided not to come. He might have drawn a blank and headed home. Or he might have picked up on her skepticism. She phoned his number again. Nothing. He wasn't coming.

At last, she gave up on Fearby. She put food in the cat's bowl, and then she walked to Number 9 for coffee. As she was returning, she saw a figure walking toward her. Something about the heavy-footed, purposeful stride was familiar.

"Yvette?" she said, as they drew close to each other. "What is it? Why are you here?"

"I've got to talk to you."

"What's happened?"

"Can we go inside?"

She led Yvette into the house. Yvette took off her jacket and sat down. She was wearing black jeans with a hole in the knee and a button-down man's shirt that had seen better days. Clearly, she wasn't on duty.

"So what is it? Is it something about the Lennoxes?"

"No. I'm taking a well-earned break from that bloody circus. You wouldn't believe—but anyway. That's not why I'm here."

"So why are you?"

"I had to tell you: I'm on your side."

"What?"

"I'm on your side," Yvette repeated. She seemed close to tears.

"Thank you. But on my side against who?"

"All of them. The commissioner. That wanker Hal Bradshaw."

"Oh, that."

"I needed you to know. I know you had nothing to do with it, but if you had—well, I'd still be on your side." She gave a crooked, emotional smile. "Off the record, of course."

Frieda stared at her. "You think I might have done it," she said at last.

Yvette flushed. "No! That's not what I was saying at all. But it's not a secret that you and Dr. McGill were angry with him. You had every reason. He shafted you. He was just jealous."

"I promise you," Frieda said, softly, "that I haven't been near Hal Bradshaw's house."

"Of course you haven't."

"It was a monstrous thing to do. And I know that Reuben wouldn't do that, however angry he was."

"Bradshaw said something else as well."

"What?"

"You know what he's like, Frieda. Insinuating."

"Just tell me."

"He said that he had some dangerous enemies, even if they didn't do their own dirty work."

"Meaning me?"

"Yes. But also that he has some powerful friends."

"Good for him," said Frieda.

"Don't you care?"

"Not so much," said Frieda. "But what I want to know is why you do."

"You mean why should I care?"

She looked steadily at Yvette. "You haven't always looked after my best interests."

Yvette didn't look away. "I have dreams about you," she said, in a low voice. "Not the kind of dreams you'd expect, not dreams where you're nearly killed or stuff like that. These are odder. Once I dreamed we were at school together—though we were our real age—and sitting next to each other in class, and I was trying to write neatly to impress you, but I just kept smearing the ink and couldn't form the letters correctly. They were crooked and childish and kept sliding off the page, and yours were perfect and neat. Don't worry, I'm not asking you to interpret my dreams. I'm not so stupid I can't do that myself. In another dream, we were on holiday and were by a lake surrounded by mountains that looked like chimneys, and I was really nervous because we were about to dive into the water and I didn't know how to swim. Actually, I can't really swim—I don't like getting my head underwater. But I couldn't tell you because I thought you'd laugh at me. I was going to drown so I didn't look like a fool in front of you."

Frieda was about to speak, but Yvette held up a hand. Her cheeks were crimson. "You make me feel completely inadequate," she said, "and as if you can look into me and see through me and know all the things I don't want people to see. You know I'm lonely and you know I'm jealous of you and you know I'm crap at relationships. And you know . . ." Her cheeks burned. "You know I've got a schoolgirl crush on the boss. The other night I got a bit drunk, and I kept imagining what you'd think of me if you could see me stumbling around."

"But, Yvette—"

"The fact is that I nearly let you get killed, and when I'm not having dreams, I've been lying awake and wondering if I did it out of some pathetic anger. And how do you think that makes me feel about myself?"

"So you're making amends?" Frieda asked, softly.

"I guess you could call it that."

"Thank you."

Frieda held out her hand and Yvette took it, and for a moment the two women sat across the table from each other, holding hands and gazing into the other's face.

FIFTY-SIX

F rieda was dreaming about Sandy. He was smiling at her and holding
out his hand to her, and then Frieda, in her dream, realized it wasn't
Sandy at all—that it was actually Dean's face, Dean's soft smile. She
woke with a lurch and lay for several minutes, taking deep breaths and waiting for the dread to subside.

At last, she rose, showered, and went into the kitchen. Chloë was already
sitting at the table. There was a mug of untouched tea and what looked like
a large album in front of her. She was bedraggled, her hair unbrushed and
her face grimy with yesterday's mascara. She looked as though she had
hardly slept for nights. She was like an abandoned waif—her mother was
going through a messy crisis and barely thought about her, her friends had
been taken away from her, and her aunt had absented herself at her time of
need. She lifted her smudged, tear-stained face and stared blindly at her.

Frieda took a seat opposite her. "Are you OK?"

"I guess."

"Can I get you some breakfast?"

"No. I'm not hungry. Oh, God, Frieda, I can't stop thinking about it all."

"Of course not."

"I didn't want to wake you."

"How are you feeling?"

"I was lying in bed, and I kept imagining what they were feeling at that
very moment. They've lost everything. Their mother, their father, their belief
in their past happiness. How do they ever get back to an ordinary kind of life
after this?"

"I don't know."

"What about you?"

"I didn't sleep so well either. I was thinking about things." Frieda walked
across the kitchen and filled the kettle. She looked at her niece, who had her
head propped on her hand and was dreamily staring at the pages of the album in front of her.

"What is that?" she asked.

"Ted left his portfolio. I'll give it back to him, but first I've been looking through it. He's an amazing artist. I wish I was just a tenth, a hundredth as good as he is. I wish—" She stopped and bit her lip.

"Chloë. This has been hard for you."

"Don't worry," she said harshly. "I know he just thinks of me as a friend. A shoulder to cry on. Not that he does cry on it."

"And probably," said Frieda, "your own feelings are rather complicated because of everything he's been through."

"What d'you mean?"

"I mean there's something extremely attractive about a young man who's so surrounded by tragedy."

"Like I'm a grief tourist?"

"Not exactly."

"It's all over now," said Chloë. Her eyes filled with tears, and she went on staring at the book in front of her.

Frieda leaned over her shoulder as she turned the large pages. She saw a beautifully exact drawing of an apple, a bulbous self-portrait as reflected in a convex mirror, a painstakingly precise tree. "He's good," she said.

"Wait," said Chloë. "There's one I want to show you." She leafed over page after page until she was almost at the end. "Look."

"What is it?"

"Look at the date. Wednesday, the sixth of April, nine thirty a.m. That's the still life drawing he had to do for his mock A level. It's also the drawing he did on the day his mother was killed. It almost makes me cry just to look at it, to think of what was about to happen."

"It's beautiful," said Frieda, and then she frowned, turning her head slightly. She heard the kettle click behind her. The water had boiled. But she couldn't attend to it. Not now.

"It bloody is," said Chloë, "it—"

"Wait a moment," said Frieda. "Describe it to me. Tell me what's in it."

"Why?"

"Just do it."

"All right. There's a watch and a bunch of keys and a book and an electric plug thing and then . . ."

"Yes?"

"There's something leaning on the book."

"What is it?"

"I can't tell."

"Describe it."

"It's sort of straight and notched, like a sort of metal ruler."

Frieda concentrated for a moment in silence, so hard that her head hurt. "Is that what it is?" she said, finally. "Or what it looks like?"

"What do you mean?" said Chloë. "What's the difference? It's just a drawing." She slammed the portfolio shut. "I need to take it into school," she said. "To give to Ted."

"He won't be at school," said Frieda. "And, anyway, I need that book today."

Karlsson stood in front of her, but he didn't look at her. "I wasn't expecting you," he said at last.

"I know. This won't take long."

"You don't understand, Frieda. You shouldn't be here. The commissioner doesn't want you here. And you'll not make your case any better with Hal Bradshaw if you start hanging round the station. He already thinks you're an arsonist and a stalker."

"I know. I won't come again," said Frieda, steadily. "I want to see the murder weapon."

"As a favor? But you've called in the favor, Frieda. And I'm in huge trouble now. I won't bother you with the details."

"I'm very sorry," said Frieda. "But I need to see it. And then I'll go away."

He stared at her, then shrugged, and led her down the stairs into a basement room, where he opened a metal drawer.

"This is what you want," he said. "Don't put fingerprints on it, and let yourself out when you've finished."

"Thank you."

"By the way, Elaine Kerrigan has confessed to the murder of Ruth Lennox."

"What?"

"Don't worry. I think Russell Lennox is about to confess as well. And the Kerrigan sons. The whole station will be full of people confessing, and we still won't know."

And he left.

Frieda pulled on plastic gloves and lifted out the large cog, placing it on the table in the center of the room. It looked as if it should be in the machinery of a giant clock, but the Lennoxes had had it on their mantelpiece as a sort of sculpture.

She opened Ted's art book at the page dated Wednesday, April 6, and put it on the table as well. She stared from cog to drawing so hard that everything began to blur. She stood back. She walked round the table so that she could see the cog from every angle. She squatted on the floor and squinted up at it. Very delicately, she tipped the object, swiveled it, held it so that it flattened out in her view.

And then at last she had it. Viewed at a certain angle, tilted back and twisted, the hefty object looked like a straight, notched line. The same straight and notched line that she could see among the items that Ted had drawn for his mock art A level, on the morning of Wednesday, April 6.

Frieda's face became expressionless. At last, she gave a small sigh, put the cog back into the metal drawer, which she slid shut, pulled off the gloves, and left the room.

FIFTY-SEVEN

L ouise Weller and her family lived in Clapham Junction, in a narrow redbrick terraced house set slightly back from the long straight road, lined with plane trees and regulated by speed humps. The bow windows downstairs had lace curtains, to prevent anyone looking in, and the door was dark blue with a brass knocker in the middle. Frieda rapped on it three times, then stood back. The spring weather had turned cooler, and she felt a few welcome drops of rain on her hot skin.

The door opened and Louise Weller stood in front of her, holding a baby to her chest. Behind her, the hall was dark and clean. Frieda could smell drying clothes and detergent. She remembered Karlsson telling her about the sick husband and imagined him lying in one of the rooms upstairs, listening.

"Yes? Oh—it's you. What are you doing here?"

"Can I come in, please?"

"This is probably not a good time. I'm about to feed Benjy."

"It's not you I've come to see."

"They don't need to be disturbed. They need stability now, a bit of peace."

"Just for a moment, then," said Frieda, politely, and stepped past Louise Weller into the hall. "Are they all here?"

"Where else would they be? It's a bit cramped, of course."

"I mean, all here at the moment."

"Yes. But I don't want them troubled."

"I'd like a word with Ted."

"Ted? Why? I'm not sure that's appropriate."

"I'll be brief."

Louse Weller stared at her, then shrugged. "I'll call him," she said stiffly. "If he wants to see you. Come through into the drawing room."

She opened the door beside them, and Frieda stepped into the front room with the bow window. It was too hot and had too much furniture in it, too many little tables and straight-backed chairs. There was a doll's buggy parked by the radiator, with a flaxen-haired blue-eyed doll propped in it. She found it hard to breathe.

"Frieda?"

"Dora!"

The girl's face had a greenish pallor, and there was a cold sore at the corner of her mouth. Her hair wasn't in its usual plaits but hung limply around her face. She was wearing an old-fashioned white blouse and looked, thought Frieda, like a figure in a Victorian melodrama: pitiable, abandoned, acutely distressed.

"Have you come to take us away?" Dora asked her.

"No. I've come to see Ted."

"Please can we go to your house?"

"I'm sorry. It's not possible." Frieda hesitated, taking in Dora's scrawny frame and her pinched, dejected face.

"Why?"

"Your aunt is your guardian. She'll take care of you now."

"Please. Please don't let us stay here."

"Sit down," said Frieda. She took Dora's hand, a parcel of bones, between both hers and gazed into the girl's eyes. "I'm so very sorry, Dora," she said. "I'm sorry about your mother, and I'm sorry about your father. I'm sorry you're here, not with people you love—though I'm sure your aunt loves you in her way."

"No," whispered Dora. "No. She doesn't. She tells me off about messes, and she makes me feel like I'm in her way all the time. I can't even cry in front of her. She just tuts at me."

"One day," said Frieda, slowly, feeling her way, "one day I hope you'll be able to make sense of all this. Now it must just feel like a terrible nightmare. But I want to tell you that these bad days will pass. I'm not telling you that it will cease to be painful, but the pain will become bearable."

"When will Dad come back?"

"I don't know."

"Her funeral's next Monday. Will you come to it?"

"Yes. I'll be there."

"Will you sit with me?"

"Your aunt—"

"When Aunt Louise talks about her, she makes this horrible face. As if there's a bad taste in her mouth. And Ted and Judith are so angry about her. But—" She stopped.

"Go on," said Frieda.

"I know she had an affair. I know she did wrong and cheated on Dad. I know she lied to us all. But that's not how I think of her."

"Tell me how you think of her."

"When I was ill, she used to sit on my bed and read to me for hours. And in the mornings, when she woke me up, she'd always bring me a cup of tea in my favorite mug and put her hand on my shoulder and wait till I was properly awake. Then she'd kiss me on my forehead. She always had a shower in the morning and she smelled clean and lemony."

"That's a good memory," said Frieda. "What else do you remember?"

"When I was being bullied, she was the only person in the world I could talk to about it. She made me feel less ashamed. Once, when it was really bad, she let me stay home from school and she took the day off herself and we spent hours in the garden, deadheading the roses together. I don't know why it made me feel better, but it did. She told me about how she was bullied at school. She said I had to go on being who I was, being kind and nice."

Dora stopped. Tears stood in her eyes.

"I think she sounds like a lovely mother," said Frieda. "I wish I'd met her."

"I miss her so much I want to die. I want to *die*."

"I know," said Frieda. "I know, Dora."

"So why did she—"

"Listen to me now. People are very complicated. They can be lots of different people at the same time. They can cause pain and yet still be kind, sympathetic, good. Don't lose your memories of your mother. That's who she was to you and that's real. She loved you. She may have been having an affair, but that doesn't alter the way she felt about her children. Don't let anyone take her away from you."

"Aunt Louise says—"

"Fuck Aunt Louise!"

Ted was standing in the doorway. His hair was greasy and lank, and his face looked mushroomy in its unhealthy pallor; there were violet smudges under his eyes and a prickling rash on his neck. Small sprouts of a young man's beard were beginning to appear on his chin. He was wearing the same clothes as yesterday. Frieda wondered if he'd even been to bed, let alone slept. As he approached, she could smell sweat and tobacco, a yeasty unwashed aroma.

"What are you doing here? Couldn't keep away?"

"Hello, Ted."

Ted jerked his head at Dora. "Louise wants you."

Dora got to her feet, still holding Frieda's hand. "Will you come and see us?" she asked urgently.

"Yes."

"Promise?"

"I promise."

The girl left the room, and Frieda was left with Ted. She held up his portfolio. "I've brought you this."

"You thought I might be worrying about where it was? I've had other things on my mind."

"I know. DCI Karlsson told me that your father has confessed to the manslaughter of Zach Greene and he's under suspicion of murdering your mother."

His face twisted violently, and he turned away from her. His thin, dirty figure reeked of misery and wretchedness.

"I've also been told that Elaine Kerrigan has confessed, though I think she might be trying to protect her sons."

"Jesus," he muttered.

"I'd like to say something, but maybe we can get out of here for a bit," suggested Frieda.

"There's nothing to say."

"Please."

They went outside together. Frieda thought she saw a face staring at them out of a high window, but perhaps she was imagining things. She waited until they turned off the road onto a narrower street, which ran along a deserted playground and then beside a small gray church, before speaking.

"I was looking at your art," she said. "You're good."

"That's what my mum used to say. 'Ted, you've got a gift.' Is that what you've come to tell me?"

"I saw the still life you did for your mock exam. On the morning your mother died."

Ted said nothing. They continued walking in silence down the street. It felt like everybody had gone away and only they were left.

"There was a strange object I didn't recognize at first," said Frieda. Her voice sounded dry and scratchy. She cleared her throat. "You'd drawn it from an interesting angle, so it took me some time to see what it was. I went to the evidence room to check."

Ted had slowed. He dragged his feet as though they were too heavy for him.

"You can only see the cog as it appears in your drawing if you tip it sideways and back. Then it flattens out, into what looks more like a ruler."

"Yes," said Ted, in what sounded more like a shudder than a word. "We had riddle books like that when I was a boy. I used to love them. *I Spy . . .*"

Frieda put her hand on Ted's shoulder, and he looked at her. "Your father knew you'd taken the cog to school that morning. When it turned up as the murder weapon, he knew it couldn't have been there until you brought it back."

"He never said." Ted spoke in a dull voice. "I thought it could be all right, that nobody would ever know."

"You discovered about your mother's affair?"

"I'd suspected for ages," Ted said drearily. "I followed her that day, on my bike. I saw her go to the flat and a man open the door. I left her there, and I wandered around for ages, in a kind of fog. I couldn't really think, and I felt sick. I thought I would be sick. I went home, and I was putting the fucking cog back on the mantelpiece when she came in." He put one hand up to his face for a moment, touching his skin. "When I was little, I thought she was the best person in the whole wide world. Safe and kind. She'd tuck me into bed every night, and she always had the same smell. She looked at me and I looked at her, and I knew she knew that I'd found out. She didn't say anything at once, and then she gave me this odd little smile. So I swung the thing in my hand and it hit her, *smack*, on the side of her head. I can still hear the sound it made. Loud and dull. For one moment, it seemed like nothing had happened and she was still looking at me and I was looking at her and there was this funny smile on her face and then—she seemed to explode in front of my eyes. Blood everywhere and she didn't look like my mother anymore. She was lying on the floor and her face was mashed up and I was still holding the cog and it was all . . ."

"So you ran away."

"I went to the park, and I was sick. I was so sick, and I've felt sick ever since. Every moment. Nothing takes the taste away."

"And then Judith gave you an alibi?"

"I was going to confess. What else could I do? But then the murder weapon had gone, and everyone was saying it was a burglary gone wrong, and Judith was begging me to say I'd been with her that afternoon. So I went along with it. I didn't work anything out in advance."

"You do understand that your father planned Zach's murder, don't you, Ted? It wasn't manslaughter. It was murder. Once Judith came to him and told him about her affair and that she'd been with Zach on the day your mother died, he knew your alibi would be broken. Zach would say he'd been with Judith that afternoon."

"He killed Zach to save me," said Ted, in a low voice.

"If he wasn't caught, your alibi was safe. If he was, he could say he did it in an argument."

"What will happen to him now?"

"I don't know, Ted."

"Is he going to say he killed Mum as well, to save me?"

"I think he will if he has to. It's all a bit of a muddle at the moment, because of Elaine Kerrigan's intervention."

"Will you tell the police?"

"No," said Frieda, thoughtfully. "I don't think I will."

"Why?"

Frieda stopped and turned to him. She looked at him with her dark eyes. "Because you are going to."

"No," he whispered. "I can't . . . I never meant to . . . I can't."

"What's it been like?" said Frieda. "These last weeks."

"Like being in hell," he said, the words barely audible.

"That's where you'll be forever unless you speak the truth."

"How can I? My mother. I killed my mother." He jerked to a pause, and then dragged the words back again. "I killed my mother. I can see her face." He repeated the words wildly: "I can see her face, her smashed-in face. All the time."

"This is the only way. It won't make things better. You will always be the person who killed his mother. You will always carry that with you, until the day you die. But you have to admit what you did."

"Will I go to prison?"

"Does that matter?"

"I wish I could tell her—"

"What would you tell her?"

"That I love her. That I'm sorry."

"You can tell her."

The street had swung round in a crescent, and now they were back on the road where Louise Weller lived. Ted stopped and drew a deep, unsteady breath.

"We don't need to go back in there," said Frieda. "We can just go to the station."

He stared at her, his young face stricken with dread. "Will you come with me?"

"Yes."

"Because I don't think I can do it alone."

Frieda had walked through London many times, but she couldn't remember a walk so ghostly and so strange. It felt as if crowds separated as they passed, and their footsteps rang out in the fugitive gray light. After a while, she put her arm through Ted's, and he drew closer to her, like a child with his mother. She thought of Judith and Dora in that dark, tidy, airless house, their father locked away, their brother too—this young, horror-struck man. Everyone alone in their own terror and grief.

At last they were there. Ted drew apart from her. Beads of sweat had sprung up on his forehead, and there was a dazed expression on his face. Frieda put a hand on the small of his back.

"This is it," she said. And they went inside together.

Karlsson had just gone back in to Russell Lennox, when Yvette put her head round the door and beckoned him out again.

"What is it?"

"I thought you should know at once. Frieda's here, with the Lennox boy."

"With Ted?"

"Yes. She says that he has something important to say to you."

"OK. Tell them I'll come now."

"And Elaine Kerrigan is still insisting she did it."

Karlsson went back into the room. "I'll be back shortly," he said to Russell Lennox. "But apparently your son's here to see me."

"My son? Ted? No. No, he can't be. No—"

"Mr. Lennox, what is it?"

"I did it. I'll tell you everything. I killed my wife. I killed Ruth. Sit down. Turn on the tape recorder. I want to confess. Don't go. I did it. No one else. It was me. You have to believe me. I murdered my wife. I swear to God it was me."

Ted lifted his burning eyes and stared at Karlsson full in the face. For the first time, Karlsson felt a stillness about him, a sense of concentrated purpose. The boy took a breath and then said in a clear and ringing voice: "I am here to confess to the murder of my mother. Who I loved very much . . ."

FIFTY-EIGHT

Josef was sitting in the kitchen with Chloë, playing some card game that involved lots of shouting and slapping of cards one on top of another, when Frieda returned. Even as she was considering how to break the news to her niece, she had time to wonder why Chloë was in her house when she should have been at school, and think of how, from being her secure retreat from the world, it had become a casual meeting place for everyone, a place of disorder and grief. Perhaps, she thought, she would replace all the locks when this was over. She looked at Josef. "Could Chloë and I have a moment?" she asked.

Josef seemed puzzled. "Moment?"

"Yes," said Frieda. "Could you go out of the room?"

"Yes, yes," said Josef. "I go to Reuben now anyway. Poker for the guys."

He picked the cat off his lap and, holding it against his broad chest, backed out.

As Frieda told Chloë, she watched the succession of emotions on the young girl's pale face: confusion, shock, distress, disbelief, anger. When Frieda had finished, there was a silence. Chloë's eyes flickered from side to side.

"Is there anything you want to ask me?" she said.

"Where is he?"

"At the police station."

"In a cell?"

"I don't know. They were going to take a statement, but they'll keep him in."

"He's only a child."

"He's eighteen. He's an adult."

There was another pause. Frieda saw that Chloë's eyes were glistening. "Tell me," she said.

"You were supposed to look after him."

"I think I *was* looking after him."

"What do you mean?"

"He had to own up to what he did."

"Even if it meant ruining his life."

"It's his only hope of *not* ruining his life."

"In your opinion," said Chloë, bitterly. "In your fucking professional opinion. I brought him to you. I brought him to you so that you could help him."

"Helping people isn't simple. It's—"

"Shut up. Shut up shut up shut up. I don't want to hear you talk about taking responsibility and fucking autonomy. You've betrayed him and you've betrayed me. That's what you've done."

"He killed his mother."

"He didn't mean to!"

"And that will be taken into account."

"I'm going."

"Where?"

"Back home. Mum might be a head case and the house might be a slum, but at least she doesn't send my friends to prison."

"Chloë—"

"I'll never forgive you."

It was finished, she told herself. She had finished. The feverishness of the last few weeks could abate; the strangeness could fade, like a violent bruise fades until at last it is just a faint ache, invisible to anyone else. The Lennox murder was solved. The Lennox children had gone to their different kinds of prison. Chloë had gone. Frieda had betrayed her friendship with Karlsson. The wild quest for a girl she had never known was over, and already it had the quality of a dream. She wondered if she would ever see Fearby again, with his staring eyes and his silver hair.

She started clearing up, putting objects back where they belonged, wiping stains off surfaces, rubbing beeswax polish onto the little chess table by the window. That afternoon she would go and see Thelma Scott, and dip the bucket down into the dark well of thoughts, but perhaps later on she could play through an old chess game, let the wooden pieces click their way across the board, while silence settled around her again. She would have to call Sandy too. In her tumult, she had let him go. The two days in New York seemed distant, unreal. Now at last she let herself dwell upon the way he'd held her that night and the words he had said. Remember.

Remember. Halfway up the stairs, Frieda stopped dead. Something had come into her mind, setting her heart racing. What was it? Fearby.

Something about Fearby, and his last message to her, before he'd disappeared out of her life. Frieda sat down on the step and tried to recall exactly what he'd said in his message. Most of it wasn't important, but he'd obviously had an idea that seemed worth following up. He'd said he'd looked over the files of the girls. She remembered that bit clearly enough. Then he'd said something else. That we'd been thinking about them in the wrong way. Yes, and that he was going out to take another look.

Was there anything else? Yes: they hadn't heard the engine—what did that mean, for God's sake? It sounded like a slightly mad metaphor for the way the mind works. Frieda thought so hard that it almost hurt. No, that was all, except that he'd said he'd come round and tell her what he found. So that was all. It didn't seem much. The files of the girls. We'd been thinking about them in the wrong way. What had he meant by that? How could it be the wrong way? Was there some sort of connection they'd missed? He'd said "we." In what way had Fearby and she been thinking together about the girls? She thought about the rest of the message. He was going to take another look. Another. What did that mean? Was he going to go back to one of the girls' families? It was possible.

But then Frieda thought, No. There had been three parts to what he'd said. The girls. "We" had thought wrongly about them—and he hadn't heard the engine. And he was going to take another look. That must mean—mustn't it?—that he was going to a place the two of them had been together.

Was he going to the horse sanctuary to talk to Doherty? No, that didn't make sense. Then he would have said he was going to talk to someone. His message was about a place. That must mean he'd been going back to Croydon. To take another look. But what could be the point of that? The police had been to the house. They had searched it. What could there possibly be to take another look at? She thought again about the message, as if it were a machine she was taking apart and laying out on the table. The girls. We had the wrong idea about them. Taking another look. The first bit was clear enough. The girls. The third bit seemed obvious. Another look. That must be Croydon. The problem was the second bit, the middle. We had the wrong idea about them. We. That was clear enough: Fearby and Frieda. What did Fearby and Frieda have the wrong idea about? Them. The engine. They hadn't heard the engine. What bloody engine?

And then, quite suddenly, it was as if Frieda had walked out of a dark tunnel into light so dazzling that she could hardly see.

Them. What if "them" wasn't the girls? What if the engine wasn't a metaphor at all—because, after all, Fearby didn't talk in metaphors. He made lists; he focused on objects, facts, details, dates. The engine was the one that Vanessa Dale had heard, the day she was attacked, just before Hazel Barton had been killed. Vanessa Dale, through her panic, when her attacker's hands were round her throat, had heard an engine revving.

That meant her attacker hadn't been acting alone. Someone else had been sitting in the car, revving the engine, waiting to drive them away. Not one person. Two. A pair of killers.

FIFTY-NINE

Everything had a steely clarity now, icy, hard-edged. She found Thelma Scott's number and dialed it.

"Dr. Scott? This is Frieda Klein. I've got to cancel."

There was a pause.

"Do you have a moment to talk?"

"Not really. I've got something to do. Something that can't wait."

"Frieda, are you quite well?"

"Probably not, just at the moment. But there's something important. It overrides everything."

"It's just that you don't sound quite well."

"I'm so sorry. I've got to go."

Frieda hung up. What did she need? Keys, jacket, her hated phone. That was all. She was just pulling on her jacket when the doorbell rang. It was Josef, dusty from work.

"I'm on my way out. I've got no time. Not even to talk."

Josef took her by the arm. "Frieda, what is happening? Everyone phoning everyone. Where is Frieda? What she doing? You never phoning. Never answering."

"I know, I know. I'll explain. But not now. I've got to get to Croydon."

"Croydon? The girls?"

"I don't know. Maybe."

"Alone?"

"I'm a big girl."

"I take you."

"Don't be ridiculous."

Josef looked stern. "I take you or I hold you here and phone to Reuben."

"You want to try it?" said Frieda, fiercely.

"Yes."

"All right, drive me, then. Is this yours?"

Behind Josef was a battered white van.

"Is for work."

"Then let's go."

It was a long, long drive, first across to Park Lane, then Victoria and over Chelsea Bridge into south London. Frieda had the map open on her lap, guiding Josef and thinking about what she was going to do. Battersea. Clapham. Tooting. Should she be calling Karlsson? And saying what? Suspicions about a man whose name she didn't know? Whose address she didn't know? About a girl nobody was looking for? And after their last awful encounter? Now they were in parts of south London with names she barely recognized. The instructions got more complicated and then, finally, Frieda steered Josef just a little past Lawrence Dawes's house.

"So," said Josef, expectantly.

Frieda thought for a moment. Lawrence and his friend, Gerry. Them. She didn't know Gerry's second name and she didn't know where he lived. But she knew something. Upstream. That was what Lawrence had said. He lived upstream, which meant he was on the same side of the road, and she remembered that when she had stood in the garden with her back to the house, the river flowed from right to left. So Gerry's house was up to the right. And it probably wasn't next door. Lawrence would have said "my next-door neighbor." And hadn't he talked about next door being used for refugees? She got out of the car. She would start with the house next door but one. Josef got out as well.

"I'm fine," said Frieda.

"I come with you."

Lawrence Dawes lived at number eight. Frieda and Josef walked up the path of number twelve. Frieda rang the bell. There was no response. She rang again.

"No people home," said Josef.

They walked back onto the pavement and up to the door of number fourteen and rang the bell.

"This is for what?" said Josef, puzzled, but before Frieda could answer, the door was opened by a white-haired old woman.

Frieda was momentarily at a loss. She hadn't thought of what she was going to say. "Good afternoon," she said. "I'm trying to drop something off for a friend of a friend. He's called Gerry. He's in his sixties. I know he lives in one of these houses but I'm not sure which one."

"It might be Gerry Collier," said the woman.

"Early sixties?" said Frieda. "Brown hair going gray?"

"That sounds like him. He lives along there. Number eighteen."

"Thanks so much," said Frieda.

The woman closed the door. Frieda and Josef walked back to the van and got inside. Frieda looked at the house. A two-story, semidetached house, gray pebbledashed exterior, aluminum window frames. Ornate front garden, with a little white brick wall, yellow, blue, red, white flowers spilling over.

"And now?" said Josef.

"Wait a moment," said Frieda. "I'm trying to think what to do. We can—"

"Stop," said Josef. "Look."

The door of number eighteen opened, and Gerry Collier stepped out. He was wearing a gray windbreaker and carrying a plastic shopping bag. He walked out onto the pavement and set off along the road.

"I wonder if we should follow him," said Frieda.

"Follow the man?" said Josef. "Is no good."

"You're right. He's probably going to the shops. We've got a few minutes. Josef, can you help me break inside?"

Josef looked bemused and then he grinned. "Break into the house? You, Frieda?"

"Now, this minute."

"This not a joke?"

"It's really, really not a joke."

"OK, Frieda. You ask. Questions later." He picked up his work bag, from which he grabbed a heavy wrench and two large screwdrivers. They left the van and walked up to the front door of number eighteen.

"We need to be quick," said Frieda. "And quiet. If you possibly can."

Josef ran his fingers over the lock with a certain delicacy. "Which is most important? Quick or quiet?"

"Quick."

Josef pushed one screwdriver into the gap between the door and the frame. He flexed it, and the gap widened slightly. Then he pushed the other screwdriver into the gap about a foot farther down. He looked at Frieda. "All right?"

She nodded. She saw him silently mouth the words, one, two, *three*, and pull the two screwdrivers sharply toward him, at the same time leaning hard on the door. There was a splintering sound and the door swung inward.

"Where now?" said Josef, in a hoarse whisper.

Frieda had seen Lawrence Dawes's house. Where was possible? She pointed downward. Josef put down his bag, and they walked softly along the hallway, by the left side of the staircase, Josef in front. He stopped and nodded to the right. There was a door leading back under the stairs. Frieda nodded and Josef gently opened it. Frieda saw the beginning of stairs leading down into darkness. There was a smell, something slightly sweet that she couldn't quite identify. Josef fumbled along the wall and switched on a light.

With a start, Frieda saw that a figure was sitting at the bottom of the flight, on the floor, back against the brick wall, half lost in shadow. Whoever it was didn't look round. Josef hissed at Frieda to stop, but she walked decisively down the steps. She had only taken a few steps before she knew who it was. She recognized the jacket, the white hair, the bent frame. When she reached the cellar floor, Jim Fearby was looking up at her with open, unblinking, unseeing, yellow dead eyes. His mouth gaped open as well, as if in surprise, and there was a large brown stain extending from his scalp down one side of his face. Frieda was going to lean down and check if he was dead but she stopped herself. There was no point. She felt a jolt of nausea that was overtaken by an intense aching sadness as she gazed down at this abandoned, dear man, who had finally been proved right.

Josef was coming down the stairs, and Frieda was turning to speak when she heard a sound, like the whimper of an animal, somewhere farther in the cellar, where it went under the pavement. She looked and saw a movement. She stepped forward and in the semidarkness a figure took shape. A person, female, young, propped upright against the wall, arms splayed, legs splayed. Frieda saw matted hair, staring blinking eyes, taped mouth. She stepped forward and saw that the woman was secured by wire around her wrists and ankles, waist and neck. She was whimpering. Frieda put her finger to her lips. She tried to pull at the wire around one wrist but then Josef was beside her. He took something from his tool bag. She heard a click of pliers and one hand was free. The other wrist, the neck, the waist and then the woman fell forward. Frieda supported her, fearing she might break her ankles. Josef knelt down and cut her free and the woman fell to her knees.

"Call for help," said Frieda to Josef.

Josef took out his phone.

"Upstairs for signal," he said.

"Nine, nine, nine," said Frieda.

"I know it," said Josef.

Frieda looked into the woman's face. "Sharon? I'm going to pull the tape off. You'll be fine but keep quiet. Gerry has gone out but we have to move." Another whimper. "You'll be all right. But this will sting." Frieda got some purchase on the tape and pulled it off. The skin underneath was pale and raw and smelled of decay. Sharon made sounds like an animal. "It's all right," said Frieda, soothingly. "I told you. He's gone."

"No," said Sharon, shaking her head. "Other man."

"Fuck," said Frieda, turned round and started to run up the stairs. "Josef."

As she ran, she heard a clattering and banging, like furniture falling downstairs, and as she emerged from the cellar door, she saw shapes moving and heard shouts. She couldn't make anything out clearly and her foot slipped. The floor was wet, sticky. Then there was a mess of impressions: the figures moving and flexing, flashes of metal, cries, splashes, bangs, impacts so that the floor shook under her feet. Her focus became narrow, as if she were looking at the world through a long thin tube. Her thoughts became narrow as well. They seemed slow and time seemed slow and she knew that she must not collapse because then it would all have been for nothing. She found something in her hand—she didn't know what it was or how it got there, but it was heavy, and she was hitting with it, as hard as she possibly could, and then the scene became clearer, as if the light had gradually been turned up. Lawrence Dawes was lying facedown on the hall floor and a dark red pool was spreading out from him, and Josef was leaning back against the wall, panting and groaning, and Frieda herself was leaning against the wall opposite, and she realized that the wet sticky stuff on her hands and clothes was blood.

SIXTY

F rieda? Frieda, *Frieda*." Josef seemed to have lost his English; her name was all that he could say, over and over.

Frieda crossed to him. She felt suddenly clear and light and calm, a sense of purpose and energy coursing through her. She saw that he had a violent gash running down his face and neck, and one of his arms was hanging in an odd way. His face was horribly pale under the grime.

"It's all right, Josef," she said. "Thank you, my very dear friend."

Then she stooped down beside Lawrence Dawes. There was a matted red patch on his head where she had hit him, but she could see that he was breathing. She looked at the object she was still holding: it was one of Josef's heavy wrenches, which must have tumbled from his bag, and it had red smeared across it.

"Take this," she said to Josef. "If he comes round, hit him again. I'll be back in a minute."

She ran into the kitchen and started pulling drawers open. Gerry Collier was a very organized man: everything had its proper place. She found a drawer full of string, masking tape, pens, and took out a roll of washing line. That would do. She returned to the two men and, bending down, brought Lawrence Dawes's hands together and rapidly bound the line round them multiple times, before bringing it down and wrapping it round his ankles as well, until he was trussed.

She pulled her phone out of her pocket with fingers that were not trembling and dialed the emergency services. She said she needed the police, lots of them, and ambulances and gave the address, repeating it to make sure they had it. She gave her name, and heard it as if it belonged to someone else. She told them they should be quick. Then she put her phone back into her pocket. She could hear Josef's labored breathing beside her and, turning, saw the pain on his drawn face. She took the wrench out of his hand and touched him lightly on the shoulder.

"Wait there for one more minute," she said, and kissed him on his clammy forehead.

She ran down the cellar stairs. At the bottom, she stopped briefly to put two thumbs on Fearby's lids, closing them. She smoothed his hair off his face, then went to where Sharon Gibbs was still on her knees, her head cradled on her arms. She was making guttural little cries, like those of an animal in pain. She was wearing a bra that barely covered her shallow breasts and some filthy drawstring trousers; her feet were bare and torn. Frieda could see in the dim light that she was covered with bruises and what looked like cigarette burns.

She squatted beside her and put a hand under her elbow. "Can you get up?" she asked. "Let me help. Here." She took off her jacket and wrapped it around the girl's emaciated frame. Her ribs stood out starkly, and her collarbone. She smelled of rot and decay. "Come with me, Sharon," Frieda said gently. "It's over, and you're safe. Come out of here."

She half led and half carried the girl, past Fearby and up out of the cellar that had been her torture chamber, into the light that was fading now. Sharon gave a little cry of pain at the dazzle and bent over, almost falling, coughing up dribbles of vomit. Frieda got her to the doorway, out of the accursed house and into the clean air, and sat her on the steps.

Josef shambled over. Frieda took off her cotton scarf and wrapped it around his neck, where blood was running thickly. He made to sit on the step, but Sharon shrank from him.

"It's OK," Frieda said. "This man is good. He rescued you, Sharon. We both owe him our lives."

"I was coming to find Lila. I wanted to see Lila."

"It's all right now. Don't talk yet."

"Is she dead?"

"Yes. I'm certain she is. She must have found out about her father, so he killed her. But you are alive, Sharon, and you're safe now."

She stood beside the two of them. There was the smell of honeysuckle wafting to them from the neighboring garden, and three doors down Frieda could see the old woman watering her tiny front garden with a hose. It was a beautiful late spring evening. She fixed her eyes on the road—looking not just for the flashing blue lights of the police and the ambulances but also for the figure of Gerry Collier. It was only minutes since she and Josef had watched him leave, but it seemed like hours, days—another world. Behind them, the door was wrenched off its hinges, and in the cellar lay Jim Fearby, his long task over.

At last they came, sirens and lights shattering the soft evening. She heard them before she saw them, blue arcs swinging over the street before the cars and ambulances arrived, a screech of brakes, a sudden rush of men and women, voices speaking urgently, orders and exclamations, people bending toward them, stretchers, oxygen masks. Neighbors gathering on the road, a sudden sense of being at the center of a world closing in on them.

There was a man standing in front of her, asking her something. She couldn't make out his questions, but she knew what she had to say.

"My name is Frieda Klein." She heard her voice, calm and clear. "I made the call. This is Josef, who is hurt. And Sharon Gibbs, who has been missing for weeks. She has been held in the cellar by the man tied up inside, Lawrence Dawes. Be careful with her. You can't know what she's been through. A second man is at large, Gerry Collier. You have to find him."

"Gerry Collier, you say?"

"Yes. He owns this place. And a man called Jim Fearby is dead, inside the house. You're too late for him."

Faces hovered above her, blurred, anonymous, mouths opening and stretching, eyes large and staring. Someone was saying something, but she pressed on.

"There will be bodies in the garden." She could no longer tell if she was speaking quietly or shouting, as if from a pulpit. "Or bodies in the cellar."

Sharon Gibbs was lifted from her crouched position on the steps to a stretcher. Her huge eyes gazed imploringly at Frieda from her pinched, dirty face. Now Lawrence Dawes was carried from the house, still tangled in the washing line. His eyes were flickering, and they opened briefly on Frieda. For a moment they stared at each other, into each other, and then he turned his head away.

"Please can someone tell Karlsson?" Frieda continued.

"Karlsson?"

"DCI Malcolm Karlsson."

A woman was wrapping a blanket around Josef's shoulders, unwrapping Frieda's bloody scarf from his neck. He stood up, bulky and dazed, staggering slightly. Frieda put her arms round him, careful of his dangling arm, and pressed her head against his chest. She could feel his heart hammering and smell his sweat and his blood. "You'll be fine now," she said. "You've done well, Josef."

"I?"

"Yes. I will write to your sons to tell them. They will be very proud of you."

"Proud?"

"Yes, proud."

"But you—"

"I'll come and see you very soon." She looked at the woman. "Where are you taking him?"

"St. George's."

Now Josef was gone, and Fearby's body was being carried out of the house. His face was covered, but Frieda could still see his fine white hair. His feet poked out of the blanket at the other end; the shoes were old and scuffed, and on one the lace was undone.

The ambulances slid away, and suddenly she was alone. There were gathering crowds in the street, and in the house the light was unnaturally bright and full of noises, voices. But here, on this small patch of soil, she was by herself at last. The door gaped behind her, like a foul, hot mouth; she could smell its sickening stench.

"Frieda Klein?"

A man was in front of her, blocking out the light.

"Yes."

"I need to talk to you urgently. I will be a few more minutes. Would you wait for me here, please?"

He left her again. Her mobile rang. She looked at it—Sandy—but didn't answer. Then she turned it off.

Without thinking what she was doing, she stood up and went into the house. No one stopped her or even seemed to notice. She stepped out of the back door into the garden. It was the same size and shape as Lawrence Dawes's garden and was full of flowers. Bright, sweet, fragrant flowers: peonies and roses and tall foxgloves. Perhaps they were feeding on the bodies, she thought. Perhaps that was why they were so strong and bright and colorful. She walked down the lawn, past a well-tended vegetable plot, until she was standing by the shallow brown River Wandle. She could see the pebbles on its bottom, and a few tiny dark fish. Behind her, there was the roar of the world, but here just the trickle of water; she could hear its faint gurgle. A swallow dipped past her, low and fast, then up into the evening sky.

She knew she had to go home. She thought of something she had read in a book when she was a child. If you're lost in the jungle, find a stream and follow it downhill, and it will reach a larger river or the sea. This little brook would take her home.

She took off her sandals, rolled up her jeans, and stepped into the water.

It rose to her ankles. She walked delicately along the stony bed until she was standing outside Lawrence Dawes's garden. They'd drunk tea together there, and he'd shown her this little river. She could hear his voice now, mild and amiable: *We used to make little paper boats and put them on the stream and watch them float away. I used to tell them that in three hours' time, those boats would reach the Thames and then, if the tide was right, they'd float out to sea.*

Frieda crossed to the other side and stepped out onto a narrow, overgrown path, pulling her sandals back onto her wet feet. Here it was green, tangled and wild—a place of nettles and Queen Anne's lace, a smell of grass, mulched leaves, and moisture. She started to walk.

The secret river narrowed to a ribbon of brown water. Frieda kept pace with its flow, watching the bubbles beading and bursting on its surface. She saw Jim Fearby's face. She saw his dead eyes staring at her. What had his last thoughts been? She wished so much that he had stayed alive long enough to know he had won. She saw Josef's face. He would lay down his life for her, but she would lay down hers for no reason at all, except that it seemed a cursed thing.

A short distance away in the opposite direction, the Wandle disappeared underground forever, into a network of springs, burrowing its way under the earth. Here it wound north, the path following it almost closed over now with nettles that stung her feet and hanging branches that stroked her cheeks, so that Frieda felt she was in a tunnel of green light. She smelled something sweet and nasty; there must be the carcass of an animal or bird rotting nearby. This little river had worked so hard in its time and carried so much shit and poison and death, a sclerotic artery clogged with waste. There would have been water mills once, and tanning factories, lavender fields, and watercress ponds, litter and chemicals and flowers. All gone now, demolished and lying buried under concrete and housing estates. To her left, Frieda could see through the tangle of weeds a deserted warehouse, a rash of light industrial units, a deserted car park, a rubbish dump rising out of the dusk. But the little river flowed on, quick and clear, leading her out of the labyrinth.

The water widened again, slowed. There were faces she could see in its swirling course, rising up at her. Faces of young women. Weeds for hair. Calling out for help. Too late. Only Sharon Gibbs had been saved: Frieda could hear her animal cries and smell her dying flesh. In the darkness, rats with yellow teeth—what had been done to her, and what had she felt?

Drinking tea in the garden, smiling. Shaking his hand—what had that hand done? His daughter. Lily. Lila. Wild child. All those wild children. Lost young women. How many more were there, in their own underworlds?

She saw Ted's young face, then Dora's and Judith's—motherless, fatherless children, hungry for love and for safety. Lives wrecked. Homes torn apart. What had she done? How could she bear the damage she had caused and carry the burden through the rest of her days?

Now the river was channeled between concrete banks, tamed. And suddenly the path was a road that ran alongside a redbrick, buttressed wall. For a moment, she felt that she was in a country village long ago. There was a gray church beside her, surrounded by a huddle of graves. Frieda looked at one of the names, a teenage boy dead in the Great War. She thought she saw a shape rise up from the ground, but it was only a trick of the dying day. She didn't know what time it was. She didn't want to turn on her mobile to see. It didn't matter anyway. She could walk through the evening and into the night. She could walk for days and never stop. The pain in her legs and her lungs was good; better than pain in her heart.

But where was her river? It had disappeared. They had taken it away from her. She stumbled, feeling sharp pebbles under her soles. Ahead, a park stretched out, an avenue of great trees. She walked toward it and after a while saw a small stone bridge. She had found it again and it took her to a pond. Dragonflies in the dusk. A child's sandal on the bank. But it led her to a road and then disappeared, and a car sped by with the bass thump of music coming from it, and then a man in black leather crouched low on his motorbike, and Frieda was lost in a dingy corridor of houses and flats. But she walked in the direction it had been flowing, and after a few minutes there it was, merry and leaping, as if it had been teasing her. Past buildings, cottages, an old mill, and once more she was on an overgrown path, leaving the road behind. The surface of the city dropped away as she walked along its hidden corridor. You could stand ten feet away and not know it was there. You could hide there, seeing but unseen. Like a ghost.

Too many ghosts. Too many dead people in her life. Already a crowd of them behind her. The ghost of herself, young and eager. You start on your journey full of ignorance and hope. Her father. Sometimes she still saw him, not just in her dreams but among the faces she passed on the streets. There was something she wanted to tell him, but she could no longer remember what it was. Darkness was gathering round her. Her head was filled with the colors of pain.

Past an old deserted warehouse, painted an ugly blue and covered with graffiti. Shattered windows. You could hide there. Perhaps it, too, was full of dead people, or of lost people. You couldn't look everywhere. There isn't an end, there are always others, and she was tired. Not a soft, blurred tiredness but one that was sharp and insistent. Tiredness like a knife, a millstone grinding. Sharon Gibbs was alive, but Lila was dead. The others were dead. Bones in the rich soil that fed a garden full of flowers.

The path broadened out into a wide track. The river was slow and brown. If she lay down here, would she ever get up? If Sandy were here, would she tell him? If Sasha were here, would she cry at last? Or sleep. When would she ever sleep? To sleep was to let go. Let go of the dead, let go of the ghosts, let go of the self.

Cranes. Great thistles. A deserted allotment with crazy little sheds toppling at the edge of the river. A fox, mangy, with a thin, grubby tail. Swift as a shadow into the shadows. She liked foxes. Foxes, crows, owls. A bird flitted by, and she realized it must be a bat. It was night at last. How long had it been? Her river was still showing her the way and a moon rose and everyone she knew stood a long way off. Reuben, Sasha, Olivia, Chloë, Josef, Sandy, Karlsson. Her patients were reduced to a crouched figure in a chair, asking her to rescue them from themselves. Dean Reeve stood in a corner; he looked in at a window; she heard his footsteps when no one was there; and he left behind him the sickly smell of lilies and death. He was more real than anyone.

It was hard to know any longer why she put one foot in front of the other, one foot in front of the other, and kept breathing in and out, as if her body had the willpower her spirit no longer possessed. She was spent. Her waters were run dry.

But then the river widened and the path opened out and there was a fence, an iron bell hanging in a metal cage. The Wandle had guided her and now it opened out into its own small estuary and poured itself at last into the great thoroughfare of the Thames. Frieda was standing on a stone walkway, looking out at the lights of the city. She wasn't lost anymore, and somewhere in those pulsing lights lay home.

SIXTY-ONE

This was not a night for sleep. Thoughts burned in Frieda's brain; images pulsed behind her eyes. She sat upright in her armchair and stared into the empty grate, where she saw the well-tended garden in Croydon. Now they would be pushing spades into the loamy soil, pulling the house apart. She remembered the two of them, Dawes and Collier, sitting in the garden. She felt sick and closed her eyes, but the pictures wouldn't go away. She thought the stench of lilies still hung in the air.

At last, she rose and went upstairs. She put the plug into the bath—Josef's bath—and turned the taps, poured in bath lotion until the water foamed. She peeled off her dirty clothes and cleaned her teeth, avoiding looking at herself in the little mirror over the basin. Her limbs felt heavy and her skin stung; she was all used up. At last she climbed into the fragrant, scorching water and let herself sink beneath the surface. Perhaps she could lie here until day, her hair floating on the surface and her blood pounding in her ears.

At last she got out. It was still dark, but there was a faint band of light on the horizon. A new day was starting. She dressed and went downstairs. There were things she needed to do.

First, she made a phone call, one she should have made days ago. He didn't reply at once, and when he did his voice was thick with sleep.

"Sandy?"

"Frieda? What? Are you all right?"

"I don't think so. I'm sorry."

"Hang on." There was a pause. She imagined him sitting up, turning on the light. "Why are you sorry?"

"I'm just sorry. I'm so sorry. I should have told you."

"Told me what?"

"Can you come over?"

"Yes. Of course."

"I mean, now."

"Yes."

That was one of the things she loved about him—that he would make a decision like that, without hesitation or a flurry of anxious questions that she wouldn't be able to answer, knowing she would only ask out of extreme need. He would get up at once, book a flight, make arrangements with his colleagues, be with her before the day was out because she had turned to him at last.

"Thank you," she said simply.

She made herself a bitterly strong cup of coffee and fed the cat, watered the plants in her backyard, breathing in the intense fragrance of hyacinths and herbs. Then she put on her jacket and left the house. It was a fresh, damp dawn; later it would be warm and bright. The sweetness of spring. The shops were all still shut, but she could smell bread baking in the little bakery on the corner. Lights were coming on in flats and houses; metal shutters rattled up in newsagents and corner shops; a bus rumbled by with a single passenger staring out of the window. A postman pulling his red cart passed her. The great life of London starting up again.

Frieda reached Muswell Hill and consulted her *A–Z*, then turned off into a wide residential street full of handsome detached houses. Number twenty-seven. From the outside, the damage wasn't immediately obvious—just darkened bricks, some charred woodwork, a broken window on the first floor and, as she drew closer, the acrid smell that caught in the back of her throat. She hesitated, then stepped into the front garden with its graveled pathway and its tub of red tulips that had survived the blaze. From here, she could see through the large bay window into the front room, where the devastation was obvious. She pictured the fire raging through the orderly spaces, gobbling tables, chairs, pictures, doors; licking ashy blackness up the walls. Dean had done this—casually pushed a petrol-soaked rag through the letter box, dropped a match after it. *We couldn't let him get away with it.* In a way, Bradshaw was right: this was her fault.

There was a side door to the left of the house, and when she pushed at it, it opened onto the garden at the back. She stepped through into a green space, and now she was looking in at what had once been a conservatory and kitchen but was now a ruin. She was about to turn away when she saw something that stopped her.

Hal Bradshaw was in there, stooped over the scorched remains. He squatted, pulled out what had obviously once been a book, held it up to examine, then dropped it again. He was wearing a crumpled suit and Wellington boots and stepped softly through the silt of ashes that stirred as he walked, lifted in dark petals around him. Frieda saw his face, which was tired and defeated.

He seemed to sense her presence because he straightened up. Their eyes met and his expression tightened. He pulled himself back into the Hal Bradshaw she knew: controlled, knowing, defended.

"Well," he said, coming toward her. "Quite a sight, isn't it? Come to assess the damage?"

"Yes."

"Why?"

"I needed to see it. What were you looking for?"

"Oh." He smiled mirthlessly, lifted his sooty hands, then let them drop. "My life, I suppose. You spend years collecting things and then—*poof,* they're gone. I wonder now what they all meant."

Frieda stepped into the ruin and picked up the remains of a book that crumbled at her touch. She watched words dissolve into ash and dust.

"I'm very sorry," she said.

"Is that an admission?"

"A regret."

As she made her way toward the Underground, Frieda turned on her mobile and looked at all the messages. So many, from people she knew and people she didn't. She was walking toward uproar, questions and comments, the dazzle of attention that she dreaded, but for now she was alone. Nobody knew where she was.

But there was someone she did have to call.

"Karlsson. It's me."

"Thank God. Where are you?"

"I'm on my way to Tooting, to the hospital."

"I'll meet you there. But are you all right?"

"I don't know. Are you?"

He met her in the lobby, striding toward her as he came in through the revolving door, putting one hand briefly on her shoulder as he stared into her face, looking for something there.

"Listen—" he began.

"Can I say something first?"

"Typical." He tried to smile, his mouth twisting. He looked exhausted and stricken.

"I'm sorry."

"You're sorry!"

"Yes."

"But you were right. Frieda, you were horribly right."

"But I did wrong too. To you. And I apologize."

"Oh, Jesus, you don't need to—"

"I do."

"OK."

"Have you been there?"

"Yes."

"Have they found the missing girls?"

"It'll take more than one night. But yes."

"How many?"

"It's too early to say." He swallowed hard. "Several."

"And have you found . . ."

"We have. Gerald Collier isn't saying anything. Nothing at all. But we don't need him to. They were in his cellar."

"Poor Fearby," said Frieda, softly. "It was him, you know, not me. I would have given up, but he never did."

"An old drunk hack." Karlsson's voice was bitter. "And a traumatized therapist. And you solved a crime we didn't even know existed. We'll be tremendously efficient now, of course. Now that it's too late. We'll identify the remains and we'll inform the poor bloody relatives and we'll go back over their lives and we'll find out everything there is to be discovered about those two fucking bastards who got away with it for so many years. We'll update computers and conduct an inquiry as to how this could have happened. We'll learn from our mistakes, or that's what we'll tell the press."

"His own daughter," said Frieda. "She was the one I was looking for."

"Well, you found her."

"Yes."

"You'll need to answer a lot of questions, I'm afraid."

"I know. I'll come to the station later. Is that all right? But first I'm going to see Josef. Have you seen him?"

"Josef?" A tiny smile broke through Karlsson's wintry expression. "Oh, yes, I've seen him."

Josef had a room to himself. He was sitting up in bed, wearing oversized pajamas, with a bandage round his head and his arm encased in a plaster cast. A nurse stood by his side with a clipboard. He was whispering something to her and she was laughing.

"Frieda!" he cried. "My friend Frieda."

"Josef, how are you?"

"My arm is broken," he said. "Bad break, they say. But clean snap so good recovery. Later you write on arm. Or draw one of your pictures maybe."

"Does it hurt?"

"Drugs take away pain. I have eaten toast already. This is Rosalie, and she is from Senegal. This is my good friend Frieda."

"Your good friend who nearly got you killed."

"Is nothing," he said. "A day's work."

There was a knock at the door, and Reuben came in, followed by Sasha, who was bearing a bunch of flowers.

"I'm afraid you aren't allowed flowers," said Rosalie.

"He's a hero," said Reuben, decisively. "He has to have flowers."

Sasha kissed Josef on his bristly cheek, then put her arm around Frieda, gazing at her with beseeching concern.

"Not now," said Frieda.

"I've brought you some water." Reuben drew a little bottle out of his pocket and gave Josef a meaningful look.

Josef took a gulp, flinched, and offered it to Frieda. She shook her head, withdrew to the chair by the window, which looked out onto another wall and a narrow strip of pale blue sky. She could see the vapor trail of a plane, but it was too soon for it to be Sandy's. She was aware of Sasha's eyes on her, heard Reuben's voice and Josef's boisterous replies. A junior doctor came in and then left. A different nurse entered, wheeling a trolley; the creak of shoes on linoleum. Doors opening, doors closing. A pigeon perched on the narrow sill and stared in at her with a beady eye. Sasha said something to her, and she replied. Reuben asked her a question. She said yes, no, that she would tell them everything later. Not now.

Sandy took her in his arms and held her against him. She could feel the steady beat of his heart and his breath in her hair. Warm, solid, strong. Then he drew away and looked at her. It was only when she saw the expression on his face that she began to understand what she had come through. It took a great effort not to turn away from his pity and horror.

"What have you done, Frieda?"

"That's the question." She tried to laugh, but it came out wrong. "What *have* I done?"

SIXTY-TWO

Frieda had the strange feeling that she was onstage, but that she was playing the wrong part. Thelma Scott was sitting in what should have been Frieda's chair, and Frieda was pretending to be a patient. They were facing each other, and Thelma was looking straight at her with a kind, sympathetic expression, an expression that said there was no pressure: anything could be said, anything was allowed. Frieda knew the expression because it was one she used herself. She felt almost embarrassed that Thelma was trying it out on her. Did she think she would be so easily fooled?

Frieda kept her own consulting room deliberately austere, with neutral colors, a few pictures deliberately chosen not to send out any precise signals. Thelma Scott's room was quite different. She had busy, patterned wallpaper, blue and green tendrils intertwined, here and there a bird perched on them. The surfaces were crowded with little objects, knickknacks. There were miniature glass bottles, porcelain figurines, a glass vase with pink and yellow roses, pill boxes, china mugs, a set of plates decorated with wildflowers. But there was nothing personal, nothing that told you about Thelma Scott's life or personality, except that she liked little objects. Frieda hated little objects. They felt like clutter. She would have liked to sweep them all into a trash bag and put them out on the pavement for the binmen to take away.

Still Thelma looked at her with her kind, accepting expression. Frieda knew what it was to sit there, to wait for the first step that would mark the beginning of the journey. Sometimes Frieda had sat for the entire fifty minutes with a patient failing to say a single word. Sometimes they would just cry.

Why was she here? What, really, was there to talk about? She'd already gone through it all, all the choices, all the permutations, the roads she had taken and the roads she hadn't taken, while lying awake at two, three, four in the morning. Because of her intervention, Russell Lennox's attempt to protect his son had failed, and Ted was now in custody. The thought of him in prison and all he might be going through was painful, but he had committed a terrible act of violence, and against his own mother. His only hope was to acknowledge what he had done and take the consequences. The legal system might be merciful. With the right defense, he might escape a murder conviction.

Some people might think that Ted would have stood a better chance if he had remained free. Human beings have an ability to survive by burying the past, making themselves forget. Ted might have found his own way of atoning. But Frieda couldn't make herself believe that. You had to face the truth, however painful, and move on from there. Burying it didn't make it die, and in the end it would claw its way out of the earth and come for you. But was that just an opinion, and was Ted paying the price for it?

And were Dora and Judith paying the price as well? As she thought of them, the image came into her mind of the funeral that she had attended just two days ago. There had been music and poems and hundreds of people, but what she had seen from her position at the back had been the two girls, one on either side of their grimly virtuous aunt. Both had had their hair cut for the occasion: Dora now had a severe fringe and Judith's wild curls had been shorn. They seemed limp and defeated, utterly wretched. Judith had seen Frieda; her remarkable eyes had blazed briefly, and then she had turned away.

The truth: Jim Fearby had lived for it and sacrificed everything for it, his family, his career, and his life. In those last moments, when Lawrence Dawes and Gerry Collier had killed him, did he briefly realize he had found the truth? Did he feel justified? And was it her fault? She had tried to help Fearby, and he had died. She had traveled with him, talked with him, planned with him. She had abused her friendship with Karlsson to get him involved, but she had failed Fearby. Fearby had made the connection with Dawes, but should Frieda herself have realized that he couldn't have acted alone? He had gone ahead of her into that underworld, and she hadn't been able to save him.

Sharon Gibbs had been rescued and restored to her family, and that was something. If she and Josef hadn't burst in, Sharon Gibbs would have joined the others. They had found them buried in the cellar. Frieda was haunted by their names and by their faces in the photographs Fearby had shown her. Happy family snapshots of young girls, who didn't know what was ahead of them. Hazel Barton and Roxanne Ingatestone and Daisy Crewe and Philippa Lewis and Maria Horsley and Lila Dawes. And there was a seventh. The police had found another body in the cellar, the skeletal remains of a young female. Unidentified. Fearby had missed her somehow, and the police had the names of too many missing girls. Karlsson said they had a DNA sample and might strike lucky. All those lost girls, but Frieda couldn't stop thinking about the unknown one. It was like staring into an abyss and being lost there.

Frieda wanted to feel guilty about what she'd done to Josef as well, but that was harder. She suspected at first that his cheerful stoicism might be concealing post-traumatic stress. It could emerge much later; that was what the literature said. But really there was no sign of it at all. He was enjoying the attention, and when Karlsson had said there was some possibility of an award for bravery, he seemed to enjoy it even more. His account of the event seemed to become more embroidered with each retelling, but even Frieda couldn't detect signs of emotional distress.

And there was Dean Reeve. He was like an obscene kind of lover, someone who wanted to observe everything she did, feel everything she felt, accompany her to places no one else would go. The memory, the smell of the charred ruin, of Hal Bradshaw's house haunted her. Had Dean Reeve done it to punish Bradshaw or to punish her? Had he sensed, in a way nobody else could, her hostility toward Bradshaw, then acted it out in a way she never would have? This is you, he was telling her. This is who you really are, and you and I are the only people who truly recognize that. I am your twin, your other self.

So much wreckage, so much damage she had left trailing behind her.

Frieda lifted her eyes. She had almost forgotten where she was. Thelma was looking at her, full in the face.

"I'm sorry," said Frieda. "I can't put this into words."

Thelma gave a slow nod. "That sounds like the place to begin."

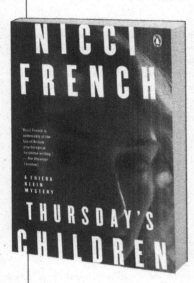

AVAILABLE FROM PENGUIN

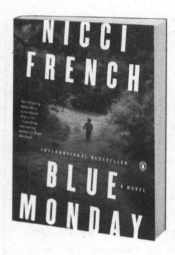

Blue Monday

When five-year-old Matthew Farraday is abducted, psychotherapist Frieda Klein cannot ignore the fact that his photograph perfectly matches the boy one of her patients describes from his fantasies. With Detective Chief Inspector Karlsson, Frieda finds herself at the center of a desperate race to find the kidnapper.

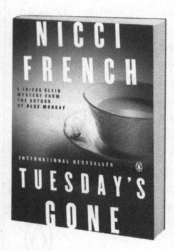

Tuesday's Gone

A London social worker discovers her psychotic client serving tea to a naked, decomposing corpse. Inspector Karlsson asks Frieda for help in uncovering the man's identity. But Frieda can't help feeling that man was killed in order to embroil her in the investigation. If so, is Frieda herself the next victim?

PENGUIN BOOKS

P.O. 0003688848